Japanese

London Oriental and African Language Library

The LONDON ORIENTAL AND AFRICAN LANGUAGE LIBRARY aims to make available reliable and up-to-date analyses of the grammatical structure of the major Oriental and African languages, in a form readily accessible to the non-specialist. With this in mind, the language material in each volume is in roman script, and fully glossed and translated. The series is based at the School of Oriental and African Studies of the University of London, Europe's largest institution specializing in the study of the languages and cultures of Africa and Asia. Each volume is written by an acknowledged expert in the field who has carried out original research on the language and has first-hand knowledge of the area in which it is spoken.

For an overview of all books published in this series, please see *http/benjamins.com/catalog/loall*

Editors

Theodora Bynon
David C. Bennett
School of Oriental and African Studies
University of London

Masayoshi Shibatani
Kobe University, Japan
Rice University, Houston, Texas, USA

Advisory Board

James Bynon
Bernard Comrie
Gilbert Lazard
Christian Lehmann

James A. Matisoff
Christopher Shackle
Andrew Simpson

Volume 17

Japanese. Revised edition
by Shoichi Iwasaki

Japanese
Revised edition

Shoichi Iwasaki
UCLA

John Benjamins Publishing Company
Amsterdam / Philadelphia

The paper used in this publication meets the minimum requirements of the American National Standard for Information Sciences – Permanence of Paper for Printed Library Materials, ANSI z39.48-1984.

Cover illustration: Children dancing around a raised drum stage at a summer festival, Tokyo. Photo: Shoichi Iwasaki, 2006.

Library of Congress Cataloging-in-Publication Data

Japanese / Shoichi Iwasaki. -- Rev. ed.
  p. cm. (London Oriental and African Language Library, ISSN 1382-3485 ; v. 17)
Text in English and Japanese.
Includes bibliographical references and index.
1. Japanese language--Grammar. I. Title.
PL533.I97   2013
495.6'5--dc23   2012030916
ISBN 978 90 272 3817 7 (Hb ; alk. paper)
ISBN 978 90 272 3818 4 (Pb ; alk. paper)
ISBN 978 90 272 7314 7 (Eb)

© 2013 – John Benjamins B.V.
No part of this book may be reproduced in any form, by print, photoprint, microfilm, or any other means, without written permission from the publisher.

John Benjamins Publishing Co. · P.O. Box 36224 · 1020 ME Amsterdam · The Netherlands
John Benjamins North America · P.O. Box 27519 · Philadelphia PA 19118-0519 · USA

To My Parents

Table of contents

Preface — XV

Romanization and text presentation — XVII

List of abbreviations — XXI

CHAPTER 1
Overview — 1
1. Language varieties 1
2. Genetic relationships with other languages 3
3. Historical periods and important changes in the language 6
4. Typological features of Japanese 11

CHAPTER 2
Writing system — 18
1. Early history 18
2. The current system 20
3. *Kanji*: Chinese characters 21
4. *Kana* 24

CHAPTER 3
Sounds — 29
1. The inventory of sounds 29
    - 1.1 Vowels 29
    - 1.2 Consonants 31
        - 1.2.1 Phonetic inventory 31
        - 1.2.2 Phonemic analysis 33
        - 1.2.3 Syllable-initial clusters 36
        - 1.2.4 Special phonemes 37
2. Sound modification 39
    - 2.1 High vowel devoicing 39
    - 2.2 Sequential voicing (*Rendaku*) 39
3. Syllable, mora, and foot 42
4. Accent 46
5. Intonation 49

CHAPTER 4
Words 54
1. Vocabulary strata 54
2. Word classes 57
    2.1 Major word classes 57
        2.1.1 Nouns 57
        2.1.2 Adjectives 61
        2.1.3 Nominal adjectives 62
        2.1.4 Verbs 63
    2.2 Minor word classes 63
        2.2.1 Adverbs 63
        2.2.2 Conjunctions 64
        2.2.3 Adnouns 65
        2.2.4 Auxiliaries 65
        2.2.5 Copula 65
        2.2.6 Particles 66
        2.2.7 Affixes 67
        2.2.8 Interjections 68
3. Some notable word classes 68
    3.1 Sound-symbolic words 68
    3.2 Numerals and numeral-classifiers 72
        3.2.1 Numerals 72
        3.2.2 Numeral classifiers and numeric phrases 74

CHAPTER 5
Morphology 78
1. Morphology of the inflectional category 78
    1.1 Verb morphology 78
        1.1.1 Verb types 78
        1.1.2 *Onbin* (sandhi) 83
        1.1.3 Transitive-intransitive opposition 85
    1.2 Adjective morphology 86
    1.3 Copula morphology 87
    1.4 Polite register inflection paradigms 89
2. Word-formation processes 90
    2.1 Noun equivalents (Lexical nominalization) 90
    2.2 Affixation 92
    2.3 Compounding 95
    2.4 Reduplication 99
    2.5 Clipping and blending 100

CHAPTER 6
Argument structures   104
1. Argument structure types   104
   1.1 Argument structures with stative predicates   105
   1.2 Argument structures with dynamic predicates   109
   1.3 Argument structure for the reportative verbs   116
2. Adjunct noun phrases   116
3. Syntactic roles and clausal structures   120
   3.1 Subjects   120
   3.2 Objects   125

CHAPTER 7
Tense and aspect   126
1. Tense   126
2. Aspect   132
   2.1 Perfect (anterior) aspect: -ta   132
   2.2 Perfective aspect   133
   2.3 Imperfective aspect: Progressive and resultative   133
       2.3.1 -te-iru   134
             2.3.1.1 Canonical cases   136
             2.3.1.2 Extended uses   139
       2.3.2 -te-aru   142
       2.3.3 Summary   143
   2.4 Marked aspects   143
       2.4.1 Completive aspect   145
             2.4.1.1 [Verb$_{INF}$]-owaru/oeru   145
             2.4.1.2 -te-shimau   145
       2.4.2 Preparatory aspect: -te-oku   146
       2.4.3 Exploratory aspect: -te-miru   147
       2.4.4 Inceptive aspect: (INF) -hajimeru/-dasu   147
       2.4.5 Inchoative aspect   148
             2.4.5.1 (ni/-ku) naru   148
             2.4.5.2 -te-kuru and -te-iku   149
       2.4.6 Summary   152

CHAPTER 8
Grammatical constructions   153
1. Passive construction   153
   1.1 Eventive passives   153
       1.1.1 Direct passives: -(r)are- as a "voice converter"   153

        1.1.2   Indirect passives: *-(r)are-* as a "valence increaser"   158
        1.1.3   Psychological affect (Adversity)   160
    1.2   Stative Passives: *-(r)are-* as a "stativizer"   162
2.   Spontaneous constructions   164
3.   Potential constructions   165
4.   Causatives   168
    4.1   Lexical causatives   168
    4.2   Morphological causatives   170
        4.2.1   Intransitive-based morphological causatives   171
        4.2.2   Transitive-based morphological causatives   176
    4.3   Periphrastic causatives   177
    4.4   Causative-passives   178
5.   Benefactives   179
    5.1   Basic structure   179
    5.2   "Malefactive" interpretation   183
    5.3   Causative-benefactives and passive-benefactives   184
6.   Reciprocals   187
    6.1   Lexical reciprocals   187
    6.2   Morphological reciprocals   189
    6.3   Periphrastic reciprocals   193
7.   Numeric phrases   194

CHAPTER 9

Noun phrase structures   198

1.   Genitive and associative phrases   198
2.   Simple attributive phrases   199
3.   Clausal noun modification   201
    3.1   "Cased head" type (Relative clause)   202
    3.2   "Adverbial head" type   208
    3.3   "Relational head" type   209
    3.4   "Content label head" type (Appositive clause)   210
4.   Some syntactic characteristics   212
    4.1   The *ga-no* conversion   212
    4.2   Relative clause formation in English and Japanese   216

CHAPTER 10

Quotation and complementation   219

1.   Quotation: Quoted speech and thought   219
2.   Complementation   223
    2.1   The object complement   224
    2.2   The subject complement   227

3. Internally headed relative clauses (IHRs) 229
4. Integrated adverbial clauses 234
5. Summary 236

CHAPTER 11
Information structure and the sentence form 237
1. The topic-comment structure 238
   1.1 Identifiability, activation and discourse 239
   1.2 The "eel" sentence 241
   1.3 The -wa -ga sentence structure 242
2. The contrastive structure 243
3. The focus structure 247
   3.1 Presupposition and assertion 247
   3.2 Obligatory focus interpretation 249
   3.3 The cleft argument focus construction 250
4. The topic-less sentence 252
   4.1 The exclamatory sentence 252
   4.2 The presentational sentence 255
5. The mixed-type sentence 256

CHAPTER 12
Clause combining 259
1. Conjoining 259
   1.1 Coupling 259
   1.2 Contrast 261
2. Adverbial subordination 263
   2.1 Temporal clauses 263
       2.1.1 "When" (General time) 263
       2.1.2 "Before" 264
       2.1.3 "After" 265
       2.1.4 "While" 266
   2.2 Conditionals 266
       2.2.1 Reality conditionals 266
       2.2.2 Unreality conditionals 267
       2.2.3 Concessive conditionals 268
   2.3 Cause/reason 269
   2.4 Counter expectation 269
   2.5 Purpose 270
   2.6 Circumstantials 270
3. Clause chaining and continuity marking 271
4. The "open clausal structure" and discourse organization 274

CHAPTER 13
Reference system in discourse 276
1. Personal pronouns, reflexive pronouns, and logophoric pronouns 276
2. Nominal ellipsis (zero anaphora) 279
3. Demonstratives as discourse deixis 283
    3.1 Nominal reference 283
    3.2 Discourse reference 285

CHAPTER 14
Pragmatics 287
1. Subjectivity concerns 287
    1.1 Internal state expressions 287
    1.2 Deictic expressions 290
        1.2.1 Demonstratives: The *ko-so-a-do* words 290
            1.2.1.1 Spatial use 290
            1.2.1.2 Cognitive use 292
            1.2.1.3 Affective use 293
        1.2.2 Movement and transaction expressions 294
2. Modality expressions 296
    2.1 Epistemic modality 297
        2.1.1 Conjectural and inferential 297
        2.1.2 Evidentials 299
    2.2 Evaluative modality 301
3. Pragmatic particles 302
    3.1 Markers of the "territory of information" 303
    3.2 Markers of illocutionary act 304
    3.3 Markers of unassimilated information 305
4. Conversation and language 306
    4.1 Pragmatic particles and *aizuchi* 306
    4.2 Discourse markers and discourse connectives 308

CHAPTER 15
Speech styles and registers 314
1. Personal indexical terms 314
2. Predicate forms 318
3. Direct vs. indirect dimensions 318
4. Honorifics 320
5. Gendered speech 325
6. Speech register creation 329

CHAPTER 16
Sample texts 331
1. Newspaper article 331
2. Folk tale 333
3. First person narrative ("Air Raid") 339
4. Conversation (1): "The Northridge earthquake" 349
5. Conversation (2): "Australia" 354

References 358

Index 375

Preface

This is a significantly expanded, revised version of *JAPANESE*, a part of the *London Oriental and African Language Library* series, originally published in 2002. The main purpose of this book is to provide an introductory, but comprehensive, overview of major aspects of the Japanese language for students and researchers. It is my hope that readers of this book find it to be an entry point to sub-fields of Japanese linguistics, broadly defined. The book covers such topics as the historical background, typological characteristics, the writing system, phonetics, phonology, vocabulary strata, morphology, argument structures, tense and aspect, major grammatical constructions, noun phrase structures, quotation and complementation, the information structure, clause combining strategies, reference tracking systems in discourse, pragmatics, and speech styles. At the end of the book, samples of written and spoken discourse are presented. Since it is also my goal to present the most updated, accurate descriptions of the language, I have adopted an eclectic approach, which allows me to refer to significant insights gained from the diverse descriptive and theoretical frameworks of modern Japanese linguistics, including those developed both in Japan and in the West. Notwithstanding this goal, I must point out that in some chapters I have tried to provide more functional explanations, especially in chapters on tense and aspect (Chapter 7), the major grammatical constructions (Chapter 8), noun phrase structures (Chapter 9), and the information structure (Chapter 11). Compared to the original version, I have greatly expanded on the topics of pragmatics and speech styles (Chapters 14 and 15). Readers who are interested in an alternative formal approach to phonology, morphology, and syntax can supplement this book with Tsujimura (2007) who introduces some of the phenomena from a generative grammar perspective. Those who are interested to know more about the phonetics and phonology of Japanese introduced in this book (Chapter 3) should consult Vance (2008), which I cite numerous times. Other "classic" resources that I have consulted extensively include Miller (1967), Kuno (1973), Martin ([1975] 1991), Hinds (1986), Teramura (1982, 1984), and Shibatani (1990). Hudson (2009) and Lurie (2011) are new resources that provide insightful discussions on the language from the perspectives of archeology and the history of writing, respectively.

Much progress has been made in the field of Japanese linguistics during the ten years that have elapsed since the publication of the original version. This new edition of *JAPANESE* includes a summary of these recent accomplishments published in journals, proceedings, edited books and monographs. As a result, the reference and the footnote sections have been expanded significantly. One of the most valuable resources that I consistently relied on was the volumes of *Japanese/Korean Linguistics*, a conference proceedings published by the *Center for the Study of Language and Information* (CSLI). I am fortunate that I have been one of the continuing standing committee members who assist in annual conferences which produce the conference proceedings. Another valuable resource is the graduate students at UCLA with whom I could discuss issues of Japanese linguistics. I have included some of the insights that I gained from their dissertations and published papers. Undergraduate students' questions always challenged me to describe linguistic phenomena more clearly and concisely.

For writing this book and for many other projects, I owe a great deal to Professor Masayoshi Shibatani. I express my gratitude for him with my deepest respect. Professors Theodora Bynon and David Benett, the other editors of the series, also gave me warm encouragement for the first edition of the book. Hiroyuki Nagahara, Timothy Vance, John Haig, Tsuyoshi Ono, Yasuhiro Shirai, Kaoru Horie, Foong Ha Yap, Yoshiko Matsumoto, and Hajime Hoji also provided me valuable help. To prepare the revised version, I have received many critical comments from Chisato Koike, Emi Morita, Yumiko Kawanishi, Michiko Kaneyasu, Noriko Yoshimura, and Maggie Camp. Also Maggie Camp and Jori Lindley edited the current version of the book. Finally, I would like to thank Isja Conen of John Benjamins Publishing Co., without whose help (and extreme patience!) I could not have finished this project.

While I was preparing the new edition, both of my parents passed away. My father, Kenjiro Iwasaki, left us on April 18, 2005 and my mother, Suzu Iwasaki, followed him on March 23, 2011. I acknowledge the enormous debts that I owe them. This book is dedicated to my parents.

Romanization and text presentation

1. The system of Romanization used in this book is a modified Hepburn system with five vowels, two semi-vowels, and 17 consonants including those represented by two letter combination, *ts*, *ch*, and *sh*.

Vowels:		*a*	*i*	*u*	*e*	*o*			
Semi-vowels:		*y*	*w*						
Consonants:									
voiceless									
	p	*t*	*k*	*f*	*s*	*sh*	*h*	*ts*	*ch*
voiced									
	b	*d*	*g*		*z*	*j*			
sonorant									
	m	*n*	*r*						

2. Palatalized consonants (before vowels *a*, *u*, *o*) are represented by an added *y*, as in *kya*, *kyu*, and *kyo* (except for *ja*, *ju*, *jo*).

3. A consonant (*p*, *k*, *ch*, *sh*, *b*, *g*, *j*, *n*, *m* and *r*) may be followed by any of the five vowels. Others are followed by a restricted number of vowels as shown below.

t	is followed by	*a*			*e*	*o*
ts				*u*		
s		*a*		*u*	*e*	*o*
h		*a*	*i*		*e*	*o*
f				*u*		
d		*a*			*e*	*o*
z		*a*		*u*	*e*	*o*

4. The 100 basic moras are arranged below as found in the traditional table of *kana* symbols.

Vowels

a	i	u	e	o

Consonant + Vowels

ka	ki	ku	ke	ko	ga	gi	gu	ge	go
sa	shi	su	se	so	za	ji	zu	ze	zo
ta	chi	tsu	te	to	da	–	–	de	do
na	ni	nu	ne	no					
ha	hi	fu	he	ho	ba	bi	bu	be	bo
					pa	pi	pu	pe	po
ma	mi	mu	me	mo					
ya	–	yu	–	yo					
ra	ri	ru	re	ro					
wa									

Palatalized Consonant + Vowels

kya	kyu	kyo	gya	gyu	gyo
sha	shu	sho	ja	ju	jo
cha	chu	cho			
nya	nyu	nyo			
hya	hyu	hyo	bya	byu	byo
			pya	pyu	pyo
mya	myu	myo			
rya	ryu	ryo			

5. Moraic nasal is represented as *n* though their actual pronunciation varies depending on the following consonant (see Chapter 3 §1.2.4). When the moraic nasal is followed by a vowel, an apostrophe is added to separate them (e.g. *shin'ai* 'dear') to distinguish a sequence of a nasal consonant /n/ followed by a vowel (e.g. *shinai* 'do not do').

6. Geminate consonants are represented by a sequence of two identical consonants (e.g. *kitte* 'stamp', *happi* 'a *happi* coat') except when the gemination involves *ch*, which is preceded by *t* (e.g. *matchi* 'match').

7. Diphthongs and long vowels are represented by a sequence of two vowels (e.g. *aa, ai, au, ae, ao; ia, ii, iu, ie, io* etc.). However, the sequences, *ei* and *ou*, are spelt as *ee* (e.g. *eega* 'movie') and *oo* (e.g. *oosama* 'king'), respectively (see Chapter 3 §1.1).

8. In addition to the above basic syllables, innovative combinations may be used to represent recent loan words and onomatopoetic words.

fa as in	*famirii* 'family'	*fi* as in	*firumu* 'film'
fe	*feminisuto* 'feminist'	*fo*	*fooku* 'folk/fork'
she	*sherii* 'sherry'	*che*	*chekku* 'check'
ti	*tii* 'tea'	*di*	*diizeru* 'diesel'
je	*jetto* 'jet'		

9. In examples shown in chapters of this book, no capitalization is used; neither the initial letter of the first word in a sentence nor that of a proper noun is capitalized (e.g. *nihon* 'Japan', *jon* 'John'). Japanese personal and place names used in the translation and descriptive portion of text, however, are spelt according to the normal convention. Thus *tookyoo* is used in an example but it is spelt as *Tokyo* in a translation.

10. A hyphen may be used to separate a suffix (e.g. *ip-pon* 'one-classifier suffix'), and bases in a compound (e.g. *gakusee-undoo* 'student movement'). However, for compounds which have been firmly established in the lexicon as single words are not broken up (e.g. *kokuban* 'blackboard' < *koku* 'black' + *ban* 'board'), except when such boundaries are crucial in the discussion as in the section on word formation. A hyphen is also used to separate a verbal noun from *suru* (*benkyoo-suru* 'study'), and the *-te* form and the following auxiliary (*tabete-iru* 'is eating'). A hyphen is also added when a certain clitic is added as in *itta-n desu* (go:PAST-SE COP) where *-n* is a short (clitic) form of the sentence extender, *no*. However, unless it is crucial for the discussion (e.g. Chapter 5 §1), a hyphen is not used to separate the roots/stems from affixes: e.g. *yom-a-na-i* (root ('read') – stem forming suffix – negative suffix – adjectival ending) or *yomi-kaki* (reading-writing) are normally spelt as *yomanai* and *yomikaki*.

11. In presenting clauses/sentences, words are separated by spaces. Particles (case particles and others) can be regarded as enclitics, but for the sake of simplicity and readability (and in accordance with the tradition), a space is put to separate a word from the following particle (except for Chapter 1), as if particles were regular, independent words, e.g. *boku wa koko de hon o katta.* (I TOP here INS book ACC bought) 'I bought a book here.'

12. The glosses which are accompanied to examples taken from other authors have been adjusted to conform to the present glossing system.

List of abbreviations

ABL	ablative	MOD	modal expression
ACC	accusative	NEG	negative
ADV	adverbial form	NEGIMP	negative imperative form
ALL	allative	NML	nominalizer
ASP	aspect	NOM	nominative
ATT	attributive form	NONPAST	nonpast
AUX	auxiliary	PAST	past
BCH	backchannel expression	PFX	prefix
CAU	causative suffix	PL	plural
CLS	classifier	POL	polite suffix
COM	comitative	POT	potential suffix
COND	conditional form	PP	pragmatic particle
COP	copula	PRO	pronoun
DAT	dative	PSS	passive suffix
DES	desiderative form	PURP	purposive
DO	direct object	Q	question marker
EMPH	emphasis marker	QT	quotative particle
F	female	QTF	quantifier
FRG	fragments	RCP	reciprocal suffix
GEN	genitive	REP	representative
HES	hesitation	S	subject
HON	(respect) honorific	SE	sentence extender
HUM	humble honorific	SFX	suffix
IHR	internally-headed relative clause	SOF	softener
IMP	imperative form	SPON	spontaneous suffix
INF	infinitive form	SSW	sound-symbolic word
INJ	interjection	TE	-te (conjunctive) form
INS	instrumental	TMP	temporal
IO	indirect object	TERM	terminal
LK	linker	TOP	topic marking particle
M	male	VOL	volitional suffix

CHAPTER 1

Overview

Japanese[1] is currently spoken by approximately 127 million people in Japan. It is the ninth largest language in the world in terms of the number of first-language speakers out of the close to seven thousand languages listed in *Ethnologue* (Lewis 2009). The country with a land area of 377,944 km^2 is 62nd among the world's countries in terms of land size; it is slightly smaller than the state of California in the United States of America and slightly larger than Germany. The four major islands of *Hokkaidō* (北海道), *Honshū* (本州), *Shikoku* (四国) and *Kyūshū* (九州), as well as over six thousand smaller islands,[2] lay parallel to the eastern coast of the Asian continent, stretching approximately 3,000 km from northeast to southwest, defining the western edge of the Pacific Rim. (See the map of Japan on the next page.)

1. Language varieties

The language described in this book is a variety of Japanese generally referred to as the "common" language (*kyōtsū-go* 共通語) or "standard" language (*hyōjun-go* 標準語) – as was formally established by the government in the early part of the 20th century – and is based on the dialect spoken in part of Tokyo, the capital city of Japan. Presently, the common language is used for education and mass communication, and is understood throughout the country. For daily purposes, however, distinct regional dialects may be used, especially among speakers from older generations.

Japanese dialects are first divided into two major groups: the east and west. The boundary shown by the dotted vertical line on the map on the next page coincides with the line of the Northern and Central Japanese Alps cutting across from north to south almost exactly at the mid point of the largest island of *Honshū* (Hirayama 1968: 74; Onishi 2008: 59). The eastern dialect group spreads in the eastern and northeastern parts of *Honshū* and

---

1. The Japanese language is normally referred to as *koku-go* (国語) 'national language' within Japan, especially as the name of a school subject. It is also referred to as *nihon-go* (日本語) 'Japanese language' when it is contrasted with other languages. See Gottlieb (2005: 15–6) for more discussion on *koku-go* and *nihon-go*.

2. The statistics of number of islands is based on a report by the Ministry of Land, Infrastructure, Transport and Tourism available at: http://www.mlit.go.jp/crd/chirit/ritoutoha.html.

Map 1. Map of Japan

the northern most island of *Hokkaidō*. This dialect group includes the approximately 12 million speakers of the Tokyo dialect, close to 10% of the total population of Japan. The western dialect group includes the vibrant Kyoto and Osaka dialects, and is found in the west and southwest areas of *Honshū* and also on *Shikoku* and *Kyūshū*, though *Kyūshū* can be separated as a southern dialectal group contrasting with the eastern and western groups (Hirayama 1968:75). Though many dialectal forms are clearly distributed along the east vs. west/south division (e.g. the negative morpheme, -*nai* in the east and -*nu* in the west/south), there are also forms whose distribution is defined instead by the central vs. peripheral division. That is, form A (say, a new name for 'snail') is found in the old capital of Kyoto while a different form B referring to the same object (an older form for 'snail') may be found in both the west and east sides of the ancient capital. This pattern is described as a new form pushing older forms outward in different directions (Yanagita 1908; Shibatani 1990:201–2). This central-periphery division together with the east-west division make the pattern of dialectal variation very complex.

Besides Japanese, two other indigenous languages should be recognized in Japan: Ryukyuan and Ainu. Varieties of the Ryukyuan language are spoken on islands of the Okinawa Prefecture and on a few islands of the Kagoshima Prefecture. Though Ryukyuan is sometimes classified as the forth dialect group of Japanese, it can be aptly considered a sister language to Japanese under the common Japonic language family (Serafim 1994, 1999; Bentley 2008). This language with its own four major dialect groups (Nakasone 1961) is spoken on the islands of the Ryukyu archipelago which extends from the south of *Kyūshū* down to the east of Taiwan between the East China Sea and the Philippine Sea. The Ryukyuan language is believed to have separated from Japanese, sometime between the mid 3rd and early 6th centuries CE (Hattori, 1954).[3] The Ryukyuan language has diverged significantly from the Japanese branch, and is completely unintelligible to speakers of any dialects of Japanese. The current number of residents on the islands is over 1,300,000 (about 1% of the total population in Japan), but the number of native speakers of the original Ryukyuan has been rapidly diminishing over the last hundred years or so due to a massive language shift instigated partly by the government's language policy (Shinzato 2003). At present, fluent speakers are mostly sixty years old or older, and children are not learning the ancestral vernaculars. Ainu is the third language found in Japan. Its homeland is the island of *Hokkaidō*, but its genetic affiliation is yet to be determined (see below). While the Ainu ethnicity is gaining political recognition in recent years, and the efforts to revive the culture and language is being rigorously pursued, the language is close to complete extinction with only ten to twenty fluent native speakers remaining (Vovin 1993: 1).

2. Genetic relationships with other languages

Japan has a long pre-historical period, which prevents unequivocal explanation of the genesis of its language. The archeological evidence shows that Japan was inhabited by people of the *Jōmon* (縄文) culture between 7,500 to 400 BCE, though there are indications of much earlier pre-*Jōmon* inhabitants as early as 35,000 years ago or much earlier.[4] Though the language of the *Jōmon* people is not known, two hypotheses for the early state of the language situation have been rigorously pursued. The first is part of a larger "Altaic hypothesis" which attempts to place Japanese (and Korean) under the Tungusic branch of the Altaic language family with Turkic and Mongolic as two other main branches. The

---

3. Later, Hattori (1976) pushed the range slightly earlier to span from the 1st century BCE to the late 5th century CE. Hokama (2007: 17, 294), on the other hand, proposes the range from the 2nd / 3rd to the 6th / 7th centuries CE. See Serafim (2003) for a further discussion.

4. The estimate of the *Jōmon* period given here (7,500 to 400 BCE) is a traditional one. More recent studies have pushed back the beginning of the period substantially. Based on the new data from radiocarbon dating (Habu 2004: 37–42), some have proposed the period between 14,500 BCE and 400 BCE. The date of the earliest inhabitants in Japan is also not conclusive. See Lurie 2011: 20–21, 367.

second is the "southern hypothesis," which searches for the origin of the language in the Austronesian languages.[5]

According to a version of the first hypothesis (Miller, 1971, 1980, 1986a, 1986b), several waves of Altaic language speakers arrived in Japan during the Jōmon period. These waves of Altaic languages provided the basis for the proto-Japanese, from which all the dialectal forms later derived. This hypothesis is attractive, as Japanese shares many features with Altaic languages: an agglutinating verb morphology; modifier-head constituent order; the use of postpositions rather than prepositions; a lack of articles, gender and relative pronouns; a lack of initial consonant clusters and initial *r* in their indigenous vocabulary. It is also believed by some that Japanese used to share the system of vowel harmony widely found in Altaic languages and middle Korean. Notwithstanding these similarities, the hypothesis is not without problems; compared to the simpler phonological system of Japanese, the phonological systems of Altaic languages are much more complex, and not much similarity in basic lexical and grammatical items can be found between Japanese and Altaic languages (Vovin 2003:18). The view of successive waves of Altaic population movement is also challenged by the archeological record (Hudson 1999b:86–7). Though constructing a larger Altaic hypothesis is problematic, it may still be possible to consider a more local genetic tie between Japanese and Korean. This is reasonable as Korean is the most similar language to Japanese in the area outside of the Japonic family (Martin 1966; Whitman 1985; Unger 2001). Although their relationship is marred by the same problems discussed above for the larger Altaic hypothesis, some experts believe that this is one of the most fruitful hypotheses to pursue (Vovin 2003:26).

The southern hypothesis considers Austronesian languages to have contributed to the formation of Japanese. This is a plausible hypothesis, as Japanese shares many features with Austronesian languages, such as a phonological simplicity, the use of prefixes and reduplication, and the typicality of open syllables (Polivanov 1924/1974). One version of this hypothesis is the Austronesian "substratum hypothesis," according to which Japanese is argued to be genealogically related to the Altaic language family but also incorporated lexical items from the Austronesian languages (Izui [1953] 1985). In other words, the Altaic language is the superstratum language and the Austronesian language a substratum language which provided loanwords to the former. Another version is the "hybrid language hypothesis," which considers that Japanese was formed with the Altaic and Austronesian stocks equally contributed (e.g. Polivanov 1924; Maruyama 1976; Sakiyama 1990) to become a kind of creole language (Sakiyama 2001).

---

5. Austronesian languages of the modern world include the Philippine languages (e.g. Tagalog, Illocano, Cebuano), Malaysian, Indonesian, Javanese, and many other languages spoken throughout the islands of Southeast Asia (e.g. Sumatra, Borneo) and the Pacific (e.g. Fiji, Tonga, Samoa).

The linguistic mixture of Altaic and Austronesian elements in Japanese proposed in both subtypes of the southern hypotheses can be supported by findings obtained independently by biological anthropologists. Based on cranial, dental and other biological evidence, Hanihara (1991) proposes a "dual structure model" for the population history of Japanese. According to this model, the first occupants in the Japanese archipelago came from southeast Asia sometime during the Upper Paleolithic Age roughly between 10,000 and 50,000 years ago. The earliest skeletal remains thought to be related to the *Jōmon* population have been dated to 18,000 years old. The second group of people arrived from northeast Asia during the *Yayoi* (弥生) period (between 400 BCE and 250 CE).[6] These two population groups started to intermix and eventually became the mainland Japanese. The mixture is still ongoing even in the present time. In addition, Hanihara further proposes that Ryukyuan and Ainu are more closely related to the *Jōmon* population than to the modern mainland Japanese (pp. 12–15).[7]

Both the Altaic and southern hypotheses assume a continuous development of the Japanese language from the *Jōmon* period (cf. Unger 2001:89). However, a recent development in archeology provides a reason against such a view and suggests that the *Jōmon* language, whatever it may have been, was replaced by a new language brought over by a migrant population from the Korean peninsula at the beginning of the *Yayoi* period (between 400 BCE and 250 CE). Using the farming-language dispersal model (Bellwood and Renfrew 2002), Hudson (1997, 2002) proposes that a large immigrant population who arrived in north *Kyūshū* from the Korean peninsula at the beginning of the *Yayoi* period brought both the new technology of rice cultivation and a new language (proto-Japanese). The new language quickly replaced the old *Jōmon* language as the farming *Yayoi* population moved into the other parts of Japan during the Early to Middle *Yayoi* period (ca. 400 BCE–1 CE). The farming technology and the new

---

6. Like the estimate of the *Jōmon* period, the estimate of the *Yayoi* period given here (400 BCE and 250 CE) is more of a traditional one. Though still disputed, the new estimate sets the *Yayoi* period between 900 BCE and 250 CE. See Lurie 2011:21, 368.

7. Omoto and Saitou (1997), however, based on the "genetic difference analysis" using such data as blood groups, red cell enzyme systems, and serum protein systems proposed a modified dual structure model. They first found that within the larger world population, mainland Japanese, Ryukyuan, and Ainu belong to a northeast Asian group together with Korean, Mongolian, and Tibetan. In the comparison among Japanese, Ryukyuan, Ainu, and Korean, they found that Japanese and Korean cluster together while Ryukyuan and Ainu cluster together. Their results suggest that the Japanese population originated with a group from northeast Asia. Though not conclusive, they suggest that the *Jōmon* population gave rise to 'the modern Ainu and probably also the Ryukyuan populations' (p. 444). Their proposal gives a credit to the theory of waves of Altaic immigrants proposed by Miller (1971, 1980, 1986a, 1986b).

language did not affect the Ainu people in *Hokkaidō* (Hudson 1999b: 133).[8] In the case of the Ryukyus, agriculturalists' migration was much delayed, probably no earlier than 900 CE (according to Asato and Doi 1999, as cited in Serafim 2003: 466).[9] As for the language (proto-Japanese) which the migrants from the Korean peninsula assumed to have brought, it is considered by some to have been derived from the proto-Korean-Japanese in the Korean peninsula, which may have been a Tungusic language (Unger 2001: 88). The debate over the "origin" of Japanese is still unsettled, but new collaborations between linguists, archeologists and other scientists may lead to interesting new discoveries.

3. Historical periods and important changes in the language

The 3rd century Chinese document *Gishi Wajin Den* (魏志倭人伝) provides important information about the people who resided in part of the Japanese archipelago in the late *Yayoi* period during the 3rd century. According to this document, a powerful queen named *Himiko* ruled *Yamatai* and other polities in *Kyūshū* (or some argue it may be in the *Kinai* area near Kyoto).[10] After *Yayoi* came the *Kofun* (古墳) period from the mid 3rd through the late 6th centuries CE and the *Asuka* (飛鳥) period from the late 6th until the early 8th century CE. During these periods, the *Yamato* state was gaining

---

8. This view suggests that Ainu may be more closely related to the language(s) of *Jōmon* than to Japanese (cf. Hudson 1999a: 275). Furthermore, if the *Jōmon* people came from southeast Asia as Hanihara (1991) proposes, then it is not unreasonable to consider that Ainu has a southeast Asian connection. This is indeed explored by Vovin (1993: 163–74) who compares Proto-Ainu and Proto-Austroasiatic languages.

9. If both the archeological estimate and Hattori's estimate of the split of the Ryukyuan from Japanese at mid 3rd and early 6th centuries CE are correct, then proto-Ryukyuan first developed outside the Ryukyus (most likely in *Kyūshū*), which was then carried by the agriculturalists from the original location. This seems consistent with the view presented in Bentley (2008: 26–7), which shows that Proto-Japanese first split between Early *Kyūshū* and Early Old Japanese branches, and then the Early *Kyūshū* branch split between the Ryukyuan and *Kyūshū* branches.

10. 魏志 (*Gishi* in Sino-Japanese reading/*Weizhi* in Chinese reading) is one of the three sections of the Chinese historical document *Sangokushi/Sanguazhi* (三國志) compiled in the 3rd century CE. The final section of *Gishi* is traditionally referred to as *Wajinden* (倭人伝), which describes the people of *Wa* 倭 (the name used by Chinese to refer to Japanese people at that time). According to the document, *Himiko* established a tributary relationship with 魏 (*Gi/Wei*) (220–265 CE). One controversy surrounding *Gishi Wajin Den* is the location of *Yamatai*. *Gishi Wajin Den* is important not only for historians but also for linguists as personal (*Himiko* etc.) and place names (*Yamatai* etc.) in indigenous Japanese at that time can be assessed.

power near present-day Nara in central Japan, and began to take control over a large part of the archipelago. Both Confucianism and Buddhism spread to Japan from China during this time.

Though some records of the language are available from earlier periods (Chapter 2), it is from the 8th century that substantial records started to appear. The language from the eighth century represent what is now referred to as Old Japanese. In the subsequent period Old Japanese was followed by Late Old Japanese (9th–12th centuries), Middle Japanese (12th–16th centuries), Early Modern Japanese (17th–mid 19th centuries) and Modern Japanese (mid 19th century to present). In Table 1, the names of the stages of language are listed at the top, and each stage is aligned with the corresponding centuries and political periods.

Table 1. Different stages of Japanese and historical periods

Old J	Late OJ	Middle J	Early Mod. J	Mod. J
8	9–10–11–12	12–13–14–15–16	17–18–mid 19	mid 19 – present
Nara	Heian	Kamakura/Muromachi	Edo	Meiji/Taisho/Showa/Heisei

Modern Japanese has retained many important structural properties since the time of Old Japanese, such as SOV word order, modifier–head order, the use of case particles, agglutinating verb morphology, and an open syllable structure. Many changes, however, also took place throughout history, especially during the *Muromachi* period (14th–16th century). Several changes, described below, are especially noteworthy as they separate the older form of language from the newer modern form.

First, the language underwent several phonological modifications. Old Japanese is believed to have had eight vowels (*a*, *u*, and two varieties each of *i*, *e*, and *o*).[11] But by the period of Late Old Japanese, the distinction between the two varieties of *i*, *e*, and *o* had disappeared, and consequently the number of vowels had been reduced to the five we see in Modern Japanese. Also between Late Old Japanese and Middle Japanese, several syllables merged. The syllable /wi/ was merged to the vowel /i/, while the syllable /we/ was merged to /ye/, which was further merged to the vowel /e/ in Modern Japanese. Some plosive consonants became affricates before high vowels: [ti] > [cɕi], [di] > [ɟzi], [tɯ] > [tsɯ], [dɯ] > [dzɯ]. The voiced variety of the new sound [ɟzi] became indistinguishable with [zi], and so did and [dzɯ] with [zɯ]. Other phonological changes that occurred during the same time period include the firm establishment of moraic nasal (n in *yo<u>n</u>de* < *yomite*)

---

11. Although the precise phonetic values of the two varieties are not known, Ohno (1980) suggests that the two varieties of vowels *i*, *e*, and *o* are the plain and centralized vowels.

and geminate (*tt* in *ta**tt**e* < *tachite*) consonants,¹² and an increase in the number of words with initial /r/ and voiced consonants. Toward the end of Middle Japanese, the labiality of bilabial fricatives became weakened, initiating a series of changes. In the intervocalic environment, it changes as follows:

ɸ¹³ > w (> ø)
(kaɸa > kawa 'river'; iɸe > iwe > ie 'house')

In the word initial environment, it changes to *h* as follows:

ɸ > h   (ɸa > ha 'leaf')

Second, the Middle Japanese period also saw many significant morphological modifications. In this period verbs and auxiliary verbs started to undergo many changes; notably their conjugation categories and paradigms became greatly simplified. In the earlier stage, many auxiliary verbs were used to encode various aspectual and modal information: perfective (*tsu, nu, tari, ri*), retrospective (*ki, keri*), desiderative (*tashi*), conjectural (*kemu, ramu, mu, beshi, rashi, mashi*), visual evidential (*meri*), and auditory evidential (*nari*). Most of these auxiliaries disappeared. Surviving auxiliaries include the perfective -*tari*, a predecessor of the Modern Japanese past-tense/perfect auxiliary -*ta* (Chapter 7) and the desiderative -*tashi* (Classical form) > -*tai* (Modern form).¹⁴

Third, a classical grammatical construction known as the *kakari-musubi* (係り結び) 'focus concord' in Late Old Japanese disappeared (see, for example, Ohno 1993). While a regular independent sentence is concluded with a verb or auxiliary verb in the conclusive form, a sentence containing a special *kakari* particle (focus particle) such as *zo, namu, ya,* and *ka* required a verb or auxiliary verb in the attributive form concluding it. Both of the sentences below mean 'X existed.' The first sentence is ended with the conclusive form of the retrospective auxiliary *keri* suffixed to the verb root, *ari* 'exist.' In contrast, the second

---

12. The origin of these special moras has been debated by the specialists. In one opinion, these types of mora emerged as the language adopted many words from Middle Chinese which contains closed syllables with the final /p, t, k/ and /m, n, ŋ/. In other words, the foreign phonology influenced the indigenous phonology. On the other hand, some believe that such special moras were already in existence in Japanese as emphatic epenthetic consonants, though not widely recognized in writing. For example, Watanabe (2001: 78–89) considers that the geminate /pp/ appeared as an emphatic version of the exclamation word /aɸare/ before mid-*Heian* period: /aɸare/ > /aɸɸare/ > /appare/. See Note 13 directly below.

13. The bilabial fricative, /ɸ/, is further reconstructed as *p for proto-Japanese. Many Ryukyuan dialects still retain this consonant as in *pa* 'leaf' and *pana* 'flower', which are *ha* and *hana* in Modern Japanese, respectively.

14. Also the retrospective -*ker*- has been fossilized as *kke* in Modern Japanese as a sentence-final particle of recollection in question form (Martin 1975: 937–8); *kore nan da kke* (this what COP *kke*) 'What was this?' See also Chapter 7, Note 9.

sentence focuses X with the *kakari* particle *namu*, and is concluded with the attributive form *keru*.

> normal sentence: X *ari-keri*   'X existed'
> focus sentence: X *namu ari-keru* 'It is X that existed.'

During the Middle Japanese period, however, the attributive ending became the *de facto* sentence final form even for regular independent sentences, thereby making the original conclusive form obsolete (Iwasaki 1993c, 2000).[15]

Fourth, while many features of older Japanese were disappearing, new features also started to emerge in Middle Japanese. One such feature is a structural division for the use of the particles *ga* and *no*. The particles were both used to mark the nominative case in a nominalized clause as well as the genitive case in a noun phrase in Old and Late Old Japanese (Shibatani 1990: 348; Yanagida & Whitman 2009). In the latter function, *ga* mostly occurred with a noun denoting the speaker, the hearer, the person close to the speaker, the narrative protagonist, and others, while *no* occurred with high rank person, indefinite animate nouns, and inanimate nouns (Kobayashi 1938, Takeuchi 1999: 159–60). This semantic distinction was replaced with a more structural one; the nominative case function of *no* was weakening, and *ga* was losing its genitive marking function. In Modern Japanese, thus, *no* generally functions as the genitive case particle and performs as a nominative case marker only in the subordinate clause, while *ga* works as the nominative particle in both subordinate and non-subordinate environments, but it does not appear as a genitive marker except in a few frozen expressions (e.g. *wa ga ya* (I – GEN – house) 'my house').

Fifth, another notable change during Middle Japanese was the complication of the honorific system, reflecting changes to the social structure brought on by the new warrior class who had ascended to political power. This emerging class also employed a large amount of Sino-Japanese vocabulary (i.e. Chinese loan words), especially in their writing. As a consequence the written language became significantly different from the spoken language which employed more native vocabulary.

Between the 9th and 16th centuries, Kyoto was the seat of the Imperial court and recognized as the center of the country. However, in 1603, the Shogun Government was established in Edo (present-day Tokyo), which controlled Japan for over 250 years until it returned the power to the Emperor in 1868. During the earlier part of the Edo period, the Kyoto dialect was still regarded as standard. However, different dialect speakers started to mingle in Edo, in part due to the "alternate attendance system" imposed by the government upon local loads who were required to move their residency between their homelands and

---

15. The *kakari musubi* sentence structure is still found in some varieties of the Ryukyu language (Shinzato & Serafim 2003; Serafim & Shinzato 2005, 2009, forthcoming; Shinzato forthcoming.) However, see also Karimata (2011).

Edo periodically, and to the migratory move of the merchants and craftsmen from Kyoto, Osaka, and other places to Edo (Hirayama 1968: 28–9). At the same time, different socially stratified varieties started to emerge to give distinct features to the speeches of the *samurai* class, merchant class, and women. Many modern linguistic elements were introduced during this period, including honorific expressions (*irassharu* 'come/go/exist,' *ossharu* 'say,' *kudasaru* 'give,' *nasaru* 'do'), politeness suffixes (*-masu, -gozaimasu, -desu*), and plain copula verbs (*dearu, da*) (Yamaguchi 2006: 159–163, see Chapter 15). The Edo dialect became a vibrant language and the basis for the Tokyo dialect in the following Meiji era.

After the Meiji Restoration in 1868, Japan was faced with several language related issues. First, since Japan needed to catch up with Western civilization to become part of the modern world as quickly as possible, scholars started to translate Western books which had been inaccessible during over two hundred years of the "closed door" policy of the Edo Shogunate.[16] Translators took advantage of the long tradition of Chinese translation which had been developing in Japan over the centuries, and coined many Sino-Japanese compounds to render Western concepts, e.g. 科学 *kagaku* 'science,' 心理学 *shinrigaku* 'psychology,' 価値 *kachi* 'value,' 可能 *kanoo* 'possibility,' and 広告 *kookoku* 'advertisement' (Chapter 4 §1). These new words were quickly absorbed in the language, many of which were subsequently exported back to China. Second, the government needed to establish a standard national language in order to disseminate knowledge throughout Japan efficiently and evenly. Educators and opinion leaders advocated one variety of Tokyo speech to serve as the model for such a standard language. The government published the first nationally edited textbook in 1902 in the Meiji era, and adopted the language of educated Tokyo speakers as the "standard language" in 1913 during the Taisho era. After World War II (1939–1945), the name was changed to the "common language" to avoid the prescriptive overtone of "standard" and to acknowledge regional varieties as part of Japanese. Third, the government needed to regulate the use of Chinese characters which were hindering the spread of new knowledge through written language across a wider audience. Prior to the Meiji Restoration, in 1866, Maejima Hisoka (前島密), a scholar and politician, had already proposed that Chinese characters be abolished from the language while Fukuzawa Yukichi (福澤諭吉), an educator and a writer, proposed a limit to the number of characters. Still others proposed using roman letters or *kana* syllabary exclusively to write sentences in Japanese. Eventually, the government adopted a policy limiting the use of characters, the policy still in effect today. Fourth, the style of writing needed to be changed as official documents had been written in pure or modified Chinese until the Edo period. Many people, especially translators of Western documents and progressive writers, noticed that

---

16. During the time when Japan closed its doors to the West, the Shogun government allowed limited trading with Dutch and Chinese merchants. During this period some scholars had already translated Dutch books on medicine and physics, and toward the end of the Edo period some started to translate books written in English, French and German as well.

the gap between spoken and written modes of language was large for Japanese compared to Western languages and felt the need to bring the written language closer to the spoken language in order to make writing more accessible. A group of writers experimented with different styles under the name of *genbun-itchi* (言文一致) 'unification of spoken and written languages,'[17] and their effort finally brought about the modern style of Japanese toward the end of the Meiji era.

4. Typological features of Japanese

Japanese can be characterized by distinctive typological features, as described in this section.

4.1   Japanese is an SOV language, which places the order of the subject, direct object and a verb in a typical transitive sentence as in (1) below. The SOV order is one of the two most common orders found among languages. In Dryer (2008a), SOV type languages slightly outnumber SVO type languages such as English, and the two types of language together make up 76% of the 1228 sampled languages.

(1)   *inu-ga   ringo-o   tabeteiru*   'a dog is eating an apple'
       dog-NOM   apple-ACC   eat:ASP
       [S]   [O]   [V]

Constituents in a ditransitive sentence with a direct object (DO) and an indirect object (IO) are arranged as S-IO-DO-V (Chapter 6 §1.2(1)).

(2)   *hanako-ga   inu-ni   ringo-o   yatta*
       (name)-NOM   dog-DAT   apple-ACC   give:PAST
       [S]   [IO]   [DO]   [V]
       'Hanako gave an apple to the dog.'

4.2   Japanese is a "case marking" and a "dependent marking" language (cf. Nichols 1986; Blake 1994: 9, 13–15). In sentences like (1) and (2) above, it is the noun phrases ("dependent constituents") that are marked with a case particle to indicate their relationship to the predicate ("head"). In (1) and (2), *ga* is a case particle which shows that the preceding noun phrases, *inu* 'dog' and *hanako* (name), respectively, have a nominative case relationship with the verb, *tabeteiru* 'is eating' and *yatta* 'gave,' respectively, while the case particle *o* shows that the noun phrase *ringo* 'apple' in both

---

17.   Credit for the first novel that used the spoken style is usually given to Futabatei Shimei 二葉亭四迷 who published *Ukigumo* 浮雲 'The Drifting Cloud' in 1887–9. Many writers tried to experiment with new and different styles. Ozaki Kōyō 尾崎 紅葉 is credited with the use of the *de aru* copula style, which defines the new written mode and was widely accepted by the writers who followed.

sentences has an accusative case relationship with the verb. (In this section, a hyphen is added between the noun and particle to show their interdependency, but in the rest of the book the hyphen notation is not adopted.) Other cases, such as locative and instrumental, are also indicated by an array of case particles (see Chapter 6). The verb is marked for aspect ("progressive aspect," -te i-) and tense ("present," -ru and "past," -ta), but not for any information about the noun phrase, *inu*, *hanako*, or *esa*.

4.3 Japanese is a nominative-accusative language which codes the subjects of transitive and intransitive sentences in an identical manner. Thus, in (3), the intransitive subject *inu* is marked with *ga* in the same manner in which the transitive subject *inu* is marked in (1).

(3) inu-ga   hasshitteiru 'a dog is running'
     dog-NOM run:ASP
     [S]   [V]

4.4 Japanese is a "subject-prominent and topic-prominent" language (Li & Thompson 1976). This means that the language is sensitive both to the syntactic notion of subject (Chapter 6 §3) and the more pragmatically oriented notion of topic (Chapter 11), and the distinction can be marked by different particles, *ga* and *wa*, respectively. Thus, while *hanako-ga* in (2) above only functions as a subject for the predicate, *hanako-wa* in (4) below functions as a topic, about which the comment that follows is providing a remark. One of the crucial properties of a topic noun is that it must represent identifiable/definite information. The function of topic is discussed in detail in Chapter 11.

(4) [hanako-wa] [inu-ni   ringo-o   yatta]
     (name)-TOP   dog-DAT apple-ACC give:PAST
     [TOPIC]   [COMMENT]
     'As for Hanako, she gave an apple to the dog.'

One particular type of sentence available in a topic-oriented language is exemplified in (5).

(5) zoo-wa   hana-ga   nagai
     elephant-TOP nose-NOM long
     [TOPIC]   [Sub.   Pred.]_{COMMENT}
     'The elephant; its nose is long.'

The adjective, *nagai* 'long,' is a predicate for the subject *hana* 'nose.' The proposition '(the) nose is long' is then taken as a clausal comment for the topic *zoo* 'elephant.' Topic prominence is widely observed in many Asian languages (Chapter 11 §1.3).

4.5 Japanese is a language that allows abundant ellipsis (Chapter 13 §2; Hinds 1986; Fry 2003), or a "pro-drop" language in some linguistic theory. As discussed in 4.2 above, Japanese is a dependent marking language, and no co-referencing of arguments is coded in the verb complex. It is a remarkable fact, then, that Japanese allows an abundance of ellipsis. In fact, pragmatically retrievable information is, more often than not, unspecified in a sentence. Noun phrase ellipsis is the most common type of ellipsis and can be found in both written and spoken modes of the language. (6) shows the ellipsis of subject and direct object.

(6) A: *mita   no ?* 'Have (you) seen (it)?'
       see:PAST SE
    B *mita   yo.*   '(I)'ve seen (it).'
       see:PAST PP

Verbal ellipsis and case particle ellipsis are also found in speech and informal writing. In (7), the verb does not appear, but the accusative particle clearly anticipates a verb such as *mochimashita* 'had.' In (8), no postposition appears after *boku* 'I' (a casual first person male pronoun) and *kore* 'this.'

(7) (from Hinds 1986: 22)
    donna   fuu-na   inshoo   o?
    what.kind   appearance-LK   impression   ACC
    'What kind of impression (did you have)?'

(8) *kore boku morau   yo*
    This   I   receive:NONPAST PP
    'I'll take this, okay?'

4.6 As described already, the basic constituent order of Japanese is S-O-V and S-IO-DO-V. However, in actual use, the order can be adjusted for various pragmatic reasons. Notice that the constituent order in (8) above is O-S-V. Now compare the order of the constituents presented in (2) in 4.1 above and the order with the direct object pre-posed in (9) below.[18] The pre-posed element is often topicalized with the topic marker *wa*. The accusative *o* is always replaced by *wa* as in (10), but the dative *ni* may be retained before *wa* as in (11) (Chapter 11).

(9) *ringo-o   hanako-ga   inu-ni   yatta*
     apple-ACC   (name)-NOM   dog-DAT   give:PAST
     'The apple, Hanako gave it to the dog.'

(10) *ringo-wa   hanako-ga   inu-ni   yatta*
     apple-TOP   (name)-NOM   dog-DAT   give:PAST
     'The apple, Hanako gave it to the dog.'

(11) *inu-ni-wa   hanako-ga   ringo-o   yatta*
     dog-DAT-TOP   (name)-NOM   apple-ACC give:PAST
     'To the dog, Hanako gave an apple.'

---

18. Moving constituents around at the abstract level of sentence structure is called "scrambling" in the generative theory of Japanese (e.g. Saito 1985).

Permutation of words as shown above is possible both in written and spoken language. Furthermore, in spoken language, a noun phrase can also appear after the predicate, as shown in (12) and (13) below (Ono & Suzuki 1992).

(12) moo   yatta   yo aitsu-ni
     already give:PAST   PP that.guy DAT
     '(I) already gave it to that guy.'

(13) moo   yatta   yo ringo
     already give:PAST   PP apple
     '(I) already gave an apple (to that guy).'

This phenomenon is referred to as "right dislocation" or "postposition," and is motivated by the speaker's desire to add information as an afterthought. The phenomenon is also referred to as "increment" in the literature of interactional linguistics and Conversation Analysis (CA). This means that an utterance is produced and the speaker expands her turn in conversation by adding extra materials to the utterance produced so far (see Koike 2001; Couper-Kuhlen & Ono 2007).

4.7 A polar question (or a "yes/no" question) is formed without the change of constituent order like in English. It is constructed by attaching the question particle *ka* at the end of the sentence, when the verb contains the polite suffix, as in (14). Among the world's languages, the Japanese style is much more common than the English style (Dryer 2008e).

(14) hanako-wa   ken-ni   hon-o   yarimashita   ka
     (name)-TOP   (name)-DAT   book-ACC   give:POL:PAST   Q
     'Did Hanako give the book to Ken?'

With the abrupt verb form (i.e. the form without the polite suffix), the nominalizer *no* (or "sentence extender," glossed as SE) with a rising intonation is more common than *ka*, as in (15).

(15) hanako-wa   ken-ni   hon-o   yatta   no↗
     (name)-TOP   (name)-DAT   book-ACC   givePAST   SE
     'Did Hanako give the book to Ken?'

4.8 A content question (or an information question) is formed similarly to the polar question with the question particle *ka* and an appropriate question word *in situ*, i.e. a question word appears in the same position as a corresponding non-question word in a non-question sentence. The question word, *nani* 'what' in (16) below appears in the same position as *hon* 'book' in (14) above. Compare also the positions of *ken-ni* 'to Ken' in (14) and *dare-ni* 'to whom' in (17). This type of language is more common than the English type of language which requires an interrogative noun to appear at the beginning of a question (Dryer 2008c).

(16) *hanako-wa ken-ni   **nani-o**   yarimashita   ka*
     (name)-TOP (name)-DAT what-ACC give:POL:PAST Q
     '**What** did Hanako give to Ken?'

(17) *hanako-wa **dare-ni** hon-o   yarimashita   ka*
     (name)-TOP who-DAT   book-ACC give:POL:PAST Q
     '**To whom** did Hanako give a book?'

When the question word corresponds to the subject, the topic marker *wa* cannot be used. This is because, as noted earlier, *wa* requires the noun phrase be identifiable/definite, but the referent of a question word is by definition non-identifiable/indefinite.

(18) ***dare-ga*** *ken-ni   hon-o   yarimashita   ka*
     who-NOM   (name)-DAT book-ACC give:POL:PAST Q
     'Who gave a book to Ken?'

Alternatively, (18) may be expressed by a cleft focus construction (Chapter 11 §3.3), as shown in (19).

(19) *ken-ni   hon-o   yatta   no wa **dare** desu ka*
     (name)-DAT book-ACC give:PAST NML TOP who   COP   Q
     'Who gave a book to Ken?'
     (lit., 'The one who gave a book to Ken is who?')

4.9 Japanese is a consistent "head final language." The verb is the head with respect to its arguments. Thus, in sentences with the basic constituent order, the verb appears at the end of the sentence. The noun is the head in a noun phrase. Thus an adjective and a relative clause precede the head noun as shown in (20) and (21) below. This type of language is common among the OV type languages like Japanese, though OV languages which put a modifier after the head noun (i.e. the [Noun–Adjective] and [Noun–Relative clause]) are equally common (Dryer 2008b, 2008d). Notice also there is no relative pronoun in a relative clause construction in (21). (See Chapter 9 for these and other noun modification constructions.)

(20) *[takai]   [hon]*
     expensive book
     'an expensive book'

(21) *[hanako ga   katta]   [hon]*
     (name)   NOM buy:PAST book
     'the book which Hanako bought'

4.10 Japanese is an "agglutinative language," and has developed a rich array of verbal suffixes. The tense and negative polarity are such suffixes. (22) is a past, affirmative sentence, while (23) is its negative counterpart. Here each suffix is separated with a hyphen.

(22) *kono inu-wa sakana-o tabe-**ta***
This dog-TOP fish-ACC eat-PAST
'This dog ate fish.'

(23) *kono inu-wa sakana-o tabe-**na-katta***
This dog-TOP fish-ACC eat-NEG-PAST
'This dog did not eat fish.'

Suffixes also code such information as voice and modality among other things, and they can be stacked upon each other as shown in (24) (Chapter 5).

(24) *tabe-sase-rare-taku-nakat-ta*
eat-CAU-PSS-DES-NEG-PAST
'(I) did not want to be made to eat.'

4.11 Japanese employs compositional expressions for "obligation," "permission," and "prohibition." In other words, while these meanings are expressed in a mono-clausal construction with modal verbs in English such as 'may' and 'must,' in Japanese they are expressed in a bi-clausal construction. In these compositions, actions are expressed by a clausal proposition (affirmative or negative) with the *-te* form and followed by an adverbial particle *wa* or *mo*. The sentence is concluded by an evaluative predicate (cf. Akatsuka & Clancy 1993; Clancy et al. 1997; Kurumada & Iwasaki 2011). Some of these have more colloquial alternatives.

(25) **Obligation**
[*ikanakute wa*] [*naranai/ikenai*]
go:NEG:TE TOP become:NEG:NONPAST/go:POT:NEG:NONPAST
'(One) must go.' (Lit. '(One's) not going is no good.')

cf. (colloquial form): *ikanakucha.*
go:NEG:TE:TOP
'(I) must go.'

(26) **Permission**
[*itte mo*] [*ii*]
go:TE also good:NONPAST
'(You) may go.' (Lit. '(Your) going is also good.')

(27) **Prohibition**
[*itte wa*] [*naranai/ikenai*]
go:TE TOP become:NEG:NONPAST/go:POT:NEG:NONPAST
'(You) mustn't go.' (Lit. '(Your) going is no good.')

cf. (colloquial form): *itcha dame.*
go:TE:TOP no.good
'(You) shouldn't go.'

Conditional forms are also used in similar constructions.

(28) **Opinion**
[*ittara*]   [*komaru/dame*]
go:COND   inconvenienced/no.good
'Don't go.'
(Lit. 'If (you) go, I would be inconvenienced/it would be no good.')

[*ittara/ikeba/ikuto*]   [*ii*]
go:COND/go:COND/go:COND   good
'Why don't go.'
(Lit. 'If (you) go, it would be good.')

4.12   Japanese is a "clause chaining language" (Chapter 12 §3). Several medial clauses (e.g. clauses ending in the *-te* form) may be strung together and concluded by a final clause containing tense information. In (29) below, three medial clauses are chained together before the sentence is concluded by the final clause. Notice also in (29) that the noun phrase *boku* 'I' (the agent of the four actions) is mentioned only once, and is subsequently not mentioned (i.e. ellipsis).

(29)   *boku-wa   kinoo   asa   roku-ji   ni   okite,*
       I(male)-TOP   yesterday   morning   six-o'clock   DAT   get up:TE

ha-o   migaite,
tooth ACC   brush:TE

koohii-o   nonde,
coffee ACC   drink:TE

sugu   dekaketa
immediately   go.out:PAST

'Yesterday, I got up at 6 in the morning, brushed my teeth, drank coffee, and went out right away.'

The sentence above is of a spoken register and uses the *-te* form (*okite, migaite, nonde*) for clause combining. In the written register, a different medial form, the infinitive form (*oki, migaki, nomi*) can also be used.

CHAPTER 2

Writing system

1. Early history

Japanese learned how to write down information linguistically from China,[1] which had a fully developed writing system by the late Shan dynasty (14th–11th century BCE) (Norman 1988:58). Chinese characters started to appear in the Japanese archipelago as early as the 1st and 2nd centuries CE. First, they came in the form of inscriptions on coins and official seals brought over from Chinese continent, and later on bronze mirrors and swords (Oshima 2006:3–4, 18–38; Lurie 2011:17–20, 83–105).[2] With assistance from Korean scribes, the Japanese began to harness characters for their own purposes during the *Kofun* period (mid 3rd–late 6th centuries), especially after the 5th century. In the process of domestication of characters, the Japanese developed a system of *kundoku* (訓読) to read and understand the text produced in China (e.g. Kin 2010:12–91; Lurie 2011:169–212).[3] The practice of *kundoku* had substantial influence on the development of the writing system that emerged in Japan.

---

1. The labels "Japan/Japanese" and "China/Chinese" are employed in this section as an abbreviated means to refer to the geographical areas of parts of present-day Japan and China and the peoples who lived there, though they are not appropriate in a strictly historical context.

2. The coins that were brought to Japan were made in *Qin* and *Han* dynasties (the 3rd century BCE through the 3rd century CE) of China. The most famous seal from the early period is an official seal given to the king of *Na* of *Wa* (an early Chinese name for Japan) by the *Han* Dynasty. Bronze mirrors (*dookyoo* 銅鏡) were also brought in from China, and played an important role for introducing characters to Japan. They were later produced in Japan. The front side is polished for reflection, but on the back side were inscribed various designs and words noting the place and year of production, the name of the producer, and also, in some cases, auspicious words. Inscribed swords dating from the late 4th century to the 5th century have been found from *Kyūshū* to the eastern part of *Honshū* (Lurie 2011:85–95). A particularly important sword (late 5th century) was discovered at the *Inariyama Kofun* 稲荷山古墳 (grave mound) in Saitama Prefecture near Tokyo. It bears a description of a long genealogy of an indigenous king's subject in 115 characters, providing crucial information about the pronunciation of Japanese names during that period.

3. *Kundoku* is a kind of simultaneous interpretation. A reader receives sentences written in Chinese as an input and produces Japanese sentences as an output. Lurie describes *kundoku* in terms of the following three simultaneous processes: "(1) associate logographs of Chinese origin with Japanese words and (2) transpose the resulting words into Japanese order while (3) adding necessary grammatical elements, thereby producing an actual or imagined vocalization

By the mid 7th century, the Japanese were using characters more widely and for varied purposes. This is attested by *mokkan* (木簡) 'wooden tags', rectangular pieces of wood (10–30 cm × 3–4 cm), which were first produced during the pre-Nara period (before the 8th century). On *mokkan*, such materials as work orders, receipts, brief notes between officials, dictionary entries, and poems were recorded (Inukai 2006: 20–21; Kinsui et al. 2008: 43; Lurie 2011: 121–5). As many *mokkan* pieces were from the pre-Nara period, they provide vital information about the initial stage of the development of writing in Japan in the original (rather than copied) forms.

By the 8th century, characters were employed in writing texts of substantial length. *Kojiki* (古事記) 'Records of Ancient Matters' (712 CE) and *Nihon Shoki* (日本書紀) 'Chronicles of Japan' (720 CE) are records of histories and myths surrounding the birth of Japan. From the point-of-view of a history of writing in Japan, this is a period of experimentation. At the time these texts were compiled, the indigenous *kana* syllabaries (§4) had not yet been developed, thus Chinese characters were not only used to write texts in the Chinese style, but also used for writing texts according to the Japanese syntax. While *Nihon Shoki* predominantly followed literary Chinese both syntactically and stylistically, *Kojiki* (except for the introduction which follows the literary Chinese style) was written with a mixture of Japanese and Chinese syntactic patterns with characters occasionally used as phonetic symbols (see §3 below) (Miller 1967: 31–32; Lurie 2011: 230, 237).[4] *Man'yōshū* (万葉集) 'Collection of Myriad Leaves' (759 CE) is an anthology of poems with more than four thousand entries. All the poems are written in a Japanese style following the Japanese word order, but recorded with characters, each of which represents either a syllable of Japanese without a meaning attached (i.e. the "sound" of *ya*) or a meaning/reading unit in Japanese (e.g. the "word" *yama* 'mountain').[5] These systems associated with characters are taken up in §3 and §4 in more detail.

---

in Japanese" (2011: 175). The second process was necessary because the word orders are different between the two languages. While Chinese is an SVO language, Japanese is an SOV language. When Japanese writers wrote their sentences, they gradually shifted the word order from SVO to SOV through the practice of *kundoku*, i.e. from Chinese to Japanese syntax. In some cases, both word orders were mixed in one text, showing Japanese writers' attempt to harness a writing system developed in a foreign country to suit their own language. See note 4 directly below and §4.

4. The mixed style found in *Kojiki* is traditionally called *hentai kanbun* 変体漢文 (modified Chinese sentences), but more recently the label, *kanshiki wabun* 漢式和文 (Japanese sentences in Chinese style) is gaining popularity among specialists. The new term acknowledges that these sentences are an early attempt to write Japanese sentences using Chinese characters, though with varying success (Yamaguchi 2006: 48).

5. According to Lurie (2011: 271), only about a quarter of the poems in *Man'yōshū* use characters phonetically (i.e. *Man'yōgana* – see below).

2. The current system

The current Japanese writing system is built upon three major sets of symbols, *kanji* (Chinese characters), *hiragana*, and *katakana*. *Kanji* is a written symbol representing a word (morpheme), while *hiragana* and *katakana*, collectively known as *kana*, are phonetic based symbols. Not only does Japanese have the three sets of symbols, but also, and more significantly, it mixes them systematically in normal writing. The mixed use is a consequence of an initial adoption of Chinese characters and the subsequent developments of *hiragana* and *katakana* based on those characters. The *kanji-kana* mixed writing system has a long history going back over thirteen hundred years. Both *kanji-katakana* and *kanji-hiragana* mixtures were employed until the mid 20th century, but the current practice is a *kanji-hiragana* mixture with the supplementary use of *katakana*. As described below, it is a general rule in modern Japanese that content words either of native or Sino-Japanese origins are written in *kanji*, function words such as case particles and inflectional endings in *hiragana*, and non-Chinese loan words and most, if not all, sound-symbolic words such as onomatopoeia in *katakana*. To a much lesser degree, the Roman alphabet may also be employed, especially for abbreviations such as "DNA," "DVD," and "ASEAN" (Association of Southeast Asian Nations). Numbers are written either in *kanji* (一、二、三、四、五 ...) or Arabic numerals (1, 2, 3, 4, 5 ...) depending on the orientation of the text presentation (vertical or horizontal, respectively).

Sentences are written vertically from top to bottom, and each line is read from right to left ((a) in Diagram 1). This mode of writing has been used throughout the history of Japanese and is still used in most types of modern writing including newspapers, magazines, and novels, but it is also possible to use the Western style of arrangement, with sentences being written horizontally from left to right, especially in scientific writings and some textbooks ((b) in Diagram 1). The horizontal system is also used for text messages on the mobile phone and some other text communication devices.

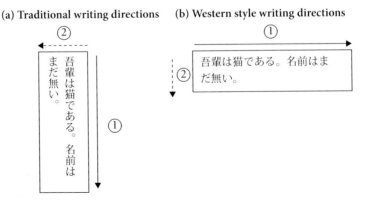

Diagram 1. Directions of writing in modern Japanese

The horizontal orientation is adopted in the example sentences in this chapter as shown below.

兄は新しい家具を買った。
'My elder brother bought new furniture.'

There are no spaces inserted between words in a sentence. However, the sequence of a noun written in *kanji* followed by a grammatical particle written in *hiragana* can, to some extent, indicate phrasal boundaries. The above sentence is repeated below with transliteration in *romaji* (Roman letters). Here, **BOLD CAPITAL LETTERS** indicate *kanji*, small letters indicate *hiragana*, spaces show word boundaries, and square brackets phrasal units.

兄は　　　　新しい　　　　家具を　　　　買った。
[ANI wa]　　[ATARAshii]　[KAGU o]　　[KAtta]
[eld.bro. TOP]　[new]　　　[furniture ACC]　[buy:PAST]
'My elder brother bought new furniture.'

As already noted, *kanji* are usually employed to write content words either of native or Sino-Japanese origins. This includes nouns (e.g. *ANI* 'elder brother' (native) and *KAGU* 'furniture' (Sino Japanese)), and the unchanging parts of verbs (e.g. *KA-* as in *KA-tta* 'bought') and adjectives (e.g. *ATARA-* in *ATARA-shii* 'new'). *Hiragana* symbols are used, as also noted above, to write function words such as particles (e.g. *wa* and *o*) and inflectional endings (e.g. *-shii* in *ATARA-shii* and *-tta* in *KA-tta*). It was noted above that *katakana* symbols are employed in modern Japanese to write words (mostly nouns) of non-Chinese foreign origin (mostly English), such as ***roketto*** 'rocket,' as well as sound-symbolic (onomatopoeic) words such as ***byuun*** (noise of a fast moving object). In the following example, *katakana* words are represented in **bold small underlined letters**, *kanji* in **BOLD CAPITAL LETTERS** and *hiragana* in small letters. (NOM = nominative case marker; SSW = sound-symbolic word; QT = quotative marker).

ロケットが　　ビューンと　　飛び立った
[**roketto** ga]　[**byuun** to]　[TObi-TAtta]
[rocket NOM]　[SSW QT]　　[fly-depart:PAST]
'A rocket flew off with the sound of *byuun*.'

3. *Kanji*: Chinese characters

The use of *kanji* in Japanese is significantly complicated compared to their use in the Chinese language. The first reason for this is that the Japanese have adopted a writing system designed for a foreign language which has very different phonological and morphosyntactic features. Chinese characters are symbols that represent words (or morphemes), and package both semantic and phonetic values. For example, the Chinese character 毛

means 'hair' and is pronounced as /moo/.⁶ In one method, Japanese directly imported the original semantic-phonetic pairing from Chinese, which is represented here as; 毛 = {hair : /moo/}. This method is known as the *on* reading, and paved the way for many borrowings from Chinese throughout the history of the Japanese language. In another method, characters' meanings were paired up with Japanese words (sounds). The meaning of 'hair' is signified by the word (sound) /ke/ in Japanese. Thus this semantic-phonetic pairing structure can be represented as; 毛 = {hair : /ke/}. This method is known as *kun* reading. In yet another method, the semantic value is completely stripped off and only the sound value of a character is adopted through the principle known as "rebus" (Miller 1967:98–9).⁷ This can be represented by the structure, 毛 = {___ : /moo/}.⁸ The characters used in this third way are called *Man'yōgana* (万葉仮名), because they were used frequently in the *Man'yō-shū* (万葉集) anthology of poems. In summary, 毛 can be given three different structures as follows.

	character		meaning	:	sound
Kun reading	毛	=	{hair	:	/ke/}
On reading	毛	=	{hair	:	/moo/}
Rebus reading	毛	=	{___	:	/moo/}

In general, the *on* reading is chosen when *kanji* characters appear in compounds. In the example sentence given earlier, 家, which is part of the compound 家具, is read as *ka* (the *on* reading). The *kun* reading is chosen when a *kanji* character stands in isolation, so in the sentence on the next page, the same character 家 is read as *ie* with the *kun* reading, which means 'house'. In fact all the *kanji* used in this sentence are read with the *kun* reading, since they stand alone and not in a compound.

---

6. /moo/ is an approximation of the original Chinese pronunciation, cf. Modern Mandarin /máo/, Modern Cantonese /mou/ with low falling tone.

7. The rebus principle, for example, takes a symbol such as 👁 to represent the homophonous word "I." In this process the meaning of 'eye' (a body part) is completely ignored and only its sound is borrowed to represent an unrelated word 'I.' A more elaborate use of rebus known as *gisho* 戯書 'playful writing' was also adopted in the early times. For example, 十六 represents number 16, but is used to represent 'a lion.' This is because 16 is the product of 4 × 4, and 4 in *on* reading is *shi*. Thus, 4 × 4 can be read as *shi shi* which is homophonous with 'lion' (cf. Kinsui et al. 2008:37).

8. Reading 毛 as /moo/ is based on the character's *on* reading. The rebus principle may also use the *kun* reading of a character, though not as frequently as the *on* reading based rebus. One interesting example is 庭, the meaning of which is 'garden,' and the *kun* reading of which is /niwa/. The meaning is ignored to render a particle sequence of /ni wa/ (locative particle + topic marking particle) (Miller 1967:98; Habein 1984:12).

兄は　　　　　新しい　　　　家を　　　　　買った。
[ANI wa]　　　[ATARAshii]　[IE o]　　　　[KAtta]
[eld.bro. TOP]　[new]　　　　[furniture ACC]　[buy:PAST]
'My elder brother bought a new house.'

The second source of complication for the use of *kanji* in the Japanese context is the fact that the same *kanji* may have been introduced to Japan at several different times in history. The three distinct historical/geographical groups of *kanji* are *Go-on* (呉音) (from the Wu dialect of southern China in the 5th through 6th centuries), *Kan-on* (漢音) (Tang Dynasty, 7th through 9th centuries), and *Tōsō-on* (唐宋音) (Hangchow dialect, 14th through 16th centuries) (Miller 1967: 101–12). *Kan-on* is the most significant variant for the Japanese system. In contrast, the number of *Tōsō-on* is extremely small compared to the other two. The character 家, for example, had been introduced as *ke* (*Go-on*) in the 5th through 6th centuries before it was (re-)imported as *ka* in the Tang Dynasty period (*Kan-on*).[9] The older pronunciation is kept in some compounds, such as 家来 *ke.rai* 'a retainer, or a subordinate *samurai*.' The *Tōsō-on* variety was brought over by Japanese Buddhist monks who went to China to study Zen Buddhism. The character 行 'go,' for example, has three *on* readings: *gyoo* (*Go-on*), *koo* (*Kan-on*), and *an* (*Tōsō-on*) in addition to its *kun* readings. The table below shows some examples of various *on* readings and one or more *kun* readings. It shows the true complexity of *kanji* as used in the Japanese writing system.

Table 1. Different readings of *Kanji* characters

	Go-on (5th–6th C.)	*Kan-on* (7th–9th C.)	*Tōsō-on* (14th–16th C.)	*Kun*
家 (house)	ke	ka	–	ie
日 (sun, day)	nichi	jitsu	–	hi
人 (person)	nin	jin	–	hito
行 (go)	gyoo	koo	an	ik-u/okona-u
京 / 經 (capital/sutra)	kyoo	kee	kin	
子 (child)	shi	shi	su	ko

It should be also noted that only about 60% of the regularly used *kanji* (see the next paragraph) have both *on* and *kun* readings, and about 38% have only an *on* reading and 2%

---

9. The character 家 had the sound value of /kǎ/ in the *Chang-an* dialect of the *Tang* Dynasty (618–906 CE), cf. modern Mandarin /jiā/; modern Cantonese /ga/ with high tone.

only a *kun* reading.[10] The writer/reader, thus, must have a comprehensive knowledge of all *kanji* in order to write/read them properly.

Together with the complications in *kanji* use noted above, the very large number of *kanji* employed in the language makes the writing system extremely demanding. The new *Jōyō Kanji* (常用漢字) List (the List of Characters of General Use) published in 2010 recommends 2136 characters be used in general publication. In addition, a set of close to one thousand *kanji* are allowed for personal and place names, and even some that are not on these lists are used in specialized writings. Although it is reported that if one knows the 500 most frequently used *kanji*, one can understand 75% to 80% of the content of newspaper articles (Saiga 1995), the use of *kanji* seems to be on the rise due in part to easier production of *kanji* via increasingly sophisticated computer technology. Currently the Japanese Industry Standard (JIS) lists nearly seven thousand characters that can be used on computers and word processors.[11]

4. *Kana*

Kana includes two types of syllabaries known as *hiragana* and *katakana*. They developed from *man'yōgana*, which, as noted earlier, are the characters used according to the rebus principle. *Man'yōgana* allowed writers to represent any indigenous Japanese words using the sound of appropriate characters. For example, the Japanese word, *iro* 'color' was written as 伊呂 because the first character has a sound similar to *i* (Mandarin 'yī'; Cantonese 'yi' with high tone) and the second a sound similar to *ro* (Mandarin 'lǚ'; Cantonese 'leui' with low rising tone). *Man'yōgana* was also necessary to write grammatical particles and auxiliary verbs, which are not present in Chinese (Oshima 2006: 53, 86). This use of *man'yōgana* made it possible for writers to write sentences and poems according to the Japanese syntax more easily. At the beginning, a variety of characters were selected to represent a syllable; e.g. 阿, 安, 英, 足 all have similar sound to *a*, and were used to represent this sound. Out of *man'yōgana* came two different *kana* systems, *hiragana* and *katakana*. As these new systems matured, one character came to exclusively represent a particular

---

10. The 2% of characters that have only *kun* reading are mostly *kokuji* (国字), those characters devised in Japan based on the principles of character design. Some examples are: 峠 *tooge* 'mountain pass,' 榊 *sakaki* '(a type of tree), 畑 *hatake* '(agricultural) field.' However, there are some *kokuji* that have an *on* reading, 働 'work' *hatara(ku)* (*kun* reading); *dou* – (*on* reading).

11. The other side of the coin is the decline in ability to produce *kanji* characters among Japanese (Gottlieb 2000: 96–104).

syllable in each syllabary.[12] *Hiragana* letters were developed through the cursive writing of *man'yōgana* (e.g. hiragana あ 'a' is based on the cursive writing of the *kanji* 安), and was mainly used by women writers to write poems, Japanese style narratives and diaries. In contrast to *hiragana* which was based on the whole character, *katakana* letters were based on a portion; the *katakana* ア 'a' is based on the left side component of the *kanji* 阿.[13] *Katakana* was developed as a practical device used by Buddhist monks mainly to supply particles and verbal endings when reading sutras written in Chinese, which lack such morphemes. Note the *kanji* 安 has the meaning of 'peace' and 阿 of 'hills, bent shape' among others, but the two *kana* symbols have nothing to do with these meanings; they simply represent the sound *a* which is associated with the *kanji*, i.e. the rebus reading.

Hiragana and *katakana* are both syllabaries. This means that each symbol represents a syllable-like unit of "mora," i.e. either a single vowel (V) or a consonant-vowel combination (CV) (see Chapter 3 §3 for more details). In modern Japanese there are 46 basic symbols in each set of *hiragana* and *katakana* (see Appendixes at the end of this chapter). The symbols in each set are traditionally organized in the "Chart of 50 Sounds (*gojuu-on-zu* 五十音図)," a five by ten grid.[14] The chart is believed to be based on the principle of Indic phonological arrangements which was introduced by Buddhist monks in the 11th century. The chart starts with the five vowel symbols (あ, い, う, え, お, – *a, i, u, e, o*, respectively) followed by thirty nine symbols that represent the CV syllables.[15] In addition to these there is one special vowel symbol, を, which is pronounced identically as お 'o' in modern Japanese, but used exclusively to write the accusative case marking particle. Finally, there is one symbol (ん) that represents a moraic nasal (/N/), which can stand alone as an independent mora. (Chapter 3, §1.2.4).

The *kana* symbols with the voiceless consonants, e.g. /t, k, s, h/, will take a diacritic (two dots on the right shoulder of the symbol) to represent moras with voiced consonants, /d, g, z, b/, respectively: e.g. か /ka/ → が /ga/; た /ta/ → だ /da/. Due to the historical sound mergers between [ʑi] and [zi], and [dzu] and [zu] as described in Chapter 1, the symbols じ and ぢ have the same sound values as /ji/, and ず and づ as /zu/. (Normally the first

---

12. Actually the process of selection took a long time, and it was only 100 years ago when one *kana* came to represent one particular mora (syllable) exclusively (Takashima 2001:93).

13. Some *katakana* such as モ are based on the whole character, 毛. This character was also the basis of *hiragana* も.

14. The number of symbols was never 50, but it is nevertheless called the "Chart of 50 sounds" to reflect the five rows and ten columns.

15. The consonants are ordered as follows: k, s, t, n, h, m, y, r, w. The last three (y, r, w) are non-nasal sonorants. The first six consonants are arranged from those pronounced at the back of the mouth to front of the mouth; velar (k)-alveolar (s/t/n)-bilabial ('h'/m). From the historical evidence, 'h' can be interpreted as 'p' (bilabial).

member of the pairs is used to write these syllables. See Chapter 3 for detailed phonetic descriptions of these sounds.) Another diacritic, or a small circle on the right shoulder of a symbol, may be added only to an *h*-initial *kana* to convert it to a *p*-initial sound: は /ha/ → ぱ /pa/. The special treatment of the *h*-initial *kana* is the result of a series of sound changes involving these phonemes (Chapter 1 §3). When the two dots are added to は, the sound changes to a voiced sound, ば /ba/. Other notable conventions include the use of reduced size や (ya) for palatalized consonants (e.g. きゃ kya, きゅ kyu, きょ kyo) and the use of reduced size つ (tsu) for geminate consonants (e.g. あった atta, まっか makka).

Unlike English alphabetic symbols where the same letter may be pronounced differently, e.g. the letter *i* can be read in different ways as in *i*sland, h*i*t; or the letter *a* can be read differently in f*a*ther, h*a*te, w*a*nted, m*a*ny, vill*a*ge and b*a*d, etc. each *kana* symbol has a one-to-one correspondence to a specific sound; the hiragana い is always pronounced as [i]. The only exceptions to this very general rule are the use of *hiragana* as grammatical particles. The topic marking particle and the directional marking particles are pronounced *wa* (わ) and *e* (え), respectively. However, they are represented by *hiragana* that are pronounced as *ha* (は) and *he* (へ), respectively. In addition, the accusative marking particle pronounced as *o* is written by the special hiragana を. These irregularities are due to historical sound changes.

As noted several times already, *katakana* is used to write loan words, mostly from English (Chapter 4 §1), e.g. カメラ (*ka me ra*) 'camera,' コーヒー (*ko o hi i*) 'coffee' and mimetic words (Chapter 4 §3.1), e.g. キーン (*ki i n*) '(sharp sound),' ボチャン (*bo cha n*) '(splashing sound).' The tradition of using *katakana* to write foreign words began in the early Meiji period with some experimental structures. One way is to spell Western words in *katakana* and to provide the meaning in Sino-Japanese (Ezaki 2010; Seeley 1991: 137); '(government) minister' is written as "ミニストル (大臣)" in which the first spelling gives the original pronunciation, (*mi ni su to ru*), and the second Chinese compound, 大臣 (*dai jin*) is a semantic translation. Another is to write a concept using *kanji* and to provide the original pronunciation of a Western word in *katakana* on top of the character; 眞理 (the *kanji* is read as (*shin ri*) 'truth' but the *katakana* reading-guide forces this to be read as *toruusu*.

The mimetic category is a completely open class, and in the recent years a large number of new mimetic words have been created as the popularity of comic books that use many such words is on the rise (see Chapter 4 §3.1). *Katakana* also provides an easy entryway of foreign words into Japanese, and many new foreign words are now in use due to the increased intensity of globalization in Japan. This is inevitable, but some Japanese have started to become concerned about the unregulated use of foreign words written in *katakana*, especially when they are used for the purpose of public welfare. The National Institute for Japanese Language and Linguistics (国立国語研究所) suggested alternatives to *katakana* words using *kanji*, whose meanings are more accessible to Japanese readers.[16] In the next two examples, the item to the left of the arrow is a *katakana* rendition of an English word, and the item to the right of the arrow is a recommended writing using Sino-Japanese vocabulary using Chinese characters.

ケア (ke a) 'care' → 手当て *te – ate* (hand – apply)
     or 介護 *kai – go* (assist – protect)
インフォームドコンセント (i n fo o mu do ko n se n to)
     'informed consent'
     → 納得診療 *nat.toku-shin.ryoo* (satisfaction – medical treatment)
     or 説明と同意 *setsu.mee to doo.i* (explanation and consent)

Appendix A (Hiragana chart)

	basic 46 symbols						symbols with diacritics				
	a	i	u	e	o		a	i	u	e	o
	あ	い	う	え	お						
k-	か	き	く	け	こ	g-	が	ぎ	ぐ	げ	ご
s-	さ	し	す	せ	そ	z-	ざ	じ	ず	ぜ	ぞ
t-	た	ち	つ	て	と	d-	だ	***ぢ	***づ	で	ど
n-	な	に	ぬ	ね	の						
h-	は	ひ	ふ	へ	ほ						
						b-	ば	び	ぶ	べ	ぼ
						p-	ぱ	ぴ	ぷ	ぺ	ぽ
m-	ま	み	む	め	も						
y-	や		ゆ		よ						
r-	ら	り	る	れ	ろ						
w-	わ	*(ゐ)		*(ゑ)	**を						
	***ん										

---

16. See http://www.ninjal.ac.jp/gairaigo/

Appendix B (Katakana chart)

	basic 46 symbols							symbols with diacritics				
	a	i	u	e	o			a	i	u	e	o
	ア	イ	ウ	エ	オ							
k-	カ	キ	ク	ケ	コ		g-	ガ	ギ	グ	ゲ	ゴ
s-	サ	シ	ス	セ	ソ		z-	ザ	ジ	ズ	ゼ	ゾ
t-	タ	チ	ツ	テ	ト		d-	ダ	****ヂ	****ヅ	デ	ド
n-	ナ	ニ	ヌ	ネ	ノ							
h-	ハ	ヒ	フ	ヘ	ホ							
							b-	バ	ビ	ブ	ベ	ボ
							p-	パ	ピ	プ	ペ	ポ
m-	マ	ミ	ム	メ	モ							
y-	ヤ		ユ		ヨ							
r-	ラ	リ	ル	レ	ロ							
w-	ワ	*(ヰ)		*(ヱ)	**ヲ							
	***ン											

*ゐ/ヱ, ヰ/ヱ are no longer used as the syllables they represent (/wi/, /we/) have disappeared from the language.

**を/ヲ (/o/, same pronunciation as お/オ, used only as accusative marker).

***ん/ン (/N/, mora nasal; see Chapter 3 §1.2.4).

****ぢ/ヂ (/ji/, same pronunciation as じ/ジ; see Chapter 3 §1.2.2).

****づ/ヅ (/zu/, same pronunciation as ず/ズ; see Chapter 3 §1.2.2)

CHAPTER 3

Sounds

This chapter first provides inventories of vowels, consonants and semivowels based on their articulatory properties (phonetics) and on their phonemic analysis (phonology). Then it discusses two important sound modifications of high vowel devoicing (phonological) and sequential voicing (morphophonological). Also discussed are the structures of syllables, moras, and feet, as well as the suprasegmental phenomena of pitch accent and intonation.[1]

1. The inventory of sounds

1.1 Vowels

There are five short vowels in modern Standard Japanese.

Table 1. Japanese vowels

Phonemic Representation	Phonetic Representation	Romanization
/i/	[i]	*i*
/e/	[e]	*e*
/a/	[a]	*a*
/o/	[o]	*o*
/u/	[ɯ]	*u*

Circles on the chart of cardinal vowels on the next page indicate the relative positions of the Japanese vowels. These five vowels have the following phonetic characteristics: (i) [e] and [o] are articulated with a slightly lower tongue position compared to their corresponding cardinal vowels, (ii) the low back vowel [a] is produced at a slightly more forward

---

[1] This chapter assumes basic familiarity with phonetics and phonology, and the concepts and terminologies used in these fields, including the IPA (International Phonetic Association) symbols. Refer, among others, to International Phonetic Association (1999), Radford et al. (1999), Ladefoged (2001), Hayes (2009), for a general introduction, and Tsujimura (2007) and Vance (2008) for Japanese. Tsujimura (2007: 106–7) gives a useful reading list for Japanese phonetics and phonology.

position than the cardinal vowel, (iii) lip rounding for [o] is weak, and (iv) the high back vowel [ɯ] is unrounded but with compressed lips and without spreading, and is produced at a significantly more forward position than the cardinal vowel (Okada 1999: 118, Vance 2008: 54–5).

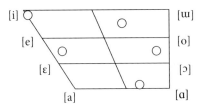

Figure 1. Japanese vowels compared to the cardinal vowels

Vowel length is phonemic, and thus can indicate meaning differences. The symbol [:] represents lengthening of the preceding sound, and the /H/ symbol lengthening of the preceding vowel phoneme.

Table 2. Short and long vowels

/ki/	[ki]	'tree'	/kiH/	[ki:]	'key'
/ke/	[ke]	'hair'	/keH/	[ke:]	'small size car'
/ka/	[kɑ]	'mosquito'	/kaH/	[kɑ:]	'(crow's cry)'
/ko/	[ko]	'child'	/koH/	[ko:]	'in this way'
/ku/	[kɯ]	'nine'	/kuH/	[kɯ:]	'air, space'

All combinations of different vowels are possible (e.g. /ao/ 'blue', /uo/ 'fish', /ie/ 'house', /oi/ 'nephew'). However, a few facts should be noted.

– Some combinations such as /o/-/u/ are very rare within a morpheme boundary. Though some words have a *kana* spelling that suggests an /o/-/u/ sequence, the actual pronunciation, even in careful speech, is always /oH/ [o:].[2] In the following examples, a morpheme boundary is indicated by a period; e.g. *ou* おう /oH/ [o:] 'king' and *kousui* こうすい /koH.sui/ [ko:sui] 'fragrant.water > perfume'.
– The /o/-/u/ sequence, however, can appear freely across a morpheme boundary; e.g. *koushi* こうし /ko.uši/ [kouši] 'baby.cow > calf', which clearly contrasts with *koushi* こうし /koH.ši/ [ko:ši] 'lecture.teacher > lecturer'.

---

2. Vance notes that *souru* ソウル /souru/ [soɯrɯ] 'Seoul' is one of the rare examples that contains the [ou] segment within the morpheme boundaries, though many speakers pronounce this word with a long vowel, /soHru/ [so:rɯ] (2008: 67–8).

- Additionally, the combination, /o/-/u/, appears regularly in the verb citation form, which consists of the verb root and the nonpast tense suffix -*u*; e.g. *ou* おう /o.u/ [oɯ] 'to chase,' *sou* そう /so.u/ [soɯ] 'to be or stay beside.' Thus, though /oH/ 'king' and /o.u/ 'chase' are spelled identically in *kana* (*ou* おう), they are not homonyms.
- When the sequence is /a/-/i/, it is always [ɑi] whether they appear within or across a morpheme boundaries. Vance notes that *haisha* 歯医者/ha.i.ša/ (tooth.medicine. person) 'dentist' and *haisha* 敗者/hai.ša/ (loose.person) 'defeated person' are homonyms as both /a.i/ and /ai/ are produced identically.
- In contrast, /ei/ may fluctuate between [ei] and [e:] even in careful pronunciation within morpheme boundaries; e.g. *heiwa* 平和 /hei.wa/~/heH.wa/ ([he̞iwɑ]~[he̞:wɑ]) 'peace,' *suiei* 水泳 /sui.ei/~/sui.eH/ ([sɯie̞i]~[sɯie̞:]) 'swimming,' *keiki* 刑期 /kei.ki/~/keH.ki/ ([ke̞iki]~[ke̞:ki]).
- However, monomorphemic loan words such as *keeki* ケーキ 'cake' are usually not pronounced with [ei], but with a long vowel; *keeki* ケーキ /keHki/ [ke:ki] 'cake.' Thus, *keiki* けいき（刑期）'prison term' and ケーキ *keeki* 'cake,' can be distinguished in principle, but when 'prison term' is pronounced as /keHki/ [ke:ki], the distinction will vanish (cf. Vance 2008: 63–4).
- It should be noted further that as in the case of the /o/-/u/ sequence, the vowel lengthening does not happen across a morpheme boundary for /e/-/i/; *tameiki* 溜め息 /tame.iki/~*/tame.Hki/. Thus, *meiru* 滅入る /me.i.ru/~*/me.H.ru/ 'feel depressed' and *meeru* メール /meHru/ 'e-mail' are not homonyms.
- There is one further complication. There seems to be a trend to pronounce monomorphemic loan words such as *meeku* メーク /meHku/ [me:kɯ] 'make-up' as /meiku/ [meikɯ]. This attests to the unstable status of the /e/-/i/ sequence in Japanese phonology.

1.2 Consonants

1.2.1 *Phonetic inventory*

The twenty-thee consonants and two semivowels (glides) used in modern Standard Japanese are listed with IPA symbols in Table 3 on the next page. Some minor allophonic variants are excluded.[3] The symbol to the left of the slash (/) in this table is a voiceless

---

[3] Vance (2008: 236) lists twenty five consonants and two semivowels. The alveopalatal fricative [z] is not included in Vance's list of consonants (but see the discussion on this consonant below). The three consonants that Vance includes, but are not included here, are palatalized allophones of velar consonants; [kʲ, gʲ, ʲ]. These will be included in the phonemic analysis of the velar consonants in §1.2.2.

consonant and the symbol to the right is the voiced counterpart. The symbol (–) indicates a gap in the Japanese phonology.

Table 3. Phonetic inventory of consonants and glides

	Bilabial	Alveolar	Alveo-palatal	Palatal	Velar	Uvular	Glottal
stops	p / b	t / d			k / g		
fricatives	ɸ / –	s / z	ɕ / ʑ	ç / –			h / –
affricates		ts / dz	tɕ / dʑ				
tap		– / ɾ					
nasals	– / m	– / n	– / ɲ		– / ŋ	– / N	
semivowels				– / j	– / ɰ		

Brief descriptions of notable features of some consonants are given below.

- The voiceless stop consonants, [p, t, k], in Japanese are articulated with less aspiration at the beginning of a word compared to their English counterparts; e.g. [t⁽ʰ⁾ai] 'sea bream' (Japanese) vs. [tʰai] 'tie' (English) (Okada 1999: 118).
- The voiceless bilabial fricative [ɸ] is produced by blowing out air through a narrow opening made by bringing the lips close together, e.g. *hude* [ɸɯde] 'brush.' This can be contrasted with the English [f] (voiceless labio-dental fricative), which is produced by bringing the lower lip close to the upper teeth.
- The consonant, [ɕ], is a voiceless "predorso-alveopalatal" fricative found in the initial consonant of the word *shita* [ɕita] 'below.' This is close to the "post-alveolar" fricative, [ʃ], found in the initial consonant of the English word 'she,' but its constriction is made across the entire area between the post-alveolar and palatal regions, in comparison to [ʃ] which is made at the post-alveolar region (Vance 2008: 14).
- The voiceless predorso-alveopalatal [ɕ] is also very close to the dorso-palatal fricative [ç]. It is found in the final consonant of the German word 'ich,' but in Japanese it only occurs as the initial consonant of a syllable ending in [i], as in *hito* [çito] 'person.'[4]
- The voiced predorso-alveopalatal fricative [ʑ] also exhibits a constriction area larger than the post-alveolar [ʒ].

---

4. Because some speakers in the area known as *shimtamachi* in Tokyo produce [ɕ] very close to the palatal fricative [ç], confusion between a pair like *hiroi* [çiroi] 'wide' and *shiroi* [ɕiroi] 'white' could occur.

- The alveopalatal affricates [cc̦] (e.g. *cha* [cc̦a] 'tea') and [ɟz] (e.g. *juu* [ɟzɯː] 'ten') are similarly close to the post-alveolar affricate, [tʃ] (e.g. English '<u>ch</u>oke') and [dʒ] (e.g. English '<u>j</u>oke'), respectively.
- The symbol [ɾ] represents the apico-alveolar tap, e.g. *ringo* [ɾĩŋgo] 'apple,' *nori* [noɾi] 'seaweed.' To produce this sound, the tip of the tongue moves from a relaxed position not touching anywhere in the mouth and makes a single quick "tapping" motion against the alveolar region. This can be contrasted with [d] (e.g. English 'dingo') for which the tip of the tongue is placed at the alveolar ridge at the onset of pronunciation. The tap appears for a word-internal 't' in American English (e.g. 'naugh<u>t</u>y,' 'bu<u>tt</u>er').
- The uvular nasal [ɴ] is produced by making a closure at the uvular with the back of the tongue and letting the air flow from the nose. This only appears at the end of a word before a pause as in *hon* [hõɴː] 'book.'
- The velar semivowel, [ɰ], has no associated lip rounding.

1.2.2 *Phonemic analysis*

The consonants and semivowels in Table 1 can be organized into distinct phonemes through phonemic analysis. There are nineteen regular phonemes and three special phonemes. The special phonemes are /H/, /N/, and /Q/. The phoneme /H/ which indicates a long vowel has been already mentioned in the section on vowels above, and the other two will be analyzed separately in detail below (§1.2.4).

/ p, t, c, č, k, b, d, g, s, š, f, h, z, ǰ, r, m, n, y, w, H, N, Q /

Table 4 on the next page shows all nineteen regular phonemes along with allophonic variants and their phonological environments. All regular consonants can appear as the initial consonant of a syllable. It accounts for both conservative and innovative pronunciations, the latter of which includes commonly used loanwords. Older speakers may only operate within the conservative variety while younger generations utilize both varieties. However, the table excludes rare sounds that only appear in extremely special vocabulary, such as transliteration of foreign names (see Vance 2008: 74–93, for a more detailed description of the distribution of phones). Some description of selected phonemes follow the table.

- [p] and [b] appear before all five vowels.
- [t] and [d] only appear before [a], [e], and [o] in the conservative variety of the language, but [ti]/[di] and [tɯ]/[dɯ] are possible in the more innovative system. In Table 4, parentheses are used to indicate recent syllable status, so [i] and [ɯ] in the parentheses show that they appear only in recent loanwords; [paːti̠ː] 'party,' [tatɯː] 'tattoo,' [ci̠di̠ː] 'CD,' 'Hindu' [çĩnːdɯː], and the French loan, 'deux' [dɯː] as in 'un-deux-trois.'

Table 4. Phonemes and allophones

Phonemic Rep.	Phonetic Rep.	Romanization	Examples in Romanization	Meaning
/p/	[p] //_ ɑ, i, ɯ, e, o	p	*paipu*	'pipe'
/b/	[b] //_ ɑ, i, ɯ, e, o	b	*ba*	'place'
/t/	[t] // _ ɑ, (i), (ɯ), e, o	t	*ta*	'rice field'
/d/	[d] // _ ɑ, (i), (ɯ), e, o	d	*dare*	'who'
/k/	[k] // ɑ, ɯ, e, o [kʲ] // - i	k k	*kami* *kimi*	'hair' 'you'
/g/	[g] // ɑ, ɯ, e, o [gʲ] // - i [ŋ] (sporadically observed word internally)	g g g	*ga* *gimu* *shitagi*	'moth' 'obligation' 'underwear'
/h/	[h] // _ ɑ, e, o [ç] // _i	h h	*haha* *hito*	'mother' 'person'
/f/	[Φ] // _(ɑ), (i), ɯ, (e), (o)	f	*furo*	'bath'
/s/	[s] // _ɑ, ɯ, e, o	s	*sake*	'rice wine'
/š/	[ɕ] //_ ɑ, i, ɯ, (e), o	sh	*shako*	'garage'
/c/	[ts] // _ ɯ	ts	*tsume*	'finger nail'
/z/	(word initial, after N or Q) [dz] // # _ ɑ, ɯ, e, o (word internally) [z] // V _ ɑ, ɯ, e, o	z z	*zaru* *kazaru*	'basket' 'to decorate'
/č/	[cɕ] //_ ɑ, i, ɯ, e, o	ch	*cha*	'tea'
/j/	[ɟʑ] //_ ɑ, i, ɯ, e, o ([ʑ] sporadically observed word internally)	j	*jimi* *kujaku*	'dull tone' 'peacock'
/r/	[ɾ] //_ ɑ, i, ɯ, e, o	r	*rajio*	'radio'
/m/	[m] //_ ɑ, i, ɯ, e, o	m	*mata*	'again'
/n/	[n] //_ ɑ, ɯ, e, o [ɲ] // _ i	n n	*natsu* *ninjin*	'summer' 'carrot'
/y/	[j] // _ ɑ, ɯ, o	y	*yama*	'mountain'
/w/	[ɰ] // _ ɑ	w	*waki*	'side'

- The phonemes /k/ and /g/ have plain [k]/[g] and palatalized [kʲ]/[gʲ] allophones, the latter of which appears before the vowel [i] and semivowel [j].
- The phoneme /g/ is pronounced unequivocally as [g] at the word-initial position (e.g. *gakkoo* /gaQkoH/ [gɑk::o:] 'school'). It is also pronounced as such in the intervocalic environment, but some speakers may pronounce it as [ŋ] (e.g. *shoo-gakkoo*

/šoHgaQkoH/ [ɕo:ɡak::o:] ~ [ɕo:ŋak::o:] 'elementary school') (Hibiya 1995; Vance 2008: 214–222).[5]
- As will be discussed below, [ŋ] also appears at the end of a syllable as an allophone of the moraic nasal, /N/.
- The phoneme /h/ can be established for three allophones in the conservative phonological system; [h] before [a], [e], [o] ([ha] 'tooth,' [he] 'fart,' [ho] 'sail'); [ç] before [i] or a palatal glide [j] ([çi] 'fire,' [çjo:] 'leopard'); and [ɸ] before [ɯ] ([ɸɯne] 'boat').
- However, [ɸ] may appear before other vowels in recent loan words; e.g. [ɸaito] 'fighting spirit,' [ɸi:to] 'feet,' [ɸeminĩ:n] 'feminine,' [ɸõn:to] 'font.' Thus, in the innovative variety of the language, [ɸ] is given the status of phoneme, /f/, as shown in Table 4.
- The phoneme /s/ is realized as [s] before [a], [ɯ], [e], and [o], and as [ɕ] before [i]. The syllable [si] is a foreignism even in a more innovative system. Thus, one of the above examples is [ɕi:di:], not *[si:di:] 'CD.'
- However, [ɕ] can also appear before other vowels though the syllable [ɕe] can only appear in loan words, and thus is given the status of a phoneme /š/. e.g. /šamiseN/ [ɕamiseN] (a three string instrument), /šumi/ [ɕɯmi] 'hobby,' and /šodoH/ [ɕodo:] 'calligraphy,' and /šepaHdo/ [ɕepa:do] 'shepherd (dog) – a loan word.'
- The affricate [ts] appears only before [ɯ], and is given the status of the phoneme /c/. English phonotactics does not allow this consonant to appear at the syllable-initial position,[6] but Japanese only allows it in this environment, /cuki/ [tsɯki] 'moon,' /cunami/ [tsɯnami] 'tidal wave.'[7]
- [dz] and [z] are allophones of the phoneme /z/. They both appear before all vowels except [i]. However, the affricate [dz] appears word-initially or immediately following /N/ or /Q/ (e.g. zoo /zoH/ [dzo:] 'elephant,' *hon-zan* /hoNzaN/ [hõn:dzãn:] 'main

---

5. There are three types of speaker with respect to the use and non-use of the word medial, syllable initial velar nasal [ŋ] (Vance 2008: 214–222). Consistent nasal speakers always pronounce *shoo-gakkoo* as [ɕo:ŋak::o:], while consistent stop speakers always pronounce it as [ɕo:ɡak::o:]. Non-consistent speakers could use either form. Many Tokyo dialect speakers used to be consistent nasal speakers, but younger speakers are mostly consistent stop speakers. This change is believed to have started with those who were born around 1930 because the speakers in this age group were relocated out of Tokyo during the Pacific War (1941–45) to the area where [g] rather than [ŋ] appears in the relevant phonological environment. See Hibiya 1995 and Kindaichi 1942 for a historical discussion of this change.

6. A famous example of the syllable initial [ts] in English is found in the loanword, 'Tsetse fly.'

7. In a more innovative variety, other vowels appear with [ts]. An Italian loanword, *kantsōne* [kantso:ne] 'Canzone' is a famous example that contains the combination of [ts] and [o] (Vance 2008: 84). However, the other syllables, [tsa], [tsi], [tse], may be found only in transliteration of foreign names, as in [tse:tse:bae] 'Tsetse fly.' See Note 6 above.

mountain'), while [z] appears in other word-medial environments (e.g. *ko-zoo* /kozoH/ [kozo:] 'baby elephant').⁸

- The affricates [cɕ]/[ɟʑ] appear before all five vowels, and are given the status of the phoneme, /č/ and /ǰ/, respectively.
- The phoneme /ǰ/ is realized in all environments as [ɟʑ] in careful pronunciation; *jika* /ǰika/ [ɟʑika] 'current price,' *kaji* /kaǰi/ [kaɟʑi] 'fire'; *juu* /ǰuH/ [ɟʑɯː] 'ten,' *shinju* /šiNǰu/ [ɕinːɟʑɯ] 'pearl.'
- However, /ǰ/ may be realized as [z] in a rapid speech by at least some speakers; /kuǰira/ [kɯɟʑiɾa] ~ [kɯziɾa] 'whale,' /kuǰaku/ [kɯɟʑakɯ] ~ [kɯzakɯ] 'peacock.'
- The tap [ɾ] /r/ appears before all five vowels.
- While the bilabial nasal [m] /m/ appear before all five vowels, [n] and [ɲ] are in complementary distribution; [ɲ] before [i] and [n] elsewhere. ([ɲ] also appears as an allophone of the special phoneme /N/. See below, §1.2.4.)
- The two semivowels (or glides) have defective distributions; the palatal semivowel [j] (phonemically /y/) appears only before the vowels /a, u, o/ (/yama/ [jama] 'mountain'), and the velar semivowel, [ɰ] (phonemically /w/) only appears before /a/ (/kawa/ [kaɰa] 'river').

1.2.3 *Syllable-initial clusters*

Japanese does not allow consonant clusters, but it does allow the combination of a consonant and the palatal semivowel [j] at the syllable-initial position, represented as C[j]. The consonant (C) is one of the following phones: [p, b, t, (d), k, g, (ɸ), ç, m, ɲ, r].⁹ As mentioned before, the velar consonants, [k]/[g], are palatalized before [j] and [i], and pronounced as [kʲ]/[gʲ]. In fact, any consonants preceding [i] or [j] will be under the influence of palatalization, but such effect is negligible on consonants with places of articulation other than velar, and thus the [ʲ] notation is often excluded for non-velar stops in broad transcription (Vance 2008: 92). Thus, phonetically the syllable-initial cluster, C[j], will be represented as [pj, bj, tj, (dj), kʲj, gʲj, (ɸj), çj, mj, ɲj, rj]. Phonemically the cluster, C/y/, is represented as /py, by, ty, (dy), ky, gy, (fy), hy, my, ny, ry/. C[j] can only be followed by [a], [ɯ], or [o] due to [j]'s defective distribution mentioned earlier. In *kana* spelling, this cluster is represented by an /i/ ending syllable followed by

---

8. The variation, however, may be conditioned more strongly by the time allotted for articulation; /z/ is realized as [dz] even in the non-initial environment if enough time is provided for pronunciation, e.g. *ko-zoo* /kozoH/ [kodzo:] 'baby elephant' (Maekawa 2010: 373).

9. Phones [d] and [ɸ] may form the C[j] cluster with the vowel [ɯ], but the distribution is extremely limited; /dyuetto/ [djɯet:o] 'duet' and /fyuHzyoN/ [ɸjɯːɟʑoNː] 'fusion' are rare examples.

a small-size symbol for /ya/, /yu/ or /yo/; *ki* き followed by small *ya* や will produce *kya* きゃ /kya/.

きゃく	/kyaku/	[kʲjakɯ]	'guest'
ぎゃく	/gyaku/	[gʲjakɯ]	'opposite'
びゃくい	/byakui/	[bjakɯi]	'(doctor's) white robe'
みゃく	/myaku/	[mjakɯ]	'pulse'

Kana spelling (e.g. しゃ *shi* – small *ya*, ちゃ *chi* – small *ya*, じゃ *ji* – small *ya*) also suggests that the same cluster appears with alveopalatal consonants, [ɕ, ʑ, cɕ, ɟʑ], but as these consonants are already near the palatal region, palatalization is non-effective, and the [ʲ] and /y/ notations are inappropriate. Also, unlike other consonants, these consonants allow all five vowels following them. For example, as noted earlier, [ɕ] can appear in [ɕa, ɕi, ɕɯ, ɕe, ɕo], though [ɕe] is only found in loan words.

しゃしん	/šašiN/	[ɕaɕĩN:]	'picture'
しんじゅ	/šiNju/	[ɕĩN:ɟʑɯ]	'pearl'
しゅじん	/šujiN/	[ɕɯʑĩN:]	'husband'
シェパード	/šepaHdo/	[ɕepa:do]	'Sheppard' (loanword)
しょどう	/šodoH/	[ɕodoH:]	'calligraphy'
ちゃいろ	/čairo/	[cɕairo]	'brown'
チェック	/čeQku/	[cɕek::ɯ]	'check' (loanword)
ジェット	/jeQto/	[ɟʑet::o]	'jet' (loanword)

1.2.4 *Special phonemes*

In addition to the consonants given in Table 4, there are three special phonemes; /H/, /N/, and /Q/, which appear at the end of a syllable. The vowel-lengthening phoneme /H/ was introduced in §1.1, and /N/ and /Q/ were briefly mentioned in §1.2.2. This section discusses /N/ and /Q/ further. To do so, a preliminary discussion of mora is in order, though a more complete discussion of mora is given in §3 below. A mora is a unit of measure conceived to be constant in temporal duration. A syllable consisting of a single vowel (V), a consonant-vowel (CV), or a consonant-semivowel cluster with a vowel (C/y/V) all constitute one mora. Thus, /a/, /ma/ and /mya/ would have the same duration in time (at least psychologically perceived so) and constitute one mora each.

The special phoneme /N/, known as the moraic nasal, constitutes a mora by itself. It has six allophonic variants, [N:, n:, m:, ɲ:, ŋ:, ũ̃:], which nasalizes the preceding vowel.[10] A long consonant notation with [:] reflects the full mora length.

---

10. [ŋ] will be palatalized as [ŋʲ] before a palatalized consonant, /hoNki/ [hoŋʲ:kʲi].

Table 5. Moraic nasal

$$/N/ \rightarrow \begin{cases} [\text{N:}] & // \_ \# \\ [\text{n:}] & // \_ [\text{t, d, n, ɾ, ts, dz}] \\ [\text{m:}] & // \_ [\text{p, b, m}] \\ [\text{ɲ: }] & // \_ [\text{cç, ɟʑ}] \\ [\text{ŋ:}] & // \_ [\text{k, g}] \\ [\text{ɰ̃:}] & // \_ [\text{s, z, ɕ, ç, h, ɸ }]; // \_ \text{vowel} \end{cases}$$

The moraic nasal is pronounced as a uvular nasal ([N]) before a pause. Thus, /saN/ 'three' is pronounced as [sãN:] in an isolated environment. When followed by a stop, tap, affricate, or another nasal consonant, it becomes a nasal consonant with its place of articulation assimilated to that of the following consonant; [n:, m:, ɲ:, ŋ:]. Note that the syllable will carry an extra length when the following consonant is a nasal sound (compare [sãm:bai] and [sãm::ai]).

/saN/	=	[sãN:]
three		
/saN/ + /dai/	=	[sãn:dai]
three classifier for large machines		
/saN/ + /bai/	=	[sãm:bai]
three classifier for glassfuls of liquid		
/saN/ + /mai/	=	[sãm::ai] 'three sheets'
three classifier for flat object		
/ saN / + /čaku/	=	[sãɲ:cçakɯ] 'the third place'
three classifier for arrival order		
/saN/ + /gai/	=	[sãŋ:gai] or [sãŋ:ŋai]
three classifier for floors		

When /N/ is followed by a fricative or vowel, it is generally pronounced as the long nasalized dorso-velar semivowel, [ɰ̃:] (Vance 2008: 97–9). This sound is similar to the uvular nasal ([N:]), but unlike the uvular nasal, it allows air flow through the oral cavity as well as the nasal cavity. The moraic nasal never syllabifies with the following vowel or semivowel. Thus, /saN + i/ 'the third place' is pronounced as [sãɰ̃:i] with three moras, but never becomes [sa ni] with two moras.

/saN/ + /i/	=	[sãɰ̃:i]	'the third place'
three classifier for rank			
/saN/ + /eN/	=	[sãɰ̃:ẽN:]	'three *yen*'
three yen (Japanese currency)			
/saN/ + /sai/	=	[sãɰ̃:sai]	'three years old'
three classifier for age			

The other special phoneme is the moraic obstruent represented by /Q/. This phoneme corresponds to the initial part of a geminate consonant, as found in ke*kk*a 'result,' and ki*pp*u 'ticket,' which are phonemically transcribed as /keQka/ and /kiQpu/, respectively. In other words, /Q/ is realized as the same consonant as that which follows /Q/. This phoneme corresponds to the duration of a mora. In other words, like /N/, /Q/ is represented as a long consonant in the phonetic transcription; e.g. [p:], which has the same length as [pa]. Thus, the word /haQpa/ 'leaf' has three moras, [ha] – [p:] – [pa], and is transcribed as [hap::a]. In *kana* spelling, the moraic obstruent is represented by a reduced size つ *tsu*.

はっぱ	/haQpa/	[hap::a]	'leaf'
ばった	/baQta/	[bat::a]	'grass hopper'
あっち	/aQči/	[ac::ɕi]	'over there'
みっつ	/miQtu/	[mit::sɯ]	'three'
がっき	/gaQki/	[gak::i]	'musical instrument'
ほっさ	/hoQsa/	[hos::a]	'seizure'
ざっし	/zaQši/	[dzaɕ::i]	'magazine'

2. Sound modification

2.1 High vowel devoicing

The short high vowels [i] and [ɯ] tend to be devoiced in the following two environments in Tokyo Japanese: (i) between two voiceless consonants and (ii) between a voiceless consonant and a pause. It should be noted that this sound modification is not absolute, and there are many variations that can occur in these environments (Vance 2008: 206–14). The devoiced vowels are represented by [i̥] and [ɯ̥] in the following list of words.

/hito/	[ç i̥ to]	'person'
/huta/	[ɸ ɯ̥ ta]	'lid'
/šuto/	[ɕ ɯ̥ to]	'capital city'
/čikyuH/	[cɕ i̥ kʲɯ:]	'earth'
/kutu/	[k ɯ̥ ts ɯ̥]	'shoes'
/kiči/	[kʲ i̥ cɕ i̥]	'military station'
/kiši/	[kʲ i̥ ɕ i̥]	'shore'
/kuši/	[k ɯ̥ ɕ i̥]	'comb'

The palatalization on [kʲ] before [i] is retained even if the vowel becomes devoiced, thereby maintaining distinct auditory impressions between the last two words above (Vance 2008: 209).

2.2 Sequential voicing (*Rendaku*)

Sequential voicing, known as *rendaku* 連濁 in the Japanese scholarship, refers to a phenomenon in which a voiceless consonant becomes voiced when morphemes are combined. More specifically, the initial voiceless consonant of the second morpheme of a compound word or that of a prefixed base become voiced under certain circumstance (Vance 1987: 133–148). For example, the word, /keri/ 'kick' becomes /-geri/ in the compound /mawaši-geri/ 'turn kick,' and /taiko/ 'drum' becomes /-daiko/ in the prefixed word /ko-daiko/ 'small dram.' There are five patterns of sequential voicing as shown below.

/k/ → /g/
/t/ → /d/
/c/, /s/ → /z/
/č/, /š/ → /ǰ/
/h/ → /b/

The last pattern above involves the change of /h/ to /b/ instead of the expected change of /p/ to /b/. This is because the original form of the modern Japanese /h/ is believed to have been /p/ (e.g. Yanagida 1975: 103–8, see also Chapter 1 §2). In the examples below, the affected consonants are underlined and boldfaced.

/k/ → /g/: /moči/   + /kome/   = /moči +gome/
            'rice cake' 'rice'   'sticky rice'

/t/ → /d/: /ama/   + /tare/   = /ama+dare/
            'rain'   'drop'   'rain drop'

/c/ → /z/: /oboro/   + /cuki/   = /oboro+zuki/
            'haze'   'moon'   'hazy moon'

/s/ → /z/: /mesu/   + /saru/   = /mesu+zaru/
            'female'   'monkey'   'female monkey'

/č/ → /ǰ/: /hana/   + /či/   = /hana + ǰi/
            'nose'   'blood'   'nose bleeding'

/š/ → /ǰ/: /neko/   + /šita/   = /neko + ǰita/
            'cat'   'tongue'   'sensitive to hot food'

/h/ → /b/: /koi/   + /hito/   = /koi+bito/
            'love'   'person'   'lover'

Although the process of sequential voicing is not a totally regular morphophonological process, a few conditions that trigger or prohibit the process have been identified. Lyman's Law states that a voiced obstruent in the second member of a compound or the prefixed base inhibits the process. Notice that the voiced obstruent /g/ in /kagi/ and /z/ in /kaze/ block sequential voicing in the examples below.

/ai/   + /kagi/   = /ai+kagi/   (S.V. blocked)
'matching'   'key'   'duplicate key'
cf./aka/   + /kumi/   = /aka+gumi/   (S.V. applied)
'red'   'group'   'red group'

/oo/	+	/<u>k</u>aze/	=	/oo+kaze/	(S.V. blocked)
'big'		'wind'		'strong wind'	
cf. /oo/	+	/<u>k</u>oe/	=	/oo+goe/	(S.V. applied)
'big'		'voice'		'loud voice'	

However, there are some exceptions to Lyman's Law, as with /nawa+**b**ašigo/ 'rope ladder' (= /nawa/ + /<u>h</u>ašigo/) (Vance 1987: 137). Because of the voiced obstruent /g/ in /hašigo/, the process should fail, but it in fact proceeds. On the other hand, /kumi/ 'group, class room' does not contain a voiced obstruent, but a compound with /ni/ '#2' will not add voicing to /k/, /ni + kumi/ (not */ni + gumi/) 'class room #2'. (cf. /san-nin + kumi/ 'threesome' > /san-nin + gumi/).

Another condition is that the process applies mainly to the native vocabulary (N_{at}). Thus, if the second element is a Sino-Japanese (SJ) or foreign (F) word, the process will be blocked. See the examples below.

/biNboH/	+	/<u>s</u>amurai/	=	/biNboH + **z**amurai/ (S.V. applied)
'poor (SJ)'		'warrior (N_{at})'		'*samurai* with no money'
cf. /biNboH/	+	/<u>š</u>ačo/	=	/biNboH + šačo/ (S.V. blocked)
'poor (SJ)'	'comp. president (SJ)'			'a president with no money'
cf. /biNboH/	+	/<u>s</u>anta/	=	/biNboH + santa/ (S.V. blocked)
'poor (SJ)'	'Santa Claus (F)'			'Santa Claus with no money'

This condition, however, is by no means absolute. To a lesser degree, the voiceless consonant of a second Sino-Japanese compound element undergoes sequential voicing (Vance 1996).

/wata/	+	/<u>k</u>aši/	=	/wata + **g**aši/
'cotton (N)'		'candy (SJ)'		'cotton candy'
/otama/	+	/<u>š</u>akuši/	=	/otama + **j**akuši/
'ball (N)'		'dipper (SJ)'		'tadpole'
/suimiN/	+	/<u>h</u>usoku/	=	/suimiN + **b**usoku/
'sleep (SJ)'		'lack (SJ)'		'lack of sleep'

In addition, as briefly noted earlier, and the following examples further show, the same native compound element or homophonous words may or may not undergo the process.[11]

/nori/	+	/<u>k</u>oši/	=	/nori + **k**oši/ (not */nori + goši/)
'ride (N)'		'passing (N)'		'riding beyond one's destination'
/yoi/	+	/<u>k</u>oši/	=	/yoi + **g**oši/ (not */yoi + koši/)
'evening (N)'	'passing (N)'			'overnight'

---

11. Some linguists also note another condition called the "Right-Branch Condition." This condition applies to compounds consisting of three or more bases. See Otsu (1980) and Ito and Mester (1986).

/hito/	+	/k̲oe/	=	/hito + k̲oe/ (not */hito + g̲oe/)
'one (N)'		'voice (N)'		'a single call'
/hito/	+	/k̲oe/	=	/hito + g̲oe/ (not */hito + k̲oe/)
'people (N)'		'voice (N)'		'people's voice'
/ika/	+	/s̲aši/	=	/ika + s̲aši/ (not */ika + z̲aši/)
'squid (N)'		'pierce (N)'		'squid *sashimi*'
/me/	+	/s̲aši/	=	/me + z̲aši/ (not */me+s̲aši/)
'eye (N)'		'pierce (N)'		'dried sardines strung together'

Some family names have two versions.[12]

/yama/	+	/s̲aki/	=	/yama + s̲aki/
/yama/	+	/s̲aki/	=	/yama + z̲aki/
'mountain (N)'		'top (N)'		'Mr. Mountaintop (surname)'

3. Syllable, mora, and foot

Phonological segments such as vowels and consonants are combined to form a larger phonological entity. To analyze larger phonological entities, three different prosodic units have been proposed and used in Japanese phonology. The most familiar unit is the syllable, though its precise definition is unclear, and its significance in Japanese phonology is sometimes disputed (Labrune 2012: 147–161). A syllable can be seen as consisting of three parts: "onset," "nucleus" and "coda." The only obligatory element in the syllable is the nucleus, which is a vowel, either short, long or diphthongal. A syllable can be either an open or closed type. English words such as 'cap' and 'big' consist of one closed syllable each, while words such 'pie' and 'key' consist of one open syllable each. Japanese syllables are mostly of the open type, but the moraic nasal /N/ and the moraic obstruent /Q/ can stand as the coda to form a closed syllable; e.g. *kin* /kiN/ 'gold' consists of one closed syllable and *kitto* /kiQto/ 'surely' consists of one closed syllable /kiQ/ and one open syllable /to/. In the English syllable structure, the nucleus and the coda constitute a unified constituent called a "rhyme," which plays a crucial role in creating metric structures in poetry and songs.

In Japanese the structure of syllable seems important also, as the coda influences the quality of nucleus in some cases. The nasal assimilation triggered by the coda /N/ is one such example; the nuclear vowel [a] will be nasalized in the word 'three' /saN/ [sã̃ɴ:]

---

12. There is an informal report on the distribution of *Yamazaki* and *Yamasaki* based on the telephone directory entries. According to the report, *Yamazaki* with the *rendaku* is found more frequently in eastern Japan while *Yamasaki* without *rendaku* more in the western Japan. This trend is also apparent for the contrast between *Nakajima* and *Nakashima* (Nikkei Shinbun, 4/20/2012, http://www.nikkei.com/).

(§1.2.4). However, Labrune (2012:152) notes that this kind of anticipatory assimilation is not only triggered by a coda element but also by any subsequent segment. For example the nasal consonant will undergo place assimilation triggered by the onset consonant [b] in the following syllable in *san-bai* 'three bottles' /saNbai/ [sãm:bɑi]. A more convincing argument for the importance of syllable will be discussed in conjunction with the accent placement rule (§4 below).

In addition to the open and closed syllable types, another distinction can be made for Japanese syllable structure, the short versus long syllables. A short syllable (also known as "light syllable") consists of an optional onset consonant, either a simple consonant (C), or a consonant-semivowel cluster (C/y/), and an obligatory vowel (this vowel may be a diphthong – see below). For presentational purposes, in this section, C stands for both C and C/y/. The parentheses around C show that C is optional.

    Short syllable structure:
    (C)   V

In contrast, a long syllable (or "heavy syllable") includes an additional final element, which is either /N/, /Q/, /H/, or /V_j/ (a different vowel from the nucleus) (Vance 2008:118).[13]

    Long syllable structure:
    (C) V_i /N, Q, H, or V_j/

Words like *pan* /paN/ 'bread' and *hou* /hoH/ 'cheek' have one long syllable each. The word, *kitto* /kiQto/ 'surely' consists of one long syllable (/kiQ/) and one short one (/to/). A crucial question arises when the sequence of V_i and V_j is examined because the sequence can be analyzed either as a sequence of two short syllables or a single long syllable. In other words, what is the proper analysis of words such as *kai* 'shellfish,' *koe* 'voice,' *gia* 'gear,' *kao* 'face,' and *kau* 'to buy'? According to Vance (2008:133–8), when the second vowel is a high vowel, /i/ or /u/, the sequence tends to form a diphthong. Thus, *kai* and *kau* are words with one short syllable with a diphthongal vowel, /kai/ and /kau/, respectively, while the others are words with two short syllables, i.e. /ko-e/, /ka-o/, and /gi-a/.

The syllable can be further analyzed by the second type of analytical unit known as "mora". Mora is a temporal unit conceived to be constant in temporal duration (§1.2.4). It consists of the non-optional vowel (V) preceded by an optional consonant, which is of either the palatalized (C/y/) or non-palatalized (C) variety. A mora may also consist solely of a moraic nasal (N), or a moraic obstruent (Q). These three types of mora can be represented as follows. Again, C stands for both C and C/y/.

---

[13]   There are also the extra long syllables which consist of one additional element at the end., e.g. *hoon* /hoHN/ 'horn'.

Mora structure:
   a. (C) V
   b. N
   c. Q

What this means is that the five words mentioned above (*kai* 'shell fish,' *koe* 'voice,' *gia* 'gear,' *kao* 'face,' and *kau* 'to buy') all consist of two moras (i.e. *ka-i, ko-e, gi-a, ka-o,* and *ka-u*) despite the fact that some are one-syllable words (i.e. *kai, kau*) and others two syllable-words (*ko-e, gi-a, ka-o*).

The significance of moras is readily seen in the way the *kana* symbols are structured. That is, one mora corresponds to one *kana* syllabary symbol (e.g. あ, か, ん, the small sized っ), except when it contains a cluster with /y/, in which it is spelled using a combination of one *kana* (e.g. き) and one reduced-size *kana* representing *ya, yu* or *yo* (e.g. きゃ – §1.2.3 above and Chapter 2).[14] The mora is used in the metric system of traditional Japanese poetry such as *haiku* and *waka*, which require a specified number of moras per line. The *haiku*, for example, is composed of three lines containing five, seven and five moras, respectively. This is shown in the *haiku* below, by the master *haiku* poet, Matsuo Basho (1644–1694).

ふるいけ や		
fu ru i ke ya	(5 moras)	An old pond
old pond PARTICLE		
かわず とびこむ		
ka wa zu to bi ko mu	(7 moras)	a frog jumps in
frog jump into		
みず の おと		
mi zu no oto	(5 moras)	the resonance of water
water GEN sound		

The next is a non-literary piece that takes advantage of the 5-7-5 metric pattern to create poetic illusion. Note that in this piece the 5-7-5 mora pattern can be achieved only if /N/, /Q/ and /H/ are counted as one mora.

ホームラン		
hoHmuraN	(5 moras)	Homerun!
homerun		
やきゅうしょうねん		
yakyuH šoHneN	(7 moras)	A baseball boy
baseball boy		

---

14. Recent loanwords use reduced-size *kana* other than *ya, yu* or *yo*. The following words contain the reduced-size ア (a), イ (i), ウ (u), エ (e) and オ (o); *famirii* ファミリー 'family,' *fiito* フィート 'feet,' *tatuu* タトゥー 'tatoo,' *weetoresu* ウェートレス 'waitress,' *wokka* ウォッカ 'vodka.' Each combination, ファ /fa/ etc. in these examples, constitutes one mora.

にっこりと
<u>niQkori to</u>　　　　　　　　(5 moras)　　smilingly
smilingly

As shown in the analyses of the above *haiku* and non-literary piece, a word may or may not contain the same number of moras and syllables.

かわず
/kawazu/　　　'frog'
3 syllables:　| k-a | w-a | z-u |
3 moras:　　| ka | wa | zu |

ホームラン
/hoHmuraN/　'homerun
3 syllables:　| h-oo | m-u | r-a-N |
5 moras:　　| ho | H | mu | ra | N |

にっこりと
/niQkorito/　　'smilingly'
4 syllables:　| n-i-k | k-o | r-i | t-o |
5 moras:　　| ni | Q | ko | ri | to |

やきゅう
/yakyuH/　　'baseball'
2 syllables:　| y-a | ky-uu |
3 moras:　　| ya | kyu | H |

In Japanese phonology, a third type, or level, of unit has been proposed (Poser 1990). This is the unit of "foot" (or "bimoraic foot") which is made up of two moras (Labrune 2012: 161–174). The foot is a useful unit to account for the "minimality condition" which states that a word must be at least two mora in length. This does not mean that no monomoraic words exist in Japanese; they do (i 'stomach, *ka* 'mosquito'). But the significance of foot can be attested in many phonological phenomena (Tsujimura 2007: 94–104). One is a natural lengthening of a single mora in recitation of numbers. The number 'two,' 'four,' and 'five' are monomoraic words *ni* (2), *shi* (4), and *go* (5), respectively. In recitation, however, the speaker would pronounce them as two-mora words, *nii* (2), *shii* (4), and *goo* (5), respectively; *ichi-nii-san-shii-goo...* '1-2-3-4-5...' The word, *kaoiro* 'facial color,' for example, is a word with two sets of bimoraic foot: *(ka-o) (i-ro)*. The diagram on the next page shows an example of structural analysis using this word. [F = foot, μ = mora].

Crucially, this structural analysis, (ka-o) (i-ro), is different from the one using the syllable as an analytical unit; (ka) – (o) – (i) – (ro). The importance of the notion of foot becomes clearer when a morphological process known as "clipping and compounding" is discussed in Chapter 5 §2.5.

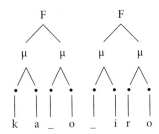

Figure 2. Foot and mora structures for 'kaoiro'

4. Accent

Japanese is a pitch accent language which specifies a tone pattern (or an arrangement of tones in sequence) for an entire word rather than assigning a specific tone for each syllable in a word, as found with a tone language like Mandarin. A pitch accent language like Japanese is similar to a stress accent language like English in that in both types of language the location of accent can be identified within a word. The difference between the two is that a pitch accent language uses the fall in pitch as a marker of accent while a stress accent language uses the stress as a marker of accent locus. For example, the Japanese word for 'rain' is *ame*, which has a pitch fall between the first and second moras. The accent location can be specified by the notation (ˈ) as shown in [aˈme] 'rain.' The English word, 'rainbow,' on the other hand, has the (primary) accent on the first syllable, and is normally specified as [ˈreɪnboʊ]. A word in a tone language, on the other hand, does not have an accent locus, but each syllable is specified with an inherent tone. For example, Thai, being a tone language, specifies a tone for each of the syllables in [fǒn tòk] 'rain fall' with the rising tone on the first syllable and the low tone on the second.

Pitch patterns are one of the most important elements in dividing the Japanese language into different dialects. In the Tokyo accent system, high (H) and low (L) tones are phonemically distinctive.[15] Tones are associated with moras, and an accent is defined as a pitch fall from a high (H) mora to a low (L) mora. The H mora from which a pitch falls is the locus of an accent. If a word is unaccented, there is no pitch fall. In the following discussion, as already noted, an accent fall mark (ˈ) is inserted after the accented mora, as in /kaˈgaku/ 'science' in which the first mora /ka/ bears an accent and the pitch falls from H to L between /ka/ and /ga/. Tone patterns have the function of discriminating otherwise homophonous words (e.g. /aˈme/ 'rain' with H on the first mora and L on the second is distinguished from the unaccented word /ame/ 'candy' which has the opposite tone

---

[15]. The Tokyo accent type is found not only in and around Tokyo, but also in Hokkaido, a large part of northern Honshu, southwestern Honshu, and northeastern Kyushu (Hirayama 1968).

assignments), but, due to a limited number of possible patterns (see below), the functional load of an accent is not very high; /koꜜi/ 'carp,' /koꜜi/ 'love,' /koꜜi/ 'dark (color),' and /koꜜi/ 'Come!' all have the same HL pattern, and cannot be distinguished by accent.[16]

The following four rules will determine the tone patterns of a noun automatically; (i) the initial mora is always L, except when it is itself the locus of an accent, (ii) the tones of the initial and the second moras must be distinct, (iii) there can be at most one accent ("pitch fall") in an accented word, the location of which is lexically specified, and (iv) *all* moras after the locus of the accent bear the L tone, i.e. once the tone goes down to L, it will never rise within the accentual phrase boundary. A four-mora sequence, for example, must be either LHHH, LHLL, LHHL, or HLLL, and the patterns such as *LHLH, *HLHL, or *HLLH are not allowed.[17]

Among the different lexical categories, nouns show the most varied accent patterns (see Vance 2008: 162–180 for a discussion of the accent patterns for verbs and adjectives). For any *n* mora nouns, there are always *n* + 1 possible pitch patterns. (This will be slightly modified shortly.) The following examples show four possible patterns for three-mora words. In addition to the notation in terms of H and L, a numeric notation is also given. For example, (−1) means that the accent locus is the first mora from the end of a word, and (−2) the second mora from the end (penultimate) of a word, and so forth. The unaccented pattern is indicated by (0).

/iꜜnoči/	HLL	(−3)	'life'
/amaꜜdo/	LHL	(−2)	'shutter'
/hukuroꜜ/	LHH	(−1)	'bag'
/miyako/	LHH	(0)	'capital'

Among the examples of three-mora nouns given above, the last two nouns, /fukuroꜜ/ (−1) and /miyako/ (0), have identical tone patterns (LHH). The difference becomes apparent when they are followed by the nominative case marking particle *ga* or the topic marking particle *wa*.

| /fukuroꜜ ga/ | LHHL | 'bag + nominative particle' |
| /miyako ga/ | LHHH | 'capital + nominative particle' |

The difference between the tone patterns (−1) and (0) becomes more evident when comparing two one-mora quasi-homophones such as *hi* /hiꜜ/ 'fire' (−1) vs. *hi* /hi/ 'sun' (0).

---

16. These homophones are distinguished in writing with different Chinese characters; 鯉、恋、濃い、来い, respectively.

17. The description of accentual patterns given here is a traditional one. See Pierrehumbert and Beckman (1988: 25–56), Kubozono (1993: 75, 92), and Vance (2008: 142–198) for more recent accounts of these patterns.

These words cannot be distinguished in isolation. Only when they are followed by a particle such as *ga*, does the distinction emerge.

| /hiˀ ga/ | H L | 'fire + nominative particle' |
| /hi ga/ | L H | 'sun + nominative particle' |

The two notions of mora and syllable discussed in §3 become important when describing pitch patterns in Japanese. First, although a mora bears an accent, the accent-bearing mora must be the nucleus of a syllable. Thus, though special phonemes, /N/, /Q/, and /H/, have the status of a mora, they cannot be the locus of an accent. This means that while a three-mora noun normally allows four possible accentual patterns, as described above, a three-mora noun containing /N/, for example, shows only three possible patterns; a word shape of μ–N–μ (where μ represents a mora, and /N/ a moraic nasal), *LHL is not a possible pattern. However, if the notion of syllable is adopted, a regularity can be captured more easily: an *n*–"syllable" noun always allows *n+1* different accentual patterns. Compare a "two mora, two syllable" word (μ–μ) and a "three mora, two syllable" word (e.g. μ–N–μ). Both have three possible accentual patterns: for the former, (μˀ–μ), (μ–μˀ), or no accent are possible, and, for the latter, (μˀ–N–μ), (μ–N–μˀ), or no accent are possible (i.e. (μ–Nˀ–μ) is not possible).

Second, the second vowel in a vowel sequence can bear an accent only when the two vowels appear in different syllables. Compare *tameiki* 溜め息 /tame.iki/ 'sigh' and *chimeido* 知名度 /či.mei.do/ 'reputation.' Both are four-mora words, but while the former has four syllables, the latter has only three. The initial vowel, /i/, of the second morpheme of *tame.iki* can bear an accent because /e/ and /i/ are in two separate syllables, while /i/ in /mei/ of *chi.mei.do* cannot because /i/ is the second vowel within the same syllable. These facts show the importance of the concept of syllable when considering accent patterns in Japanese.

The next data set also demonstrates the significance of the concept of syllable in Japanese phonology. When the two-mora suffix *-ten* /teN/ 'a (branch) store' is attached to a place name, the last mora of the place name becomes the locus of the accent (i.e. (−3) is automatically assigned for the compound noun), regardless the original locus of accent in the place name, as shown below.

/roQpoNgi/ (0) /-teN/	= /roQpoNgiˀ -teN/ (−3)	'Roppongi Branch'
/seˀto / (−2) /-teN/	= /setoˀ -teN/ (−3)	'Seto Branch'
/toˀčigi/ (−3) /-teN/	= /točigiˀ -teN/ (−3)	'Tochigi Branch'

However, when the last mora of a place name is one of the special moras discussed earlier, the accent shifts to the mora on the left, resulting in a (−4) pattern. This rather complicated situation can be simplified greatly when employing the notion of syllable. It is possible to restate the description more simply; the last "syllable" (rather than the last "mora") of a place name receives the accent when suffixed by *-ten*, and the accent locus is placed on the nucleus of the syllable. It's crucial to note that the accent shifts to the left from the coda within a syllable when the coda is a special mora. If the concept of syllable is not used, the leftward movement is not motivated.

/hoˈNzaN/ (−4)   /-teN/ = */ho N za Nˈ -te N/
  → hoN zaˈN -teN (−4)   'Honzan Branch'

/yuHraˈkučoH/ (−4)   /-teN/ = *yu H ra ku čo Hˈ -te N
  → yuH ra ku čoˈH –teN (−4) 'Yuurakuchoo Branch'

In addition, the notion of syllable simplifies the description of the accent patterns of verbs. Verbs are either accented or unaccented. If accented, the pitch fall occurs either after the penultimate (−2) mora (e.g. /tabeˈru/ 'eat') or the antepenultimate (−3) mora (e.g. /toˈHru/ 'pass'). Using the syllable as a unit, however, these patterns can be simply restated as a pitch fall occurring after the penultimate (−2) "syllable"; |ta| |beˈ| |ru|, |toˈH| |ru|.

5. Intonation

The term 'intonation' is used in at least two different ways in recent studies of Japanese phonetics and phonology. First, it can be considered to be pitch movements which add various meanings and functions to an utterance. Intonation with this definition is termed here the "tail pitch movement (TPM)" or distinct patterns of pitch change observable on the final syllable of an utterance in Japanese (Nagahara and Iwasaki 1995). There are five major distinct tail pitch movements, "setting," "rising," "fall-and-rise," "level," and "rise-and-fall" (cf. Koyama 1997: 99; Venditti 2005: 181–4); these movements are indicated by the notations, (↘), (↗), (∨), (,), and (∧), respectively. Setting intonation, otherwise known as a natural falling intonation, marks an utterance as a statement, while rising intonation indicates a question. For example, the loan word /doˈmino/ '(the game of) dominos' with the instrumental case particle *de* has its inherent accentual pattern, HLL-L. (The sentence *domino de asobu* means '(I) played the game of dominos.') This word may be used as (a) a declarative utterance with a natural falling intonation *domino de(↘)*, '(I tell you I played the game of) dominos,' or (b) as a question with a rising intonation *domino de(↗)*, '(You played the game of) dominos?' If it is uttered with a fall-and-rise pitch movement (∨) as in *domino de(∨)*, it adds an affective overtone of disbelief, or incredulity, 'Really (you played the game of) dominos?' (See Figure 3).[18] The question and incredulity TPMs are also distinguished by the vowel lengthening on the latter.

---

18. The pitch tracks shown in this section were obtained by Praat (http://www.fon.hum.uva.nl/praat/) designed and developed by Paul Boersma and David Weenink of the University of Amsterdam. The pitch displays are presented to give visual impressions of pitch movements only, and are not intended for detailed phonetic analyses.

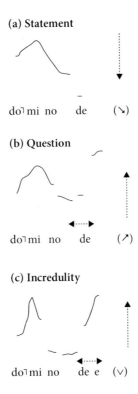

Figure 3. Tail pitch movements (1)

One of the functions of 'rise-and-fall' (∧) pitch movement, especially when accompanied by vowel lengthening, is to signal continuation of a conversational turn (Hashimoto 2009); *domino de* (∧) *asonde* (∧)….'With dominos, we played, and …' This TPM is particularly popular with younger speakers. Level movement (,) is an unmarked movement for continuation which encodes no particular grammatical or affective information; *domino de* (,) *asonde* (,)…; 'With dominos, we played, and …' (Figure 4). Tail pitch movements often appear on the pragmatic particles (*ne, yo, sa* etc.) and other sentence final elements (*deshoo, janai* etc.) (Chapter 14 §3.2). Interaction between these markers and intonation creates various subtle pragmatic indices (Koyama 1997; Vance 2008: 195–8).

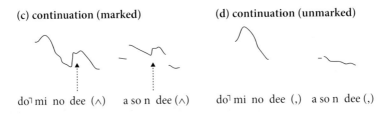

Figure 4. Tail pitch movements (2)

Second, "intonation" may refer to an overall pitch contour covering a larger speech unit, as seen in a study of "intonation phrasing" (Pierrehumbert & Beckman 1988; Kubozono 1993; Venditti 2005).[19] In this line of research, intonation is analyzed as a sequence of smaller prosodic units, such as the accentual and intonation phrases. For example, two accentual phrases, {maʾria no} (girl's name GEN) and {oneʾesan} 'older sister' may be combined to become one intonation phrase when no break is inserted between the genitive phrase and the head noun, [{maʾria no} {oneʾesan}] 'Maria's older sister.' (The curly brackets indicate an accentual phrase and the square bracket an intonation phrase.) Each accentual phrase is shaped by different pitch configurations specified by the accentual patterns of the words involved, but there is always an initial rise at the beginning of an accentual phrase (Kubozono 1993:91; Venditti 2005:175).[20] The pitch rises to a high point on the accented mora, and falls gradually to a low point within an accentual phrase. Thus one accentual phrase has a general pitch configuration as in (a) below.

(a)

Several accentual phrases can be strung together like (b).

(b)

But when they are strung together in one breath, they form an intonation phrase, and the constituent accentual phrases show a stair-like stepping down, as shown in (c). This is due to a mechanical declination which lowers the overall pitches along the time axis.

(c)

When there is a minor break between two accentual phrases, such as a short pause, the one after the break may begin a new intonation phrase as shown in (d). Here, the height of the high pitch in the third accentual phrase is higher than that in the second one.

(d)

---

19. This research program has developed its own system of transcribing the intonation and prosodic structure of spoken utterances, known as ToBI (Tones and Break Indices). See Jun (2005) for details.

20. This rise at the beginning of an accentual phrase can be observed even when the initial word has the accent (H) on the initial mora, as seen in the pitch track of /doʾmino/ in figures above.

The above made-up pitch contours can be described as follows with the curly brackets indicating an accentual phrase and the square bracket an intonation phrase.

(a) [{   }]

(b) [{   }] [{   }] [{   }] [{   }]

(c) [{   } {   } {   } {   } }]

(d) [{   } {   }] [{   } {   }]

Figure 5. Different phrasing patters

Pattern (b) could appear, for example, when one utters the numbers 'one' through 'four' one by one slowly; *ichi*(↘) *nii*(↘) *san*(↘) *shii*(↘). Pattern (c) would appear when one utters the four numbers in one breath; *ich-nii-san-shii* (↘). Pattern (d) would appear when one utters the four numbers in two breath groups; *ich-nii* (↘) *san-shii*(↘).

An intonation phrase is defined as a domain of "accent reduction" (McCawley 1968; Kubozono 1993; Koori 1997).[21] When two accented words appear in sequence within an intonation phrase, the second accent is reduced. Thus, the high pitch on the second mora of *one˺esan* 'older sister' is lowered significantly when following a phrase with an accented word, e.g. *ma˺ria no* (girl's name GEN), compared to when it follows a phrase with an unaccented word, such as *morio no* (boy's name GEN). Compare the pitch peak on *ne* of *one˺san* with respect to that of the initial part of the first phrase, *maria* and *morio* in Figure 6 below.

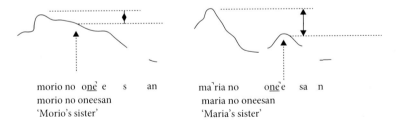

morio no one e   s   an
morio no oneesan
'Morio's sister'

ma˺ria no   one˺e   sa   n
maria no oneesan
'Maria's sister'

Figure 6. Different patterns of accentual phrases within one intonation phrase

In actual speech, speakers produce utterances in terms of the intonation phrase. The intonation phrase, or more commonly known as "intonation unit (IU)" by discourse

---

21. Alternatively, it is defined as a domain of "catathesis" (a down step, or a lowering of pitch range after an accented word) (Poser 1984; Pierrehumbert & Beckman 1988).

oriented researchers (Du Bois et al. 1992; Chafe 1987, 1994; Iwasaki 1993a, 2009), may be marked by the distinct tail pitch movement discussed above (Nagahara and Iwasaki 1995). Figure 7 below shows an overall pitch contour for one long utterance produced by a female speaker, who has started to share her memory of the day when the Japanese Emperor declared defeat in the Pacific War over a radio broadcast: *atashi wa ne, uchi de kiita no ne↗ sono are wa ne↗ hoosoo wa ne↗ kazoku de↘* 'I, you know, heard it at home, you know, that thing, you know, the broadcast (of the Emperor's announcement of the end of the war), you know, with my family.'

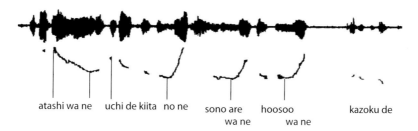

Figure 7. Pitch contours in one long utterance

There are five intonation units in this utterance. The second one consists of two accentual phrases, but each of the rest consists of a single accentual phrase. Each intonation unit is marked by a tail pitch movement, and the entire utterance moves gradually to a lower pitch level due to a mechanical declination. In the representation below each intonation unit is presented on a separate line, and the double slash at the end of the entire string indicates the finality of a long sequence of intonation units.

[{atashi wa ne (,)}]	'I, you know?'
[{uchide} {kiitano ne (↗)}]	'heard it at home, you know?'
[{*sono are wa ne*(↗) }]	'that thing, you know?'
[{ *hoosoo wa ne*(↗) }]	'the broadcast, you know?'
[{*kazoku de* (↘)}] //	'with my family.'

'I heard that thing, the broadcast (of the Emperor's announcement of the end of the war) at home with my family.'[22]

---

22. This utterance, when all segments are put together, represent a semantically coherent speech, which can be rendered prescriptively as in a written sentence like *watashi wa sono hoosoo wa kazoku to uchi de kiita* (I – that broadcast – with my family – heard). This exemplifies the great difference between how a written and spoken sentences are organized.

CHAPTER 4

Words

1. Vocabulary strata

The Japanese lexicon consists of three major strata, namely the native, the Sino-Japanese, and the foreign (mainly Western) loan vocabulary. These three layers of vocabulary are different not only for their respective source languages, but also for their phonological characteristics and modes of written representations. Phonologically, for example, native words rarely begin with a voiced consonant or the consonant *r* except in sound-symbolic words; Sino-Japanese words tend to contain geminate and moraic nasal consonants, and only foreign words can have voiced geminate consonants such as *-dd-* as in *beddo* 'bed'. Sino-Japanese words are normally written in Chinese characters (*kanji*), while non-Chinese foreign words are written in *katakana*. Native nouns and verbs are usually written in *kanji*, but function words are written in *hiragana*. In addition to the three major strata, there is also a special class of sound-symbolic words, which are undoubtedly native words, but are often written in *katakana*, and show distinct phonological features (§3.1).

Native and Sino-Japanese words together occupy about 80–90% of the total lexicon according to a survey of vocabulary use in 90 different magazines conducted by the National Language Research Institute (国立国語研究所 *Kokuritsu Kokugo Kenkyuujo*) (1964). In this report, it was found that Sino-Japanese words (47%) outnumber native words (36%) in distinct word count, by which words are counted on their first appearance only. The frequency order reverses in the total token count, i.e. words are counted each time they appear – Sino-Japanese (41%) and native words (53%). This reversal order of frequency can be accounted for by the fact that those which appear repeatedly in the same form are of native origin; this group of words includes grammatical particles, conjunctions, and demonstratives.

An important semantic characteristic of native vocabulary is its position in the taxonomy of concepts; single bases of native vocabulary are found abundantly at the level of basic concepts (genera), especially those relating to nature (Morioka 1987:95–7), with which subordinate concepts are created. Thus *kaze* 'wind' is the basic word and *oo-kaze* 'strong wind' and *aki-kaze* 'autumn wind' are derived words. The next show some examples of native words (see also §2.1.1 below).

Nature	*haru* 'spring'	*aki* 'autumn'	*sora* 'sky'	*hi* 'sun'
	tsuki 'moon'	*hoshi* 'star'	*ame* 'rain'	*kawa* 'river'
Animates	*hito* 'human'	*ushi* 'cow'	*inu* 'dog'	*neko* 'cat'
	tori 'bird'	*uo* 'fish'	*hebi* 'snake'	*mushi* 'insects'

Sino-Japanese words are almost always nouns, including verbal nouns (§2.1.1) and nominal adjectives (§2.1.3), often referring to more abstract or super-ordinate concepts (e.g. 自然 *shi.zen* 'nature,' 精神 *see.shin* 'spirit,' and 動物 *doo.butsu* 'animals'). Many Sino-Japanese words are a compound word consisting of two bases written by two separate characters; the period within each example word just given shows the morpheme boundary between the two characters, and each component has its own meaning: 自*shi* (self) + 然 *zen* (manner) = nature, 精 *see* (pure) + 神 *shin* (god) = spirit, 動 *doo* (move) + 物 *butsu* (thing) = animal.

Sino-Japanese words can be added to the lexicon rather freely in order to accommodate the names of new objects and concepts, and to provide alternative expressions for things which already have names. From the time the Japanese adopted the Chinese writing system (5th century CE.), they have continuously borrowed Chinese words. Miller (1967: 244) calls this aggressive pattern of borrowing the principle of "total availability," according to which "potentially any morpheme or any word existing in Chinese of any variety at any period in the history of the language has in theory always been available as a potential loan word in Japanese." By the 19th century, Sino-Japanese words had been well entrenched in the Japanese vocabulary. Thus when the Japanese translators translated new concepts from the West before and after the Meiji Restoration (1868), they could make use of their knowledge of compound formation in Sino-Japanese vocabulary. Sometimes the translators sought ancient Chinese compounds and revived them, and other times they created completely new compounds (Chinese vocabulary manufactured in Japan). Many new Sino-Japanese words created by this process were eventually exported back into the Chinese language. The following are just a few examples of revived and newly created Chinese compounds. As before, a period placed within the example words indicates a morpheme boundary that corresponds with the boundary between characters. A meaning for each component word is given separately in parentheses, and the total concept is defined to the right.

Revived ancient Chinese words:

解放	*kai.hoo* (release + liberate)	'liberation'
絶対	*zet.tai* (excellent + opposite)	'absolute'
法則	*hoo.soku* (law + rule)	'rules (of nature)'
経済	*kee.zai* (organize + clear)	'economy'
交流	*koo.ryuu* (mingle + flow)	'interaction'
供給	*kyoo.kyuu* (offer + give)	'supply'

Japan-manufactured Chinese vocabulary

自由	*ji.yuu* (self + by)	'freedom'
自然	*shi.zen* (self + manner)	'nature'
文学	*bun.gaku* (letters + study)	'literature'
心理	*shin.ri* (heart + rule)	'psychology'
古典	*ko.ten* (old + document)	'classics'
工業	*koo.gyoo* (manufacture + industry)	'industry'

Foreign loan words are those words borrowed from foreign languages other than Chinese. The survey by the National Language Research Institute mentioned earlier reports that the foreign words comprise about 10% in the distinct word count, but only about 3% in the total token count. This means that a variety of loan words are used, but only a few recur with any frequency in the 90 magazines surveyed. Foreign loans are similar to Sino-Japanese words in that they are morphologically nouns and assist to incorporate new words into the Japanese vocabulary. Compared to Sino-Japanese words, they tend to refer to concrete objects (e.g. ビール *biiru* 'beer,' カメラ *kamera* 'camera,' and セーター *seetaa* 'sweater'), though more abstract concepts such as エレガンス *eregansu* 'elegance' and インテリ *interi* 'intelligentsia (from Russian)' also exist (Chapter 2 §3 for abstract concepts written in *katakana*). The earliest loan words are from Portuguese (カッパ *kappa* 'raincoat' < *capa*, パン *pan* 'bread' < *pão*, タバコ *tabako* 'cigarette' < *tabaco*) and Dutch (e.g. コーヒー *koohii* 'coffee' < *koffie*, ゴム *gomu* 'rubber' < *gom*) and date back to the mid sixteenth century, when Japan first had contact with the Western world.[1] While Japanese has borrowed from other Western languages such as German, French, and Italian, the major source especially after World War II is English. More recently, however, Asian (including Chinese) and European languages have also supplied new loan words, e.g. キムチ *kimuchi* < *kimch* (Korean), ドリアン *dorian* < *durian* (Malay), トムヤムクン *tomu yamu kun* < *tom yam kung* soup (Thai), ラオチュー *raochuu* < *lǎojiǔ* liquor (Mandarin), カプチーノ *kapuchiino* < *cappuccino* (Italian), フォアグラ *foagura* < *foie gras* (French). The flexibility of incorporating foreign loan words seems to suggest that the principle of "total availability" Miller mentioned for Sino-Japanese can now be applied to this category of words in modern Japanese. Undoubtedly, the existence of *katakana* makes this process easier.

When loan words are introduced into the language, phonological adjustments are often made in order to make them pronounceable according to the Japanese phonological system. Sometimes, however, loan words introduce innovative pronunciation not available in the native or Sino-Japanese phonological system. For example, the sound [ɸ] only appears before [ɯ] in the native phonology, but it appears before all other vowels in the foreign loan words; e.g. ファイト *faito* [ɸito] 'fight,' フィルム *firumu* [ɸirumu] 'film,' フェミニスト *feminisuto* [ɸeminisuto] 'feminist,' and フォント *fonto* [ɸonto] 'font' (Chapter 3 §1.2.2). Loan words do not always carry the same semantic content as their counterparts in the original languages. For example, the word just mentioned above *feminisuto* doesn't usually mean a person who fights for women's causes, but means a male person who is unusually kind to women. Like Sino-Japanese words, loan words are usually introduced as nouns, but some are used as verbs with *suru* 'do,'

---

1. Some older loan words have been entrenched in Japanese and can be written in Chinese characters; *kappa* 'raincoat' > 合羽, *tenpura* 'temporas' (from Portuguese) > 天麩羅, *koohii* 'coffee' > 珈琲.

e.g. ゲットする *getto-suru* 'get (an object, idea etc.)' < get-do; アップする *appu-suru* 'raise; upload' < up-do; デートする *deeto-suru* 'date' < date-do; アルバイトする *arubaito-suru* 'work part time' < Arbeit (from German)-do), and others as adjectives with *na*, and adverbs with *ni*: e.g. ドライな/に *dorai na/ni* 'businesslike (way)' < (with semantic change) dry; スムーズな/に *sumuuzu na/ni* 'smooth/ly' < smooth; スマートな/に *sumaato na/ni* 'stylish/ly' < (with semantic change) 'smart.' Once loan words have established themselves firmly in the Japanese lexicon, they may start to provide resources to innovate the vocabulary system by invoking some derivational processes, producing the so-called "Japan-made English" (e.g. *arubaitaa* 'part-time worker < Arbeit + er; *mai baggu* 'eco friendly bags (to avoid using disposal plastic bags)' < my + bag; *hai sensu* 'stylish' < high + sense; *raibu hausu* 'club with live music' < live (music) + house). A foreign word may be fused with a native morpheme to create a hybrid word especially in the domain of slang (in the following examples, -*ru* is a native verbal suffix for nonpast tense, and SL indicates "slang"); サボる *sabo-ru* 'to slack off' (< sabotage –*ru*), ミスる (SL) *misu-ru* 'to make a mistake' (< mistake –*ru*), トラブる (SL) *torabu-ru* 'to encounter a problem' (< trouble –*ru*), ググる (SL) *gugu-ru* 'to do Google search' (<Goog -*ru* < Google -*ru*). However the derivational productivity of foreign loan words is completely marginal when compared to that of the Sino-Japanese words, as mentioned above.

2. Word classes

The major word classes in Japanese are nouns, nominal adjectives, adjectives, and verbs, which play the role of argument and/or predicate. The minor word classes are adverbs, conjunctions, adnouns, auxiliaries, the copula, particles, affixes, and interjections.

2.1 Major word classes

Nouns and nominal adjectives belong to the non-inflectional category, while adjectives and verbs belong to the inflectional category.

2.1.1 *Nouns*

This open class category consists of many free morphemes with several sub-types. They do not inflect for case, but their role in the clause is coded by an array of case particles (Chapter 6). Though Japanese does not require a noun to be marked for number, plural marking is possible for human nouns; *gakusee-tachi, gakusee-ra* 'students.' The same plural markers are used for the associative plural meaning, i.e. X and his/her associates, when a noun is identifiable/definite animate; *yoshiko-tachi, yoshiko-ra* 'Yoshiko and her friends.' This applies to first and second personal pronouns as well; *boku-tachi, boku-ra* 'me and my friends'; *kimi-tachi, kimi-ra* 'you guys.' For third person pronouns, *kare-ra* 'he and his associates' is more common than *kare-tachi*; but *kanojo-ra* and *kanojo-tachi* 'she and her associates' are used with equal frequency. The suffix *–gata* is an honorific form, so *sensee-gata* 'teachers,' *gofujin-gata* 'ladies,' and *tono-gata* 'gentlemen' are natural. However, this form (*-gata*) does not allow associative meaning, **tanaka-sensee-gata* 'Prof. Tanaka and his associates.' Plurality is also expressed with duplication in some limited cases (Chapter 5 §2.4). When a noun appears as the predicate, it can be supported by the copula, as in *America.jin da* (American COP) '(He's) an American.'

Proper nouns: Proper nouns include names referring to specific individuals, places, events etc. (e.g. *Kurosawa Akira*, *Tokyo*, or *Shunbun no Hi* 'the Vernal Equinox Day').[2]

Common nouns: Common nouns refer to physical entities or abstract concepts. There is no countable-uncountable distinction. They are either simple, compound, or derived ones with affixation. They may be native, Sino-Japanese, or of foreign origin. Some compound and affixed nouns are hybrids of two or more components of different origins. (As before, a period within the multi-morpheme word indicates a morpheme boundary.)

Native Nouns

筆	*fude*	'brush'
桜	*sakura*	'cherry blossom'
貝	*kai*	'shell fish'
そよ風	*soyo.kaze*	(soft + wind) = 'breeze'
小麦	*ko.mugi*	(small + wheat) = 'wheat'
大麦	*oo.mugi*	(large + wheat) = 'barley'

Sino-Japanese Nouns

愛	*ai*	'love'
円	*en*	'circle; Japanese currency'
式	*shiki*	'ceremony; mathematic formula'
言語	*gen.go*	(speech + word) = 'language'
科学	*ka.gaku*	(classify + study) = 'science'
法律	*hoo.ritsu*	(law + order) = 'legislation'

---

2. In the case of personal names and place names, the more inclusive category precedes the subordinate category. For personal names, the family name appears before the given name as in *Kurosawa Akira*, where *Kurosawa* is the family name and *Akira* is the given name. Place names also start from the larger geopolitical unit and move to the smaller one; in the address, *Tokyo-to, Mitaka-shi, Osawa, 3-choome*. *Tokyo-to* is the largest municipality organization within Japan, *Mitaka-shi* is one of the cities in Tokyo, *Osawa* is one of the areas within the city, and *3-choome* is the local block within *Osawa*.

Foreign Nouns

カメラ	kamera	'camera'
コーヒー	koohii	'coffee'
オートバイ	ooto.bai	(auto + bicycle) = 'motorcycle'
バターミルク	bataa.miruku	'butter milk'
ポケットナイフ	poketto.naifu	'pocket knife'
スマートフォン	sumaato.fon	'smart phone'

Hybrid Nouns:

アメリカ人 *america.jin*	F-SJ	'American people'
バス停 *basu.tee*	F-SJ	'bus stop'
ロココ風 *rokoko.fuu*	F-SJ	'Rococo style'
インサイダー取引 *insaidaa.torihiki*	F-N	'insider trading'
薬品メーカー *yakuhin.meekaa*	SJ-F	'pharmaceutical company < medicine + producer'
胃カメラ *i.kamera*	N-F	'gastric endoscope' < stomach + camera
鳥インフルエンザ *tori.infuruenza*	N-F	'bird flu' < bird + influenza
水商売 *mizu.shoo.bai*	N-SJ-SJ	'water business' (= business related to serving clients with food and beverages, e.g. bars, clubs and the like)
手数料 *te.suu.ryoo*	N-SJ-SJ	'fees'

Personal pronouns: Pronouns have the special functional characteristic of being a substitutive expression for an identifiable referent, but they are morphosyntactically indistinguishable from common nouns. A large inventory is one characteristic feature of Japanese pronouns, and the most appropriate form is selected according to sociolinguistic concerns. The diagram below shows some first and second personal pronouns available for a particular level of speech and politeness. Although *kare* 'he' and *kanojo* 'she' are known as third person pronouns, they are not usually used for one's seniors. Those marked with (M) and (F) are used by male and female speakers, respectively, in normal situations. See Chapter 15 §1 for further discussion.

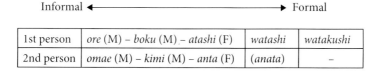

Informal ← → Formal

| 1st person | *ore* (M) – *boku* (M) – *atashi* (F) | *watashi* | *watakushi* |
| 2nd person | *omae* (M) – *kimi* (M) – *anta* (F) | (*anata*) | – |

Diagram 1. Speech levels and 1st and 2nd person pronominal forms

The reflexive pronoun is *jibun* 'self' (Chapter 13 §1).

Demonstrative pronouns: This type of pronoun is a substituting deictic expression. Three distinctions are made in this type of pronoun depending on the location of the object with respect to the speaker and the addressee: *kore* (speaker proximal demonstrative), *sore* (addressee proximal demonstrative), and *are* (distal demonstrative). Traditional grammar identifies these expressions together with their interrogative form, *dore* 'which,' as *ko-so-a-do* words (こそあど言葉). Demonstrative pronouns, especially *sore*, may be used anaphorically in text (Chapter 13 §3). *Are* can be used in discourse when the referent is mutually accessible, or the speaker speaks in the monologic mode with a particularly strong emotional attachment to the referent (Chapter 14 §1.2.1.2, §1.2.1.3; cf. Kuno 1973: 282–90; Kinsui & Takubo 1992).

Interrogative nouns: This type of noun takes the place of a noun whose identity is unknown. Many of them are the *do*-words in the *ko-so-a-do* series just mentioned above.[3]

dore	'which among more than three'
dochira/dotchi	'which between two'
doko	'where'
dare	'who'
donate	'who' (honorific)
nani	'what'
itsu	'when'

Verbal nouns: Verbal nouns are nouns which refer to an action or event. Some verbal nouns are semantically transitive while others intransitive. Verbal nouns take the verb *suru* 'do' to function as verbs. Many verbal nouns are Sino-Japanese, but native (e.g. *temaneki* 'beckon') and foreign (e.g. *tesuto* 'test,' *getto* 'get') verbal nouns also exist (Martin [1975] 1991: 869–80).

Verbal Noun		Verbal use	
benkyoo	'study'	*benkyoo-suru*	'study (transitive)'
tesuto	'test'	*tesuto-suru*	'test (transitive)'
jisatsu	'suicide'	*jisatsu-suru*	'commit suicide (int.)'
futtoo	'boil'	*futtoo-suru*	'boil (intransitive)'
temaneki	'taste'	*temaneki -suru*	'beckon (intransitive)'

Semantically transitive verbal nouns can function as a transitive verb with a direct object specified by the accusative particle *o*. Alternatively they can function as the direct object for *suru* with the accusative particle *o*. In this case, a noun which constitutes the patient can appear as a modifier for the verbal nouns along with the particle *no*.

---

3. Some question words are excluded in this list as they are not nominals; *doo* (adverbial) 'how,' *naze/dooshite* (adverbial) 'why,' and *donna* (adnoun) 'what type, what kind.'

[nihongo]	o	benkyoo-suru →	[nihongo *no* benkyoo] o suru
Japanese	ACC	study-do	Japanese GEN study ACC do
'to study Japanese'			'to do studying of Japanese'

[enjin]	o	tesuto-suru →	[enjin *no* tesuto] o suru
engine	ACC	test-do	engine GEN test ACC do
'to test an engine'			'to do testing of an engine'

Formal nouns: Formal nouns have little or no semantic content in themselves, and thus are always modified by another word or a clause. Particularly important formal nouns are *tokoro, koto,* and *no*, which make complement clauses (see Chapter 10 §2).

Adverbial clause forming nouns: Some nouns construct adverbial phrases and clauses. Some examples follow (Chapter 7 §1, Chapter 12 §2.1).

Reason	*tame (ni), okage (de), see (de)* 'because of/thanks to/due to'
Manner	*toori (ni)* 'as' *kawari (ni)* 'instead of' *hoka (ni)* 'besides' *mama (ni)* 'as it is' *tsuide (ni)* 'at the same time; while doing something'
Time	*toki (ni)* 'when' *aida (ni)/uchi (ni)* 'while' *ato (ni/de)* 'after' *mae (ni)* 'before'
Others	*ippoo (de)/hanmen* 'on the other hand' *kekka* 'as a result' *kagiri* 'as long as' *kuse (ni)* 'though (with an emotional tone)'

2.1.2 Adjectives

Japanese has two morphologically identifiable types of adjectives: verbal adjectives and nominal adjectives. Verbal adjectives are inflecting words like verbs, and are identified by the final *-i* in the nonpast affirmative form (e.g. *ooki-i* 'big'). Verbal adjectives must be distinguished from stative verbs whose citation form ends in *-(r)u* rather than *-i*, e.g. *deki-ru* 'be capable of.' (Verbal adjectives are henceforth referred simply as "adjectives"). All major semantic types of adjective are attested (Dixon 1977: 31).

Dimension	*ooki-i* 'big'	*chiisa-i* 'little'	*naga-i* 'long'
	mijika-i 'short'	*atsu-i** 'thick'	*usu-i* 'thin' ...
Physical property	*atsu-i** 'hot'	*tsumeta-i* 'cold'	*kata-i* 'hard, tough, firm'
	yawaraka-i 'soft'	*ama-i* 'sweet' ...	
Color	*kuro-i* 'black'	*shiro-i* 'white'	*aka-i* 'red' ...
Human propensity	*ureshi-i* 'happy'	*kanashi-i* 'sad'	
	kashiko-i 'clever'	*zuru-i* 'tricky' ...	
Age	*atarashi-i* 'new'	*waka-i* 'young'	*furu-i* 'old (inanimate)' ...

Value	*i-i* 'good' *waru-i* 'bad' *subarashi-i* 'excellent' …
Speed	*haya-i* 'fast, early' *oso-i* 'slow, late' *noro-i* 'slow' …

atsu-i* 'thick' and *atsu-i* 'hot' are different words with different pitch accent. The former has an accent on the second mora, and the latter has no accent.

In addition to these adjectives that refer to properties and qualities, some words are also identified as adjectives based on the morphological shape; *hoshi-i* 'want (something),' *tabe-tai* 'want to eat,' *tabe-nai* 'do not eat' etc.

Adjectives inflect for tense and polarity (Chapter 5 §1.2), but do not inflect for the comparative and superlative degrees. These meanings are expressed periphrastically; *A-ga B-yori ookii* (A- NOM B-from big) 'A is bigger than B'; *X-no naka-de A -ga ichiban ookii* (X-GEN among-LOC A-NOM first big) 'Among X, A is the biggest.'

2.1.3 *Nominal adjectives*

Nominal adjectives are semantically like adjectives in that they describe the state of an entity. At the same time, they are morphologically like nouns because they do not inflect and require the copula to become a predicate. Notice that predicate adjectives appear without the copula in the plain register.

Nominal Adjective:	*kiree*	*da*	'(It's) beautiful.'
	beautiful	COP	
Noun:	*gakusee*	*da*	'(She's) a student.'
	student	COP	
Adjective:	*ookii*	(**ookii da*)	'(It's) big.'
	big	big COP	

However, nominal adjectives are different from both nouns and adjectives in that, when used as a modifier, they require a special attributive form of the copula, *na* (nouns take *no*), while adjectives do not require any copula in the informal register (§2.2.5 below).

Nominal Adjective:	*kiree-**na***	*hito*
	beautiful-COP:ATT	person
	'a beautiful person'	
Noun:	*nihonjin-**no***	*hito*
	Japanese-COP:ATT	person
	'a Japanese person'	
Adjective:	*wakai*	*hito*
	young	person
	'a young person'	

The boundary between nominal adjectives and nouns is not always clear because some words allow either *na* or *no* when modifying a noun. This indicates the continuous nature of these word classes (Teramura 1982:62–75; Uehara 1998).

Nominal Adjective:	*heewa-**na***	*jidai*	'a peaceful time'
	peaceful-COP:ATT	time	
Noun:	*heewa-**no***	*shirushi*	'a sign of peace'
	peaceful-COP:ATT	sign	
Nominal Adjective:	*wazuka-**na***	*okane*	'a little money'
	little-COP:ATT	money	
Noun:	*wazuka-**no***	*okane*	'a little money'
	little-COP:ATT	money	

2.1.4 Verbs

Verbs are inflecting words and are identified morphologically by the final *-(r)u* in the nonpast affirmative form; e.g. *tabe-ru* 'eat' and *nom-u* 'drink' (Chapter 5 §1.1.1). A major semantic division can be made between the dynamic and stative classes, and this division has some consequences in tense-aspect interpretation in a sentence (Chapter 7). Another important division is the morphosyntactic distinction of transitivity (Chapter 5 §1.1.3). The intransitive verb requires only one argument which appears with the nominative case particle *ga* (*hon ga <u>ochiru</u>* 'a book <u>falls</u>'), while the transitive verb requires an additional argument marked by the accusative particle *o* (*kodomo ga hon o <u>otosu</u>* 'a child <u>drops</u> the book'). The ditransitive verb, on the other hand, requires a third argument marked by the dative particle *ni* (*sensee ga kodomo ni$_i$ hon o <u>yaru</u>$_j$* 'a teacher <u>gives</u>$_j$ a book <u>to a child</u>$_i$') (Chapter 1 §4.1, Chapter 6 §1.2). The third important division is made on the basis of self-controllability and volitionality. Some events are under the agent's control and volition, as in *kodomo ga <u>tobioriru</u>* 'a child <u>jumps down</u>,' while others are not, as in *kodomo ga <u>korobu</u>* 'a child <u>falls down</u>.' This distinction is relevant to causative constructions (Chapter 8 §4) as well as aspect (Chapter 7 §2.3).

2.2 Minor word classes

2.2.1 Adverbs

Adverbs are non-inflecting words whose function is to modify verbs, adjectives, nominal adjectives, other adverbs, as well as sentences. Some adverbs are identical in form to the *-k-u* (infinitive) form of an adjective: *hayak-u* 'fast/early,' *oishik-u* 'deliciously.' Others are derived from nominal adjectives by means of *ni*; *kiree-ni* 'beautifully/cleanly,' *shizuka-ni* 'quietly' (§2.2.5 below). Yet some others are adverbs proper.

Adverbs can be sub-classified according to their specific functions. Manner adverbs describe the mode of action, such as *yukkuri* 'slowly,' *gussuri* 'soundly (sleeping),' *jitto* 'patiently,' *iyaiya* 'unwillingly.' There are many Sino-Japanese and sound-symbolic words that belong to this class of adverbs. Some adverbs take the adverbial suffix *to*, either optionally or obligatorily. Some examples of S-J manner adverbs are: *doodoo-to* 'magnificently,' *heezen-to* 'calmly,' *mokumoku-to* 'quietly.' Examples of sound-symbolic manner adverbs include: *fuwafuwa-to* 'in a light manner (for floating),' *hirahira-to* 'in a light manner (for falling),' and *bishibishi-to* 'strictly.' (See §3.1 below for more discussion of the sound-symbolic words.) There are also *ko-so-a-do* adverbs; *koo* 'in this manner,' *soo* 'in that manner,' *aa* 'in that manner,' and *doo* 'in what manner.'

Degree adverbs indicate the extent of a certain state: *totemo* 'very,' *sukoshi* 'a little,' *zenzen* 'not at all,' *wari-ni/wari-to* 'rather,' *zutto* 'far more,' *motto* 'more,' and *kekkoo* 'rather.' Quantity adverbs include *takusan* 'much,' *dossari* 'much,' *ippai* 'much,' *hotondo* 'most,' and *daitai* 'most.' Degree and quantity adverbs overlap with each other, but while degree adverbs modify adjectives (e.g. *sukoshi takai* 'a little expensive'), quantity adverbs modify verbs (e.g. *sukoshi tabe-ta* 'ate a little.') The degree adverb *zenzen* 'not al all' is a negative polarity item, and must co-occur with a negative form (*zenzen oishkunai* 'not delicious at all'), but recently it has come to be used with affirmative form as well (*zenzen oishii* 'very delicious'). Frequency adverbs include *itsumo* 'always,' *tokidoki* 'sometimes,' *taitee* 'almost always,' and *yoku* 'often.' The last example, *yoku*, is the adverbial form of adjective *i-i*, and may also be used as a degree adverb with the meaning of 'well' as in *yoku shitte-iru* 'know well.'

Temporal adverbs refer to a certain point on the temporal axis. Some of these adverbs are identical to temporal nouns such as *kinoo* 'yesterday,' *kyoo* 'today,' and *ashita* 'tomorrow,' while others are adverbs proper: *katsute* 'previously' and *sugu* 'soon.' Aspect adverbs refer to the temporal aspect of an event and they include: *moo* 'already,' *sude-ni* 'already,' *mada* 'not yet,' *tootoo* 'finally,' *tadachini* 'immediately,' and *mazu* 'first of all.'

Sentence adverbs express the speaker/writer's modal stance and judgment towards the proposition and speech act: *zehi* 'by all means,' *ittai* 'what on earth,' *kesshite* 'never (a negative polarity item),' *osoraku* 'probably,' *tabun* 'probably,' *kitto* 'definitely,' *masaka* 'on no account,' and *toozen* 'naturally.'

2.2.2 Conjunctions

Conjunctions are free words which connect clauses, sentences, or paragraphs in various types of relationships. Some are only used in formal writing, e.g. *shikaruni* 'therefore,' but some are used in both writing and speech, *shikashinagara* 'however,' *shikashi* 'but,' and *aruiwa* 'or.' In addition to pure conjunctions such as *mata* 'and' and *nao* 'further more,' there are many that have derived from other types of words. Some are from nouns (e.g. *yue-ni* 'therefore' < *yue* 'reason'), and others are from verbs (e.g. *suru-to* 'then' < *suru* 'do' + conjunctive particle). One important type of conjunction is built upon the deictic word *so-* (< *sore* 'deictic expressing referring to the previous context'): *sokode* 'so,' *sorede* 'and then,' *soreni* 'and what's more,' *soshite* 'and then,' and *sorekara* 'and then.' Another important type of conjunction is built upon the copula. The element *da* in the following example is the copula: *dakara* 'so,' *dattara* 'in that case,' *datoshite* 'provided that,' *dakedo* 'however,' and *daga* 'but.' Another significant type of conjunction is derived from bound conjunctive particles, including *ga* 'however' and *keredomo* (and its shorter versions, *keredo* and *kedo*) 'however.' (See Chapter 12, Note 4; also "discourse markers" and "discourse connectives" in Chapter 14 §4.2).

2.2.3 Adnouns

A group of words called adnouns have the sole function of modifying a noun (e.g. *aru* 'certain' in *aru hi* 'one day'). They are similar to adjectives and nominal adjectives in their modifying function, but they do not inflect like adjectives or require a special attributive form of the copula like nominal adjectives. Neither do they form a predicate like adjectives and nominal adjectives. This group includes words derived from other words: from the attributive form of verbs: *aru* 'certain,' *arayuru* 'every,' *iwayuru* 'so-called,' *kitaru* 'upcoming,' and *saru* 'in the past'; from the past tense form of verbs: *taishita* 'quite impressive,' *tonda* 'unexpected (negative connotation),' and *chottoshita* 'of some significance'; from adjectives: *chiisana* 'small,' *ookina* 'big,' *okashina* 'funny,' *komakana* 'fine,' *doodoo-taru* 'magnificent,' and *bibi-taru* 'insignificant.' Some adnouns modify numeric phrase: *tatta* 'only,' *yaku* 'approximately,' and *seezee* 'at the most.' There are also adnouns belonging to the *ko-so-a-do* class: *kono* 'this,' *sono* 'that,' *ano* 'that over there,' and *dono* 'which'; *konna* 'this type,' *sonna* 'that type,' *anna* 'that over there type,' and *donna* 'which type.'

2.2.4 Auxiliaries

Auxiliaries are of two types. The first type is modal auxiliaries which do not inflect. They follow different verb forms as shown in the parentheses.

(nonpast) *mai*:	negative conjecture/will
(nonpast) *beki*:	obligation (Chapter 15 §3)
(inf.) *-soo*:	visual evidential (Chapter 14 §2.1.2)
(plain) *soo*:	hearsay evidential (Chapter 14 §2.1.2)
(plain) *daroo*:	conjecture (Chapter 14 §2.1.1)
(plain) *hazu da*:	logical inference (Chapter 14 §2.1.1)
(plain) *yoo da/rashii/mitai da*:	evidential (Chapter 14 §2.1.2).

Mai is a negative conjecture auxiliary with the third person subject, e.g. *kare wa iku mai* (he TOP go AUX) '(I think) he will not go.' It is a negative will auxiliary with the first person subject, e.g. *boku wa iku mai* (I TOP go AUX) 'I will not go'). For other auxiliaries listed above, refer to the chapters and sections noted.

The second type contains those words which have been grammaticalized from verbs, and thus conjugate. They follow the *-te* form of verbs, and indicate aspects, benefactivity, and various other modal information.

Aspectual:	*-te-iru, -te-aru, -te-shimau, -te-iku/-te-kuru*
	-te-oku, -te-miru etc. (Chapter 7 §2)
Benefactive:	*-te-yaru, -te-ageru, -te-morau, -te-kureru* (Chapter 8 §5)
Modal:	*-te-hoshii, -te moraitai* 'want someone to do something'

2.2.5 Copula

The copula is an inflecting word that assists nouns and nominal adjectives, both of which do not inflect, in forming a predicate. It typically appears in a topic-comment sentence (Chapter 11 §1) such as follows.

michiko	wa	gakusee	*da*		'Michiko is a student.'
(name)	TOP	student	COP		
kono	ko	wa	genki	*da*	'This child is healthy.'
this	child	TOP	healthy	COP	

The copula is the only inflecting category in modern Japanese which has an attributive form distinct from the conclusive form. While the conclusive form is *da*, the attributive form is *no* when following a noun, or *na* when following a nominal adjective.[4] See Chapter 5 §1.3 for its inflectional pattern.

gakusee-*no*	michiko	'Michiko, who is a student'
student-COP:ATT	(name)	
genki-*na*	kodomo	'healthy child'
healthy-COP:ATT	child	

The copula also appears as *ni* with a nominal adjective used as an adverb (§2.2.1).

kiree-*ni*	kaku	'to write beautifully/neatly'
beautiful-COP:ADV	write:NONPAST	
kiree-*ni*	naru	'to become beautiful/clean'
beautiful-COP:ADV	become:NONPAST	

There are two other stylistic variants of copula; *desu* and *dearu*. The latter appears only in formal written texts, while the former is the general polite variant and more versatile than *da* in that it can appear after an adjective.

kyoo	wa	atsui	**da / desu / *dearu*	'Today is hot.'
today	TOP	hot	*COP / COP / *COP	

2.2.6 Particles

Particles are postpositional words attached mainly to noun phrases. They supply various kinds of syntactic, semantic and pragmatic information.

Case particles: These particles supply information about the relationship between a noun phrase and the predicate: *ga* (nominative), *o* (accusative), *ni* (dative), *de* (locative/instrumental), *to* (comitative), *kara/yori* (ablative), *e* (allative), *made* (terminal). In addition, *no* (genitive), which specifies the relationship between two noun phrases, is included in this type of particle. (See Chapter 6 for more discussion).

Topic marking particles: A topic marking particle shows that a noun phrase in a sentence has the special pragmatic status of topic. When the topic overlaps with a nominative or accusative noun phrase (and sometimes a dative noun phrase), the topic marking particle

---

4. The attributive *no* should not be confused with the genitive case particle (see Chapter 9 §2).

replaces these case particles. Otherwise it follows the case particle (e.g. *de wa* 'INS TOP'). The most typical particle in this group is (topical/thematic) *wa*, but others such as *nara*, *-ttara*, and *-tte* may also function in this capacity. (See "topic-comment sentences" in Chapter 11 §1).

Adverbial particles: These particles foreground one part of a proposition described in a sentence. They add contrast (contrastive *wa*), as well as other meanings, such as 'also' (*mo*), 'even' (*sae, demo, sura, datte, made*), 'only' (*dake, bakari, nomi, shika*), 'emphatically' (*koso*), 'for example' (*nado, nanka, nante, kurai*).

Conjunctive particles: Conjunctive particles conjoin either two noun phrases or two predicates/clauses. For the former *to* 'and' is used for complete listing, *ya* 'and' for representative listing, *mo* for 'both… and…', *ni* for 'in addition', and *ka* for 'or'. For the latter, *shi* 'and' is used (Chapter 12 §1.1).

Quotative particles: *To* and *tte* follow quoted material with verbs of speech and thought (Chapter 10 §1).

Pragmatic particles: There are two distinct types of pragmatic particles. The first type, the sentence final particle, appears at the end of a complete sentence and expresses the speaker's stance towards the referential information: *ka, kashira* (interrogative), *sa* (judgment), *ne, na* with high tone (confirmation), *yo, zo, ze, wa, yo* (assertion), *kke* (memory confirmation), and *na* with low tone (prohibition). The second type, the interjective particle, appears after a phrase or clause, and solicits involvement from the addressee: *ne/nee* and *sa/saa* both function similarly to the English expression 'you know' as in 'Yesterday, you know, I met this guy' (Chapter 14 §3).

Complex adjunct phrases and complex postpositional phrases: These phrases function similarly to those simple particles mentioned above (e.g. case particles), but they consist of a simple particle and other elements. Complex adjunct phrases consist of a particle and the *–te* form of a verb: *ni taishite* 'against', *ni kanshite* 'in regards', *ni yotte* 'by', *ni kawatte* 'in place of', *ni tsuite* 'regarding' (Matsumoto 1998). Complex postpositional phrases consist of a genitivized noun and a particle: *no tame ni* 'for the sake of', *no kawari ni* 'in place of', and *no okage de* 'thanks to'.

2.2.7 Affixes

An affix attaches to and modifies a base (Chapter 5 §2.2). The prefix and suffix are the two types of affixes found in Japanese, of which the latter is more numerous in variety. A noun may be modified by either a prefix (e.g. *mu-* in <u>mu</u>-*imi* 'meaningless') or a suffix (e.g. *-sa* in *akaru*-<u>sa</u> 'bright<u>ness</u>'), or by both (e.g. <u>mu</u>-*imi*-<u>sa</u> 'meaning<u>lessness</u>', *hi-seesan*-<u>teki</u> '<u>non</u>produc<u>tive</u>'). An important subclass of prefixes is the polite prefix *o-/go-*. The former precedes native words (e.g. *o-namae* '*o-*name = your name') and the latter Sino-Japanese words (e.g. *go-juusho* 'go-address = your address'). An important subclass of suffixes is the numeral classifier, which follows a numeral (§3.2 below). Verbs are modified by a derivational and inflectional suffix (Chapter 5 §1.1 for details). Verbal prefixes are rare, but some verbs may be modified by prefixes of intensity or vulgar connotation (e.g. *bun-naguru* 'hit someone hard' < *naguru* 'hit someone,' *but-tobasu* 'beat up, drive fast' < *tobasu* 'make something fly,' *kat-tobasu* 'hit (a) ball)' < *tobasu* 'make something fly,' and *kas-sarau* 'steal away' < *sarau* 'snatch'). Both prefixes and suffixes may be of native or Sino-Japanese origin. Only a few, however, are of foreign origin: *posuto-* as in *posuto-koizumi* 'poast-Koizumi (*Koizumi* is a name of a former prime minister of Japan), *-izumu* as in *waseda-izumu* 'Wasedaism' (*Waseda* is a name of a famous private university in Japan), and *-chikku* as in *otome-chikku* 'yong-feminine-like (*otome* means young females).

2.2.8 *Interjections*

There are several subgroups in this word class, but they all express the speaker's attitude towards a specific situation or information. Many interjections express surprise: *a!, aa!, are!?, arya!?, hee!,* and *wa(a)!* (see Chapter 11 §4.1, Chapter 14 §1.1). This group also includes the so-called back channeling expressions (Chapter 14 §4.1): *nn, ee,* and *hai*; reactive expressions: *naruhodo* 'I see,' *honto* 'Really?', *ussoo* 'You're kidding!', *maji* 'Are you serious?', and *saa* 'Well...'; positive and negative responses: *hai/ee* 'Yes,' and *iie/iya* 'No'; fillers: *anoo, sonoo, eeto,* and *maa*; and vocative expressions: *anoo, oi, nee,* and *hora*.

3. Some notable word classes

3.1 Sound-symbolic words

Sound-symbolic words, also known as mimetic words, are words that imitate natural sounds (i.e. onomatopoeia) or symbolize manners and states (including psychological states) in an expressive fashion. These words constitute an important word class in Japanese, as attested by many published dictionaries dedicated just to this class of words, with well over 1,000 entries. Though sound-symbolic words are indigenous words, they exhibit phonological characteristics not shared by the core native vocabulary; for example, the voiceless bilabial stop, /p/, which does not appear word-initially in the native vocabulary in modern Japanese, is one of the most common consonants in this position in sound-symbolic words; palatalization, a restricted phenomenon in the native vocabulary, is widespread in sound-symbolic words; and a glottal stop, which is not part of the regular inventory of sounds, can be observed. Orthographically, they are usually written in *katakana*, not in *hiragana*, again showing their special status among native words (Tsujimura 2007: 85–94).

Semantically, sound-symbolic words can be classified into three types: (1) phonomimes (the onomatopoeia proper) with *gi-on-go* 擬音語 'sound mimicking words' and *gi-see-go* 擬声語 'voice mimicking words' as two sub-types; (2) phenomimes (*gi-tai-go* 擬態語 'manner mimicking words'), and (3) psychomimes (*gi-joo-go* 擬情語 'psychological/physiological-state mimicking words') (Shibatani 1990: 153–7). Some examples of surface forms are shown below with their [roots] presented in square brackets; N indicates a moraic nasal, and Q a moraic obstruent or glottal stop (Chapter 3 §1.2.4). (The analysis below is largely based on Hamano 1998).

Phonomimes

boN [*bo-*]	(sound of explosion)
pakaQ-pakaQ [*paka-*]	(sound of a horse trotting)
zaa-zaa [*za-*]	(sound of rain or flowing water)
bochaN [*bocha-*]	(sound of splashing)
dokaaN [*doka-*]	(sound of loud explosion)
nyaa-nyaa [*nya-*]	(sound of cat's meowing)
buu [*bu-*]	(sound of a car, or crying of a pig)
bagyuuN [*bagyu-*]	(sound of firing a pistol)

Phenomimes

pikaQ [*pika-*]	(manner of shining e.g. of a diamond)
kiraQ [*kira-*]	(manner of shining e.g. of a sharp sword)
puQ [*pu-*]	(manner of pouting)
chibi-chibi [*chibi-*]	(manner of performing an action in small increments as when one drinks *sake* little by little)
yura-yura [*yura-*]	(shaking motion of a large structure such as a building during an earthquake)
guzu-guzu [*guzu-*]	(slow, lazy movement)
hira-hira [*hira-*]	(light flying, or falling movement)
fuwa-fuwa [*fuwa-*]	(light floating movement, or state of soft material like cotton)
fuwari [*fuwa-*]	(light floating movement)
tsuuN [*tsu-*]	(indignant, cold attitude, cf. also see below as a psychomime)

Psychomimes

kyuuN [*kyu-*]	(acute romantic experience)
kaaQ [*ka-*]	(acute emotional upsurge)
tsuuN [*tsu-*]	(acute olfactory experience)
uki-uki [*uki-*]	(happy mood)
uto-uto [*uto-*]	(drowsy)

Morphologically, sound-symbolic words are built on either CV or (C)VCV roots, as indicated by the square brackets in the above examples, which may be reduplicated, or suffixed by the moraic nasal, N, or a moraic obstruent (glottal stop), Q. A vowel (V_i) may be followed by another identical V_i, resulting in a long vowel (e.g. /aa/), or in a CV root word, the V_i may be followed by a different V_j, resulting in one of the three diphthongs, /ai/, /oi/ or /ui/. In addition, a (C)VCV root may insert an intensifying infix (N or Q) between the two moras, or may be suffixed by -*ri* (Hamano 1998: 106–7). Q represents a consonant that is identical to the one that follows (see Chapter 3 §3). These processes create a variety of forms.

CV root
[*pi-*] (tension or high pitched sound):
    piN piQ pii   piiN   piiQ piQ-piQ pii-pii
[*gu-*] (strong motion):
    guN guQ guiQ gui-gui gui-guiQ guN-guN

(C)VCV root
[*pata-*] (light falling sound)
    pataN pataQ pata-pata
[*kuru-*] (rolling movement):
    kuruN kuruQ kuru-kuru
[*doshi-*] (heavy sound)
    doshiN   doshi-doshi   doshiN-doshiN
    do-Q-shiN   do-Q-shi-ri
[*pata-*] (light falling sound)
    pataN pataQ pata-pata

Not all sound-symbolic words are clearly iconic. However, there are a few phonological and morphological correlates of the events and states depicted. First, reduplication, a very common morphological characteristic of sound-symbolic words, indicates repeated actions or continuous states. Thus, *baN* may be referring to a single gun shot, but *baN-baN* or *baN-baN-baN* may be referring to multiple gun shots. Similarly, *pikaQ* refers to a single flicker of light, but *pika-pikaQ* refers to multiple flickering rays.[5] Second, vowel-lengthening is another common iconic characteristic which indicates a prolonged event; *suQ-to* or *saQ-to* depicts, for example, a quick and quiet movement, such as someone suddenly appearing and moving away; *suuQ-to* or *saaQ-to* with the lengthened vowel depicts the same situation, but the movement is registered as a longer one. Third, the voiced-voiceless contrast of the (initial) obstruent is also conspicuous; the formula "voiceless (p/t/s/k) = light, small, fine, thin" and "voiced (b/d/z/g) = heavy, large, coarse, thick" is generally observed (Hamano 1998: 83, 125). There are also other more subtle sound-meaning correspondences. The vowel /e/, which appears least frequently

---

5. Also *pika-pika* refers to the state of a shining object; *kono kutsu wa pika-pika da* (this shoe TOP shiny COP) 'These shoes are shiny.' In this case *pika-pika* is re-lexicalized as a noun functioning as the predicate of a sentence. More discussion on word formation processes is at the end of this section.

among the five vowels in Japanese, is often associated with vulgar, inelegant actions and states; *bero-bero* depicts a crude way of licking, or a state of extreme drunkenness; *hera-hera* mimics an unpleasant way of laughing, or describes the personal trait of not being serious or trustworthy. The intensifying infixes, N or Q, as noted earlier, can appear with a (C)VCV root to indicate an event or state that is more forceful or extreme than usual; *zudooN* is a phonomime depicting a loud sound produced by firing, e.g. a canon, but *zuQdooN* depicts an even louder noise. In contrast, the *-ri* suffix appearing with a (C)VCV root, indicates softness, quietness and smoothness; *goroN* describes the rolling motion of a person in the act of lying down, while *gorori* refers to the same action but emphasizes more smoothness. Also between the two members of the pairs such as *bataN-batari* and *doshiN-doshiri* (all depicting the manner of falling down), the first with /N/ gives a somewhat larger, louder, and forceful impression compared to the second member with *-ri*.

Syntactically, sound-symbolic words are most typically used as adverbs. In this use, the quotative particle *to* (and sometimes *te*) follows either obligatorily or optionally.

mizu   ga   zaaQ to   nagare-dashita
water   NOM   SSW   QT   flow-begin:PAST
'Water began to flow <u>with force</u>.'

choocho   ga   hira-hira (to)   matte-iru
butterfly   NOM   SSW   (QT) dance:TE-ASP:NONPAST
'Butterflies are dancing about <u>flutteringly</u>.'

pokiQ to   eda   o   otta
SSW   QT   branch ACC   break:PAST
'(I) broke a (small) branch <u>with a snap</u>.'

bokiQ to   eda   o   otta
SSW   QT   branch ACC   break:PAST
'(I) broke a (large) branch <u>with a loud crack</u>.'

The adverbial function plays an especially important role when details of an event or state need to be made explicit since many native Japanese verbs are often very general. Thus, for example, the difference between 'laugh' and 'smile' will be made by different sound-symbolic expressions with the same verb, *warau*; while *gera-gera warau* means to 'laugh out loud,' *niko-niko warau* means 'smile' (Shibatani 1990: 155). Similarly, the difference between '(it) flashes,' '(it) twinkles' and '(it) glares' may be made with different sound-symbolic expressions with the verb *hikaru* 'shine'; *pikaQ to hikaru* 'flash,' *kira-kira hikaru* 'twinkle,' and *gira-gira hikaru* 'glare.'

Sound-symbolic words play a non-trivial role in the grammar of Japanese by participating in various word-formation processes. First, it should be noted that the sound-symbolic word *kira-* just mentioned can be suffixed with *-mek-* (appearance of an elegant/mild feature – Chapter 5 §2.2), to produce a compound verb, *kira-mek-u* 'to twinkle' (Hamano

1998: 57). The verbs *yoro-meku* 'to sway unintentionally and softly' and *doyo-meku* 'to stir, as in an audience or group making a noise in a soft, restrained manner' are also made by the same process. Second, some sound-symbolic words behave like verbal nouns, helping to enrich the verbal inventory of native words. Some examples are:

gyoQ-to suru	'be surprised/frightened'
bikuQ-to suru	'be frightened, scared'
dokiQ-to suru	'be surprised, have a heart-stopping experience'
kura-kura suru	'feel dizzy'
nechi-nechi suru	'be pertinacious (negative connotation)'
haki-haki suru	'be articulate'
haQkiri suru	'become clear'

Third, some sound-symbolic words have related nouns, compound nouns, verbs and adjectives. Sound symbolic words are underlined.

<u>wan</u>-<u>wan</u>	'dog' (baby talk)
<u>poN</u>-<u>poN</u>	'tummy' (baby talk)
<u>butsu</u>-<u>butsu</u>	'protruded object (such as pimples)'
<u>boro</u>-ya	'run-down (= SSW)-house'
<u>bara</u>-maku	'scatter (= SSW)-throw'
<u>hikar</u>-u (< *pika-*)	'shine' (< a phenomime for shining)
<u>noro</u>-i (<*noro-*)	'slow' (< a phenomime for slow movement)

3.2 Numerals and numeral-classifiers

3.2.1 *Numerals*

Two numeral systems are used in modern Japanese: the native and Sino-Japanese numeral systems. They are summarized in the table on the next page. The native system stops at ten, and beyond that mostly Sino-Japanese numbers are used (11 *juu-ichi*, 12 *juu-ni*, 13 *juu-san*, 20 *ni-juu* etc.). However, the native number for 20 is used for age (*hatachi* 'twenty years old') and for days (*hatsuka* 'the 20th day'). Also 30 is normally *san-juu*, and the 30th day of a month is *san-juu-nichi*, but occasionally called *mi-so-ka*.[6] The numbers ending 4 and 7 can combine with either the native or Sino-Japanese numbers; 14 (*juu-shi*, *juu-yon*), 24 (*nijuu-shi*, *nijuu-yon*) and 37 (*sanjuu-shichi*, *sanjuu-nana*), 97 (*kyuujuu-shichi*, *kyuujuu-nana*) etc. The Sino-Japanese system is also used for larger numbers; *hyaku* (100),

---

6. The suffix *-so* is a native suffix for ten; *mi-so* '30', *yo-so* '40', *ya-so* '80' etc. However, these are not used productively. Only fixed expression are available; *mi-so-ka* (30th day of a month), *mi-so-ji* (30 years old), *mi-so-hito-moji* (31 letters – the number of moras used to compose a *waka* poem).

Table 1. Native and Sino-Japanese numbers

	Native Series		Sino-Japanese Series
	free form	*bound form*	
1	hi	hito-	ichi
2	fu	futa-/futsu-	ni
3	mi	mi-	san
4	yo/yon	yo-	shi
5	itsu	itsu-	go
6	mu	mu-/mui-	roku
7	nana	nana-/nano-	shichi
8	ya	ya-/yoo-	hachi
9	kokono	kokono-	kyuu/ku
10	too	too-	juu
11			juu ichi
12			juu ni
13			juu san
14			juu shi/juu yon
20		(hata-/hatsu-)	ni juu
30		(mi-so-)	san juu
100			hyaku
1,000			sen
10,000			ichi man (= 1 man)
100,000			juu man (= 10 man)
1,000,000			hyaku man (= 100 man)

sen (1000), *ichi-man* (1 × 10000 = 10 thousand), *juu-man* (10 × 10000 = 100 thousand), *hyaku-man* (100 × 10000 = 1 million), *ichi-oku* (10^8), and *it-choo* (10^{12}).[7]

Most native numerals have identical free and bound forms, but for 'one' and 'two,' the forms are distinct, *hi* (free) and *hito-* (bound) and *fu* (free) and *futa-* (bound), respectively,

---

7. There are native numbers for 100 (*momo*), 1000 (*chi*), and 10000 (*yorozu*). They only appear in fixed expressions; *momo-tose* (100 years old), *chi-tose-ame* (1000 year candy – candy used for cerebration of children's healthy growth at the age of 3, 5 and 7), *chi-yo* (1000 reigns – as used in the national anthem of Japan), *ya-o-yorozu no kamigami* (8,000,000 gods, i.e. many gods).

e.g. *hito-ri, futa-ri* (1 person, 2 persons) and *hito-tsu, futa-tsu* (1 item, 2 items). Some bound forms have alternate forms for different suffixes (e.g. *futa-ri* 'two people' and *futsu-ka* 'two days'; *mu-ttsu* 'six items'– and *mui-ka* 'six days'). For 'ten', *too-ka* 'ten days / the tenth day' exists, but to count ten items, *too* is used without the -*tsu suffix*. The 'first day' and 'one day' are special (*tsuitachi* and *ichi-nichi*, respectively) (see Miller 1967: 337 and Downing 1996: 35–51 for more information on the native numeral system). Because there are very few numbers in the native system, only Sino-Japanese numerals are employed for mathematical and computing purposes. Either system may be used when reciting numbers up to ten, but the important function of both of these numeral systems is to construct a numeric phrase with measure words, quantifiers, and numeral classifier suffixes (§3.2.2 below).

3.2.2 *Numeral classifiers and numeric phrases*

A numeric phrase consists of a numeral suffixed by one of the three types of counters: measure words, quantifiers, and numeral-classifiers. Measure words literally measure objects and concepts according to an established unit. Some examples of measure words are given below. Each example of a measure word is preceded by the gloss SJ (Sino-Japanese) or N (native), indicating the type of numeral that accompanies it. There is a strong tendency to replace the SJ *shi* (4) and *shichi* (7) with their native counterparts, *yon* and *nana*, respectively. Thus, for example, '4 meters' is *yon-meetoru* rather than **shi-meetoru*. The avoidance of these SJ numbers is often attributed to their unpleasant homophones, *shi* 'death' and *shichi* ≈ *shitsu* 'loss.' Also note that *shichi* (7) is phonetically similar to *ichi* (1) and confusing, especially when the high vowel /i/ is devoiced (Chapter 3 §2.1).

Measure words

SJ-*meetoru*	'meters'
SJ-*guramu*	'grams'
SJ-*kiro*	'kilograms, kilometers'
SJ-*nen* (*kan*)	'years'
SJ-*kagetsu* (*kan*)	'months'
SJ-*shuukan*	'weeks'
SJ-*jikan*	'hours'
N-*ka* (*kan*)	'days' (from 2–10 days; *ichi-nichi* for 'one day')
SJ-*nichi* (*kan*)	'days' (over 11 days except 14, 20, 24 days)[8]

The functions of measure words and of quantifiers and classifiers are quite different: while measure words describe an object's length, weight, volume, or the duration of time, quantifiers and classifiers "enumerate" objects. Quantifiers are usually used to quantify objects with no delineating boundaries in terms of containers (e.g. *glasses* in *two glasses*

---

8. The words for 14, 20, 24 days are *juu-yo-kka* (*kan*), *hatsu-ka* (*kan*), and *nijuu-yo-kka* (*kan*), respectively.

of water is a quantifier in English). There are also two quantifiers (*-kai/-do*) that count the frequency of events. Some examples of quantifiers are given below. Native numerals tend to be restricted to represent very small numbers such as 'one' and 'two.' The quantifier *-hako* 'box' usually appears with native numerals, 1–4, and appears with SJ numerals bigger than 5. Below are examples of quantifiers, with numbers 1–3 shown in parentheses.

Quantifiers

SJ-*hai/-pai/-bai*	'cups of'	(*ip-pai, ni-hai, san-bai*)
SJ-*hon/-pon/-bon*	'bottles of'	(*ip-pon, ni-hon, san-bon*)
N/SJ-*hako*	'boxes of'	(*hito-hako, futa-hako, mi-hako*)
N-*kan*	'cans of'	(*hito-kan, futa-kan*) for 1 and 2 only
N-*saji*	'spoonfuls of'	(*hito-saji, futa-saji, mi-saji*)
N-*fukuro*	'bags of'	(*hito-fukuro, futa-fukuro, mi-fukuro*)
SJ-*kai /-do*	'times'	(*ik-kai, ni-kai, san-kai*) (*ichi-do, ni-do, san-do*)

In contrast to quantifiers, numeral classifiers are words used exclusively when counting objects with clear, delineating boundaries. While numerals can directly modify a noun in a language like English, as in "3 DOGS," classifier languages like Japanese must use a numeric phrase, which consists of a numeral and a classifier to modify it, e.g. "3-CLASSIFIER (for animal) + DOG." While measure words and quantifiers can be found in many languages of the world, numeral classifiers are generally found only in languages that do not display obligatory formal number distinctions in nouns (Greenberg 1972). Indeed Japanese does not indicate grammatical numbers obligatorily in nouns (there is no distinction between the singular 'dog' and the plural 'dogs'), but make use of classifiers when such a distinction must be made.

Classifiers are more complex and numerous than quantifiers. There are over 150 classifiers in Japanese, but only less than 30 are regularly used (Downing 1996). The fifteen most commonly used classifiers in the Japanese system are shown on the last page of this chapter. As seen in the table, classifiable objects are first separated into "Animate" and "Inanimate." Under "Animate," "Human" and "Non-human" are distinguished. The native human classifier, N-*ri*, is used for one and two people, *hito-ri* and *futa-ri*, respectively, as noted earlier, and the SJ suffix SJ-*nin* is employed for over 3 people (e.g. *san-nin* '3 people'). In addition SJ-*mee* is employed in more formal situations, especially in writing. Animals and fish are categorized together, but normally the larger species (e.g. horses, elephants, whales) are counted with SJ-*too*, and the smaller ones with SJ-*hiki*, or its variant forms, -*piki* or -*biki* (rabbits, dogs, snakes, and also insects). Birds have their own special classifier, SJ-*wa* (-*ba* for three), though -*hiki/-biki/-piki*, used for small animals, may be also used by some speakers. Under "Inanimate," "Machine" and "Non-machine" are separated. Airplanes (as a type of machine) are counted with SJ-*ki*, and boats are counted with either SJ-*seki* (for a larger type) or SJ-*soo* (generally for a smaller type). Cars are counted with SJ-*dai*, and so are other machines regardless of their size (bulldozers, computers, calculators, smart phones). "Non-machine" inanimate objects are classified according to the shape of the object. Long cylindrical objects such as pens, bottles, cigarettes, and trees are counted with SJ-*hon*, or its variants, -*pon* or -*bon*; thin, flat objects such as paper, CDs, photos, stamps, shirts, are counted with SJ-*mai*; bound objects such as books, photo albums, notebooks are counted with SJ-*satsu*. Small objects with a "roughly equivalent extension in all three dimensions" (Downing 1996: 20), such as apples, erasers, pebbles, and nuts, are counted using SJ-*ko*. Objects with other shapes are usually counted with the general native classifier, N-*tsu* (e.g. mountains, chairs, hats) up to ten, and the Sino-Japanese numerals without a classifier beyond ten. There are also more specialized classifiers such as SJ-*ken* for small buildings (e.g. houses and shops); SJ-*soku* for pairs of shoes, socks etc.; SJ-*zen* for sets of meals, or pairs of chopsticks; SJ-*tsubu* for small grains. Sometimes different classifiers are selected for the same object according to the shape in which it appears; an individual banana is counted with -*hon* (the classifier for cylinder shape object), but a bunch of bananas is counted with -*fusa* (the classifier for bunches of fruit), or according to the conceptual image; as noted -*ken* is used for shops when they are perceived as something similar to houses, but they are counted with -*ten* when viewed as business enterprises.

A crucial syntactic difference between quantifiers (QTF) and classifiers (CLS) is that the former may be preceded by a specifier (SPC), which refers to the type of container used for enumeration; *koppu* (cup = SPC) *ni-hai* (2-QTF) *no* (GEN) *mizu* (water) 'two glasses of water.' A classifier cannot be preceded by a specifier. This difference is attributed to the fact that the classifier directly counts the item denoted by the noun, while the quantifier can do so only indirectly. What a quantifier counts is actually the container, and this container is what the appositive quantifier phrase refers to. When a numeric phrase with either quantifier or classifier modifies a noun, it is followed by the genitive case particle, *no*. Some examples follow.

Quantifier

```
[[(SPC -)   #-QTF]    -GEN   - NOUN]
  koppu     ni-hai     no     mizu        'two glasses of water'
  glass     two-QTF    GEN    water

  tokkuri   san-bon    no     sake        'three bottles of sake'
  bottle    3-QTF      GEN    rice.wine
```

Classifier

```
[[#-CLS]    -GEN   - NOUN]
 san-biki    no     ko-buta      'three little pigs'
 3-CLS       GEN    little.pig

 go-nin      no     heeshi       'five soldiers'
 five-CLS    GEN    soldier
```

Numeric phrases appear in different syntactic positions. This is discussed in Chapter 8 §7 under the heading "numeric phrases."

Chapter 4. Words 77

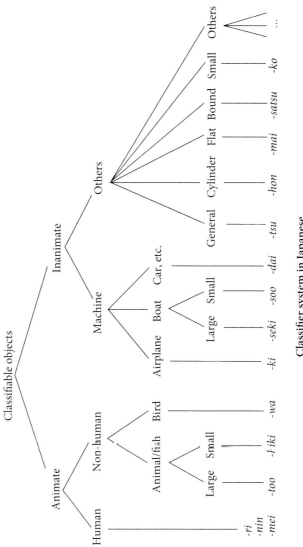

Classifier system in Japanese

CHAPTER 5

Morphology

This chapter concerns morphological structures of both inflectional and non-inflectional categories. The important morphological process of the inflectional categories is "agglutinating suffixation," while two major word-formation processes for the non-inflectional categories are "affixation" and "compounding." Other minor word-formation processes such as "reduplication," "clipping," and "blending" are also discussed. (See Nomura 1977: 245–284; Shibatani 1990: 215–256; Tsujimura 2007: 114–201 for additional discussion.).

1. Morphology of the inflectional category

There are three inflectional categories in Japanese, verbs including auxiliary verbs, adjectives, and the copula. Verb morphology is the most complex, with a large number and variety of suffixes. Adjectives also inflect with their own suffixes. The copula is a bound morpheme with its own inflectional paradigm.

1.1 Verb morphology

1.1.1 *Verb types*

Verbs are classified into three groups according to their morphological structures: the consonant root verb, vowel root verb, and irregular root verb. (These will be referred to hereafter as consonant verbs, vowel verbs, and irregular verbs, respectively.) The root of consonant verbs ends in one of the following consonants *k, s, t, r, b, g, m, n* or the semi-vowel *w* (the semi vowel *w* only appears before the vowel *a*). The root for the consonant verbs 'drink' and 'speak,' for example, are represented by *nom-* and *hanas-*, respectively. In contrast, the vowel verb root ends in either *e* or *i*. Thus the roots for the vowel verbs 'eat' and 'see/watch,' for example, are represented by *tabe-* and *mi-*, respectively. There are only two members in the irregular verb category. They are 'do' and 'come' and have various root-allomorphs as described later in this section.

The root is followed by a stem forming suffix (SFS) to form a stem. An SFS is null (represented by "ø") for vowel verbs and one of the five vowels for consonant verbs. A stem is followed by one or more auxiliary suffixes (Aux Suffixes) to construct a verb form, as shown below. (See Vance (1987: 175–208) and Shibatani (1990: 221–235) for different theoretical models proposed by various linguists for Japanese verb morphology.)

Chapter 5. Morphology

Each auxiliary suffix requires a specific stem-forming suffix (SFS) to be present in the preceding stem. The following table lists the different suffixes that follow each of the five stem-forming suffixes for consonant verbs. (*nom-* is the root for the verb 'drink.')

Table 1. Consonant verb forms

	Root	SFS	AUX SUFFIX
I	nom=	=a-	-ser-/-s- (CAUSATIVE)[a] -rer- (PASSIVE) -na=(i) (NEGATIVE)[b]
II	nom=	=i-	-ø (INFINITIVE)[c] -soo$_1$ (EVIDENTIAL)[d] -ta=(i) (DESIDERATIVE)[b] -niku=(i), -yasu=(i), -zura=(i) etc. (TOUGH)[b] -mas- (POLITE)[e] -nagara, -tsutsu (SIMULTANEOUS) -ta (PAST)[f] -te (CONJUNCTIVE)[f] -tara (CONDITIONAL)[f] -tari (REPRESENTATIVE)[f]
III	nom=	=u-	-ø (NON-PAST) -mai (NEGATIVE VOLITIONAL/CONJECTURE) -yoo, -soo$_2$[d] -rashii (EVIDENTIAL) -na (NEGATIVE IMPERATIVE)
IV	nom=	=e	-ba (CONDITIONAL) -ø (IMPERATAIVE)
V	nom=	=o	-o (VOLITIONAL)

(a) There are also innovative causative forms, which will be discussed in Chapter 8.3.
(b) The verb forms with *-na=(i)*, *-ta=(i)*, *-niku=(i)*, *-yasu=(i)*, and *-zura=(i)* conjugate as adjectives (§1.2 below).
(c) The stem with the *=i-* suffix is the infinitive form.[1] It has three distinct functions. First, it is used as a noun equivalent in the word formation process (§2.1 below). Second,

---

1. The term "infinitive" is due to Martin ([1975] 1991: 392–401). This form is known as *ren'yoo-kee* (連用形) in traditional grammar, and is rendered in various ways in English, including "adverbial" form (Shibatani 1990) and "continuative" form (Kuno 1973), suggesting a wide range of functions.

it is used as a medial verb form in the system of clause chaining (Chapter 12 §3).[2] Third, and most importantly, it combines with numerous other suffixes to code various types of information such as aspectual information, e.g. -hajimeru 'begin,' as in *nom=i-hajimeru* 'begin to drink,' (Chapter 7 §2). Martin ([1975] 1991: 392–475) lists more than fifty suffixes that appear after the infinitive form.

(d) There are two -soo evidentials. One (soo_1) follows the =i- to code immediate evidence including visual evidence, and the other (soo_2) follows the =u- to code hearsay evidence (Chapter 14 §2.1.2).

(e) -mas- is the polite register suffix, and has its own conjugation paradigm (§1.4 below).

(f) The *t* initial suffixes such as the past tense suffix -ta and the conjunctive -te form[3] triggers the process of *onbin* "sandhi" (§1.1.2 below).

Some of the auxiliary suffixes for vowel verbs exhibit allomorphy with an extra syllable, as shown in the capital letters in the table below, e.g. SA for causative, RA for passive, and so forth. As examples of vowel ending root, *tabe-* 'eat' and *mi-* 'see/watch' are used.

Table 2. Vowel verb forms

	ROOT	SFS	AUX SUFFIX
I	tabe=; mi=	=ø-	-SAser-/-SAs- (CAUSATIVE) -RArer- (PASSIVE)
II	tabe=; mi=	=ø-	– same as for the consonant verb –
III	tabe=; mi=	=ø-	-RU (NON-PAST) -RU mai (NEGATIVE VOLITIONAL/CONJECTURE) -RU yoo, soo, rashii (EVIDENTIAL) -RU na (NEGATIVE IMPERATIVE)
IVa	tabe=; mi=	=ø-	-RE-ba (CONDITIONAL)
IVb	tabe=; mi=	=ø-	-RO (IMPERATAIVE)
V	tabe=; mi=	=ø-	-YOo (VOLITIONAL)

The paradigm for the irregular verb *kuru* 'come' partially overlaps with those for the vowel and consonant verbs. However, this verb has three different root forms, as shown in the table below.

---

2. Though the "nominal equivalent" and "clause chaining forms" appear to be identical, their accentual patterns may differ. For example, the accentual pattern for *yom-i* as the nominal equivalent is LH, but that for as the clause chaining form is HL (Martin [1975] 1991: 883).

3. The form referred to here as the "conjunctive form" (or the *-te* form) is also called the "gerund" or the "gerundive form" (Martin [1975] 1991: 475). It has similar functions as the infinitive form (Note 1 above), and connects two predicates (Chapter 4 §2.2.4) and two clauses (Chapter 12 §3) with various semantic relationships (cf. Hasegawa 1996).

Table 3. Irregular verb forms (1)

	ROOT	SFS	AUX SUFFIX
I	ko=	=ø-	– same as for the vowel verb –
II	ki=	=ø-	– same as for the consonant and vowel verb –
III	ku=	=ø-	– same as for the vowel verb –
IVa	ku=	=ø-	– same as for the vowel verb –
IVb	ko=	=ø-	-i (IMPERATAIVE)
V	ko=	=ø-	– same as for the vowel verb –

The other irregular verb, *suru* 'do' also shows an overlapping paradigm with the vowel and consonant verb paradigms, but again it has three different root forms.

Table 4. Irregular verb forms (2)

	ROOT	SFS	AUX SUFFIX
Ia	sa=	=ø-	-ser-/-s- (CAUSATIVE) -rer- (PASSIVE)
Ib	shi=	=ø-	-na=(i) (NEGATIVE)
II	shi=	=ø-	– same as for the consonant verb –
III	su=	=ø-	– same as for the vowel verb –
IVa	su=	=ø-	– same as for the vowel verb –
IVb	shi=	=ø-	– same as for the vowel verb –
V	shi=	=ø-	– same as for the vowel verb –

Auxiliary suffixes mentioned in the above tables can be categorized into four different classes according to their function; voice derivational suffix, termination suffix 1 and 2, and conjunctive suffix.

Voice derivational suffixes: There are four voice derivational suffixes. The causative and passive suffixes must follow the consonant verb's stem forming suffix, *a*, and the desiderative and "tough" sentence (Inoue 1976: 137–150) marking suffix must follow *i*. Three of these suffixes can be combined as in *-sase-rare-ta-(i)* 'want to be cause to do' and *-sase-rare-niku-(i)* 'hard to be cause to do' in these orders to form a complex verb form. A significant characteristic of these forms is that they affect argument structure, e.g. *A ga B o tabe-ru* 'A eats B' vs. *A ga B ga tabe-ta-i* 'A wants to eat B.'; *A-ga B-o taberu* 'A eats B' vs. *B-ga A-ni tabe-rareru* 'B is eaten by A.'

Termination suffixes: The termination suffix can end a sentence. Termination suffix 1 can be further suffixed, but termination suffix 2 cannot. From the functional point of view, termination suffixes 1 marks tense and polarity, while termination suffixes 2 aspect, mood

Table 5. Termination and conjunctive auxiliary suffixes for verbs

Voice Derivational Suffix	Termination Suffix 1	Termination Suffix 2
-(sa)ser-/-(sa)s- (CAUSATIVE)	-na=(i) (NEG)	-(yo)o (VOLITIONAL)
-(ra)rer- (PASSIVE)	-ta (PAST)	-mai (NEG VOLITIONAL)
-ta=(i) (DESIDERATIVE)	-ø /-RU (NON-PAST)	-yoo, -soo$_2$, -rashii (EVID)
-niku=(i) etc. (TOUGH)		- ø/RO (IMPERATIVE)
		-na (NEG IMPERATIVE)
		-mas- (POLITE)
		-soo$_1$ (EVIDENTIAL)
	Conjunctive Suffix	
	-ø (INFINITIVE)	
	-te (CONJUNCTIVE)	
	-tara (CONDITIONAL)	
	-tari (REPRESENTATIVE)	
	-nagara, -tsutsu (SIMULTANEOUS)	
	-(re)ba (CONDITIONAL)	

and modality. Termination Suffixes 2 require a specific form in the preceding element. Evidential suffixes, *-yoo, -soo$_2$, rashii*, can follow all three Termination Suffixes 1 (note *nom=i-ta* becomes *nonda* 'drank' through the *onbin* process, next section), while *-mai* and *–na* follow only the non-past suffix. The other four follow the verb stem directly; e.g. *nom=i-mas-, nom=i-soo$_1$, nom=o-o,* and *nom=e-ø*.

Table 6. Co-occurring patterns of termination suffixes

Stem	Termination Suffix 1	Termination Suffix 2
nom=a ; tabe=ø	-na=(i)	-yoo, -soo, -rashii
nom=i ; tabe=ø	-ta*	-yoo, -soo, -rashii
nom=u; tabe=ø	-ø /-RU	-yoo, -soo, -rashii; -mai; -na
nom=i; tabe=ø		-mas-; -soo
nom=o; tabe=ø		-(yo)o
nom=e; tabe=ø		- ø/RO

Conjunctive suffixes: These suffixes follow a stem to form various adverbial clauses.

Table 7. Co-occurring patterns of conjunctive suffixes

Stem	Conjunctive Suffix
nom=i; tabe=ø	-te*, -tara*, -tari*, -ø, -nagara, -tsutsu
nom=e; tabe=ø	-(re)ba

All except for one require the stem to contain the =*i* stem-forming suffix to be preceding if the verb is a consonant verb; *nom-i-te* (> *non-de*), *nom-i-tara* (> *non-dara*), *nom-i-tari* (> *non-dari*), *nom-i*, *nom-i-nagara* and *nom-i-tsutsu*, the first three of which undergo the process of *onbin* 'sandhi' (next section). The only conjunctive suffix that requires the =*e* stem-forming suffix for consonant verbs is the –*ba* conditional form; *nom-e-ba*.

Different suffixes can concatenate to form a long verb form.

    [mat=a] –[se]-[rare]-[ta=ku]-[na=katta]-[rashii]
    [Root=SFS]-VDS-VDS-VDS-TS1-TS2
    [wait]-[CAUS]-[PSS]-[DES=ADV]-[NEG=PAST]-[EVI]
    '(he) seems to have not wanted to be made to wait'

    [tabe=ø] -sase-rare-tara
    [Root-SFS]-VDS-VDS-CS
    [eat]-[CAUS]-[PSS]-[COND]
    'if (he) is made to eat'

[=*ku* is the adverbial form and =*katta* the past tense form of an adjective (§1.2 below); VDS= voice derivational suffix, TS = termination suffix, and CS = conjunctive suffix.]

1.1.2 Onbin (sandhi)

In the foregoing discussion, reference was made to the process of *onbin* (音便). This is usually translated as "sandhi" or "sound euphony," a morphophonemic process in which the sound is modified under the influence of an adjacent sound for easier and/or pleasing pronunciation. More specifically, it refers to a series of changes prompted by a deletion of the = *i* stem forming suffix. From a historical point of view, it created rare phonemes such as the syllabic nasal and geminate consonants in Japanese. These special phonemes are believed to have become wide-spread when the language imported massive numbers of Chinese words which contain them during the late Old to Middle Japanese periods (9–13 century CE), although they may have been present earlier in the form of sound-symbolic words and emphatic phonology (cf. Chapter 1 Note 12; Watanabe 2001: 78–93). In the context of modern Japanese verb morphology, the *onbin* process applies when the infinitive form of a consonant verb (or the stem ending with =*i*) attaches to a *t* initial inflectional suffix (i.e. -*ta*, -*te*, -*tara*, and -*tari*). Depending on the type of the final consonant of the root, three different *onbin* processes occur, as shown separately below with the conjunctive suffix -*te* as an example. The patterns shown here are only for expository purposes and are not intended to precisely reflect historical development. (See Miller (1967: 203) for a discussion of the historical process.)

As shown in Table 8 on the next page, with roots ending in -*t*, -*r*, -(*w*), the stem forming suffix, -*i*-, elides, then the final consonant of the root assimilates to the *t*, yielding a geminate consonant.[4]

---

4. Note -*t* appears as -*ch* (/č/, [cc]) before *i* in *kach=i-te* /kačite/ [kaccite] in Table 8. The -*t* final consonant verbs conjugate as follows: *kat=a*- /kata/ [kɑta], *kach=i*- /kači/ [kacci], *kats=u* /kacu/

Table 8. The "*onbin*" process for consonant verbs ending in *-t*, *-r*, *-(w)*

	kach=i-te	fur=i-te	ka(w)=i_ -te
i deletion	kach_ -te	fur_-te	ka(w)_ -te
Assimilation	kat-te	fut-te	kat -te
	'win'	'fall'	'buy'

With roots ending in *-n*, *-m*, *-b*, as shown in Table 9 below, the inflectional ending, *-i-*, clides as well. For the *-n* ending root, *t* assimilates to the voicing of *n* and becomes *d*. For the *-m* ending root, *m* first becomes *n* by assimilating to the place of articulation of *t*, then proceeds like the *-n* ending root. For the *-b* ending root, *b* is replaced by the corresponding nasal, and proceeds like the *-m* ending root afterwards. These processes create the syllabic nasal *n*. The proposed processes are summarized below.

Table 9. The "*onbin*" process for consonant verbs ending in *-n*, *-m*, *-b*

	shin=i-te	nom=i-te	asob=i-te
i deletion	shin_-te	nom_-te	asob_-te
Nasalization	–	–	asom-te
Assimilation	–	non-te	ason-te
Voicing	shin-de	non-de	ason-de
	'die'	'drink'	'play'

As shown in Table 10 below, with roots ending in *-k* and *-g*, the following *-i-* palatalizes the preceding consonant. This consonant, represented as k^y and g^y, remains after *i* deletion. Then the voicing of *t* occurs if the ending is the voiced g^y, but it does not occur if the ending is the voiceless k^y. And the palatalized consonant, k^y or g^y, is replaced by the vowel *i*.

Table 10. The "*onbin*" process for consonant verbs ending in *-k*, *-g*

	kak=i-te	kag=i-te
Palatalization	kak^y=i-te	kag^y=i-te
i deletion	kak^y-te	kag^y-te
Voicing	–	kag^y-de
Vowelization	kai-te	kai-de
	'write'	'smell'

[kɑcɯ], *kat=e* /kate/ [kɑte], *kat=o* /kato/ [kɑto]. Also note that the *-w* in the *-w* ending consonant verbs, e.g. *ka(w)=u* 'buy,' appears only before '=a,' so the conjugation pattern is as follows: *kaw=a-* /kawa/ [kɑwɑ], *ka=i-* /kai/ [kɑi], *ka=u* /kau/ [kɑɯ], *ka=e* /kae/ [kɑe], *ka=o-* /kao/ [kɑo].

The verb *ik-* 'go' is the only exception to the *onbin* process. It does not follow the expected pattern just described for the *-k* ending root, but follows the pattern of the root ending *-t, -r, -(w)* mentioned earlier. See Table 11.

Table 11. The "*onbin*" process for *iku* 'go'

	iki-te
i deletion	*ik_-te*
Assimilation	*it-te*
	'go'

The remaining consonant root verbs, i.e. verbs with the *s* ending root, as well as vowel verbs do not trigger the *onbin* process.

hanashi-te tabe-te mi-te
'speak'   'eat'   'see'

1.1.3 *Transitive-intransitive opposition*

One important characteristic of verb morphology in Japanese is the existence of a large set of transitive-intransitive verb pairs (about 350 pairs are listed in Jacobsen 1992: 258–268). Transitive 'open,' for instance, is *ake-ru* while its intransitive counterpart is *ak-u*. Given in Table 12 on the next page are five of the 16 types in Jacobsen (ibid.)'s list with selected examples. To highlight the segment in focus in this section, the following special convention is used; the segment in focus is preceded by an underline and followed by an equal sign, as in _e=.

The productivity of these transitive-intransitive oppositions is limited, and transitivity cannot be established solely on the basis of the morphological form of a verb. However, it is possible to observe some systematic morphological relations between the two verbs in each pair, e.g. in Group (i) the intransitive members are all *-e* ending vowel verbs while the transitive members are all consonant verbs; in Group (ii) the situation reverses. More significant patterns are found in Groups (iii) through (v). In these groups, the transitive members contain *-s* in the root, and for (iv) and (v) the intransitive members contain the consonant *-r* in the root. These associations are rather constant in a large part of the transitive-intransitive sets with only a few exceptions. Crucially, this distinction is similar to the distinction between the passive *-(r)ar-* and the causative *-(s)as-*. In other words, a significant number of transitive verbs contain in their roots the causative element *-s* and a significant number of intransitive verbs contain the passive element *-r*, suggesting some productive morphological process of transitivity marking in an earlier stage of the language. However, this process seems to have ceased before the eighth century when written documents first became available.

Table 12. Intransitive vs. transitive verb pairs

	Intransitive	Transitive	
(i)	_e=	_ø=	
	kir_e=ru	kir_ø=u	'become cut' vs. 'cut'
	muk_e=ru	muk_ø=u	'become peeled' vs. 'peel'
	chigir_e=ru	chigir_ø=u	'become torn' vs. 'tear'
(ii)	_ø=	_e=	
	ak_ø =u	ak_e=ru	'open$_{INT}$' vs. 'open$_{TR}$'
	itam_ø =u	itam_e=ru	'hurt' vs. 'injure'
	sodats_ø =u	sodat_e=ru	'grow up' vs. 'bring up'
(iii)	_ø=	_as=	
	a(w)_ø=u	aw_as=u	'meet' vs 'bring together'
	her_ø=u	her_as=u	'decrease$_{INT}$' vs. 'decrease$_{TR}$'
	odorok_ø=u	odorok_as=u	'surprise$_{INT}$' vs. 'surprise$_{TR}$'
(iv)	_r=	_s=	
	hita_r=u	hita_s=u	'soak$_{INT}$' vs. 'soak$_{TR}$'
	modo_r=u	modo_s=u	'return$_{INT}$' vs. 'return$_{TR}$'
	shime_r=u	shime_s=u	'wet$_{INT}$' vs. 'wet$_{TR}$'
(v)	_re=	_s=	
	hana_re=ru	hana_s=u	'move away' vs. 'separate from'
	kaku_re=ru	kaku_s=u	'hide$_{INT}$' vs. 'hide$_{TR}$'
	kobo_re=ru	kobo_s=u	'spill$_{INT}$' vs. 'spill$_{TR}$'

1.2 Adjective morphology

The adjective is another inflectional category in Japanese. Its internal organization can be compared to that of the verb, but its conjugation pattern is much simpler than verbs with fewer auxiliary suffixes.

```
           ←——————— ADJECTIVE FORM ———————→
              ←——— STEM ———→
           [ [   ROOT = SFS   ]  -Aux Suffix  -Aux Suffix]
```

The adjectival root ends in any vowel except *e*. Thus the root for 'high/expensive' and 'hot,' for example, are represented as *taka=* and *atsu=*, respectively. There are five stem-forming suffixes; =*ka-*, =(*k*)*i-*, =*ku-*, =*ke-* and =ø-.

Table 13. Adjective forms

	Root	SFS	AUX SUFFIX
I	atsu=	=ka-	-tta (PAST) -ttara (CONDITIONAL) -ttari (REPRESENTATIVE)
II	atsu=	=ki- > =i-(a)	-ø (NONPAST) -yoo, -soo$_2$, -rashii (EVIDENTIAL)
III	atsu=	=ku-(b) (>=u-)(c)	-ø (INFINITIVE) -na-(i) (NEGATIVE)(d) -te (CONJUNCTIVE)
IV	atsu=	=ke-	-reba (CONDITIONAL)
V	atsu=	=ø-	-soo$_1$ (EVIDENTIAL) -gar=(u) (REVEALING)(e)

(a) The suffix =ki- has gone through a historical change (*onbin*) and *k* is always deleted in the modern language: *atsu=ki > atsu=i*.
(b) The =ku- suffix turns an adjective into an adverb (e.g. *taka-ku* 'highly'). It is also used as a clause chaining form (e.g. 'high and') and as a noun equivalent (§2.1 below).
(c) The suffix =ku- may appear as =u- in the hyper polite adjective form, *atsuku-gozaimasu > atsuu-gozaiamasu* 'it is hot (hyper polite).' This form is found in the common morning greeting expression *o-hayoo gozaimasu* 'Good Morning' (haya*ku* > haya*u*> hayoo). The change from =ku- to =u- is common in the Western dialect.
(d) The -na-(i) is the negative auxiliary suffix which must follow =ku- mentioned above. However, it may be a free morpheme rather than a suffix (a) bound morpheme since a topic particle *wa* can intervene between it and the stem, as in *atsuku wa nai* 'it is NOT expensive.' (Timothy Vance – personal communication).
(e) The -*garu* revealing suffix is used only with emotion and sensation adjectives such as *ureshii* 'happy', *sabishii* 'lonley' *atsui* 'hot,' and *samui* 'cold' to code an internal state of an animate being. See Chapter 14 §1.1. It conjugates as a *r*- ending consonant verb.

The tense, negative, and "revealing" suffixes (Termination Suffix 1) may be followed by one of the evidential suffixes (Termination Suffix 2). The immediate evidential (-soo$_1$) follows the root directly. The suffixes, –ø, -te, -ttara, -ttari, and -reba are conjunctive suffixes.

1.3 Copula morphology

The copula is a word which helps to form a predicate with a noun or nominal adjective. Besides the forms listed below, it has a separate polite register conjugation (see the section which immediately follows).

Table 14. Termination and conjunctive auxiliary suffixes for adjectives

ROOT	Termination Suffix 1	Termination Suffix 2
atsu=	=ku-na=(i) (NEG) =ka-tta (PAST) =i (NONPAST) = ø-gar=(u) (REVEALING)	-yoo, -soo$_2$, -rashii (EVID)
atsu=		-soo$_1$ (EVIDENTIAL)
	Conjunctive Suffix	
atsu=	=ku-ø (INFINITIVE) =ku-te (CONJUNCTIVE) =ka-ttara (CONDITIONAL) =ka-ttari (REPRESENTATIVE) =ke-reba (CONDITIONAL)	

Table 15. Copula forms

Nonpast	da
Past	datta
Conjecture	daroo
Negative	de wa na-i/ja na-i
Past Negative	de wa na-katta/ja na-katta
Conjunctive (TE)	de
Attributive	no/na
Adverbial	ni

The *de* in the negative form is the conjunctive, TE, form of *des-u* and is followed by the topic/contrast particle *wa*. In normal speech *de wa* will be contracted to *ja*. The copula is unique among inflectional categories in that it retains the (non-past) conclusive-attributive distinction that has been lost for both verbs and adjectives. Contrast *da* and *no* for attributive nouns, and *da* and *na* for attributive nominal adjectives in the following examples (Chapter 9 §2).

(ano hito wa) nihonjin <u>da</u> that person TOP Japanese COP	'(He) is Japanese.'
nihonjin -<u>no</u> hito Japanese COP:ATT person	'a Japanese person'
(ano hito wa) kiree <u>da</u> that person TOP beautiful COP	'(She) is beautiful.'
kiree -<u>na</u> hito beautiful COP:ATT person	'a beautiful person'

Also *ni* is the adverbial form of the copula in the following words (Chapter 4 §2.2.5).

kiree-ni   'beautifully/cleanly'
kantan-ni   'easily'

1.4 Polite register inflection paradigms

All three inflectional categories have a secondary paradigm in the polite register with the past/nonpast and affirmative/negative oppositions. The verbal paradigm is constructed with the *-mas-* suffix, which must follow the infinitive form, e.g. *nom=i-*. The next table shows the paradigm for *nom=i-* 'drink.'

Table 16. Polite register forms – verbs

	Nonpast	Past
Affirmative	*nom=i-mas-u*	*nom=i-mash-ita*
Negative	*nom=i-mas-en*	*nom=i-mas-en deshita*

The polite register paradigm for the copula is shown below with the noun *hana* 'flower.' Note that *arimasen* is the polite/negative form of an existential verb *arimasu* '(inanimate object) exists.'

Table 17. Polite register forms – copula

	Nonpast	Past
Affirmative	*hana des-u*	*hana desh-ita*
Negative	*hana de wa ari-masen*	*hana de wa ari-masen deshi-ta*
	hana ja ari-masen	*hana ja ari-masen deshi-ta*

The adjective's secondary formal register paradigm is shown below with the adjective *taka-* 'high/expensive.'

Table 18. Polite register forms – adjectives

	Nonpast	Past
Affirmative	*taka-i des-u*	*takak-atta des-u (?taka-i desh-ita)*
Negative (1)	*taka-ku-na-i des-u*	*taka-ku-na-katta des-u*
Negative (2)	*taka-ku-arimasen*	*taka-ku- ari-masen desh-ita*

Basically the polite paradigm is constructed by adding the non-inflecting *des-u* to the informal adjective paradigm. The past-affirmative form *deshi-ta* is sometimes added to the -i ending in the past as shown in parentheses (?*taka-i desh-ita*), but its use is infrequent and has not yet been incorporated in the language (Alfonso 1966: 141). Note that the informal copula, *da*, cannot replace *des-u* in this paradigm, e.g. *takai da (Chapter 4 §2.1.2). There are two negative forms, among which Negative (2) is standard. Negative (2) uses the *arimasen* and *arimasen deshita* forms from the copula paradigm.

2. Word-formation processes

A word may be a simple word consisting of one lexical base. Alternatively it may be a composite word formed by combining two or more lexical bases ("compounding"), or a base and one or more affixes ("derivation"). Words may be constructed through more minor processes such as "reduplication," "clipping," or "blending."

2.1 Noun equivalents (Lexical nominalization)

In the process of word formation, noun equivalents are employed extensively.[5] Noun equivalents are made from adjectives (A), nominal adjectives (NA) and verbs (V). The adjective based noun equivalent is the same as the adjective's root (e.g. *aka* 'red'). Though some adjectives (e.g. *aka=i* 'red') have actual nominal counterparts (e.g. *aka* 'red'), most do not. The adjective based noun equivalents are never used as independent nouns; they merely participate in the word-formation process; *atsu-kan* (*atsui* 'hot' + *kan* 'warming of *sake*') > hot *sake*' (§2.3 below); *usu-giri* (*usui* 'thin' + *kiru* 'cut, slice') > 'thin-cut (e.g. thinly sliced bread)'. Adjective based noun equivalents may be reduplicated; *atsu-atsu* 'hot-hot > 'deeply in love,' *taka-daka* 'high-high' > high up in the sky.'

Table 19. Adjectives and their noun equivalents

Adjective (A)	Noun (N)	Noun Equivalent
aka=i (red)	*aka*	
shiro=i (white)	*shiro*	
atsu=i (hot)		*atsu-*
usu=i (thin)		*usu-*

---

5. Lexical nominalization should be distinguished from grammatical nominalization with formal nouns such as *koto* and *no*. Grammatical nominalization will be discussed as the process of complementation in Chapter 10:2. See Shibatani (2009) and Shibatani (to appear) for a distinction between the two types of nominalization.

There is no formal difference between the nominal adjective and its noun equivalent. Some nominal adjectives are used as nouns directly in the process of word formation (e.g. *kenkoo-tai* 'healthy body' ← (*kenkoo* 'healthy (NA)' + *tai* 'body (N)'; *suki-kirai* 'likes and dislikes.'

Table 20. Nominal adjectives and their noun equivalents

Nominal Adjective (NA)	Noun Equivalent
suki (like)	*suki* (liking)
genki (healthy/vigorous)	*genki* (health/vigor)
heewa (peaceful)	*heewa* (peace)

Verbs in their nonpast form with the *-(r)u* inflection, and infinitive forms with the *-i* inflection, can be used as noun equivalents in word formation.

Table 21. Verbs and their noun equivalents

Verb (V)	Noun Equivalent (nonpast form)	Noun Equivalent (infinitive form)
ik= (go)	*ik=u*	*ik=i*
kaer= (return)	*kaer=u*	*kaer=i*

Nominalization with a nonpast form, shown underlined in the following examples, is not very productive and is found only in fixed expressions (Martin [1975] 1991: 889–904; Horie 1997).

> <u>nigeru</u>   ga   kachi
> fleeing   NOM   winning.
> 'Nothing is better than fleeing.' (← 'Fleeing is winning.')
>
> <u>miru</u>   to   <u>kiku</u>   to   wa   oochigai   da
> seeing and   listening and   TOP   big.difference COP
> 'Seeing something is far different from hearing about it.'
>
> <u>naguru</u>   <u>keru</u>   no   bookoo   o   uketa (Chapter 16 §1, line 1.3)
> hit   kick   GEN   assault ACC   receive:PAST
> '(They) were beaten and kicked in an assault on them.'

By contrast, nominalization with the infinitive form is very productive (Martin [1975] 1991: 886). See a few examples below. (The location of pitch fall associated with accent, if any, is shown with an arrow (⌐) in this table.)

Nominalization with the infinitive form shown in the table above involves many cases of compound noun formation to be discussed shortly. In the remainder of this chapter, a "nominalized verb" refers to a noun equivalent derived by this process. Also, in the

Table 22. Nominalized verbs

Nominalized Verb	Non-past Form
ugoki˥ (movement)	← ugo˥k-u (move)
hanashi˥ (story)	← hana˥s-u (speak)
odori (dance)	← odor-u (dance)
tsuri (fishing)	← tsur-u (fish)
hirameki (sudden realization)	← hirame˥k-u (realize)

following discussion, the collective term "noun equivalent" refers to words used as nouns that are derived from adjectives (Na) or verbs (Nv).

2.2 Affixation

Affixation in Japanese is a process that combines a bound morpheme, either a prefix or suffix, with a lexical base to create a new word. In this section, the following notations are used: Sino-Japanese (underlined), **loan words** (boldface); N = Noun, V = Verb, A= Adjective, NA = Nominal Adjective, Adv. = Adverb, SSW = sound symbolic word.

Prefixes: The most productive native noun prefix is the "polite prefix," *o-*, which precedes native nouns and nominalized verb bases. This prefix also occasionally precedes Sino-Japanese words, but the *go-* prefix is more common in this case. These prefixes often precede food/beverage names and things belonging to the addressee. Words with the prefix *o-/go-* are employed more often by women than men in the polite speech register (Chapter 15 §5).

Polite prefix		
o-[Native N]	o-kome	'raw rice'
	o-sake	'rice wine'
	o-karada	'(your) body/health'
	o-tearai	'bath room'
	o-kane	'money'
go-[SJ N]	go-fujin	'ladies'
	go-kigen	'state of mind'
o-[Nv]	o-share	'dressing up'
	o-dekake	'(your) going out'

Emphatic and size/degree prefixes appear with a noun or nominalized adjective base.

Emphatic prefix		
ma-[N]	*ma-hiru*	'in the midst of the day'
	ma-yonaka	'midnight'
	mas-shiro	'pure white'
ma-[Na]	*mak-kura*	'pitch dark'
	mak-ka	'deep-red'
Size/degree prefixes		
oo-	*oo-arashi*	'heavy storm'
	oo-genka	'big fight'
ko-	*ko-goe*	'whisper'
	ko-ishi	'pebbles'
*do-**	*do-erai*	'extremely problematic'
	do-shirooto	'extremely inexperienced person'

*(*do-* is very colloquial and vulgar.)

Prefixes do not generally change the word class of the base, but productive Sino-Japanese (S-J) negative prefixes often (though not always) change nouns into nominal adjectives. The difference can be assessed the attributive form of copula that a word takes; nouns (N) take *no* while nominal adjectives take *na* (Chapter 4 §2.1.3).

Negative prefix		
<u>*mu-*</u>	<u>*mu-tenka*</u> (N)	'non-addition'
<u>*fu-*</u>	<u>*fu-keeki*</u> (NA)	'economic slump'
<u>*hi-*</u>	<u>*hi-jooshiki*</u> (NA)	'lack of common sense'
<u>*mi-*</u>	<u>*mi-happyoo*</u> (N)	'non public, unpublished'

Other common S-J prefixes are as follows.

Other S-J prefixes		
<u>*han-*</u> 'anti/opposite'	<u>*han-taisee*</u> (N)	'anti-establishment'
<u>*jun-*</u> 'pure'	<u>*jun-bungaku*</u> (N)	'pure literature'
<u>*zen-*</u> 'all'	<u>*zen-sekai*</u> (N)	'all over the world'
<u>*choo-*</u> 'super'	<u>*choo-nooryoku*</u> (N)	'super mental power, ESP'

Suffixes: Suffixes are more numerous in kind and more productive than prefixes in Japanese. The base to which suffixes are attached is either a noun or a noun equivalent. A suffix may or may not change the lexical category of the base. The next is a non-exhaustive list of common suffixes classified according to the type of lexical category they attach to; the symbol to the left of the arrow is the category of the word without the suffix, and the one to the right of the arrow is its category with the suffix.

N → N (no lexical category change)

(a) Title suffixes (Chapter 15 §1)

-*san* (a general polite title)	*yamada-san*	'Mr./Ms. Yamada'
-*shi* (formal title)	*yamada-shi*	'Mr./Ms. Yamada'
-*kun* (familiar male title)	*yamada-kun*	'Mr. Yamada'
-*chan* (diminutive title)	*taroo-chan*	'Dear Little Taro'

(b) Plural & Associative-Plural (Chapter 4 §2.1.1)

-*tachi* (neutral)	*kodomo-tachi*	'children'
	yoshiko-tachi	'Yoshiko and others'
-*ra* (general)	*kodomo-ra*	'children'
	aitsu-ra	'those guys'
-*gata* (honorific)	*sensee-gata*	'teachers'

(c) Agent suffixes (person who does/is X)

-*ka*	*shihon-ka*	'financier'
-*sha*	*shiki-sha*	'conductor'
-*nin*	*annai-nin*	'guide'
-*jin*	*gaikoku-jin*	'foreigner'
-*te*	*hataraki-te*	'worker'

(d) Others

-*fuu*	'style/like'	*nihon-fuu*	'Japanese-style'
-*yoo*	'use'	*gakusee-yoo*	'for students' use'
-*ryoku*	'power'	*settoku-ryoku*	'power to convince'
-*darake*	'full of'	*kizu-darake*	'cuts and bruises'

N → A

-*rashii*	'like'	*otoko-rashii*	'manly'
		kodomo-rashii	'child like'
-*poi*	'like'	*onnap-poi*	'feminine'
		kodomop-poi	'childish'

N /A/ etc. → NA

-yaka	'appearance/manner'	tsuya-yaka	'glossy'
		yuru-yaka	'gentle'
		hiso-yaka	'quiet'
		ade-yaka	'charming'
<u>teki</u>	'like'	<u>jishu-teki</u>	'independent'
		<u>kojin-teki</u>	'privately'

A/NA → N

-sa (nominalizer)		naga-sa	'length'
		reesee-sa	'calmness' 'offensiveness'
-mi (nominalizer)		iya-mi	'weakness'
		yowa-mi	

A → NA

-ge	'appearance'	ureshi-ge	'happy appearance'
		sabishi-ge	'sad appearance'

V → N

-kata	'method'	tsukai-kata	'how to use'
		nomi-kata	'way of drinking'

NA/A/V → N

-ke 'feeling'		iya-ke	'aversion'
		samu-ke	'feeling cold'
		haki-ke	'nausea'

N/NA/A/Adv. → V

-meku	'become'	iro-meku	'become tinged'
		kira-meku	'shine'
-tsuku	'become'	zawa-tsuku	'become noisy'
		gata-tsuku	'become shaky'
-buru	'pretend'	iiko-buru	'pretend to be a good kid'
-garu	'show signs of'	arigata-garu	'showing gratitude'
		kawai-garu	'showing affection'

2.3 Compounding

Compounding is a very productive process in Japanese. Among compound words, compound nouns are far greater in number than compound verbs or adjectives. The lexical category is determined by the head which always appears as the right-most element in a compound.

Compound verbs: A compound verb consists of a verbal head which combines with either a noun or a noun equivalent (Nv = nominalized verbal base; Na = nominalized adjective base). When the lexical meaning of V in the Nv + V structure becomes weakened, auxiliary verbs can be derived; e.g. the aspectual auxiliary, -*dasu* with the original meaning of 'put out' has become an "inceptive aspect" marker as in *furi-dasu* '(rain) starts to fall' (Chapter 7 §2).

N + V

ki-zuku 'notice' (*ki* 'spirit' + *tsuku* 'turn on' cf. *ki ga tsuku* 'notice')
na-zukeru 'name' (*na* 'name' + *tsukeru* 'attach' cf. *na o tsukeru* 'attach a name')

Nv + V

| *uchi-otosu* | 'shoot down' | (*utsu* 'shoot' + *otosu* 'drop') |
| *haki-dasu* | 'spit out/sweep out' | (*haku* 'vomit/sweep' + *dasu* 'put out') |

Na + V

| *ao-zameru* | 'become pale' | (*aoi* 'blue' + *sameru* 'cool off') |
| *naga-biku* | 'prolong' | (*nagai* 'long' + *hiku* 'draw') |

Compound adjectives: A compound adjective consists of an adjectival head which combines with either a noun or a noun equivalent.

N + A

haba-hiroi 'wide' (*haba* 'width' + *hiroi* 'wide', cf. *haba ga hiroi* 'width is wide')
na-dakai 'famous' (*na* 'name' + *takai* 'high', cf. *na ga takai* 'name is high')

Nv + A

| *mushi-atsui* | 'humid' | (*musu* 'steam' + *atsui* 'hot') |
| *mawari-kudoi* | 'roundabout' | (*mawaru* 'circle' + *kudoi* 'verbose') |

Na + A

| *atsu-kurushii* | 'sweltering' | (*atsui* 'hot' + *kurushii* 'tormenting') |
| *hoso-nagai* | 'slender' | (*hosoi* 'narrow' + *nagai* 'long') |

Compound nouns: Compound nouns with two bases consist of a nominal head with another nominal element. Some compound nouns are hybrid (Chapter 4 §2.1.1). Since each base of a two-member compound noun can be a noun (N) or a noun equivalent (Nv or Na), there are nine logically possible patterns. Among them, the N+N is the most productive pattern.

N + N		
kabe-gami	'wall paper'	(kabe 'wall' + kami 'paper')
<u>eeyoo</u>-busoku	'malnutrition'	(eeyoo 'nutrition' + fusoku 'lacking')
<u>eegyoo</u>-**man**	'sales person'	(eegyoo 'sales' + man 'man')
nyuusu-<u>bangumi</u>	'news program'	(nyuusu 'news' + bangumi 'program')

The second most productive pattern is N+Nv. The first element, N, in this pattern most often is the direct object or the intransitive subject to the Nv, but it may also be in some adverbial relation to the Nv. Referent types of these compounds vary; they may be an event (*ame-furi* 'raining'), a person (*kane-mochi* 'rich person'), an instrument (*kan-kiri* 'can opener'), or a product (*tamago-yaki* 'omelet'). (See Kageyama 1982; Shibatani 1990: 237–247.)

N + Nv (1)		N (Subject)
hi-atari	'sunlight'	(hi 'sun' + ataru 'hit')
ame-furi	'rain'	(ame 'rain' + furu 'fall')
ne-agari	'price hike'	(ne 'price' + agaru 'rise')
N + Nv (2)		N (Direct Object)
kane-mochi	'rich person'	(kane 'money' + motsu 'have')
sake-nomi	'drinker'	(sake 'liquor' + nomu 'drink')
hito-goroshi	'murder/murderer'	(hito 'person' + korosu 'kill')
N + Nv (3)		N (Adverbial)
nama-goroshi	'killing alive'	(nama 'raw' + korosu 'kill')
shita-gi	'underwear'	(shita 'bottom' + kiru 'wear')
toranpu-uranai	'fortune-telling by cards'	(**toranpu** 'cards' + uranau 'tell fortune')

The next most productive pattern is Nv + Nv. Some of these noun compounds have verbal compound counterparts (e.g. *hanashi-ai* 'negotiation' < *hanashi-au* 'negotiate'), but others don't (e.g. *hiki-nige* 'hit-and-run' < *hiki-nigeru 'hit and run') (Ohta 1994).

Nv + Nv		
kui-nige	'dine and ditch'	(kuu 'eat' + nigeru 'escape')
nozoki-mi	'peeping'	(nozoku 'peep' + miru 'watch')
uchi-awase	'staff meeting'	(utsu 'beat' + awaseru 'put together')
tachi-yomi	'reading a book standing in a book-store'	(tatsu 'stand' + yomu 'read')

The next most productive combination is Nv + N.

Nv + N		
deki-gokoro	'sudden impulse'	(*dekiru* 'come out' + *kokoro* 'mind')
yake-ato	'ruins of a fire'	(*yakeru* 'be burnt' + *ato* 'remains')

Other less productive combinations are as follows.

N + Na	sake-zuki	'alcohol lover'	(*sake* 'liquor' + *suki* 'like')
Na + N	furu-kabu	'old timer'	(*furui* 'old' + *kabu* 'stump')
Na + Nv	haya-oki	'early rising/riser'	(*hayai* 'early' + *okiru* 'get up')
Na + Na*			
Nv + Na	hanashi-beta	'unskillful speaker'	(*hanasu* 'tell' + *heta* 'unskillful')

*(See "Coordinate compounds" below).

In addition to the nine possible combinations for noun compounds, there is also a type of nominal compound consisting of a sound-symbolic (SSW) or other adverbial expressions with a noun head.

SSW/adverbial + N		
kankan-deri	'intense sunlight'	(SSW + *teru* 'shine')
dotabata-kigeki	'slapstick comedy'	(SSW + *kigeki* 'comedy')
chotto-mi	'glimpse'	(*chotto* 'a little' + *miru* 'look')
ukkari-mono	'absent-minded person'	(*ukkari* 'absentminded' + *mono* 'person')

Coordinate compounds (or "dvandva" compounds), which are numerous in Japanese, are those consisting of two semantically opposing elements (i.e. *asa-yuu* 'morning and night') and those consisting of semantically related elements (e.g. *eda-ha* 'branches and leaves'). The compound, *eda-ha*, just mentioned, literally means "a tree's branches and leaves," but also means "minute details" figuratively. Some coordinate compounds have both literal and metaphorical usage. Metaphorical meanings are indicated after an arrow in parentheses in the next table.

N + N		
joo-ge	'up and down'	
dan-jo	'man and woman'	
oya-ko	'parent and child'	
fuu-fu	'husband and wife'	
zen-aku	'good and bad'	
kyoo-jaku	'strong and weak'	(→ 'rhythm')
me-hana	'eyes and nose'	(→ 'shape of a matter')
o-hire	'tail and fin'	(→ 'exaggeration')

Na + Na

suki-kirai	'likes and dislikes'	(→ 'preference')
yoshi-ashi	'good and bad'	(→ 'quality')
ama-kara	'sweet and spicy'	(→ 'various experiences in life')

Nv + Nv

dashi-ire	'taking out and putting in'	
kashi-kari	'lending and borrowing'	
yomi-kaki	'reading and writing'	
de-hairi	'leaving and entering'	(→ 'foot traffic')
uki-shizumi	'floating and sinking'	(→ 'up and down, fluctuation')

Multiple bases may be compounded variously.

[[***pan – kui***] – *kyoosoo*]]   'bread eating competition'
[[bread - eat] – competition]

[[*shirooto*]– [*nodo-jiman*]]   'amateur singing contest'
[[amateur – [throat – proud]

2.4 Reduplication

Reduplication is a special type of compounding in which two identical bases are combined. Though not very productive, reduplication is sometimes used to indicate the plurality of a noun base. In the following examples, the non-reduplicated form (e.g. *yama*) is ambiguous between the singular and the plural meanings, but when it is reduplicated, it has only the (emphatic) plural meaning.

yama-yama 'mountains'   *hito-bito* 'people'   *ki-gi* 'trees'
hi-bi 'days'   *sumi-zumi* 'every corner'

Reduplication also creates adverbial and/or adjectival expressions with different types of bases. The most productive reduplication of this type is observed in sound-symbolic words (Chapter 4 §3.1).

fura-fura   'groggy/-ily'
doki-doki   'nervous/ly'
mero-mero   'infatuated/ly'

Reduplication of a noun or noun equivalent also creates adjectival and/or adverbial expressions.

N + N		
iro-iro	'various/ly'	(*iro* 'color')
sama-zama	'various/ly'	(*sama* 'appearance')
Na + Na		
karu-garu	'lightly/effortlessly'	(*karui* 'light')
chika-jika	'soon'	(*chikai* 'close')
Nv + Nv		
hore-bore	'fondly'	(*horeru* 'fall in love')
omoi-omoi	'in different ways'	(*omou* 'think')
naki-naki	'cryingly'	(*naku* 'cry')

The reduplication of a verb's nonpast form produces a limited set of expression, as seen in the following examples.

kawaru-gawaru	'one after another'	(*kawaru* 'change')
yuku-yuku (wa)	'in the future'	(*yuku* 'go')
miru-miru (*uchini*)	'in a short period of time'	(*miru* 'watch')
osoru-osoru	'carefully/timidly'	(*osoruru* 'fear')

2.5 Clipping and blending

Clipping is a shortening process whereby part of a word is cut off. It may be used to create slang (SL) expressions (first three words below), but more often than not it is used to shorten loan words which tend to contain multiple moras in the non-clipped form. It is usually the latter part of a longer word that is clipped but, in some cases, it is the beginning part (Kubozono 2002: 81–111; Tsujimura 2007: 141).[6]

---

6. Shortened words tend to have one (bimoraic) foot, e.g. *suto* 'strike' (Chapter 3 §3). When they are longer than one foot length, they tend to form the syllable structure definable as [long-short]. Thus, *panku* 'puncture' is analyzed as having *pan* (a long syllable) and *ku* (short syllable). Similarly, *paama* 'permanent wave' is analyzed as having *paa* (a long syllable) and *ma* (short syllable). The reverse order is not allowed. This explains why the clipped form of *rokeeshon* 'location' is *roke*, not **rokee* (the word *roke* means 'a movie shooting' from the original meaning of 'location of a movie shooting'). Similarly, the clipped form of *gyarantii* 'guaranteed fees' is *gyara*, not **gyaran* as the latter would contain a short syllable (*gya*) followed by a long syllable (*ran*) (Kubozono 2002: 94–102).

maji	'serious' (SL)	(*maji*[*me*])
kiza	'obnoxious' (SL)	(*kiza*[*wari*])
satsu	'police' (SL)	([*kee*]*satsu*)
suto	'(labor) strike'	(*suto*[*raiki*])
demo	'demonstration'	(*demo*[*nsutoreeshon*])
panku	'puncture'	(*panku*[*chaa*])
paama	'permanent (wave)'	(*paama*[*nento*])
baito	'temporary/part time job'	([*aru*] *baito*=*Arbeit* (from German))
hoomu	'platform in a railway station'	(= [*puratto*] *hoomu*)
intoro	'introduction'	(*intoro*[*daku.shon*])

Clipping also applies to Sino-Japanese and loan word compounds.

suupaa	'super market'	(*suupaa.* [*maaketto*])
konbini	'convenience store'	(*konbini* [*ensu. sutoaa*])
basuke	'basketball'	(*basuke* [*tto. booru*])
<u>*koosoku*</u>	'highway'	(<u>*koosoku.*</u>[*dooro*])
<u>*keetai*</u>	'mobile phone'	(<u>*keetai.*</u>[*denwa*])

A related process is the "clipping and compounding," a process that can be applied to longer (usually) four character Sino-Japanese compounds. A four character word (e.g. *too.kyoo-dai.gau* 東京大学 'University of Tokyo') usually consists of two lexical bases (東京 and 大学), each of which is comprised of two characters (東 and 京; 大 and 学). In the "clipping and compounding" process, the first character of each base (東 and 大) is selected and then put together (too-dai 東大). Since many Sino-Japanese bases are of two mora length, the resultant clipped form is more often than not a four mora word, i.e. two sets of a bimoraic foot (Chapter 3 §3). Using a period (.) to represent the boundary between the two characters making up each base, and a hyphen to show the boundary between the two bases, the process can be represented as: [A.B – X.Y] > [A – X]. The last example below is a case of a five character word undergoing the same process: [A.B.C – X.Y] > [A – X]. In this case, too, the resulting word has two characters and four moras.

<u>*nichi-gin*</u>   'Bank of Japan'
日銀 < 日本銀行 (*ni.hon* 'Japan' – *gin.koo* 'bank')

<u>*koku-ren*</u>   'United Nations'
国連 < 国際連合   (*koku.sai* 'international' – *ren.goo* 'union')

<u>*gaku-wari*</u>   'student discount'
学割 < 学生割引   (*gaku.see* 'student' – *wari.biki* 'discount')

<u>*gen-patsu*</u>   'nuclear power generation'
原発 < 原子力発電 (*gen.shi.ryoku* 'nuclear power' – *hatsu.den* 'power generation')

The method of "clipping and compounding" is also applied to longer loan words, especially to produce slang expressions (Ito 1990). Though loan words are unlike Sino-Japanese words in that they do not show internal morpheme boundaries within a base, the resultant word also tends to be a four mora length (two sets of "bimoraic foot"). Thus, リモート-コントロール (*rimooto-kontorooru*) 'remote control' becomes リモ-コン (rimo-kon). (However, see an example of a three-mora word shown in the last example below).

rimo-kon	'remote control'
	(= *rimo[oto]* 'remote' + *kon[torooru]* 'control')
paso-kon	'personal computer'
	(= *pa[a]so[naru]* 'personal' + *kon[pyuutaa]* 'computer')
tsua-kon	'tour conductor'
	(= *tsua[a]* 'tour' + *kon[dakutaa]* 'conductor')
suke-boo (SL)	'skate board'
	(= *suke[eto]* 'skate' + *boo[do]* 'board')
poke-mon	'Pocket Monster' (name of video game)
	(= *poke[tto]* 'pocket' + *mon[staa]* 'monster')
suma-ho	(SL) 'smart phone'
	(= *suma[ato]* 'smart' + [*tere*]*ho[n]* 'telephone')

"Clipping and compounding" is also applied to the hybrid compounds shown below.

bat-te	'batting glove'
	(= *bat[tingu]* 'batting' + *te[bukuro]* 'glove')
kara-oke	'sing-along'
	(= *kara* 'empty' + *o[o]ke[sutora]* 'orchestra')
kawa-jan	'leather jacket'
	(= *kawa* 'leather' + *jan[paa]* 'jumper')
natsu-mero	'oldies'
	(= *natsu[kashii]* 'reminiscing' + *mero[dii]* 'melody')
joshi-puro	'female pro (golfer)'
	(= *joshi* 'female' + *puro.[gorufaa]* 'pro-golfer')
datsu-sara	'escape from a salaried man post'
	(= *datsu* 'escape' + *sara[riiman]* 'salaried employee'); referring to the phenomenon whereby company employees quit their jobs and start their own businesses.

"Blending" is another process similar to, but distinct from, the "clipping and compounding" process. This process takes the first part of one word and combines it with the latter half of another, i.e. [A.B – X.Y] > [A – Y]. The most famous word derived by this process is *gojira* 'Godzilla.' The first part *go* is from *gorira* 'gorilla' and the second part *jira* is from *kujira* 'whale.' Likewise, a famous magician in Japan calls himself Mr. Marikku, which is made up of *ma* from *majikku* 'magic' and *rikku* from *torikku* 'trick' (Kubozono 2002: 38–44).

CHAPTER 6

Argument structures

The term "argument structure" refers to the organization of a predicate and the minimum number of arguments necessary to complete the information which the predicate is designed to express. A predicate is either a verb, an adjective, a nominal adjective with copula, or a noun phrase (NP) with copula. A motion verb, for example, requires an entity that moves and the goal toward which it moves. A verb of giving, on the other hand, requires a giver, a recipient and something that is transferred between them. Arguments are distinguished by their positions with respect to each other in the linear organization of argument structures, as well as their marking by postpositional case particles. A predicate takes one to three arguments and is represented as the last element in the structure: [[NP Prt.]$_1$ ([NP Prt.]$_2$ ([NP Prt.]$_3$)) Pred.]. The case particle *ga* (NOM = Nominative) is always present regardless of argument structure and, with only one exception to be discussed later, appears in the first constituent, i.e. [NP Prt.]$_1$.

In order to maintain the argument structure as an abstract concept sheltered from any pragmatic influence, in this chapter, three adjustments have been made in presenting the data. First, although the particle *ga* (the first *ga* if there is more than one) is often realized as *wa* in actual discourse due to its pragmatic saliency (Chapter 11), it is retained as *ga* as it appears in a context sheltered from pragmatic effect, such as in an embedded environment like a relative clause. Second, the predicate is exclusively presented in the nonpast form in order to show that it is not tied to any specific time frame. Consequently, the notation, NONPAST, is not used in the inter-linear gloss in this chapter. Third, neither a capital letter at the beginning of a clause nor a period at its end is used in the free translation to remind the reader that it is a clause in its abstract form.

1. Argument structure types

Argument structure types will be classified according to the following three criteria: (i) the dynamicity of the predicate, (ii) the valency of the predicate, and (iii) the arrangement of noun phrases (NPs) with specific particles associated with them. The first criterion classifies argument structures into stative or dynamic types. The dynamic predicate in its nonpast tense form can refer to future time (e.g. *taberu* 'will eat'), while the stative predicate in this tense form cannot and only refers to present time (e.g. *dekiru* 'can do (now)'). Also the dynamic predicate allows the *-te iru* aspectual form (e.g. *tabete-iru* 'is eating'), while the stative predicate does not (e.g. **dekite-iru* *'can be doing') (Chapter 7 §2). The second criterion, or the valency of the predicate, classifies predicates into a one-, two- or three-argument type. The third criterion, the arrangement of the NPs, classifies argument structures into specific sub-types.

Table 1. Classification of argument structure types

Number of Arg.	Stative			Dynamic			
1	(a) NP_1 ga		Pred.	(f) NP_1 ga			Pred.
2	(b) NP_1 ga $\quad$ NP_2 ga		Pred.	(g) NP_1 ga	NP_2 o		Pred.
	(c) NP_1 ni $\quad$ NP_2 ga		Pred.	(h) NP_1 ga	NP_2 ni		Pred.
	(d) NP_1 ga $\quad$ NP_2 ni		Pred.	(i) NP_1 ga	NP_2 e		Pred.
	(e) NP_1 ga $\quad$ NP_2 to		Pred	(j) NP_1 ga	NP_2 to		Pred.
3				(k) NP_1 ga	NP_2 o	NP_3 ni	Pred.
				(l) NP_1 ga	NP_2 ni	NP_3 o	Pred.
				(m) NP_1 ga	NP_2 to	NP_3 o	Pred.

Table 1 above summarizes all 13 possible argument structure types, which are categorized into two major groups of stative and dynamic predicate types. The stative sentence describes a property or an experience of the referent coded in the first constituent. The semantic role of the first constituent, therefore, is either Experiencer or Proprietor of an identity or characteristic. The dynamic sentence, on the other hand, encodes description of an event, and the major semantic role of its first constituent is either Agent or Undergoer.

1.1 Argument structures with stative predicates

(a) NP_1 ga Pred.

Equational construction: Most adjectival, nominal adjectival, and nominal predicates take only one argument.

fuji-san   ga   utsukushii
Mt. Fuji   NOM   beautiful   'Mt. Fuji is beautiful'

mona   ga   kiree   da
(name)   NOM   beautiful   COP   'Mona is beautiful'

jon   ga   gakusee   da
(name)   NOM   student   COP   'John is a student'

(b) NP_1 ga NP_2 ga Pred.

i. This is the "double nominative" construction in which two nominative noun phrases appear. Most predicates showing this pattern are adjectives or nominal adjectives of sensation, desire, emotion, preference and ability, and the lack thereof. This pattern and pattern (d) below will be discussed again in §3.

boku[1]	ga	atama	ga	itai	
I (male)	NOM	head	NOM	painful	'I have a headache'

hanako	ga	hebi	ga	kowai	
(name)	NOM	snake	NOM	fearful	'Hanako is afraid of snakes'

boku	ga	koinu	ga	hoshii	
I (male)	NOM	puppy	NOM	want	'I want a puppy'

jon	ga	merii	ga	suki	da	
(name)	NOM	(name)	NOM	fond	COP	'John is fond of Mary'

jon	ga	nihongo	ga	nigate	da	
(name)	NOM	Japanese	NOM	poor	COP	'John is poor at Japanese'

ii. There are also a few noun predicates which take two *ga*-marked arguments.

wain	ga	furansu	ga	honba	da
wine	NOM	France	NOM	real-place	COP

'the home of wine is France'

dorian	ga	mareeshia	ga	sanchi	da
durian	NOM	Malaysia	NOM	producing-place	COP

'the growing place of durian is Malaysia'

(See Chapter 11 §1 for the *-wa-ga* sentence developed from this pattern.)

> (c) NP$_1$ *ni* NP$_2$ *ga* Pred.

This pattern is the only argument structures in which a *ga*-marked NP is not placed at the initial position of the structure.

(i) "Dative subject" construction: The *ni*-marked phrase in the dative subject construction represents a human possessing "ability, needs, or emotion," and the *ga*-marked phrase specifies the type of ability, need, or emotion. All the potential predicates (e.g. *hanas-e-ru* 'speak-POT-NONPAST') follow this pattern. The particle *ni* on the first NP may be replaced by *ga*, which turns this argument structure into the "double nominative" (b-i) type above (Sadler 2007).

jon	ni	nihongo	ga	dekiru	/ wakaru	/ hanas-e-ru
(name)	DAT	Japanese	NOM	capable	/ understand	/ can speak

'John can do (=speak)/understand/can speak Japanese'

---

1. *Boku* 'I' is a casual male first-person pronoun (Chapter 15), which is used in many of the examples in this chapter. The sentence with *boku* sounds more natural to this author (male) in many cases, but can be replaced with the more common first-person pronoun *watashi*.

jon   ni   okane ga   iru   / hitsuyoo da
(name) DAT   money NOM   need / need   COP
'John needs money'

jon   ni   obake no   hanashi ga   kowai   / tanoshii
(name) DAT   ghost GEN story   NOM fearful / enjoyable
'John is afraid of/enjoys ghost stories'

(ii) Existential construction: The location NP with *ni* appears before a *ga*-marked NP indicating a person or an object that exists at that location. A notable feature of the existential construction in Japanese is that different verbs must be selected for animate and inanimate referents; the existential verb *iru* (affirmative) and *inai* (negative) are used for animates while *aru* (affirmative) and *nai* (negative) are used for inanimates. Adjectives of quantity, such as *ooi* 'many,' and *sukunai* 'few,' also belong to this pattern. (See also Chapter 11 §4.2 for a discussion of presentational sentences.)

kono heya ni   isu   ga   aru   / nai
this room LOC   chair NOM exist / exist:NEG
'there are/are not chairs in this room'

asoko   ni   inu ga   iru   / inai
over.there   LOC dog NOM exist / exist:NEG
'there is/is not a dog over there'

kyooto   ni   furui tera   ga   ooi
(place name) LOC   old   temple NOM   many
'there are many old temples in Kyoto'

(iii) Possessive construction: The possessor is expressed as the *ni* phrase and the possessed as the *ga* phrase. The possessed can be either a human or non-human. Unlike the existential expression, *aru* may be employed as an alternative when the possessed is a human noun (see first example).[2]

---

2. When the possessed is inanimate, another construction can be used with *motsu* 'have, hold.' Thus, [(Person) *ni* (Object) *ga aru*] can be changed to [(Person) *ga* (Object) *o motsu*] (Pattern (g) below).

kanojo ga   ookii ie   o   motsu
she   NOM   big   house ACC have   'she has a big house'

This construction normally cannot be used when the possessed is human. But if the possessor-possessed relationship is between the parent and the child or the husband and the wife, *motsu* is allowed.

boku   ni   koibito   ga   iru   / aru
I (male) DAT lover   NOM   exist / exist   'I have a girlfriend'

kanojo ni   kane   ga   aru
she   DAT   money   NOM   exist   'she has money'

kono inu   ni   nomi   ga   ooi
this dog   DAT   flee   NOM   many   'this dog has many fleas'

(d) NP₁ *ga* NP₂ *ni* Pred.

(i) Predicates that indicate a subject lacking or being rich in something (with *ni*) take this argument structure. This structure may be changed into the "NP-*ni* NP-*ga*" structure like (c–ii) above.

nihon ga   ten'nen-shigen   ni   fusoku-suru
Japan NOM   natural-resource   DAT   be.short.of
'Japan is short of natural resources'

cf. *nihon ni   ten'nen-shigen   ga   fusoku-suru*
    Japan LOC natural-resource NOM   be.short.of
    'Natural resources are in short supply in Japan'

kono otoko ga   kyooyoo   ni   kakeru
this man   NOM   intelligence   DAT   lack
'this man lacks intelligence'

(ii) Predicates indicating a match between two items may code the two items with *ga* and *ni*.

yoshio ga   hanako ni   fusawashii / pittari   da
(name)   NOM   (name) DAT   suitable   / perfect   COP
'Yoshio is suitable/perfect for Hanako'

kono fuku   ga   kimi ni   au
this clothing NOM   you DAT   match
'this clothing becomes you'

minna   ga   boku   ni   sansee da
everybody NOM   I(male) DAT   agree   COP
'everyone is in agreement with me'

---

kanojo ga   rippana musuko o   motsu
she   NOM   fine   sone   ACC   have   'she has a fine son'

In actual speech, they are most likely modified with the *-te iru* aspectual auxiliary, e.g. *motte-iru*.

(iii) Some predicates may take a *ni* phrase to specify the object to which a description applies.

> *yoshiko ga   hoshi no   namae ni   kuwashii*
> (name) NOM   star GEN   name DAT   knowledgeable
> 'Yoshiko is knowledgeable regarding the names of the stars'

(e) NP₁ *ga* NP₂ *to* Pred.

The *to*-marked phrase indicates a reference point against which the *ga*-marked phrase is measured for its "similarity or difference." Some "similarity" sentences such as the first (but not the second) example below can use *ni* (DAT) instead of *to* (COM), but "differences" can be only expressed with *to* (COM), as in the last sentence below.

yumi   ga   hahaoya to   sokkuri   da
(name) NOM mother COM resemble COP
        (*hahaoya ni* is also acceptable)
'Yumi resembles her mother'

kono ji   ga   sono ji   to   onaji da
this character NOM that character COM same COP
'this character is the same as that character'
        (**sono ji ni* is not acceptable)

kono kao ga   shashin to   chigau
this face NOM picture COM different
'this face is different from the picture'
        (**shashin ni* is not acceptable)

1.2 Argument structures with dynamic predicates

(f) NP₁ *ga* Pred.

This is the typical intransitive pattern. Two sub-types, the "volitional intransitive" and the "non-volitional intransitive," are distinguished on the basis of the volitionality, intention, control, or lack thereof, ascribed to the referent of the noun phrase. This distinction echoes the syntactic notion of the unergative-unaccusative distinction (e.g. Perlmutter and Postal 1983; Miyagawa 1989). The distinction becomes crucial when the aspectual expression *-te-i(ru)* is interpreted; it is interpreted as resultative if used with non-volitional predicates, as in (i), and as progressive (in the unmarked case) if used with volitional ones, as in (ii) (Chapter 7 §2.3.1.1).

(i) Non-volitional intransitive
   mado   ga   wareru
   window NOM break   'a window breaks'

oyu	*ga*	*waku*	
hot.water	NOM	boil	'water boils'
roopu ga		*kireru*	
rope	NOM	cut	'the rope becomes severed'
taroo	*ga*	*taoreru*	
(name)	NOM	fall	'Taro falls'

(ii) Volitional intransitive

kodomo ga		*tobiagaru*	
child	NOM	jump	'a child jumps'
taroo	*ga*	*hashiru*	
(name)	NOM	run	'Taro runs'
hanako ga		*oyogu*	
(name)	NOM	swim	'Hanako swims'

(g) NP$_1$ *ga* NP$_2$ *o* Pred.

There are five sub-types of the pattern that marks the second noun phrase with the accusative case marker *o*.

(i) Transitive Event: This is the typical transitive structure. There are various semantic types of accusative-marked noun phrases, such as the physically affected patient, the physically non-affected patient, and the object of creation, represented by the three examples below, respectively.

tanaka	*ga*	*nakamura o*	*naguru*	
(name)	NOM	(name) ACC	beat	'Tanaka beats up Nakamura'
tanaka	*ga*	*eega o*	*miru*	
(name)	NOM	movie ACC	see	'Tanaka watches a movie'
tanaka	*ga*	*isu o*	*tsukuru*	
(name)	NOM	chair ACC	make	'Tanaka makes a chair'

(ii) Transversal movement: The area which is covered by a movement is marked by *o*. Some verbs belonging here are also classified as volitional intransitives.

inu ga	*kooen o*	*aruku*		
dog NOM	park ACC	walk		'a dog walks in the park'
shoonen ga	*umibe o*	*hashiru*		
boy NOM	beach ACC	run		'a boy runs on the beach'
kodomo ga	*hashigo o*	*oriru*		
child NOM	ladder ACC	descend		'a child descends a ladder'

(iii) Departure movement: The location from which the agent leaves may be marked by *o*. Some verbs belonging here are also classified as volitional intransitives. The time needed for an activity depicted by the verb in this type is brief compared to that needed for an activity in (ii) immediately above. Notice the two different meanings associated with the verb *oriru* in (ii) above and (iii) here.

jiroo	ga	heya	o	deru	
(name)	NOM	room	ACC	leave	'Jiro leaves the room'
kodomo	ga	densha	o	oriru	
child	NOM	train	ACC	get.off	'a child gets off the train'

(iv) Emotion and cognition movement: The target of cognition or emotion is marked by the accusative case *o*.

hanako ga toshio o nikumu / uramu / konomu[3]
(name) NOM (name) ACC hate / resent / like
'Hanako hates/resents/likes Toshio'

roojin ga mukashi no koto o omou / natsukashimu
old.man NOM old.days GEN thing ACC think / reminisce
'an old man thinks/reminisces about the old days'

kodomo-tachi ga sensoo no kowasa o kangaeru
child-PL NOM war GEN horrors ACC think
'children think about the horrors of war'

(v) Speech event: Some speech event verbs code the linguistic message with the accusative marker. See also §1.3 below.

jiroo ga hen'na koto o iu
(name) NOM strange thing ACC say
'Jiro says strange things'

jiroo ga betonamu-go o hanasu
(name) NOM Vietnamese ACC speak
'Jiro speaks Vietnamese'

jiroo ga hen'na uwasa o kiku
(name) NOM strange rumor ACC hear
'Jiro hears a strange rumor'

---

3. Though semantically these verbs are like stative verbs, their core meaning is still dynamic. Only when these predicates are marked with the *-te iru* aspectual auxiliary do they become stative predicates, e.g. *A-ga B-o nikunde-iru* 'A hates B' (Chapter 7).

jiroo   ga   hana   no   namae   o   kiku
(name) NOM flower GEN name   ACC ask
'Jiro asks the name of the flower'

> (h)   NP$_1$ ga   NP$_2$ ni Pred.

The dative particle *ni* indicates the goal of a real or abstract movement. The goal may be (i) place, (ii) a person/object, or (iii) a different state.

(i) Movement towards a place

mogura ga   ana   ni   hairu
mole   NOM hole DAT enter
'a mole enters a hole'

gakusee ga   kootee   ni   atsumaru
student NOM school.yard DAT gather
'students gather in the school yard'

densha ga   eki   ni   tomaru
train   NOM station DAT stop
'a train stops at the station'

(ii) Movement towards a person/object

yoshiko ga   taroo   ni   au
(name)   NOM (name) DAT meet
'Yoshiko meets Taro'

torakku ga   densha ni   butsukaru
truck   NOM train   DAT collide
'a truck collides with a train'

minna   ga   boku   ni   sansee-suru
everyone NOM I(male) DAT agreement-do
'everyone agrees with me'

koinu ga   shoojo   ni   amaeru
puppy NOM little.girl DAT show.affection
'a puppy shows affection towards the little girl'

(iii) Movement towards a different state

shingoo   ga   aka ni   kawaru
traffic.light NOM red DAT change
'the traffic light changes to red'

otamajakushi ga   kaeru ni   naru
tadpole   NOM frog   DAT become
'a tadpole becomes a frog'

ken   ga   otona ni   naru   (*otona to* is also acceptable)
(name) NOM adult DAT become
'Ken becomes an adult.'

(i) NP₁ ga NP₂ e Pred.

A direction is marked by the allative marker *e* for verbs of motion. The *e* may freely be replaced by *ni*. (See Chapter 9 §2 for the environment where this is not allowed.)

kodomo-tachi ga doobutsuen e   iku
child-PL   NOM zoo   ALL go
'children go to the zoo'

ryuugakusee   ga   kuni   e   kaeru
exchange.students NOM country ALL return
'exchange students go back home'

gakusee ga   tsukue o   migi e   ugokasu
student NOM   desk   ACC right ALL move
'students move the desk to the right'

(j) NP₁ ga NP₂ to Pred.

Reciprocal verbs require that the noun phrase indicating a partner be marked by *to* as an argument.[4] See also (m), below. (Chapter 8 §6 for a detailed discussion of reciprocal verbs).

taroo   ga   hanako to   kekkon-suru
(name) NOM   (name) COM   marriage-do
'Taro marries Hanako/Taro gets married to Hanako'

taroo   ga   hanako to   wakareru
(name) NOM   (name) COM   separate
'Taro separates from Hanako'

gunshuu ga   keekan to   arasou
mob   NOM police COM fight
'the mob fights with the police'

(k) NP₁ ga NP₂ o NP₃ ni Pred.

(i) Verbs of placement require an agent (*ga*), a transferred object (*o*), and a destination (*ni*).

kodomo ga   ringo o   sara ni   noseru
child   NOM apple ACC plate DAT place
'a child places the apple on a plate'

---

4. Some directional verbs such as *au* 'meet' (Pattern (h-ii) above) can take *to* instead of ni with a marked difference in interpretation. Compare *yoshiko ga taroo ni au* 'Yoshiko meets Taro' and *yoshiko ga taroo to au* 'Yoshiko meets with Taro.' Reciprocity is emphasized with *to*.

jiroo ga okane o saifu ni ireru
(name) NOM money ACC wallet DAT put
'Jiro puts the money in the wallet'

okaasan ga taoru o mizu ni hitasu
mother NOM towel ACC water DAT soak
'Mother soaks the towel in water'

(ii) Verbs of transitive change require an agent (*ga*), an entity before a change (*o*), and an entity after the change (*ni*).

ryokoosha ga doru o en ni kaeru
traveler NOM dollar ACC yen DAT change
'a traveler exchanges dollars for yen (lit. changes dollars into yen)'

hon'yakuka ga nihongo o eego ni suru
translator NOM Japanese ACC English DAT make
'a translator translates (lit. makes) Japanese into English'

(l) NP$_1$ ga NP$_2$ ni NP$_3$ o Pred.

(i) Verbs of giving are like "verbs of placement," (k-i) above, in that they require an agent, a transferred object, and a destination. However, the destination in this case must be a human recipient and appears before the accusative-marked phrase in the argument structure. Also the transferred object may be an abstract concept with certain verbs of giving.

taroo ga otooto ni jitensha o yaru
(name) NOM y.brother DAT bicycle ACC give
'Taro gives his younger brother a bicycle'

taroo ga kyooko ni hana o ageru
(name) NOM (name) DAT flower ACC give
'Taro gives Kyoko a flower'

sensee ga kodomo ni sansuu o oshieru
teacher NOM child DAT arithmetic ACC teach
'the teacher teaches the children arithmetic'

taroo ga hanako ni jiroo o shookai-suru
(name)$_1$ NOM (name)$_2$ DAT (name)$_3$ ACC introduce
'Taro$_1$ introduces Jiro$_3$ to Hanako$_2$.'

(ii) Verbs of communication are like "verbs of giving" above. The accusative noun phrase here, however, is a message rather than an object.

shachoo ga yamada ni tenkin o meejiru
president NOM (name) DAT relocation ACC order
'the company president orders Mr. Yamada to relocate'

kokumin ga   daitooryoo ni   jinin   o   yookyuu-suru
people   NOM president   DAT resignation ACC demand-do
'the people demand the President's resignation'

(iii) Verbs of receiving take the same argument structure as (i) and (ii) above with a transferred object being marked by *o*. They differ from (i) and (ii) in that they require the goal of transaction, i.e. a receiver, to appear first with *ga* before the source, i.e. a sender, which is marked with *ni*. Both receiver and sender are usually human. The sender noun phrase may also be marked by the ablative maker *kara*.

taroo   ga   jiroo   ni   jisho   o   morau
(name) NOM (name) DAT dictionary ACC receive
'Taro receives a dictionary from Jiro'

yoshiko ga   sensee   ni   sansuu   o   narau
(name) NOM teacher DAT arithmetic ACC learn
'Yoshiko learns arithmetic from the teacher'

heeshi   ga   gunsoo   ni   meeree o   ukeru
soldier NOM sergeant DAT order   ACC receive
'the soldier receives an order from the sergeant'

(iv) Verbs of mixing and attaching require two patients, coded by *ni* and *o*. Unlike the construction with verbs of giving, communication, and receiving described above, the *ni*-marked phrase has an inanimate referent.

kagakusha ga   sanso   ni   chisso   o   mazeru
scientist NOM oxygen DAT nitrogen ACC mix
'a scientist adds nitrogen to oxygen'

suidooya ga   ano paipu ni   kono paipu o   tsunagu
plumber   NOM that pipe   DAT this pipe   ACC connect
'a plumber connects this pipe to that pipe'

kodomo ga   akai himo   ni   shiroi himo o   musubu
child   NOM red string DAT white string ACC tie
'a child ties the white string to the red string'

The particle *ni* in the above sentences may be replaced by *to* freely, but this is distinct from the reciprocal pattern shown in (m) below, because here *to* conjoins two patients, while in (m) *to* connects two agents. Some other verbs do not allow the *ni/to* alternation, as in the following examples.

sakkyoku-ka ga   sono shi   ni   kyoku o   tsukeru
composer   NOM that poem DAT music ACC attach
'a composer puts music to the poem'

kangofu-san ga   kizuguchi ni   gaaze o   ateru
nurse   NOM wound   DAT goze ACC place
'a nurse places a gauze onto the wound'

gaka   ga   kabe ni   iro   o   nuru
painter NOM wall DAT color ACC paint
'a painter colors the wall with paint'

(m) NP$_1$ ga NP$_2$ to NP$_3$ o Pred.

This is the reciprocal pattern similar to (j) above, but contains an additional *o*-marked argument. The examples below are the comitative construction with the *-ga -to* pattern, which can be changed into the plural subject pattern with the *-to -ga* pattern (see Chapter 8 §6).

taroo   ga   hanako to   shookin   o   wakeru
(name) NOM (name) COM prize.money ACC divide
'Taro divides the prize money with Hanako'

yoshiko ga   hanako to   fuku   o   torikaeru
(name)   NOM (name) COM clothe ACC   exchange
'Yoshiko exchanges the clothes with Hanako'

1.3 Argument structure for the reportative verbs

In addition to the types of argument structures presented above, there is the "reportative" structure distinct from the "speech event" structure in (g-v) above. The reportative structure adds quotative marker *to* after the quoted material for verbs like *iu/yuu* 'say' or *omou* 'think'. If the verb is that of question (e.g. *kiku* 'ask,' *tazuneru* 'inquire') and conjecture (e.g. *omou* 'think,' *utagau* 'doubt'), the quoted material is first followed by *ka* (a) question particle) before *to*. This pattern is discussed fully in Chapter 10:1.

[[NP$_1$ ga] [... (ka) to] Pred.]

boku   ga   [...   to]   omou / iu
I (male) NOM   [...   QT]   think / say
'I think/say that [...]'

boku   ga   [...   ka to]   omou / kiku
I (male) NOM   [...   Q QT]   think / say
'I conjecture/ask if [...]'

2. Adjunct noun phrases

Argument structures are abstract constructs, which supply the source for clauses and sentence formation. When a clause/sentence is formed based on the argument structure, some optional phrases, i.e. adjunct phrases, may be present to further modify a predicate. Some of the particles, *ni* and *to*, specifically, used for argument structure discussed above are also used as adjunct markers for certain predicates. The list of all the adjunct particles is given in Table 2 below.

Table 2. Adjuncts

Case	Particle	Semantic roles
DATIVE (DAT)	*ni*	(a) purpose, cause, specification of time etc.
LOCATIVE (LOC)	*de*	(b) location of action
INSTRUMENTAL (INS)	*de*	(c) instrument, means, cause for event, limit
COMITATIVE (COM)	*to*	(d) partner
TERMINAL (TERM)	*made*	(e) terminal goal
ABLATIVE (ABL)	*kara/yori*	(f) source
TEMPORAL (TMP)	*madeni*	(g) specification of time
GENITIVE (GEN)	*no*	(h) possessor

(a) Dative *ni*: Dative *ni* appears in many argument structures discussed in the prior section. This particle is also extremely versatile for marking various types of adjuncts such as purpose, cause, source, opponent, and various domains of application. Whether the *ni* phrase is obligatory or not varies for particular predicates in particular situations.

ane   ga   haikingu ni   iku   (purpose)
o.sister NOM hike   DAT go
'my elder sister goes on a hike'

koneko ga   mono-oto ni   odoroku   (source/cause)
kitten NOM noise   DAT surprised
'a kitten is surprised by a noise'

kono rikishi   ga   ano rikishi   ni   katsu   (opponent)
This wrestler NOM that wrestler DAT win
'this wrestler wins over that wrestler'

kodomo ga   michi ni   mayou   (applicable domain)
child   NOM street DAT get.lost
'a child gets lost in (his sense of) direction'

chichi ga   sake   ni   you   (applicable domain)
father NOM liquor DAT get.drunk
'my father gets drunk with liquor'

ani   ga   okane ni   komaru   (applicable domain)
o.brother NOM money DAT be.troubled
'my elder brother is in trouble with regard to money'

>   *tanaka ga   josee   ni   yowai*   (applicable domain)
>   (name) NOM female DAT   weak
>   'Tanaka is weak willed when it comes to women'

Another important function of this particle is to mark a specific time at which an activity occurs.

>   *kodomo ga   ku-ji   ni   neru*   (temporal)
>   child   NOM 9-o'clock DAT   sleep
>   'the child goes to bed at 9'

(b) Locative *de*: This marks the location of an action. This can be contrasted with locative *ni* which marks the location of a stationary entity, as seen in the "existential structure" of (c–ii) in Section 1,

>   *kodomo-tachi ga   ano kooen de   yakyuu   o   suru*
>   child-PL   NOM   that park   LOC   baseball ACC   do
>   'children play baseball in that park'

The particle *de* also marks the domain for a superlative degree.

>   *doobutsu no   naka   de   kujira ga   ichi-ban ookii*
>   animal   GEN   inside INS   whale   NOM   first   big
>   'among animals, the whale is the biggest'

(c) Instrumental *de*: Instrumental *de* marks the instrument and means of an action.

>   *nihonjin ga   hashi   de   gohan o   taberu*
>   Japanese NOM   chopsticks INS   rice   ACC   eat
>   'Japanese people eat rice with chopsticks'

>   *michi ga   jitensha de   gakkoo e   iku*
>   (name) NOM bicycle   INS   school ALL   go
>   'Michi goes to school by bicycle'

Instrumental *de* also marks the cause for an event.

>   *neko ga   byooki de   shinu*
>   cat NOM illness INS   die
>   'a cat dies of illness'

Finally, instrumental *de* marks the limit of quantity.

>   *supiichi ga   go-fun   de   owaru*
>   speech   NOM   five-minute INS   finish
>   'the speech ends in five minutes'

>   *kodomo ga   hitori   de   asobu*
>   child NOM one:CLS   INS   play
>   'a child plays by himself'

(d) Comitative *to*: The use of comitative *to* with arguments of reciprocal verbs such as *kekkon-suru* 'get married' is mentioned in (j) in §1 and Chapter 8 §6, but it is also used to mark adjunct phrases of non-reciprocal verbs.

> *boku   ga   kimiko   to   issho-ni   eega   o   miru*
> I(male) NOM   (name)   COM   together   movie   ACC   see
> 'I see a movie (together) with Kimiko'

The adjunct use of *to* allows for the adverbial phrase *issho-ni* 'together' to co-occur as in the above example. This is not possible with argument phrases (cf. Chapter 9 §3.1).

> *boku   ga   kimiko   to   (*issho-ni)   wakareru*
> I(male) NOM   (name)   COM   (*together)   separate
> 'I separate from Kimiko'

(e) Terminal *made*: This particle specifies the spatial or temporal end point of an action.

> *demo-tai   ga   seemon   made   aruku*
> demonstrator   NOM   main.gate   TERM   walk
> 'the demonstrators walk all the way to the main gate'

> *demo-tai   ga   san-ji   made   aruku*
> demonstrator   NOM   3-o'clock   TERM   walk
> 'the demonstrators walk until 3 o'clock'

(f) Ablative *kara* specifies the spatial and temporal inceptive point of an activity.

> *hanako   ga   getsuyoo   kara   kin'yoo   made   hataraku*
> (name)   NOM   Monday   ABL   Friday   TERM   work
> 'Hanako works from Monday until Friday'

> *taroo   ga   rosu   kara   sanfuranshisuko   made   aruku*
> (name)   NOM   Los Angeles   ABL   San Francisco   TERM   walk
> 'Taro walks from Los Angeles to San Francisco'

For some predicates, such as those below, *kara* is more central, and thus may mark an argument rather than an adjunct.

> *kodomo   ga   hee   kara   tobioriru*
> child   NOM   wall   ABL   jump
> 'a child jumps off the wall'

> *mogura   ga   ana   kara   haideru*
> mole   NOM   hole   ABL   come.out
> 'a mole comes out of the hole'

> *taroo   ga   ginkoo   kara   okane   o   kariru*
> (name)   NOM   bank   ABL   money   ACC   borrow
> 'Taro borrows money from the bank'

Another ablative, *yori*, is archaic if used in place of *kara*. However, it is used regularly to mark the standard in a comparison. *Kara* cannot replace *yori* in the comparison sentence.

> taroo   ga   jiroo   yori ookii
> (name) NOM (name) ABL   big
> 'Taro is bigger than Jiro'

(g) *madeni*: This is a combination of two particles, *made* and *ni*, and specifies the time by which something is done.

> chichi ga   roku-ji   madeni kaeru
> father NOM six-o'clock TMP   return
> 'my father comes home by six'

(h) *no*: Genitive *no* marks a possessor and other modifying concept in a noun phrase (see Chapter 9 §1 for more information).

> boku   no   jitensha
> I(male) GEN bicycle   'my bicycle'
>
> nihon   no   hata
> Japan GEN flag   'Japanese flag'

3. Syntactic roles and clausal structures

The discussion so far has focused on the surface patterns of how arguments are arranged with respect to a predicate. This section adds to it the important aspect of clausal structure by addressing the issue of syntactic roles, especially the notion of subject, and clausal structures. The two argument structures, (b) [NP_1 *ga* NP_2 *ga* Pred.] and (c) [NP_1 *ni* NP_2 *ga* Pred.] will have a special place in this discussion.

3.1 Subjects

Subject seems an intuitively clear concept, but is a notoriously difficult one to define cross-linguistically. In general, it is identified as a noun phrase privileged over others in a clause. Syntactically, a privileged noun phrase is often a controller of such processes as "reflexivizations," "coreferential deletions," "backward pronominalizations," "switch reference" and so forth (Keenan 1976: 314; Foley & van Valin 1984: 109–11). In English, the subject noun phrase is the only noun phrase that triggers verb agreement.

In Japanese, a privileged noun phrase can be initially identified as the one that is marked with the case particle *ga*, as such a noun phrase appears in all argument structures, and in most cases appears at the beginning of an argument structure. However, there are two argument structures that challenge this first approximation. In pattern (b) [NP_1 *ga* NP_2 *ga* Pred.], two *ga*-marked noun phrases appear, thereby making it difficult to decide which noun phrase is the subject if there cannot be more than one subject (this point will be discussed later). In pattern (c) [NP$_1$ *ni* NP$_2$ *ga* Pred.], the *ga*-marked phrase appears in the second position, and the initial noun phrase is marked with *ni*. It is, therefore, important to carefully examine these two argument structures in the attempt to define subject in Japanese.

There are a few syntactic processes that refer to a privileged noun phrase, i.e. subject, in Japanese. The first involves reflexivization, in which the reflexive pronoun *jibun* (Chapter 13 §1) selects a certain noun phrase over others as its antecedent. Consider the following sentences (Shibatani 1977, 1978b).

(1) taroo$_i$ ga   jiroo$_j$ o   jibun-no$_{i/*j}$ heya de   settokushita
    (name) NOM (name) ACC self GEN   room LOC convince:PAST
    'Taro$_i$ convinced Jiro$_j$ in self's$_{i/*j}$ room.'

(2) taroo$_i$ ga   hanako$_j$ ni   jiroo$_k$ o   jibun$_{i/j/*k}$ no heya
    (name) NOM (name) DAT (name) ACC self   GEM
    de   settokus-aseta
    room LOC convince-CAU:PAST
    'Taro$_i$ had Hanako$_j$ convince Jiro$_j$ in self's$_{i/j/*k}$ room.'

In (1), *jibun* selects *taroo*, but not *jiroo*, as its antecedent. That is, antecedent selection is not random, and the noun phrase that serves as an antecedent for *jibun* is a privileged noun phrase, i.e. the subject. In (2), *jibun* refers to either *taroo* or *hanako*, but not to *jiroo*. This means that both *taroo* and *hanako* are subjects. Indeed, while *taroo* can be analyzed as a matrix subject, *hanako* is the subject of the embedded verb *settokus-* 'convince' in the causative construction. Jiro is not a subject for any predicate element. This sentence is understood to have the structure as follows.

(2)' taroo$_i$ [hanako$_j$ jiroo$_k$ jibun$_{i/j/*k}$ no heya de settokus]-aseta
     Mx subj. [Embd. subj. Obj. "in self's room" "convince"]- CAUS

Although the nominative case marker *ga* and the subject-hood of the noun marked by this particle coincide well in most argument structures, sentences such as (3) below are problematic due to their "double nominative" argument structure with two nominative case particles. It turns out that *jibun* clearly picks *taroo* as its antecedent, showing that *taroo*, but not *hanako*, is the subject.

(3) taroo$_i$ ga   hanako$_j$ ga   jibun$_{i/*j}$ no kurasu no naka de
    (name) NOM (name) NOM self GEN   class   GEN in   LOC
    ichiban suki da
    1st   like COP
    'Taro$_i$ likes Hanako$_j$ best in self's$_{i/*j}$ class.'

Like the process of reflexivization, the process of one type of honorification also refers to a particular noun phrase in a sentence, and this privileged noun phrase is conventionally called the subject. This type of honorification is called "subject-honorifics" (Chapter 15 §4). Consider the following sentences (cf. Shibatani 1978a, 1978b; Tsujimura 2007: 272).

(4) yamada sensee$_i$ ga   miki$_j$ ni
    (name) teacher NOM (name) DAT
    jibun$_{i/*j}$ no tegami o   miseru (→ o-mise-ni naru)
    self   GEN   letter ACC show   (→ show:HON)
    'Prof. Yamada shows self's letter to Miki.'

(5) miki$_i$ ga yamada sensee$_j$ ni
    (name) NOM (name) teacher DAT
    jibun$_{i/*j}$ no tegami o   miseru (→ *o- mise -ni naru)
    self   GEN book   ACC send   (→ *show:HON)
    'Miki shows self's letter to Prof. Yamada.'

The reflexive pronoun *jibun* identifies *yamada sensei* in (4) and *miki* in (5) as a subject. Both (4) and (5) include a person (Prof. Yamada) worthy of respect. However, only (4) allows the honorific verb *o-mise-ni naru*. This shows that subject-honorification can be achieved only when the subject, as identified by reflexivization in this case, coincides with a person worthy of respect. This fact further helps to identify a *ni*-marked noun phrase as a subject in the "possessive construction" in (6) and "dative subject construction" in (7).

(6) yamada sensee ni   wa   shakkin ga   takusan aru (→ o-ari-ni naru)
    (name) teacher DAT TOP debt   NOM much   exist (→ exist:HON)
    'Prof. Yamada has lots of debt.'

(7) yamada   sensee ni   miki   no   kimochi ga
    (name) teacher DAT (name) GEN feeling NOM
    wakaranai   (→ o-wakari-ni naranai)
    understand:NEG (→ understand:NEG:HON)
    'Prof. Yamada does not understand Miki's feeling.'

These sentences clearly show that the use of honorific verb forms (*o-ari-ni naru* and *o-wakari-ni naranai*) are due to the *ni*-marked noun phrase *yamada sensei* 'Professor Yamada' as it is the only possible trigger for honorification in these sentences. Thus, despite its *ni*-marking, *yamada sensee* is identified as the subject.[5] However, (8), an "existential construction" which shares the same surface structure as "possessive

---

5. Besides the processes of reflexivization and subject-honorification, a subject can be also identified as one of the triggers involved in the process of "quantifier float," or the process in which a quantifier "moves out" of a noun phrase (see Shibatani 1978a, b, 1990: 280–306, and Chapter 8 §7).

construction" and "dative subject construction" does not identify the *ni*-marked phrase as a subject, but it is the *ga*-marked noun phrase which triggers honorification and thus is the subject.

(8) Existential Construction
 ano heya ni   yamada sensee ga   iru   (→ *irassharu*)
 that room LOC (name) teacher NOM exist (→ exist:HON)
 'Prof. Yamada is in that room.'

To summarize the discussion so far, although (i) "dative subject construction," (ii) "existential construction", and (iii) "possessive construction" are listed under the same argument structure, (c) [NP$_1$ *ni* NP$_2$ *ga* Pred.], (ii) is distinct from (i) and (iii) in terms of the location of the subject.

The fact that it is possible to identify a privileged noun phrase (subject) in argument structures morphologically through *ga*-marking and syntactically with some syntactic processes afford Japanese to be classified as a subject-prominent language. However, Japanese is also categorized as a "topic prominent language" (Li & Thompson 1976), and thus it is necessary at this point to inspect this aspect. Interestingly, the two argument structures that present challenges to the identification of subject, i.e. (b) [NP$_1$ *ga* NP$_2$ *ga* Pred.] and (c) [NP$_1$ *ni* NP$_2$ *ga* Pred.] will clarify the nature of subject and topic in Japanese.

The reason why the structures (b) and (c) present challenges to the identification of subject seems to be related to their special internal organization, identified here as a "layered structure." Namely, they involve an inner clause with its own (internal) subject marked by *ga* embedded in an outer clause with its (external) subject marked by *ga* or *ni*. The subject identified in the previous paragraphs, thus, strictly speaking, refer to external subjects in the layered clause structure. This layered structure can be schematized as follows (cf. Langacker 1999; Shibatani 2000):

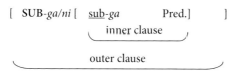

Argument structures with the layered clause structure have special semantic characteristics; the 'external' subject is a human noun and the predicate is lower in transitivity, i.e. adjectival, nominal adjectival, or stative verb predicates.

(9) Double nominative construction
 [*taroo   ga*   [*atama ga   ookii*]]
 (name) NOM head NOM big
 'Taro has a big head'

(10) Dative subject construction
[taroo   ni   [furansu-go ga   dekiru]]
(name) DAT   French   NOM   can.do
'Taro can speak French'

(11) Possessive construction
[yamada-san ni   [okane ga   takusan aru]]
(name)-Mr   DAT money NOM much   exist
'Mr. Yamada has lots of money'

Though the internal clause may be syntactically complete with its (internal) subject and predicate, it must be semantically anchored to an extra argument in order to become fully meaningful. In other words, the external subject sets the domain in which the described state of affairs is obtained (Shibatani 2000). It should be noted that this characterization of external subject is similar to that of topic. Chafe (1976: 50) referring to a construction in Chinese that is similar to the Japanese structures (9)–(11) above states that "[w]hat topics appear to do is to limit the applicability of the main prediction to a certain restricted domain." It is thus natural that the argument structures (9)–(11) above can develop into the -wa -ga sentence pattern by substituting ga or ni attached to the external subject with wa (Chapter 11 §1), as shown in (9′)–(11′) below. These sentences are in fact much less marked for Japanese, and are a hallmark of a topic-prominent language.

(9′) Double nominative construction
[taroo   wa   [atama ga   ookii]]
(name) TOP head   NOM big
'Taro has a big head'

(10′) Dative subject construction
[taroo   wa   [furansu-go ga   dekiru]]
(name) TOP French   NOM   can.do
'Taro can speak French'

(11′) Possessive construction
[yamada-san wa   [okane ga   takusan aru]]
(name)-Mr   TOP money NOM much   exist
'Mr. Yamada has lots of money'

Note that an existential sentence such as (8) discussed earlier, a subtype of argument structure (c), [NP_1 ni NP_2 ga Pred.], on the other hand, will not replace ni with wa, but adds wa to ni to form a combined particle string (ni wa), suggesting that this sentence does not have a layered clause structure, but a simple one-layered structure. This is consistent with the earlier finding that it is NP_2 ga (and not NP_1 ni) that is the subject.

(8′) Existential Construction
 ano heya <u>ni</u> <u>wa</u> yamada sensee ga iru
 that room LOC TOP (name) teacher NOM exist
 'Prof. Yamada is in that room.'
 cf. (8″) ?*ano heya <u>wa</u> yamada sensee ga iru[6]

3.2 Objects

The direct object is a more elusive syntactic category than the subject. Direct passivization (Chapter 8 §1.1.1) identifies a subset of accusative (*o*)- and dative (*ni*)-marked noun phrases as the direct object. As for the indirect object, there is one syntactic test to identify it. In the context of a verb of giving, it is the noun phrase marked with the dative case particle (*ni*), which determines the choice of lexical verb; if the *ni*-marked noun phrase is the first person, *kureru/kudasaru* 'give' must be selected, but if it is the second or third person *yaru/ageru/sashiageru* 'give' is selected (for more details, see Chapter 14 §1.2.2 and Kindaichi 1988: 181–2). Of course, it is hardly the case that all dative-marked noun phrases are indirect objects.

---

6. Example (8′) is grammatical, while (8″) is marked, if not completely ungrammatical. It should also be noted that the possessive construction such as in (11) can have the *ni wa* after the first noun phrase. Compare (11′) with (11″) below.

(11″) Possessive construction
 [yamada-san ni wa [okane ga takusan aru]]
 (name)-Mr DAT TOP money NOM much exist
 'Mr. Yamada has lots of money'

Both (11′) and (11″) are equally grammatical. This can be contrasted with the much lower acceptability of *taroo <u>ni wa</u> furansugo ga dekiru* compared to the completely acceptable sentence *taroo <u>wa</u> furansugo ga dekiru*. The table below summarizes the degree of acceptability of the relevant structures under discussion.

(b) Double nominative	-ga –ga	*- ga wa – ga	-wa –ga
(c-1) Dative subject	-ni –ga	?*-ni wa –ga	-wa –ga
(c-3) Possessive	-ni –ga	-ni wa –ga	-wa –ga
(c-2) Existential	-ni –ga	-ni wa –ga	?*-wa –ga

CHAPTER 7

Tense and aspect

Tense refers to a grammatical system which codes a sequential relationship between the time of the situation (event, action or state) referred to and some other time, usually the time of speech (Comrie 1976: 1–2). In contrast, aspect is defined as the "different ways of viewing the internal temporal constituency of a situation" (Comrie 1976: 3). Put another way, tense codes an objective relationship between two points along the temporal axis, while aspect codes a temporal interpretation of a situation viewed from the speaker's perspective. Aspect could further include more subjective interpretation of a situation derived from the temporal structure of a situation, such as an action done in preparation for a future situation.

1. Tense

In Japanese, tense is expressed by two opposing inflectional suffixes, -(r)u vs. -ta for verbs, -i vs. -katta for adjectives and da vs. datta for the copula. Here, the first member of each opposing pair is called the "nonpast form," and the latter the "past form." The table on the next page shows the tense forms of the three types of predicates.[1] Roughly speaking, the nonpast form refers to the present and/or future time and the past form the past time. But in order to provide a more accurate description of tense forms in Japanese, they must be examined from the following three different perspectives: the nature of the sentence (generic/habitual vs. specific sentence types), the nature of the predicates (dynamic vs. stative), and the nature of the clauses (main vs. subordinate).

A generic/habitual sentence represents a statement about someone or something which is true over an unspecified period of time. The past form of a generic/habitual sentence reports a situation which was true over an unspecified period of time in the past, but is not true at present. Examples (1a) and (1b) are generic/habitual sentences with dynamic predicates in the past form (*tabeta* 'ate'). They reveal the past eating habits of John and of the people of some country, respectively. Similarly, Examples (2a) and (2b) have stative predicates in the past form (*mazushikatta* 'was poor'), and describe their past economic

---

1. The verb's nonpast negative form (-*nai*) which shares the identical form (-*i*) with the adjective follows the adjectival conjugation paradigm. Compare *tabe-nai* 'does not eat' > *tabe-nakatta* 'did not eat' vs. *akaku-nai* 'is not red' > *akaku-nakatta* 'was not red.'

Table 1. Tense forms of verbs, adjectives and the copula

	Nonpast form	Past form
Verb	-(r)u	-ta
Adjective	-i	-katta
Copula	da	datta

conditions, respectively. An adverbial phrase such as *mukashi wa* 'in the past' may be included in all of these cases.[2]

(1) a. jon   wa   mukashi wa   yoku   karee o   <u>tabeta</u>
       (name) TOP old.days TOP often curry ACC eat:PAST
       'John ate curry often in the past.'

   b. kono kuni   no   hitobito wa   mukashi wa   karee o   <u>tabeta</u>
      this country GEN people   TOP old.days TOP curry ACC eat:PAST
      'People in this country used to eat curry.'

(2) a. jon   wa   mukashi wa   <u>mazushikatta</u>
       (name) TOP old.days TOP poor:PAST
       'John used to be poor.'

   b. kono kuni   no   hitobito wa   mukashi wa   <u>mazushikatta</u>
      this country GEN people   TOP old.days TOP poor:PAST
      'People in this country used to be poor.'

The nonpast form in the generic/habitual interpretation asserts that a situation exists in the present as a continuation from the past and will continue to exist in the future, i.e. a stable state. Some adjectives (e.g. *takai* 'tall') inherently denote a stable state.

---

2. Past habitual actions ('used to do something') can be expressed overtly in a periphrastic construction involving nominalization with *mono* 'thing' followed by the copula. The tense form of the copula may be either past or nonpast with no meaning difference. The adverb *yoku* 'often' particularly resonates well in this type of sentence. This construction can be added to verbal sentences (1a,b), but not to the adjectival sentences, (2a,b).

(1) a'. jon   wa   mukashi wa   yoku   karee o   <u>tabeta</u> <u>**mono datta**</u>
        (name) TOP old.days TOP often curry ACC eat:PAST   thing COP:PAST
        'John often used to eat curry in the past.'

    b'. kono kuni   no   hitobito wa   mukashi wa
        this country GEN people   TOP old.days TOP

        karee o   <u>tabeta</u> <u>**mono datta**</u>
        curry ACC eat:PAST   thing COP:PAST
        'People in this country used to eat curry.'

(3) a. *jon   wa karee o   taberu*
       (name) TOP curry ACC eat:NONPAST
       'John eats curry.'

   b. *kono kuni no hitobito wa karee o   taberu*
       this country GEN people TOP curry ACC eat:NONPAST
       'People in this country eat curry.'

(4) a. *jon   wa se   ga   takai*
       (name) TOP back NOM high:NONPAST
       'John is tall.'

   b. *kono kuni no hitobito wa minna se   ga   takai*
       this country GEN people TOP all   back NOM high:NONPAST
       'People in this country are all tall.'

What the examples above demonstrate is that the type of predicate (dynamic or stative) does not affect the temporal interpretation of the tense form in generic/habitual sentences. In contrast, different readings occur in specific statements, which report one particular event. Some stative predicates (e.g. *byooki da* 'being sick') always denote a specific temporary state.

(5) a. *jon   wa (senshuu)   karee o   tabeta*
       (name) TOP (last week) curry ACC eat:PAST
       'John ate curry (last week).'

   b. *jon   wa (senshuu)   byooki datta*
       (name) TOP (last week) sick   COP:PAST
       'John was sick (last week).'

(6) a. *jon   wa (ashita)   karee o   taberu*
       (name) TOP (tomorrow) curry ACC eat:NONPAST
       'John will eat curry (tomorrow).'

   b. *jon   wa (*ashita)   byooki da*
       (name) TOP (tomorrow) sick   COP:NONPAST
       'John is sick.' (not 'John will be sick (tomorrow).')

Both specific sentences with a dynamic predicate in the past form, as in (5a), and those with a stative predicate in the past form, as in (5b), refer to the past. However, specific sentences with the nonpast form render different interpretations depending on the type of predicate; (6a) can only refer to a future event, while (6b) can only refer to the present state. Compatibility with an adverb such as *ashita* 'tomorrow' demonstrates this point.[3]

---

3. Stative predicates in the nonpast form may indicate the future if the state reported is the result of a scheduled event (Yasuhiro Shirai – Personal communication).

The table below summarizes the different possible interpretations of the tense forms discussed so far. The past form always refers to an event or state in the past time, but the nonpast form's temporal reference varies depending on the type of sentence (generic/habitual or specific) and the type of predicate (stative or dynamic). The gaps in the table are filled by means of other resources available in the grammar; Gap 1 may be expressed by the *naru* 'become' construction (§2.5.5.1 below) or by modals such as *daroo* and *kamoshirenai* 'maybe' (Chapter 14 §2.1.1). Gap 2 may be expressed by an aspectual form, *-te-iru* (§2.3.1 below).

Table 2. Tense forms and their meanings

	Past time	Present (Speech) time	Future time
Generic/Habitual			
– Stative	Past form	←————Nonpast form————→	
– Dynamic	Past form	←————Nonpast form————→	
Specific			
– Stative	Past form	Nonpast form	(Gap1)
– Dynamic	Past form	(Gap2)	Nonpast form

Tense forms in subordinate and main clauses show that the Japanese tense system is (partially) relative. That is, the tense form of the main clause is based on the relation between the event time and speech time (absolute tense), but that of the relative clause and adverbial subordinate clause is determined by the temporal relation of the subordinate clause event to the main clause event (relative tense), not to the speech event. First consider the tense form in the relative clause with respect to the main clause in the next two examples. The examples are from McGloin (1989: 10–11).

(7) [[*ashita gakkoo e kita*] *hito ni agemasu*]
    tomorrow school ALL come:PAST person DAT give POL:NONPAST
    'I will give (it) to those who come tomorrow'

(8) [*kinoo* [*gakkoo e iku*] *hito o mita*]
    yesterday school ALL go:NONPAST person ACC see:PAST
    'I saw a person going to school yesterday.'

(i) *ashita tookyoo ni imasu*
    tomorrow Tokyo DAT be:NONPAST
    '(I) will be in Tokyo tomorrow.'

(ii) *taroo wa ashita ichinensee da*
    (name) TOP tomorrow first.grade COP:NONPAST
    'Taro will be a first grader tomorrow.'

Agemasu in the main clause of (7) is the nonpast tense form of a dynamic verb referring to the future time. *Kita* in the relative clause in this sentence is the past tense form which indicates, not the absolute past time, but the relative prior time with respect to the time of giving in the main clause. In contrast, past tense in the main clause (8) indicates the past time, but the nonpast tense form in the relative clause (*iku*) does not point to the absolute future time, but the future with respect to the time of seeing (*mita*).

Now consider the following four specific sentences with an adverbial 'when' clause (cf. McGloin 1989: 18).

(9) [[*nihon ni iku toki*] *kamera o kau*]
Japan DAT go:NONPAST when camera ACC buy:NONPAST
'(I) will buy a camera when (= before) (I) go to Japan.'

(10) [[*nihon ni itta toki*] *kamera o kau*]
Japan DAT go:PAST when camera ACC buy:NONPAST
'(I) will buy a camera when (= after) (I) go to Japan.'

(11) [[*nihon ni iku toki*] *kamera o katta*]
Japan DAT go:NONPAST when camera ACC buy:PAST
'(I) bought a camera when (= before) (I) went to Japan.'

(12) [[*nihon ni itta toki*] *kamera o katta*]
Japan DAT go:PAST when camera ACC buy:PAST
'(I) bought a camera when (= after) (I) went to Japan.'

The interpretation of these sentences must be as follows. First, the position of the event of the main clause (E-main) is located with respect to speech time (S) on the time axis, indicating the whole event either will take place in the future or took place in the past. Assuming that time flows from left to right, the nonpast form locates the main event (E-main) to the right (future) of speech time (S), while the past form locates the main event (E-main) to the left (past) of S. Then, the position of the event of the subordinate clause (E-sub) is located with respect to the position of main event (E-main). The nonpast form locates the subordinate event (E-sub) to the right of main event (E-main), while the past form locates it to the left of main event (E-main).

In (10) above, for example, the main clause tense is nonpast (*kau*), so *kau* 'to buy a camera (E-main)' is designated as a future event, with respect to the time of speech (S), as shown in the following diagram.

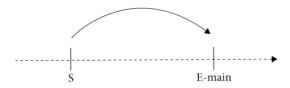

Figure 1. Tense form interpretation (1)

Then the past form (*itta*) in the subordinate clause places its event (E-sub) to the left of E-main, i.e. the subordinate event (E-sub) is interpreted as a "past" event in comparison to the main event (E-main). See the following diagram.

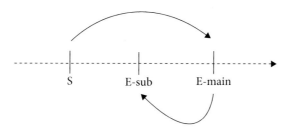

Figure 2. Tense form interpretation (2)

In the final analysis, (10) asserts that 'buying a camera' (E-main) will take place after the agent goes to Japan (E-sub), i.e. he will buy a camera in Japan.[4]

This relative tense interpretation readily accounts for a predetermined tense form for certain types of adverbial clauses (Chapter 12 §2.1).

(Type I) *mae(ni)* 'before' *tabi (ni)* 'every time' *uchi (ni)* 'while' …
(Type II) *ato (de)* 'after' *nochi (ni)* 'after' *kiri* 'once and for all'
             ageku 'after' …

Type (I) adverbial clause-forming formal nouns situate the subordinate event (E-sub) either after the main event (E-main) (relative future), or concurrent with the main event (E-main). That is, irrespective of the main verb tense, the tense of the subordinate event (E-sub) clause must be nonpast. In contrast, Type (II) adverbial clause-forming formal nouns situate the subordinate event (E-sub) before the main event (E-main) (relative past), and thus the tense for the subordinate event (E-sub) clause must be past, again irrespective of the main clause tense form. Here are a few examples.

(13) heya   ni   <u>hairu</u>   /*haitta   **mae**   ni   ashi o   <u>aratta</u>
      room DAT enter:NONPAST / *PAST before DAT foot ACC wash:PAST
      '(I) washed my feet before entering the room.' (Relative future)

---

4. When the main clause tense is past and the subordinate clause predicate is stative, such as *iru* 'stay' or *sunde-iru* 'live' (but not an adjective or predicate nominal), the subordinate clause tense form can be either past or nonpast with the same interpretation. See Chapter 12, §2.1.1.

(1) berurin ni   sunde-iru / -ita   toki   doitsugo o   naratta
     Berlin LOC live-ASP:NONPAST/PAST when German ACC learn:PAST
     '(I) learned German when I lived in Berlin.'

See also Josephs (1971) and Kuno (1973) for more discussion on the tense form in subordinate and relative clauses.

(14) heya ni _hairu_   /*_haitta_ **mae** ni ashi o _arau_
     room DAT enter:NONPAST /*PAST   before DAT foot ACC wash:NONPAST
     '(I) will wash my feet before entering the room.' (Relative future)

(15) amerika ni _iru_   /*_ita_ **uchi** ni eego   ga   joozu
     US   LOC stay:NONPAST /*PAST   while   DAT English NOM skillful

     ni   natta
     COP:ADV become:PAST
     '(I) became fluent in English while (I) stayed in America.' (Concurrent)

(16) shokuji o   *suru   / _shita_   ato de kono kusuri
     Meal   ACC do:NONPAST   / do:PAST   after LOC this medicine

     o   nomu
     ACC drink:NONPAST
     '(I) will take this medicine after eating.' (Relative past)

(17) ie   o   *deru   / _deta_   kiri
     house ACC leave:NONPAST / leave:PAST once

     zenzen modotte-konakatta
     at.all return:TE-come:NEG:PAST
     'Once (he) left the house, (he) never came back.' (Relative past)

2. Aspect

As noted, aspect refers to "different ways of viewing the internal temporal constituency of a situation," and is different from tense, which "relates the time of the situation referred to to some other time, usually to the moment of speaking" (Comrie 1976: 1–3). Aspect is normally divided between "perfective" and "imperfective." The perfective aspect "indicates the view of a situation as a single whole, without distinction of the various separate phases that make up that situation" (*ibid.* p. 16). No special form is used in English to code this aspect (e.g. "She swam in the river"). In contrast, the imperfective aspect "pays essential attention to the internal structure of the situation (*ibid.*). The *be V-ing* construction is used in English to signal this aspect (e.g. "She was swimming in the river"). Using a visual metaphor, a perfective viewpoint views a star from a distance and sees it as a dot in the sky, while an imperfective zooms in and observes it as a complex celestial object with geological details.

2.1 Perfect (anterior) aspect: -*ta*

Before discussing perfective and imperfective aspects, "perfect" (also known as "anterior") aspect should be mentioned. This aspectual meaning is to indicate "that the situation occurs prior to reference time and is relevant to the situation at reference time" (Bybee, Perkins, & Pagliuca 1994: 54). In Japanese, this aspect can be signaled by the past tense marker -*ta*. (Another possibility will be discussed in §2.3.1.2 below). The fact that -*ta* is used for both past tense and perfect is not surprising because it has developed historically from the classical completive suffix -*tar*-. The perfect (anterior) interpretation is compatible with certain adverbs such as *moo* 'already.' Thus (18) is a sentence with a perfect (anterior) interpretation while (19) with the past temporal adverb *kesa* 'this morning' is a sentence with a past tense interpretation.

(18) *moo   gohan   tabeta ?*
     already meal   eat:PAST
     'Have you eaten already?'

(19) *kesa   gohan   tabeta ?*
     this.morning   meal   eat:PAST
     'Did you eat this morning?'

Though the verb forms in both of these sentences are identical, the temporal information is clearly distinct, as seen in the negative responses to these questions (Nakau 1976: 427–8; Teramura 1984: 120–1).

(18′) *iya, mada tabete-(i)nai*
      no   yet eat:TE-ASP:NEG:NONPAST
      'No, (I) haven't eaten yet.'

(19′) *iya, tabenakatta*
      no   eat:NEG:PAST
      'No, (I) didn't eat (this morning).'

The -*te-(i)nai* in (18′), to be discussed below, is an aspectual expression (here the negative perfect) indicating that the event of eating has not taken place yet. In contrast, -*nakatta* is a simple negative past.

2.2   Perfective aspect

As with English, Japanese does not have a special marker for the perfective, and the simple verb forms such as *oyogu* 'swim' and *oyoida* 'swam' are used for this type of aspect. For example, *hanako wa kawa de oyoida* 'Hanako swam in the river' simply presents Hanako's swimming activity as a "dot" in the temporal universe.

2.3   Imperfective aspect: Progressive and resultative

Imperfective aspect in Japanese is divided into the two major types of "progressive" and "resultative." These aspectual meanings are signaled by the interaction between verb semantics and the morphological structure, -*te-iru/-aru*. The auxiliaries -*iru* and -*aru* have developed from the lexical verbs *iru* 'be/stay (for animate subjects),' and *aru* 'be/stay (for inanimate subjects),' respectively. According to Kindaichi ([1950] 1976), verbs are classified into "stative," "continuative," "instantaneous," and "Type IV." A "stative" verb ('to know her name') refers to a static condition that holds over time with no inherent initial and final point. A "continuative" verb refers to a process which starts at one point and progresses over time ('to run in the park'), while an "instantaneous" verb codes an event that starts and ends simultaneously ('to die'). The Type IV is a special category (to be discussed in §2.3.1.2 below). Kindaichi's four-way verb classification is echoed by Vendler's (1957) four-way verb classification and to Smith's (1991) five-way classification of situation types. Kindaichi's taxonomy can be matched with Smith's as follows: [Stative–Stative], [Continuative–Activity/Accomplishment], and [Instantaneous–Semelfactive/Achievement]. An "activity" ('She *strolled* in the park') has no natural ending point though it can be terminated or stopped at any time. On the other hand, an "accomplishment" ('She *built* a house') will come to a natural end when a specific ending point is reached. (This type of situation is called "telic" in the discussion of verb semantics.) In addition, it will produce a natural resultant state (e.g. a house will be in existence). "Semelfactives" and "achievements" are both instantaneous events. "Semelfactive" situations refer to a single occurrence action such as 'to cough,' 'to knock,' 'to jump' (Smith 1991:55–58). "Achievements" ('She wins the race'), on the other hand, have a natural ending point like "accomplishments" (i.e. telic), and have a phase leading to the event and the phase resulted by the occurrence of the event. Thus, before 'someone won the race,' she was engaged in a race, and after the event, she became a winner. In what follows, the terms used by Kindaichi will be used, but terms used by Smith are also used whenever they will make the discussion clearer. The table on the next page shows some examples for each verb type (Kindaichi ([1950] 1976:9–11). It should be noted here that many verbs may be classified across different types because a verb may interact with elements in a sentence to code different situation types.

2.3.1 -te-iru

The aspectual construction *-te-iru* presents "a state of affairs as existing in a homogeneous, unchanging fashion over a given interval of time" (Jacobsen 1992:200, see also Shirai 1998).[5] Schematically, the *-te-iru* expression refers to the area shown by the darker line in Fig. 3 on the next page (Note CS is "the point at which a change-of-state occurs," and R is "the reference time.") State A changes into State B at the CS, and *-te-iru* points to the homogeneous, unchanging portion that persists after CS. This general meaning will

---

5. The form *-te-iru* has gone through a phonological reduction and the shorter form *-te-ru* is widely used in colloquial speech.

Chapter 7. Tense and aspect

Table 3. Verb types

Stative (· = intransitive).

aru ·	'to exist'	dekiru ·	'can do'	wakaru* ·	'know'
kireru ·	'can cut'	mieru ·	'can see'	yoo suru ·	'need'
iru ·	'need'	atai suru ·	'be equal'	ooki-sugiru ·	'be too big'

*The verb *wakaru* 'know' is stative when it is used in *nihongo ga wakaru* 'to know Japanese', but it can also be an instantaneous/achievement type in the sense of 'understanding', as in *yatto wakatta* 'I just got (understood) it.' The form, *wakatte-iru*, gives a resultative interpretation.

Continuative (Activity) (· = intransitive, + = also Accomplishment).

yomu	'to read'	kiku	'to listen'	hashiru ·	'to run'
kaku	'to write'	taberu	'to eat'	oyogu ·	'to swim'
warau ·	'to laugh'	nomu	'to drink'	hataraku ·	'to work'
naku ·	'to cry'	osu+	'to push'	kangaeru	'to think'
shaberu ·	'to talk'	hiku+	'to pull'	furu ·	'to fall (rain)'
utau	'to sing'	chiru ·+	'to scatter'	benkyoo-	'to study'
soru+	'to shave'	aruku ·	'to walk'	suru	

Continuative (Accomplishment) (no intransitive).

wataru	'to cross'	kowasu	'to destroy'	yorokobasu	'to amuse'
mageru	'to bend'	yogosu	'to spoil'	uchi-otosu	'shoot down'
uru	'to sell'	kau	'to buy'	chigiru	'to tear off'

Instantaneous (Achievement) (· = intransitive).

shinu ·	'to die'	nokoru ·	'to remain'	wasureru	'to forget'
tsuku ·	'to arrive'	yameru ·	'to quit'	sotsugyo-suru	'to graduate'
kieru ·	'to be out'	hajimaru ·	'to begin'	(me ga)-sameru ·	'to wake up'
kimaru ·	'to be decided'	owaru ·	'to finish'		
kekkon-suru ·	'to get married'	yamu ·	'to stop (rain)'		
		mitsukaru ·	'to be found'		

Instantaneous (Semelfactive) (· = intransitive).

tataku ·	'to tap'	tobiagaru ·	'to jump'	seki o suru ·	'to cough'
hoeru ·	'to bark'	kamitsuku ·	'to bite'	(hik)kaku ·	'to scratch'
tataku ·	'to tap'	tobiagaru ·	'to jump'	seki o suru ·	'to cough'
hoeru ·	'to bark'	kamitsuku ·	'to bite'	(hik)kaku ·	'to scratch'

produce either a progressive reading ('he is eating') when State A ('non-eating') changes to State B ('eating') or a resultative reading ('the statue is standing at the corner') when State A ('erecting a statue') changes State B ('a statue erected').

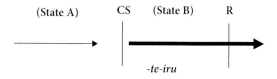

Figure 3. Interpretation of *-te-i*

2.3.1.1 *Canonical cases.* The *-te-iru* construction shares great deal of similarities with the English *be V-ing* construction as the table below shows.

Table 4. Comparison of *be V-ing* in English and *-te-iru* in Japanese

Verb types	Aspectual meanings	be V-ing	-te-iru
Stative	–	–	–
Continuative	Progressive	'is eating x'	'x o tabete-iru'
Instantaneous	Inceptive	'is dying'	–
	Resultative	'is standing'	'tatte-iru'
		–	'shinde-iru'

Neither *be V-ing* nor *-te-iru* can be used with stative verbs, and both create the progressive meaning with continuative verbs. The difference arises for the instantaneous verbs. English instantaneous verbs usually refer to the inceptive phase leading up to the point of event, but they may also refer to the resultant phase with "position" and "location" verbs (Smith 1991: 115). On the other hand, Japanese counterpart can only refer to the resultant phase. The English sentence, 'my goldfish is dying' refers to the initial stage of the fish's dying, and 'a statue is standing at the corner' refers to the resultant state after the statue was erected at the corner. In contrast, *sakana ga shinde-iru* (fish NOM die-*te-iru*) and *doozoo ga tatte-iru* (statue NOM stand-*te-iru*) both have the resultative meanings, 'the fish (has died and) is dead (now)' and 'the statue (has been erected and) is standing (now).' It is important to note that the former never means 'the fish is dying.'

Progressive. The progressive focuses on "the internal stages of durative, non-stative situations" (Smith 1991: 222). On the diagram presented in Figure 3 on the previous page, CS can be seen as corresponding to the initial point of State B, which is continuing at the reference time (R). Continuative verbs that refer to an event with internal stages of a situation are compatible with the progressive meaning. These verbs tend to be transitive and volitional, and their *-te-iru* form often describes a "dynamic, temporary, and/or volitional" event (Smith 1991: 223). However, also, volitional intransitive verbs (i.e. "unergative verbs"), intransitive verbs of emotion-induced human behaviors, such as *naku* 'cry' and *warau* 'laugh,' as well as those of meteorological phenomena, such as (*ame/yuki ga*) *furu* '(rain/snow) falls' and (*kaze ga*) *fuku* '(wind) blow,' may produce the progressive meaning with the *-te-iru*. (cf. Kindaichi [1950] 1976: 22–23, Okuda 1978a, 1978b).

(20) (Transitive Verb)
 ani wa honbako o tsukutte-iru
 o.brother TOP bookcase ACC make:TE-ASP:NONPAST
 'My elder brother is making a bookcase.'

(21) (Intransitive, Unergative Verb)
 taroo wa umibe o hashitte-iru
 (name) TOP beach ACC run:TE-ASP:NONPAST
 'Taro is running on the beach.'

(22) (Intransitive, Verb of an emotion-induced human behavior)
 akachan ga waratte-iru
 (name) NOM laugh:TE-ASP:NONPAST
 'A baby is laughing.'

(23) (Intransitive, Verb of a meteorological phenomenon)
 ame ga futte-iru
 rain NOM fall:TE-ASP:NONPAST
 'It is raining.'

The aspectual meaning known as "iterative" is conceptually close to progressive. Iterative means "multiple-event activities" consisting of "an unbroken series of sub-events which are conceptualized as a single, ongoing event." In other words, they represent "repetitions with an arbitrary end point" (Smith 1991:85). This meaning is signaled when a particular type of instantaneous verb called "semelfactive" verbs appear with the *-te-iru* construction. For example, *seki o suru* (cough ACC do) 'cough' is a one time event, but *seki o shiteiru* means that the same event occurred repeatedly.

(24) (Transitive, Instantaneous (Semelfactive) Verb)
 taroo ga sakki kara seki o shiteiru
 (name) NOM a.while.ago from cough ACC do:TE-ASP:NONPAST
 'Taro has been coughing since a while ago.'

Resultative. The resultative meaning "focuses an interval that follows the change of state" (Smith 1991:225). In contrast to the progressive interpretation, CS on the diagram presented in Fig. 3 earlier can be seen as corresponding to the final point of State A, the result of which is relevant at the reference time (R). The nonpast tense form of *-iru* in the resultative *-te-iru*, thus, indicates the "current state" resulted from a "past action." This contrasts with the nonpast tense form of *-iru* in the progressive *-te-iru* which indicates the "current state" of the "current action." The change of state is a crucial feature that is required for the resultative meaning, and verbs that include the change of state as part of their semantic property are eligible for this meaning. The most natural type of verbs that signal the resultative meaning are instantaneous (achievement type) verbs, e.g. *shinu* 'die' and *ochiru* 'fall.' Unlike continuative verbs, this type of verb does not have duration, so a progressive aspect interpretation is not possible; the only possible interpretation is the resultative aspect. See examples in (25) below.

(25) (Intransitive, Instantaneous (Achievement) Verb)
 kingyo ga shinde-iru
 goldfish NOM die:TE-ASP:NONPAST
 'The goldfish died (and now) is dead.'

>
> *saifu ga ochite-iru*
> wallet NOM fall:TE-ASP:NONPAST
> 'A wallet has fallen (and, is lying on the ground).'

Transitivity and aspect. There is a skewed association between the aspectual meaning and transitivity of verbs (Kindaichi op.cit., Jacobsen 1992: 157–203). This can be seen clearly in the two members of a transitive-intransitive pair (Chapter 5 §1.1.3). Transitive members such as *taosu* 'make (something) fall' are usually continuative (accomplishment) verbs with a volitional agent and durative time span. Thus, they naturally impart the progressive meaning. On the other hand, their intransitive counterparts such as *taoreru* '(something) falls down' are usually instantaneous (Achievement type) verbs with non-volitional, inanimate participant, and indicate a resultative meaning.[6]

(26) Transitive member + -*te-iru* = Progressive
taroo ga ki o taoshite-iru
(name) NOM tree ACC make.fall:TE-ASP:NONPAST
'Taro is felling the tree'

(27) Intransitive member + -*te-iru* = Resultative
ki ga taorete-iru
tree NOM fall:TE-ASP:NONPAST
'A tree has fallen (and, is lying on the ground).'

Although this pattern is not completely watertight, there are many such pairs. Some more examples are listed below.

---

6. Marginally, (27) can be interpreted with the progressive meaning; 'The tree is falling (very slowly).' Also noteworthy is the resultative interpretation of the transitive -*te* with -*iru*, as shown in (i) (Emi Morita - personal communication). See §2.3.1.2 below for more discussion.

(i) (Transitive -*te-iru* with a resultative interpretation)
ano hito wa hiruma demo itsumo heya no denki
that person TOP day.time even always room GEN light
o tsukete-iru
ACC turn.on:TE-ASP:NONPAST
'That person always leaves the lights on even during the day.'

Compare (i) with (ii) below.

(ii) (Intransitive -*te-iru* with a resultative interpretation)
kono heya no denki wa hiruma demo itsumo tsuite-iru
this room GEN light TOP day.time even always turn.on:TE-ASP:NONPAST
'The light in this room is always on, even during the day.'

Table 5. Transitivity and Aspectual meanings

Transitive -te-iru = Progressive (Accomplishment)		Intransitive -te-iru = Resultative (Achievement)	
akete-iru	'is opening'	aite-iru	'is open'
shimete-iru	'is closing'	shimatte-iru	'is closed'
tsukete-iru	'is turning on (the light)'	tsuite-iru	'is turned on'
keshite-iru	'is turning off (the light)'	kiete-iru	'is turned off'
mazete-iru	'is mixing'	mazatte-iru	'is mixed'
hodoite-iru	'is untying'	hodokete-iru	'is untied'
kuzushite-iru	'is crushing'	kuzurete-iru	'is crushed'
watte-iru	'is breaking'	warete-iru	'is broken'

2.3.1.2. *Extended uses.* In the previous section, the unmarked meanings of the *-te-iru* form with different types of verbs were presented. However, marked, extended meanings may also emerge when a specific context is provided. This includes the resultative meaning coded by the continuative and semelfactive with *te-iru*, which normally produces the progressive or iterative meanings, respectively.

Resultative. The resultative aspect may emerge when *-te-iru* modifies the continuative verbs (both Accomplishment and Activity types) in the context like (28) below.[7] Example (28) uses an Accomplishment verb.

(28) ani   wa   honbako o   moo   nijuk-ko mo   tsukutte-iru
     o.brother TOP bookcase ACC already 20-CLS   also make:TE-ASP:NONPAST
     'My elder brother has already made as many as 20 bookcases.'

Example (29) with an activity verb is interpreted to mean that Taro's running has been completed before the reference (= speaking) time as preparation for an up-coming race.

(29) taroo   wa   shiai   no   mae   ni   moo
     (name) TOP   competition GEN   before DAT   already

   juubun   hashitte-iru
   enough   run:TE-ASP:NONPAST
   'Taro has run enough before the race.'

---

7. The reason why the progressive is unmarked and the resultative marked for *-te-iru* is seen in the fact that for the latter meaning to emerge extra information needs to be supplied from adverbs and other extra information in a sentence and/or from discourse. Note that (28) without the extra information provided by words such as *moo* 'already' and *nijuk-ko mo* 'as many as twenty,' the resultative information is difficult to obtain.

The semelfactive type of instantaneous verbs can also be interpreted with the resultative aspect given the right environment. Here the adverb *sudeni* 'already' and the specific number of knocks give the extra information.

(30) *mari   wa   sudeni   doa   o   san-kai   tataite-iru*
     (name) TOP   already   door   ACC 3-times   knock:TE-ASP:NONPAST
     'Mari has knocked the door three times already.'

Though continuative verbs tend to produce the progressive meaning with *-te-iru*, some verbs (e.g. "clothing verbs") do not have the skewed aspectual association, and both aspectual readings are equally available for the *-te-iru* expression. That is, while (31) with verb *migaku* 'polish' (continuative/achievement) is more naturally interpreted with the progressive meaning, (32) with a clothing verb, *haku* 'wear,' is interpreted equally with either meaning.[8]

(31) *mari   wa   akai   kutsu   o   migaite-iru*
     (name) TOP   red   shoe   ACC polish:TE-ASP:NONPAST
     'Mari is polishing (her) red shoes.'   (Progressive)

(32) *mari   wa   akai   kutsu   o   haite-iru*
     (name) TOP   red   shoe   ACC wear:TE-ASP:NONPAST
     'Mari is putting on red shoes.'   (Progressive)
     OR 'Mari is wearing red shoes.'   (Resultative)

Perfect (anterior). The resultative meaning associated with *-te-iru* has a sense of relevance at the time of speech. When this relevance is particularly strong, the perfect (or anterior) is a more proper aspectual meaning. In this case, the actual time interval between the termination of an event and the speech time can be quite long. Put differently, the *-te-iru* form can instruct the recipient of the information to assume present relevance of a situation.

---

8. Another factor that influences the aspectual interpretation of *-te iru* is 'reflexibility.' To understand the significance of this concept at issue here, consider the following pair. (The examples and explanation are due to Shibatani – personal communication.)

(i) *otooto   wa   (jibun no)   hige   o   sotte-iru*
    younger.brother TOP   (self GEN)   mustache ACC shave:TE-ASP:NONPAST
    'My younger brother is shaving his mustache.'
    OR 'My younger brother has his mustache shaved.'

(ii) *otooto   wa   oyaji   no   hige   o   sotte-iru*
     younger.brother TOP   dad   GEN   mustache ACC shave:TE-ASP:NONPAST
     'My younger brother is shaving dad's mustache.'

While (ii) has the non-reflexive interpretation of 'shaving,' and hence has only the progressive meaning, (i) has the reflexive interpretation, and the meaning is ambiguous between progressive and resultative interpretations.

(33)   *yamada wa 1960 nen ni kookoo*
       (name) TOP 1960 year DAT high school

       o   sotsugyoo-shite-iru
       ACC graduate-do:TE-ASP:NONPAST

       'Yamada graduated high school in 1960.'

The time lag between the year Yamada graduated from high school and the time at which (33) is uttered does not prevent the *-te-iru* from making the event relevant at the time of speech. In fact, this kind of *-te-iru* is used frequently when the speaker or writer tries to evaluate past events in order to understand the current situation; thus it is often found in detective stories, biographies, analytical comments of sports events, and so forth (Teramura 1984: 135).

Iterative. If an instantaneous verb (both achievement and semelfactive types) has a plural subject, the aspectual interpretation becomes iterative. (34) is an example of iterative aspect with the achievement verb, and (35) is that with the semelfactive verb. These sentences indicate that many instances of an event happen sequentially and/or simultaneously.

(34)   Achievement with a plural subject
       wakamono   ga   sensoo de   takusan shinde-iru
       young.people NOM   war   INS   many   die:TE-ASP:NONPAST
       'Many young people are dying in the war.'

(35)   Semelfactive with a plural subject
       kodomo-tachi ga   oozee seki o   shiteiru
       child-PL   NOM   many cough ACC   do:TE-ASP:NONPAST
       'Many children have been coughing.'

Derived Stative. As noted earlier, intransitive, non-volitional, dynamic verbs such as *taoreru* '(something) falls' may appear with the *-te-iru* aspectual form to indicate the resultative aspect, but these verbs also appear regularly without it as the form of perfective, *kaze de ki ga takusan taoreta* 'many trees fell because of the wind.' However, there is a group of non-volitional, dynamic verbs which appear more often than not with the *-te-iru* form rather than the perfective form, e.g. *shitte-iru* 'know.' This is because, though they are still dynamic verbs lexically, it is their resultant state that is almost always at issue rather than their dynamic activities. This is what Kindaichi calls the Type IV verbs. In other words, this group of verbs has a propensity to behave like stative verbs, but still needs the help of *-te-iru* to actually be considered as such. This group includes: *shitte-iru* 'know,' *sobiete-iru* '(mountain) towering high,' *sugurete-iru* 'outstanding,' and *unuborete-iru* 'stuck up,' *zubanukete-iru* 'excellent,' *arifurete-iru* 'ordinary,' *nite-iru* 'resemble' (see Kindaichi

[1950] 1976). Some verbs are moving towards this category, and show both stative and resultative readings with the *-te-iru* construction; *kono michi wa magatte-iru* 'This road bends' (stative) and *kono harigane wa magatte-iru* 'This wire has been bent' (resultative) (cf. Teramura 1984: 137–144; Jacobsen 1992: 164).

2.3.2 *-te-aru*

The *-te-aru* aspectual form expresses only the resultative aspect and, to some extent, is similar to the *-te-iru* expression with its resultative meaning. Thus the aspectual meaning of *-te-aru* coincides with the thick line of Fig. 3 presented earlier for the *-te-iru* expression. However, while the *-te-iru* form appears with either volitional or non-volitional verbs, the *-te-aru* form only appears with volitional (transitive, continuative) verbs. Example (36) below is similar to an earlier example, (27), repeated here, in its aspectual interpretation. The minimal distinction between (27) and (36) is that the *-te-aru* form in (36), with a transitive volitional verb, implies an agent involvement in the event (i.e. someone's effort of bringing a tree down), while (27), with an intransitive non-volitional verb, does not (i.e. it simply describes the stative situation.) Another implied meaning of *-te-aru* is its future purpose. That is, (36) strongly implicates that the action of knocking down a tree was performed for some purpose, e.g. so that it will not fall down accidentally onto the house roof during a storm etc. Finally, (36) should be compared with another earlier example, (26), repeated here, in which a transitive verb is followed by *te-iru* and gives the progressive meaning.

(36) Volitional (Transitive, Contituative) Verb + *-te-aru*
 ki   ga   taoshite-aru
 tree NOM fell:TE-ASP:NONPAST
 'The tree has been felled.'

 cf. (27) Non-volitional (Intran., Achievement) Verb + *-te-iru*
 ki   ga   taorete-iru
 tree NOM fall:TE-ASP:NONPAST
 'A tree has fallen (and, is lying on the ground).'   (Resultative)

 cf. (26) Volitional (Transitive, Continuative) Verb + *-te-iru*
 taroo   ga   ki   o   taoshite-iru
 (name) NOM tree ACC fell:TE-ASP:NONPAST
 'Taro is felling the tree.'   (Progressive)

Towards the end of §2.3.1.1 above, a contrast between [Transitive + *-te-iru*] and [Intransitive + *-te-iru*] was made. The former is associated with the progressive meaning while the latter resultative. Some transitive verbs, e.g. *kaku* 'write,' do no have their intransitive counterparts. In this situation, the [Transitive + *-te-aru*] plays the role of creating a related resultative meaning as shown in the table below.

Table 6. -te-iru and -te-aru and their aspectual meanings

Transitive -te-iru = Progressive		Transitive -te-iru = Resultative	
kaite-iru	'is writing'	kaite-aru	'is written'
yonde-iru	'is reading'	yonde-aru	'has been read'
tsukatte-iru	'is using'	tsukatte-aru	'has been used'
hanashite-iru	'is speaking'	hanashite-aru	'has been told'

The relationship between -te-iru and -te-aru can be summarized as follows. The secondary interpretations are placed in the parentheses.

Table 7. A summary of -te-iru and -te-aru

	Transitive (taosu)	Intransitive (taoreru)
-te-iru	Progressive (Resultative$_1$) Example 32	Resultative$_3$, Example 33
-te-aru	Resultative$_2$, Example 34	–

The difference between the three types of resultatives in the table are attributed to the identity of the agent. The agent can be clearly indicated for resultative$_1$, but can only be inferred for resultative$_2$. No agent is implied for resultative$_3$.

2.3.3 *Summary*

Compared to the perfective aspect, the imperfective aspect consists of a complex array of aspectual meanings. Both -te-iru and -te-aru constructions refer to "a state of affairs as existing in a homogeneous, unchanging fashion over a given interval of time." Table 8 on the next page shows all the aspectual meanings and their relation to the verb and aspectual auxiliary types. The -te-iru appears with all types of verbs except for stative to create progressive, resultative, or iterative meanings. In contrast, -te-aru appears only with volitional continuative verbs to signal a resultative interpretation. Semelfactive is a minor type associated with the instantaneous verb, and its te-iru form creates an iterative form, which is conceptually similar to a progressive meaning. On the other hand, the other instantaneous verb, the achievement verb, will mark the resultative with -te iru.

2.4 Marked aspects

In addition to the basic aspectual forms and meanings discussed above, Japanese has a number of marked aspect forms and meanings. These marked aspects focus on either the

Table 8. Aspectual meanings with different verbs and auxiliary verbs

Verb type	-te-iru		-te-aru (Volit. V. only)
	(Primary)	(Secondary)	
Stative	N/A		N/A
Continuative			
– Activity	Progressive	Resultative	Resultative
– Accomp.	Progressive	Resultative	Resultative
Instantaneous			
– Semelfactive	Iterative (≈Progressive)	Resultative	N/A
– Achievement	Resultative	N/A	N/A

beginnings, middles, or endings of a situation (cf. Smith 1991: 75), or add more subjective coloring to a situation. The two major morphological structures involved for marked aspect marking are; [Verb$_{INF}$]-AUX$_{TYPE1}$ and [Verb$_{CONJ}$]-AUX$_{TYPE2}$. There are strict selectional restrictions between the verb form and the type of auxiliary suffix. AUX$_{TYPE1}$ require the preceding verbs to be the infinitive form, and AUX$_{TYPE2}$ the conjunctive -te form.[9] (The forms -te-iru and -te-aru discussed already belong to the latter type of construction.) All aspectual auxiliary suffixes have been grammaticalized from lexical verbs. While some of the AUX$_{TYPE1}$ suffixes retain the meaning of their lexical source to some degree,[10] AUX$_{TYPE2}$ suffixes have been completely grammaticalized to breach out the original verbal meanings, and in some cases, have acquired more subjective meaning, such as the speaker's evaluation of an event (Chapter 14 §2.1.3). Some of the important auxiliaries are listed below.

---

9. In Classical Japanese, specific aspectual suffixes were productive. Among six such aspectual suffixes, only two have survived in Modern Japanese with modification: the completive -tar- has survived as -ta with both the past tense and perfect interpretations (see §1, §2.1 in this chapter), and the residue of the reminiscent suffix -ki is found in the "retrospective" particle kke (see an example of this particle glossed as PP below), which denotes 'thinking back, recollecting oneself, or questioning oneself about some situation to be recalled' (Martin [1975] 1991:937).

   kyoo nan-nichi da   kke
   today what-day COP PP
   'What is today ('s date)?'

10. In cases where the verb following the infinitive form retains the original meaning, the form should be analyzed as a compound verb. However, no attempt has been made to make a clear distinction here.

AUX$_{TYPE1}$ with the verb *taberu* 'eat' (see Martin [1975] 1991:451–452).

tabe-hajimeru / - dasu	'begin to eat'
tabe -owaru / -oeru /	'finish eating'
(also *-yamu* as in *naki-yamu* 'stop crying')	
tabe-kakeru	'just begin to eat'
tabe-kiru	'finish eating completely'
tabe-tuzukeru	'continue eating.'
tabe-makuru	'madly keep eating'
tabe-tsukusu	'finish eating completely'
tabe-toosu	'continue eating without stopping'

AUX$_{TYPE2}$ with the verb *taberu* 'eat' for the first five examples, and *naru* 'become' for the last two (the original lexical meaning is specified in the parentheses).

tabete -iru	'is eating' (< 'exist – animate) cf. §2.3.1
tabete -aru	'has been eaten' (< 'exist – inanimate') cf. §2.3.2
tabete -oku	'eat in advance' (< 'put, place, set aside')
tabete -shimau	'finish eating' (< 'put away')
tabete -miru	'try eating' (< 'see')
natte -kuru	'become' (< 'come')
natte -iku	'will become' (< 'go')

AUX$_{TYPE1}$ and AUX$_{TYPE2}$ (*-te-iru*) may be combined in this order, e.g. *tabe-hajimete-iru* (eat:INF-begin:TE-ASP) 'has started eating.' The reverse order does not occur, e.g. * *tabete-i-hajimeru* (eat:TE-ASP-begin).

2.4.1 *Completive aspect*

2.4.1.1 [Verb$_{INF}$]-*owaru/oeru*. The "completive" aspect is expressed by *-owaru* and *-oeru* following the infinitive form. These auxiliary verbs have derived from the main verbs, *owaru* (intransitive) and *oeru* (transitive), both of which mean 'finish, end.' Continuative (activity and accomplishment) verbs are compatible with them (*hashiri-owaru/-oeru* 'finish running,' *tsukuri- owaru/-oeru* 'finish building'), but instantaneous (achievement and semelfactive) and stative verbs are not (*ochi-owaru 'finish falling,' *tataki-owaru 'finish knocking,' *wakari-owaru 'finish understanding'). The two forms, *-owaru* and *-oeru*, may be interchangeable, but *-oeru* is more literal compared to *-owaru*.

2.4.1.2 *-te-shimau*. The completive aspect is also expressed by *-te-shimau*. The auxiliary *-shimau* has developed from the lexical verb *shimau*, which means 'put away.'[11] *-Te-shimau*

---

11. A different verb, *sumafu* 'finish', is suggested as an alternative lexical source (cf. Yoshida 1971:554).

has developed the colloquial form -*chau* (-*zyau*), which is used extensively in colloquial speech; *tabete-shimau* > *tabe-chau*; *yonde-shimau* > *yon-zyau* (Yoshida 1971:558). Unlike the -*owaru*/-*oeru* suffixes, -*te-shimau* is compatible with both continuative and instantaneous (achievement and semelfactive) verbs (but not with stative verbs). Thus, with the activity verbs such as *yomu* 'read,' either -*owaru*/*oeru* or -*shimau* suffix convey a similar meaning, as shown in (37), but only -*shimau* is allowed with an achievement verb, such as *shinu* 'die,' as shown in (38).

(37) *kono hon wa zenbu yonde-shimatta/yomi-owatta/-oeta*
this book TOP all read:TE-ASP:PAST
'This book, I have already finished reading it.'

(38) *kingyo ga shinde-shimatta/shini-*owatta/-*oeta*
goldfish NOM die:TE-ASP:PAST
'The goldfish has died.'

When -*te-shimau* appears with achievement verbs as in (38) above, it forces an interpretation of a prolonged process with the ultimate end point, though this is not the case of the "leading up" interpretation of the English sentence, 'the goldfish is dying.' But rather the sentence indicates that an event has reached a culminating point where a reversal is not possible. This irreversible situation adds a particular overtone of speaker's negative feeling, or "frustrative" meaning (Ono 1992:376–378) (similar to the English expression 'end up doing something') as a result of subjectivization in the process of semantic change (Chapter 14 §2.1.3, cf. Traugott & Dasher 2005). Thus, even with a typical continuative (activity) verb such as *yomu* 'read' mentioned above, the negative overtone can be inserted in a specific context; Ken or the speaker feels that it is a regrettable fact that Ken has read Mami's diary in (39) below with *te-shimatta*. On the other hand *yomi-owatta*/-*oeta* simply indicate a completed action, and do not have this subjective overtone.

(39) *ken wa mami no nikki o yonde-shimatta*
(name) TOP (name) GEN diary ACC read:TE-ASP:PAST
'Ken read Mami's diary, (which I think is a bad thing).'

In this case, -*te shimau* shifts the activity verb, such as *yomu* 'read,' to an achievement verb, like *shinu* 'die,' and conceives the activity as an instantaneous event. When the two aspectual forms -*owaru*/-*oeru* and -*shimau* are combined as shown in (40), the negative tone gets weakened considerably and the pure completive aspect is emphasized.

(40) *ken wa mami no nikki o yomi-oete-shimatta*
(name) TOP (name) GEN diary ACC read:INF-ASP:TE-ASP:PAST
'Ken finished read Mami's diary.'

2.4.2 *Preparatory aspect: -te-oku*

The "preparatory" aspect auxiliary -*oku* has developed from the lexical verb *oku*, which means 'put, place, set aside.' The aspectual form -*te-oku* can be reduced to -*toku/doku*;

tabete-oku > *tabet-oku*; *nonde-oku* > *nond-oku*. This aspect indicates agent's action in preparation for a future situation, e.g. opening the door so that someone can come in later, or so that the room will not get too hot. Thus, this suffix requires a volitional verb. This aspect can be seen as a stage that leads to the state expressed by *-te-aru* (§2.3.2 above). One turns on the light ((41) below) for some purpose, and as a result the light is now on ((42) below).

(41) *denki o   tsukete-oku*
     light ACC   turn.on:TE-ASP:NONPAST
     '(Someone) has turned on the light (for future).'

(42) *denki ga   tsukete-aru*
     light NOM   turn.on:TE-ASP:NONPAST
     'The light has been turned on.'

2.4.3 *Exploratory aspect: -te-miru*

The "explorative" aspect auxiliary *-miru* has developed from the lexical verb *miru* 'see, look at.' It codes the meaning of 'doing X to see, trying X to see.'[12]

(43) *kono botan o   oshite-miru*
     this button ACC   push:TE-ASP:NONPAST
     '(Someone) tries pushing this button (to see the effect).'

The meaning shares some similarity to that of *-te oku* (the preparatory aspect) just described above in that both are a future oriented aspect, i.e. 'do something (X) to create a result (Y).' The difference is that the agent knows Y in the case of *-te oku*, but he does not in the case of *-te miru*. For example, *kono botan o oshite-oku* 'I will push this button (so that, e.g. the washing machine will start two hours later)' vs. *kono botan o oshite-miru* 'I will push this button (to find out what will happen).' The *-te miru* auxiliary form takes only volitional verbs as is the case with the *-te oku* form. Also like *-te oku*, the information coded in this aspectual form is more subjective in the sense that it codes the agent's intention, as compared to *-te-iru* and *-te-aru*.

2.4.4 *Inceptive aspect: (INF) -hajimeru/-dasu*

The "inceptive" aspect focuses on "the entry into an action" (Smith 1991:35), and is expressed by *–hajimeru* or *–dasu* following the infinitive form. These auxiliary verbs have derived from the main verbs, *hajimeru* ('begin' – transitive) and *dasu* ('put out' – transitive). Continuative (activity and accomplishment) verbs are compatible with these

---

12. This meaning entails the success in performing an action, e.g. *tabete-miru* entails that one actually succeeds in eating. This meaning should be distinguished from an unsuccessful attempt of 'trying to do, attempting to do,' which is expressed by [*-(yo)o* suffix + *to* + *suru*]; *tabe-yoo-to suru* 'try/attempt to eat,' *nom-o-o to suru* 'try/attempt to drink.'

auxiliary verbs (*hashiri-hajimeru/-dasu* 'start running,' *tsukuri-hajimeru/-dasu* 'start making'). They may be interchangeable in some cases, but since *-dasu* invokes a more sudden initiation of an action or event, it is more appropriate in such expressions as *kyuuni okori-dasu* 'get mad suddenly.' In contrast, a more gradual starting is compatible with *-hajimeru*; *akachan ga aruki hajimeru* 'the baby has started to walk (recently).' When appearing with an achievement verb, it depicts an iterative interpretation with plural subjects; *murabito ga shini-hajimeru* 'villagers start to die' (see "iterative" in §2.3.1.2 above). It is generally impossible to use it for a stative verb.[13] For this type of verbs, the inchoative aspect is used (see below).

2.4.5 Inchoative aspect

2.4.5.1. (ni/-ku) naru. The "inchoative" aspect means a "change of state," or more specifically "the coming about of a state (without agentive intervention)" (Smith 1991: 35). The word *naru* is mainly used to code the inchoative aspect of adjectives (stative predicates). In this sense, it is different from the other aspectual forms described in this chapter, which concern the aspect of verbs. *Naru* is a verb meaning 'become' (*sensee ni/kiree-ni naru* = teacher DAT/beautiful-COP:ADV become = 'to become a teacher/beautiful'). As an aspectual auxiliary expression, *naru* follows the infinitive (*-ku*) form of an adjective and that of the negative form of a verb (the *-naku* form in (46)) to show a change-of-state.

(44) *kodomo ga   ookiku-naru*
     child   NOM big:INF-become:NONPAST
     'The child will start to grow.'

(45) *nedan ga   takaku-natta*
     price NOM expensive:INF-become:PAST
     'Prices have begun to rise.'

(46) *wakaranaku-natta*
     understand:NEG:INF-become:PAST
     '(I) have become confused.'

When *naru* is used with a nominal adjective, the adverbial form of copula *ni* must be inserted before *naru*, (47) below. Another use of *naru* is with the potential form of a verb, (48) below. In this case, the potential verb is followed by a formal noun *yoo* (coded below as NML=nominalizer) and *ni* is inserted before *naru*. Note here that 'becoming able' does not entail agent intervention, but refers to a result of a natural process.

---

13. One counter example to this generalization is *wakari-hajimeru* (but not *wakari-dasu) 'start to understand.' However, this type of *wakaru* may be used as an achievement verb. See Table 3 (p. 135). Also see Example (52) later in this section.

(47) kiree   ni   natta
    beautiful COP:ATT   become:PAST
    '(It) has become beautiful.'

(48) kega-nin   ga   arukeru-yoo-ni   natta
    injured-person NOM   walk:POT- NML-COP:ATT   become:PAST
    'The injured person has become able to walk.'

2.4.5.2. *-te-kuru* and *-te-iku*. The auxiliary verbs in *-te-kuru* and *-te-iku* (or *-te-ku* with *i* deleted), which are derived from *kuru* 'come' and *iku* 'go,' respectively, also show the inchoative aspect. The original use of these expressions is directional (Chapter 14 §1.2.2), signaling a movement towards the speaker for *-te-kuru* and away from the speaker for *-te-iku*; e.g. *tori ga tonde-kita* (bird NOM fly-came) 'Birds came flying towards me.'; *tori ga tonde-itta* (bird NOM fly-went) 'Birds went flying away from me.' However, these same expressions have been metaphorically extended to the domain of temporal expressions as a way of coding the inchoative aspect (cf. Hasegawa 1996: 107–148). When used as aspectual forms, they refer to the intermediary stage bounded by the beginning and end of a change, with the implication of a gradual process (CS = the point of state change; R = reference time).

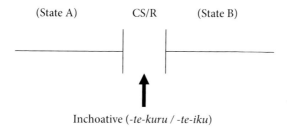

Figure 4. Interpretation of the inchoative aspect

Three types of verbs appear with the *-te-kuru* expression, all indicating some change-of-state. First, perception verbs with the *-te-kuru* expression indicate the gradual process of perceiving something.

(49) kumo-ma   kara   yama   ga   miete-kita
    clouds-between ABL   mountain   NOM   see:TE-come:PAST
    'The mountains have come to be visible between the clouds.'
    i.e. 'I can now see the mountains between the clouds.'

(50) nami   no   oto   ga   kikoete-kita
    wave   GEN   sound   NOM   hear:TE-come:PAST
    'The sound of the waves has come to be heard.'
    i.e. 'I can now hear the sounds of the waves.'

(51) iya-na   yokan   ga   shite-kita
    bad-COP:ATT premonition NOM   do:TE-come:PAST
    'A bad premonition has started to emerge.'
    i.e. 'I now have a bad feeling.'

Second, spontaneous and potential verbs with -te-kuru indicate the gradual process of obtaining a result.

(52) kanojo no   kimochi ga   dandan   wakatte-kita
    She   GEN feeling NOM gradually understand:TE-come:PAST
    '(I) have gradually come to understand her feelings.'

(53) kare ga   hannin   da   to   omo-ete-kita
    he   NOM culprit COP QT think-POT:TE-come:PAST
    '(I) have gradually come to believe that he is the culprit.'

(54) dandan   jisho   nashi   de   genbun
    Gradually dictionary without COP:TE original

    ga   yom-ete-kita
    NOM   read-POT:TE-come:PAST
    'Gradually, (I) have come to be able to read the originals without a dictionary.'

Third, the change-of-state verbs with -te-kuru indicate a process of change.

(55) kono machi mo   zuibun kawatte-kita
    this town also very   change:TE-come:PAST
    'This town has changed a lot, too.'

(56) kono mura   wa   kore kara   dondon
    this village TOP this ABL   rapidly

    hatten   shite-kuru   daroo
    develop do:TE-come:NONPAST   MOD
    'This village will probably develop rapidly from now on.'

(57) kono kuni   no   jinkoo   ga
    this country GEN population NOM

    mata   hette-/fuete-kita
    again decrease/increase:TE-come:PAST
    'This country's population has decreased/increased again.'

Verb complexes comprised of the inchoative expression *naru* with the adjectives or nominal adjectives mentioned above are used frequently to indicate change-of-state, and can appear quite naturally with the -te-kuru expression.

(58) koinu wa   dondon   ookiku-natte-kita
    puppy TOP rapidly big:INF-become:TE-come:PAST
    'The puppy has become big rapidly.'

(59) wareware no   seekatsu mo
    we   GEN life   also
    daibu benri-ni-natte-kita
    very convenient-COP:ADV-become:TE-come:PAST
    'Our lives have become very convenient.'

Compared to the -te-kuru expression, the range of applicability of the inchoative expression -te-iku (or -te-ku with i deleted) is restricted. Only the change-of-state verbs can appear with either expression. Examples (49)–(54) which include perception and spontaneous/potential verbs are completely incompatible with the -te-iku expression. Though either -te-kuru or -te-iku may be used with the change-of-state expressions such as (56), there are some restrictions. Most importantly, their point of views are different. The lexical semantics of the original verbs kuru 'come' focuses on the end point of a movement, and thus when it is used as an auxiliary, it focuses on the end point of a change, as in (60) below. The lexical semantics of the original verbs iku 'go' focuses on the starting point of a movement, and thus when it is used as an auxiliary, it focuses on the initial point of a change, as in (61) below.

(60) hatten   shite-kuru
    develop do:TE-come:NONPAST
    '(It) will become developed.'

(61) hatten   shite-iku
    develop do:TE-go:NONPAST
    '(It) will go on developing.'

However, when used in the past form, the interpretation is different. Due to the end point orientation of the -te-kuru, (62) takes the present resultative aspect interpretation, and due to the initial point orientation, (63) refers to a "future change" seen from the past.[14]

(62) hatten   shite-kita
    develop do:TE-come:PAST
    '(e.g. The city) has become developed.'

(63) hatten   shite-itta
    develop do:TE-go:PAST
    '(e.g. The city) went on developing.'

---

14. Another interesting difference between these sentences is that the -te-kuru expression signals higher speaker involvement in the situation, and the -te-iku expression lower speaker involvement (Shibatani 1990:382–3). Thus the mayor of a city would utter (62) but not (63). (63), on the other hand, is more suitable for an objective statement in the historical description of a city (Yasuhiro Shirai – personal communication.)

2.4.6 Summary

Aspect is coded in various constructions, but that with the -*te* conjunctive is most productive. The seven aspectual forms with the -*te* conjunctive including -*te-iru* and -*te-aru* is summarized in Table 9 in terms of their compatibility with transitive and intransitive verbs and volitional and non-volitional verbs. This table indicates that -*te-iru* and -*te shimau* are used in many different contexts (e.g. have higher type frequency than others). These forms also show a more varied aspectual interpretation as discussed above. The -*te-iru* suffix may indicate either a progressive, iterative, or resultative aspect, and the -*te shimau* may indicate a completive aspect and a subjective ('frustrative') overtone. In contrast, -*te kuru* and -*te iku* have been grammaticalized less for aspectual meanings as their primary grammatical function is to indicate directional information. Thus they appear with a narrow range of verbs (perception, spontaneous/potential and change of state verbs for -*te kuru*, and only the change of state verbs for -*te iku*.).

Table 9. Summary of aspectual forms

	Tr.-Vol.	Tr.-non-Vol.	Int.-Vol.	Int.-non-Vol.
-te-iru	√	√	√	√
-te-aru	√			
-te shimau	√	√	√	√
-te oku	√		√	
-te miru	√		√	
-te kuru				√
-te iku				√

CHAPTER 8

Grammatical constructions

This chapter analyzes some of the key grammatical constructions in Japanese by examining how morphosyntactic features such as verb morphology and case marking patterns are deployed to encode specific meanings in a sentence. Specifically, the chapter analyzes the following seven constructions: passive, potential, spontaneous, causative, benefactive, reciprocal, and sentences with numeral phrases.

1. Passive construction

The passive sentence (known as *ukemi-bun* 受け身文) is built upon a predicate with the auxiliary suffix *-(r)are-*. Predicates compatible with this suffix are non-stative predicates, so stative predicates such as *aru* 'exist,' *dekiru* 'be able,' *wakaru* 'understand,' *niru* 'resemble,' *iru* 'be in need of' cannot enter into a passive construction. Passive sentences are first divided into the type which depicts events (eventive passives) and that which depicts static situations (stative passives). The eventive type is further divided into direct and indirect passives.

1.1 Eventive passives

1.1.1 *Direct passives: -(r)are- as a "voice converter"*
A transitive event may be expressed either in an active or a passive sentence. As shown in (1) a prototypical active sentence codes the agent of an action as the syntactic subject with the nominative marker *ga* (or the topic marking particle *wa*), and the patient as the direct object with the accusative marker *o*. The same event may be represented by a direct passive, as in (2), in which the patient is coded as the subject with *ga* (or *wa*) and the agent is coded as a *ni* phrase. Thus in this type of passive, the suffix *-(r)are-* converts the active voice to the passive voice.

(1) Active Sentence
   [Agent/SUB]   [Patient/OBJ]   [Verb]
   neko ga (or wa)   sakana o   tabeta
   cat NOM (TOP)   fish ACC   eat:PAST
   'The cat ate the fish.'

(2) Passive (direct) Sentence
   [Patient/SUB]   [Agent/*ni* phrase]   [Passivized Verb]
   sakana ga (or wa)   neko ni   tabe-*rare*-ta
   fish   NOM (TOP)   cat DAT   eat-PSS-PAST
   'The fish was eaten by the cat.'

In the following examples, (a) sentences are active and (b) sentences are passive.

(3) a. *kodomo-tachi ga   kame o   ijimete-iru*
       child-PL   NOM turtle ACC bully:TE-ASP:NONPAST
       'The children are teasing a turtle.'

   b. *kame ga   kodomotachi ni   ijime-rarete-iru*
       turtle NOM child-PL   DAT bully-PSS:TE-ASP:NONPAST
       'The turtle is being teased by the children.'

(4) a. *keesatsu ga   sono shoonen o   taiho-shita*
       police   NOM that boy   ACC arrest-do:PAST
       'The police arrested that boy.'

   b. *sono shoonen ga   keesatsu ni   taiho-s-are-ta*
       that boy   NOM police   DAT arrest-do-PSS-PAST
       'That boy was arrested by the police.'

(5) a. *taroo   wa   mata jiroo   o   damashita*
       (name) TOP again (name) ACC cheat:PAST
       'Taro cheated Jiro again.'

   b. *jiroo   wa   mata taroo   ni   damas-are-ta*
       (name) TOP again (name) DAT cheat-PSS-PAST
       'Jiro was cheated by Taro again.'

Some active sentences with the object marked with the dative *ni* instead of the accusative *o* may be also converted to passive sentences (Examples (6) and (7) below). However, sentences with verbs that can replace the dative *ni* with the comitative marker *to* (e.g. *au* 'meet') can not be passivized (Example (8) below). That is, the former type of *ni* phrase is a direct object, but the latter type is not (Chapter 6 §3.2).

(6) a. *yopparai   ga   taroo   ni   butsukatta / hanashikaketa*
       drunkard NOM (name) DAT bump:PAST / accost:PAST
       'A drunkard bumped/accosted Taro.'

> b. *taroo ga yopparai ni butsukar-**are**-ta / hanashikake-**rare**-ta*
> (name) NOM drunkard DAT bump-PSS-PAST / accost-PSS-PAST
> 'Taro was bumped/accosted by a drunkard.'

(7) a. *inu ga kodomo ni kamitsuita*
dog NOM child DAT bite:PAST
'The dog bit the child.'

> b. *kodomo ga inu ni kamitsuk-**are**-ta*
> child NOM dog DAT bite-PSS-PAST
> 'The child was bitten by the dog.'

(8) a. *ichiroo ga hanako ni atta*
(name) NOM (name) DAT meet:PAST
'Ichiro met Hanako.'

> b. **hanako ga ichiroo ni aw-**are**-ta*
> (name) NOM (name) DAT meet-PSS-PAST
> 'Hanako was met by Ichiro.'

When the verb refers to donatory acts (e.g. *ataeru* 'bestow,' *okuru* 'send), the recipient (9b) or the transferred object (9c) will become the subject of a passive sentence. The agent in such a passive sentence is often marked by the ablative marker *kara*. This does not apply, however, to the most common donatory verbs such as *ageru, yaru,* and *kureru*, all of which mean 'give.' That is, there are no such forms as **age-rare-ru, *yar-are-ru,* and **kure-rare-ru*.

(9) a. *gakuchoo ga sono gakusee ni shoojoo o okutta*
school.president NOM that student DAT certificate ACC send:PAST
'The school president presented that student with a certificate of merit.'

> b. *sono gakusee ga gakuchoo kara (*ni) shoojoo*
> that student NOM school.president ABL (*DAT) certificate
>
> *o okur-**are**-ta*
> ACC send-PSS-PAST
> 'That student was presented with a certificate of merit by the president.'
>
> c. *shoojoo ga gakuchoo kara (*ni) sono gakusee*
> certificate NOM school.president ABL (*DAT) that student
>
> *ni okur-**are**-ta*
> ACC send-PSS-PAST
> 'That student was presented with a certificate of merit by the president.'

The choice of an active or a passive sentence depends on the perspective that the speaker takes for the event she describes. In the unmarked case the speaker describes an event from the agent's point of view using an active sentence, but in the marked case she describes it from the patient's point of view using the passive sentence (Kuno & Kaburaki 1977). Adopting the patient's point of view is especially natural when the patient is human/animate and the agent is non-human/inanimate, as shown in the (b) versions of the following examples.

(10) a. *basu ga taroo o haneta*
bus NOM (name) ACC hit:PAST
'A bus hit Taro.'

b. *taroo ga basu ni hane-rare-ta*
(name) NOM bus DAT hit-PSS-PAST
'Taro was hit by a bus.'

(11) a. *nami ga kodomo o saratta*
wave NOM child ACC take.away:PAST
'A wave swept away a child.'

b. *kodomo ga nami ni saraw-are-ta*
child NOM wave DAT take.away-PSS-PAST
'A child was swept away by a wave.'

However, this general rule does not apply when the human/animate patient (e.g. *Taro*) is marked with *ni* in the active sentence as shown in (12) below. Compare (12) with (6).

(12) a. *booru ga taroo ni butsukatta*
ball NOM (name) DAT bump:PAST
'A ball hit Taro.'

b. **taroo ga booru ni butsukar-are-ta*
(name) NOM ball DAT bump-PSS-PAST
'Taro was hit by a ball.'

When both participants in a transitive sentence are inanimate and one of them can be interpreted as having some agency in a particular context, both active and passive sentences are possible. In this case, their comparative discourse saliency will determine the sentence type. In the next examples, *kaze* 'wind,' *mizu* 'water,' and even *tsuki no hikari* 'moonlight' can be construed to have some agency.

(13) a. *kaze ga kami o tobashita*
wind NOM paper ACC blow:PAST
'The wind blew the paper away.'

b. *kami ga kaze ni tobas-are-ta*
paper NOM wind DAT blow-PSS-PAST
'The paper was blown away by the wind.'

(14) a. *mizu ga doro o oshi-nagashita*
water NOM mud ACC push-flow:PAST
'The water carried the mud away.'

b. *doro ga mizu ni oshi-nagas-are-ta*
mud NOM water DAT push-flow-PSS-PAST
'The mud was carried away by the water.'

(15) a. tsuki no hikari ga   furu-ike o   terashi-dashita
        moon GEN light NOM old-pond ACC shine-reveal:PAST
        'The moonlight illuminated an old pond.'
    b. furu-ike ga   tsuki no hikari ni   terashi-das-**are**-ta
        old-pond NOM moon GEN light DAT shine-reveal-**PSS**-PAST
        'The old pond was illuminated by the moonlight.'

One modification that can be made in the (b) sentences above is to use *ni-yotte* instead of *ni* to mark the inanimate agent. The *ni-yotte* marking will suppress the degree of agency associated with the noun phrase to which it is attached, and change the noun phrase from an "agent" to a "cause" noun phrase. If a passive sentence has a *ni-yotte*-marked noun with no agency attached, it has no active counterpart. *Shimin no bokin* 'citizen's donation' in (16b) is a cause rather than an agent.

(16) a. (active sentence, non existent)
    b. kono kooen wa   shimin no bokin   ni-yotte tsukur-**are**-ta
        this park NOM citizen GEN donation by   make-**PSS**-PAST
        'This park was constructed by the citizen's donation.'

The *ni-yotte* passive is also used when the discourse saliency of an inanimate patient overrides the natural tendency to focus on an animate agent (Inoue 1976; Kuroda 1979a; see also Kinsui 1997 for the historical development of the *ni-yotte* passive). Human noun phrases in the following examples still retain some degree of agency, and therefore, both active and passive sentences are possible.

(17) a. shichoo ga   hanabi o   uchiageta
        mayor NOM fire.work ACC launch:PAST
        'The mayor launched fireworks.'
    b. hanabi ga   shichoo ni-yotte uchiage-**rare**-ta
        fire.work NOM mayor by   launch-**PSS**-PAST
        'Fireworks were launched by the mayor.'

(18) a. yamada-hakase ga   kono sekihi   o hakken-shita
        (name)-Dr.   NOM this stone.monument ACC discover-do:PAST
        'Dr. Yamada discovered this stone monument.'
    b. kono sekihi   wa yamada- hakase
        this stone.monument TOP (name)-Dr.
        ni-yotte hakken-s-**are**-ta
        by   discover-do-**PSS**-PAST
        'This stone monument was discovered by Dr. Yamada.'

In the above sentence, the patient is inanimate and is somehow physically affected. However, when it is not, an active sentence cannot be turned into a passive sentence.

Although *toodai* (the University of Tokyo) is marked with *o* in the active sentence in (19a), it is not physically affected. Thus (19b) is impossible.

(19) a. *yamada-kyooju ga   toodai   o   yameta*
       (name)-prof. NOM U.of.Tokyo ACC quit:PAST
       'Prof. Yamada quit the University of Tokyo.'

   b. **toodai   ga   yamada-kyooju ni/ni-yotte yame-**rare**-ta*
       U.of.Tokyo NOM (name)-prof.   DAT/by   quit-PSS-PAST
       '*The University of Tokyo was quit by Prof. Yamada.'

All the examples so far are specific sentences, but generic statements can also be expressed in the passive sentence.

(20) a. *oya   wa   taitee   kodomo o   amayakasu*
       parents TOP usually   child   ACC spoil:NONPAST
       'Parents usually spoil their children.'

   b. *kodomo wa   taitee   oya   ni   amayakas-**are**-ru*
       child   TOP usually   parents DAT spoil-PSS-NONPAST
       'Children are usually spoiled by their parents.'

(21) a. *kamakiri wa   mesu   ga   osu   o   taberu*
       mantis   TOP female NOM male ACC eat:NONPAST
       '(As for) the mantis, the female eats the male.'

   b. *kamakiri wa   osu   ga   mesu   ni   tabe-**rare**-ru*
       mantis   TOP male NOM female DAT eat-PSS-NONPAST
       '(As for) the mantis, the male is eaten by the female.'

1.1.2   Indirect passives: -(r)are- as a "valence increaser"

The indirect passive is a type of passive whose subject is not directly involved in the event (and is thus thematically/semantically extra), but is instead indirectly affected by the event (Shibatani 1995). In this type of passive, the *-(r)are-* suffix increases the valence of the verb complex. Below is a comparison between active, direct passive, and indirect passive sentences.

(22) **Active Sentence**
   neko ga   sakana o   tabeta
   cat   NOM fish   ACC eat:PAST
   'The cat ate the fish.'

(23) **Direct Passive Sentence**
   *sakana ga   neko ni   tabe-**rare**-ta*
   fish   NOM cat   DAT eat-PSS-PAST
   'The fish was eaten by the cat.'

(24) **Indirect Passive Sentence**
yamada-san wa neko ni sakana o tabe-rare-ta
(name)-Mr. TOP cat DAT fish ACC eat-PSS-PAST
'Mr. Yamada was adversely affected by the cat's having eaten the fish.'

The three types of sentences are schematically summarized below.
[A = Agent, P = Patient, X = extra argument].

ACTIVE	A-ga/wa		P-o (-ni)	Verb-active
DIRECT PASSIVE	P-ga/wa	A-ni		Verb-passive
INDIRECT PASSIVE	X-ga/wa	A-ni	P-o	Verb-passive

The above comparison reveals two distinctions between direct and indirect passives. First, in the direct passive the patient is marked by *ga* or *wa* (it is marked by *o* in the active sentence), but in the indirect passive it is still marked by *o* (hence this direct object in the indirect passive is called the "retained" object.) Second, the indirect passive contains an extra argument (shown as X), but the direct passive does not. In Example (24) above, *yamada-san* 'Mr. Yamada' is an extra argument, not part of the argument structure of *taberu* 'eat,' which is only associated with an agent (*neko* 'cat') and a patient (*sakana* 'fish'). Mr. Yamada, however, is pragmatically relevant to the scene depicted by the rest of the sentence, indexing a special meaning of psychological affect (see 1.1.3 below). In the examples follow the (a) sentences are active while the (b) sentences contain indirect passives. The pragmatically relevant extra argument is underlined in each indirect passive sentence.

(25) a. kodomo ga mado o watta
child NOM window ACC break:PAST
'The child broke the window.'

b. <u>hanako</u> <u>wa</u> kodomo ni mado o war-**are**-ta
(name) TOP child DAT window ACC break-PSS-PAST
'Hanako was adversely affected by the child's having broken the window.'

(26) a. hyooron-ka ga shojosaku o shoosan-shita
critic NOM first.novel ACC praise-do:PAST
'The critic praised (his) first novel.'

b. <u>kimura</u> <u>wa</u> hyooron-ka ni shojosaku o shoosan-s-**are**-ta
(name) TOP critic DAT first.novel ACC praise-do-PSS-PAST
'Kimura was positively affected by the critic's having praised his first novel.'

Another significant structural difference between direct and indirect passive is that indirect passives can be formed from intransitive verbs. This can be done by introducing a new subject whose referent was not originally part of the semantics of the verb.

(27) a. *inu ga hoeta*
dog NOM bark:PAST
'A dog barked.'

b. <u>*boku wa*</u> *inu ni hoe-**rare**-ta*
I TOP dog DAT bark-PSS-PAST
'I was barked at by a dog.'

(28) a. *ame ga futta*
rain NOM fall:PAST
'It rained.'

b. <u>*shoojo wa*</u> *ame ni fur-**are**-ta*
girl TOP rain DAT fall-PSS-PAST
'The girl was rained on.'

(29) a. *kingyo ga shinda*
goldfish NOM die:PAST
'The goldfish died.'

b. <u>*sono ko wa*</u> *kingyo ni shin-**are**-ta*
that child TOP goldfish DAT die-PSS-PAST
'The child was adversely affected by the goldfish's having died on him.'

1.1.3 *Psychological affect (Adversity)*

The indirect passive depicts some psychological impact, usually identified as "psychological adversity," experienced by the human referent denoted by the passive subject. It is qualitatively different from the mere adversity communicated via semantics of the verb; verbs such as *naguru* 'beat up' and *keru* 'kick' convey the adversity meaning even in an active sentence, *jiroo wa taroo o nagutta* 'Jiro beat up Taro,' or a direct passive such as *taroo wa jiroo ni nagurareta* 'Taro was beaten up by Jiro.' The affect indexed by indirect passives is psychological in nature. Consider also the following.

(30) a. *taroo wa boku ga tobaku o shiteiru*
(name) TOP I(male) NOM gamble ACC do:TE:ASP:NONAST
no o mita
NML ACC see:PAST
'Taro saw me gambling.'

b. *boku wa taroo ni tobaku o shiteiru*
I(male) TOP (name) DAT gamble ACC do:TE:ASP:NONAST
no o mi-rare-ta
NML ACC see-PSS-PAST
'I was seen gambling by Taro.'

The active sentence (30a) simply states the fact that 'Taro saw me when I was gambling'. The passive counterpart (30b), on the other hand, clearly adds the negative emotion experienced when the speaker found out that "I had been watched."

The degree of psychological adversity increases counter-proportionally to the degree of physical involvement of the referent of the passive subject in the event depicted. This is because direct involvement implies potential control over the action. If one is not directly involved, one cannot exert control and can thus only experience indirect effects of the action. Consider the following indirect passive sentence with two different interpretations (modified from Washio 1993: 53).

(31) taroo   wa   hanako   ni   kami   o   kir-**are**-ta
      (name)   TOP   (name)   DAT   hair   ACC cut-**PSS**-PAST
      (i) 'Taro was adversely affected by the fact that Hanako had cut **his** hair.'
      (ii) 'Taro was adversely affected by the fact that Hanako had cut **her** hair.'

In the example above, *kami* 'hair' may belong to Taro or Hanako as the two translations indicate. It is natural that Taro's involvement in the event is greater when the hair belongs to Taro than when it belongs to Hanako. Thus the degree of psychological adversity in question is comparatively lower in (i) and higher in (ii). The next examples also show the same point.

(32) a. sensee   ga   kodomo   o   hometa
         teacher   NOM   child   ACC   praise:PAST
         'The teacher praised the child.'

      b. yoshiko   wa   sensee   ni   kodomo   o   homer-**are**-ta
         (name)   TOP   teacher DAT   child   ACC   praise-**PSS**-PAST
         'Yoshiko was affected by the fact that the teacher praised (her) child.'

      c. yoshiko   wa   sensee   ni   yamada-san   no   kodomo
         (name)   TOP   teacher DAT   (name)-Mr.   GEN   child

         o   homer-**are**-ta
         ACC   praise-**PSS**-PAST

         'Yoshiko was (negatively) affected by the fact that the teacher praised Mr. Yamada's child.'

Examples (32b) and (32c) are indirect passives with Yoshiko being an extra argument, entailing some kind of psychological effect. The type of psychological impact depicted in (32b) can be positive due to the semantics of the verb *homeru* 'praise' (but it may also be a negative one, if, for example, Yoshiko was embarrassed by the fact), but the type of impact shown in (32c) is definitely negative ("adversative"). To ascertain the adversity interpretation, the aspectual form *-te shimatta* (see Chapter 7 §2.4.1.2) can be added; *homerarete shimatta* 'was negatively affected.' The point here, however, is that Yoshiko is not directly involved in the event depicted in (32c) whereas she was somewhat involved in the event depicted in (32b) since her own child was involved. Thus the degree of psychological affectedness is stronger in (c) than (b) (Washio 1993: 52).

1.2 Stative Passives: -(r)are- as a "stativizer"

In contrast to the eventive passives considered so far, which refer to some events, the stative passive refers to stative situations. Consider the following examples.

(33) a. *takusan-no   ki   ga   kono   kooen*
    many-COP:ATT tree NOM this park

    o   kakonde-iru
    ACC surround:TE-ASP:NONPAST

    'Many trees surround this park.'

   b. *kono kooen wa takusan no   ki*
      this park TOP many   GEN   tree

      ni   kakom-arete-iru
      DAT surround-PSS:TE-ASP:NONPAST

      'This park is surrounded by many trees.'

(34) a. *wakamono ga   kono hon o   yoku yonde-iru*
       youth   NOM this book ACC well read:TE-ASP:NONPAST
       'Many young people read this book.'

   b. *kono hon wa   wakamono ni   yoku yom-arete-iru*
      this book TOP youth   DAT well read-PSS:TE-ASP:NONPAST
      'This book is read by many young people.'

(35) a. *kono kudamono wa   bitamin shii o*
       this fruit   TOP vitamin C   ACC

       takusan fukunde-iru
       much   contain:TE-ASP:NONPAST

       'This fruit contains a lot of vitamin C.'

   b. *kono kudamono ni   wa   bitamin-shii ga*
      this fruit   DAT TOP vitamin-C   NOM

      takusan fukum-arete-iru
      much   contain-PSS:TE-ASP:NONPAST

      'A lot of vitamin C is contained in this fruit.'

The stative passive is different from the eventive passive in several distinct ways. First, the stative passive always depicts situations that range over a period of time. That is why the stative passive takes the stative *-te-iru* form. Second, while the eventive passive usually requires an animate subject, with some exceptions noted earlier, there is no such restriction on the stative passive. Third, while the eventive passive concerns the relationship between its subject and the scene depicted, the stative passive describes an attribute of its subject. That is, semantically the subject in a stative passive is not an affected party in the event but simply the target of description. Thus the particle *wa* is much more natural than *ga* in this type of passive.

Structurally, the stative passive sentence may take any of the forms available to the eventive passive.[1] (36b) below is structurally identical to the indirect passive. In (37b), the "agent" can be marked either with the dative *ni* or the ablative *kara*, and in (38b) the "agent" is marked with *ni-yotte* as well as the dative *ni* or instrumental *de*.

(36) a. *ooku no hito ga kono e no na*
many GEN people NOM this painting GEN name

o shitte-iru
ACC know:TE-ASP:NONPAST

'Many people know the name of this painting.'

b. *kono e wa ooku no hito ni na*
this painting TOP many GEN people DAT name

o shir-arete-iru
ACC know-PSS:TE-ASP:NONPAST

'(As for) this painting, its name is well known among people.'

(37) a. *seeto ga michiko sensee o aishite-iru*
pupil NOM (name)- teacher ACC love:TE-ASP:NONPAST
'The pupils love Ms. Michiko.'

b. *michiko sensee wa seeto ni/kara ais-arete-iru*
(name)- teacher TOP pupil DAT/ABL love-PSS:TE-ASP:NONPAST
'Ms. Michiko is loved by her pupils.'

(38) a. *ip-pon no boo ga sono furukabe o sasaete-ita*
one-CLS GEN stick NOM that old.wall ACC support:TE-ASP:PAST
'One beam was supporting that old wall.'

---

1. A dative marked phrase in an active stative sentence cannot be turned into the subject of a stative passive.

(i) *kono heya ga umi ni menshite-iru*
this room NOM ocean DAT face:TE-ASP:NONPAST
'This room faces the ocean.'

(ii) **umi wa kono heya ni mens-arete-iru*
ocean TOP this room DAT face-PSS:TE-ASP:NONPAST
'*The ocean is faced by this room.'

b. sono furukabe wa ippon   no   boo
   that old.wall   TOP one-CLS GEN stick

   de/ni/ni-yotte   sasae-rarete-ita
   INS/DAT/DAT by   support-PSS:TE-ASP:PAST

   'That old wall was supported by one beam.'

2. Spontaneous constructions

A spontaneous event (known as *jihatsu* 自発) refers to "an event that automatically occurs, or a state that naturally obtains without the intervention of an agent" (Shibatani 1985: 827). Broadly speaking, this includes events depicted by "non-volitional intransitives" as in *mado ga wareru* 'a window gets broken' or *oyu ga waku* 'water gets boiled' (Chapter 6 §1.2(f)). Spontaneous meaning, however, is also expressed morphologically by the passive suffix, *-(r)are-*, or the potential suffix, *-(r)e-*. See Table 1 below.

The suffix, *-(r)are-*, has been developed from the classical suffix, *-(r)ar-*, the common suffix for the passive, spontaneous, potential and honorific. Among the four meanings expressed by the classical suffix *-(r)ar-*, the spontaneous meaning is believed to be the original source (Hashimoto [1931] 1969: 290). However, the verbs that take this suffix for the spontaneous meaning are limited in modern Japanese to those referring to mental activities and those that depict behavior which results from emotion (e.g. 'cry' and 'laugh') (Yoshida 1971: 117–8; 132–3). Most mental activity verbs use the passive suffix, while emotion-induced behavioral verbs use the potential form. The verb *omou* 'think' uses both forms.

Table 1. Verb forms for spontaneous meaning

	Basic form	Potential form V- (r)e-	Passive form V -(r)are-	English
Consonant verb	omo-u	omo-e-ru	omow-**are**-ru	'think'
	omoidas-u	–	omoidas-**are**-ru	'recall'
	omoiyar-u	–	omoiyar-**are**-ru	'consider'
	shinob-u	–	shinob-**are**-ru	'miss'
	mats-u	–	mat-**are**-ru	'long for'
	wara(w)-u	wara- *e*-ru	–	'laugh'
	nak-u	nak- *e*-ru	–	'cry'
Vowels verb	anji-ru	–	anji-**rare**-ru	'worry'
	kanji-ru	–	kanji-**rare**-ru	'feel'
	kui-ru	–	kui-**rare**-ru	'regret'
	wasure-ru	–	wasure-**rare**-ru	'forget'

(39) furuki mukashi ga   shinob-**are**-ru (*shinob-e-ru)
     Old   old.days NOM miss-SPO-NONPAST
     'The good old days come to mind.'

(40) *tooji   no   koto   ga   marude kinoo   no*
      those.days   GEN thing NOM   almost yesterday GEN

      *koto   no   yoo-ni   omoidas-**are**-ru (*omoidas-e-ru)*
      thing GEN   manner-COP:ADV   remember-SPO-NONPAST

      'Things about those old days are remembered almost as if things of yesterday.'

(41) *sono hanashi o   kiite-iru   uchi-ni*
      That story   ACC   listen:TE-ASP:NONPAST   while

      *nandaka   nak-**e**-te-kita (*nak-are-te-kita)*
      somehow   cry-SPO-TE-come:PAST

      '(I) somehow came to feel like crying while listening to the story.'

Spontaneous sentences take the argument structure of regular "non-volitional intransitives," but as shown in (42) below, when the experiencer is present, it is coded with *ni (wa)* as in the dative subject construction.

(42) *boku   ni   wa   aitsu   ga   hannin   da   to*
      I(male) DAT   TOP   that.guy NOM   culprit COP   QT

      *omow-**are**-te / omo-**e**-te   naranai*
      think-SPO-TE   / think-SPO-TE   cannot.help

      '(I) cannot help but think that he is the culprit.'

3. Potential constructions

Potential constructions (known as *kanoo* 可能) are used to express "ability" ('Taro can swim'), "circumstantial possibility" ('it's not possible to smoke here'), and middle voice ("this pen writes well."). Like with the spontaneous meaning discussed above, the potential suffix, *-e-*, and the passive suffix, *-(r)are-*, are used to express this meaning. Most consonant verbs use the potential suffix, while vowel verbs use the passive suffix. However, the distribution pattern is not completely regular, and the use of the potential suffix has been rapidly spreading to some of the vowel verbs and the irregular verb 'come.'[2] In addition,

---

2. For many vowel verbs, two potential forms (*tabe-rare-ru* and *tabe-re-ru* 'can eat') co-exist. The longer original potential form is indistinguishable from both the passive form ('be eaten') and the honorific form ('someone honorable eats'). Thus, setting up the new short form will create a stronger, if not complete, isomorphic correspondence between form and meaning. Besides this functional motivation, the emerging new paradigm is also useful for morpho-analytical simplicity. The suffix, *-e-*, is added to the consonant verb, *kak-u* 'write,' to produce the potential form, *kak-e-ru* 'can write.' The same morphological operation could be performed if the vowel verb *tabe-ru* 'eat' is reanalyzed as *taber-u* to derive *taber-e-ru* 'can eat' in line with other 'r' final consonant verbs, such as *kaer-u* 'return' (> *kaer-e-ru* 'can return'). The shift to the shorter potential form is still on going, and

the potential form for the irregular verb *suru* 'do' is expressed by a suppletive form *dekiru*.[3] See Table 2 below.

The potential and spontaneous sentences are semantically contiguous because both describe a situation in which an event or state comes out naturally with no agent-caused intervention. In fact, the suppletive form *dekiru* 'can do' (< *suru* 'do') has an etymological source, *de-kuru* < *ide-kuru* 'appear-come' (Ohno 1988: 188), suggesting an intimate relationship between "being able to obtain X without agent cause" (potential) and "X coming into being naturally" (spontaneous). This type of potential, or the "stative-potential construction," are similar semantically to the "middle voice" construction (Kemmer 1993: 147), which indicates inherent characteristics of the entity that allows some event to occur. In other words, it describes the quality of an entity coded as the subject (Teramura 1982: 259; Nakau 1991; Shibuya 1993).

Table 2. Verb forms for potential meaning

	Basic form	Potential form V- *(r)e-*	Passive form V -*(r)are-*	English
Consonant verb	kak-u	kak-e-ru	–	'write'
	yom-u	yom-e-ru	–	'read'
	hanas-u	hanas-e-ru	–	'speak'
	ik-u	ik-e-ru	ik-are-ru	'go'
Vowel verb	mi-ru	mi-re-ru	mi-rare-ru	'see'
	tabe-ru	tabe-re-ru	tabe-rare-ru	'eat'
	ki-ru	ki-re-ru	ki-rare-ru	'wear'
	kime-ru	(?kime-re-ru)	kime-rare-ru	'decide'
	kangae-ru	(?kangae-re-ru)	kangae-rare-ru	'think'
	ichizuke-ru	–	ichizuke -rare-ru	'place'
	totonoe-ru	–	totonoe -rare-ru	'prepare'
Irregular verb	ku-ru	ko-re-ru	ko-rare-ru	'come'
	su-ru	deki-ru	–	'do'

---

verbs with four or more moras such as *totonoe-ru* 'prepare' and *ichizuke-ru* 'locate' have not shifted to the shorter form yet. The new shorter form is referred to in Japan as *ra-nuki kotoba* "words with ra pulled out" as it appears to have pulled out the syllable RA from such verbs as *ta-be-RA-re-ru*. *Ra-nuki kotoba* have caused some uproar among language purists as they see it as a degenerative trend of the language. It should be noted, however, that a similar shift for the potential form took place for consonant verbs starting in the Muromachi period (14th–16th centuries); *yom-aru/yoma-reru* (passive form) > *yom-eru* (the new potential form), and the current shift is the second wave of the same language change, and is likely to be irreversible. See Yoshida 1971: 134–8; Konoshima 1973: 119–120; Martin [1975] 1991: 300 ff; Inoue 1998: 1–31 for this new form.

3. Potential meaning can be also expressed by a periphrastic construction, *V-koto ga dekiru*, e.g. *taberu koto ga dekiru* (eat NOMINALIZER NOM can.do) 'can eat.'

Stative-potential

(43) *kono tori wa tabe-**rare**-(or tabe-**re**-) nai*
    this bird TOP eat-POT-NEG:NONPAST
    'This bird cannot be eaten (= is not edible).'

(44) *kono yoofuku wa moo ki-**rare**-(or ki-**re**-) nai*
    this dress TOP already wear-POT-NEG:NONPAST
    'This dress cannot be worn anymore (= is not wearable).'

(45) *ano e wa takaku ur-e-ru (*ur-are-ru)*
    that painting TOP expensive sell-POT-NONPAST
    'This painting will sell at a high price.'

(46) *kono enpitsu wa yoku kak-e-ru (*kak-are-ru)*
    This pencil TOP well write-POT-NONPAST
    'This pencil writes well.'

Though the agent-less stative-potential sentences given above represent a semantic link between the potential and spontaneous, there are other potential sentences which describe agents' abilities ("agentive potential") and their freedom to perform an action ("circumstantial potential").

Agentive-potential

(47) *taroo wa eego ga (*hanas-**are**-ru)/hanas-**e**-ru*
    (name) TOP English NOM speak-POT-NONPAST
    'Taro can speak English.'

(48) *taroo wa sonna-ni hayaku wa oki-**rare**-/oki-**re**-nai*
    (name) TOP such fast TOP get.up-POT-NEG:NONPAST
    'Taro cannot get up so early.'

(49) *kono tori wa nagaku mizu*
    this bird TOP long.time water
    *ni (?mogur-**are**-)/mogur-**e**-ru*
    DAT dive-POT-NONPAST
    'This bird can stay under water for a long time.'

Circumstantial-potential

(50) *boku wa ashita no atsumari ni ik-**are**-/ik-**e**-naku-natta*
    I(male) TOP tomorrow GEN meeting DAT go-POT-NEG:KU-become:PAST
    'It turned out that I cannot go to the meeting tomorrow.'

(51) *koko de wa tabako wa (*suwar-e-nai)/su-e-nai*
    here LOC TOP cigarette TOP smoke-POT-NEG:NONPAST
    'One cannot smoke a cigarette here.'

When there is a direct object in an agentive-potential sentence, it is marked by *ga*, showing the double nominative construction pattern, as in (47) above (Chapter 6 §1.1(b)). However, the *ga* marking on the second noun phrase may be replaced by *o* without semantic modification of the sentence through a structural re-analysis, as in (52), in which the potential sentence models the typical transitive sentence (Sugamoto 1982: 442–3).

(52) taroo ga eego o   hanas-e-ru
                 ACC
'Taro can speak English.'

When the object is marked by *ga* as in (47) above, the subject may be marked by *ni* in its case frame as shown in (53), showing the dative subject pattern (cf. Chapter 6 §1.1 (c)).

(53) taroo ni   eego ga hanas-e-ru
       DAT
'Taro can speak English.'

4. Causatives

A prototypical causative sentence (*shieki-bun* 使役文) depicts a situation in which the agent-causer engages in some action directed towards the patient-causee, and as a consequence of this action, the causee undergoes a change of state, or engages in another action. The precise interpretation of a causative event depends on the relationship between the causer and causee, the degree of the causee's willingness or ability to comply with the causer's intent, and the nature of the action expressed by the verb. A causative sentence may take the form of a lexical, morphological, or periphrastic (*-te-morau*) causative.

4.1 Lexical causatives

Lexical causative verbs are a subset of transitive verbs meeting the definition given above. Unlike other causatives to be discussed below, they do not represent a morphologically complex predicate, but many lexical causative verbs have morphologically related intransitive counterparts (Chapter 5 §1.1.3). The table on the next page shows some examples of pairs of transitive (lexical causative) and intransitive verbs. Also shown in the table, where applicable, are intransitive (unergative)-based morphological causatives, which will be contrasted with the lexical causative in §4.2.1 below.

Chapter 8. Grammatical constructions

Table 3. Transitive, intransitive, and intransitive-based morphological causatives

Transitive (= lexical causative)		Intransitive		Intransitive-based Morph. Causative
ake-ru	'open'	ak-u	'open'	*
age-ru	'raise'	agar-u	'rise'	agar-ase-ru
kes-u	'extinguish'	kie-ru	'extinguish'	*
ki-ru	'cut'	kire-ru	'get cut'	*
kobos-u	'spill'	kobore-ru	'spill'	*
nokos-u	'leave'	nokor-u	'stay behind'	nokor-ase-ru
nose-ru	'load'	nor-u	'get on'	nor-ase-ru
oros-u	'unload'	ori-ru	'get off'	ori-sase-ru
tokas-u	'melt'	toke-ru	'melt'	(toke-sase-ru)
tome-ru	'stop'	tomar-u	'stop'	tomar-ase-ru
yak-u	'burn'	yake-ru	'be burnt'	*
wakas-u	'boil'	wak-u	'be boiled'	*

The transitive and intransitive pairs are used contrastively, as shown in the (a) and (b) versions in the following examples.

(54) **Intransitive Sentence**
a. *roopu   ga   kire-ta*
   rope   NOM   cut-PAST
   'The rope broke.'

   Transitive Sentence (= Lexical Causative)
b. *taroo   ga   roopu   o   kit-ta*
   (name) NOM   rope   ACC   cut-PAST
   'Taro cut the rope.'

(55) **Intransitive Sentence**
a. *kodomo   ga   kuruma kara ori-ta*
   child   NOM   car   ABL   get.off-PAST
   'The child got off the car.'

   Transitive Sentence (= Lexical Causative)
b. *taroo   ga   kodomo   o   kuruma kara oroshi-ta*
   (name) NOM   child   ACC   car   ABL   unload-PAST
   'Taro had the child get off the car.'

Version (a) in the above examples depicts a process or activity, and (b) is its causative counterpart which depicts this as something brought about by an agent/causer, Taro. Being ordinary transitive sentences, the (b) versions mark the causer with *ga* (or *wa*) and the causee with *o*. Semantically, the transitive, lexical causative, sentence depicts the total control of the agent-causer-subject over the patient-causee-object, and is often construed as depicting "direct causation", i.e. physical direct manipulation on the part of the causer affecting a non-volitional causee. Direct causation is also known as "manupulative causation" (Shibatani 1976b: 259–160).

4.2 Morphological causatives

The morphological causative can be productively built upon an intransitive or transitive predicate with the suffix -(s)ase-, or the shorter, colloquial form -(s)as-. These two forms are in free variation (Yoshida 1971: 95–105).[4] Additionally, a new causative form has recently emerged through a concatenation of the short and long causative suffixes (Okada 2002, 2003).[5] The new form is often used in the causative-benefactive context (§5.3 below gives a detailed analysis). Like the passive morpheme, the causative morpheme is not suffixed to stative predicates such as *aru* 'exist,' *dekiru* 'be able,' *niru* 'resemble,' and *iru* 'be necessary.'

Table 4. Morphological causative forms

Verb		Morphological Causative		
		Short form	*Long form*	*New form*
		vowel verb		
ker-u	'kick'	ker-as-u	ker-ase-ru	ker-as-ase-ru
tabe-ru	'eat'	tabe-sas-u	tabe-sase-ru	tabe-sas-ase-ru
mi-ru	'see'	mi-sas-u	mi-sase-ru	mi-sas-ase-ru
kangae-ru	'think	kangae-sas-u	kangae-sase-ru	kangae-sas-ase-ru
		consonant verb (and *kuru*)		
suwar-u	'sit'	suwar-as-u	suwar-ase-ru	suwar-as-ase-ru
kak-u	'write'	kak-as-u	kak-ase-ru	kak-as-ase-ru
wara(w)-u	'smile'	waraw-as-u	waraw-ase-ru	waraw-as-ase-ru
yom-u	'read'	yom-as-u	yom-ase-ru	yom-as-ase-ru
mats-u	'wait'	mat-as-u	mat-ase-ru	mat-as-ase-ru
ik-u	'go'	ik-as-u	ik-ase-ru	ik-as-ase-ru
kur-u	'come'	ko-sas-u	ko-sase-ru	ko-sas-ase-ru

---

4. The shorter form is actually older than the longer form. Note also that before the *-t* initial suffixes such as the conjunctive (*-te*) and the past (*-ta*) forms, the short and long causative forms are minimally distinct (*shi* vs. *se*); *tabe-sashite* (<*tabe-sas-u*) vs. *tabe-sase-te* (*tabe-sase-ru*); *yom-ashi-te* (*yom-as-u*) vs. *yom-ase-te* (*yom-ase-ru*).

5. Though the "short+long" form (*ik-as-ase-ru* 'go') is the norm in this new causative morphology, "long+short" (*owar-ase-sashi-te-* 'finish') "short + short" (*mi-sas-ashi-te* 'see') and "long+long" (*mi-sase-sase-te-* 'see') are also observed (Okada 2003: 4).

4.2.1 *Intransitive-based morphological causatives*
The intransitive-based morphological causative is called for when no related transitive verbs (lexical causative) is available. Below, x is a gap, for which an intransitive-based morphological causative is recruited.

    aku   : *akeru*   = *suwaru* : x < *suwar-aseru*
    int. 'open' : trans. 'open' = int. 'sit down' : x < morph. causative

This type of causative marks the causer-subject with *ga* (or *wa*) and the causee-object with *o* or *ni* (the difference between the *o* and *ni* marking will be discussed shortly.) In terms of the means of causation, the morphological causative is either "direct" or "indirect." While direct causation involves physical manipulation by the causer, indirect causation (also known as "directive causation") involves the causer's instruction, verbal or otherwise, to a causee who is capable of carrying out the task required (Shibatani 1976b: 259–260). Thus (56) below means either "The mother sat the child down" or something close to "The mother told the child to sit down, and the child did so accordingly."

(56)   *hahaoya ga   kodomo o   suwar-ase-ta*
      Mother   NOM child   ACC sit-CAU-PAST
      'The mother made/let the child sit down.'

Another dimension associated with the morphological causative is the degree of forcefulness; it denotes either "coercive" or "permissive/assistive" causation. The coercive interpretation is obtained when there is potential resistance on the part of the causee to comply with the causer's intention. In contrast, the permissive/assistive interpretation is obtained when there is willingness or propensity to perform the action called for by the causer. Compare (56) with (57).

(57)   *hanako ga   kodomo o   asob-ase-ta*
      (name) NOM child   ACC play-CAU-PAST
      'Hanako let the child play.'

Although the causer has authority over the causee in both (56) and (57), the exact interpretation is subtly different. That is, while (56) may be interpreted as either a "coercive" or a "permissive/assistive" causative, (57) is most naturally interpreted as "permissive." This difference comes from the nature of the verbs' lexical semantics. A more restricted interpretation is assigned to (57) because the verb *asobu* 'play' inherently indicates an action favorable to its causee (*kodomo* 'child'), and no coercion is necessary to make him/her engage in it; on the other hand, a wider range of interpretation is available for the verb *suwaru* 'sit down' because the intended action is neutral, i.e. the sentence is interpreted as coercive if the child does not want to sit down, or it is interpreted as permissive if he/she wants to do so. An "assistive" causative interpretation is obtained when a causer engages in a direct manipulative action in order to render assistance to a causee in performing an action, as in (58).[6]

(58) hanako ga   akachan o   te   o   tsunaide aruk-ase-ta
     (name) NOM   baby   ACC hand ACC take:TE   walk-CAU-PAST
     'Hanako let the baby walk by holding hands.'

As mentioned above, the causee in an intransitive-based causative may be marked with either the accusative case particle *o* or the dative case particle *ni*. Compare now (56), repeated below, and (59).

(56) hahaoya ga   kodomo o   suwar-ase-ta
     mother NOM   child ACC sit-CAU-PAST
     'The mother made/let the child sit down.'

(59) hahaoya ga   kodomo ni   suwar-ase-ta
     mother NOM   child DAT sit-CAU-PAST
     'The mother let the child sit down.'

While (56) is ambiguous, interpretable as either a permissive or a coercive causative, (59) can only be interpreted as a permissive causative. That is, *ni* highlights higher volition on the part of the causee.[7] This explains why *ni* cannot be used with an experiencer/undergoer of uncontrollable situations expressed by "non-volitional (unaccusative) verbs" such as *warau* 'laugh,' *naku* 'cry,' *oboreru* 'drown,' *korobu* 'fall down,' *suberu* 'slip,' and *mezameru*

---

6. The "assistive" interpretation is one of the "sociative" meaning (Pardeshi 2000). Two other interpretations associated with the "sociative" meaning are "joint action" (*hahaoya ga kodomo o asobasete-iru* "Mother is making the child play") and "supervision" (*hahaoya ga kodomo ni hon o yomasete-iru* "Mother is making the child read a book" (Shibatani and Chung 2002: 36). See Note 7 below.

7. What distinguishes (56) from (59) is the notion of "sociative causation" (Pardeshi 2000, Shibatani and Chung 2002). That is, the *o*-causative clearly indicates that the causer and causee are at the same location engaging in an activity together ("sociative causation") while the *ni*-causative does not have these specifications ("indirect causation"). The distinction becomes clear when the verb is modified with the present progressive form *-te iru* as in (56′) and (59′).

(56′) asoko de   hahaoya ga   kodomo o   suwar-asete-iru
      there LOC   mother NOM   child ACC sit-CAU-PAST
      'The mother is making/letting the child sit down over there.'

(59′) ?asoko de   hahaoya ga   kodomo ni   suwar-asete-iru
      there LOC   mother NOM   child DAT sit-CAU-PAST
      'The mother is letting the child sit down over there.'

'wake up' as seen in (60).⁸ It also prevents an inanimate causee from being marked by *ni* as seen in (61) and (62).

(60) *hanako ga   jiroo   o/*ni   nak-ase-ta*
     (name) NOM (name) ACC/DAT cry-CAU-PAST
     'Hanako made Jiro cry.'

(61) *baiu-zensen/kitooshi   ga   ame o/*ni   fur-ase-ta*
     seasonal.rain-front/shaman NOM rain ACC/DAT fall-CAU-PAST
     'The seasonal rain front caused the rain to fall.'
     'The shaman made the rain fall.'

(62) *imooto ga   tamago o/*ni   kusar-ase-ta*
     y.sister NOM egg   ACC/DAT get.rot-CAU-PAST
     'My younger sister (inadvertently) let the eggs rot.'

To summarize, *o* is the unmarked particle to mark the causee noun phrase in an intransitive-based causative, but when the causee's volition and/or ability to respond to the causer's intention becomes an issue, the higher degree of causee volition/ability may be indicated by the choice of *ni*.

The prototypical definition of the causative given at the outset includes the causer's active engagement in bringing about the result, either by physical manipulation ("direct causative") or direction ("indirect causative"). In some less prototypical situations, a causer may actually not perform an action. Thus in (62) above, it is the lack of activity rather than a performed activity that brings about the resultant state. This type of sentence is identified as a "non-interventive" causative. When non-intervention applies to animate causees, as in (63) below, the causative sentence conveys a strong sense of adversity in relation to an unfortunate event. Thus, this type of causative is called an "adversative" causative (Oehrle & Nishio 1981; Washio 1993). In an adversative causative, the "causer" has only a nominal status and is, in actuality, a victim of the situation, similar to the subject of an adversative passive like (64), in which the referent of the passive subject suffers some negative effect (§1.1.3 above). Thus (63) below with the non-interventive interpretation means that the father, who may have been at his son's side, did not do anything to prevent him from dying (e.g. 'The father let his son die peacefully'). The same sentence with the

---

8. The *ni*-marking becomes possible in (60) in two situations. One situation is the case of the "movie director causative" (cf. Shibatani 1976b: 260), in which the causer is a movie director and the causee an actor who performs the desired act. In this situation, *naku* 'cry' is used as a controllable verb. In the other situation, the causee's action is not the result of some action initiated by the causer, but of spontaneous process (e.g. the causee has a strong desire to cry for some reason, and the causer lets him cry). This latter case is the "non-interventive" type of causative, which will be discussed shortly. See (63) and (64), and Note 9 directly below.

adversative causative interpretation means that the father was only involved psychologically, not physically, in the unfortunate event, just as in the adversity passive (64).⁹

(63) **Adversative Causative Sentence**
chichioya ga kodomo o shin-ase-ta
father NOM child ACC die-CAU-PAST
'The father let his son die.'
OR 'The father had his son die.'

(64) **Adversative Passive Sentence**
chichioya ga kodomo ni shin-are-ta
father NOM child DAT die-PSS-PAST
'The father had his son die on him.'

The final point about the intransitive-based morphological causative concerns a comparison between it and the lexical causative (see Table 3 in §4.1 above). Earlier, it was mentioned that a morphological causative is called for when no lexical causative is available. However, in some cases the morphological causative is used even when there is a perfectly well formed lexical causative available. In such a situation, the division between "direct" and "indirect" causation becomes clear. Compare (65a) and (65b).

(65) **Lexical, "Direct" Causative**
a. chichioya ga kodomo o sono jitensha ni nose-ta
father NOM child ACC that bicycle DAT ride-PAST
'The father put his child on that bicycle.'

Intransitive-based Morphological, "Indirect" Causative
b. chichioya ga kodomo o/ni sono jutensha ni nor-ase-ta
father NOM child ACC/DAT shoulder DAT ride-CAU-PAST
'The father made/let his child climb onto his shoulder.'

(65a) above refers to a direct manipulative situation in which the father actually carries the child and puts her onto a bicycle. The causee does not have any discretion in bringing about the resultant situation. When the morphological causative, (65b), is used instead,

---

9. It is natural for the adversative sentences in (63) and (64) to take the completive aspectual auxiliary suffix *shimau* which indicates the speaker's regret towards the event (Chapter 7 §2.4.1.2).

(63′) chichioya ga kodomo o shin-asete-shimatta
father NOM child ACC die-CAU:TE-ASP:PAST
"The father let his son die."

(64′) chichioya ga kodomo ni shin-arete-shimatta
father NOM child DAT die:TE-ASP:PAST
"The father had his son die on him."

it indicates a indirect "directive" causation. Thus in (65b), the father uses some direction, verbal or otherwise, to order his child to climb onto a bicycle.[10] Marking the causee by *ni* instead of *o* in (65b) indicates higher causee volition as mentioned earlier, and imparts the permissive causation interpretation.

When a lexical causative is available, a morphological causative is not employed with inanimate causees, which cannot take orders, as shown by (66b) below.

(66) **Lexical, "Direct" Causative**
  a. taroo   ga   hon   o   tana   ni   nose-ta
     (name) NOM book ACC shelf ALL load-PAST
     'Taro put the book on the shelf.'

  Intransitive-based Morphological, "Indirect" Causative
  b. *taroo   ga   hon   o/ni   tana   ni   nor-ase-ta
     (name) NOM book ACC/DAT shelf ALL put.up-CAU-PAST
     'Taro had the book go up on the shelf.'

What the above restriction means is that those intransitive verbs which always require an inanimate subject such as *kireru* '(e.g. a string) gets cut' and *waku* '(e.g. water) gets boiled' can never form a morphological causative. The lack of a morphological causative for some verbs in Table 3 (§4.1) above reflects this fact. It should be noted, however, that in some

---

10. The reason why the morphological causative has a directive ("indirect") causative interpretation is often assumed to be related to its syntax. This type of causative is usually interpreted as containing a complement clause as shown in (i) below (see, e.g. Kuroda 1965; Shibatani 1976b; Inoue 1976). Argument case particles such as the nominative or accusative are not yet inserted at this level of representation.

  (i) [chichioya [kodomo   jitensha   ni   nor]   -ase-ta]
      [father [child   bicycle   DAT   ride]   -CAU-PAST]

The noun phrase, *kodomo* 'child,' in this representation is within the complement clause, and is not a direct argument of the causative morpheme. In other words, it is not completely "bound" (in the sense of Givón 1980) by the causative morpheme. This structure reflects that *kodomo* is not completely controlled by another person's (here the father's) action, but is rather the independent, free-willed agent of the action represented by the embedded verb *nor-*. In other words, the morphological causative is a means to encode a greater degree of freedom associated with the causee. In contrast, a "lexical causative" does not contain such an embedded clause. (ii) may be construed as an "underlying" representation for (65a).

  (ii) [chichioya   kodomo   jitensha   ni   noseta]
       [father   child   bicycle   DAT   load:PAST]

In this structure, *kodomo* is completely bound and controlled by the matrix causative verb *noseta* 'load,' and does not represent an independent agent. That is why the lexical causative is usually interpreted as a direct manipulative causative.

limited cases, the inanimate causee may appear in a morphological causative even though a lexical causative is available with a marked pragmatic interpretation. Thus (67) refers to the normal use of a key when the causer has a total control, but (68) refers to some unusual use (e.g. "throwing the key into the engine so as to cause the engine to jam" (McCawley 1978:58)).

(67) kii de   enjin o   tome-ta
     key INS engine ACC stop-PAST
     '(I) stopped the engine with a key.'

(68) kii de   enjin o   tomar-ase-ta
     key INS engine ACC stop-CAU-PAST
     '(I) stopped the engine with a key.'

Various types of causatives described so far are summarized below.

Table 5. A summary of lexical and intransitive-based morphological causatives

	Lexical causative	Morphological causative
Direct Causation	Manipulative	Manipulative (Assistive or Coercive)
Indirect Causation	N/A	Directive (Permissive or Coercive) Non-interventive Adversative

4.2.2 Transitive-based morphological causatives

Example (69a) below is a transitive sentence with a transitive verb *yom-u* 'read,' where the subject is marked by *ga* and the direct object by *o*. (69b) is a causative sentence with the same verb, in which the causer is marked with *ga* and the causee with *ni*, while the direct object of *yom-* is still marked with *o*.

(69) a. taroo   ga   hon   o   yom-u
        (name)   NOM book ACC read-NONPAST
        'Taro reads a book.'

     b. hanako   ga   taroo   *o/ni   hon   o   yom-ase-ru
        (name)   NOM (name) ACC/DAT   book ACC read-CAU-NONPAST
        'Hanako forces Taro to read the book.'
        'Hanako allows Taro to read the book.'

As shown in (69b), transitive-based causatives do not have the option of marking the causee with *o* due to a general constraint prohibiting multiple occurrences of this particle in a causative sentence (the "double-*o* constraint," Harada 1973). Thus the exact interpretation of such a causative, coercive or permissive, depends solely on the context in which it is found. Also unlike the intransitive-based morphological causative, the transitive-based morphological causative does not contrast with the lexical causative because the latter does not exist.[11]

4.3 Periphrastic causatives

In a prototypical causative situation, the causer is someone who has natural authority over the causee. In contrast to this, in some unconventional situations, a person or persons who normally do not have authority play the role of causer. When a morphological causative is used for this kind of situation, the sentence conveys an unusually strong sense of coercion (Miyagawa 1983: 156). (70) and (71) below are interpreted to mean that the students, who typically do not have authority over their professors, resorted to threat or violence in order to make the professors sit down and sign, respectively. (This actually occurred during the student movements on the university campuses of Japan in the 70's.)

(70) *gakuseetachi ga   kyooju-tachi o   suwar-ase-ta*
      student-PL   NOM professor-PL ACC sit-CAU-PAST
      'The students forced the professors to sit down.'

(71) *gakuseetachi ga   kyooju-tachi ni   shomee   o   s-ase-ta*
      student-PL   NOM professor-PL DAT signature ACC do-CAU-PAST
      'The students forced the professors to sign (the document).'

In order to avoid such an implication of violent causation, a different causative sentence structure is available. This is the periphrastic causative, which is made up of the *-te* form of a verb and the auxiliary verb of receiving (*-morau* or its honorific counterpart *-itadaku*). This construction is discussed in § 5.3 below.

---

11. There are a few exceptions to this statement. Some "clothing" verbs have two transitive forms (cf. McCawley 1978; Shibatani 1976b). The following verbs all mean 'wear'; *kiru* 'wear' (a shirt, etc.), *kaburu* 'wear (a hat),' and *haku* 'wear (a pair of pants, etc.).

Transitive	Lexical Causative	Morphological Causative
ki-ru	kiseru	ki-sase-ru
kabur-u	kabuseru	kabur-ase-ru
hak-u	hakaseru	hakas-ase-ru

When this contrast is available, the lexical causative refers to a manipulative ("direct") causation (i.e. 'The mother puts a shirt on her son'), and the morphological causative refers to a directive ("indirect") causation; i.e. 'The mother ordered her son to put on a shirt.' This is the same pattern observed for the intransitive-based causative and its related lexical causative. It should be noted that *hakaseru* listed under the lexical causative is actually a morphological causative (*hak-ase-ru*) made from the transitive *hak-u*, but it seems to have been reanalyzed as the lexical causative.

4.4 Causative-passives

The causative and passive suffixes can be concatenated in this order, -(s)ase-rare-. The shorter causative form, -as-are-, and the new combined causative form -as-ase-rare- are available for consonant verbs, although the latter is considered substandard by some speakers.

Table 6. Causatives-passive forms

Verb		Causative-Passive		
		Short form	Long form	New form
vowel verbs (and *kuru*)				
tabe-ru	'eat'	*tabe-sas-are-	tabe-sase-rare-	*tabe-sas-ase-rare-
mi-ru	'see'	*mi-sas-are-	mi-sase-rare-	*mi-sas-ase-rare-
tobiori-ru	'jump'	*tobiori-sas-are-	tobiori-sase-rare-	*tobiori-sas-ase-rare-
kur-u	'come'	*ko-sas-are-	ko-sase-rare-	*ko-sas-ase-rare-
consonant verbs				
aruk-u	'walk'	aruk-as-are-	aruk-ase-rare-	aruk-as-ase-rare-
yom-u	'read'	yom-as-are-	yom-ase-rare-	yom-as-ase-rare-
kak-u	'write'	kak-as-are-	kak-ase-rare-	kak-as-ase-rare-
wara(w)-u	'smile'	waraw-as-are-	waraw-ase-rare-	waraw-as-ase-rare-
ik-u	'go'	ik-as-are-	ik-ase-rare-	ik-as-ase-rare-
mats-u	'wait'	mat-as-are-	mat-ase-rare-	mat-as-ase-rare-

The causee in a causative sentence becomes the subject in a causative-passive sentence.

(72)
a. **Causative**
sensee   wa   kodomo o   juk-kiro   aruk-ase-ta/aruk-asase-ta
teacher TOP   child   ACC   10-kilometer   walk-CAU-PAST
'The teacher made the children walk 10 kilometers.'

b. **Causative-Passive**
kodomo wa   sensee   ni   juk-kiro
child   TOP   teacher DAT   10-kilometer

aruk-as-are-ta/aruk-ase-rare-ta/aruk-as-ase-rare-ta
walk-CAU-PSS-PAST

'The children were made to walk 10 kilometers by the teacher.'

(73)
a. **Causative**
okaasan ga   boku   ni   yasai   o   tabe-sase-ta
mother   NOM   I(male) DAT   vegetable   ACC   eat-CAU-PAST
'My mother made me eat vegetables.'

b. **Causative-Passive**

boku   wa   okaasan ni   yasai   o
I(male) TOP mother   DAT vegetable ACC

tabe-sase-rare-ta/*tabe-sas-ase-rare-ta
eat-CAU-PSS-PAST

'I was made to eat vegetables by my mother.'

5. Benefactives

5.1 Basic structure

A benefactive sentence consists of a one noun phrase indicating a benefactor (the one who performs an act for someone's sake), another indicating a beneficiary (the one who receives the benefit), and the benefactive verb complex. The benefactor noun phrase is coded as a subject. The beneficially noun phrase is coded with the special beneficiary marking complex postpositional phrase *X no tame ni* (X GEN sake/benefit-DAT) 'for the sake of X' though there are some constraint for its use. The benefactive verb complex consists of the main verb in the *-te* form and an auxiliary derived from the verb of giving with an outward (*-yaru, -ageru, -sashiageru*) or inward orientation (*-kureru, -kudasaru*). When the speaker (or someone who is close to the speaker) is the beneficiary, a verb of giving with inward orientation is used as in (74). Otherwise, a verb of giving with outward orientation is used as in (75) (Chapter 14 §1.2.2).

(74) *ane   wa   watashi   -no-tame-ni   baasudee-keeki*
      o.sister TOP I-GEN-sake- DAT   birthday-cake

      o   yaite-kureta
      ACC bake:TE-give:PAST

      'My elder sister baked a birthday cake for me.'

(75) *watashi wa   ane-no-tame-ni   baasudee-keeki o   yaite-ageta*
      I   TOP o.sister-GEN-sake-DAT   birthday-cake ACC bake:TE-give:PAST
      'I baked a birthday cake for my elder sister.'

In the sentences above, the benefactor is *ane* 'elder sister' in (74) and *watashi* 'I' in (75). The beneficiary, which is *watashi* in (74) and *ane* in (75), is marked by *X no tame ni* (X GEN sake/benefit-DAT) 'for the sake of X.' When this complex postpositional phrase is present, the benefactive verb complex *-te-ageru* can be omitted as in (76) below, which thus is identical in content to (75). However, when the beneficiary is the speaker, even with the postpositional phrase, *-te-kureru* is strongly called for, so (77) is odd.

(76) *watashi wa   ane-no-tame-ni   baasudeekeeki o   <u>yaita</u>*
      I   TOP o.sister-LK-sake-DAT birthday-cake ACC bake:PAST
      'I baked a birthday cake for my elder sister.'

(77) ?ane   wa   watash-no-tame-ni   baasudee-keeki o   <u>yaita</u>
     o.sister TOP I-GEN-sake-DAT   birthday-cake ACC   bake:PAST
     'My elder sister baked a birthday cake for me.'

The *X no tame ni* cannot be used with a verb that includes the sense of benefit for someone in its semantics, e.g. *homeru* 'praise.' In the following sentences, the referent of the non-subject noun phrases marked by accusative *o* and dative *ni* are pragmatically interpretable as the beneficiary.

(78) *hanako wa   inu no   pepaa   o   homete-yatta*
     (name) TOP dog COP:ATT (name)   ACC praise:TE-give:PAST
     'Hanako praised Pepper.' (Beneficiary = Pepper, the dog)

(79) *chichioya wa   kowagaru musume   o   dakishimete-yatta*
     father   TOP scared   daughter ACC hug:TE-give:PAST
     'The father hugged his frightened daughter.'
     (Beneficiary = daughter)

(80) *hanako wa   boku   ni   hohoende-kureta*
     (name) TOP I(male) DAT smile:TE-give:PAST
     'Hanako smiled at me.' (Beneficiary = I)

(81) *hanako wa   boku   ni   atte-kureta*
     (name) TOP I(male) DAT meet:TE-give:PAST
     'Hanako took the trouble to meet me.' (Beneficiary = I)

In comparison to the verbs with implicit beneficiary in its semantics used in sentences (78) through (81) above, verbs without such implication may restructure the argument structure with a benefactive verb complex. In other words, the benefactive auxiliary brings out the recipient role to make it a part of the new argument structure for the benefactive verb complex. As (82a) shows, a beneficiary is usually not part of the two-place predicate argument structure for the verb *kau* 'buy.' But the implicit beneficiary role (e.g. *kodomo* 'the child') can be made manifest with the help of the benefactive auxiliary, as in (82b). (82b) can be changed into a sentence with the explicit beneficiary phrase as in (82c). (83) demonstrates the same point.

(82) a. *?taroo wa   kodomo ni   ehon   o   katta*
        (name) TOP child   DAT picture.book ACC buy:PAST
        'Taro bought a picture book for the child.'

     b. *taroo wa kodomo ni ehon o katte-yatta*
                                    buy:TE-give:PAST
        'Taro bought a picture book for the child.'

     c. *taroo wa <u>kodomo no-tame-ni</u> ehon o katte-yatta*
        'Taro bought a picture book for the child.'

(83) a. *michiko wa tomodachi ni sono peeji o kopii-shita.
       (name) TOP friend   DAT that page ACC copy:PAST
       'Michiko copied that page for her friend.'

   b. michiko wa tomodachi ni sono peeji o kopii-shite-yatta
                                              copy:TE-give:PAST
      'Michiko copied that page for her friend.'

   c. michiko wa tomodachi-no-tame-ni sono peeji o kopii-shite-yatta
      'Michiko copied that page for her friend.'

A human participant represented as the indirect object of a three place predicate such as *kasu* 'lend' is naturally taken as the beneficiary noun phrase when such a verb is used in a benefactive verb complex. In the following, *hanako* 'Hanako,' *watashi* 'I,' and *sensee* 'the teacher,' are easily construed as beneficiaries. The '*X no tame ni*' phrase is awkward in these sentences as they implicitly include the beneficiary role (see Examples (78) through (81) above).

(84) taroo wa hanako ni okane o   kashite-ageta
     (name) TOP (name) DAT money ACC lend:TE-give:PAST
     'Taro lent some money to Hanako.' (Beneficiary = Hanako)

(85) sono josee ga watashi ni kippu o watashite-kureta
     that woman NOM I   DAT ticket ACC hand:TE-give:PAST
     'That woman handed the ticket to me.' (Beneficiary = I)

(86) watashi wa sensee ni shashin o misete-sashiageta
     I   TOP teacher DAT photo ACC show:TE-give:HON:PAST
     'I showed the photo to the teacher.' (Beneficiary = teacher)

In the examples with two- and three-place predicates mentioned thus far, the sense of a concrete object being transferred is very strong. With other types of two-place predicates, a more abstract kind of transfer is implied. In (87) and (88) what is transferred is the "content" of a song and a book, respectively, to the audience-recipient.

(87) boku wa kodomo-tachi ni uta o utatte-yatta
     I   TOP child:PL   DAT song ACC sing:TE-give:PAST
     'I sang a song to/for the children.'

(88) sensee wa seeto ni hon o yonde-yatta
     teacher TOP pupil DAT book ACC read:TE-give:PAST
     'The teacher read a book to/for the pupils.'

When neither concrete nor abstract transfers to a recipient is construable, the benefactive sentence is judged to be unacceptable, as (89) below shows.

(89) *boku wa mami ni hon o fuite-yatta
I TOP (name) DAT book ACC wipe:TE-give:PAST
'I wiped the book for Mami.'

The judgment of the construability mentioned above is pragmatic in nature rather than strictly semantic. Compare the two sentences below (from Shibatani 1994: 67).

(90) a. boku wa hanako ni to o akete-yatta
I(male) TOP (name) DAT door ACC open:TE-give:PAST
'I opened the door for Hanako.'

b. *boku wa hanako ni to o shimete-yatta
close:TE-give:PAST
'I closed the door for Hanako.'

(91) a. hanako wa boku ni to o akete-kureta
(name) TOP I(male) DAT door ACC open:TE-give:PAST
'Hanako opened the door for me.'

b. *hanako wa boku ni to o shimete-kureta
close:TE-give:PAST
'Hanako closed the door for me.'

The above (a) and (b) sentences are minimally distinct in the main verb, but the (a) sentences are judged to be more readily acceptable than the (b) sentences. The reason is that the passage created by the action of opening is more easily construed as something transferable to a beneficiary than the absence of space effected by the action of closing (Shibatani 1994: 67–8).

One-place predicates are more restricted than two-place predicates in the marking of an implicit beneficiary with *ni* (cf. (82) and (83) above). Thus (92) through (95) are all ungrammatical.

(92) *watashi wa haha ni ichiba e itte-ageta
I TOP mother DAT market ALA go:TE-give:PAST
'I went to the market for mother.'

(93) *yamada wa tsuma ni shinde-yaru koto ni shita
(name) TOP wife DAT die:TE-give:NONPAST NML COP:ADV do-PAST
'Yamada decided to die for her (e.g. so that he won't be a burden to her).'

(94) *hanako wa boku ni otooto to asonde-kureta
(name) TOP I(male) DAT y.brother COM play:TE-give:PAST
'Hanako played with my younger brother for me.'

(95) *hanako wa boku ni waratte-kureta
(name) TOP I(male) DAT laugh:TE-give:PAST
'Hanako laughed for me (when I told her a joke).'

What should be noted about these sentences is that they become grammatical when the beneficiary phrases marked with *ni* are removed from the sentence (Shibatani 1994:61). Consider the following.

(96) *haha   ga   isogashikatta node*
 mother NOM busy:PAST   because

 watashi ga   kawari-ni ichiba e   itte-ageta
 I   NOM instead   market ALA go:TE-give:PAST

 'I went to the market for my mother because she was busy.'

(97) *tsuma no   koto o   omoi yamada wa*
 wife GEN thing ACC think (name) TOP

 shinde-yaru   koto ni   shita
 die:TE-give:NONPAST   NML COP:ADV do-PAST

 'Thinking about his wife, Yamada decided to die for her (e.g. so that he won't be a burden to her.)'

(98) *boku   ga   isogashikatta   node*
 I(male) NOM busy:PAST   because

 hanako ga   otooto   to   asonde-kureta
 (name) NOM y.brother COM play:TE-give:PAST

 'Since I was busy, Hanako played with my younger brother.'

(99) *boku   no   joodan ni   hanako dake ga   waratte-kureta*
 I(male) GEN joke   DAT (name) only NOM laugh:TE-give:PAST
 'Only Hanako laughed at my joke.'

In the above examples, the beneficiaries are not explicitly included in the benefactive sentences. This means that the benefactive verb complex is not inherently a valence increasing structure, unlike the causative verb complex.

5.2 "Malefactive" interpretation

The same benefactive verbal complex may express a "malefactive meaning," i.e. some action performed in order to negatively affect someone (cf. Kindaichi 1988:203–4). Compare the following two sentences.

(100) *taroo wa   jiroo   o   nagusamete-yatta*
  (name) TOP (name) ACC console:TE-give:PAST
  'Taro consoled Jiro.'

(101) *taroo wa   jiroo   o   naguritsukete-yatta*
  (name) TOP (name) ACC beat:TE-give:PAST
  'Taro beat Jiro.'

(100) is a benefactive sentence with Taro being the benefactor and Jiro being the beneficiary. (101) is ambiguous. It may be a benefactive sentence if the beneficiary is someone unexpressed in the sentence (i.e. a revenge on behalf of someone) or if it is Jiro who enjoys Taro's beating him (i.e. the masochistic interpretation). Alternatively it may be interpreted as malefactive if Jiro is a victim of Taro's beating. However, the malefactive sentence is only a slightly special case of the benefactive sentence, with the beneficiary coinciding with the subject (i.e. Taro satisfied his own desire by beating Jiro). As in (101), a wider range of interpretation becomes possible when the main verb is more or less of the negative nature. A couple more examples follow.

(102) ore   wa   aitsu   o   kenashite-yatta
       I(male, informal) TOP that.guy ACC condemn:TE-give:PAST
       'I condemned that guy (to my satisfaction).'

(103) boku   wa   kodomo o   donaritsukete-yatta
       I(male) TOP child   ACC yell:TE-give:PAST
       'I yelled at the kid (to release my frustration).'

To summarize the discussion so far, the benefactive meaning is expressed via the verbal complex with a benefactive auxiliary (e.g. -te-yaru etc.) but beneficiary is expressed in different ways. In fact, sometimes the grammatical coding of the beneficiary is not possible. In all benefactive sentences, the beneficiary must be pragmatically construed. The malefactive meaning can be understood as a special case of benefactive when the beneficiary coincides with the subject rather than a non-subject argument.

5.3 Causative-benefactives and passive-benefactives

The benefactives examined so far are constructed with the benefactive auxiliaries -yaru and -kureru and their variants. The third benefactive construction is formed with the auxiliary verb -morau 'receive/get' and its humble form -itadaku. This type of benefactive sentence is distinct from the other benefactive constructions in a number of ways. First, the beneficiary is always coded as the subject, while the benefactor is coded with the ni phrase. So while it is not always possible to include the beneficiary in, e.g. the yaru benefactive sentence without the 'X no tame ni' phrase (see (92) through (99) above), it is always possible to include it in the morau benefactive.

(104) watashi wa   haha   ni   ichiba   ni   itte-moratta
       I   TOP mother DAT   market   DAT   go:TE-get:PAST
       'I got my mother to go to the market.'

Second, the -te-morau sentence has a causative or passive meaning which overlays the benefactive meaning. The exact meaning depends on the degree of agency associated with the subject; if it is high, it is interpreted as causative-benefactive, and if it is low, passive-benefactive. Consider the following.

(105) *musuko wa chichioya ni jitensha o katte-moratta*
son TOP father DAT bicycle ACC buy:TE-get:PAST
'The son had his father buy a bicycle.'

(106) *kanja wa kangofu ni karada o fuite-moratta*
patient TOP nurse DAT body ACC wipe:TE-get:PAST
'The patient had the nurse wipe his body.'

(107) *gakusee wa sensee ni kite-itadaita*
student TOP teacher DAT come:TE-get:H.HON:PAST
'The students had their teacher come.'

In one interpretation of these examples, the subject referents requested that some action be performed (agentive subjects with the causative-benefactive interpretation). Regular causative sentences cannot be employed to express the kind of situations represented in (105) through (107), since the causers (the son, the patient, the students) do no possess any authority and/or physical power over the causee (the father, the nurse, the teacher) – see §4.3 in this chapter. Thus the *-te-morau* structure is the only way to express these situations. When the caused event is a non-self-controllable one such as laughing or stumbling, the *-te-morau* periphrastic causative may not be used. This construction is also incompatible with an inanimate causee because it is not plausible to consider that an inanimate object has more power than the animate causer. A possible exception to this statement is when the causee is a natural phenomenon. Rain, anthropomorphically interpreted, may be considered to have some power over the human in the sentence below.

(108) *ano toki ame ni futte-moratte, tasukatta*
that time rain DAT fall:TE-get:TE be.saved:PAST
'(We) were saved when the rain fell for us at that time.'

In the second interpretation of the *-te-morau* construction, the subject referent does not request that a particular action be performed. Instead, the referent of the *ni*-marked phrase takes initiative and acts on his own accord (the passive-benefactive interpretation). For example, in (105) above, the son may not have done anything to cause his father to buy a bicycle, but the father initiated the action by himself to surprise the son. Example (109), modified from Masuoka (1981:71), is more naturally interpreted as a passive-benefactive than a causative-benefactive. (110) is a passive sentence which is identical in meaning to (109).

(109)   *jiroo   wa   minna   ni   sono koto de   yorokonde-moratta*
        (name)   TOP   everyone DAT that thing INS delight:TE-get:PAST
        'Jiro was appreciated by everyone for that.'

(110)   *jiroo wa minna ni sono koto de yorokob-are-ta*
                                            delight-PSS-PAST
        'Jiro was appreciated by everyone for that.'

Finally, the periphrastic *-te-morau* causative may be combined with the lexical or morphological causatives.

(111)   *taroo   wa   hanako   ni   denki   o   keshite-moratta*
        (name)   TOP   (name)   DAT   light   ACC   turn.off:TE-get:PAST
        'Taro had Hanako turn of the light.'

(112)   *taroo   wa   hanako   ni   nikki   o   yom-asete-moratta*
        (name)   TOP   (name)   DAT   diary   ACC   read-CAU:TE-get:PAST
        'Taro had Hanako allow him to read her diary.'
        i.e. 'Taro was allowed by Hanako to read her diary.'

There are two layers of causation involved in these sentences. The outer layer of causation is expressed periphrastically by *-te-moratta* (Taro had Hanako do X), and the internal layer is expressed by the lexical causative in (111) (Hanako turned off the light) and by the causative morphology in (112) (Hanako let Taro read her diary).

The new causative form with doubling of causative suffixes mentioned in §4.2 is used frequently in the causative-benefactive construction especially with the humble benefactive auxiliary, *itadakimasu*. The following are from Okada (2003: 2).

(113)   *honjitsu shikai o   yar-**as-ase**-te itadakimasu*
        today   host   ACC   do-CAU-CAU-TE-get:H.HON:PAST
        'Allow me to be your host today.'

        *otayori yom-**as-ase**-te-itadakimasu*
        letter   read-CAU-CAU-TE-get:H.HON:PAST
        'Allow me to read your letters.'

        *tsugini ik-**as-ase**-te-itadakimasu*
        next   go-CAU-CAU-TE-get:H.HON:PAST
        'Allow me to move on.'

These utterances were recorded from a live TV show in which an entertainer made an announcement. Doubling of a causative suffix seems to correspond to an elevated level of politeness. It should also be noted that the *-(s)ase-te-moraitai*, or *-(s)as-ase-te-moraitai* 'want to be caused to do X' is often employed as a polite request expression (i.e. 'I'd like to do X') (Chapter 15 §3).

6. Reciprocals

Reciprocal events are events in which two (or more) participants act concurrently as both agent and patient; in reciprocal states the two participants relate to each other, by describing the other and at the same time being described by the other.[12]

6.1 Lexical reciprocals

Situations that, by their nature, require two participants are depicted by lexically reciprocal verbs, and to a limited extent by adjectives and other parts of speech. Some examples are listed below, separated by several semantic sub-types.

'Marriage' type
    kekkon-suru   'to get married'
    musubareru   'to be joined (as husband and wife)'
    issho-ni-naru   'to be joined together'
    gooryuu-suru   'to merge together'
    deeto-suru   'to go on a date'

'Divorce' type
    rikon-suru   'to get divorced'
    wakareru   'to break up or part'

'Fighting' type
    kenka-suru   'to fight verbally/physically'
    tatakau   'to fight physically'
    (shiai o) suru   'to have a (sports) match'
    (sumoo o) toru   'to have a *sumo* (wrestling) match'
    shoototsu-suru   'to collide'

'Joining' type
    kuttsuku   'to get stuck (together)'
    tsunagaru   'to get conjoined'
    tonariau   'to be located next to each other'

'Resembling' type
    niru   'to resemble one another'
    hitoshii (Adj.)   'to be equal'
    onaji (Adnoun)   'to be the same'
    tooka (Nominal Adj.)   'to be of equal value'

---

[12] Reciprocal situations may include more than two participants. However, in this section, only reciprocals with two participants are considered. See Nishigauchi (1992: 158–9) for cases involving more than two participants.

The participants may appear conjoined in the "conjoined subject construction."[13]

(114) taroo   to   hanako ga   kekkon-shita
       (name)   and (name) NOM   marriage-do:PAST
       'Taro and Hanako married.'

(115) taroo   to   hanako ga   wakareta
       (name)   and (name) NOM   part:PAST
       'Taro and Hanako broke up.'

(116) torakku to   basu   ga   shoototsu-shita
       truck   and bus   NOM   collision-do:PAST
       'A truck and a bus collided.'

(117) kono e   to   ano   e   ga   nite-iru
       this picture and that picture NOM   resemble:TE-ASP:NONPAST
       'This picture and that picture resemble each other.'

Alternatively, the participants may be split into a subject and a comitative argument in the "comitative construction."

(114′) taroo   ga   hanako to   kekkon-shita
       (name)   NOM   (name) COM   marriage-do:PAST
       'Taro married Hanako.'

(115′) taroo   ga   hanako to   wakareta
       (name)   NOM   (name) COM   part:PAST
       'Taro broke up with Hanako.'

(116′) torakku ga   basu   to   shoototsu-shita
       truck   NOM   bus   COM   collision-do:PAST
       'The truck collided with a bus.'

(117′) kono e   ga   ano   e   to   niteiru
       this picture NOM   that picture COM   resemble:NONPAST
       'This picture resembles that picture.'

Conceptually, while the conjoined subject construction depicts the reciprocal situation as a whole and a bi-directional situation, the comitative construction represents only one half

---

13. Some of the conjoined subject sentences are ambiguous in that they could be interpreted either as an example of noun phrase conjoining, or an example of sentence conjoining (Kuno 1973:112–123). (114), for example, may mean either that 'Taro and Hanako got married to each other' (phrasal-conjoining, i.e. the reciprocal) or that 'Taro got married to someone, and Hanako got married to someone else' (sentence-conjoining). (115) and (116) also have these two-way meanings. Some others have only the phrasal conjoining interpretation (e.g. (117)). The unmarked interpretation of all sentences with the conjoined subject construction, however, is that of the noun phrase conjoining, i.e. the reciprocal.

of the whole situation, described from one participant's point of view. See the diagrams on the next page.

Diagram 1. "Conjoined subject construction" (left) and "comitative construction" (right)

It should also be noted that reciprocal sentences employing the comitative construction must be distinguished from ordinary comitative sentences such as the following.[14]

(118) taroo   ga   hanako to   benkyoo-shita
       (name) NOM (name) COM study-do:PAST
       'Taro studied together with Hanako.'

The adverbial phrase *issho-ni* 'together' can be added to an ordinary comitative sentence, (118), but not to a reciprocal sentence, (114) (Chapter 9 §3.1).

(118′) taroo   ga   hanako to   issho-ni benkyoo-shita
       (name) NOM (name) COM together study:PAST
       'Taro studied together with Hanako.'

(114″) *taroo   ga   hanako to   issho-ni kekkon-shita
       (name) NOM (name) COM together marriage-do:PAST
       'Taro got married with Hanako.'

6.2 Morphological reciprocals

Some transitive situations involve a human actor and a human patient or a body-part of the latter, such as the following.

(119) taroo   ga   jiroo o   hagemashita
       (name) NOM (name) ACC encourage:PAST
       'Taro encouraged Jiro.'

(120) taroo   ga   hanako no   me o   mitsumeta
       (name) NOM (name) GEN   eye ACC stare:PAST
       'Taro looked into Hanako's eyes.'

---

14. (118) and (118′) can both be expressed in a conjoined subject construction as well.

    taroo   to   hanako ga   issho-ni benkyoo-shita
    (name) COM (name) NOM together study-do:PAST
    'Taro and Hanako studied together.'

While transitive situations such as those shown above are unidirectional events, reciprocal events are bi-directional. When a reciprocal situation is built on a transitive verb, the suffix, -au, derived from the verb, au 'meet,' is employed (cf. Nishigauchi 1992). Below are examples of such reciprocal sentences in conjoined subject constructions and comitative construction.

(121) taroo to jiroo ga hagemashi-atta   (Conjoined Sub.)
(name) and (name) NOM encourage-RCP:PAST
'Taro and Jiro encouraged each other.'

(121') taroo ga jiroo to hagemashi-atta   (Comitative)
(name) NOM (name) COM encourage-RCP:PAST
'Taro and Jiro encouraged each other.'

(122) taroo to hanako ga me o mitsume-atta   (Conj. Sub.)
(name) and (name) NOM eye ACC stare-RCP:PAST
'Taro and Hanako looked into each other's eyes.'

(122') taroo ga hanako to me o mitsume-atta   (Comitative)
(name) NOM (name) COM eye ACC stare-RCP:PAST
'Taro and Hanako looked into each other's eyes.'

Examples of morphologically reciprocal verbs are shown below, to the right of the arrow.

'Physical' Type

naguru	'hit, beat up'	→	naguri-au
(te o) toru	'take (hands)'	→	(te o) tori-au
nigiru	'hold'	→	nigiri-au
mitsumeru	'stare'	→	mitsume-au
ubau	'take, steal'	→	ubai-au
kubi o shimeru	'strangle'	→	kubi o shime-au
daku	'embrace'	→	daki-au

'Psychological' Type

nagusameru	'console'	→	nagusame-au
tashikameru	'ascertain'	→	tashikame-au
motomeru	'seek/long for'	→	motome-au
kizutsukeru	'hurt'	→	kizutsuke-au
aisuru	'love'	→	aishi-au

'Human Relations' Type

sonkee-suru	'respect'	→	sonkee-shi-au
keebetsu-suru	'despise'	→	keebetsu-shi-au
hihan-suru	'criticize'	→	hihan-shi-au
kenasu	'condemn'	→	kenashi-au

'Discussion' Type
- *hanasu*   'talk'   →   *hanashi-au*
- *soodan-suru*   'consult'   →   *soodan-shi-au*
- *giron-suru*   'discuss'   →   *giron-shi-au*

Lexical reciprocals and morphological reciprocals are similar in that two or more participants engage in one coherent event, but they differ from each other in a crucial way (cf. Kemmer 1993:95–127). The lexical reciprocal with a conjoined subject (*A to B ga kenka-suru* 'A and B fight') conceives a situation as a single event or state with two equally involved participants; an action is executed simultaneously by the two participants, or more generally a situation is conceived as bounded (see Diagram 2 below). In contrast, the morphological reciprocal (e.g. *A to B ga naguri-au* 'A and B hit each other') conceives an event as consisting of multiple components with two participants acting independently; the situation is conceived as less bounded, and the components of an event are often construed as being executed sequentially by the two participants (see Diagram 2 below).

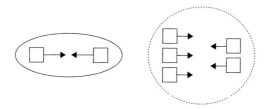

Diagram 2. "Lexical reciprocal" (left) and "morphological reciprocal" (right)

Morphological reciprocals (but not lexical reciprocals – see below) may be further modified by the adverbial phrase *otagai-ni* 'each other'.[15]

(121″)   taroo   to   jiroo   ga   otagai-ni   hagemashi-atta
       (name) and (name) NOM each.other encourage-RCP:PAST
       'Taro and Jiro encouraged each other.'

(122″)   taroo   to   hanako   ga   otagai-ni   me   o   mitsume-atta
       (name) and (name) NOM each.other eye ACC stare-RCP:PAST
       'Taro and Hanako looked into each other's eyes.'

The *otagai-ni* adverbial phrase highlights two identical, but separate, events which are reciprocated (but see below for the "parallel reading"). Thus it is generally not compatible with lexical reciprocals, which conceptualize one bounded, simultaneous event.

It should be noted that though the comitative construction is possible with a morphological reciprocal, as shown below, it does not allow (or only marginally allows) the

---

15. *O-* in *otagai* is a polite prefix, and is often, if not always, optional.

otagai-ni adverbial phrase. This confirms, first, that the comitative construction only represents part of a reciprocal event, and, second, that *otagai-ni* requires two events that take place sequentially.

(121‴)   taroo   ga   jiroo   to   hagemashi-atta
         (name)   NOM (name)   COM   encourage-RCP:PAST
         'Taro and Jiro encouraged each other.'

   cf. * taroo   ga   jiroo   to   otagai-ni   hagemashi-atta
         (name) NOM   (name)   COM   each.other   encourage-RCP:PAST

(122‴)   taroo   ga   hanako   to   me   o   mitsume-atta
         (name) NOM   (name)   COM   eye   ACC   stare-RCP:PAST
         'Taro and Hanako looked into each other's eyes.'

It should also be added here that *otagai-ni* actually is more general than a pure reciprocal adverbial phrase, as the following examples show (Hoji 1997).

(123)   taroo   to   hanako   ga   otagai-ni   ude   o   kisoi-atta
        (name) and   (name)   NOM   each.other   arm   ACC   race-RCP:PAST
        'Taro and Hanako competed (with each other) in a competition.'

(124)   taroo   to   hanako   ga   otagai-ni
        (name) and   (name)   NOM   each.other

        (*sorezore jibun no*)   yume   o   motte-iru
        (each   self   GEN) dream   ACC have:TE-ASP:NONPAST
        'Taro and Hanako both have their own dreams.'

(125)   *otagai-ni   ganbaroo!*
        each.other   do.best:VOL
        'Let's both do our best.'

(126)   (taken from *Noruwee no Mori* by Murakami Haruki, 1991: 136)
        (in this sentence *otagai* appears without *ni*)

        shibaraku   mise   o   shimete
        a.while   shop   ACC   close:TE

        otagai   suki-na   koto   o   shiyoo   tte
        each.other   like-COP:ATT thing   ACC   do:VOL   EVD

        '(She said) "Let's close the shop for a while, and let's both do whatever we each like."'

(127)   *toire   wa   otagai-ni   kiree-ni   tsukai-mashoo* (Public Notice)
        toilet   TOP   each.other   clean-ADV   use-POT.VOL
        'Let's use our public toilet cleanly.'

These sentences refer to similar parallel events, but unlike the canonical reciprocal event, the participants do not act upon each other (Hoji 1997). This interpretation of *otagai-ni* is, thus, similar to the collective interpretation of reciprocal markers in some languages (Kemmer 1993: 98–100).

6.3 Periphrastic reciprocals

The phrase *otagai-ni* discussed above is an adverbial phrase, but *otagai* by itself may be integrated as an argument. In the latter case, *otagai* may be interpreted as a reciprocal pronoun. The adverbial use is represented by the hyphen between *otagai* and *ni*, while the use as an argument is indicated by *otagai* followed by a case particle, *ga, o,* or *ni* without a hyphen. When the use is ambiguous, the notation *otagai(-)ni* is used. In (128) below, *otagai* appears with the accusative case marker in a conjoined subject construction. In these cases, the reciprocal suffix, *-au*, is optional.[16]

(128) taroo   to   jiroo   ga   otagai   o
      (name) and (name) NOM   each.other ACC
      hagemashita   / hagemashi-atta
      encourage-:PAST / encourage-RCP:PAST
      'Taro and Jiro encouraged each other.'

In this case, the comitative construction is not possible, again confirming that *otagai* requires an event to have multiple, sequential components.

(129) *taroo ga   jiroo   to   otagai   o
      (name) NOM (name) COM each.other ACC
      hagemashita   / hagemashi-atta
      encourage-:PAST / encourage-RCP:PAST
      'Taro and Jiro encouraged each other.'

In (128) above, *otagai* is a direct object. When the antecedent is retrievable from the context, *otagai* may appear as the subject.

(130) otagai   ga   moo   sukoshi rikai-shi-aeba
      each.other NOM more a.little understanding-do-RCP:COND
      koto   wa   sugu   kaiketsu-suru
      matter TOP immediately resolve-do:NONPAST
      'If they understand each other, the matter will resolve (itself) immedieately.'

Otagai may even appear as both subject and object in a single sentence, if the context warrants such an interpretation.

---

16. *Otagai* is often referred to as a "reciprocal anaphor" in the generative grammar literature, but its precise nature is controversial (Hoji 1997).

(131)   *otagai   ga   otagai   o   semete-ite-wa*
         each.other NOM   each.other ACC   accuse:TE-ASP:TE-TOP

         doo   ni   mo   naranai
         how   COP:ADV   also   become:NEG:NONPAST

         'If they both accuse each other, nothing will be resolved.'

The reciprocal pronoun *otagai* may also appear as part of a genitive phrase, *otagai no*, especially when the possessed is an alienable object and the verb is modified with *-au*.

(132)   *taroo   ga   hanako   to   otagai   no   nikki   o*
         (name)   NOM   (name)   COM   each.other   GEN   diary   ACC

         kookan-shita   / kookan-shi-atta
         exchange-do:PAST   / exchange-do-RCP:PAST

         'Taro and Hanako exchanged diaries.'

When a verb requires three arguments, *otagai* appears with *ni*. In this case, it is not clear if *otagai(-)ni* is an adverbial phrase or a recipient argument phrase.

(133)   *taroo   to   hanako   ga   otagai(-)ni   shookin   o*
         (name)   and   (name)   NOM   each.other   prize.money   ACC

         waketa   / wake-atta
         divide:PAST   / divide-RCP:PAST

         'Taro and Hanako divided the prize money with each other.'

(134)   *taroo   to   hanako   ga   otagai(-)ni   chokoreeto   o*
         (name)   and   (name)   NOM   each.other   chocolate   ACC

         okutta   / okuri-atta
         send:PAST   / send-RCP:PAST

         'Taro and Hanako sent chocolates to each other.'

7. Numeric phrases

Numeric phrases (Ch4 §3.2.2) appear in different syntactic positions (cf. Martin [1975] 1991: 777). Most typically, they appear either as a pre-nominal genitive phrase, as in (A), or as an independent adverbial phrase separated from the noun phrase it quantifies, as in (B).

(A)   Pre-nominal:
      [[***futa-ri***]   *no*   [*gakusee*]]   *ga/o/ni/kara/to* etc.   VERB
      two-CLS   GEN   student   NOM/ACC/DAT/ABL/COM etc.

(B)   Adverbial:
      [*gakusee*]   *ga/o/(ni)*   [***futa-ri***]   VERB
      student   NOM/ACC/(DAT)   two-CLS

One crucial morphosyntactic difference between (A) and (B) is the case-marking particles that the constructions can take; while a noun phrase in pattern (A) may be followed by any case particle, a noun phrase separated from its adverbial numeric expression in pattern (B) can only be followed by the nominative *ga* or accusative *o*. The dative *ni* may also appear with certain predicates. Dative *ni* is shown below in both a pattern (A) sentence, (135), and a pattern (B) sentence, (136).

(135)   sensei   ga   **futa-ri**   no   **gakusee**   **ni**   pen   o   yatta
        (name)   NOM   two-CLS   GEN   student   DAT   pen   ACC give:PAST
        'The teacher gave pens to two students.'

(136)   sensei   ga   **gakusei**   **ni**   **futa-ri**   pen   o   yatta
        (name)   NOM   student   DAT   two-CLS   pen   ACC give:PAST
        'The teacher gave pens to two students.'

Generative grammar explains the relationship between (135) and (136) using the term "quantifier float" (Miyagawa 1989; Tsujimura 2007: 307–313). That is, the quantifier *futa-ri* 'two-CLS' in (136) is considered to have 'floated' out of the genitive phrase, *futari-no gakusee* in (135).[17] The examples below are also pattern (B) sentences with the quantifier floated out.

(137)   hanako   ga   wain   o   **san-bon**   motte-kita
        (name)   NOM   wine   ACC three-CLS   hold-come:PAST
        'Hanako brought three bottles of wine.'

(138)   kinoo   guuzen   shinjuku   de
        yesterday   accidentally   (place name)   LOC

        kookoo-jidai   no   tomodachi   ni   **futa-ri**   deatta
        high.school-days   GEN   friend   DAT   two-CLS   meet:PAST
        'Yesterday I accidentally ran into two friends from my high school days.'

---

17. Miyagawa (1989: 28–37) posits the mutual c-command condition to account for the fact that only the core argument subscribed by a verb allows the adverbial construction. He also claims that the ergative/accusative distinction of verbs structurally explains the different possible positions of numeric phrases. (Miyagawa (1989: 23–7) and Downing (1996: 234–243) for a summary of the issues surrounding the case marking of noun phrases quantified by an adverbial numeric expression.) It should be added that not all allegedly floated-out numeric phrases have a corresponding pre-nominal form (A). As noted in the translation, these sentences refer to different situations, thus (i) is not derived from (ii).

(i)   kangofu   ga   kizuguchi   ni   **san-kasho**   kusuri   o   nutta
       nurse   NOM   wound   DAT   three-CLS   medicine   ACC   apply:PAST
       'A nurse applied medicine to the three spots on the wound.'

(ii)   kangofu   ga   **san-kasho**   **no**   kizuguchi   ni   kusuri   o   nutta
                         three-CLS   GEN
       'A nurse applied medicine to the three wounds.'

Normally, it is suggested that a *ni*-marked dative subject does not allow quantifier floating, as the next example shows (Shibatani 1978: 264).

(139) *_gakusee ni_ **san-nin** furansugo ga wakaru
Student DAT three-CLS French NOM understand:NONPAST
'These three students understand French.'
cf. **san-nin** no _gakusee ni_ furansugo ga wakaru (gramatical)

The pre-nominal form (Pattern A) is used whether the nominal referent it modifies is definite/identifiable or not. In contrast, the adverbial numeric phrase (Pattern B) cannot appear when the nominal referent is definite/identifiable. Thus, it is suited for a noun phrase which is mentioned for the first time (Downing 1996: 245). Notice that (140a) and (140b) are both possible as the opening in a narrative, while (141a), but not (141b), is possible as a subsequent sentence.

(140) a. *mukashi mukashi aru mura ni*
old.days old.days certain village LOC
[[**san-biki**] no *kobuta*] ga *sunde-imashita*
3-CLS GEN small.pig NOM live:TE-ASP:POL:PAST
'Once upon a time, there were three little pigs who lived in a village.'

b. *mukashi mukashi aru mura ni*
old.days old.days certain village LOC
[*kobuta*] ga [**san-biki**] *sunde-imashita*
small.pig NOM 3-CLS live:TE-ASP:POL:PAST
'Once upon a time, there were three little pigs who lived in a village.'

(141) a. *sono* [[**san-biki**] no *kobuta*] ga/wa...
that 3-CLS GEN small.pig NOM/TOP

b. **sono kobuta* ga/wa [**san-biki**]...
that small.pig NOM/TOP 3-CLS

(142) and (143) below are further examples to contrast patterns A and B: (142) with an adverbial phrase could be said by an employer when ordering the layoff of (any) three workers, perhaps to cut costs. In (143), on the other hand, the employer is ordering to fire three specific/identifiable workers, perhaps for their tardiness. In fact, a demonstrative, e.g. *sono* 'that/those,' would accordingly be quite appropriate before the genitive phrase in (143).

(142) [*arubaitaa*] o [**san-nin**] *kubi-ni-shiro*
part.time.worker ACC three-CLS fire:IMP
'Fire three part-timers.'

(143) *sono* [[**san-nin**] no *arubaitaa*] o *kubi-ni-shiro*
That three-CLS GEN part.time.worker ACC fire:IMP
'Fire those three part-timers.'

Though less typical than the pre-nominal and adverbial numeric phrases, there are also numeric phrases that appear in three other positions, as shown in (C), (D), and (E) below.

(C) Preposed Adverbial:
[*futa-ri*] (...) [*gakusee*] *ga/o/(ni)*   VERB
   two-CLS   student   NOM/ACC/(DAT)

(D) Appositive:
[[*gakusee*] [*futa-ri*]] *ga/o/ni/kara/to*   VERB
   student   two-CLS   NOM/ACC/DAT/ABL/COM

(E) Summation Appositive:
[[A (*to*) B] (*no*) [*futa-ri*]] *ga/o/ni/kara/to*   VERB
   A (and) B   (GEN) two-CLS   NOM/ACC/DAT/ABL/COM

The preposed adverbial construction, as shown in (C), is a variant of the adverbial construction presented in (B), but places the adverbial numeric phrase before the noun phrase it modifies. Though superficially similar to the pre-nominal construction in (A), (C) is not the result of deleting the genitive particle from (A). This can be shown by the fact that intervening material (e.g. *kinoo* 'yesterday') can appear between the numeric expression and the noun phrase in (C), whereas this type of intervening material cannot appear either before or after the genitive particle in (A). Further evidence that (C) is not related to the pre-nominal (A) but rather to the adverbial (B) can be found in the types of particles (*ga, o* and possibly *ni*) that are able to follow the noun phase.

The appositive construction presented in (D) puts the noun phrase in the appositive relation to the numeric phrase. Here, the noun phrase (i.e. *gakusee* in the example) must be definite/identifiable. That is, this is the opposite of the adverbial construction (B) in terms of the textual quality of the noun phrase. (E) is what Downing (1996: 230-3) calls the "summation appositive." This is similar to the appositive construction of (D) in that the noun phase is definite/identifiable, but is dissimilar in other respects. First, the noun phrase must contain a list of individuals, and second, the genitive case particle *no* is optionally placed between the numeric phrase and the noun phrase. As the name suggests, this construction's numeric phrase summarizes the number of individual members listed in the noun phrase. And, unlike any other construction discussed so far, its noun phrase does not refer to a category or a group, but refers to specific members.[18]

---

18. When the noun phrase refers to a category or a group, as in (D), and the genitive case particle follows the noun phrase, as in (E), the numeric expression may be interpreted as a partitive construction; e.g. *gakusee no futari* 'two of the students.' Martin ([1975] 1991:777) calls this type an "appositive ellipsis," since it is possible to say *100-nin no gakusee no futari* 'two of the 100 students,' and delete the modifier *100-nin no*. Contrast the appositive ellipsis with the regular appositive, *gakusee futari* 'the two students,' cf. **100-nin no gakusee _ futari*.

CHAPTER 9

Noun phrase structures

A noun phrase may be a simple or a compound noun, or may consist of a head noun and its modifier. The modifier may be a genitive/associative phrase, a simple attributive phrase, or a clause, and it always precedes the head noun.

1. Genitive and associative phrases

A genitive or associative phrase appears with the genitive particle *no* before the head noun as in:

[[NP   *no*]   NP]
  Genitive/Associative   Head Noun
  Phrase

The two NPs in this construction can be connected through a variety of semantic relations, with the genitive (possessive) being the most important type (cf. Li & Thompson 1981: 113), as shown in (1).

(1) taroo   no   e
    (name) GEN painting
    'Taro's picture (e.g. a picture that Taro owns, that he painted, that portrays Taro, etc.)'

(2) and (3) are examples of genitive phrases that semantically indicate the possessor of the head noun.

(2) watashi no   haha
    I   GEN mother
    'my mother'

(3) kono e   no   namae
    this painting GEN name
    'the name of this painting'

(4) though (7) are examples of various other associative meanings.

(4) suugaku   no   sensee
    Mathematics GEN teacher
    'a math teacher'

(5) igaku   no   shinpo
    medical.science GEN   advancement
    'the advancement of medical science'

(6) kaji no   gen'in
    fire GEN cause
    'the cause of the fire'

(7) kono kanji   no   kakikata
    this Chinese.character GEN   way.of.writing
    'the way to write this *kanji*; how to write this *kanji*'

2. Simple attributive phrases

All major word categories can serve as a simple attributive phrase for a head noun.

[[Adj./V/NA + COP; N + COP]   NP]
  Attributive Phrase   Head Noun

Adjectives and verbs do not have distinct attributive forms.[1] In (8) below an adjective *shiroi* 'white' modifies *hana* 'flower.' The past tense form and the resultative form of certain verbs may be used as modifiers. In (9) and (10) below, *kawatta* (the past tense form of *kawaru* 'change'), and *kawatte-iru* (the resultative form of the same verb) are used, respectively, to indicate the notion "unusual."

Adjective
(8) shiroi hana
    white flower
    'a white flower'

Verb
(9) kawatta   hana   'an unusual flower'
    change:PAST flower

(10) kawatte iru   hana   'an unusual flower'
     change:TE-ASP:NONPAST flower

The copula is the only inflecting category which distinguishes conclusive and attributive forms. The conclusive form is *da*, and the attributive form is *na* for nominal adjectives and *no* for nouns (see Chapter 5 §1.3).

---

1. Since the attributive and conclusive (finite) forms are distinctive in many languages (e.g. Keenan 1985:161), the Japanese case here is rather unusual. This typological uncommonality is a result of the paradigm leveling that took place in pre-modern Japanese (Chapter 1 §3).

(11) kiree- **na** hana
    beautiful-COP:ATT flower
    'a beautiful flower'

(12) aka- **no** hana
    red-COP:ATT flower
    'a red flower'

This distinction, however, is maintained only in the affirmative, non-past form; for the past, negative and negative-past forms, the attributive and conclusive forms are identical. For example, *kiree-janai* 'beautiful COP:NEG' can be used both as the attributive and predicative forms.

An attributive phrase using a noun, such as (12) above, is similar in appearance to the genitive construction discussed in § 1 above. However, while the first NP must be referential (or generic) in the genitive construction, it must be non-referential/non-generic in attributive constructions. Thus, (13) containing a referential noun (*taroo*, a personal name) is a genitive construction while (14) containing a non-referential noun an attributive construction.

(13) taroo no sensee
    (name) GEN teacher
    'Taro's teacher (= genitive interpretation)'

(14) sensee-no taroo
    teacher-COP:ATT (name)
    'Taro, who is a teacher (= an attributive interpretation)'

Some phrases, such as the one which follows, can have either a genitive or attributive interpretation, depending on how the first NP is interpreted. If *nihonjin* 'Japanese person(s)' refers to a particular Japanese person or persons, or is used as a generic term, (15) is interpreted as a genitive construction. If it does not refer to any particular person(s), (15) is interpreted as an attributive construction.

(15) nihonjin(-)no tomodachi
    Japanese GEN/-COP:ATT friend
    'the Japanese people's friends (= genitive interpretation)'
    'friends who are Japanese (= attributive interpretation)'

There are also two other notable types of attributive constructions. One is a construction with postpositional phrase, which takes the form of:

[[[NP - Case Prt]-*no*]   NP]
   Attributive Phrase   Head Noun

Any particles except for those used with the three major cases, i.e. nominative (*ga*), accusative (*o*), and dative (*ni*), can appear in this construction. Thus, note that normally the allative *e* and dative *ni* are interchangeable to mark a goal (Chapter 6 §1.1(i)), *ni* is not allowed to replace *e* in (16) below.

(16) [[*sanhose e*]-*no*]   *michi*
      (place name) ALL -COP:ATT   way
      'the way to San Jose'

(17) [[*shinjuku de*]-*no*]   *deeto*
      (place name) LOC -COP:ATT   date
      'a date in Shinjuku'

(18) [[*yoshiko to*]-*no*]   *yakusoku*
      (name) COM-COP:ATT   promise
      'a promise with Yoshiko'

The other is a construction which uses numerals with a classifier (Chapter 4 §3.2.2, Chapter 8 §7). It takes the form of:

[[[Numeral-Classifier]-*no*]   NP]
         Attributive Phrase   Head Noun

(19) *hi-tori-no*   *josee*   'one woman'
      one-CLS-COP:ATT   woman

      ni-satsu-no   *hon*   'two books'
      two-CLS-COP:ATT   book

      san-biki-no   *kobuta*   'three little piggies'
      three-CLS-COP:ATT   piggy

3. Clausal noun modification

Clausal noun modification takes the form of a modifying clause followed by a head noun:

[Modifying Clause] [Head Noun]

Based on the types of relationship that exist between the head noun and a modifying clause, four types of clausal noun modifications are identified.[2]

(a) "Cased Head" Type (Relative Clause): the head noun bears some case relation to the predicate in the modifying clause
(b) "Adverbial Head" Type: the head noun bears an adverbial relation to the information expressed in the modifier

---

2. This classification, by and large, corresponds to Matsumoto's (1997b) three-part classification: (a) and (b) correspond to her "clause" host, (c) her "clause-noun" host, and (d) her "noun" host structures, respectively.

(c) "Relational Head" Type: the head noun and the modifier form some sort of interdependent relationship
(d) "Content Label Head" Type (Appositive Clause): the head noun serves as a label for the content expressed in the modifier

3.1 "Cased head" type (Relative clause)

Noun modification with a cased head noun is commonly known as the "relative clause" construction, consisting of a relative clause (RC) and a head noun. The case of the head noun with respect to the predicate in the relative clause can be nominative (subject), accusative (direct object), dative (indirect object), or oblique.[3] Each type of relative clause is termed "subject relative," "direct object relative" and so forth.

In the examples below a relative clause (RC) is shown in brackets and a head noun is underlined. The symbol ø in Examples (20) through (22) indicates the original location of the head noun with respect to the predicate in the relative clause. The source sentence that relates to a RC construction is shown in the parentheses at the end of each RC construction. Since the head noun of a RC construction is necessarily identifiable, the demonstrative *sono* 'that' is attached to the noun phrase in the associated source sentence except when the noun phrase is a proper noun.

(20) Subject Relative
[ø   inu   o   katte-iru]   *kimura-san*
    dog ACC keep:TE-ASP:NONPAST (name)-Mr.
'the Mr. Kimura who has a dog (as opposed to the other Mr. Kimura who doesn't)'
or 'Mr. Kimura, who has a dog'
(cf. *kimura-san ga* inu o katte-iru)

(21) Direct Object Relative
[kimura-san ga/no/*wa   ø   katte-iru]   *inu*
  (name)-Mr. NOM/GEN/TOP   keep:TE-ASP:NONPAST dog
'the dog that Mr. Kimura has'
(cf. *kimura-san ga/*no/wa sono inu* o katte-iru)

(22) Indirect Direct Object Relative
[kimura-san ga/*no/*wa   ø   inu o ageta]   *kodomo*
  (name)-Mr. NOM/GEN/TOP   dog ACC gave   child
'the child to whom Mr. Kimura gave a dog'
(cf. *kimura-san ga/*no/wa sono kodomo* ni inu o ageta)

---

3. In this chapter, the case relations and syntactic roles are loosely correlated in order to make some typological comparison. See Chapter 6 §3 for a discussion of syntactic roles.

There are several important features of Japanese relative clauses. First, the Japanese relative clause construction does not make a morphosyntactic distinction between restrictive and non-restrictive relative clauses, as the English translation of (20) above shows. Second, the verb form must be informal, plain form. If the verbs in the above examples are changed to *katte-imasu* 'has (polite)' and *agemashita* 'gave (polite),' the expressions will become ungrammatical.[4] Third, as seen in (21), the subject, if present in the relative clause, can be marked by the nominative marker *ga* or the genitive marker *no*.[5] This phenomenon, i.e. interchangeability of *ga* and *no*, is known as the '*ga-no* conversion' though the process is not completely regular as (22) shows. This phenomenon will be taken up again in § 4.1 later in this chapter. (cf. Harada 1971; Inoue 1976; Bedell 1972; Yoshimura & Nishina 2010). Fourth, as seen in (21) and (22), the topic marking particle *wa* cannot appear within a relative clause. In contrast, in the source sentences for (21) and (22), the subject can be marked with either *ga* or *wa*, but not by *no*.

Fifth, the Japanese relative clause is formed by means of the "gapping" strategy. The "gap" refers to the lack of pronominal elements such as a relative pronoun (e.g. '*who*,' and '*whom*' in English) that specifies the case relation of the head noun. The "gapping" strategy is found in such English relative constructions as '<u>the woman</u> [I met]' and '<u>the school</u> [I graduated from],' in which no pronominal element is present to identify the case role of the head noun in the relative clause. Though English also has the relative pronoun strategy such as '<u>the woman</u> [whom I met]' and '<u>the school</u> [which I graduated from], Japanese has only the "gapping" strategy. That is, there is no overt marking of the case relation between the head and the predicate in the RC. Thus the case relation must be assessed by examining the head noun and the predicate and other information expressed in the RC.[6]

Formation of the RC construction in Japanese is sensitive to Keenan & Comrie (1977)'s "Noun Phrase Accessibility Hierarchy" as shown below. In addition to the subject, direct object, and indirect object, Japanese can also relativise, as discussed shortly, an oblique noun phrase, allowing the first four positions of the "Noun Phrase Accessibility Hierarchy." On the other hand, the genitive (GEN) and the "object of comparison (OCOMP)" are either impossible or subject to restrictions as discussed below.

---

4. In the hyper-polite register, the polite form may be allowed; [*watakushi ga senjitsu ookuri shimashita*] *tegami* 'the letter which I sent to you the other day.'

5. Both *ga* and *no* were allowed to mark the subject in the nominalized clause in classical Japanese. Later *ga* became a particle used to code a subject both in main and relative clauses. On the other hand, *no* became a genitive case marker and lost its subject marking function, except in relative clauses. See more discussion in Section §4.1.

6. English has another gapping strategy with the complementizer *that*, as in *the woman that I met*. The complementizer is different from a relative pronoun in that the former does not have the property of a pronoun which shows such information as the case and animacy distinctions.

Noun Phrase Accessibility Hierarchy
SU > DO > IO > OBL > GEN > OCOMP

The "object of comparison (OCOMP)" is generally impossible to relativize as shown in (23), though it may become possible with a resumptive pronoun in restricted cases (see below).

(23) * [*kimura-san ga*   ø   *hayaku hashiru*] <u>*inu*</u>
      (name)-Mr. NOM   fast   run   dog
'the dog which Mr. Kimura runs faster than'

(cf. *kimura-san ga*   <u>*sono inu yori*</u>   *hayaku hashiru*)
    (name)-Mr. NOM   that   dog   than   fast   run
'Mr. Kimura runs faster than that dog.'

The genitive noun phrase (GEN) can be relativized, but only if its syntactic head is an inalienable part of the genitive phrase (that is, something that cannot be detached from the possessor; in Japanese this category also includes clothing items), as in (24) and (25) below. That is, *ashi* 'foot' is an inalienable body part of the possessor 'dog', in (24); *mado* 'window' is an inalienable part of the possessor 'car' in (25), and *booshi* 'hat' is a clothing item belonging to the possessor 'friend' in (26). Otherwise it cannot be relativized as (27) demonstrates.

(24) [*kimura-sa ga*   *ashi o*   *funda*]   <u>*inu*</u>
      (name)-Mr. NOM   foot ACC   step.on:PAST   dog
'the dog whose foot Mr. Kimura stepped on'
(cf. *kimura-san ga* <u>*sono inu no ashi*</u> *o funda*)
'Mr. Kimura stepped on the dog's foot.'

(25) [*yakuza ga*   *mado   o   kowashita*]   <u>*kuruma*</u>
      gangsterNOM   window ACC   break:PAST   car
'the car whose window a gangster broke'
(cf. *yakuza ga* <u>*sono kuruma no mado*</u> *o kowashita*)
'a gangster broke the car's window'

(26) [*taroo   ga*   *booshi o*   *nakushita*]   <u>*tomodachi*</u>
      (name) NOM   hat   ACC lose:PAST   friend
'the friend whose hat Taro misplaced'
(cf. *taroo ga* <u>*sono tomodachi no booshi*</u> *o nakushita*)
'Taro misplaced that friend's hat'

(27) * [*taroo   ga   kooen de   inu o   mita*]   *tomodachi*
      (name) NOM   park   LOC   dog ACC   see:PAST   friend
'a friend whose dog Taro saw in the park'
(cf. *taroo ga kooen de* <u>*sono tomodachi no inu o mita*</u>)
'Taro saw that friend's dog in the park'

Other positions (SU, DO, IO, OBL) can be rather freely relativized, though, as already discussed, the exact case relation is not coded for the head noun due to the gapping strategy.

Goal/Locative *ni*
(28) [taroo   ga   mainichi   kayotta]   kissaten
     (name)   NOM   everyday   go:PAST   coffee.shop
     'the coffee shop to which Taro went every day'
     (cf. *taroo ga mainichi sono kissaten **ni** kayotta*)
     'Taro went to that coffee shop every day.'

(29) [taroo   ga   suwatte-iru]   isu
     (name)   NOM   sit:TE-ASP:NONPAST   chair
     'the chair in which Taro is sitting'
     (cf. *taroo ga sono isu **ni** suwatte-iru*)
     'Taro is sitting in the chair.'

Locative *de*
(30) [taroo   ga   benkyoo-shita]   daigaku
     (name)   NOM   study-do:PAST   university
     'the university at which Taro studied'
     (cf. *taroo ga sono daigaku **de** benkyoo-shita*)
     'Taro studied at that university.'

Temporal *ni*
(31) [taroo   ga   gakkoo   o   yasunda]   hi
     (name)   NOM   school   ACC   absent:PAST   day
     'the day when Taro was absent from school'
     (cf. *taroo ga sono hi **ni** gakoo o yasunda*)
     'Taro was absent from school on that day.'

Instrumental *de*
(32) [kodomo   ga   inu   o   butta]   boo
     child   NOM   dog   ACC   hit:PAST   stick
     'the stick with which the child hit the dog'
     (cf. *kodomo ga sono boo **de** inu o butta*)
     'The child hit the dog with that stick.'

Allative *e*
(33) [shoojo   ga   aruite-itta]   eki
     girl   NOM   walk:TE-go:PAST   station
     'the station to which the girl went walking'
     (cf. *shoojo ga sono eki **e** aruite-itta*)
     'The girl walked to that station.'

Comitative (with reciprocal verb) *to*
   (34) [*taroo ga*   *kekkon-shita*]   *josee*
         (name) NOM marriage-do:PAST woman
         'the woman whom Taro married'
         (cf. *taroo ga sono josee **to** kekkon-shita*)
         'Taro married that woman.'

A comitative *to* phrase is relativizable when used with a reciprocal verb as seen (34) above (Chapter 8 §6). In contrast, it cannot be relativised when used with non-reciprocal verbs, as (35) below shows. However, with the adverb, *issho-ni* 'together,' in the relative clause, it becomes acceptable (see Matsumoto 1997b: 98 and citation therein).

   (35) *[*kimura-san ga*   *benkyoo-shita*] *tomodachi*
         (name)-Mr. NOM study-do:PAST friend
         'the friend with whom Mr. Kimura studied'
         (cf. *kimura san ga sono tomodachi **to** benkyoo-shita*)
         'Mr. Kimura studied with that friend'

   (36) [*kimura-san ga*   ***issho –ni***   *benkyoo-shita*] *tomodachi*
                        together
         'the friend with whom Mr. Kimura studied'

Because it does not overtly mark the case relation of the head noun, the gapping strategy sometimes presents problems in case identification. For example, the case of the head noun *kooen* 'park' in (37) can be interpreted in two ways, because *dete-kita* 'came out' can be associated with either a place 'from which' and a place 'in which' something appeared.

   (37) [*kuma ga*   *dete-kita*]   *kooen*
         Bear NOM out-come:PAST park
         a. 'the park from which a bear appeared'
         b. 'the park in which a bear appeared'

To avoid this type of ambiguity, the "resumptive pronoun" strategy may be employed. A resumptive pronoun is a pronoun that appears in a relative clause and refers to the head noun. In the next examples, the demonstrative pronoun, *soko* 'there' refers to *kooen* 'park' and is used as a resumptive pronoun.

   (37') a. [***soko kara*** *kuma ga*   *dete-kita*]   *kooen*
             there ABL bear NOM out-come:PAST park
             'the park **from which** a bear appeared'
        b. [***soko ni*** *kuma ga*   *dete-kita*]   *kooen*
             there DAT bear NOM out-come:PAST park
             'the park **in which** a bear appeared'

This strategy may be also employed to relativize the object of comparison which is usually unrelativizable, as seen earlier. The expression *sore* 'that' in the example below refers to 'the minimum balance' (John Haig – personal communication).

(38) [*sore yori hikuku-naru-to tesuuryoo ga*
 that than lower:KU-become-TO fee NOM
 kaserareru] *saitee-zandaka*
 impose:PSS minimum-balance
 'the minimum balance at which a fee is imposed'

The gapping strategy may also be problematic for non-oblique (i.e. arguments) heads with a three-place predicate in the RC. For example, the predicate *okutta* 'sent' in (39) requires three arguments, one of which is not expressed, and the missing argument may be either a nominative (subject) or dative (indirect object) phrase, as the English translation indicates. (See also Matsumoto, 1997b: 40.)

(39) [*tegami o okutta*] *josee*
 Letter ACC send:PAST woman
 a. 'the woman who sent a letter (to someone)'
 b. 'the woman to whom (someone) sent a letter'

The resumptive pronoun strategy cannot be used in this case. If a nominative-marked phrase is put in the relative clause as in (40), the head noun is invariably interpreted as the argument not found in the modifier, i.e. the dative (indirect object). Likewise, if a dative-marked phrase is inserted as in (41), the head noun must be interpreted as the nominative-subject.[7]

(40) [*kanojo/sono hito ga tegami o okutta*] *josee*
 she/that person NOM letter ACC send:PAST woman
 'the woman to whom she/that person sent a letter'
 NOT 'the woman who sent a letter (to someone)'

---

7. The selective interpretation shown in the English translation for (40) and (41) is a consequence of pragmatic preference which builds up complete and reasonable information based on what is available at hand. The process may be summarized as follows: the predicate 'send' requires two human participants, agent (sender) and recipient; and if the head noun and an overt argument in an RC both refer to human participants, these participants will be distributed between the agent and recipient. So the argument in the RC of (40) is interpreted as the agent because it is a *ga*-marked noun phrase, and by default the head noun is interpreted as the recipient. The reverse interpretation is observed in (41). This suggests that semantics and pragmatics, in addition to syntax, play significant roles in forming and interpreting the relative clause in Japanese.

(41) [kanojo/sono hito ni tegami o okutta] josee
    she/that person DAT letter ACC send:PAST woman
    the woman who sent a letter to her/that person
    NOT 'the woman to whom (someone) sent a letter'

3.2 "Adverbial head" type

In the relative clause construction discussed above, the head noun and the modifying clause bear some clear case relation. In some situations, however, the case relation is less obvious, and the connection between them must be construed pragmatically for an appropriate interpretation. First, observe the head nouns in (42) and (43) below which may still be considered as case heads; in (42) the head noun *kakegoto* 'gambling' can be interpreted as the instrumental relationship (i.e. cause), and in (43) the head noun *heasutairu* 'hair style' may be interpreted as having either the nominative or instrumental (i.e. cause) relationship.

(42) [zaisan o nakushita] kakegoto
    property ACC lose:PAST gamble
    'the gamble (because of which) (he) lost (his) property'
    (cf. *sono kakegoto de zaisan o nakushita*)

(43) [watashi-rashisa o ikasu] heasutairu
    I-becoming ACC highlight:NONPAST hair.style
    'the hair style which highlights my true self'
    (cf. *sono heasutairu ga watashi-rashisa o ikasu*)
    'the hair style with which I (can) highlight my own self'
    (cf. *sono heasutairu de watashi-rashisa o ikasu*)

However, it is difficult to assign a case head interpretation for the head noun in (44) below. Note that *yoku-naru* 'become good' is an intransitive predicate and its subject (*atama* 'head') is already in the RC. The head noun, *sono hon* 'that book,' can be semantically interpreted as a cause (i.e. an "adverbial" head), but as the related source sentence shows, it cannot be included with the instrumental particle *de*. It is possible to use a transitive counterpart, *yoku suru* 'to make it good,' instead of *yoku naru* 'become good' to construct a subject relative construction, *atama o yokusuru hon* 'the book that makes your head good (=intelligent).' However, as a Japanese RC, (44) is much more natural compared to the subject relative construction.

(44) [atama no yoku-naru] hon   (Matsumoto 1997b: 104)
    head GEN good-become:NONPAST book
    'the book (which by reading) (one's) head gets better
    [= one becomes more intelligent]'
    (cf. **sono hon de atama ga yokunaru*)

The next two examples are similar to (44).

(45) [namida ga dete-kuru] eega
tears NOM come.out-come:NONPASAT movie
'the movie (which by seeing) (one's) teas come out'
(cf. *sono eega **de** namida ga dete-kuru)

(46) [kii o osanakute-ii] keetai
keys ACC push:NEG:TE-good:NONPAST cell.phone
'a cell phone (for which) (one) doesn't have to press keys'
(cf. *sono keetai **de** kii o osanakute-ii)

The kind of pragmatic relationship involved between the head and the clausal modifier in the examples above is a "cause-effect/entailment" relationship. (See Matsumoto (1997b: 103–132) for more discussion.) When this kind of relevant relationship is recognized, the phrase is comprehended and determined to be acceptable.

3.3 "Relational head" type

Some head nouns are relational nouns whose meaning is completely dependent on some other concept. Thus 'a/the year' is not a relational noun, but 'the next year' is, because it requires another year from which it is measured; likewise 'a/the desk' is not a relational noun, but 'the front (of a/the desk)' is, because it requires a fixed location from which the front is positioned. Temporal nouns and noun phrases which are relational nouns include *yokunen* 'the next year,' *yokujitsu/tsugi-no-hi* 'the next day,' *x-jikan-go* 'after x hours,' *x-shuukan-mae* 'x weeks before.' Spatial nouns and noun phrases which are relational nouns include *mae* 'front,' *ushiro* 'back,' *ue* 'up,' *shita* 'down,' *migi* 'right,' and *hidari* 'left.' In (47) and (48) *yokunen* 'the next year' and *mae* 'front' are relational heads, respectively. (see Teramura (1980: 262); Matsumoto (1997b: 149–162) for further examples).

(47) [taroo ga tookyoo e itta] yokunen
(name) NOM Tokyo ALL go:PAST next.year
'the year after Taro went to Tokyo'

(48) [yoshiko ga suwatte-iru] mae
(name) NOM sit:TE-ASP:NONPAST front
'in front of where Yoshiko is sitting'

Those concepts that refer to "contingent results," or necessary consequences of some act, comprise another type of relational noun. Examples of this include *nokori* 'remainder,' *kaeri* 'return,' *otsuri* 'returned change,' and *kekka* 'result.' In (49) below, *otsuri* 'the received change' (in the head noun) is the money contingent on the act of buying of bread (as described in the modifier) with a large bill. In (50), *kekka* 'result' is the consequence of "partying too hard all night."

(49) [pan o   katta]   otsuri
     bread ACC buy:PAST change
     'the change received from buying bread'

(50) [yoasobi   shisugita]   kekka
     night.play   do.excessively:PAST result
     'the result of partying too hard all night'

3.4 "Content label head" type (Appositive clause)

The last type of clausal noun modification takes a "content label" head and is usually known as the "appositive construction." A "content label" head serves as a label for some complex information expressed in the modifier. Sub-classification of typical content label nouns are shown below.

Table 1. Types of content nouns

(a) linguistic communication	*kotoba* 'words,' *uwasa* 'rumor,' *nyuusu* 'news,' *meeree* 'order,' *shirase* 'report,' *tegami* 'letter,' …
(b) facts	*koto* 'fact,' *jijitsu* 'fact/truth,' *jiken* 'incident,' *jootai* 'situation,' *kekka* 'result,' *gen'in* 'cause,' …
(c) thoughts and feelings	*kangae* 'thought,' *soozoo* 'imagination,' *yume* 'dream,' *utagai* 'doubt,' *kanji/ki* 'feeling,' *ito/tsumori* 'intention,' *yakusoku* 'promise,' *yokan* 'premonition' …
(d) stimulus source (visual)	*kakkoo/sugata* 'appearance,' *metsuki* 'a look (in eye),' *kao* 'facial expression,' *e* 'painting,' *shashin* 'photograph,' *kuse* 'habit,' *ato* 'trace,' …
(e) stimulus source (non-visual)	*nioi* 'smell,' *oto* 'sound,' *koe* 'voice,' *kanshoku* 'sensation,' …

Note that most content label nouns are simultaneously regular nouns or relational nouns. For example, *nyuusu* 'news' may be a regular noun or a content label noun, and *kekka* 'result' is a relational noun, but can also be a content label noun, depending on the construction in which it appears. In other words, content nouns are those nouns which have the potential to be further commented on for their content. The classification shown in Table 1 is based on semantics of the head noun, but is co-related with the use of the complementizer derived from a hearsay expression *to yuu* (Quotative marker + 'say'). While it is obligatory for type (a) nouns, it is not used with type (e) nouns. It is optionally used with types (b), (c) and (d) nouns.

Type (a) nouns represent concepts, objects, or events related to linguistic activities. The next examples show how the type (a) label head appears with a complementizer, *to yuu*.

(51) [sakura   ga   saita   to-yuu] tegami
     cherry.blossom NOM bloom:PAST COMP   letter
     'a letter saying that cherry blossoms are in bloom'

(52) [taroo   ga   okane   o   nusunda   to-yuu] uwasa
     (name) NOM money ACC steal:PAST   COMP   rumor
     'the rumor that Taro stole some money'

(53) [otoko wa   gun'eki   ni   fukusu beshi to-yuu] fukoku
      man   TOP military.duty DAT fulfill MOD   COMP   announcement
     'the announcement that men should fulfill their military duty'

As shown in the last example above, a noun modifying clause with *to yuu* may contain main clause elements such as the topic marking particle *wa* and the modal expression *beshi* 'should,' which are not allowed in a noun modifying clause without *to yuu*. This means that *to yuu* provides an environment in which information supplied by some other source besides the proximate speaker can be included directly.

The content label nouns listed in (b) 'facts' designate information which can be obtained ether from hearsay or from more direct perception. When the information is hearsay information, *to yuu* is obligatory. Otherwise, it is not. Thus, the expressions with *to yuu* in (54) and (55) below indicate that the speaker is presenting the information as if he heard it, while the versions without it indicate that the speaker is presenting the fact as if he had observed it more directly (cf. Kuno 1973: 218–9; Terakura 1983; Masuoka 1994).

(54) [taroo   ga   okane   o   nusunda   (to yuu)] jiken
     (name) NOM money ACC steal:PAST   (COMP)   incident
     'the incident in which Taro stole some money'

(55) [inu   ga   akanboo o   kanda   (to yuu)] jijitsu
     dog   NOM baby   ACC bite:PAST (COMP)   fact
     'the fact that the dog bit the baby'

The content label nouns listed in (c) 'thoughts and feelings' and (d) 'visual stimulus' also optionally take *to yuu*. But in this case, *to yuu* does not mark the distinction between hearsay and direct evidence, but a lower degree of certainty. Thus, the *to yuu* expression has become generalized from the hearsay marker to indicate the speaker's weaker conviction/confidence towards the proposition (i.e. a "challengeable information" marker, Givón 1982) presented in the modifier. So the version with *to yuu* in (56) that contains a type (c) word, for example, may be used when the speaker wants to express that his prediction that 'a big earthquake will occur' is tentative, unfounded, or not readily accepted. The version with *to yuu* in (57) that contains a type (d) word, on the other hand, indicates speaker's weak conclusion about the appearance of a person in question compared to the stronger conviction that expressed by the version without *to yuu*.

(56) [ookina   jishin   ga   okiru   (to yuu)]
     big   earthquake   NOM   occur:NONPAST   (COMP)
     yokan   (ga suru)
     premonition   (NOM do:NONPAST)
     '(I) have a feeling that a big earthquake will occur.'

(57) [tooi   tabi   ni   deru   (to yuu)]   kakkoo
     far   journey   DAT   depart:NONPAST   (COMP)   appearance
     'the appearance that (he) is leaving for a long journey'

Type (e) nouns refer to a "non-visual perception stimulus" including *nioi* 'smell,' *oto* 'sound,' *koe* 'voice,' and *kanshoku* 'sensation.' This type of content label head rarely takes *to yuu*, because the information is not linguistic and is accessed more immediately.

(58) [sakana   ga   kogete-iru]   nioi
     fish   NOM   burn:TE-ASP:NONPAST   smell
     'the smell of fish being burnt'

(59) [inu   ga   hoeru]   koe
     dog   NOM   bark:NONPAST   voice
     'the sound of a dog barking'

(60) [senaka   o   tsumetai   yubi   de   furerareru]   kanshoku
     back   ACC   cold   finger INS   feel:PSS:NONPAST   sensation
     'the sensation that the back is being touched by a cold finger'

4. Some syntactic characteristics

4.1 The *ga-no* conversion

In the main clause, the subject can be marked by the nominative case particle *ga*, but not by the genitive marker *no*, as shown in (61a) below. However, as introduced in § 3.1, the subject can be marked with either of these particles in the "case head" type noun modification (the relative clause), as shown in (61b). This alternation is known as the *ga-no* conversion in the generative tradition of Japanese linguistics (Bedell 1972; Shibatani 1975; Harada 1976; cf. Mikami 1953).

(61) a. in the main clause
         kimura-san {ga/*no}   *biiru   o   nonde-iru*
         (name)-Mr.{NOM/*GEN}   beer   ACC   drink:TE-ASP:NONPAST
         'Mr. Kimura is drinking beer.'

     b. [*kimura-san {ga/no}*   *nonde-iru*]   *biiru*
         (name)-Mr. {NOM/GEN}   drink:TE-ASP:NONPAST   beer
         'the beer that Mr. Kimura is drinking'

The conversion can be applied to the so-called "objective *ga*" (Kuno 1973) as well. The noun phrases, *biiru* 'beer' is marked by the "objective *ga*," but not by *no* in the main clause as shown in (62a). However, both *ga* and *no* are possible in the relative clause structure, as shown in (62b).

(62) a. objective *ga* in the main clause
watashi wa biiru {ga/*no} nomitai
I TOP beer {NOM/*GEN} drink:DES
'I want to drink beer'

b. [[*biiru {ga/no} nominai*] *hito*] *wa dare desu ka*
[[beer NOM/GEN drink:DES] person] TOP who COP Q
'Who are those people wanting to drink beer?'

Example (63a) is a double nominative sentence with two nominative particles appearing in a main clause (Chapter 6 §1.1(b)). Neither of them can be changed into *no*. However, the *ga-no* conversion is possible in a relative clause, as shown in (63-b), modified from Yoshimura & Nishina (2010: 11).[8]

(63) a. double nominatives in the main clause
boku {ga/*no} wain {ga/*no} suki da
I {NOM/*GEN} wine {NOM/*GEN} like COP

b. double nominatives in the relative clause
[[*boku {ga/no} wain {ga/no} sukina*] *riyuu*]
[[I(male) NOM/GEN wine NOM/GEN like:ATT] reason]
o shitte-imasu ka
ACC know Q
'Do you know the reason I like wine?'

The conversion appears in other types of noun modification with varying degrees of acceptability. The *ga-no* conversion works in (64) through (66).

(64) (= (43)) "Adverbial Head" Type
[*atama {ga/no} yoku-naru*] *hon*
[head NOM/GEN good-become:NONPAST] book
'the book (which by reading) (one's) head gets better [= one becomes more intelligent]'

(65) (= (48)) "Relational Head" Type
[*yoshiko {ga/no} suwatte-iru*] *mae*
(name) NOM/GEN sit:TE-ASP:NONPAST front
'in front of where Yoshiko is sitting'

---

8. In (63b), all four patters, *-ga -ga, -ga -no, -no-no,* and *-no-ga,* are possible. However, the last pattern, *-no-ga,* seems least favored. The reason for this may be related to the fact that *boku no wain ga sukina riyuu* may be more easily interpreted as 'the reason why (someone) likes my wine.'

(66) (= (51) "Content Label Head" Type (a)
[sakura   {ga/no}   saita   to-yuu] tegami
cherry.blossom NOM/GEN   bloom:PAST   COMP   letter
'a letter saying that cherry blossoms are in bloom'

In the three sentences above, *N ga/no* appears before an intransitive verb. However, in the following sentences in which *N ga* appears before another noun such as a direct object of a transitive verb, the '*ga-no*' conversion is not readily observed.

(67) (= (52)) "Content Label Head" Type (a)
[taroo   {ga/?no}   okane o   nusunda   to-yuu] uwasa
(name)   NOM/GEN   money ACC   steal:PAST   COMP   rumor
'the rumor that Taro stole some money'

(68) (= (55)) "Content Label Head" Type (b)
[inu   {ga/?no}   akanboo o   kanda   (to yuu)] jijitsu
dog   NOM/GEN   baby   ACC bite:PAST   (COMP)   fact
'the fact that the dog bit the baby'

(69) (= (22)) Indirect Direct Object Relative
[kimura-san   {ga/?no}   inu   o   ageta]   *kodomo*
(name)-Mr.   NOM/GEN   dog   ACC   gave   child
'the child to whom Mr. Kimura gave a dog'

(70) (=(25) Oblique (Genitive) Relative
[yakuza   {ga/?no}   mado   o   kowashita]   *kuruma*
gangster   NOM/GEN   window   ACC   break:PAST   car
'the car whose window a gangster broke'

(71) (= (47) "Relational   Head" Type
[taroo   {ga/?no}   tookyoo e   itta]   yokunen
(name)   NOM/GEN   Tokyo   ALL   go:PAST   next.year
'the year after Taro went to Tokyo'

It may be first speculated that these sentences are less acceptable with *no* because the first and the second nouns inadvertently form a noun phrase with the genitive marker, i.e. *taroo no okane* 'Taro's money,' *inu no akanboo* 'the dog's baby,' and *kimura-san no inu* 'Mr. Kimura's dog,' *taroo no tookyoo* 'Taro's Tokyo,' producing unintended meanings. However, if the phrases are scrambled as below to avoid such unwanted interpretations, the genitive marking becomes even less acceptable.

(67′) [okane o   taroo   {ga/*no}   nusunda   to-yuu]   *uwasa*
      money   ACC   (name)   NOM/GEN   steal:PAST   COMP   rumor
      'the rumor that Taro stole some money'

(68′) [akanboo o   inu   {ga/*no} kanda   (to yuu)] <u>jijitsu</u>
     baby   ACC dog   NOM/GEN   bite:PAST (COMP)   fact
     'the fact that the dog bit the baby'

(69′) [inu o   kimura-san {ga/*no} ageta] <u>kodomo</u>
     dog   ACC (name)-Mr.   NOM/GEN   gave   child
     'the child to whom Mr. Kimura gave a dog'

(70′) [mado o   yakuza   {ga/*no} kowashita] <u>kuruma</u>
     window ACC gangster NOM/GEN   break:PAST   car
     'the car whose window a gangster broke'

(71′) [tookyoo e   taroo   {ga/*no} itta] <u>yokunen</u>
     Tokyo   ALL (name)   NOM/GEN   go:PAST   next.year
     'the year after Taro went to Tokyo'

Finally the *ga-no* conversion is observed not only in the noun modification context, but also in complement clauses marked by *no* and *koto* as in (72) and (73), respectively below, as well as a noun phrase headed by a pronominal *no* as in (74). The following examples are from Yoshimura & Nishina (2010:11). See also Watanabe (1996) and Hiraiwa (2002) for more discussions.

(72) [[taroo {ga/no} wain {ga/no} sukina] <u>no</u>] o
     (name)   NOM/GEN   wine NOM/GEN like:ATT   COMP] ACC
     shitte-imasu   ka
     know:TE-ASP:POL   Q
     'Do you know the fact that Taro loves wine?'

(73) [[taroo {ga/no} kekkon-shita] <u>koto</u>] ga   minna   ni   bareta
     (name)   NOM/GEN marry-do:PST]   COMP] NOM   everyone DAT   reveal:PAST
     'The fact that Taro got married has been leaked out to everyone'

(74) [[musuko {ga/no}   kaita]   <u>no</u>] ga   nyuushoo-shita
     son   NOM/GEN   draw:PST] PRO] NOM win.a.prize-do:PAST
     'The one that my son drew won a prize.'

Temporal adverbial clauses also allow the conversion.[9]

---

9. Other types of sentences have been also proposed for the context for the *ga-no* conversion. The following examples are from Hiraiwa (2002:547) with some modification.

   (i) [boku ga/no   omou ni]   jon wa marii ga suki ni-chigainai
       I (male) NOM/GEN think:NONPAST DAT (name) TOP (name) NOM like certainly
       'I think John likes Mary.'

(75) [[taroo {ga/no}   kaette-kita]   toki]   minna
     (name) NOM/GEN   return-come:PST   when]   everyone

   moo   nete-ita
   already   sleep:TE-AUX:PAST

   'When Taro came home, everyone was already sleeping.'

(76) [[taroo {ga/no}   kaette-kuru]   made]   minna   matte-ita
     (name) NOM/GEN   return-come:PST   till] everyone wait:TE-AUX:PAST
   'Everyone was waiting until Taro came home'

4.2 Relative clause formation in English and Japanese

Japanese relative clause formation is not subject to all the constraints that restrict English relative clause formation (cf. Ross 1967). In English, noun phrases within a relative clause cannot be further relativized, but this is allowed in some cases in Japanese. Both the nominative subject and the accusative direct objects can be extracted as a head noun from a deeply embedded clause. Examples (77) and (78) are possible (Haig 1996: 60).

(77) [[__i __j kawaigatte-ita]   inu_j   ga   shinde-shimatta]   kodomo_i
         cherish:TE-ASP:PAST   dog   NOM   die:TE-ASP:PAST   child
   '*that child who the dog that __i was keeping __j died'

(78) [[__i __j kawaigatte-ita]   hito_i   ga   nakunatta]   sono inu_j
         cherish:TE-ASP:PAST   person NOM   die:TE-ASP:PAST that dog
   '*that dog that the person who __i was keeping __j died'

A noun phrase from other types of clausal noun modification, especially if it is the subject, may also be extracted. The following examples involve the relational head and content label head, respectively.

(79) [[__ suwatte-iru]   mae   ga   aite-iru]   hito
         sit:TE-AUX:NONPAST front NOM   empty:TE-ASP:NONPAST   person
   '*the person who the front of which (she) is sitting is empty'

(ii) [jon   ga/no   kuru to   konai   to]
     (name) NOM/GEN   come:NONPAST and   come:NEG:NONPAST   and

   de   wa   oochigai   da
   COP:TE   TOP   big.difference COP

   'It makes a great difference whether John comes or not.'

However, the embedded clauses in these sentences are nominalized clauses without a nominalizer. It is possible to insert *no* as in [*omou no ni*] and [*kuru no to konai no to*], respectively.

(80) [[__ okane   o   nusunda   to   yuu]   uwasa   ga
          money ACC steal:PAST QT say   rumor NOM
     nagarete-iru]   hito
     flow:TE-NONPAST person
     '*the person who the rumor that (he) stole some money is spreading'

Another important difference between Japanese and English is the possibility of including an interrogative word within a modifying clause (Hasegawa 1989). (81) is possible as a Japanese sentence, but its English translation is not.[10]

(81) [dono   shoosetsuka ga   kaita]   hon   desu ka
       which novelist   NOM write:PAST book COP   Q
      '*Is it the book [that which novelist wrote] ?'
      (intended meaning: Which novelist wrote (this) book?)

This structure is allowed not only in relative clauses but also in other types of clausal modifiers. In the following, a question word is embedded in the modifying clause for an adverbial head, a relational head, and a content head.

---

10. An explanation for embedded interrogative words as seen in (81)–(84) may be related to the information structure allowed in Japanese. Both (ii) and (iii) are possible translations of (i).

   (i)   Which   novelist wrote   this   book?

   (ii)   dono   shoosetsuka ga   kono hon   o   kaita   no.
          which novelist   NOM this book ACC write:PAST SE

   (iii) kono hon   wa   dono   shoosetsuka ga   kaita   no
          this book TOP which novelist   NOM write:PAST SE

The head noun generally has a sentence topic relationship with the relative clause (Kuno 1973). In other words, the sentence topic (kono) hon '(this) book' in (iii) is qualified as the head noun for the relative clause dono shoosetsuka ga kaita 'which novelist wrote.' That is, if 'X wa Y' is possible, then the noun modification, [Y] X, is also possible. It should be noted, however, the reverse is not always possible. Head nouns in some clausal noun modifications (mostly non-relative clause types) cannot be rendered into a sentence topic in the topic-comment sentence. The following is one example (Yoshiko Matsumoto, personal communication).

   (iv)   [kono hon   o   hon'yaku-shita]   okane
          this   book ACC translate-do:PAST money
          the money (I received from) translating this book

   (v)   * sono okane   wa   kono hon   o   hon'yaku-shita
            that money   TOP this book ACC translate-do:PAST

(82) [dare ga   yuumee ni   natta]   sakuhin ga   shoo o
       who NOM famous COP:ADV become:PAST work   NOM prize ACC

  moratta   no
  receive:PAST Q

  '*The work (because of which) who became famous received a prize ?'
  (intended meaning: Whose novel that made (the author) famous won
  the prize?)

(83) [dare ga   suwatte-iru]   mae   ga
       who NOM sit:TE-AUX:NONPAST   front NOM

  aite-ita   no
  empty:TE-ASP:PAST   Q

  '*In front of which who is sitting is empty ?'

(84) [dare ga   okane o   nusunda   to yuu]
       who NOM money ACC steal:PAST   COMP

  uwasa ga   nagarete-iru   no
  rumor NOM flow:TE-NONPAST   Q

  '*The rumor that who stole some money is spreading ?'

CHAPTER 10

Quotation and complementation

This chapter begins by discussing the grammatical systems of "quotation" and "complementation" and ends with an analysis of "internally headed relative clauses" and "integrated adverbial clauses." In these structures, an embedded clause (or a sentence in a limited number of cases) functions as the constituent of a larger syntactic unit. Quotation embeds a clause or sentence as an adjunct of a larger clause/sentence to represent speech and thought with various degrees of similarity to the original. Complementation is a strategy used to integrate a clause as an argument of a larger clause/sentence. The internally headed relative clause is similar to complementation in structure, but functions more like relative clauses. In turn, the integrated adverbial clause is similar to the internally headed relative clause, but its function is closer to that of adverbial clauses.

1. Quotation: Quoted speech and thought

A clause or sentence may be embedded within a sentence using the quotative marker *to*, or its informal variety *tte*, for quoting another's or one's own speech. In a quotation, two different speakers must be identified, "the proximate speaker" (or "the immediate speaker") who does the quoting and "the prime speaker" (or "the original speaker") whose speech is being quoted (cf. Du Bois 1986: 322). Likewise, "the proximate addressee" in the immediate speech context and "the prime addressee" who is the recipient of the original speech material can be separately identified. The quotation is, then, a structure that embodies the following schema with Taro as the prime speaker and Michiko the prime addressee when 'I' (Proximate Speaker) am talking to 'you' (Proximate Addressee).

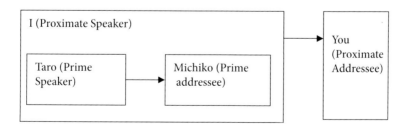

To quote Taro's original utterance addressed to Michiko in (1), for example, the proximate speaker may use different quoting strategies. In the following, the quoted materials are underlined and in bold. Here, Maki is Michiko's sister. Sentences (2) through (4) are quotation sentences based on Taro's direct speech in (1). In these sentences, the proximate speaker (I) is not coded linguistically whereas the "prime speaker," Taro, is coded as a subject noun phrase with *wa* and the "prime addressee," Michiko, is coded as a dative noun phrase.

(1) Direct speech: Taro to Michiko
kimi no imooto-san ni zehi aitai naa
you GEN y.sister-Ms DAT really meet:DES PP
'(I) really want to see your younger sister, you know.'

(2) *taroo wa michiko ni*
(name) TOP (name) DAT
kimi no imooto-san ni zehi aitai naa *to itta*
you GEN y.sister-Ms. DAT really meet:DES PP QT say:PAST
'Taro said to Michiko, "(I) really want to see your younger sister, you know."'

(3) *taroo wa michiko ni*
(name) TOP (name) DAT
maki ni zehi aitai *to itta*
(name) DAT really meet:DES QT say:PAST
'Taro said to Michiko that (he) really wanted to see Maki.'

(4) *taroo wa michiko ni* **_maki ni aitai_** *to itta*
(name) TOP (name) DAT (name) DAT meet:DES QT say:PAST
'Taro said to Michiko that (he) wanted to see Maki.'

Both subject and dative noun phrases appear before the quoted material in (2) through (4), but it is also possible for either or both to appear after the quotation and before the verb. For example, (3) may appear as (3′).

(3′) **_maki ni zehi ai-tai_** *to (taroo wa michiko ni) itta*
(name) DAT really meet:DES QT (name) TOP (name) DAT say:PAST
'Taro said to Michiko that (he) really wanted to see Maki.'

Furthermore, due to the prevalent tendency of noun phrase ellipsis, the speaker and addressee noun phrases (put in the parentheses in the above example) may not appear at all on the surface, leaving only the quoted material with *to* and the quoting verb.

One of the notable facts about quotation in Japanese is the fuzzy division between direct and indirect quotation. This is due, first, to the identical syntactic frame employed for both; "____" *to itta* for direct quotation; ___ *to itta* for indirect quotation. Notice that in both frames the quotative particle *to* appears after the quoted material. This sharply contrasts with English, which uses two distinct frames, with *that* only appearing in the indirect quotation; *He said,* "___" for direct quotation and *He said that* ___ for indirect quotation. Second, in Japanese written discourse, quotation markers may be employed to demarcate the material directly quoted, but their use is not always obligatory (Maynard 1986: 180). Third, Japanese lacks the sequence of tense rule found in English. Both in direct and in indirect quotation, the tense form used in the original quotation is maintained. Notice that the same nonpast tense form *aitai* 'want to meet' is used in the original (1) and in all quoted sentences (2)–(4). In fact, the use of the past tense form *aitakatta* 'wanted to meet' would be unacceptable due to the "relative tense" interpretation between the tenses in the main clause and the subordinate clause (see Chapter 7 §1 for the discussion of the "relative tense.").

Among the three example quotations given above, (2) is direct quotation, reporting (1) verbatim; it includes the pragmatic (or sentence final) particle *naa*, a marker of the prime speaker's exclamation and the polite suffix *-san* for *imooto* 'younger sister.' In (3) the proximate speaker replaces the original term *kimi no imooto-san* with the referent's name, Maki, showing his control over the prime speaker's utterance. In (4), the proximate speaker does not include the sentential adverb *zehi* 'by all means,' reducing the prime speaker's utterance down to the mere propositional content, and thus approaching the prototypical indirect quotation. Said differently, (4) shows the highest degree of syntactic integration of the quoted material into the larger sentence, (2) the lowest, and (3) is intermediate.

The verb used to report speech in Examples (2) through (4) is *itta* 'said' (← *yuu* 'say'), and this is the word for reporting speech communication (This verb is orthographically spelled as *iu* いう but pronounced as *yuu*.) A number of other verbs which report verbal activities may be used in place of *yuu* 'say'; some specify the manner of utterance (e.g. *sakebu* 'shout,' *donaru* 'yell,' *tsubuyaku* 'say to oneself softly'; while some others specify the type of speech action (e.g. *tsugeru* 'inform,' *noberu* 'state,' *jihaku-suru* 'confess,' *kotaeru* 'answer,' *aizuchi o utsu* 'send an acknowledging token').

Besides statements, quotations can report orders and questions. For orders, more specific verbs, such as *meezuru/meejiru* 'order,' *tanomu* 'request,' and *susumeru* 'urge,' may be used in addition to the verb *yuu* 'say.' Orders must contain the imperative verb form (e.g. *akero* 'open!'), as in (5), or request expressions (e.g. *kashite /kashite-kudasai/kashite-kure* 'please lend me'), as in (6). An order may be more indirectly quoted with the purposive construction, *yoo-ni* 'fashion-COP:ADV' as in (7). In this case, the quotative marker *to* is often absent.

(5) *chichioya wa kodomo ni mado o akero to itta*
father TOP child DAT window ACC open:IMP QT say:PAST
'The father told the child, "Open the window."'

(6) *taroo wa hanako ni okane o kashite-kure to tanonda*
(name) TOP (name) DAT money ACC lend:TE-give QT say:PAST
'Taro asked Hanako to lend him some money.'

(7) chichioya wa kodomo ni mado o shimeru
father TOP child DAT window ACC close:NONPAST

yoo-ni (to) meejita
fashion-COP:ADV (QT) order:PAST

'The father ordered the child to close the window.'

Questions are quoted with such verbs as *kiku/tazuneru/shitsumon-suru* 'ask.' Since there is no difference in word order between statements and questions in Japanese, quoted questions follow the same word order as the original question. A quoted question, however, is always followed by the question particle *ka*. The quotative marker *to* may follow, but is more often than not dropped. A quoted "yes/no" question may be followed by an expression such as *doo ka* 'or not' (= lit. 'how Q'), as in (9) below.

(8) michiko wa taroo ni donna eega ga
(name) TOP (name) DAT what.kind movie NOM

suki ka (to) kiita
like Q (QT) ask:PAST

'Michiko asked Taro what kind of movie (he) likes.'

(9) michiko wa taroo ni sono kai ni iku ka
(name) TOP (name) DAT that meeting DAT go:NONPAST Q

(doo ka) (to) tazuneta
(how Q) (QT) ask:PAST

'Michiko asked Taro if (he) will go to that meeting.'

(10) jiroo wa sensee ni kanbojia no shuto wa
(name) TOP teacher DAT Cambodia GEN capital TOP

doko ka (to) shitsumon-shita
where Q (QT) question-do:PAST

'Jiro asked the teacher where the capital of Cambodia is.'

In a similar manner to speech quotation, people's thoughts can be quoted (though there is no prime addressee, and thus no dative phrase to code such a participant). The quotative particle is *to*, the other variety *-tte* is only marginally acceptable. The most common verb used is *omou* 'think.' In the following, the past tense form *omotta* 'thought' is used for both first person and third person subjects.

(11) boku wa aitsu ga hannin da to omotta
I TOP that.guy NOM culprit COP QT think:PAST

'I thought that guy was the culprit.'

(12) taroo wa hanako mo sono kai ni
(name) TOP (name) also that meeting ALL

>   *deru*   *to*   *omotta*
>   participate:NONPAST QT think:PAST
>   'Taro thought that Hanako would also participate in that meeting.'

The nonpast form of *omou* refers to the present time and usually requires a first person subject. A third person subject, on the other hand, usually requires the *-te-iru* (progressive/resultative) aspectual form (Iwasaki 1993b). For (13), because of the *omotte-iru* form, the subject is inferred to be the third person, Taro. For (14), because of the *omou* form, the subject is inferred to be the first person, which is not overtly coded.

(13)   *taroo*   *wa*   *tensai*   *da*   *to*   *omotte-iru*
        (name)   TOP   genius   COP   QT   think:TE-ASP:NONPAST
        'Taroi thinks that (hei) is a genius.'

(14)   *taroo*   *wa*   *tensai*   *da*   *to*   *omou*
        (name)   TOP   genius   COP   QT   think:NONPAST
        '(I) think that Taro is a genius.'

In addition to using *omou* 'think,' quotations of thought can be reported by such verbs as *kangaeru* 'think,' *shinjiru* 'believe,' *utagau* 'doubt.' Some of the verbs of speech and thought can take a complement rather than the quotative clause. This will be described in the next section.

2. Complementation

Complementation refers to the process in which a clause is embedded as either an argument (the subject or object) or adjunct in a larger clause/sentence. Structurally it consists of a complement clause followed by a complementizer: *koto, no,* or *tokoro*. Complementizers in Japanese are nominalizers, which are formal nouns, i.e. nouns in form only without much semantic content; the semantic content is null in the case of *no* or extremely weak in the case of *koto* (= abstract things) and *tokoro* (= place); they cannot stand alone and must always be modified. In this section, only the object and subject complements are surveyed. Schematically, the sentence with a complement is represented as follows (Comp Cl = Complement Clause).

> Object Complement
> [Subj.] *wa/ga* [Comp Cl]-(*to yuu*) koto /no/tokoro   o/ni   [Pred.]
>
> Subject Complement
> [Comp Cl]-(*to yuu*) koto /no   wa   [Pred.]

The *to yuu* expression which may optionally appear after a complement clause is a marker of "challengeability" (Givón 1982), which expresses that either the speaker himself or the addressee, according to the speaker's assessment, has lower certainty about the complement information (see Chapter 9 §3.4). The choice of complementizer, *koto*, *no*, or *tokoro*, is determined by the degree of abstractness of the information expressed in the complement; *koto* for the most abstract, *no* for less abstract, and *tokoro* for the least abstract (and thus most vivid) information not yet fully integrated in the speaker's cognitive structure (cf. Kuno 1973:221; Josephs 1976; Akatsuka-McCawley 1978; Suzuki 1997).

2.1 The object complement

There are several types of verbs that take an object complement. The first type is a subset of verbs of speech and thought. These verbs take either the quotative clause (see §1 above) or a complement clause object which refers to speech or thought. The (a) versions in the next examples are quotative constructions and the (b) versions are complement constructions. The complementizer is usually *koto*. The complement clause is marked by the square brackets.

(15) a. *taroo wa [hanako ga iede-shita] to nageita*
        (name) TOP (name) NOM leave.home-do:PAST QT grieve:PAST
        'Taro grieved that Hanako had run away from home.'

   b. *taroo wa [hanako ga iede-shita] koto o nageita*
        (name) TOP (name) NOM leave.home-do:PAST NML ACC grieve:PAST
        'Taro grieved over the fact that Hanako had run away from home.'

(16) a. *hannin wa [jibun ga yatta] to jihaku-shita*
        Culprit TOP self NOM do:PAST QT confession-do:PAST
        'The culprit confessed that he did (it).'

   b. *hannin wa [jibun ga yatta] koto o jihaku-shita*
                                       NML ACC
        'The culprit confessed to the fact he did (it).'

Though what the (a) and (b) versions communicate is similar, there is a clear "factivity" difference between them (Kuno 1973; Josephs 1976; Akatsuka-McCawley 1978). "Factivity" is a property of verbs which presupposes the truth of the information provided by the complement or quoted material according to the proximate speaker, or person who is uttering the sentence (cf. Kiparsky and Kiparsky 1971); the complement is a factive clause while the quotation is not. It is thus assumed that the proximate speaker of (15b), for example, believes that Hanako ran away from home. However, such a conclusion does not follow from (15a); according to its proximate speaker, Hanako may or may not have actually run away from home, though the prime speaker, Taro, obviously believes so. An important trait of factive sentences is that even if they are negated (e.g. "Taro didn't grieve over the fact that Hanako had run away from home" or its Japanese counterpart), the truth value of the complement remains intact.[1]

Some complement taking verbs in Japanese are inherently factive and always take the complement construction (e.g. *omoidasu* 'remember' and *wasureru* 'forget'), while others are inherently nonfactive and always take the quotative construction (e.g. *kanchigai-suru* 'to make a wrong guess' and *gokai-suru* 'to form an incorrect notion'). Still others are non-committal, in which case the choice of a complementizer determines factivity. The verbs *nageku* 'grieve,' *jihaku-suru* 'confess,' (found in Examples (15) and (16) above), and also *shinjiru* 'believe,' belong to this last group.

The second type of verb which takes an object complement refers to an activity that involves some mental process, such as *shoomee-suru* 'prove,' *kesshin-suru* 'decide,' and *akirameru* 'give up.' The complementizer is usually *koto*, though *no* may sometimes appear.

(17) keeji   wa   [taroo   ga   jiroo   o   koroshita]   koto/*no
     detective   TOP   (name)   NOM   (name) ACC kill:PAST   NML

     o   shoomee-shita
     ACC   proof-do:PAST

     'The detective proved that Taro had killed Jiro.'

(18) jon   wa   [itaria e   iku]   koto/no o   akirameta
     (name)   TOP   Italy   ALL   go:NONPAST   NML   ACC give.up:PAST
     'John gave up on going to Italy.'

The third type of verb which takes an object complement includes verbs that express non-visual perception and emotion, and verbs of accomplishment. The complementizer *koto* or *no*, but not *tokoro*, is used for this type of verbs. The complement is marked with the dative case marker.

(19) hanako wa   [taroo   ga   mada   akiramenai]   koto/no
     (name) TOP (name) NOM   not.yet give.up:NEG:NONPAST   NML

     ni   akirete-iru
     DAT   appalled:TE-ASP:NONPAST

     'Hanako is appalled by the fact that Taro won't give up yet.'

(20) boku   wa   [kare ga   itsumo hankoo-suru]   koto/no
     I(male)   TOP   he   NOM   always resist-do:NONPAST   NML

     ni   heekoo-shite-iru
     DAT   annoyance-do:TE-AUX:NONPAST

     'I am annoyed by the fact that he always resists (us).'

---

1. As "factivity" is pertinent only for complements and quotations that report past events, and generally has only limited applicability, Givón, (1980), thus, proposes to replace it with the notion of 'binding force.'

(21) katoo-san   wa   [sono yama   ni   noboru]   koto/no
     (name)-Mr. TOP that   mountain DAT climb:NONPAST NML
     ni   seekoo-shita
     DAT   success-do:PAST
     'Mr. Kato succeeded in climbing that mountain.'

As noted earlier, among the three complementizers available for object complements, *koto* is used to depict an abstract fact, while *no* is used to describe less abstract information. This distinction clarifies the difference between some similar sentences, such as (22) and (23). Notice *kiku* means either 'hear (about the fact)' or 'listen (to the sound).'

(22) boku   wa   [hanako ga   piano o   hiku]   **no**
     I(male) TOP (name) NOM   piano ACC play:NONPAST   NML
     o   kiite...
     ACC listen:TE
     'I listened to Hanako playing the piano, and...'

(23) boku   wa   [hanako ga   piano o   hiku]   **koto**
     I(male) TOP (name) NOM   piano ACC play:NONPAST   NML
     o   kiite...
     ACC hear:TE
     'I heard that Hanako plays the piano, and...'

In (22) the fact that Hanako plays the piano is presented as a perceived physical event with the complementizer *no* (so *kiite* means 'listen'), while in (23) it is presented as an abstract concept with *koto* (so *kiite* means 'hear about the fact that...'). Another notable fact regarding sentences with sense perception (non-visual as well as visual) is that they never take the *to yuu* expression because they refer to information verified by perception (cf. Chapter 9 §3.4). Thus *to yuu* can be added only to (23), i.e. .. *to yuu koto o kiite*.[2] Now compare (22) above with (24) below.

(24) boku   wa   [hanako ga   piano o   hiku]   no/tokoro
     I(male) TOP (name) NOM   piano ACC play:NONPAST   NML
     o   mite
     ACC see:TE
     'I saw Hanako playing the piano, and...'

---

2. If *to yuu* is added to (22), i.e. '...*to yuu no o kite*,' the meaning of the sentence changes to that of (23).

In (24), the matrix verb, *mite* 'saw and,' expresses the most direct, visual perception. In such a case, the complementizer *no* can be replaced by *tokoro*. In other words, *tokoro* can be used when the complement depicts an immediate scene. Sentences such as (24) are similar to the "internally headed clause," which will be discussed in §3.

2.2 The subject complement

Compared to the number of predicates that can take an object complement, the number of predicates that can take a subject complement is much more restricted. Most typically, subject complements appear as the subjects of nominal, nominal adjective, or adjectival predicates to express the speaker's evaluation of the complement information. Less frequently, they appear with intransitive verb predicates, such as *shirewataru* 'become widely known.' For the subject complement, the complementizer is either *no* or *koto*, and *tokoro* never appears.

Fact-supporting predicates such as *jijitsu da* 'is a fact,' *hontoo da* 'is true,' and *tashika da* 'is certain,' show speaker support of the complement clause information. In this case, *to yuu* is optional and either *no* or *koto* can be used.

Fact supporting predicates
(25) [aitsu   ga   kane   o   nusunda]   (to yuu) koto/no wa
     that.guy   NOM   money   ACC   steal:PAST   (QT say) NML   TOP
     jujitsu   da
     fact   COP
     'It is a fact that the guy stole the money.'

(26) [hanako ga   kuni   ni   kaette-shimatta]   (to yuu)
     (name) NOM   home.town   DAT   return:TE-ASP:PAST (QT say)
     koto/no wa   hontoo da
     NML   TOP   true   COP
     'It's true that Hanako went back home.'

Proposition denying predicates such as *uso da* 'is a lie' or *kanchigai da* 'is a misconception' deny the complement clause information. In such cases, the complementizer is *no*. The *to yuu* expression is obligatory because the speaker does not believe the complement information (i.e. lower degree of certainty, Chapter 9 §3.4).

Proposition denying predicates
(27) [hanako ga   kuni   ni   kaette-shimatta]   to yuu no
     (name) NOM   home.town   DAT   return:TE-ASP:PAST QT say NML
     wa   uso   da
     TOP   lie   COP
     'It's a lie that Hanako has returned home.'

(28) [boku   ga   sore o   nusunda]   to yuu no   wa
     I(male) NOM   that ACC   steal:PAST   QT say NML   TOP

     kimi no   kanchigai   da
     you   GEN   misconception   COP

     'It's your misconception that I stole that.'

Other predicates such as *ariuru/kanoo da* 'is possible' neither support nor deny the information and are non-committal. In these cases, the complementizer is *koto*. The *to yuu* expression is obligatory because the speaker cannot support the complement information strongly.

Noncommittal predicates

(29) [aitsu   ga   kane   o   nusunda]   to   yuu koto
     that.guy   NOM   money   ACC   steal:PAST   QT   say NML

     wa   ariuru
     TOP   possible:NONPAST

     'It's possible that the guy stole the money.'

(30) [rainen   zeekin ga   agaru]   to   yuu koto wa
     next.year   tax   NOM   rise:NONPAST   QT   say NML   TOP

     kanoo   da
     possible   COP

     'It's possible that taxes will go up next year.'

Using such predicates as *toozen da* 'is natural,' or *migoto da* 'is excellent,' the speaker can also make various other comments on the information shared with his interlocutor.

Commenting predicates

(31) muri-shite-iru   kara   [byooki-ni
     excess-do:TE-ASP:NONPAST   because   sick-COP:ADV

     naru]   *koto/no wa   toozen   da
     become:NONPAST   NML   TOP   natural   COP

     'It's natural that you get sick because you do too much.'

(32) [asoko de   ichiroo ga   hoomuran   o   utta]
     then   INS   (name)   NOM   home.run   ACC   hit:PAST

     *koto/no   wa   migoto   datta
     NML   TOP   excellent   COP:PAST

     'It was excellent that Ichiro hit a home run at that time.'

(33) [ai   ga   kuni   ni   kaette-shimatta]   (to   yuu)
     (name)   NOM   home.town   DAT   return:TE-ASP:PAST   (QT   say)

     koto/no   wa   hontoo-ni   kanashii koto da
     NML   TOP   real-COP:ADV   sad   NML   COP

     'It's really sad that Ai went back home.'

(34) [taroo ga kaisha o totsuzen yameta] (to yuu)
(name) NOM company ACC suddenly quit:PAST (QT say)
koto/no wa myoo-na koto da
NML TOP strange-COP:ADV NML COP
'It's a strange thing that Taro suddenly quit his company.'

To summarize, complementation is a way to embed various types of clauses as syntactically integrated elements of a larger sentence. The choice of complementizer (*koto*, *no*, or *tokoro*) is a significant aspect of complementation in Japanese. The *koto*-complement encodes an abstract piece of information which has been assimilated into the speaker's knowledge. The *no*-complement signifies non-abstract information acquired directly. Complements with *tokoro* are even more direct than those with *no*, which report situations where the person denoted as the subject of the main clause is directly involved. The complements examined in this section function as subject or object (accusative or dative), but they may also appear as an adjunct. Even a predicate may consist of a complement, as the next example shows. (35), below, is a pseudo-cleft sentence with two complement clauses, one as a subject/topic and the other as the predicate.

(35) [daredemo shitte-iru] no wa
anyone know:TE-ASP:NONPAST NML TOP
[ningen wa itsuka wa shinu] to yuu koto da
man TOP someday TOP die:NONPAST QT say NML COP
'What everyone knows is the fact that people eventually die.'

3. Internally headed relative clauses (IHRs)

The "internally headed relative clause (IHR)," also known as the "headless relative" or a "pivot independent relative" (Kuroda 1974), modifies a head noun which is contained in the modifier itself. It consists of a clause followed by a nominalizing complementizer, *no* or *tokoro* (but not *koto*), and functions as a constituent of a larger sentence. Despite the structural similarity between the internally headed relative clause and noun complementation (see the end of § 2.1), these structures must be kept distinct. Example (36) below contains an IHR whose head (*taroo*) is selected by the matrix verb (*tsukamaeta* 'caught') but contained within the embedded clause itself. Example (37), on the other hand, contains a complement, and the matrix verb (*kitai-suru* 'hope for') cannot select a head noun in it. It is possible to turn the head noun *taroo* in (36) into a normal relative clause head, as shown in (36′), but it is not possible to do so with *taroo* in (37), as shown in (37′).

(36) boku   wa   [taroo   ga   heya   kara   dete-kuru]
    I(male) TOP   (name)   NOM   room   ABL   come.out:TE-come:NONPAST
    tokoro/no   o   tsukamaeta
    NML   ACC catch:PAST
    'I caught Taro coming out of the room.'

(37) boku   wa   [taroo   ga   heya   kara   dete-kuru]
    I(male) TOP   (name)   NOM   room   ABL   come.out:TE-come:NONPAST
    koto/no   o   kitai-shita
    NML   ACC expect:PAST
    'I expected Taro to come out of the room.'

(36') boku   wa   [heya   kara   detekuru]   taroo
     I(male) TOP   room   ABL   come.out:TE-come:NONPAST (name)
     o   tsukamaeta
     ACC   catch:PAST
     'I caught Taro, who was coming out of the room.'

(37') *boku   wa   [heya   kara   detekuru]   taroo
      I(male) TOP   room   ABL   come.out:TE-come:NONPAST (name)
      o   kitaishita
      ACC   expect:PAST
      'I expected Taro, who was coming out of the room.'

Other typical examples of IHRs are (38) and (39). (The examples are modified from Kuroda 1992b: 157, 160).

(38) taroo   wa   [*aoi*   *ringo*   ga   sara   no   ue   ni   aru]
    (name)   TOP   unripe   apple   NOM   plate   GEN   TOP   DAT   exist:NONPAST
    no   o   totte…
    NML   ACC   take:TE
    'Taro took an unripe apple which was on the plate, and…'

(39) taroo   wa   [*sensee*   ga   hikoojoo   ni   o-tsuki-ni-natta]
    (name)   TOP   teacher   NOM   airport   DAT   arrive:HON:PAST
    no   o   sassoku   kuruma   de   hoteru   e   o-tsure-shita
    NML   ACC   immediately   car   INS   hotel   ALL   take:HON:PAST
    'Taro took the teacher, who had just arrived at the airport, to the hotel by car.'

The complementizer *no* appearing with internally headed relatives should be distinguished from a homophonous pronominal. *No* as a pronominal has a peculiar non-honorific overtone. The cases of *no* in (40) and (41) below are examples of the pronominal usage. When it refers to a student, as in (40), the sentence is acceptable, but when it refers to a teacher, as in

(41), it is not (despite the fact that in this latter case, both the matrix and embedded verbs are in the honorific form). This is because the pronominal *no* carries a non-honorific tone.

(40) *gakusee no naka de kuruma o motte-iru*
     student GEN among LOC car ACC have:TE-AUX:NONPAST
     no ni eki made okutte-moratta
     one DAT station ALL send:TE-give:PAST
     '(I) had one of the students who had a car give me a ride to the station.'

(41) **sensee no naka de kuruma o motte-irassharu*
     student GEN among LOC car ACC have:TE-AUX::HON:NONPAST
     no ni eki made okutte-itadaita
     one DAT station ALL send:TE-give:PAST
     '(I) had one of the teachers who had a car give me a ride to the station.'

However, *no* appearing in an internally headed relative clause lacks this non-honorific tone and can appear in a sentence like (39) in which an honorific person (e.g. *sensee* 'teacher') is involved.

Though the IHR functions similarly to the relative clause (RC), it has several features not shared with the normal relative clause. First, an RC does not have any restrictions on the syntactic role of the head noun with respect to the matrix clause as shown below in (42). However, acceptable syntactic roles for the IHR are limited to the direct object and, marginally, the subject, as shown in (43).

(42)
Subj. [*ki no ue ni ita*] *risu ga*
       tree GEN top LOC exist:PAST squirrel NOM
       kyuuni tobiorite-kita
       suddenly jump.down-come:PAST
       'A squirrel which was in the tree suddenly jumped down (towards me).'

D.O. *taroo wa* [*ki no ue ni ita*] *risu*
     (name) TOP tree GEN TOP LOC exist:PAST squirrel
     o uchiotoshita
     ACC shoot.down:PAST
     'Taro shot down the squirrel which was in the tree.'

I.O. *taroo wa* [*ki no ue ni ita*] *risu ni esa o yatta*
                                         DAT food ACC give:PAST
     'Taro gave some food to the squirrel which was in the tree.'

Obl. *taroo wa* [*ki no ue ni ita*] *risu de hakusee o tsukutta*
                                         INS specimen ACC make:PAST
     'Taro made a stuffed specimen out of the squirrel which had been in the tree.'

Obl.	*taroo wa [ki no ue ni ita] risu kara*	
	ABL	

junban-ni shashin o   totta
in.order photo ACC take:PAST

'Taro took photos of squirrels starting with the one which had been in the tree.'

(43)
Subj.	?[*risu ga ki no ue ni ita*] *no ga kyuuni tobiorite-kita*
D.O.	*taroo wa* [*risu ga ki no ue ni ita*] *no o uchiotoshita*
I.O.	* *taroo wa* [*risu ga ki no ue ni ita*] *no ni esa o yatta*
Obl.	* *taroo wa* [*risu ga ki no ue ni ita*] *no de hakusee o tsukutta*
Obl.	* *taroo wa* [*risu ga ki no ue ni ita*] *no kara junban-ni shashin o totta*

Second, there must be a strict "relevancy condition" between the content of an IHR and the matrix clause (Kuroda 1992b: 147). This is most readily seen in the temporal overlap or contiguity between the events expressed by the two clauses.

(44) *taroo   wa   [hanako ga   keeki o   futatsu ni   kitta]   no*
      (name) TOP (name) NOM cake   ACC two   DAT cut:PAST NML

o   totte   tabeta
ACC   take:TE   eat:PAST

'Taro took the cake which Hanako had just cut into two, and ate it.'

(45) **taroo wa [hanako ga kinoo keeki o futatsu ni kitta] no o*
                              yesterday

sakki   totte tabeta
just.now

'Taro took the cake which Hanako cut into two yesterday, and ate it just now.'

(46) (Normal relative clause, cf. (45))
      taroo wa [hanako ga kinoo futatsu ni kitta] keeki o sakki totte tabeta.
      'Taro took the cake which Hanako cut into two yesterday, and ate it just now.'

In (44), Taro eating the cake must immediately follow Hanako cutting it. If there is a time lapse between the two events, a sentence with an IHR, such as (45), is unacceptable. A normal relative clause does not pose any such constraint, as the grammatical (46) demonstrates.

The third characteristic of the IHR is its inability to specify the semantic head. As mentioned in Chapter 9 (§3.1), the case relationship between the head noun and the relative clause predicate cannot be overtly specified. In the case of IHRs, this problem does not arise, since the head noun retains its case particle within the clause. However, the semantic head of the IHR is not overtly marked in any way, so its identification becomes problematic when there is more than one potential candidate. In (47) there are two noun phrases (*jiroo* and *taroo*), and indeed this sentence is ambiguous, as the three possible translations indicate.

(47) *keekan   wa [jiroo   ga   taroo   o*
     police.man TOP (name)   NOM   (name) ACC

   nigasoo-to   suru]   no/tokoro o   toriosaeta
   free:VOL-ADV do:NONPAST NML ACC   arrest:PAST

   'The policeman arrested Jiro when he was trying to free Taro.'
   'The policeman arrested Taro when Jiro was trying to free him.'
   'The policeman arrested Jiro and Taro when Jiro was trying to free Taro.'

Most of the examples so far use the complementizer *no* (but see (47) just above). This complementizer is most suitable when the internal head refers to a static object. When it refers to an animate engaging in a more dynamic activity, the complementizer *tokoro* is preferred (Horie 1993: 130). The following examples demonstrate this point.

(48) *keeji   wa [taroo ga   kenjuu o   tsukue no   ue ni*
     detective TOP (name) NOM   gun   ACC desk   GEN TOP LOC

   *oita]   no/*tokoro o   totte...*
   put:PAST NML   ACC take:TE

   'The detective took the gun which Taro had placed on the desk, and...'

(49) *keeji   wa [taroo ga   kenjuu o*
     detective TOP (name) NOM   gun   ACC

   *nagetsuketa] no/*tokoro o   uketomete...*
   throw:PAST   NML   ACC catch:TE

   'The detective caught the gun which Taro had thrown (at him), and...'

(50) *keeji   wa [taroo ga   kenjuu o*
     detective TOP (name) NOM   gun   ACC

   tukue no   ue ni   oita]   no/tokoro o   toriosaeta
   desk GEN top LOC put:PAST NML   ACC arrest:PAST

   'The detective arrested Taro who had placed the gun on the desk.'
   (see Chapter 12 §2.6)

(51) *keeji wa [taroo ga nemurikonde-ita]   no/tokoro*
                       sound.asleep:TE-ASP:PAST   NML

   o   kenkyo-shita
   ACC make.arrest:PAST

   'The detective made an arrest of Taro who had fallen asleep.'

Although there are two potential semantic heads for the IHRs in these examples, the choice is unambiguously 'gun' in (48) and (49) because the matrix verbs, *toru* 'take' and *uketomeru* 'receive,' pick an inanimate entity for their direct object. For such inanimate semantic heads, the complementizer is always *no*. On the other hand, the matrix verbs in (50) and (51), *toriosaeta* 'arrested' and *kenkyo-shita* 'made an arrest,' pick a human for their direct object, so the head for these examples is *taroo* 'Taro.' When these animate semantic heads perform certain activities, the complementizer can either be *tokoro* or *no*.

4. Integrated adverbial clauses

The "integrated adverbial clause" is similar to the *tokoro* marked IHR which specifies the circumstantial situation (i.e. the circumstance in which the matrix event takes place) like (50) and (51) above, but also differs from it in the mismatch between its case marking and the matrix verb's argument structure. Example (52) was taken from Harada (1973: 122), (53) from Kuroda (1978: 44), and (54) is from Shibatani (personally communication).

(52) taroo   wa   [kanningu o   shite-iru]   no/tokoro o
     (name)   TOP   cheating ACC   do:TE-ASP:NONPAST   NML   ACC
     sensee   ni   mitsukatta
     teacher DAT   be.found:PAST
     'Taro was spotted by the teacher when he was cheating (during the exam).'

(53) taroo   wa   [moo   sukoshide   oboreru]
     (name)   TOP   more   a.little   be.drowned:NONPAST
     no/tokoro o   yatto   booto   e   oyogi-tsuita
     NML   ACC finally   boat   ALL   swim-arrive:PAST
     'Taro had almost drowned by the time he finally reached the boat.'

(54) taroo   wa   [ie   o   deru]   *no/tokoro o   osowareta
     (name)   TOP   house ACC   leave   NML   ACC   attack:PSS:PAST
     'Taro was attacked when he was leaving the house.'

The main predicates in (52) and (53) are intransitive verbs and that in (54) is the passive predicate, all of which do not take an *o*-marked complement. These sentences can be paraphrased by substituting *tokoro o* with the adverbial *toki* 'when.' Further examples are given below. (56) is modified from Martin ([1975] 1991: 980).

(55) takashi   wa   [isogashii]   tokoro/no o
     (name)   TOP   busy   NML   ACC
     wazawaza   mimai   ni   kite-kureta
     expressly   visit   DAT   come:TE-give:PAST
     'Takashi took the trouble to visit (me at the hospital) though he was busy.'

(56) [hajime   fuufu   futari datta]   <u>tokoro/no</u> ga
     beginning husband.wife two   COP:PAST NML   NOM

   kodomo ga   dekite...
   child NOM be.made:TE

   'At the beginning they were only husband and wife; then a child was born, and...'

(57) [sore made ikizumatte-ita]   <u>tokoro/no</u> ga
     then ALL reach.limit:TE-ASP:PAST NML   NOM

   sono hon o   yonde   ii   kangae ga   hirameita.
   that book ACC read:TE good idea   NOM strike:PAST

   'Until then (I) was stuck, but (I) read that book, and hit upon a good idea.'

In (55) the main predicate is a complex verb phrase, *mimai ni kite-kureta* 'came to see (me at the hospital),' which may take a direct object. In fact the direct object, if expressed, should be *boku o* 'me.' Notice, however, the accusative marking in this sentence is on the *tokoro/no* clause. If this were to be analyzed as an IHR, the internal head must be the subject of *isogashii* 'busy,' which is *takashi*. This would produce the wrong interpretation: *Takashi came to visit himself who was busy. In these examples, *tokoro/no* may no longer be pure complementizers, but may function as conjunctions. (Indeed, *tokoro-ga* has already become a proper conjunction with the meaning of 'however,' which can start a sentence.) Examples (55) through (57) can be rephrased with regular adverbial clauses.

(55′) takashi wa   isogashikatta <u>keredo</u>
      (name) TOP busy:PAST   but

   wazawaza   mimai ni   kite-kureta
   expressly visit DAT come:TE-give:PAST

   'Takashi took the trouble to visit (me at the hospital) though he was busy.'

(56′) hajime   fuufu   futari data   <u>ga</u>
      beginning husband.wife two   COP:PAST but

   kodomo ga   dekite...
   child NOM be.made:TE

   'At the beginning they were only husband and wife; then a child was born, and ...'

(57′) sore made ikizumatte-ita   <u>ga</u>
      then ALL reach.limit:TE-ASP:PAST but

   sono hon o   yonde   ii   kangae ga   hirameeta.
   that book ACC read:TE good idea   NOM strike:PAST

   'Until then (I) was stuck, but (I) read that book, and hit upon a good idea.'

The original versions with complementizers and those with adverbial clauses do not present much semantic difference, though the former are a syntactically more integrated way of presenting the adverbial information (cf. Horie 1997).

5. Summary

Among the four processes described here, the quotative construction is the process which embeds a clause/sentence in the least integrated way. Or, said differently, this process gives the most independence to the embedded material. Noun complementation is a more syntactically integrated process of embedding a clause which functions as a subject or object for the matrix verb. The internally headed relative clause is structurally similar to the noun complement, but they are distinguished from one another based upon the ability (or lack thereof) of the matrix verb to select the head noun. Another difference is that the internally headed relative clause is marked either by *no* or *tokoro*, while the complement is marked by *no* or *koto* (and *tokoro* in some limited cases). The internally headed relative clause is functionally similar to the normal relative clause in that both have head nouns that are constituents of the matrix clause. However, compared to the normal relative clause, the internally headed relative clause is much more restricted both syntactically and semantically. The integrated adverbial clause is similar to the internally headed relative clause structurally, but it does not serve as an argument for the matrix verb even though it is marked by a case particle. It has acquired the function of adverbial clause.

CHAPTER 11

Information structure and the sentence form

Though Argument Structure (Chapter 6) is the basis for understanding the structure of a sentence, more is necessary for a fuller appreciation of how a sentence is composed. This is because a sentence is a construct which receives a significant amount of influence form discourse and other pragmatic factors, with information structure being one of the most crucial. The information structure of a sentence refers to the "formal expression of the pragmatic structuring of a proposition in a discourse" (Lambrecht 1994:5). In Japanese, the particle *wa* in a sentence and the lack thereof plays a crucial role for information structuring. Relevant concepts for information structure include "topic" "contrastiveness," "focus," "new vs. given information," "assertion vs. presupposition," "challengeable vs. non-challengeable information," "identifiability," "activation and salience of a concept."

Topicalization and contrastivization are processes in which a sentence constituent is made into a topic or a contrast constituent through *wa* marking. Particles *ga* and *o* do not appear with *wa*, while adjunct particles such as *to*, *de* and others do appear with *wa*. Particle *ni* may or may not appear with *wa*. (See below.) According to a survey of magazine articles (written language) by *Kokuritsu Kokugo Kenkyuujo* (the National Language Research Institute) (1964), among different types of noun, a subject noun is most likely to receive *wa* marking (61.1%), and an object is a distant second (4.7%). All other types of nouns comprise only 4.5%. (In the survey's remaining 30% or so, *wa* appears with adverbs and verbs.) Also in conversation the subject noun is marked by *wa* far more frequently than any other types of nouns (Fry 2003:158).[1]

Non-topicalized/Contrastivised		Topicalized/Contrastivised
NP-*ga*	→	NP-*wa*
NP-*o*	→	NP-*wa*
NP-*ni*	→	NP-*wa* or NP-*ni wa*
NP-*to*	→	NP-*to wa*
NP-*de*	→	NP-*de wa*
etc.		

---

1. Fry shows that when a noun is the subject of a sentence, it is marked by *wa* 12% of the time, by *ga* 31%, and by zero 33%; a direct object is marked by *wa* 6% of the time, by *o* 18%, and zero 53%. In his data a locative noun phrase is slightly more likely to be marked by *wa* (9%) than a direct object.

1. The topic-comment structure

The topic-comment structure consists of a *wa*-marked topic and the comment that follows. Functionally, a topicalized constituent is an entity about which a comment is provided. The structure (1) is a schematic representation of topic-comment sentences, (2) and (3).

(1) [TOPIC – *wa*]   [COMMENET]

(2) [*taroo - wa*] [*gakusee da*]
    (name) TOP student COP
    'Taro is a student.'

(3) [*taroo - wa*] [*uta o   utatta*]
    (name) TOP song ACC sing:PAST
    'Taro sang songs.'

Though the comment may be a single predicate, it may also consist of multiple predicates (Iwasaki 1987: 131–135). In the examples in (4), the comment portion consists of two predications.

(4) Subject-topic
    [*jon   wa*] [*jibun de piano o   hiki,   uta o   utatta*]
    (name) TOP self by piano ACC play:INF, song ACC sing:PAST
    'John played the piano and sang a song himself.'

   Object-topic
   [*kono uta   wa*] [*jon   ga sakkyoku shi,   pooru ga*
   this song TOP (name) NOM compose do:INF, (name) NOM
   sakushi shita]
   write. lyrics:PAST
   'This song, John composed, and Paul wrote lyrics.'

   Dative-topic
   [*sono ko ni wa*] [*jon   ga hana o   okuri,   pooru ga*
   this child DAT TOP (name) NOM flower ACC send:INF, (name) NOM
   uta o   uttatta]
   song ACC sing:PAST
   'To this child, John sent flowers, and Paul sang a song.'

   Dative-/Adverbial topic
   [*shuumatsu (ni) wa*] [*jon   ga uta o   utai,   pooru ga*
   weekend   (DAT) TOP (name) NOM song ACC sing:INF, (name) NOM
   piano o   hiku]
   piano ACC play:NONPAST
   'On weekends, John sings songs and Paul plays the piano.'

1.1 Identifiability, activation and discourse

The topic-comment sentence is a canonical declarative sentence which proclaims the speaker/writer's modal judgment about the relationship between the entity expressed by the *wa*-marked noun phrase (topic) and the state of affairs predicated on it (comment). Kuroda (1984, 1992b: 23) described this as a particular type of mental process called "double (or categorical) judgment," which refers to the process of "apprehending something as substance and attributing to it a certain property perceived in a situation." (See also Morishige 1965, 1971.) When this explanation is applied to a topic-comment sentence used in a communicative setting, however, it is necessary to re-interpret "apprehension" as "mutual apprehension" between the speaker and addressee (cf. Kurumada 2009; Tomasello 2003). That is to say, the topic-comment sentence cannot be used unless the speaker believes the entity to be coded as the topic is "identifiable" to the addressee.

The identifiability does not simply mean first-hand knowledge of an entity (this is not actually necessary); rather it means the speaker's belief in the addressee's ability to pick out ("identify") the referent the speaker has in mind from the other possible candidates which might be categorized in the same way (Chafe 1976: 33–8; Lambrecht 1994: 77–92). For example, a particular car is identifiable if it is coded as *boku no kuruma* 'my car.' This is not because the addressee knows this car (she may or may not), but because the addressee is expected to isolate one particular car from others as it is clarified by the genitive phrase *boku no* 'my.' On the other hand, if a particular car is simply coded without any introduction as *kuruma* 'car,' the addressee cannot discriminate the particular car that the speaker has in mind from others because *kuruma* 'car' can refer to any car; thus it is unidentifiable. Unique referents as defined in (a) below are always identifiable by default.

a. items that exist uniquely in the shared universe of the interlocutors, e.g. *the sun, the moon, the President of the United States, my mom*, "*John*" between two people who share a particular "*John*" as a mutual acquaintance.

Entities can be also made identifiable through lexical, syntactic, semantic, or pragmatic processes such as those described in (b) through (f).

b. Items that are deictically anchored are always identifiable, e.g. *watashi* 'I,' *anata* 'you,' *kore* 'this,' *are* 'that,' *kyoo* 'today,' *kinoo* 'yesterday.'
c. Items can be made identifiable through grounding with a modifier, e.g. *boku no kuruma* 'my car,' *weetoresu* 'waitress,' in a phrase such as *kinoo itta resutoran no weetoresu* 'the waitress of a restaurant I went to yesterday.'
d. Items may become identifiable through the use of a "frame" (Fillmore 1982) as a supercategory, e.g. "*the passport*" may become identifiable as soon as an overseas trip is mentioned.

e. Items may become identifiable after being introduced through "presentational" sentences (§4.2), *obaasan* 'old lady' becomes identifiable after an introduction by a sentence such as *mukashi mukashi aru tokoro ni hitori no obaasan ga sunde-imashita* 'Once upon a time there lived an old woman.'
f. A generic noun phrase (e.g. the concept of 'elephant,' the concept of 'love') is always identifiable as long as the category which it refers to is mutually recognizable between the speaker and hearer. For example, the generic noun *zoo* 'elephant' is always identifiable as any competent Japanese speaker knows what it means, or to what it refers. However, when the speaker knows a concept (e.g. *kabutogani* 'horseshoe crab') but the addressee doesn't, it is not an identifiable generic noun.

In contrast, certain other nouns are inherently non-identifiable. Interrogative words such as *dare* 'who' or *nani* 'what,' non-referential, indefinite nouns such as *dareka* 'someone' and quantified expressions such as *takusan no hito* 'many people' are such words, and they cannot appear as topics with *wa*. (Replacing *wa* with *ga* makes all the sentences below grammatical.)

(5) **dare wa kimashita ka*
    who TOP come:POL:PAST Q
    'Who came?'

(6) **dareka wa kimashita ka*
    anyone TOP come:POL:PAST Q
    'Did anyone come?'

(7) **takusan no hito wa iru*
    many GEN people TOP exist:NONPAST
    'There are many people.'

Although identifiability is a crucial feature of the nominal referent for it to gain the status of topic, this is by no means the sole sufficient condition. That is, a noun with an identifiable referent is not coded with *wa* unless the speaker has reason to believe that it is sufficiently activated in the mind of the addressee, or salient in discourse.[2] In other words, topicalization (i.e. *wa* marking) is essentially a discourse process which cannot be explained fully without considering the communicative context. In a narrative, characters who have been introduced and figure prominently in a particular episode tend to be topicalized, while identifiable non-main characters are not (e.g. the "staging" effect of Maynard 1987; see also Kuroda 1987). In (8), though *obaasan* 'old woman' is introduced in line 1 and thus has become an identifiable referent, it is not topicalized in line 2. This is because the old woman is not staged as the main character in the episode.

---

2. When the concept is salient to the highest degree, it is realized as zero anaphora in Japanese (Chapter 13 §2).

(8) (Uriko Hime from Tsubota 1975: 14)
1. mukashi mukashi aru   tokoro ni
   old.days old.days certain place   DAT

   <u>ojiisan</u>   to   <u>obaasan</u>   to   ga   arimashita
   old.man COM old.woman COM NOM exist:PAST
   'Once upon a time there lived an old man and woman.'

2. aru hi <u>obaasan</u>   ga   kawa e   sentaku ni ikimashita
   one day old.woman NOM river ALL laundry DAT go:POL:PAST
   'One day, the old woman went to do the laundry at the river.'

Since topic is a global discourse notion, it operates only in the main clause. With a subject in a non-main clause, e.g. a relative clause and an adverbial clause such as the *toki* 'when' clause, *wa* marking is prohibited as shown in (9) and (10) below (Chapter 9 §3.1).

(9) [sono neko **ga/*wa**   tabete-iru]   sakana
    that cat NOM/TOP eat-ASP:NONPAST   fish
    'the fish [that that cat is eating]'

(10) [<u>pochi</u>   **ga/*wa**   <u>nigeta</u>] toki kimi wa nani o   shite-ita?
     (dog's name) NOM/*TOP flee:PAST time you TOP what ACC do-ASP:PAST
     'What were you doing when Pochi fled.'

The global nature of *wa*-marked topics explains another syntactic phenomena, witnessed in (11) below.

(11) [<u>pochi</u> <u>wa</u>], boku ga tobira o aketa   toki, [<u>nigedashita</u>]
     (dog's name) TOP I NOM door ACC open:PAST when   flee:PAST
     'Pochi fled when I opened the door.'

In this sentence, the subject-topic, Pochi, crosses over the temporal adverbial clause, 'when I opened the door,' and directly connects to the main predicate, *nigedashita* 'fled/rushed out.' Mikami (1960: 130–9) calls this phenomenon the comma crossing as the adverbial clause is often demarcated by commas in written language.

1.2 The "eel" sentence

In a sentence like (2) presented earlier (*taro wa gakusee da* 'Taro is a student'), the relationship between the topic and the comment is "logically well formed." However, the relationship is actually more of a pragmatic nature, for it may defy a strict logical interpretation. In other words, a typical topic-comment sentence like (2) is a subset of the more pragmatically anchored so-called "eel" sentence (*unagi-bun*) like (12) (cf. Okutsu 1978; Onoe 1981; Kitahara 1981).

(12) boku wa unagi da
     I   TOP eel   COP

When the relationship is not logically sensible, as in the case of (12) ("*I'm an eel"), pragmatic interpretation is called for. Thus if (12) is uttered in a restaurant, the sentence is easily interpreted as "What I will eat/order is an eel dish." If it is uttered at a meeting among biologists, it may mean "What I study is eels," among other possibilities. In fact, the interpretation of (2) may also be context sensitive. It is normally interpreted as "Taro is a student," but when school office staff members are assigning their responsibilities for different kinds of people, it may mean "Taro is responsible for taking care of students (and Hanako is responsible for teachers, and so forth)."[3]

1.3 The -wa -ga sentence structure

The -wa -ga sentence structure gives a framework in which both a topic (-wa) and a subject (-ga) co-exist in one sentence. This type of sentence, with two subject/topic-like noun phrases, is a hallmark of a topic-prominent language (Li & Thompson 1976). There are two types of sentences which take the form of -wa -ga. The first type is an expansion of a comment via clausal comment. In (13) below, a comment is provided by one-argument stative predicate, *ookii* 'big.' The comment can also be expressed by a complete clause (NP ga Pred) as shown in (14). In this case, the ga-marked phrase must represent some aspect of the category referred to by the topic (Chapter 6 §3.1). For example, in the following examples, *karada* 'body' is an inalienable part of *zoo* 'elephant'; *atama* 'head' is likewise an inalienable part of *boku* 'I'; *tai* 'sea bream' is a member of the category *sakana* 'fish,' and *tsuritate* 'freshly caught' is a state of *sakana* 'fish.'

(13) zoo   wa   ookii
      elephant TOP   big:NONPAST
      'The elephant is big.'

(14) [zoo   wa   [karada ga   ookii]]
      elephant TOP   body   NOM   big:NONPAST
      "The elephant – its body is big."

      [boku wa   [atama ga   itai]]
      I   TOP   head   NOM   painful:NONPAST
      "I have a headache."

      [sakana wa   [tai   ga   umai]]
      fish   TOP   sea.bream   NOM   delicious:NONPAST
      '(Among) fish – the sea bream is delicious.'

      [sakana wa   [tsuritate   ga   umai]]
      fish   TOP   fresh-off-the-sea   NOM   delicious:NONPAST
      '(When it comes to) fish – freshly caught is delicious.'

---

3. See Misumi (2011) for the use of 'eel' sentences in actual discourse.

The *wa*-marked noun phrases in the above examples do not have a direct case relationship with the predicate in the comment, and may be called "extra-thematic" argument (Chapter 6 §3.1, Shibatani 2000). Extra-thematic arguments may appear one after another as in the following example.

(15) [*furansu wa* [*pari ga* [*bukka ga takai*]]]
    (place) TOP (place) NOM price NOM height: NONPAST
    '(In) France, it's Paris where the prices are high.'

The second type of *-wa -ga* sentence is made with a predicate which takes two nominative-marked noun phrases in the argument structure ("double nominative"), such as *suki da* 'like' and *joozu da* 'skillful' (Chapter 6 §1(b)). In other words, these predicates are two argument predicates, and the structures involving them have forms different from those described above.

(16) [*boku wa jazu ga suki da*]
    I TOP jazz NOM like COP
    'I like jazz.'

   [*taroo wa piano ga joozu da*]
    (name) TOP piano NOM skillful COP
    'Taro is good at piano.'

A small number of nominal predicates also require two arguments. Both *honba* 'the best place' and *sanchi* 'producing place' must be specified for the place and the product.

(17) [*wain wa furansu ga honba da*]
    wine TOP France NOM best.place COP
    '(For) wine, France is the best place.'

In sum, the topic-comment sentence contains a sentence topic marked by *wa* which refers to an identifiable entity, and makes an assertion about it in the comment. The relationship between the topic and comment should be regarded as pragmatic to explain all varieties of this sentence type. The comment can be a noun or a complete clause, as in the *-wa -ga* sentence.

2. The contrastive structure

The contrastive structure resembles the topic-comment structure in which the initial noun phrase is marked by *wa*, though they are distinct in a number of ways. The unmodified noun, *inu* 'dogs,' in the next sentence is non-identifiable, and thus not a topic. However, the sentence is grammatical under the contrastive interpretation where (18) is contrasted with a proposition, e.g. *hito wa haireru* 'People can enter (but).' [The gloss TOP is used for the contrastive function in this section.]

(18) inu   wa   hairenai
    dog   TOP   enter:POT:NEG:NONPAST
    'Dogs cannot enter.'

It should be noted, however, that non-identifiability is not a requirement for the contrastive interpretation. What is crucial is the existence of a similar proposition which is to be compared. For example, if a non-identifiable *inu* 'dogs' is replaced with an identifiable, *kono inu* 'this dog,' the sentence can be interpreted as contrasting with the proposition that 'other dogs can enter.' This means that there is always ambiguity involved when a *wa*-marked constituent is identifiable. For example, whether the sentence below involves contrast or not depends entirely on the discourse context in which it appears.

(19) taroo   wa   gakusee   da
    (name) TOP   student   COP
    'Taro is a student.'

The *wa*-marked noun in (20) below is clearly a topic, as the speaker goes on to add information to this noun. In other words, a topic can be thought of as a "hitching post" to which a predication or multiple predications are added (cf. Chafe 1976; Iwasaki 1987). Mikami (1960) calls this phenomenon the "period crossing" of *wa*, since the initial NP *wa* crosses over a punctuation mark, a period, of the sentence and acts as the topic for the subsequent sentences.

(20) [taro   wa]   [gakusee   da.]
    (name) TOP   student   COP
    [mainichi   ku-ji   ni   gakkoo   ni   tsuku.]
    every.day 9-o'clock TMP   school   ALL   arrive:NONPAST
    [soshite   juu-ji   kara ...]
    and   10-o'clock ABL
    'Taro is a student. (He) gets to school at 9 every day.
    And then from 10, (he)...'

If the speaker, on the other hand, intends to put (19) against (21) below, then both (19) and (21) have a contrastive structure.

(21) mami   wa   kaikeeshi   da
    (name) TOP   accountant   COP
    'Mami is an accountant.'

The *wa*-marked noun phrases in (19) and (21) are "contrastive arguments" in this context. A contrastive argument represents an entity that is set off against another entity of the same class (e.g. a group of people consisting of Taro, Mami, and others) due to their different attributes, which nonetheless constitute a coherent set (e.g. occupation). Since affirmative and negative predicates are always two members of the same set, the polarity contrast between affirmative and negative in different *wa*-marked noun phrases is common in contrastive sentences, such as (22) below.

(22) taroo wa gakusee da ga, mami wa gakusee ja-nai
 (name) TOP student COP but (name) TOP student COP:NEG
 'Taro is a student, but Mami is not a student.'

Topicalization and contrastiveness may apply to the same noun phrase. In this case, the contrastive argument can be called a "contrastive topic." However, when a sentence contains more than one *wa*-phrase for a single predicate, the first assumes the role of topic and the second the role of contrastive argument. Consider sentence (23) below.

(23) boku **wa** kono hon **wa** yonda
 I TOP this book TOP read:PAST
 (demo ano hon wa yondeinai)
 (but that book TOP read:TE-ASP:NEG:NONPAST)
 'I read *this* book, (but (I) have not read *that* book).'

In the above sentence, the first *wa*-marked phrase, *boku* 'I,' is the topic, to which a comment is provided, but the second *wa*-marked phrase, *kono hon* 'this book,' the direct object of the verb, is the contrastive argument whose referent is distinguished from a similar referent (e.g. *ano hon* 'that book') for their different attributes ("having been read" and "not having been read"). *Kono hon* is not serving as a hitching post. The structure for (23) is understood to be as (24).

(24) [NP-*wa*] [NP-*wa* predicate]
 [ ]_{topic} [(contrastive element) predicate]_{comment}

This fact is related to another notable phenomenon of a contrastive *wa*. While topic-*wa* marking is prohibited in a relative clause as discussed earlier (see Example (9)), a contrastive *wa*-marking is allowed. (Such marking is still difficult in an adverbial clause, as seen in (10) earlier and repeated below.)

(25) [nihonjin **ga/wa** tabenai] sakana
 Japanese NOM/TOP eat:NEG fish
 'fish [that Japanese do not eat]'

(10) [*pochi* ga/*wa nigeta*] toki kimi wa nani o shite-ita?
 (dog's name) NOM/*TOP flee:PAST time you TOP what ACC do-ASP:PAST
 'What were you doing when Pochi (as opposed to Shiro) fled.'

The generalization that the first *wa*-phrase in a sentence with multiple *wa* phrases is always understood to be the topic (though it might have some element of contrastiveness in a particular context) is also applicable in sentence (26) below. In this sentence, the direct object is coded as the first *wa*-marked phrase, or topic, and the subject is coded as the second *wa*-marked phrase, or contrastive argument. Thus in this sentence, the two persons (e.g. "I" and "Taro") are contrasted for their different actions with respect to the topic, *kono hon* 'this book.'

(26) kono hon *wa* boku *wa* yonda
　　 this book TOP I   TOP read:PAST
　　 (demo taro　 wa yonde-inai).
　　 (but (name) TOP read:TE-AS:NEG:NONPAST
　　 'I read this book, (but *Taro* has not.)'

All the examples examined so far in this section deal with "contrastive arguments." However, some sentences must be interpreted as a sentence of "propositional contrast," which contrasts not a particular element in a proposition but the entire proposition with another (Kuno 1973: 46–7).

(27) kaze wa   moo   yanda   kedo mada samui
　　 Wind TOP already STOP:PAST but still cold
　　 'The wind has already stopped, but it is still cold.'

The concept *kaze* 'wind' here is not contrasted with any other meteorological phenomenon such as *ame* 'rain' or *yuki* 'snow.' What is being contrasted are the two propositions, 'The wind has already stopped (and it should be warmer)' and 'it is still cold.'

Sometimes the identifiability of a *wa*-phrase has consequences for the interpretation of elliptical arguments. Consider (28) and (29).

(28) kono hon wa   yonda   kedo mada rikai   dekinai
　　 this book TOP read:PAST but yet understanding can.do:NEG:NONPAST
　　 '(I) read this book, but (I) still cannot understand (= the book).'

(29) hon wa yonda   kedo mada   rikai   dekinai
　　 Book TOP read:PAST but not.yet understanding can.do:NEG:NONPAST
　　 'I read books, but I still cannot understand (e.g. the problem).'

In (28), the identifiable noun phrase *kono hon* 'this book,' with *wa*, is interpreted as an (object-)topic (hitching post), and multiple predicates may follow. Crucially, it is understood that the elliptical object of *rikai dekinai* 'cannot understand' is this topic. In (29), on the other hand, the nonidentifiable noun *hon* is not a topic, but part of the contrastive proposition, "reading books," which is related to some relevant proposition "I still don't understand." Here, the elliptical object of *rikai dekinai* 'cannot understand' is not *hon* 'books,' but is, for example, a complex problem that the speaker wanted to understand.

Contrastive meaning is readily available with postpositional phrases with *wa*, such as the following.

(30) a. _kyoo kara wa_ watashi ga   tannin   desu
       today ABL TOP I   NOM home.room.teacher COP
       'I will be your homeroom teacher from today.'

   b. _kare to wa_ hanashita kedo himitsu wa itte-inai
       he   COM TOP talk:PAST but secret TOP say:TE-ASP:NEG
       '(I) talked to him, but (I) have not told him (our) secret.'

   c. _hashi   de   wa_ taberarenai
       chopstick INST TOP eat:POT: NEG
       '(We) cannot eat (it) with chopsticks.'

Another notable use of contrastive *wa* is its use within a verbal and adjectival complex. To insert *wa* in a verb, a verb is split into the infinitive (*ren'yoo*) form and the dummy verb, *suru* 'do,' and *wa* is inserted between them. So, for example, the verb *kiku* 'to listen' is analyzed as '*kiki + suru*' and *wa* is inserted in the middle *kiki wa suru* '(someone) *does* listen.' This construction is used more often in the negative predicate. For adjectives, they are analyzed as the infinitive form and the dummy verb, *aru* 'exist' or its negative form *nai* 'does not exist,' and *wa* is inserted; *takai* 'expensive' > *takaku + wa + aru/nai*.

(31) a. hanashi o _kiki wa_ shitemo   nani mo jikkoo shinai
       story   ACC listen TOP do:though anything excecute:NEG
       '(He) listens to the story, but never does anything (about it.)'

   b. nondemo   _shini wa_ shinai yo
       drink:though die   TOP do: NEG PP
       'Even if you drink (this), you will not die.'

   c. _takaku   wa nai_ keredo amari   hoshikunai
       expensive TOP NEG though not.much want: NEG
       '(It's) not very expensive, but (I) don't want it really.'

3. The focus structure

3.1 Presupposition and assertion

Unmarked sentences have an information structure consisting of presupposition and assertion. Presupposition is the part that the addressee can or is willing to accept as "non-challengeable" based on various kinds of pragmatic knowledge (Givón 1982). The focus structure is closely associated with the topic structure, as a topic is (part of) the presupposition for which assertion is supplied, and assertion contains new and unpredictable information, that is, a focus. Consider the following minimal dialogue between A and B.

(32) A: jon   wa kyonen   no natsu doko e   itta ?
       (name) TOP last.year GEN summer where ALL go:PAST
       'Where did John go last summer?'

B: *(jon wa) nihon e itta.*
((name) TOP) Japan ALL go:PAST
'(He) went to Japan.'

The information structure of sentence (32B) can be described as: {presupposition, "John went to X"; assertion, "X = Japan"}. The relationship between the presupposition and the referent of the noun "Japan" is new and unpredictable on the part of the addressee. The term "focus domain" is employed here to refer to any item (e.g. "Japan" in the above) or a string of items which is not part of the presupposition in a sentence and contributes to the process of assertion. The focus domain in sentences such as (32B) overlaps with only one argument. This type of sentence is identified as a sentence with an "argument focus." (Here "argument" is used loosely to refer to both true arguments and adjunct-type constituents, cf. Chapter 6.)

The information structure cannot be gleaned from a sentence in isolation. Although (32B) above and (33B) below are identical in form, their information structures are different.

(33) A: *jon wa kyonen no natsu nani o shita?*
(name) TOP last.year GEN summer what ACC do:PAST
'What did John do last summer?'

B: *(jon wa) nihon e itta.*
((name) TOP) Japan ALL go:PAST
'(He) went to Japan.'

Since neither *itta* 'went' nor *nihon e* 'to Japan' is part of the presupposition for (33B), the focus domain is the entire comment, and this is a case of "comment focus." Notice that *nihon* 'Japan' by itself (e.g. *nihon desu* 'It's Japan') constitutes an answer for (32A), but not for (33A) (§3.3 below). The distinction between (32B) and (33B) can be summarized as follows.

Argument Focus:
(32B) = {presp., "John went to X"; assertion, "X = Japan"}
Comment Focus:
(33B) = {presp., "John did X"; assertion, "X = went to Japan"}

As seen in (32B) and (33B), an argument in the domain of the presupposition, if expressed, is marked morphologically by the particle *wa*. However, there is no special morphosyntactic markings available for a narrowly focused argument.[4] That is, an argument with a non-topic marking particle may be the focus domain itself, or it may be part of the larger

---

4. Phonologically, however, it is possible to single out the focus by assigning a focus prominence. That is, *nihon e* is pronounced with a higher pitch in (32B), while it is not in (33B).

focus domain in the comment focus structure. This is also applicable when the subject is marked with *ga*. Observe the next sentence.

(34) A: *dare ga kyonen no natsu nihon e kita?*
who NOM last.year GEN summer Japan ALL come:PAST
'Who came to Japan last summer?'

B: *jon ga kita.* (OR *jon desu*)
(name) NOM come:PAST (name) COP:NONPAST
'John came.' 'It's John.'

This is an argument focus sentence with the information structure: {presupposition, "X came to Japan"; assertion, "X = John"}. In this case the *ga*-marked noun phrase, *jon*, is the focus domain itself. Thus, *jon desu* 'It's John' is a possible response.

Now consider (35).

(35) *jon ga kita!*
(name) NOM come:PAST
'Here comes John!'

This sentence is an exclamatory sentence (§4.1 below) which conveys information that has no presupposition (i.e. "presp. = X"). The focus domain coincides with the entire sentence, and thus this is an example of a "sentence focus." Its information structure is as follows.

Sentence Focus: (35) = {presp., "X"; assertion, "X = John came"}.

The above examples indicate that non-topic marking particles (*ga, o, ni, e*, etc.) may appear with the argument that is itself the focus domain, or with an argument that is included in a larger focus domain, i.e. a comment. Although *ga* is often singled out from other non-topic marking particles as a particle of "focus," "new information," or "exhaustive listing" (Kuno 1973), it is not different from other non-topic marking particles in this respect (Shibatani 1990: 270–1). The focus reading is highlighted strongly in the case of *ga*, however, because the noun phrase marked by this particle is often the subject, and, as seen at the outset of the present chapter, the subject appears with *wa* as the topic much more frequently than any other argument. When the subject is not marked with *wa*, the discrepancy from the norm is felt much more strongly and thus projects the focus reading more forcefully.

3.2 Obligatory focus interpretation

Though it has been shown above that *ga* appears in both argument and sentence focus constructions, some sentences with *ga* are obligatorily interpreted as having an argument focus. This exclusive argument focus interpretation is the norm for sentences referring to a permanent state (e.g. 'John is a student') because such sentences in general cannot be made into an exclamatory sentence with focus over the entire sentence like (35), 'Here comes John!', above (but see §4.1 below). As a result, they are obligatorily interpreted as having an argument focus, with the (first) *ga*-marked noun phrase as the focus domain. Types of predicates involved in this situation are shown in (36) below: (a) stative verbs, (b) nominal predicates, (c) adjectival predicates, and (d) dynamic verbs in nonpast form with generic interpretation (cf. Kuno 1973; Matsuda 1997: 15–16).

(36) a. jon   ga   nihongo ga   dekiru
        (name) NOM   Japanese NOM   can.do:NONPAST
        'John (and only John) can speak Japanese.'

     b. mami   ga   kaikeeshi da
        (name) NOM   accountant COP
        'Mami is an accountant.'

     c. rosu   ga   imin   ga   ooi
        Los Angeles   NOM   immigrant NOM   many
        'In *Los Angeles* there are many immigrants.'

     d. kono inu ga   yoku nemuru
        this dog NOM well sleep:NONPAST
        '*This dog* sleeps well.'

Obligatory focus on the *ga*-marked phrase is observed even when other non-topical particles, such as *o*, co-exist with the predicate, so long as the dynamic verb indicates a generic situation, as shown in (37).

(37) <u>kono neko ga</u>   niku o   yoku taberu
     this cat   NOM   meat ACC well eat:NONPAST
     '*This cat* eats meat well.'

To focus on the *o*-marked phrase, the subject must be marked with *wa*, as in (38) below. Though (38) could be a comment focus sentence, with the appropriate pitch prominence on this constituent (either on *niku o* or only on *o*), it can be interpreted as a sentence with object argument focus. To clarify this even further, the verb may be modified with a nominalizer, *n(o)*, as in (39). This nominalization signals that the verb is part of the presupposition, and effectively marks off the *niku o* as the focus domain.

(38) kono neko wa   <u>niku o</u>   yoku taberu
     this cat TOP meat ACC   well eat:NONPAST
     'This cat eats meat well.'

(39) kono neko wa   <u>niku o</u>   yoku taberu   n(o) desu
     This cat TOP meat ACC   well eat:NONPAST   NML COP
     'This cat eats *meat* well.'

3.3 The cleft argument focus construction

The cleft sentence is a special type of sentence that isolates a focus domain. In English, the "it-cleft" (e.g. "It is Lisa who went to Japan") and "pseudo-cleft" or "WH-cleft" (e.g. "The one who went to Japan is Lisa") constructions are available. Japanese has only one type of cleft which positions the presupposed element as a topic, and the focus domain as a predicate, as in (40). This is structurally similar to the "pseudo-cleft." The Japanese cleft can isolate a noun phrase with a postposition particle, as shown in (41).

(40) nihon e itta no wa risa da
Japan ALL go:PAST NML TOP (name) COP
'It's Lisa who went to Japan.'

(41) risa ga itta no wa nihon (e) da
(name) NOM go:PAST NML TOP Japan (ALL) COP
'It's (to) Japan where Lisa went.'

The cleft sentence takes the form of "X wa Y da." X can either be a clause, as in the examples shown directly above, or a noun phrase. When X is a noun phrase, the cleft sentence superficially resembles the topic-comment sentence, but it is crucially different from it in that the *wa*-marked phrase in a cleft sentence must be non-referential and non-generic, and its predicate nominal must be referential. In contrast, and as discussed earlier, the *wa*-marked phrase in a topic-comment sentence must be identifiable, i.e. either referential or generic.

Cleft   :[non-ref./non-gen.] wa [referential NP] da
Topic-Comment :[ref./gen.] wa   NP   da

(42) below is a cleft sentence. The *wa*-marked phrase, *kyoo no pitchaa* 'today's pitcher,' is a non-referential noun phrase. (43), on the other hand, is a topic-comment sentence, because the *wa*-marked phrase is an identifiable, referential noun phrase.

(42) kyoo no pitchaa wa makoto da   (Cleft)
Today GEN pitcher TOP (name) COP
'It's Makoto who is today's pitcher.'

(43) ano pitchaa wa makoto da   (Topic-Comment)
that pitcher TOP (name) COP
'That pitcher is Makoto.'
NOT '*It's Makoto who is that pitcher.'

The cleft sentence, "X wa $\underline{Y}$ da," can be restated as "$\underline{Y}$ ga X da" by reversing the positions of X and Y, and changing the particles (i.e. argument focus). Thus (42) will render (42'). The difference is that Makoto appears as an argument focus in (42'), but as part of a comment focus in (42). However, a non-cleft sentence such as (43) cannot take this structure. See (43').

(42') makoto ga kyoo no pitchaa da
(name) NOM today GEN pitcher COP
It's Makoto who is today's pitcher.

(43') *makoto ga   ano pitchaa da
       (name) NOM that pitcher COP
       'That pitcher is Makoto.' (intended meaning)

4. The topic-less sentence

The topic-less sentence is characterized structurally by its lack of topic marking *wa*, and thus, unlike the topic-comment sentence, it does not entail the process of making a modal judgment. In other words, this type of sentence is not a prototypical declarative sentence. This also means that it does not impose the identifiability condition on the initial NP, so the non-identifiable noun phrase *dare* 'who' which cannot appear with *wa* can appear with the non-topic marking particle, *ga*, in the subject position. The speaker uses a topic-less sentence when he verbalizes his immediate perception without intending to communicate the information (exclamatory sentence), or when introducing a scene or an entity into the current discourse (presentational sentence).

4.1 The exclamatory sentence

Topic-less sentences with an exclamatory function are characterized by the deictic nature of their information and their lack of addressee. They are "self-speech, or inner-speech." It is a sentence of "thetic judgment," which represents a "direct response to the perceptual cognition of an actual situation" or "a simple recognition of the existence of an actual situation" (Kuroda 1992b: 22–23). It can be also characterized as a sentence with the sentence focus (§3 above).

In (44) below, the speaker verbalizes his perception of a dog walking as one entire scene, an unanalyzed whole. In this exclamatory sentence the process of predication, which occurs in a topic-comment sentence such as (45), is missing.

(44) inu ga   aruite-iru
      dog NOM walk:TE-ASP:NONPAST
      'There is a/the dog walking by.'

(45) inu wa   aruite-iru
      dog TOP walk:TE-ASP:NONPAST
      'The dog(, it) is walking.'

Although in the above pair the particles *wa* and *ga* seem crucial in the distinction of the two sentence types, the presence of *ga* is not actually a defining characteristic of the topic-less sentence. A *ga*-phrase appears only when the predicate requires such a node in a sentence. When a predicate does not specify a node to be coded with *ga*, the sentence does not include it. These sentences are traditionally called "one-word sentences" (*ichi-go bun* 一語文) (Mio 1948). The prefacing word *a*, *aa*, or *waa* in the following sentences is an exclamatory vocal sign (similar to the English 'look!,' 'oh,' and 'wow') and is used to clarify the exclamatory status of the sentence.

(46) *a! kaji da! / aa samui / waa kiree*
  fire COP   cold   beautiful
  'Look! Fire!' 'Oh, (I'm) cold.' 'Wow, so beautiful!'

Functionally, both one-word sentences such as (46) and sentences with *ga* such as (44) express information just perceived and new to the speaker. Such an immediate experience comes not only from perception but also from emotion and sensation. The expression of emotion is usually done with one-word sentences, and the expression of sensation and perception is done either with one-word or multi-word sentences, depending on the type of sensation or perception. Examples of emotion and sensation expressions are as follows.

(47) a. Emotion
   aa ureshii !   *aa yokatta !*
    happy:NONPAST   good:PAST
    'Oh, (I'm so) happy.' 'Oh, (I'm so) glad/relieved.'
   b. Sensation
   aa onaka ga   itai !   *aa nodo ga   kawaita*
    stomach NOM painful:NONPAST   throat NOM dry.up:PAST
    'Oh, (my) stomach hurts!'   'Oh, (I'm) thirsty.'

There are several kinds of perception: tactile (touch), gustatory (taste), equilibrium (motion), olfactory (smell), auditory (hearing), and visual (sight). For the most immediate perception of "touch," "taste," and "motion" sensations, the object stimulus cannot be directly expressed.

(48) Tactile perception
   a ! subesube !   *a ! zarazara !*
    smooth   rough
    'Oh, (it's) smooth!' (surface) 'Oh, (it's) rough!' (surface)

(49) Gustatory perception
   a!/aa karai !   *aa karakatta !*
    spicy:NONPAST   spicy:PAST
    'Oh, (it)'s spicy!'   'Oh, (it) was spicy!'

(50) Equilibrium perception
   a ! ugoita !   *a ! yurete-ru !*
    move:PAST   shake:TE-ASP:NONPAST
    'Oh, (the earth) moved!'   'Oh, (the earth's) shaking.'

In olfactory and auditory perception, it is possible to code an object stimulus with *ga* using an intransitive verb. For olfactory sensations, a semantically null verb (*suru*) is employed, and for auditory sensations, a specialized verb of auditory sensation (*kikoeru* 'hear') is also employed. Notice also that different aspectual information can be described depending on the inherent semantic make-up of the predicate.

(51) Olfactory perception
 a! hen na nioi ga suru / shite-iru
  strange COP:ATT smell NOM do:NONPAST / do:TE-ASP:NONPAST
 'Oh! (I) smell something strange./There is a strange smell here!'

 a! hen na nioi ga shita
        do:PAST
 'Oh! (I've) just smelled something strange.'

 a! hen na nioi ga shite-kita!
        do:TE-come:PAST
 'Oh! (I) can now smell something strange.'

(52) Auditory perception
 a! oto ga suru / shite-iru!
  sound NOM do:NONPAST / do:TE-ASP:NONPAST
 'Oh! (I) hear a sound.'

 a! oto ga shita
     do:PAST
 'Oh! (I've) just heard a sound.'

 a! oto ga kikoeru
     hear:NONPAST
 'Oh! (I) hear a sound.'

 a! oto ga kikoeta
     hear:PAST
 'Oh! (I've) just heard a sound.'

 a! oto ga kikoete-kita!
     hear:TE-come:PAST
 'Oh! (I) can now hear a sound.'

Visual perception may be expressed by a specialized visual perception verb *mieru* 'can see,' as shown in (53), or may also be expressed by many varieties of predicates, as in (54) and (55).

(53) Visual perception
 a! yama ga mieru
  mountain NOM see:NONPAST
 'Oh! (I) can see a mountain.'

 a! yama ga mieta / miete-kita!
  mountain NOM see:PAST / see:TE-come:PAST
 'Oh! (I) just saw/can now see a mountain.'

(54) Visual perception of states
   a! yama ga aru!
   mountain NOM exist:NONPAST
   'Oh! there's a mountain!'

   a! inu ga iru!
   dog NOM exist:NONPAST
   'Oh, there's a dog!'

   a! saifu ga ochite-iru
   wallet NOM fall:TE-ASP:NONPAST
   'Oh there's a wallet (on the ground)!'

   a! sora ga akai!
   sky NOM red:NONPAST
   'Oh, the sky is red!'

(55) Visual perception of events
   a! tori ga tobu / tonda
   bird NOM fly:NONPAST / fly:PAST/
   'Oh, a bird is going to fly!/ has just flown!'

   a! tori ga tonde-iru / tonde-kita!
   bird NOM fly:TE-ASP:NONPAST / fly:TE-come:PAST
   'Oh, a bird is flying!/ has flown over here!'

4.2 The presentational sentence

As noted in the section directly above, topic-less, exclamatory sentences are "self-speech, or inner-speech." However, a speaker may use topic-less sentences with certain modifications to externalize his self-/inner-speech for the sake of the addressee, in either the immediate or a temporally displaced context. The speaker may also use topic-less sentences to introduce non-identifiable and non-activated concepts into a discourse (Chafe 1987). These topic-less sentences are subsumed under "presentational sentences." The next examples are presentational sentences marked by interactional devices such as the addressee honorific suffix, *-masu*, and the pragmatic particle, *yo*. They communicate to the addressee the speaker's perception in the immediate temporal context in (56), or in a temporally displaced context in (57) and (58).

(56) *tori ga tonde-imasu yo*
   bird NOM fly:TE-APS:POL:NONPAST PP
   '(Look!) There is a bird flying by, you see!'

(57) *sakki gasu no nioi ga shite-imashita yo*
   moments.ago gasu GEN smell NOM do:TE-ASP:POL:PAST PP
   'There was a smell of gas moments ago, you know.'

(58) yumi   ga   bosuton ni   imashita   yo
     (name) NOM   (place) LOC   exist:POL:PAST   PP
     'Yumi was in Boston, you know.'

Presentational sentences are often found in the opening of folk tales, as in (59) or of newspaper articles as in (60).

(59) mukashi   mukashi   aru   tokoro   ni
     old.days old.days one   place   LOC

     ojiisan   to   obaasan   ga   sunde-imashita
     old.man   COM   old.woman NOM   live:TE-ASP:POL:PAST
     'Once upon a time there lived in some place an old man and an old woman.'

(60) nasa   no   uchiageta   roketto ga
     NASA   GEN   launch:PAST   rocket NOM

     kinoo   kasee   ni   toochaku-shita
     yesterday   Mars   DAT   arrival-do:PAST
     'The rocket that NASA launched arrived on Mars yesterday.'

The referents of *ojiisan to obaasan* 'old man and old woman' in (59) above are not identifiable since they are introduced in this sentence for the first time. The referent of *nasa no uchiageta roketto* 'the rocket that NASA had launched' in (60) may be identifiable, but it is not activated in the minds of the readers (If it were, it would be marked by *wa*). The presentational construction overtly introduces these referents into a discourse. From this point on, the speaker (writer) may make comments on the identifiable and activated referents using topic-comment sentences.

5. The mixed-type sentence

As demonstrated above, the exclamatory sentence has the restriction that its predicate must represent some deictically perceptible information. Because such a deictic condition is imposed on the topic-less sentence, it is not compatible, as mentioned, with generic sentences in which predicates convey permanent states. That is why (63) and (64) are not grammatical, though (61) and (62) are. ((63) without the exclamatory *a!* can be interpreted as argument-focus sentences and is then acceptable. See §2.2.)

(61) jon   wa   nihongo   ga   dekiru
     (name)   NOM   Japanese   NOM   can.do:NONPAST
     'John can speak Japanese.'

(62) hi   wa   nishi   ni   shizumu
     sun   NOM   west   DAT   sink:NONPAST
     'The sun sets in the west.'

Chapter 11. Information structure and the sentence form

(63) * a! jon   ga   nihongo ga   dekiru !
         (name) NOM Japanese NOM can.do:NONPAST
         'Oh! John can speak Japanese!'

(64) * a! hi   ga   nishi ni   shizumu !
         sun NOM west   DAT sink:NONPAST
         'Oh! The sun is going to set in the west!'

There is one strategy available, however, to express newly discovered generic states. When the speaker has suddenly realized or been informed that John can speak Japanese, he can utter (63′).

(63′) a! jon   (wa)   nihongo ga   dekiru-n   da!
           (name) (TOP) Japanese NOM can.do-SE   COP
           'Oh! John, (he) can speak Japanese!'

This kind of sentence is characterized by the deletability of the topic-marking particle and the presence of the nominalizer -n (a shortened form of no, and here glossed as SE – sentence extender) attached to the predicate. Nominalization of a sentence can work to suppress a speaker's modal judgment, which is normally associated with declarative sentences (Iwasaki 2000). Here are a few more examples.

(65) a. a! yumi   (wa)   kekkon-shite-(i)ru-n   da!
             (name) (TOP) marriage-do:TE-ASP:NONPAST-SE   COP
             'Oh! Yumi is married!'

     b. a! kimi-tachi (wa)   kyoodai-na-n   da!
             you-PL   (TOP) brother-COP-SE COP
             'Oh! You two are brothers!'

     c. a! omae (wa)   atama   ii-n   da!
             you   (TOP) head   good-COP-SE   COP
             'Oh! You are smart!'

There is another mixed-type sentence. It was noted earlier that exclamatory sentences expressing tactile and gustatory perceptions do not code the source of stimuli. The speaker may, however, identify a stimulus (with the ko series deixis), connect it with a perception predicate and express the connection. In this case, however, neither ga nor wa can be used, instead, a deictic expression is simply juxtaposed with the predicate. An interesting observation is that the order of the two parts is easily reversed, making both (66) and (67) possible (cf. Ono & Suzuki 1992).

(66) Tactile perception (S- Pred. order)
      a ! kono kami   subesube !   a ! kore atsui !
          this paper smooth   this hot
          'Oh, this paper is smooth!'   'Oh, this is hot!'

Gustatory perception (S- Pred. order)
a ! kono keeki oishii!   a ! kore karai !
    this cake delicious   this spicy
'Oh, this case is delicious!'   'Oh, this is spicy!'

(67) Tactile perception (Pred.-S order)
a ! subesube kono kami !   a ! atsui kore !
    smooth   this paper   hot   this
'Oh, this paper is smooth!'   'Oh, this is hot!'

Gustatory perception (Pred.-S order)
a ! oishii   kono keeki!   a ! karai kore!
    delicious this cake   spicy this
'Oh, this cake is delicious!'   'Oh, this is spicy!'

Although the speaker is reporting his immediate perception with these utterances, it is not pure perception. This is because the speaker has already identified the stimulus with *kore* 'this' or *kono* 'this (+ noun)', making this sentence somewhat similar to the topic-comment sentence. Similarly, some sentences expressing emotion or sensation which are normally expressed as one-word sentences may add the first person experiencer without a particle (Shibatani 1990: 368). In this case, the first person experiencer and the other constituent can also be easily reversed.

(68) Emotion
watashi kuyashii
I   mortified:NONPAST   'I'm mortified.'

(69) Sensation
boku onaka   (ga)   suita
I   stomach (NOM) empty:NONPAST   'I'm hungry.'

These mixed-type sentences show grammar's great adaptability to accommodate a speaker's need to express various kinds of information.

CHAPTER 12

Clause combining

Coordination and subordination are two commonly discussed types of clause combining strategies, but in Japanese a clear coordination strategy is lacking. Instead, the three strategies of "conjoining," "adverbial subordination," and "temporal chaining" are used quite frequently in discourse. The canonical structure of a two-clause sentence can be shown to have the following structure.

$$[\quad - \text{CCF}\,]_{\text{NFC}} \quad [\quad - \text{FF}\,]_{\text{FC}}$$
(NFC = non-finite clause; FC = finite clause; CCF = clause combining form; FF = finite form)

The reverse order of non-finite and finite clauses may occur for various pragmatic reasons, especially for the adverbial subordination type in spoken discourse. When a series of clauses are concatenated, the clause chain shows the following structure.

$$[\quad - \text{CCF}\,]_{\text{NFC1}} \quad [\quad - \text{CCF}\,]_{\text{NFC2}} \cdots [\quad - \text{FF}\,]_{\text{FC}}$$

In this chapter, conjoining and adverbial subordination are described in Sections 1 and 2, respectively, in the minimum structure consisting of one non-finite and one finite clause. Chaining and multiple clause concatenation are discussed in Section 3.

1. Conjoining

There are two types of conjoining: "coupling" and "contrast" (Longacre 1983: 82–89). The former is a non-temporal "and" relation, while the latter is a "but" relation.

1.1 Coupling

The conjunctive (-*te*) form is the most common coupling form. For adjectival and verbal predicates, the infinitive form may also be used in written discourse ((2) and (3) below).

(1) *taroo   wa   yuukan   de   kashikoi*
    (name) TOP courageous COP:TE smart
    'Taro is courageous and smart.'

(2) *kono chihoo   wa   natsu   wa   atsuku(te) fuyu   wa   samui*
    this district TOP summer   TOP hot(:TE)   winter TOP cold
    'In this district, it is hot during the summer and cold during winter.'

(3) ue   no   ko   wa tookyoo de   umarete/umare
    above COP:ATT child TOP (place) LOC   be.born:TE/be.born:INF
    shita no   ko   wa hawai   de   umareta
    bottom COP:ATT child TOP (place) LOC   be.born:PAST
    'The older child was born in Tokyo, and the younger one in Hawaii.'

Notice that when the subject of the two clauses is identical, as in (1), it must appear at the beginning of the entire sentence, and must be elided in the second clause. If a "pronoun" (e.g. *kare* 'he') is used in the second clause in (1), it usually does not refer to the subject of the first clause.[1] Thus, in a strict sense, (1) is not clause combining, but rather predicate combining, or a linkage with "core-juncture." (3) is a clearer example of clause combining with two different subjects, or a linkage with "clausal juncture" (Hasegawa 1996; Foley & Van Valin 1984). The linkage in (2) is also a clausal juncture, but the two clauses share the same topic, *kono chihoo* 'this district.'

Besides the clause (and predicate) combination with the conjunction and infinitive forms, there are also semantically more marked coupling forms. The conjunctive particle *shi* adds information with the meaning "and what's more." (1) and (2) may be re-written with *yuukan da shi* and *atsui shi*, respectively. (3) may not use *shi*, because it does not convey the "and what's more" meaning. Here is another example.[2]

---

1. This restriction is related to the *wa*'s "comma-crossing" function (Chapter 11 §1). That is, the force of *wa* extends to the end of a sentence crossing over the written punctuation of comma. This means that in an embedded context where *wa* cannot appear, as in the following example, the restriction is relaxed, and *kare* 'he' can be coreferential with *Taro*. The embedded clause is shown in brackets in the sentence below.

   [taroo ga   yuukan   de   kare ga   kashikoi] koto wa
   (name) TOP   courageous COP:TE he   NOM smart   NML TOP
   daredemo   shitteiru
   anyone   know
   'Every one knows that [Taro is courageous and he is smart].'

2. The two clauses combined with *shi* are often presented as a reason/cause for another clause. Thus, (4) may be expanded very naturally as (i).

   (i) moo   pasupooto mo   yooi-shita   shi
        already passport   also preparation-do:PAST   and
        kippu   mo   katta   kara itsudemo dekakerareru
        ticket   also buy:PAST   so   anytime   leave:POT:NONPAST
        '(I) have already prepared a passport, and what's more (I) have also bought a ticket, so I can leave anytime.'

Furthermore, the *shi* clause may simply imply the second reason/cause, and directly connect to the consequence, as in (ii) (Martin [1975] 1991:976).

(4) moo   pasupooto mo yooi-shita   shi
     Already passport also preparation-do:PAST and

   kippu mo katta
   ticket also buy:PAST

   '(I) have already gotten my passport ready, and what's more, (I) have also bought a ticket.'

Representative or repeated actions are conjoined with *-tari*. When the *-tari* form (glossed as REP) appears in a sequence, the final *tari* clause must be followed by the formal verb *suru*, as in (5) below. The *-tari* form may appear alone with *suru*. In this case, other actions are implied, as shown in (6).[3]

(5) hima-na   toki wa   hon   o   yondari   sanpo
     free-COP:ATT   time TOP book ACC read:REP walk

   o   shitari-suru
   ACC do:REP -do:NONPAST

   'When (I) have free time, (I) do such things as read books and take walks.'

(6) hima-na   toki wa   hon   o   yondari-suru
     free-COP:ATT   time TOP book ACC read:REP-do:NONPAST

   'When (I) have free time, (I) read books and so forth.'

1.2 Contrast

Contrast is expressed by *keredomo* (and its variant forms *kedomo* and *kedo*) or *ga* (cf. *no-ni* in §2.4 below). The former, especially the short form, *kedo*, is common in colloquial discourse, while *ga* is more formal and used often in written discourse. In (7) a favorable quality (the price being cheap) and an unfavorable quality (the food being poor quality) are compared. (8) is taken from a folk tale *Kabe no tsuru* 'A Crane on the Wall' by Tsubota (1975), and (9) is taken from a short story, *Hotaru-gawa, doro no kawa* 'Firefly River, Muddy River' by Miyamoto (1994: 16).

(7) ano mise   yasui <u>kedo</u>, umakunai   yo
     that restaurant cheap but   delicious:NEG PP

   'That restaurant is cheap but not very good, you know.'

(ii) moo   pasupooto mo yooi-shita   shi
      already passport also preparation-do:PAST and

   itsudemo dekakerareru
   anytime   leave:POT:NONPAST

   '(I) have already bought a ticket and so forth, so I can leave anytime.'

3. This use of the *-tari* form is typical in written discourse. In spoken discourse, it is usually used alone like (6) to add an impression of hedging (Taylor 2010).

(8) *zeni wa nai no da ga, chotto o-sake o*
Money TOP exist:NEG SE COP but, a.little PFX-rice.wine ACC
nom-asete-kudasaranai ka.
drink-CAU:TE-give:HON:NEG:NONPAST Q
'(I) don't have any money, but would you let me drink a little *sake* (anyway)?'

(9) *sadako ga yonde-ita ga nobuo*
(name) NOM call:TE-ASP:PAST but (name)
wa ugokenakatta
TOP move:POT:NEG:PAST
'Sadako was calling, but Nobuo could not move.'

Both *keredomo* (*keredomo, kedo*) and *ga* can also have a coupling meaning, instead of a contrast.[4]

(10) *aitsu wa yuukan da kedo/ga, atama mo ii*
that.guy TOP courageous COP but head also good
'That guy is courageous, and he is also smart.'

---

4. Both *keredomo* (*keredo, kedo*) and *ga* have evolved into independent conjunctives. The conjunctive particle *ga* was originally used only as a conjunctive particle bound to the predicate to its left, as in (i) below, but in modern Japanese it can also start a sentence, as in (ii). The erstwhile inflectional ending *keredomo* and its shortened forms *keredo* and *kedo* also function both as conjunctive particles and as independent conjunctives (Matsumoto 1988).

(i) *ame wa futte-iru ga, // samuku wa nai.*
rain TOP fall:TE-ASP:NONPAST but cold:INF TOP NEG:NONPAST
'It is raining, but it's not cold.'

(ii) *ame wa futte-iru. // ga samuku wa na-i.*
rain TOP fall:TE-ASP:NONPAST but cold:INF TOP NEG:NONPAST
'It is raining. However, it's not cold.'

Finally, *kedo* and *ga*, especially the former, may appear without a main clause in spoken discourse. These conjunctive particles work as a sort of pragmatic particle which weakens the force of assertion. Some of them are conventionalized expressions, as in (iii), while some others are not (Chapter 4 §2.2.2; Chapter 14 §3.2; Nakayama & Nakayama-Ichihashi 1997; Haugh 2008).

(iii) *anoo... yamada desu ga/kedo*
uhm (name) COP but
'Hello, this is Yamada, but ...'
(A common caller identification on the telephone.)

2. Adverbial subordination

The adverbial subordinate clause supplies various types of adverbial information such as time, condition, cause/reason to another clause (the reference clause). Below, adverbial clauses are listed according to the type of adverbial information they encode. There is more than one form within each type, and each conveys a slightly different meaning within the general meaning. Only the most frequently used forms are listed. Also, in the following presentation, one adverbial clause is followed by one reference clause, but in actual discourse, as briefly mentioned earlier and to be demonstrated in §1.3 below, the reference clause may be followed by another clause, creating a series of clauses.

2.1 Temporal clauses

Temporal adverbial clauses interact closely with the tense/aspect system of the language (Chapter 4 §2.1.1, Chapter 7 §1). The following adverbial clauses are described.

"when": [V:nonpast/past *toki (ni)*]
"before": [V:nonpast *mae (ni)*]; [V:non-pst, negative *uchi ni*]
"after": [V:past *ato (de/ni)*; [V:TE *kara*]
"while": [V:TE *iru uchi (ni)*]; [V:TE *iru aida (ni)*] ;
[V:INF-*nagara*]

2.1.1 "When" (General time)

The conjunction *toki* is a noun meaning 'time.' Thus structurally, the clause preceding *toki* is a clausal modifier, and the whole expression, [V-nonpast/past *toki*], is a noun phrase. Being a noun phrase, it may be followed by the particle indicating time, *ni*, and it may be also topicalized with *ni wa* or simply *wa*. When the main clause is in the past tense, the choice of tense form in the *toki* clause is influenced by the type of the verb in the *toki* clause. If it is a stative verb, either past or nonpast tense form can be used without altering the meaning, as in (11) (see Chapter 7, Note 4). However, when it is a dynamic verb, the nonpast tense form indicates that the action in the main clause occurs before the action in the *toki* clause ends, as in (12), and the past tense form indicates that the action in the main clause occurs after the action in the *toki* clause ends, as in (13) (Chapter / §1).

(11) boku   wa   tookyoo ni   iru/ita   toki
     I(male) TOP   Tokyo   DAT   stay:NONPAST/PAST   when
     yoku   kabuki   o   mi-ni   itta
     often   Kabuki   ACC   see-PURP   go:PAST
     'I went to see Kabuki often when (I) was in Tokyo.'

(12) taroo   wa   basu   o   oriru   toki   tsumazuita
     (name)   TOP   bus   ACC   get.off:NONPAST   when   trip:PAST
     'Taro tripped while he was getting off the bus.'

(13) taroo   wa   basu   o   orita   toki   tsumazuita
     (name)   TOP   bus   ACC get.off:PAST when   trip:PAST
     'Taro tripped when he got off the bus.'

Each of the example sentences shown just above have the same subject for both the adverbial and main clauses. In this case the *wa* phrase may be placed right before the main predicate in the reference clause rather than in the initial position of the entire clause chain, as shown in (11′) below.

(11′) tookyoo   ni   iru/ita   toki
      Tokyo   DAT   stay:NONPAST/PAST   when
      boku wa   yoku   kabuki   o   mi-ni   itta
      I   TOP   often   Kabuki   ACC   see-PURP   go:PAST
      'I went to see Kabuki often when (I) was in Tokyo.'

This means the proper analysis of the structure such as (11) should be the following. (See (11) in Chapter 11 §1.1).

[NP-*wa*]   [ADVERBIAL CLAUSE]   [Ref. CLAUSE]

And the variant form such as found in (11') is described as:

[ADVERBIAL CLAUSE]   [NP-*wa*]   [Ref. CLAUSE]

(See the discussion of the "comma crossing" in Note 1 for this chapter.).

2.1.2 *"Before"*

The most common conjunction to indicate 'before,' is *mae* 'before.' Like *toki*, *mae* is also a noun, and it means 'front.' The tense form in the *mae* clause is invariably nonpast (Chapter 7 §1).

(14) boku   wa   tookyoo   ni   iku   mae   (ni)
     I(male)   TOP   (place)   DAT   go:NONPAST   before   (DAT)
     yoshiko   ni   denwa-suru
     (name)   DAT   telephone-do:NONPAST
     'I will telephone Yoshiko before (I) go to Tokyo/before going to Tokyo.'

(15) boku   wa   tookyoo   ni   iku   mae   (ni)
     I(male)   TOP   (place)   DAT   go:NONPAST   before   (DAT)
     yoshiko   ni   denwa-shita
     (name)   DAT   telephone-do:PAST
     'I telephoned Yoshiko before (I) went to Tokyo/before going to Tokyo.'

The *uchi* clause (see also the 'while' clause in §2.1.4 below) with the negative nonpast form also expresses the meaning of 'before.' *Uchi* is a noun meaning 'inside,' and the particle *ni* often follows. This adverbial clause, as compared to the *mae(ni)* clause, tends to code the speaker's negative evaluation on the event expressed with the negative form and urgency for the action coded in the reference clause (McGloin 1989:9).

(16) *ame ga   furanai   uchi ni*
       rain NOM fall:NEG:NONPAST   while DAT

  hitohashiri suru/shita
  one-run   do:NONPAST/PAST

  '(I) will run/ran for a while before it rains/rained.'

2.1.3 "After"

The most common conjunction to indicate 'after,' is *ato* 'trace, behind, later.' The particle which follows *ato* is usually *de*, but sometimes *ni* (see Kuno 1973: 159–167). The tense form in the *ato* clause is invariably past (Chapter 7 §1).

(17) *boku   wa   yoshiko ni   denwa-**shita**   ato   (de)*
       I(male) TOP   (name) DAT telephone-do:PAST   after (LOC)

  *michiko ni   mo   denwa-**suru***
  (name) DAT also telephone-do:NONPAST

  'I will telephone Michiko after (I) telephone Yoshiko.'

(18) *boku wa yoshiko ni denwa-**shita**   ato   (de)*
                            telephone-do:PAST after (LOC)

  *michiko ni mo denwa-**shita***
                  telephone-do:PAST

  'I telephoned Michiko after (I) telephoned Yoshiko.'

Another important adverbial clause with the 'after' meaning is formed with the *-te* form followed by the *kara* form. (17′), for example, is equivalent to either (17) or (18).

(17′) *boku   wa   yoshiko ni   denwa-shite-kara*
       I(male) TOP   (name) DAT telephone:TE-from

  michiko ni   mo   denwa-suru   / shita
  (name) DAT also telephone-do:NONPAST / do-PAST

  'I will telephone / telephoned Michiko after telephoning Yoshiko.'

2.1.4 "While"

The most common conjunctions to indicate simultaneity are *uchi* 'inside' and *aida* 'duration.' The verb in the *uchi/aida* clause is invariably nonpast, and often takes the progressive aspect form.

(19) *kodomo ga   nete-iru   uchi/aida ni   shigoto o   shita*
       child   NOM sleep:TE-ASP:NONPAST while   DAT work   ACC do:PAST

  '(I) worked while the child was sleeping.'

The subjects of the *uchi/aida* clause and reference clause are usually different, as in (19). If the subject of 'worked' needs to be expressed in (19), *watashi wa* can be added before the adverbial clause, or before the reference clause. To express the simultaneous actions of a single agent, a different adverbial clause consisting of the infinitive (*ren'yoo*) form of a verb followed by *nagara* is used.

(20) kodomo-tachi wa uta o utai-nagara aruite-kita
 child-PL TOP song ACC sing:INF-while walk:TE-come:PAST
 'The children came, singing a song.'

2.2 Conditionals

There are four distinct conditional forms: two with the inflectional endings *-ba* and *-tara*, and two with the conditional conjunctions *nara* and *to*. Each form has a core conditional meaning, which has been extended to include other related meanings. For the most part, the core functions of the four forms are discussed here (cf. Thompson & Longacre 1985; Masuoka 1993; Akatsuka & Tsukamoto 1998).

Reality Conditionals
    Generic: *-ba/to*
    Specific: *nara*
Unreality Conditionals
    Predictive: *-tara*
    Hypothetical: *-tara (or -ba)*
    Counterfactual: *-tara (or -ba / nara)*

2.2.1 Reality conditionals

Reality conditionals place an objectively verifiable premise in the conditional clause and the resulting consequence in the reference clause. The generic conditional states a general condition under which a certain situation always follows. The *-ba* conditional expresses a universal generic conditional which specifies a law-like relationship between two situations.

(21) kono botan o oseba doa ga aku
 this button ACC push:COND door NOM open:NONPAST
 'If (one) pushes this button, the door will open.'

The *to* conditional can also express a universal generic condition (e.g. in (21) *osu to* can replace *oseba*), but it is also used for the habitual behavior of some specific individual, and in that case the *-ba* form cannot replace *to* in (22).

(22) taroo wa sake o nomu to
 (name) TOP liquor ACC drink COND
 sugu kao ga akaku-naru
 immediately face NOM red:KU-become:NONPAST
 'Taro's face immediately gets red whenever he drinks liquor.'

The specific conditional uses either present or past events as the basis for conjecture. *Nara* is used for this type of conditional. Notice that the matrix clauses are marked with modal expressions in the following sentences.

(23) ame ga futte-iru nara ha wa zenbu
 rain NOM fall:TE-ASP:NONPAST COND leaf TOP all
 ochite-shimatta daroo
 fall:TE-ASP:PAST AUX
 'If it is raining, the leaves must have all fallen.'

(24) genba ni ita nara hannin no kao o
 Location DAT stay:PAST COND culprit GEN face ACC
 mite-iru hazu da
 see:TE-ASP:NONPAST AUX COP
 'If (he) was at the scene (of the crime), he must have seen the culprit's face.'

The *nara* conditional often takes the condition given in the prior speech by the interlocutor, or in the context (Akatsuka 1985).

(25) A: oo samui
 Oh cold:NONPAST
 'Oh, I'm cold.'

 B: samui nara motto nanika kinasai
 cold:NONPAST COND more something wear:IMP
 'If it is the case that you are cold, then wear something more!'

2.2.2 Unreality conditionals

Unreality conditionals use the speaker's prediction or imagination as the basis for a conjectural statement. The type of conditional (predictive, hypothetical, or counterfactual) is determined by the degree of certainty ascribed to the adverbial clause information (Akatsuka 1985). The *-tara* conditional is the canonical form, but *nara* is used with nouns or nominal adjectives. (The *-tara* form also has a chaining function – see §3 below).

Predictive
(26) kono hon o yondara kashite-ageru yo
 this book ACC read:COND lend:TE-give:NONPAST PP
 'When (I) finish reading this book, (I) will lend it to (you).'

Hypothetical
(27) moshi takarakuji ni atattara ogotte-yaru yo
 if lottery DAT hit:COND treat:TE-give:NONPAST PP
 'If (I) win the lottery, (I) will treat (you).'

Counterfactual

(28) *moshi kimi ga kite-kurenakattara boku wa*
if you NOM come:TE-give:NEG:COND I(male) TOP

shinde-ita daroo
die:TE-ASP:PAST AUX

'If you hadn't come, I would have died.'

(29) *moshi boku ga kanemochi nara suguni mondai o*
if I(male) NOM rich.man COND immediately problem ACC

kaiketsu dekiru noni
solve can:NONPAST AUX

'If I were rich, I could solve the problem right away.'

Hypothetical and counterfactual conditionals can be headed by the adverb, *moshi* 'if,' and the counterfactual conditional must be followed by an auxiliary element such as *daroo* and *noni*.

2.2.3 *Concessive conditionals*

The *-te* form followed by particle *mo* 'also' indicates the concessive conditional ('even if') with the predictive, hypothetical, or counterfactual conditionals. Another expression, *-ta to shite* (-PAST QT do:TE), can substitute the *-te* form; *younde mo > younda to shitemo, atatte mo > atatta to shite mo, kurete mo > kureta to shite mo*. The copula, *demo*, changes to *datta to shite mo*.

(30) Predictive
hon o yonde mo wakaranai daroo
book ACC read:TE also understand:NEG:NONPAST AUX
'Even if (I) read books, (I) probably won't understand (the matter).'

(31) Hypothetical
moshi takarakuji ni atatte mo ogotte-yaranai yo
if ottery DAT hit:TE also treat:TE-give:NEG:NONPAST PP
'Even if (I) win the lottery, (I) will not treat (you).'

(32) Counterfactual
moshi kimi ga tasukete-kurete-ite mo boku wa
if you NOM help:TE-give:TE-AUX:TE also I TOP

shippai-shite-ita daroo
fail-do:TE-ASP:PAST AUX

'Even if you had helped me, I would have failed.'

(33) *moshi boku ga kanemochi demo / datta to shite mo*
if I(male) NOM rich.man COND / COP:PAST QT do:TE also

suguni	wa	mondai	o	kaiketsu	dekinai		daroo
immediately	TOP	problem	ACC	solve	can:NEG:NONPAST		AUX

'If I were rich, I could solve the problem right away.'

2.3 Cause/reason

Adverbial clauses that state the cause of an effect are marked by *node, tame (ni), see de* and so forth. *Node* is constructed from the nominalizer *no* and the particle *de*.

(34) | kyoo | wa | ame | ga | futta | node | sankasha | wa | sukunakatta |
|---|---|---|---|---|---|---|---|---|
| today | TOP | rain | NOM | fall:PAST | because | participant | TOP | few:PAST |

'There were only a few participants, since it rained today.'

Adverbial clauses which state the reason for an action are marked by *kara*. Note the form preceding *kara* is the finite form. If it is the *-te* form, the clause is an 'after' clause (§2.1.3 above).

(35) | ii | kusuri | o | **nonda** | kara | sugu | naotta |
|---|---|---|---|---|---|---|
| good | medicine | ACC | drink:PAST | because | immediately | recover:PAST |

'(I) recovered immediately since (I) took some good medicine.'

cf. | kusuri | o | **nonde** | kara sugu | neta |
|---|---|---|---|---|
| medicine | ACC | drink:TE | from immediately | sleep:PAST |

'(I) went to bed immediately after taking some medicine.'

2.4 Counter expectation

Information is presented in the matrix clause as an unexpected result or consequence ensuing from the situation presented in the *noni* adverbial clause. While the conjoining *keredo/kedo* indicates a weaker contrast, the *noni* imparts a sense of strong surprise. *Noni* (the nominalizer followed by the particle *ni*) can be contrasted morphologically and semantically with the cause/ reason adverbial clause marker, *node*, above (§2.3).

(36) | takusan | neta | noni | mada | nemui |
|---|---|---|---|---|
| lots | sleep:PAST | though | still | be.sleepy:NONPAST |

'Though (I) slept a lot, (I) am still sleepy.'

A marker of contrast *keredomo, keredo,* or *kedo* (§1.2) can substitute for *noni* in (36). However, the degree of counter expectation is stronger with *noni*, and thus the *kedo* in the earlier Example (7), repeated below, cannot be replaced by *noni*. If *noni* were used, the reference clause would have to show unexpected information, as in (37).

(7) | ano | mise | yasui | <u>kedo,</u> | umakunai | yo |
|---|---|---|---|---|---|
| that | restaurant | cheap | but | delicious:NEG | PP |

'That restaurant is cheap but not very good, you know.'

(37) ano mise   yasui *noni,* totemo umai   n da yo
     that restaurant cheap but very delicious:PP SE COP PP
     'Though that restaurant is cheap, it is very good, you know.'

2.5 Purpose

Purpose is expressed by adverbial clauses marked by [nonpast]*yoo-ni*, [nonpast]*tame-ni*, [nonpast]*(no) ni wa* and so forth.

(38) yamada-shichoo   wa kodomo-tachi ga   asob-eru
     (name)-Mayor   TOP child-PL   NOM play-POT:NONPAST
     yoo   ni   kooen o   tsukutta
     fashion COP:ADV park ACC make:PAST
     'Mayor Yamada built a park so that children can play.'

(39) kenkoo o   tamotsu   tame   ni   mainichi undo
     health ACC keep:NONPAST   purpose DAT every da exercises
     o   shite-iru
     ACC do:TE-ASP:NONPAST
     '(I) exercise everyday in order to stay healthy.'

2.6 Circumstantials

Circumstantial information may be expressed by a complement clause headed by a formal noun *tokoro* 'place' or *no* as seen in (40). (This is the same as (50) in Chapter 10, §3. See that section for a detailed discussion).

(40) keeji   wa   [taroo   ga   kenjuu o   tsukue no ue ni   oita]
     detective TOP (name) NOM gun   ACC desk   GEN top LOC put:PAST
     no/tokoro o   toriosaeta
     NML   ACC arrest:PAST
     'The detective arrested Taro when he put the gun on the desk.'

The *tokoro* complements in these sentences are structurally the direct object of the matrix verb, but functionally they provide adverbial (circumstantial) information.

3. Clause chaining and continuity marking

The coupling strategy described in §1.1 of this chapter connects two semantically similar clauses without temporal sequence. Thus reversing the two clauses will not affect the information significantly. In contrast, the clause chaining strategy is employed typically to express temporally sequenced events, and the reversal of clause order will create wrong representation of information. In clause chaining, a "medial" clause with a non-finite verb is linked to the next clause, which may be a medial clause itself or a terminal clause. Thus, a sentence using the chaining strategy consists of one or more medial clauses and one terminal clause. Schematically, a sentence with chained clauses is as below.

[MC1] ([MC2] ......) [TC]
(MC = medial clause; TC = terminal clause)

When a chain of clauses reports a series of past events, two kinds of medial verb forms are employed to mark whether the next event is a continuous or discontinuous event from the current one (Watanabe 1994). This system is reminiscent of "switch reference," a system in which the "marking clause" contains a morpheme to signal whether or not the subject of the next clause, the "reference clause," is the same as that of the marking clause (Iwasaki 1993).

In the spoken mode, the -*te* form is the most typical medial form for continuous events (with the same subject) and the -*tara* conditional form is the typical medial form for discontinuous events (with a different subject). In (41) below, an excerpt from an actual spoken narrative, three clauses are strung together with the -*te* form, and the fourth clause ends the chain with the finite verb form. The speaker explains an incident that she and her husband experienced during their trip to Eastern Europe. The excerpt starts at the end of an evening spent with a German family whom they had befriended. These four clauses report four different but continuous actions by the speaker and her husband in chronological order.

(41)
1. de   doomo-arigatoo   tte   **itte**
   then   "thank you"   QT   say:TE

2. soide **modotte**
   then   return:TE

3. **nete**
   sleep:TE

4. soide   tsugi   no   asa   itta   wake
   then   next   GEN   morning   go:PAST   SE

   '...then (we) said "thank you," and
   then (we) returned (to our tent), and
   slept, and
   then the next day (we) went (to their tent).'

In (42), an excerpt from a different narrative, the first two clauses are chained with -*te* (conjunctive form) but the third one is marked by -*tara* (conditional form) because the next clause expresses a discontinuous event with a different subject changed from the covert 'I' to *yakkosan* 'the guy.' The covert subject for clause is understood to be the 'guy' because clause 4 ends with the *-te* form.

(42)
1. *soshite hairenakute*
   then   enter:POT:NEG:TE
2. *okoshite*
   wake.up:TE
3. *de   haittara*
   then enter:COND
4. *yakkosan moo shikata-nai tte na   kanji de*
   guy   INJ no.way   QT COP:ATT manner INS
   nee okite-kite
   PP get.up:TE-come:TE
5. *soshite shawaa o   abite*
   then   shower ACC take:TE

'…then (I) couldn't enter (the room)
(and so) (I) woke him up,
then (I) entered
(then) the guy got up with a disgusted look
then (he) took a shower…'

In written discourse, the *to* conditional form is used more frequently than the *-tara* form. In (43), the *to* clause (line 1) is followed by a clause with different subject (line 2), and the *-te* clause (line 2) is followed by a same-subject clause (line 3).

(43) (from Watanabe 1994: 136)
1. *taroo   ga   soo iimasu   to*
   (name) NOM SO say:POL:NONPAST COND
   'Taro said so…
2. *baasama wa tameiki o   tsuite*
   grandma TOP sigh   ACC take:TE
   …(then) the grandma sighed…
3. *iimashita*
   say:POL:PAST
   …(and) said…'

It should be noted here that topic marking and clause chaining work collaboratively. If a noun phrase is marked by the nominative case as in (44), *sensee ga*, it functions as a subject for that clause only. In contrast, if it is marked by the topic marker as in (45), it goes beyond the initial clause. This is a case of Mikami's "comma crossing" (1960). (See Note 1 in this chapter and Chapter 11 §1.).

(44)
1. <u>sensee</u> *ga*   heya   ni   hairu   to
   teacher NOM room DAT enter:NONPAST COND
   'The teacher entered the room…

2. *megane   o*   *toridashita*
   glasses ACC take.out:PAST
   …(then) (someone) took out his glasses'

(45)
1. <u>sensee</u> *wa*   heya   ni   hairu   to
   teacher TOP room DAT enter:NONPAST COND
   'The teacher$_i$ entered the room…

2. *megane   o*   *toridashita*
   glasses ACC take.out:PAST
   …(then) (he$_i$) took out his glasses'

In written discourse, the verb's infinitive (or *ren'yoo*) form, in addition to the *-te* form, is employed for continuous events. In (46), clause 1 is marked with the infinitive form (*tsumekomi* 'pack'), and clause 2 is marked with the *-te* form (*kurunde* 'wrap').

(46) (Shibuya 1988: 107–8)
1. *okkasan   wa*   … *kuma   no   kaban   ni* …
   mother   TOP   (name) GEN   bag   DAT

   tabi   no   hitsujuhin   o   <u>tsumekomi</u>
   journey GEN necessary-goods ACC pack:INF
   'Mother packed the necessary goods for a journey in Kuma's bag,…

2. *soredemo   hairanai   bun   wa   hiroi   nuno   de   <u>kurunde</u>*
   even.so   enter:NEG portion TOP   large   cloth INS   wrap:TE
   …(and) (she) wrapped the portion which could not fit in (the bag) in a wide (piece of) cloth,…

3. *ryoohashi   o* … *kuma   no   ago   no   shita   de   musunda   no   desu*
   both.ends ACC (name) GEN chin GEN under LOC tie:PAST SE COP
   …(and) (she) tied both ends under Kuma's chin.'

In general, when both *-te* and the infinitive (*ren'yoo*) forms appear before clauses of continuous events and actions in written discourse, the *-te* form chaining shows a higher degree of continuity than the infinitive (*ren'yoo*) form connection (Kuno 1973: 196; Inoue 1983; Ono 1990).

4. The "open clausal structure" and discourse organization

As noted at the outset of this chapter, the clause chaining strategy shares an important structural similarity to conjoining and adverbial subordination; that is, all of these clause combining forms, such as *-shi, -kedo, -toki, -kara, -tara* and *-te* appear at the end of a clause. Appearance of any clause combining form, of course, entails non-closure of a sentence, and it is possible to produce non-finite clauses one after another, producing a long string of clauses (Iwasaki and Ono 1999, 2002). Sakakura (1970) attributes this discourse strategy to the "open structure" associated with the clause-combining forms. Though the open clausal structure is a distinct feature found in narrative tales written in the Late Old Japanese Period (9–12 c), such as the *Tale of Genji*, it is still seen to some extent in modern narratives, both spoken and written modes.[5] In the next excerpt of a modern Japanese oral narrative, nine clauses are combined with various clause-combining forms (the *-te* form appears four times, and *node, -tara, kedo* each appears once). In this narrative, a female speaker explains how she went out to look for her family after a heavy bombing of Tokyo during World War II. The actual narrative is presented in (48), but the clause-combining schema with minimum translation is given first in (47).

(47)

------------------ *dete*	I went out, and
------------------ *datta node*	the house was just past it, so
------------------ *ittara*	when I got there,
------------------ *yakete*	the fire engine had been burned up, and
------------------ *wakannai-n da kedo*	I could not tell whether… , but
------------------ *naranaide*	the corpse wasn't like this, but
------------------ *yatte*	it was like this, and
------------------ *tatte-n no.*	was standing up.

The actual excerpt is represented below.

(48)
244 A: *eki   no toori e   dete*
         station LK street ALL go.out:TE
         'I went out to the street in front of the station…'

---

5. In contrast to a sentence with the "open" structure, a clause with the "closed" structure tends not to continue to create a long stretch of a sentence. That is, a clause with the closed structure is self-sufficient, and completes itself immediately. A discourse with open structure clauses will definitely give different texture compared to a discourse with closed structure clauses. Sakakura claims that Japanese acquired the closed structure from the Chinese writing style. Maynard (2007:90–94) uses the term "rhetorical sentence" to refer to discourse with an open structure in modern written texts. Tanaka also discusses the same phenomena from the perspective of Conversation Analysis (1999:203–213).

245 A: *eki   yori moo   chotto saki   ga.. takahashi-san*
        station more EMPH a.little ahead NOM   (name)-Mrs.
        toko   datta-n-de
        place COP:PAST-SE-COP:TE
        '…Takahashi's house was just a little beyond the station, so…'

246 A: *eki   e   ittara*
        station ALL go:COND
        '…when I got to the station…'

247 A: *eki   no ne mae   ni ne shooboo-jidoosha ga   yakete*
        station LK PP front DAT PP fire-engine   NOM burn:TE
        '…there was a fire truck out in front, all burned up, and…'

248 A:. *soko   e   onna   ka otoko ka wa wakannai-n-da*
         ..there ALL woman or man   or TOP know:NEG:NONPAST-SE-COP
         kedo   ne
         though PP
         '…there was a body, and I couldn't tell if it was a man or woman, but…'

249 A: *are. koo   fuu-n   naranaide*
        that this appearance-COP:ADV   become:NEG:TE
        '…it wasn't like this, but…'

250 A: *chanto koo-yatte*
        neatly this.way-do:TE
        '…it was neatly like this and…'

251 A: *tatte-n   no.*
        stand.up:ASP:NONPAST   SE
        '…standing up.'

As seen in this excerpt, a sentence that occurs in discourse and has many clauses with the open structure can be quite long.

CHAPTER 13

Reference system in discourse

When a referent is introduced into discourse for the first time, it is usually expressed as a full noun. Subsequent mentions, however, tend to take different forms. Common strategies for referring to an established referent (the strategy of "referent tracking" or "anaphora") in Japanese are the use of pronouns, nominal ellipsis, and demonstratives. Demonstratives can also refer to a discourse segment.

1. Personal pronouns, reflexive pronouns, and logophoric pronouns

Pure personal pronouns used for reference tracking, such as "he, she, it, they" in the English language, do not exist in Japanese. The so-called masculine third person pronoun *kare* was historically part of the demonstrative paradigm (i.e. the system used to contain, *ko-, so-, ka-*, and *a-*) and pointed to an object physically far, yet psychologically close. The feminine counterpart *kano-jo* is a compound with *kano* (a *ka-* series adnominal demonstrative) with *-jo* (a Sino-Japanese word for female) (Kindaichi 1988: 167). *Kare/kano-jo* were established as translation equivalents of Western pronouns in the Meiji era (late 19th century). Though the younger generation uses *kare/kano-jo* more often than the previous generations, the use of these words as pure third person pronouns is still extremely limited. Instead, *kare* and *kano-jo* are used more often as nouns meaning 'boyfriend/girlfriend' (Chapter 15). (A pronominal use of *kare* will be presented below.).

The reflexive pronoun *jibun* 'self' has several characteristics. First, lexically the reflexive pronoun is not much different from regular nouns; it takes plural suffixes (e.g. *jibun-tachi, jibun-ra* 'self-PL'), can be modified (e.g. *tsukare-hateta jibun* 'exhausted self'), and can modify another noun (e.g. *jibun no heya* 'self GEN room > one's own room'). Second, syntactically, the reflexive pronoun always takes the subject as its antecedent (in fact this is used as a criterion to identify subject-hood in Japanese – Chapter 6 §3.1; Shibatani 1978a; b).

(1) taroo wa jiroo o **jibun** no heya de shikatta
(name) TOP (name) ACC **self** GEN room LOC scold:PAST
'Taro$_i$ scolded Jiro$_j$ in his$_i$/*$_j$ own room.'

When it appears in an embedded clause, *jibun* may refer to either the matrix or the embedded subject.

(2) taroo   wa   jiroo   ga   **jibun** no   heya   ni
     (name)   TOP (name)   NOM self   GEN room   DAT
     iru   to   omotta
     stay:PAST   QT   think:PAST
     'Taro$_i$ thought that Jiro$_j$ was in his$_{i/j}$ own room.'

Third, *jibun* functions in discourse as a 'logophoric pronoun,' which takes for its antecedent the participant whose consciousness, or point-of-view, is expressed. The following examples are from Kuno 1987: 138.

(3) taroo   wa   [**jibun** **ga**   tensai   da]   to   omotte-iru
     (name)   TOP self   NOM   genius   COP   QT   think:TE-ASP:NONPAST
     'Taro$_i$ thinks that he$_i$ is a genius.'

(4) ?? taroo wa   [**kare** **ga**   tensai   da]   to   omotte-iru
     (name)   TOP he   NOM   genius   COP   QT   think:TE-ASP:NONPAST
     'Taro$_i$ thinks that he$_i$ is a genius.' (intended meaning)

(3) and (4) have the identical structure of the cognition verb *omotte-iru* 'think' with a complement clause. The only difference is the choice of pronoun. The reflexive-logophoric pronoun *jibun* used in (3) clearly establishes its co-referential relationship with Taro, and the sentence is grammatical with the intended meaning. On the other hand, (4) with the so-called masculine third person pronoun *kare* would be awkward with this meaning, and *kare* would be most likely interpreted as being non-co-referential with Taro.

Consider the next excerpt taken from a detective story. *Jibun* is used not as a reflexive pronoun ('himself/myself') but as a regular pronoun ('he/I'). *Jibun* in this passage refers to the protagonist (Aida), whose consciousness is represented.[1] In this portion of the story, a detective named Aida is reflecting on a conversation with his colleague Hirase, who had just disclosed that a suspect in an extortion case may be one of their own. Aida, who is on special assignment, is cautioned not to take unnecessary hasty actions. Aida then laments the predicament he is in; he will be punished whether or not he makes a contribution to solving the case.

(5)   (Takamura 1997: 107)
   soo shita jijoo o fukunda ue de no hirase no kon'ya no monoii datta no da na to
   aida *wa sukoshi nattoku shita ga "umari kibin ni ugokarete mo" to yuu saigo no kensee wa dokoka ni iru miuchi no hanzaisha to onaji gurai fukai na mono datta*

   '**Aida** understood why Hirase talked the way he did tonight. But Hirase's final warning, "If you act too fast, (we'd be inconvenienced)," was as unpleasant as (the thought of) an unknown suspect lurking somewhere among them.'

---

1. If this *jibun* is replaced with *ore* (informal masculine first person pronoun), the text will turn into a direct representation of Aida's thought. If it is replaced by *kare* (third person pronoun), the text will turn into an objective statement by the narrator of the novel. With *jibun*, the text remains an indirect representation of his thought.

jibun	wa	katachi	bakari-no	tokumee		o
self	TOP	form	only-COP:ATT	special.assignment		ACC

otte-iru	ga
take:TE-ASP:NONPAST	but

'The self takes on a special assignment only in form, but...'

nanika	tegara	o	tateta	ga	saigo	tsubusareru.
some	merit	ACC	perform:PAST	NOM	last	crush:PSS:NONPAST

'Once (the self) cracks the case, (the self) will be crushed.'

tegara	o	tatenakereba	sono mama	massatsu-sareru.
merit	ACC	perform:NEG:COND	that situation	kill-do:PSS:NONPAST

'If (the self) doesn't crack the case, (the self) will be ignored forever.'

Jibun is also a resource for writers who describe their own actions and emotions in a story. They may use *jibun* to index the internal self while using a regular pronoun such as *watashi* (general first person pronoun) and *boku* (male first person pronoun) to index the objectively seen external self (Maynard 2007: 272–279). In the next excerpt, *boku* in line 1 is the subject of an objective sentence describing that 'I became more and more quiet.' *Jibun* in line 3, on the other hand, is the subject of a sentence describing the writer's internal thought, 'what I am thinking.'

(6) (Murakami 2002: 20)

1.
boku	wa	masumasu	mukuchi	ni	natte	itta.
I(male)	TOP	more	quiet	DAT	become:TE	go:PAST

'I became more and more quiet'

2.
kanjoo	no	kifuku	ga	kao	ni	deru	no	o
feeling	GEN	up.and.down	NOM	face	DAT	come.out	NML	ACC

dekirukagiri	osae,
as.much.as	control:INF

'(I) hid my feeling's up and down from appearing on my face.'

3.
jibun	ga	nani	o	kangaete-iru	noka...
self	NOM	what	ACC	think:TE-ASP:NONPAST	NML

kizukarenai	yoo-ni-suru	kunren	o	shita.
not.notice:PSS:NEG	in.order.to	training	ACC	do:PAST

'(I) tried to train myself to hide what **SELF** was thinking.'

this segment will be discussed again in Section 2 below.[2]

---

[2]. Reflexive pronouns are also employed by some to avoid indexical connotations such as particular speech levels and gender distinctions associated with other regular pronouns (Chapter 15 §1). For example, it is used to avoid gender specific pronouns such as *boku* (male, first person) and *atashi* (female, first person). This use is particularly popular among LGBT (lesbian, gay, bisexual, transgender) communities. See Kanamaru (1997); Abe (2004); and Camp (2009); among others.

2. Nominal ellipsis (zero anaphora)

While the use of personal pronouns is restricted in Japanese discourse, the phenomenon of "nominal ellipsis" (or "zero anaphora") is extremely common. Since Japanese does not have any co-referencing system between arguments and the predicate, the process of zero anaphora is largely pragmatic, and contextually retrievable information can be, more often than not, unexpressed (Okamoto 1985).[3] The rate of zero anaphora is especially high for the subject position. It is about 40% in written discourse (Hinds 1983), and about 70% in spoken discourse (Hinds 1983; Shibamoto 1984; Fry 2003). The zero subject tends to be the human subject of a transitive verb (Fry 2003: 84–96). In a story, once participants are introduced overtly, they immediately become candidates for zero anaphora. The next is an example.

(7) (Tsubota 1975: 9)

1. mukashi mukashi aru tokoro ni
   old.days old.days certain place LOC
   ojiisan to obaasan to ga arimashita
   old.man COM old.woman COM NOM exist:PAST
   'Once upon a time there lived an old man and woman.'

2. [Ø 1] kodomo ga nakatta   mono desu kara
          child   NOM exist:NEG: PAST NML COP so
   Because (they) did not have a child,...

3. [Ø 2] kodomo ga hoshikute hoshikute....
          child   NOM want:TE   want:TE
   ...(they) wanted a child very badly, and...

4. [Ø 3] kono koto bakari kamisama ni onegai-shite-orimashita
          this thing only gods   DAT pray-do:TE-ASP:POL:PAST
   ...(they) prayed to the gods about this matter only.'

(7) above is an introductory paragraph of a folktale. In line 1 the old man and woman are introduced. In the next three clauses, these characters, as a unit, are referred to by zero

---

3. Although the terms such as ellipsis and zero anaphora are used in this chapter, it is more accurate to state that not expressing a noun argument is an unmarked case, both in spoken and written discourse, and only pragmatic necessity such as disambiguation and initial mention requires an overt noun in discourse. Predicates and particles can also be unexpressed, but their process may be different than noun ellipsis (Hinds 1982: 47–74; 155–180; Fry 2003: 96–119). As for predicate ellipsis, it is the norm to express a predicate and unexpressed predicate is definitely a marked case. In case of particle ellipsis, it appears only in spoken language and informal written language (cf. Fujii & Ono 2000).

anaphora. The chain of zero anaphora is broken when a story crosses a discourse boundary, e.g. from an introductory paragraph to an action sequence (Hinds & Hinds 1978; Hinds 1982:76; Clancy 1980). In fact, the old man and woman in the above story are mentioned again with *wa* in the next paragraph where their actions are described. See Chapter 16 §2 for detailed analysis of another folk tale.

The zero subject is more frequent with the main predicate than with a predicate in a subordinate clause. Observe (6) from the previous section (shown as (6′) below in an abbreviated form). The subject-predicate relations are indicated by subscripts in the abbreviated sentence structure. Notice that after *boku* is spelled out in line 1, a zero pronoun is used for the main clause subject in lines 2 and 3. Subjects in the subordinate clauses, 'feelings' and 'I,' on the other hand, appear overtly with predicates within an embedded clause with the particle *ga* (cf. Iwasaki 1986).

(6′)
1. **boku**$_1$ wa.   mukuchi ni   natte-itta$_1$.
2. [Ø]$_2$ [*kanjoo no*   *kifuku*$_3$ *ga* ... deru$_3$ no]   o ...   osae$_2$,
3. [Ø]$_4$ [*jibun*$_5$ ga ..   kangaete-iru$_5$ noka]... kunren   o   shita$_4$.

1. *boku*=I$_1$ – became   quiet$_1$
2. [Ø = I]$_2$ – [*feelings*$_3$ – surface$_3$]   controlled$_2$
3. [Ø = I]$_4$ – [(*jibun* =I)$_5$ – was thinking$_5$]   trained$_4$

(8) below is a conversation between A (female graduate student) and T (male graduate student), who have just started to discuss their personal experiences of the Northridge earthquake in Los Angeles in 1994. The transcript is presented in a two-column format. There is one first person pronoun (*watashi*) on line (A-21)[4] while there are eight instances of ellipses where such a pronoun could be provided according to the argument structure of the predicates. Likewise, there are three second person subject ellipses. In the English translation, all the subjects are underlined. When they are not expressed in the original (i.e. ellipsis), they are put in parentheses and bold-faced, and the one overt first person pronoun is indicated as *I* on line A-21.[5]

---

4. Iwasaki (1997:669) notes that the overt pronoun *watashi* 'I' often appears when a new floor in conversation is initiated by a speaker.

5. Details from the original transcripts have been omitted to highlight the pattern of ellipsis, though the following conventions are maintained: period (.) = setting tail pitch movement, comma (,) = unmarked continuing tail pitch movement, circumflex (^) = rise-and-fall tail pitch movement, question mark (?) = rising tail pitch movement; three dots (...) = pause, (:) = vowel lengthening, square brackets ([) = beginning of an overlap, slash (/) = end of intonation unit boundary, (nn) = backchannel expression. See Chapter 3 §5 for the notion of tail pitch movements.

Chapter 13. Reference system in discourse

(8) Conversation about Northridge earthquake

	A	T
1	jishin no toki wa ne::.	
2	are wa mayonaka desu yo ne: ^	
3		soo desu ne.
4	toozen nete mashita?	
5	[okite mashita?	[nete mashita / nete mashita.
6		sanji da./ nanji datta n desu ka
7		are / wakannai na:.
8	are ne:./ yoji han datta n desu yo./	
9	tabun. / yoji sanjuu-ni fun ka nanka	
10	datta.	
11		nnnn
12	nn	
13		... nete mashita yo. / nn
14		are: kakure mashita?
15	… nn. ano:::,/ tsukue no shita ni	
16	chotto hairi mashita kedo, /	
17		nn
18	ano ryoo no tsukue gatchiri shite iru	
19	desho.	
20		ee ee
21	<u>watashi</u> wa ne, /jitsu wa ne, /	
22	saisho me ga sameta toki ne,/	
23	mada jishin: datte koto ga yoku	
24	wakarazu, /	
25	sugu wakatta keredomo shikashi./	
26	… shibaraku chotto./	
27	hima ga atta n desu yo.	
28		ee ee

(English translation)

	T	A
1	At the time of earthquake...	
2	That was in the middle of the night, right?	
3		That's right.
4	(You) were of course sleeping?	
5	[Or were (you) up?	[(I) was sleeping. (I) was sleeping.
6		3 o'clock? What time was it? (I)
7		don't know.
8	That was ... 4:30.	
9	Probably (it) was 4:32 or something like	
10	that.	
11		nnnn.
12	nn	
13		(I) was sleeping.
14		Did (you) hide?
15	... nn. ahm. (I) went under the desk to	
16	hide.	
17		nn
18	The desks in the dorm are sturdy, right?	
19		
20		yeah
21	*I* – to tell you the truth –	
22	when (I) woke up,	
23	(I) did not know that it was an earth-	
24	quake	
25	(I) knew it but	
26	it took	
27	a while	
28		mhm

3. Demonstratives as discourse deixis

Another productive resource for referent tracking in Japanese is the use of demonstratives as discourse deictics. A discourse deictic may refer to an object, person, place, direction, action (i.e. nominal reference), or to a piece of text (i.e. discourse reference), which has been mentioned in the previous discourse, or which, to a much lesser extent, will appear in the subsequent discourse. The *so-* series demonstrative are the most neutral and common for both nominal and discourse reference, though the *ko-* and *a-* series demonstrative may also occur under certain specific conditions. (See Chapter 14 §1.2 for more discussion of the deictic system.).

3.1 Nominal reference

The next is an excerpt from a folk tale *Hainawa Sen-taba* 'One Thousand Bundles of Ash Rope.' The demonstratives here are used as discourse deictics with nominal reference. A single underline in the text refers to 'a purple cloud,' and a double underline to 'that horse.'

(9) (Tsubota 1975: 52)
1. ten'nin ga... <u>murasaki-no kumo</u> o yobimashita.
   angel NOM purple-COP:att cloud ACC call:POL:PAST
   'The angel called a <u>purple cloud</u>.

2. <u>sore</u> ni wa <u>ryuu-no koma to yuu no</u> ga notte
   that DAT TOP dragon-COP:att horse QT say nml NOM ride:TE
   On top of it (= *sore*) was <u>a thing called a "dragon horse,"</u>...

3. wakamono o mukae-ni kimashita.
   young.man ACC invite-PURP come:POL:PAST
   ...and (it) came for the young man.

4. wakamono wa <u>sono koma</u> ni nori
   young.man TOP that horse DAT ride:INF
   ... ten no... gotten e ikimashita.
   heaven GEN palace ALL go:POL:PAST

   'The young man rode on <u>the horse</u> (= *sono koma*) and went to the palace in the heavens.'

The first *so-* series demonstrative (*sore*) in line 2 refers back to *murasaki no kumo* 'a purple cloud' in line 1, and the second *so-* series demonstrative expression (*sono koma* 'that horse') in line 4 refers back to *ryuu no koma to yuu no* 'the thing called a dragon horse' in line 2. Notice these demonstrative expressions are replaceable by their antecedents (this should be contrasted with the discourse reference to be discussed in the next section).

An important fact to note is that the use of demonstratives is prevalent in Japanese, which lacks a pronoun equivalent to English 'it.' Another point is that *sore/sono* 'that' in (9), and also generally, may be replaced by *kore/kono* 'this.' When the *ko-* series demonstratives are used as discourse deictics, this implies that the information is somehow close to the writer/speaker, while the *so-* series implies that the information is more neutral. In newspaper articles, the *ko-* series words are often found because the writer of an article has more familiarity with the information than the readers (Sakata 1992:63). In the next newspaper article, *kono seeto* 'this student' refers back to 'a first year middle school male student' mentioned in the first line.

(10)   (Yomiuri 12/17/1998)

1. ibaraki-ken... no *chuugaku*   *ichinen-no*   *danshi-seeto*   ga
  (place)   GEN middle.school 1st.year-COP:ATT male-student NOM

   "..."   to   yuu   memo   o   nokoshite
   "(quoted material)" QT say   memo   ACC   leave:te

2. jisatsushita   jiken   de
   commit.suicide:PAST incident INS

3. **kono seeto**   ga... bookoo   o   ukete-ita   koto
   this   student NOM bullying ACC receive:TE-ASP:PAST NML

   ga.... wakatta
   NOM understand:PAST

   'Regarding the incident of <u>a first year male middle school student</u> in Ibaraki Prefecture leaving a memo saying "..." and committing suicide, it was revealed that he (<u>this student</u>) had been... bullied (by his classmates).'

The substitution of *kono seeto* 'this student' with *sono seeto* 'that student' is possible, but this substitution will effect a loss in the special journalistic tone of a newspaper article. It should be emphasized, however, that the demonstrative word in (10) as well as those in (9) cannot be substituted by the *a-* series demonstratives which are constrained pragmatically; the *a-* series words are only allowed (i) when the speaker/writer and the addressee/reader have mutually established the referent in their memory (i.e. both know the referent well) (Kuno 1973: 282–290; Chapter 14 §1.2.1.2), or (ii) when the speaker is in the monologic mode (Kinsui & Takubo 1992a: 129–131; cf. Kuroda 1992a: 91–104) with strong emotional attachment to the referent (Chapter 14 §1.2.1.3). The speaker of the next spoken narrative explains an air raid in Japan during World War II to an addressee who was not alive during the war time. The speaker has an emotional attachment to the time ('sometime around May') referred to by *ano toki*.

(11)   (Bombing)

1. <u>gogatsu</u>   <u>ka</u>   <u>nanka</u>   desu   ne
   May   or   something   COP   PP

2. **ano toki** ni eki ni bakudan ga ochita-n desu
that time TMP station ALL bomb NOM drop:PAST-SE COP
'It was some time around May.
At that time a bomb fell on the station.'

3.2 Discourse reference

Discourse reference refers to textual information larger than a lexical item. The referent may be the exact wording in the previous discourse, or may be information abstracted from the previous discourse. In the following excerpt from a detective story, the speaker is proposing an idea for an extortion scheme.

(12) (Takamura 1997: 173)
1. momoi-san ga hontoo-ni yaru-n nara
(name)-Mr. NOM real-COP:ADV do:NONPAST-SE COND
'If (you) are going to do it, Mr. Momoi..,

2. ore wa kakujitsu-ni kane o toreru
I TOP sure-COP:ADV money ACC take:POT:NONPAST

hoohoo o kangaeru.
method ACC think:NONPAST
…I will think of a sure way of extorting the money.

3. zenmenteki-ni kyooryoku-suru
complete-COP:ADV cooperate-do:NONPAST
(I) will give you my complete support.

4. **sono** kawari… kakujitsu-ni kabu-ka ni eekyoo o
that instead sure-COP:ADV stock-price DAT effect ACC

oyobosu yoo-na
effect:NONPAST way-COP:ATT

hoohoo o toru.
method ACC take:NONPAST
In exchange for **that**, (we) will adopt a method that will surely affect the stock price.

5. **soo yuu jooken** de doo da
that say condition INS how COP
What do (you think of) **that condition**?'

The two demonstratives in the above excerpt are both referring to information in the immediate discourse. The first (*sono* 'that') in line 4 refers to the speaker's immediate utterance in line 3, 'I will give you my complete support,' and possibly those in lines 1 and 2 as well, 'if you are really going to do it, I will think of a sure way of extorting money.' The second demonstrative (*soo yuu jooken* 'that condition') in line 5 refers to the entire proposition that precedes this line. In this kind of demonstrative usage, again, the *so-* series is most common.

Finally, as has been mentioned in passing, the referent of a demonstrative may be found in upcoming discourse (cataphoric relation) instead of the previous discourse context (anaphoric relation). *Konna hanashi* 'this kind of story' in (13) below refers to an upcoming story that the speaker wants to relate.

(13) konna   hanashi ga   aru   no yo
     this.kind story   NOM   exist:NONPAST   SE PP
     'There is this (kind of a) story.'

CHAPTER 14

Pragmatics

Pragmatics in general refers to how speakers use language in context. In order to speak successfully in a particular situation, a speaker needs not only to be able to produce a proposition using their grammatical knowledge, but also to understand how it should be framed according to various contextual considerations. This chapter is divided into four major sections. The first section discusses the subjectivity concerns, under which internal state expressions and deictic expressions are described. The second section is about the epistemic modality, which includes conjectural, inferential, and evidential types and also about the evaluative modality. The third section deals specifically with pragmatic particles which code various pragmatic concerns. The last section discusses how speakers negotiate in conversational interaction, especially how they use pragmatic particles, discourse markers and conjunctions in real conversation.

1. Subjectivity concerns

Subjectivity here means the effect that the speaking self brings to the system of grammar. Said differently, some grammatical phenomena cannot be adequately described without referring to the notion of speaker. Three specific concerns discussed in this section are "internal states," "deixis," and "movements and transactions."

1.1 Internal state expressions

There are several types of internal state expressions, among which is the "exclamatory sentences" discussed in Chapter 11 (§4.1). Exclamatory sentences directly reveal speakers' perception (or sensation), emotion and feelings (Iwasaki to appear). Exclamatory sentences can co-occur with an exclamatory vocal sign such as *a!, aa,* or *waa* (similar to the English *oh, wow, waw*). See Table 1 on the next page.

Although exclamatory sentences always involve the speaker as an experiencer, they never code it overtly (*a! boku ga itai! 'Oh, I am in pain'); it can only be indexed indirectly through the act of exclamation. This is a crucial difference between the exclamatory sentences, e.g. *a! itai!*, and descriptive sentences, e.g. *boku mo atama ga itai* 'I also have an headache.' Also, since the exclamatory sentences are completely tied to the current speech situation (temporally deictic), the past tense form used in them is interpreted as perfect/anterior aspect (Chapter 7 §2.1), not as past tense (e.g. *a! yokatta!*

Table 1. Exclamatory sentences

Perception/sensation expressions	*a! itai!* *aa kayui!* *aa karai!*	'Ouch! (*itai* = painful)' 'Oh, itchy!' 'Oh, hot spicy!'
Emotion expressions	*aa kuyashii!* *aa zannnen!* *aa yokatta!*	'How frustrating!' 'What a pity!' 'Oh, I'm so glad!'
Feeling expressions	*aa kanashii!* *aa tsurai!* *aa natsukashii* *waa tanoshii*	'Oh, I'm so sad!' 'Oh, so painful (psychologically)' 'Oh, it brings back memories!' 'Oh, it's so much fun'

shows the speaker's relief at the time of speech.) Some of the exclamatory sentences and internal state expressions in general show peculiar morphological contrast between a speaker's own and others' experiences; the form *itai* 'painful' noted above can be used only for the speaker's sensation. It has to be modalized for someone else's pain with the suffix *-garu* in the stative form as in *itagatte-iru* 'acting as if painful,' or with an evidential suffix such as INF-*soo*$_1$ with the optional copula (see §2.1.2 below), e.g. *ita-soo-da* 'appears to be painful.' This morphological distinction is apparently motivated by difference in information accessibility; the speaker can access his own internal states such as pain, but he can access others' only through externalized evidence (Iwasaki 1993, cf. Kuroda 1973).

"Desire" is also a type of internal state, which is expressed by the adjective *hoshii* 'want (something)' and the desiderative suffix, *-tai* 'want (to do something).' See Table 2 on the next page. These forms are only available for the first person–experiencer/subject in a statement and for the second person-experiencer/subject in a question. It must be also modified with the suffix *-gatte-iru* or an evidential suffix such as INF-*soo*$_1$ with the optional copula for the third person- experiencer/subject (§ 2.1.2 below). Note also the particle that marks the desired object (e.g. *mizu* 'water') is *ga* for the first person subject with *hoshii*, but is *o* for the third person subject with *hoshi-gatte-iru*. Either particle is possible for *nomitai* 'want to drink' for the first person subject,[1] but invariably *o* for the

---

[1] The phenomenon that the *-tai* suffixed verb may allow either *ga* or *o* for its desired object is known as "the *ga-o* conversion" in the transformational framework (Kuno 1973; Inoue 1976; Shibatani 1975, 1978). A corpus study has shown that the frequency of *o* outnumbers that of *ga* substantially. Iori (1995) in his study of the use of *-o* V-*tai* and *-ga* V-*tai* in novels and essays shows 1286 tokens for the former and 52 tokens for the latter. Thus it is reasonable in the transformational framework to take *o* as the base form which will be changed to *ga* under certain conditions. It has been shown that the conversion from *o* to *ga* will be disfavored when; (i) the verb is a Sino-Japanese verb, (ii) *o* appears in a fixed expression (e.g. *ki o tsukeru* 'to be

third person subject. When the predicate is modified with INF-*soo*₁ for the third person, the particle must be *ga*.

Table 2. "Desire" expressions

1st person Experiencer	3rd person Experiencer
mizu ga hoshii '(I) want water.'	*mizu o hoshi-gatte-iru* '(He/she) wants water.'
	mizu ga hoshi-soo da '(It) looks like (he/she) wants water.'
mizu ga/o nomitai '(I) want to drink water.'	*mizu o nomita-gatte-iru* '(He/she) wants to drink water.'
	mizu ga nomita-soo da "(It) looks like (he/she) wants to drink water.'

"Mental process" expressed by the verb *omou* 'think' must also be distinguished in form for first and third person experiencers/subjects. When the subject is the speaker herself, the unmodified verb form *omou* can be employed, as in (2a), but when it is a third person, as in (2b), the verb must be stativised with the auxiliary *-iru* (see Iwasaki 1993: 12–15 for a detailed discussion).

(2) a. *watashi wa ookii jishin   ga   kuru   to   omou*
         I   TOP big   earthquake NOM come:NONPAST QT think:NONPAST
         'I think there'll be a big earthquake.'

     b. *hanako wa ookii jishin ga kuru to *omou/omotte-iru*
         (name)   think:NONPAST/think:TE-ASP:NONPAST
         'Hanako thinks there'll be a big earthquake.'

"Intention" is another type of internal states (see Table 3 on the next page). It is expressed in a number of different ways; a verb in the nonpast tense form may be modified by *tsumori* 'intention' or *yotee* 'plan,' or a verb in the volitional form may be used with the quotation structure. Here, again the first person and third person distinction must be maintained. For a sentence with a third-person subject/ experiencer, an evidential expression such as *rashii* (§2.1.2 below) must follow. Notice also here, too, the *omou – omotte-iru* distinction is made for the verb 'to think.'

---

cautious' > *ki o tsuke-tai*, *ki ga tsuke-tai), (iii) intervening material between the object and the verb is long (e.g. *sushi ga tabe-tai* '(I) want to eat sushi' > **sushi ga {Shinjuku ni aru sushiya de} tabe-tai* '(I) want to eat sushi {at a restaurant in Shinjuku}' (Shibatani 1975).

Table 3. "Intention" expressions

1st person subject	3rd person subject
iku tsumori / yotee da go intention / plan COP '(I) intend/plan to go.'	iku tsumori / yotee rashii go intention / plan MOD 'It seems that (he/she) intends/plans to go.'
ikoo to omou go:VOL QT think:NONPAST '(I) think (I) will go.'	ikoo to omotte-iru rashii go:VOL QT think:TE-ASP MOD '(I) think (he/she) will go.'

1.2 Deictic expressions

Deictic expressions encode information relevant to the speaker's here-and-now orientations. The spatial deictic system places the speaker at the absolute focal point, and uses this point to define other spatial locations.[2]

1.2.1 *Demonstratives: The* ko-so-a-do *words*

Demonstratives are deictic words with four distinct uses; spatial, cognitive, textual, and affective. In the spatial use, they point to a particular position in the physical space of the current speech event with the speaker as the absolute reference point. In the cognitive use, they point to a concept in the mental space of the speaker and addressee (Kinsui & Takubo 1992b). In the textual use, they work as a substituting words ("anaphora") to direct addressee/reader's attention to what has been referred in the current discourse. In the affective use, a demonstrative adds a peculiar overtone to the referent. In this chapter, the spatial, cognitive, and affective uses are discussed, while the textual use is discussed in Chapter 13 §3.

1.2.1.1 *Spatial use.*
There are three series of demonstratives (see Table 4 on the next page), and the distinction is marked in the first syllable of the dietetic word: *ko-*, *so-*, or *a-*. These three series of demonstrative words together with the corresponding interrogative words starting with *do-* (e.g. *dore* 'which' and *doko* 'where') are referred to as the *ko-so-a-do* words in traditional grammar.

---

2. Deictic elements do not represent a constant entity across speech situations, but rather are free variables whose content is supplied anew each time in a particular context. There are different types of deictic systems found in language. Fillmore (1975) lists personal, spatial, temporal, social, and discourse deixis. Among them, personal, temporal, and spatial deixis are three major types of deixis regularly found in languages of the world. Linguistically, the personal deixis is expressed by personal pronouns (*watashi* 'I,' *kimi* 'you'), and the temporal deixis by some temporal adverbs (*kyoo* 'today,' *ashita* 'tomorrow') and tense morphemes (*-ta* for the past tense). The spatial deictics are expressed by demonstrative words as described in this section.

Table 4. Deictic demonstrative expressions

	Speaker Proximate		Addressee Proximate		Distal (o.th = over there)	
Nominal						
object	kore	'this one'	sore	'that one'	are	'that one o.th.'
direction	kochira	'this way'	sochira	'that way'	achira	'that way o.th'
(colloq.)	kotchi	'this way'	sotchi	'that way'	atchi	'that way o.th'
place	koko	'here'	soko	'there'	asoko	'over there'
person						
(colloq.)	koitsu	'this guy'	soitsu	'that guy'	aitsu	'that guy o.th'
Adnominal	kono	'this + N'	sono	'that + N'	ano	'that + N o.th'
	konna	'this kind of N'	sonna	'that kind of N'	anna	'that kind of N o.th'
Adverbial	koo	'in this way'	soo	'in that way'	aa	'in that way o.th'

The appropriate demonstrative is selected for the object, person, direction, action, etc. being pointed to according to its relative location with respect to the speaker and the addressee. The *ko-* series demonstrative is "speaker proximate" and points to objects etc. near the speaker (i.e. within the solid line single circle in Figure 1 below), and the *so-* series demonstrative is the "addressee proximate" and points to objects etc. near the addressee (i.e. within the double line circle in the figure below). The *a-* series demonstrative is "distal" and points to objects etc. not near either the speaker or the addressee in the immediate speech environment (i.e. within the broken line circle in the figure below).

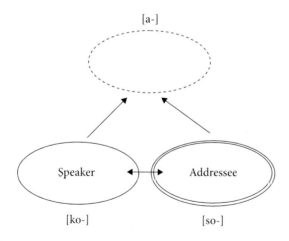

Figure 1. Spatial demonstratives

It is important to emphasize that a demonstrative is not simply selected according to the absolute distance measured from the location of the speaker. The next utterance may be used whether the distance between the speaker and addressee is either 1 meter or 100 meters.

(4) soko   o   ugoku-na !
     there   ACC move-NEGIMP
     'Don't move there!'

The above is a description of the *ko-so-a* words as used in the "face-to-face" configuration, where the speaker and addressee are facing each other. These words are also used in the "side-by-side" configuration, where the speaker and addressee are facing in the same direction. In this configuration, *so-* refers to people, objects, and locations etc. relatively closer to both the speaker and addressee, and *a-* refers to those relatively far from them (see Sakata [1971] 1992: 54–68). When a passenger in a cab directs the driver (both are facing in the same direction), she may say the following.[3]

(5) soko   no   kado   o   migi   ni   magatte-kudasai.
     there   COP:ATT corner ACC right DAT turn:TE-give:IMP
     'Turn the corner there, please.'

1.2.1.2 *Cognitive use.* The *a-* series demonstratives are used when the speaker believes that the referent is known both to speaker and addressee (Kuno 1973: 282–290). In other words, a referent must exist in the cognitive space of both speaker and addressee (Kinsui & Takubo 1992b: 129).

(6) A: yabu   tte-yuu resutoran   shitte-ru?
         (name)   COMP   restaurant know-ASP
         'Do you know the restaurant called Yabu?'

     B: nn.   asoko/ano mise   nakanaka ii   ne
         yes. there/that restaurant rather   good PP
         'Yes, that (restaurant) is very good.'

In (6), B knows the restaurant that A mentioned, so she could use *asoko* 'that place' or *ano mise* 'that restaurant.' These *a-* series words are not the spatial demonstratives describe in §1.2.1.1 above because a distal demonstrative with the spatial function must refer to a location that can be visible within the speech environment by the conversational

---

3. The use of *soko* in this sentence may be motivated by the controlling ability of an agent (the driver). That is, the "control" belongs to, or is closer to, the addressee, the driver (Yumiko Kawanishi – personal communication). This explains the use of *koko* and *soko* during a medical examination: a doctor pressing a particular area on the patient's throat might say, *koko itami masu ka?* 'Does this place hurt?' This is understandable because the doctor is pointing at something close to him. However, the patient's potential response, *iie, soko wa itaku arimasen* 'No, it does not hurt there' requires the notion of control. Though the location is close to the patient, he has to use *soko* 'there' as the action of pointing is under the doctor's control. When the patient declares without prompt, he would say, *koko ga itai-n desu* 'It hurts here' as he points to the area that hurts.

participants. If B does not know the restaurant in question in (6), she might respond, e.g. as follows.

(7) B: *iie. sore (*are)/sono (*ano) mise   doko ni aru no?*
       no. that   /that   restaurant where DAT exist Q
       'No. Where is it/that restaurant located?'

1.2.1.3 *Affective use*. The *a-* series demonstrative has a unique function to add speaker's affective stance to an utterance. This is possible when the speaker is talking to herself in an inner-speech. The next sentence is an example of an inner speech that may be produced when the speaker reminisces a past experience in solitude (Kuroda [1979b] 1992a; Maynard 2007: 251–255; see also Chapter 13 §3.1).

(8) (speaker talking to herself)
    *aa. **ano** toki **anna** koto iwanakereba yokatta!*
    oh that time that thing say:NEG:COND good:PAST
    'Oh, I should not have said **that** thing at **that** time!'

For the *a-* series demonstrative to become available, the experience must be a first hand direct experience. If it is an indirect (cognitive only) experience, the speaker cannot use *a-* (Kuroda 1979b [1992a: 97–99]). A speaker who had only heard that Yuri had said something could only use the *so-* series demonstrative as shown in (9) below.

(9) (speaker talking to herself)
    *yuri **sonna** (*annna) koto itta no ka!*
    (name) that   thing say:PAST SE Q
    'Yuri said such a thing?!'

Another affective use is found in the "modal affective" demonstratives (cf. Sawada & Sawada 2011).

(10) ***ano** hakuhoo ga   makeru nante (shinjirarenai)!*
     that (name) NOM lose   COMP (believe:POT:NEG)
     'I can't believe that the mighty Hakuho lost!'

Here the speaker expresses her surprise regarding the loss of an undefeated *sumo* wrestler, *Hakuho*, in a match. The implicature here is that *Hakuho* was expected to win, but despite this strong expectation, he lost. Unlike demonstratives used in inner speech described earlier, demonstratives used in this way must contain a strong sense of incredulity. This type of demonstrative often appears in a sentence with the specific complementizer *nante* with or without the predicate *shinjirarenai* 'can't believe' to index this incredulity. Also, note that when the referent coded with a demonstrative is a third person like *Hakuho*, the demonstrative must be an *a*-series demonstrative. In contrast, when the referent is a first person, the demonstrative must be a *ko*-series demonstrative, as shown in (11) below.

(11) *kono ore ga   makeru nante!*
    this I(male.vulgar) NOM lose COMP
    'I can't believe that I, this (mighty) person, lost!'

1.2.2 *Movement and transaction expressions*

Verbs of motion and transaction consider the position of the speaker crucial just as spatial *ko-so-a* words do. For a motion event, the appropriate verb must be selected depending on whether the speaker is the starting point or the goal of a movement. The verb *kuru* 'come' is used when, and only when, the speaker (or where the speaker is) is the goal. The English expression "I'm coming!" means that the speaker is moving away from the current position to the location of the addressee, but Japanese cannot express this idea with the verb *kuru* 'come'; rather it must be expressed with the verb *iku* 'go' (Fillmore 1966, 1972; Ohye 1975). Both *kuru* and *iku* are used very productively as directional auxiliaries as well; *V-te-kuru* indicates a direction towards the speaker, and *V-te-iku* away from the speaker (see Chapter 7 §2.4.5.2 for a discussion of these auxiliaries as aspect markers).

(12) *taroo   wa   toshoshitsu   kara   hon   o   karite-kita*
    (name) TOP reading.room ABL book ACC lend:TE-come:PAST
    'Taro borrowed a book from a reading room (towards here).'

   taroo   wa   toshoshitsu   kara   hon   o   karite-itta
    (name) TOP reading.room ABL book ACC lend:TE-go:PAST
    'Taro borrowed a book from a reading room (away from here).'

In addition, some uses of auxiliary *V-te-kuru* have been lexicalized in expressions such as those below. They indicate the direction towards the speaker, but unlike the previous examples, they do not have the *V-te-iku* counterparts.

(13) *denwa   ga   kakatte-kita*
    Telephone NOM ring:TE-come:PAST
    'There was an (in-coming) phone call.'

   ame ga   futte-kita
    rain NOM fall:TE-come:PAST
    'There was a rain fall.'

   konna   tegami o   kaite-kita
    this.kind of letter ACC write:TE-come:PAST
    '(Someone) wrote this kind of letter (to me).'

For transaction events, two different (sets of) verbs are available in Japanese depending on whether the speaker is a giver or receiver. The *yaru* group (*yaru* and its more polite forms, *ageru* and *sashiageru*) refers to a giving situation in which the speaker is the giver (i.e. the outward orientation), as shown in (14), while the *kureru* group (*kureru* and its more polite form *kudasaru*) refers to a situation in which the speaker is the receiver as in (15) (i.e. the inward orientation).[4]

(14) **boku wa** taroo ni hon o *yatta/ageta*
I TOP (name) DAT book ACC give:PAST
'I gave Taro a book.'

(15) taroo wa **boku ni** hon o *kureta*
(name) TOP I DAT book ACC give:PAST
'Taro gave me a book.'

The relationship between the giver and receiver is a relative one, as shown in Figure 2 below.

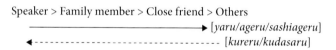

Figure 2. Direction of giving and the verb choice

If the giving direction is from left to right (the upper solid arrow in the figure above), the verb must be either *ageru* (neutral), *yaru* (to an inferior), or *sashiageru* (to a superior). If it is from right to left (the lower dotted arrow), it must be *kureru* (neutral) or *kudasaru* (honorific). Thus, when the speaker's sister (Mary) gives something to his friend (John), the appropriate verb is *ageru*, but when John gives something to Mary, it should be *kureru*. It must be also noted that the bottom arrow situation may also be described with a verb of receiving (*morau* or its humble form *itadaku*). However, the subject of a receiving verb (*morau*) is the recipient while that of a giving verb (*kureru*) is the giver. The following two sentences describe the same situation. The dative case marker *ni* can be changed into *kara* with a receiving verb, but not with a giving verb.

(16) taroo wa **boku ni** hon o *kureta*
(name) TOP I DAT book ACC give:PAST
'Taro gave me a book.'

(17) **boku wa** taroo ni/kara hon o *moratta*
I TOP (name) DAT/ABL book ACC receive:PAST
'I received a book from Taro.'

---

4. The verbs with outward orientation, i.e. the *yaru* group, are also used for neutral situations between two third persons.

The following two figures summarize the notion of movement and transaction in Japanese. Figure 3 shows a situation in which the speaker as indicated by the solid line circle is the "locus of point of view," which is coded grammatically as the "subject." The top solid line represents the motion of *iku* ('I go') and the giving of *ageru* ('I give'), while the bottom dotted line represents the receiving *morau* ('I receive'). Notice here that English 'I come' is represented by the top solid line as well ('I am coming to you'), but Japanese *kuru* cannot be used in this way.

Figure 3. Moving and giving with speaker as the point of reference

Figure 4 below, on the other hand, shows a situation in which the addressee is the "locus of the point of view," which is grammatically coded as the "subject."

Figure 4. Moving and giving with addressee as the point of reference

The motion of *kuru* ('you come') and the giving of *kureru* ('you give') are represented by the bottom solid line, while there is no verb corresponding to the top dotted line, i.e. it is not possible to put 'you' as the subject and express the dotted line. This shows that while the addressee can assume the center location, she cannot be a goal/recipient of a motion or transaction when the speaker is involved in the situation. This means that it is not possible to literally translate English sentences like 'You received money from me' (**kimi wa boku kara okane o moratta*).

To summarize the above discussion, in movement and transaction situations either speaker or addressee can be assigned the status of the locus of point-of-view, but only the speaker can assume both the point-of-view and the recipient role simultaneously, as shown in Figure 3 above. This is to confirm that the speaker has more privileges to assume different roles in grammar coding.

2. Modality expressions

Modality in the Western philosophical and linguistic tradition is divided into deontic and epistemic modalities. Deontic modality "is concerned with the necessity or possibility of acts performed by morally responsible agents" (Lyons 1977: 823), e.g. 'You must be here by 7 tomorrow.' Epistemic modality, on the other hand, concerns the degree of speaker commitment for the information conveyed (e.g. 'He must have been here before'). In English, the two types of modality are related through the use of common modal verbs, e.g. 'must,' as shown in the above examples. In the Japanese tradition, the distinction is often made between the speaker's stance towards the proposition (the "propositional modality") and that towards the interlocutor (the "interactional modality") (e.g. Maynard 1993, 2002, 2007; Horie & Taira 2002; Ide 2006; Suzuki 2006). The propositional modality is further divided into the "epistemic" and "evaluative" modalities. Section (§2.1) deals with the "epistemic modality," which is further divided into "conjectural and inferential" and "evidential" sub-types, and (§2.2) deals with the "evaluative modality" which embeds speaker's meta-comment to the propositional content. The interactional modality will be discussed in §3.

2.1 Epistemic modality

Epistemic modality is one type of propositional modality, and is concerned with the various degrees of commitment towards the proposition that is being displayed. When the speakers have the highest degree of certainty about the information, or when the information is "nonchallengeable" (Givón 1982), they can express it in a declarative statement with a finite verb form. When they do not have strong certainty, on the other hand, they have to qualify the statement as something that is unsubstantiated (conjectural), assembled based on his logical assessment (inferential), or something that have various types of evidence source (evidentials). In addition, speakers may also encode their evaluation more directly using various periphrastic constructions toward a proposition.

2.1.1 *Conjectural and inferential*
Conjectural: When speakers do not have strong bases to back up their statement with evidence, they put the information as their conjectured opinion or belief. Among such form of epistemic modality, the *kamoshirenai (kamoshiremasen*, polite form) shows the weakest degree of speaker confidence towards the proposition. If speakers believe they have some reason to back up their claim, they use the quotative construction *to omou* 'QUOTATIVE MARKER + think' (Chapter 10) and modal auxiliary, *daroo (deshoo*, polite form). Adverbs of strong conviction such as *kitto* 'certainly' or *kanarazu* 'definitely' cannot co-occur with the weakest *kamoshirenai* ending, but can appear with the other two forms of slightly stronger conviction. A person who took an exam may produce the following utterances.

(18) (*kitto/*kanarazu) ukaru kamoshirenai
 (*certainly/*definitely) pass:NONPAST MOD
 'I may pass (the exam).'

(19) *kitto/kanarazu   ukaru   daroo*
     certainly/definitely pass:NONPAST   MOD
     'I will certainly pass (the exam).'

(20) *kitto/kanarazu   urkaru   to   omou*
     certainly/definitely pass:NONPAST QT think:NONPAST
     'I think I will certainly pass (the exam).'

Inferential: *Ni chigainai* and *hazu da* are markers of logical inference. While *ni chigainai* shows a conclusion after a complex reasoning process, *hazu da* gives an inference based on a quick logical reasoning. A doctor who has just given a shot to a patient can predict that the fever would go down in one hour, (21). This does not involve a complex reasoning, so *ni chigainai* is somewhat inappropriate. Another doctor who performed various tests on an unconscious patient can conclude, and say (22). This involves more complex logical thinking, and thus *hazu da* is inappropriate.

(21) *ichi-jikan de netsu ga   sagaru hazu   da/*nichigainai*
     one-hour   in fever NOM   go.down:NONPAST   MOD/* MOD
     'The fever should go down in one hour.'

(22) *kono kanja wa   doku o   nonda   ni-chigainai/*hazu da*
     this patient TOP poison ACC drink:PAST MOD/* MOD
     'This patient must have taken some poison.'

All these expressions are preceded by the plain form of verbs or adjectives. In the square brackets in (23) and (24) below, [*kamoshirenai/daroo/to omou/ni chigainai/hazu da*] can be inserted.

(23) *taroo   wa kuru/konai [ ]*
     (name)   TOP come:NONPAST/come:NEG:NONPAST MOD
     'Taro will come/not come.'

(24) *kono e   wa takai [ ]*
     this painting TOP expensive:NONPAST
     "This painting is expensive.'

When a noun or a nominal adjective appears before these modal expressions, the copula is suppressed before *kamoshirenai*, *daroo*, and *ni chigainai*, as shown in (25) below. It appears with *da* before *to omou* and *no* (after a noun) or *na* (after a nominal adjective) before *hazu da*, as shown in (26) and (27) below.

(25) *nihonjin kamoshirenai/ daroo/ ni-chigainai*
     Japanese   MOD
     '(She) may be Japanese.'

(26) *nihonjin da   to   omou / no   hazu da*
     Japanese COP QT   think / COP:ATT MOD COP
     '(I) think (she) is Japanese.'/'(She) must be Japanese.'

(27) genki __da__ to omou/__na__   hazu da
      healthy COP QT think/COP:ATT MOD COP
      '(I) think (she) is healthy.'/'(She) must be healthy.'

2.1.2 Evidentials

When speakers have some evidence for the information, they would mark it with evidential auxiliaries. The evidence may be immediate/direct or distant/indirect/hearsay. Five common evidentials can be aligned as in Figure 5 below along the cline of directness of evidence [INF= infinitive form, INFO= informal form].

Immediate/Direct ←――――――――――――――→ Distant/Indirect/Hearsay

INF-soo_1– – INFO.-yoo – – INFO. -rashii – – INFO. - soo_2

(INFO. -mitai*)

Figure 5. Evidential forms

* -*Mitai* is an colloquial expression covering -*yoo* and -*rashii*. It will not be mentioned separately in the following discussion. Morphologically -*rashii* is an adjective, but all others including *mitai* are nominal and the copula can be added, e.g. -*yoo da*.

Among the four evidential markers under discussion, only soo_1 requires the preceding verb to be in the infinitive form (INF), and all others require informal forms (INFO) with different tenses and negative-affirmative polarities. This means, for example, with the verb *fur-* 'fall,' soo_1 can only have the form *furi-soo*, but soo_2 can have *furu-soo, futta-soo, furanai-soo, furanakatta-soo*. From the semantic/functional point of view, soo_1 indicates the most immediate and direct evidence typically obtained through visual perception and internal senses. A speaker utters (28) when he sees a book which is about to fall, and utters (29) when he feels a sensation that he is about to vomit.

(28) hon ga   ochi-soo   da
      book NOM fall:INF-EVI COP
      'It looks like the book is falling off (the shelf)'

(29) aa haki-soo
      oh vomit:INF-EVI
      'Oh, I feel like vomiting.'

With adjectives, the form must be the root (*oishi-* 'delicious'), and with the nominal adjective, the nominal adjective itself is used (*genki* 'healthy').

(30) kore wa   **oishi**-soo   da
      this TOP delicious-EVI COP
      'This looks delicious.'

(31) kare wa **genki**-soo da
     he   TOP healthy-EVI COP
     'He looks healthy.'

At the opposite end of the chart above is soo_2, which follows, as mentioned already, tense marked informal forms of a verb (*furu* 'fall', *futta* 'fell' etc.) or adjective (*oishii* 'delicious'), or the copula (*da, janai*). Soo_2 is a hearsay evidential marker used when the speaker did not witness an event himself, but simply obtained the information through a third party's account.[5]

(32) ame ga furu   soo da
     rain NOM fall:NONPAST EVI COP
     '(I) hear it will rain.'

(33) kore wa oishii   soo da
     this TOP delicious:NONPAST EVI COP
     '(I) hear this is delicious.'

(34) kare wa **genki** da soo da
     he   TOP healthy COP EVI COP
     '(I) hear that he is healthy.'

Between soo_1 and soo_2 are found *yoo* and *rashii*. These may be used interchangeably in some cases, but *yoo* tends to be used for visual evidence and *rashii* for hearsay evidence. When speakers make a comment based on their direct observation on something about the addressee, *yoo*, but not *rashii*, will be selected, as shown in (35). Notice that soo_1 cannot be used here as it requires the preceding verb form be infinitive and cannot include the aspectual information coded in *natta* 'to have become.' On the other hand, when the speaker makes a comment based on the hearsay evidence, *rashii* (but not *yoo*) will be selected, as shown in (36). (McGloin 1989: 101–104).[6]

---

5. A colloquial hearsay evidential is -*tte*. This word is related to the quotative particle *to*.

   (i) ashita   wa ame da tte
        tomorrow TOP rain COP QT
        '(I) hear it'll be rainy tomorrow.'

   (ii) ashita wa ame ga furu   tte
                   rain NOM fall:NONPAST QT
        '(I) hear it'll rain tomorrow.'

6. When a noun appears before these auxiliaries, the copula is suppressed before *rashii*, but appears as *no* with *yoo da* and as *da* with soo_2.

   kodomo __ rashii   (e.g. It seems that (the culprit) is a child.)
   kodomo <u>no</u> yoo da   (e.g. It seems that (the culprit) is a child.)
   kodomo <u>da</u> soo da   (e.g. I heard that (the culprit) is a child.)

(35) (A speaker makes a comment upon seeing a friend who has been sick.)
   kimi genki ni   natta   yoo da ne/*rashii ne/*soo da ne
   you   healthy COP:ATT become:PAST   EVI COP PP/EVI   PP/ EVI COP PP
   '(From what I see) You seem to have gotten well.'

(36) (On the phone, a speaker tries to confirm if what he heard from someone else is true.)
   kimi genki ni   natta   *yoo da ne/rashii ne/soo da ne
   you   healthy COP:ATT become:PAST   EVI COP PP/EVI   PP/EVI COP PP
   '(From what I head) You have gotten well.'

2.2 Evaluative modality

Evaluative modality is close to epistemic modality discussed above. But while the epistemic modality codes speaker's external stance vis-à-vis the proposition, the evaluative modality embeds the speaker view within the proposition. That is, while the epistemic modality deals with qualification of an event ('it looks like it rained'), the evaluative modality deals with an interpretation of an event ('unfortunately it rained'). One example of evaluative modality is the aspectual form -te-shimau, or its contracted form –chau/zyau, which shows an interpretation of 'frustration' (Chapter 7 §2.4.1.2).

(37) a. taroo ga   kega   o   shita
      (name) NOM injury ACC do:PAST
      'Taro was injured.'

   b. taroo ga kega o shite-shimatta/shi-chatta
                     do:TE-ASP:PAST
      'Oh, Poor Taro was injured.'

While (37a) simply describes the state of affairs, in (37b) the speaker's evaluation of the situation (e.g. "Oh, I feel bad.") is overlaid upon the information conveyed. It must be stressed that the evaluation is ascribed to the speaker, and not to Taro. Though Taro most likely has a similar negative opinion of the event, it is not explicitly included in the -te-shimau expression. Another grammatical resource for encoding speaker evaluation is the indirect passive which often codes adversity (Chapter 8 §1.1.3). In fact, -te shimau and indirect passives often co-occur to enhance the evaluative meaning ascribed by the speaker, (38). Of course, the speaker can encode his stance toward himself as well, (39).

Rashii has an additional meaning of stereotyping. Under this interpretation *kodomo rashii* means that '(someone) is a representative of a child (in a positive sense). *Yoo da*, on the other hand, has an additional meaning of simile; *kodomo no yoo da* can therefore mean '(someone) is/behaves like a child (often, though not always, in a bad sense), i.e. childish.'

(38) taroo   ga   ame   ni   furarete-shimatta
    (name)   NOM   rain   DAT   fall: PASS:TE-ASP:PAST
    'Poor Taro got rained on.'

(39) boku wa   aitsu   ni   aidea o   nusumarete-shimatta
    1SG TOP that.guy   DAT   idea   ACC steal: PASS:TE-ASP:PAST
    'I got my idea stolen by that guy.'

Another example of evaluative modality is the use of benefactive auxiliaries, especially with the *kureru/kudasau* variety. (40) means that the speaker received the benefit from Taro who read a book to Hanako when, e.g. the speaker was busy. (§1.2.2 above, Chapter 8 §5.1; Ohye 1975; Kuno & Kaburaki 1977).[7]

(40) taroo   ga   **hanako ni**   hon   o   yonde-kureta
    (name)   NOM   (name) DAT   book   ACC read:TE-give:PAST
    'Taro read a book for Hanako.'

3. Pragmatic particles

A group of monosyllabic words that appear often at the end of a sentence is referred to as "sentence final particles" (*shuu joshi* 終助詞). They are also known as "pragmatic" or "interactional" particles. They include: *ne, yo, sa, no, wa, ze, zo, na* and *ka*, and primarily encode the interactional modality. In particular, they mark the degree of sharedness of information (§3.1), perform illocutionary acts (§3.2), and adjust the force of an assertion (§3.3). There are also similar sentence final elements which perform some of these functions.

---

7. The other benefactive auxiliaries, *yaru/ageru* 'give' and *morau* 'receive,' are less subjective in that they can encode benefit given to a non-speaker. Compared to (40) which strongly encodes benefit for the speaker, (i) and (ii) below encode benefit for the third person, Taro, without involving the speaker. In other words, (i) and (ii) are less subjective statements compared to (40).

(i) **hanako wa**   taroo   ni   hon   o   yonde-yatta/ageta
    (name) TOP   (name)   DAT   book   ACC read:TE-give:PAST
    'Hanako read a book for Taro.'

(ii) taroo   wa   **hanako ni**   hon   o   yonde-moratta
    (name)   TOP (name) DAT   book   ACC read:TE-receive:PAST
    'Taro had Hanako read a book for him.'

3.1 Markers of the "territory of information"

Depending on which "territory" a piece of information belongs to (cf. the "Theory of Territory of Information," Kamio 1997), the sentence expressing it is marked with different particles. The particle *ne* is a marker of shared information, and it is used to mark a piece of information that presumably exists in both speaker's and addressee's territories. The speaker of (43) below assumes that the addressee has the same information as she does.

(43) moo   sugu oshoogatsu desu   ne
     already soon New.Year   COP:POL PP
     'It's almost the New Year, right?'

In contrast, the particle *yo* is a marker of unshared information. It marks a piece of information that exists in the speaker territory but not in the addressee territory, such as shown in (44). The speaker uses this particle when it is necessary to show the addressee that the information presented has strong relevance in the current speech situation (Matsui 2000). *Zo* (strong assertion) and *ze* (strong appeal) are vulgar varieties of *yo* used by men, which may be added to the informal form of the predicate (Chapter 15 §5).

(44) watashi mo eego   hanasemasu   yo
     I   also English speak:POT:POL:NONPAST PP
     'I can speak English, too, you know.'

(45) ashita   gakkoo yasumi da ze
     tomorrow school closed COP PP
     'The school is closed tomorrow, you know.' (rough sounding)

When the information has just fallen into the speaker's territory ("mirativity" – §3.3 below), and thus not shared with the addressee, the particle *wa* may be added. Male speakers and some female speakers pronounce *wa* with a low falling intonation contour (↘), and some female speakers with a rising intonation contour (↗) (Chapter 15 §5).

(46) a!   kyoo wa nichiyoobi da   wa ↘ / ↗
     oh! today TOP Sunday   COP PP M / FM
     'Oh! Today is Sunday!'

Similarly, as shown in the next example, when the information is a decision that the speaker has just made, thus not shared with the addressee, the same particle can also mark the sudden realization.

(47) ja   ore/watashi   mo iku wa ↘ / ↗
     then I(male vulgar)/I(neutral) also go   PP M / FM
     'Then, I am going, too.'

3.2 Markers of illocutionary act

Pragmatic particles may also perform a variety of illocutionary acts; *ka* for requesting an answer, *ne* for reminding the addressee of certain information, urging him to agree with the speaker, and attempting to establish a common ground (Itani 1992). The modal auxiliaries *daroo* and its polite form *deshoo* (both with a rising intonation), and the grammaticalized negative expression *janai* (rising or falling) (Kawanishi 1994; McGloin 2002) can also be used in similar ways. Intonation is indicated by the following symbols: falling (↘), rising (↗), rising-falling (∧), falling-rising (∨). Here these intonation contours are not associated with the male/female distinction.

(48) *anata wa kinoo soko ni imashita ka* ↗
you TOP yesterday there LOC exist:POL:PAST Q
'Were you there yesterday?'

(49) *anata wa kinoo soko ni imashita ne* ↗
you TOP yesterday there LOC exist:POL:PAST PP
'You were there yesterday, weren't you?'

(50) *kyoo wa atsui desu nee* ∧
today TOP hot:NONPAST COP PP
'It's hot today, isn't it?'

(51) *yamada-san wa tookyoo no umare janai* ↗ /*daroo* ↗/*deshoo* ↗
(name)-Mr. TOP (place) GEN birth PP /PP /PP
'Mr. Yamada was born in Tokyo, right?'

(52) *kono keeki oishii janai* ↘/*daroo* ↘/*deshoo* ↘
this cake delicious:NONPAST PP /PP /PP
'This cake is delicious, isn't it?'

A combined pragmatic particle, *yone(e)*, is used when speakers want to confirm the information that they believe to be true with the addressee. The tone on *ne* is rising (↗), while that on *nee* is rising-falling (∧). (The tone on *yo* is always falling (↘).)

(53) *yamada-san wa tookyoo no umare deshita yone* ↗/*yonee* ∧
(name)-Mr. TOP Tokyo GEN birth COP:PAST PP/PP
'Mr. Yamada was born in Tokyo, right?'
OR 'You were born in Tokyo, right? Mr. Yamada.'

Finally, some conjunctions have developed into a sentence final particle of politeness which lessens the force of an assertion. The concessive conjunctions *kedo* 'but' and *ga* 'but,' and the cause/reason conjunctions *kara* 'so' and *node* 'so,' may end a sentence to weaken the assertion, often creating the effect of politeness (Nakayama & Ichihashi-Nakayama 1997; Haugh 2008; cf. Mori 1999). They also signal a turn transition so that the addressee is expected to react upon hearing these particles (Chapter 12, Note 4).

(54) *suimasen yamada desu ga/kedo*
    excuse.me (name) COP but
    'Hello, this is Yamada.' (on the phone)

3.3 Markers of unassimilated information

There are some sentence final resources which mark new and unassimilated information ("mirativity"), and here the sentence final *no da* expression is the most important type (Maynard 1992; Iwasaki 1993c). *No* glossed as SE (sentence extender) in *no da* may also appear as a clitic form, *-n*. Depending on the exact kind of information, the pragmatic effect of these expressions may differ. (55) communicates the speaker's internal state, which is presented as new information for the addressee.[8] Both (56) and (57) announce unexpected information for the addressee, but the former is used as an imperative and the latter as the introduction for an anecdote.

(55) *atama ga   itai-n   desu*
    head NOM painful-SE COP
    '(I) have a headache.'

(56) *anata mo kuru-n   desu!*
    you   also come:NONPAST-SE COP
    'You, come, too!'

(57) *kinoo   yoshiko ni guuzen   atta   no yo*
    yesterday (name) DAT by.chance meet:PAST SE PP
    '(I) met Yoshiko by accident yesterday, you see.'

No may also appear without the copula, thereby making it look like a monosyllabic pragmatic particle like others. When the sentence-final *no* is uttered with a rising intonation, it marks a presupposed question.

(54) *iku   no* ↗
    go:NONPAST SE
    'Are (you/we) going?'
    (= I believe that you/we are going; Is my assumption correct?)

(55) *doko iku   no* ↗
    where go:NONPAST SE
    'Where are (you/we) going?'
    (= I know you/we are going somewhere; Where is it?)

When it is uttered with a falling intonation, it adds incredulity.

---

8. Note if the speaker utters this sentence without *-n desu*, the sentence is an internal state expression described in §1.1 in this chapter (e.g. *aa! atama itai!* 'Oh, my head hurts!')

(56) iku   no ↘
      go:NONPAST SE
      'You/we are going!'
      (= I've just realized that you/we are going; Is my assumption correct?)

4. Conversation and language

Conversation is one of the most fundamental environments in which people use language. There are linguistic resources that assist speakers to manage this social activity, and in turn this social activity helps to shape linguistic resources for the speaker. Two prominent linguistic resources are pragmatic particles (see above) and discourse markers. To understand their functions precisely, some researchers adopt as frameworks Conversation Analysis (CA) (e.g. Sacks, Schegloff & Jefferson 1974; C. Goodwin & Heritage 1990). In CA, conversational language is seen as the locus of human social interaction (see e.g. Tanaka 1999; Mori 1999; Hayashi 2003; Shimako Iwasaki 2008; Koike 2009 as examples of application of CA to Japanese).[9]

4.1 Pragmatic particles and *aizuchi*

Though some functions of pragmatic particles have been discussed in §3 above, these particles, especially *ne* and *sa*, are involved significantly in the negotiation of moves in conversation (Morita 2005). They elicit the addressee's attention and show hesitation during the communication process, much as 'you know' does in English. This function is most apparent in the phrase final as well as word final (rather than the clause/sentence final) position. Particles used in this way have been called *kantoo joshi* (間投助詞) "interjectional particle" in the Japanese linguistic tradition. As shown in (57) below (taken from Morita 2005: 40 with adjustments in glosses and translation), the speaker is figuring out how to proceed with her utterance and at the same time she delays the production of sentence so as to achieve a desirable state for interaction (Morita 2005: 40; cf. Goodwin 1981).

(57) ano ne:, ja   ne:, e:to ne:,
      uhm PP   then PP   well PP
      'uhm... then... well ...'

---

9. While many analyses of grammar in conversation use CA as a guiding principle, the main interest of CA remains to be an analysis of social action between members of a society. The grammatical resources discussed in this section are also not analyzed in the pure CA framework, but are examined in interaction in a more general framework of pragmatics informed by the CA research. This line of research has been developing as Interactional Linguistics (see Selting & Couper-Kuhlen 2001; Ochs, Schegloff & Thompson 1996.)

The following is an excerpt taken from an actual narrative. (This is the same segment used in Chapter 3 §5). Each phrase ending with *ne* is represented in a separate line. The pragmatic particle, *ne(e)*, appears after a noun phrase (lines 1, 3 and 4), and after a verb phrase (line 2).

(58) 1 *watashi wa nee,*   'I, you know …
          I   TOP PP

      2 *uchi de   kiita   no ne* ↗   …heard at home, you know.
          home LOC hear:PAST SE PP

      3 *sono are   wa   ne* ↗   …that thing, you know.
          that that TOP PP

      4 *hoosoo   wa   ne* ↗   …that broadcast, you know.
          broadcast TOP PP

      5 *kazoku de* ↘   …with my family.'
          family INS

'I heard that broadcast (= the Emperor's announcing the defeat of the war on the radio) at home with my family.'

While the speaker uses pragmatic particles to engage the conversation partner in interaction, the listener uses minimal vocal signs called *aizuchi* such as *nn* in Japanese to show his/her engagement (Mizutani 1979; Aoki 2008). It has been shown that Japanese conversationalists use such minimal vocal signs much more frequently than, say, English speakers (Maynard 1989; Clancy et al. 1996; Iwasaki 1997; Kita & Ide 2007). Two speakers in the next excerpt have been talking about their experiences in a major earthquake that hit Los Angeles (see a discussion of "Northridge Earthquake Data" in Iwasaki 1997). Here Speaker A is complaining why many of her neighbors were getting ready to leave by car though the safest place is the middle of the wide street (in front of their houses). A and B take turns, but B's utterances are all in the form of *aizuchi*.

(59) A 1 *nigeru hitsuyoo ga nai deshoo:. ano.*
      B 2   *nn nn nn*
      A 3 *… dooro ga are dake hirokute::.*
      B 4   *nn nn*
      A 5 *… ie ga ne: ^ doo taorete-kitatte dooro no mannaka wa,*
      B 6   *nn nn*
      A 7 *… daijoobu na-n da kara: ^* (while laughing during *kara*)
      B 8   *nn nn*
      A 9 *kanzen ni anzen na basho tte iu no wa dooro ni: … aru wake da kara: ^*

[: (lengthened vowel), ^ (stressed syllable with a rise-fall intonation contour), … (audible pause)]

(English translation)
A 1 there is no need to escape
B 2   nn nn nn
A 3 the streets are so wide
B 4   nn nn
A 5 no matter where a house falls down, the middle of the street is
B 6   nn nn
A 7 is safe
B 8   nn nn
A 9 the perfectly safe place is in the street

Listeners may also use "reactive tokens," which are more substantive utterances to give specific feedback (Clancy et al. 1996; Iwasaki 1997). Some examples include, *naruhodo* 'I see,' *soo desu ka* 'I see,' *honto ni* 'Really,' *maji?* "Really/No kidding?', and *masaka* 'Unbelievable!'. The next excerpt comes from the same earthquake conversation described above. B in line 2 gives an *aizuchi* and in line 4 a reactive token. The portions marked off by square brackets on lines 2 through 4 indicate the beginning of an overlapped utterances produced simultaneously by speaker A and B.

(60)   A 1 *ano toki sugu shoppingusentaa ni ikoo ka tte yuu…*
       B 2 **hai hai [hai**
       A 3   [*kangae mo atta-n desu kedo* [*nee?*
       B 4   [*naruhodo nee?*

(English translation).
A 1 at that time, I was going shopping
B 2 **yes yes [yes**
A 3   [I was thinking that but [you see?
B 4   [I see.

4.2 Discourse markers and discourse connectives

Speakers use discourse markers to manage the interaction and communication process; 'oh', 'well', 'now', 'then', 'you know', and 'I mean' are some examples of English discourse markers (Schiffrin 1986). Speakers rely on these markers as they constantly reformulate their speech during interaction, and listeners rely on them to figure out discourse level coherence. Discourse connectives such as 'and', 'but', 'or', 'so', and 'because' in English are a subset of discourse markers which link two points, [X] and [Y], in conversational interaction. Their use is motivated by the speaker's communicative needs rather than the semantic or logical ones. Japanese also uses a number of discourse markers and discourse connectives; e.g. *sorede, soide, de, nde* ('and'); *ja, jaa* ('well then'); *demo, kedo, dakedo, dakedomo* ('but'), *sorekara* ('then') (see Onodera 2004).[10]

---

10. In addition to these discourse markers and connectives, a rich array of discourse modal adverbs (*nanka* 'somehow,' *chotto* 'a little,' *yappari* 'as expected') and pragmatic particles discussed

Dakara, which was developed from a logical linker[11], is one of the most frequently used discourse connectives in Japanese (Maynard 1993; Mori 1999). In the structure, {[X] *dakara* [Y]}, *dakara* links an "afterthought clarification" in [Y] to some information [X] expressed or implied in the preceding portion of discourse. Said differently, a speaker deploys *dakara* when she finds herself in need of adding comments for something that has been said or implied earlier. From the addressee's point of view, *dakara* gives an instruction to interpret [Y] as relevant to the previous material said or implied. (61) is taken from a different conversation from the "Northridge Earthquake Data." A is explaining that she woke up when her roommate jumped onto her bed ([X] = line (1) at the time a big earthquake hit ([Y] = line 4). [The portions marked off by square brackets on lines 1 and 2 were produced simultaneously by speakers A and H.].

(61)   Earthquake Data #2; A = female, H = male
    A   1   *jibun no beddo ni batto not[tekita-n desu yo. wata]shi ga*
    H   2   *[ho h honto ni]*
    A   3   *neteru toki ni*
    A   4   **dakara** *sore de bikkurishite okita tte kanji de.*

[English translation].
    A   1   (My roommate) [jumped on] my bed, when I
    H   2   [Re- really!]
    A   3   was sleeping.
    A   4   <u>So</u> that made me wake up.

In the example above, the relationship between [X] and [Y] can be characterized as 'cause-result,' but in other cases, the relationship is reversed, i.e. 'result-cause,' as in the next example, (62) below. These diverse interpretations make it difficult to interpret *dakara* as a logical conjunction, but confirm that the function of *dakara* is most appropriately captured in terms of communication/ interactional perspective.

(62) is taken from a different earthquake conversation between two male speakers. Before the excerpt, S had told K that he was standing on the bed and trying to support

---

in this chapter provide speakers with the means to add varieties of personal stance towards the proposition and to navigate through conversational interactions.

11. *Dakara* consists of *da* (copula) and *kara* ('because/so'). As a logical linker *dakara* appears after a nominal element, including a nominalized clause with *n(o)*, as shown in (i) below.

(i)   Tawara Moeko, a female writer, recalling a childhood memory   (NHK, 10/16/2005)
[X] *anta-gata wa ne kankee nai n   **dakara***
      you-PL   TOP PP relation exist:NEG DAKARA
[Y] *deteitte kudasai to itte   itta   n desu kedo*
      leave   please   QT say:TE say:PAST SE COP but

[X] = "You are not related to us <u>so</u>
[Y] = please leave here," we said that.

the ceiling so it would not fall down on him during the earthquake. S said in lines 1 and 2 that he could not reach the ceiling after the earthquake, so K asked in line 3 if S had been standing on one foot to reach the ceiling. In line 4, S said 'no', and produced *da* (possibly a short version of *dakara*), and explained that he could reach the ceiling at that time during the earthquake (on both feet). Ignoring (or possibly because of) K's protest (*aa demo* 'yeah, but') in line 5, S deploys *dakara* on line 6 to give an afterthought explanation; he now thinks that the room was shaped like a parallelogram at that time. K gave a reactive token in line 8. Here, [X] is the fact that S could reach the ceiling during the earthquake and [Y] is a possible explanation for this fact. In other words, [X]-[Y] has the relationship of 'result-cause'. *Dakara* allowed the speaker to provide a (possible) cause in [Y] as additional information, and the addressee was fully convinced when he said 'Wow, that's something!'.

(62)   Earthquake Data #4: S = male, K = male
    S   1   *demo ima wa... beddo no ue ni agatte te nobashitara todokanai-n*
           2   *desu yo*
    K   3   *ja kataashi de isshokenmee koo yatteta tte koto na-n desu ka?*
    S   4   *iya iya iya.* **da** *ano toki wa todoiteta-n desu yo*
    K   5   *aa demo*
    S   6   **dakara** *tabun tatemono ga heekooshihenkee n*
           7   *natteta-n no ka* [*naa toka omou-n da kedo.*
    K   8   [*su.. sugoi desu nee.*

(English translation)
    S   1   but now...I could not reach the ceiling even if I got up on the bed,
           2   you see.
    K   3   You mean you were trying to reach it on one foot?
    S   4   No, no, no. <u>So</u> (*da*) I could reach it at that time.
    K   5   Yeah, but...
    S   6   <u>So</u> (*dakara*) the building was probably warped like a parallelogram,
           7   I think probably.
    K   8   Oh, my.

Speakers also rely on *dakara* when they proceed in discourse with some difficulty. In the following excerpt, P's use of *dakara* is not to provide [Y], but works as a pause filler.

(63)   Saikin no Ko (JPN Corpus)[12]
P: ...   de   kono aida   a--- ...***dakara***...   kayoobi   ni..
        and that   period   uhm – <u>so</u>   Tuesday   on

---

12. JPN Corpus was constructed by Tsuyoshi Ono (University of Alberta) and Ryoko Suzuki (Keio University).

dakara... shoonan   ni   itte:
so   (place name) DAT go: TE
'the other day… uhm… on Tuesday uhm… I went to Shonan, and…'

Datte is another frequently used discourse marker, which is similar to *dakara*, but is clearly distinctive from it. The two structures, {[X] *datte* [Y]} and {[X] *dakara* [Y]}, can be contrasted in a number of ways (Maynard 1993: 98–119; Ford & Mori 1994: 43–58; Mori 1999); (a) while *datte* is used in a context where opposition, contrast, and challenge is present in discourse, *dakara* does not require such a context, (b) thus *datte* is used when strong "self-justification" is required, while *dakara* is used simply to "add information" to further explain [X], (c) while *daraka* relies on interlocutor's cooperation in making a link between [X] and [Y], *datte* presents speaker's opinion without such a cooperation. All these give a softer impression for *dakara* and a stronger one for *datte*. In other words, *datte* gives a strong instruction to the addressee to accept [Y] as relevant explanation for the previous material said or implied.

In (64) below, *datte* is delivered in a challenged context and provides the speaker to give justification. This is a conversation between husband (H) and wife (W). Prior to this segment, they were talking about the boyfriend of their female relative. The boyfriend cancelled a trip they had planned because he decided to work over a long weekend. W had been insisting that the boyfriend is a workaholic and loves his work more than his girlfriend. H had been defending the boyfriend, and in line 1 he said "It's not that he loves the job." To this, W counters first with *ee?*, a strong sign of disagreement, and then with "But he loves it" in line 3, and then deploys *datte* to provide evidence ('he takes no vacation') in line 4 to justify her opinion ('he loves his job').

(64) Ryoko (JPN Corpus)
    H 1 *sukitte yuun ja nain da yo* [*na*].
    W 2   [*ee*]?
          3 *demo suki nan da yo.*
          4 ***datte*** *zenzen yasumi nai te itta yo.*
    H 5 … *n:n… **dakara** mawari no fun'iki toka ga aru shi ne.*

[English translation].
    H 1 It's not that he likes it.
    W 2   What?!
          3 But he likes it.
          4 Because (*datte*) (she said) he's never taken a vacation.
    H 5 … uhm… so (*dakara*) he needs to be concerned with what others think

Note also in (64) that H deploys *dakara* in line 5 to add supplementary information to his earlier claim about the boyfriend in line 1. *Dakara* gives an opportunity for the speaker to elaborate [Y] ('he needs to be concerned with what others think') on the point he made earlier, [X] ('it's not that he loves his job.').

Datte is also used as a lead to an "agreement-plus-elaboration" format when the speaker targets an utterance towards his own agreeing utterance (Mori 1999: 65). In (65) below, T was explaining how hard for a foreign student to become a medical doctor in the US. In line 3, K agrees with *soo da yo ne* 'I agree,' and adds *datte* to provide an elaboration, i.e. '(medical) terminology is difficult.' In this self-directed *datte*, there is no sense of opposition expressed.

(65)　Ryugaku (JPN Corpus)
```
    T    1    ryuugakusei ga nanchuu no?
         2    ishan naru kakuritsu wa ippaasento rashii.
    K    3    a honto ni? soo da yo ne.
    T    4    nn
    K    5    ... datte yoogo ga muzukashii mon.
```

[English translation].
```
    T    1    exchange students, what shall I say?
         2    the probability of their becoming a doctor is like about 1 percent
    K    3    Oh, really. That makes sense.
    T    4    nn (=yeah)
    K    5    ... because the terminology is difficult.
```

Finally, *dakara* and *datte* both may be used as an emotive reactive token when they are directed to an interlocutor's immediate prior utterance. While *dakara* reminds the addressee of a reason with an irritated tone ('as you should know'), *datte* gives the instruction to accept the reason without challenge ('You may not know, but you should know'). In (66) and (67), mother is urging her son to hurry up, and the son is responding to her demand. Observe the interpretation for each reaction.

(66)　Mother: *hayaku shinasai!*
　　　　　　　hurry　do:IMP
　　　　　　　'Hurry up, would you!'

　　　　Son:　*dakara　　wakatta　　　　tte:*
　　　　　　　DAKARA　understand:PAST　QT
　　　　　　　'(As you should know) I know (that I have to hurry up)!'

(67)　Mother: *hayaku shinasai*
　　　　　　　hurry　do:IMP
　　　　　　　'Hurry up, would you!'

　　　　Son:　*date　　booshi　ga　　nai-n　　　da　　mon.*
　　　　　　　DATTE　hat　　　NOM　exist:NEG　COP　SE
　　　　　　　'(You may not know, but you should know that) I can't find my hat! (That is why I am taking time).'

As shown in this section, discourse connectives allow speakers to link some information to the preceding context. This is an extremely important and useful function when speakers talk in real time and need to constantly monitor his/her own and interlocutors' utterances and make adjustments. The two discourse connectives described here make it possible for the speaker to add relevant information continuously to make the conversation meaningful.[13]

---

13. Put another way, conversational participants always perform 'repairs' (i.e. corrections), but without the resources such as discourse markers and connectives, the language communication is disrupted in a significant way. When a participant wants to make a repair, she usually does not replace what was said before with different wording, but signals minimally to alert the other participants to work out what needs to be repaired. In this way sequentiality in interaction is only minimally disrupted.

CHAPTER 15

Speech styles and registers

Speakers use various speech styles and registers while talking. Socio-cultural values associated with people's identities, their mutual relations and interactional roles, and the purpose and occasion of talk are all important factors that influence speech styles and characterize registers. As an adult member of a society, speakers must understand socio-linguistic norms associated with the way they speak (Ide 2006), but they also sometimes choose to deviate from these norms in order to create a particular effect (Maynard 2007; Jones & Ono 2008). This chapter describes speech styles and registers with a special focus on personal indexical terms, direct and indirect speech, honorifics, and gendered speech.

1. Personal indexical terms

Personal indexical terms are those words that speakers use to refer to different people in discourse. Personal pronouns are forms that are specialized for this purpose. However, Japanese personal pronouns are not like English pronouns in that they are not simply a means to refer to people, but also index the level of formality. Diagram 1 on the next page shows common first, second, and third person pronouns arranged from more informal to more formal varieties. Those marked with (M) and (F) are used by male and female speakers, respectively, in normal situations.

Across the rows in the diagram are several different pronoun forms for first, second and third persons. The diagram also indicates prescribed pairs of 1st and 2nd person pronouns; *ore-omae*, *boku-kimi* and *atashi-anta*. Though *watashi* and *anata* are often paired together, some clarification is in order. *Anata* is often used as the translation equivalent of the English second person pronoun, 'you,'[1] but its usage is much more restricted compared to its first person counterpart, *watashi*. For example, a younger

---

1. *Anata* can refer both to the "physical other," or the person whom I am speaking to, and to the "substantive other," or the person who claims to be someone. The following two examples clarify the divided "selves"; *anata ga anata de aru koto o shoomeisuru mono* 'items that prove that *anata* (physical you) is *anata* (substantive you),' a public notice found in a post office (Y. Kawanishi – personal communication, Dec. 2010) and *anata ga anata de aru tame ni* 'In order for *anata* (physical you) to be *anata* (substantive you)' (a book title).

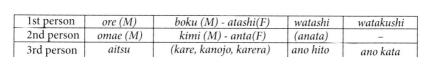

	Informal			Formal
1st person	ore (M)	boku (M) - atashi(F)	watashi	watakushi
2nd person	omae (M)	kimi (M) - anta(F)	(anata)	–
3rd person	aitsu	(kare, kanojo, karera)	ano hito	ano kata

Diagram 1. Formality and personal indexical terms

speaker who can refers to himself/herself as *watashi* is not allowed to address an older person with *anata* (Kindaichi 1988: 166). In other words, there is no second person pronoun which can be used for a socially superior person. The most typical situation in which *anata* is used is between two female adult speakers in an informal, friendly situation. Third person reference can usually be made by deictic expressions, which is also aligned along the speech level cline as shown in Diagram 1 above. They are always non-generic and referential. *Aitsu* used mostly by men in an informal setting means literally 'that guy,' and *ano hito* and *ano kata* both mean 'that person,' *kata* being more formal than *hito*. Although *kare* 'he' and *kanojo* 'she' are known as third person pronouns, they are not usually used for one's seniors. They are employed more by younger speakers as pronouns for their equals. In addition they are also used for the meanings of 'boyfriend' and 'girlfriend,' respectively.[2]

In actual conversation, a variety of other strategies can be employed to refer to different people in discourse. First, kinship terms such as *okaasan* 'Mom' and *onii-chan* '(Elder) brother' are often used for 1st, 2nd and 3rd persons. See Table 1 on the next page.[3] While any kinship terms with the senior value can be used in place of the 1st and 2nd person pronouns, those with the junior value cannot. Thus, during their childhood,

---

Until recently, *anata* was used by wives/girlfriends as an intimate term to address their husbands/boyfriends. However, this use is rapidly fading, and younger couples tend to use their first names or nicknames reciprocally (Y. Kawanishi – personal communication, Dec. 2010).

2. See Chapter 13 Note 2 for the use of the reflexive pronoun *jibun* as a personal pronoun.

3. The suffix *–chan* in *ojii-chan, obaa-chan, onii-chan* and *onee-chan* is a diminutive title suffix (Chapter 5 §2.2) which is often used among family members by both young and adult speakers. The other more formal *-san* suffix is used often to refer to a person outside of the family. To an elderly male person who seems to be in trouble, for example, one might offer help by saying *ojii-san daijoobu desuka* 'Are you alright, grandpa?' On the other hand, *-san* is the norm for 'Mom' (*Okaa-san*) and 'Dad' (*Otoo-san*). *Okaa-chan* and *otoo-chan* are only rarely heard in the Tokyo area.

an elder sister can say to her younger brother, *onee-chan ga iku yo* (elder.sister NOM go PP) 'I will go,' but a younger brother cannot say, **otooto ga iku yo* (younger.brother NOM go PP) 'I will go.' Likewise, *okaa-san ga katta no?* (mother NOM bought Q) 'Is it you (Mom) who bought it?' is fine, but **musume ga katta no* (daughter NOM bought Q) 'Is it you (daughter) who bought it?' is not. The same rule applies to the use of kinship terms as address terms. Thus, a son can call his father, *otoo-san!* 'Dad!' but the father cannot call his son, **musuko!* 'Son!' Instead, the father has to call his son by his name, e.g. *Taro!*.

Table 1. Senior and junior kinship terms

Senior kinship terms		Junior kinship terms	
ojii-chan	'grandpa'	*mago*	'grandchild'
obaa-chan	'grandma'	*musuko*	'son'
otoo-san	'dad'	*musume*	'daughter'
okaa-san	'mom'	*otooto*	'brother (younger)'
onii-chan	'brother (elder)'	*imooto*	'sister (younger)'
onee-chan	'sister (elder)'		

Second, personal names with or without a title suffix are also frequently used in place of second and third person pronouns (but not of first person pronouns[4]). Diagram 2 below shows a variety of ways a person named <u>Yamada Ken</u> (the <u>family name</u> followed by a male given name) may be referred to and addressed according to the formality cline.

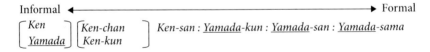

Diagram 2. Formality and use of personal names (1)

---

4. The only exception is that very young children may use their first names to refer to themselves. Thus a young girl whose nickname is *Satchan* may say *Satchan mo iku*, which literary means 'Satchan is also going,' but is understood to mean 'I will go, too.' Another notable use of reference term is the use of *boku*. This is a male first-person pronoun, but a male or female adult speaker may address a young boy with this term – *boku mo iku?* (lit. Is 'I' going?, but it is understood to mean 'Are you going?').

Each item is described in detail in Table 2 below.

Table 2. Formality and use of personal names (2)

Ken	very informal, blunt	given name alone; used among very close friends, or by an older family member to a younger member, e.g. mother to her child
Yamada	informal, blunt	family name alone; used among close male friends
Ken-chan	informal, familiar	-chan is a diminutive title suffix used for young boys and girls
Ken-kun	polite, familiar	-kun is more formal than -chan which can be attached to boy's (but not girl's) given name
Ken-san	polite, familiar	-san is more formal than -kun which can be attached to people's first name; is used between close adult speakers
Yamada-kun	polite, friendly	-kun with the family name is mostly used among adult speakers for a male referent; it may be also used for a female subordinate by her superior
Yamada-san	formal-neutral, polite	-san is also attached to a family name, and is the most common form among adult speakers
Yamada-sama	formal, polite	-sama is a formal personal title suffix that can be added to a family name in an extremely formal situation, e.g. a store attendant addressing a customer

Third, a combination of name and occupational title may also be used in place of second and third person pronouns; *Yamada sensee* (Prof. Yamada), or *Yamada shachoo* (President Yamada). For second person pronouns, bare titles such as *sensee* and *shachoo* are more natural (*sensee mo ikaremasuka* ('teacher also go') 'Are you (=teacher) going, too?').[5] The use of names and titles are particularly important as a second person reference terms at the neutral and more formal levels, where no appropriate second person pronouns exist that can be paired with *watashi* and *watakushi*, as shown in Diagram 1 on page 315 and discussed earlier above.[6]

---

5. Bare titles are normally not used for first-person indexical forms. One notable exception is the use of *sensee* 'teacher' when a teacher calls him/herself while talking to younger students (up to high school); *minna yoku dekite sensee mo ureshii* 'Everyone did very well (on the test). Teacher (I) am also happy.'

6. The use of kinship terms, names, and titles make the division between second-person and third-person ambiguous in some cases, e.g. *Yamada-san wa ikimasu ka* is ambiguous between 'Are you going, Mr. Yamada?' and 'Is Mr. Yamada going?'

2. Predicate forms

Personal reference terms define the formality level in a significant way, as described above. However, due to the liberal use of noun ellipsis in Japanese, they do not appear much in discourse. Predicates, on the other hand, appear in different forms much more frequently and thus play a more significant role in determining the formality level and characterizing a specific register. Table 3 below summarizes various forms of verbs, adjectives, and copulas in terms of their corresponding formality levels. (It should be noted that the description of these forms in this chapter is restricted to their most canonical uses. See Maynard 1991, 1993, 2008; Cook 1990, 1999; Ikuta 2008 for a pragmatic analysis of these forms.).

Table 3. Speech levels and predicate forms

Informal				Formal
Verb	*iku* *ikanai*	'go' 'not go'	*iki-masu* *iki-massen*	*irasshai-masu* *irasshai-masen*
Adjective	*samui* *samuku nai*	'cold' 'not cold'	*samui desu* *samuku arimasen*	*samuu gozaimasu* *samuku gozaimasen*
Copula	*-da* *-ja nai*	'be' 'not be'	*-desu* *-ja arimasen* *-de wa arimasen*	*-de gozaimasu* *-de wa gozaimasen*

The following two sentences both mean, "Are you going? / Is she going?" but (1) is at the informal level and (2) at the neutral level. Competent Japanese speakers know which form they are expected to use based on their relationship with the addressee and knowledge about the speech situation; cf. the notion of 'discernment' in language use in Japanese (Ide 2006).

(1) *yoshiko mo iku ?* 'Are you going, too, Yoshiko?'
    (name) also go or 'Is Yoshiko going, too?'

(2) *yamada-san mo ikimasu ka?* 'Are you going, too, Ms. Yamada?'
    (name-title) also go:NONPAST Q or 'Is Ms. Yamada going, too?'

3. Direct vs. indirect dimensions

The degree of formality of speech indexed by personal indexical terms and predicate forms intricately interacts with the degree of directness of speech to create the politeness dimension of the speech style and register. The directness of speech can be most clearly seen in the forms of speech-act related expressions, with which speakers fulfill various social needs, such as giving orders, making a request, offering assistance, expressing obligation, permission and prohibition. The speech act of making others perform a task, for example, can be achieved directly by issuing an "order," or more indirectly by making a "request." Expressing an "opinion" or giving a "suggestion" are even more indirect ways of performing a similar task. See Diagram 3 below.

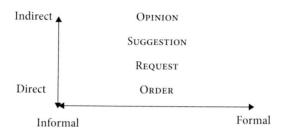

Diagram 3. Direct and indirect dimensions with different speech levels

There are different "order" expressions which can be identified along the informal-formal cline. The use of the imperative verb form (*-e* for consonant verbs, *ik-e* 'go!,' or *-ro* for vowel verbs, *nige-ro*, 'Flee!') is the most direct way of ordering the addressee to do something. The infinitive form of the verb (*ren'yoo-kee*) followed by *nasai* is rather formal (*iki-nasai, nige-nasai*), but its more abrupt form *na* (*iki-na, nige-na*) is at the informal level. Negative orders are marked by the finite form followed by *na* (*iku-na, nigeru-na*). These forms are at the level of informal style.

"Requests" fall into the medium range on the direct-indirect cline. Table 4 below contains a few examples of "Please go" (affirmative request) and "Please don't go" (negative request). Note that an affirmative request is made with the *-te* form, and a negative request with the *-naide* (the *-te* form of the negative suffix *nai*). *-Kure, -choodai,* and *-kudasai* appearing in the following request expressions all mean 'give' (see Chapter 14 §1.2.2).

Table 4. Expressions for 'Please go' and 'Please don't go'

Affirmative	Negative	
itte kure	*ikanaide kure*	informal/male; more direct
itte	*ikanaide*	informal/friendly/close; more direct
itte choodai	*ikanaide choodai*	informal/casual; more direct
itte kudasai	*ikanaide kudasai*	formal, polite command; more direct
itte itadakitai	*ikanaide itadakitai*	very formal, more literal; more indirect
itte hoshii	*ikanaide hoshii*	formal; more indirect

"Opinions" regarding other people's actions or "suggestions" may be used to indirectly issue an order. This is done with various verb forms and periphrastic constructions. The first two expressions in Table 5 below mean 'You'd better (not to) go' (opinion) and the rest mean 'Why don't you (not) go?' (suggestion).

Table 5. Expressions for 'You'd better go' and 'Why don't you go?'

Affirmative	Negative	
iku beki da	iku beki ja nai	(formal)
itta hoo ga ii	ikanai hoo ga ii	(neutral)
ikeba ii jan/ja nai	ikanakereba ii jan/ja nai	(informal, casual)
ikeba?	–	(informal, casual)
ittara?	–	(informal, casual)
ittara doo?	–	(informal)
ittara doo desuka?	–	(formal)
ittara doo deshooka?	–	(very formal)

Diagram 4 below summarizes the rich inventory of speech-act related expressions defined by the dimensions of formality and directness. Only affirmative forms are listed. They all indicate the speaker's attempt to convince the addressee to 'go' with various degrees of formality and directness.

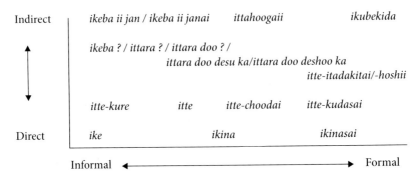

Diagram 4. Actual forms for 'Go' with various speech and directness levels

4. Honorifics

Honorifics serve to code a speaker's understanding of the hierarchical social relationship vis-à-vis the addressee and the referent (cf. Miller 1967; Martin [1975] 1991; Harada 1976). Even though the use of honorifics has been weakening since World War II (Oishi 1983: 222), certain honorifics are still quite prevalent in modern day Japan, especially in commercial and business situations (Oishi 1983: 229). The "referent honorifics" exalt a person who is part of the referential information expressed in a sentence. This can be done either by showing respect to a particular person via the "respect honorifics" (*sonkei-go* 尊敬語) or by humbling one via the "humble honorifics" (*kenjoo-go* 謙譲語). The respect honorifics place an exalted person (or the "target of honorification," after Matsumoto 2008) in the subject position, and thus it is sometimes called the "subject honorific" (Harada 1976). The subject honorific is expressed either by a special honorific verb, the passive verb morphology, or the "*o*-V(infinitive form) *ni naru*" construction. Table 6 below shows different honorific forms. Special honorific verbs are limited in number, and appear, for the most part, in complementary distribution with the periphrastic construction, "*o*-V(infinitive form) *ni naru*." The passive form is most productive, but its use as an honorific is skewed geographically: Tokyo is not among those areas that use the passive form for honorifics extensively (Inoue 1998: 13–4). It should also be noted in Table 6 that *irassharu* is used as a special honorific verb for three different verbs, *iku* 'go,' *kuru* 'come' and *iru* 'stay.' Also note that the periphrastic forms of *kuru* 'come' and *kiru* 'wear' are *o-koshi ni naru* and *o-meshi ni naru*, respectively.

Table 6. Respect honorific verbs

Non-honorific Abrupt form		Special Honorific Verb	Passive	*o*-V *ni naru*
taberu	'eat'	*meshiagaru*	*taberareru*	*o-tabe ni naru*
kuru	'come'	**irassharu**	*korareru*	***o-koshi ni naru***
iku	'go'	**irassharu**	*ikareru*	–
iru	'stay'	**irassharu**	*irareru*	–
yuu	'say'	*ossharu*	*iwareru*	–
suru	'do'	*nasaru*	*sareru*	–
kureru	'give'	*kudasaru*	–	–
kiru	'wear'	–	*kirareru*	***o-meshi ni naru***
kaku	'write'	–	*kakareru*	*o-kaki ni naru*
yomu	'read'	–	*yomareru*	*o-yomi ni naru*
matsu	'wait'	–	*matareru*	*o-machini naru*
motsu	'hold/carry'	–	*motareru*	*o-mochini naru*

In (3) and (4) below, the subject referents, *sensee* 'teacher' and *shachoo* '(company) president,' are shown respect via honorific verb morphology.

(3) *sensee wa o-sakana o meshiagaru / taberareru*
    teacher TOP PFX-fish ACC eat:HON:NONPAST / eat:PSS:NONPAST
    / o-tabe ni naru
    / PFX-eat DAT become:NONPAST
    'The teacher eats fish.'   (respect for the teacher)

(4) shachoo   wa   konna   koto   mo   osshatta / iwareta
    president TOP   such   thing   also say:HON:PAST / say:PSS:PAST
    'The (company) president said this also.'   (respect for the president)

As noted, the respect honorifics are useful only when the target of honorification coincides with the grammatical subject. When it coincides with a non-subject, the humble honorifics must be used, which lowers the status of the subject referent (the agent of the action), thereby, in effect, raising the status of the non-subject referent. The periphrastic construction "*o*-V(infinitive form) *suru*" and a limited number of suppletive humble verbs are available for this type of honorific. (See Table 7 below. Note *itadaku* is a special humble verb for both 'eat' and 'receive').

Table 7. Humble honorific verbs

Non-honorific Abrupt form		Special Humble Verb	*o*-V *suru*
taberu	'eat'	itadaku	–
morau	'receive'	itadaku	–
ageru/yaru	'give'	sashiageru	–
iku	'go'	mairu/ukagau	–
yuu	'say'	moosu/mooshiageru	–
suru	'do'	itasu	–
kaku	'write'	–	*o-kaki suru*
yomu	'read'	**haidoku suru**	*o-yomi suru*
matsu	'wait'	–	*o-machi suru*
motsu	'hold/carry'	–	*o-mochi suru*
miru	'see'	**haiken suru**	–
kariru	'borrow'	**haishaku suru**	*o-kari suru*

In (5) below, the speaker lowers the status of the subject, *imooto* 'my younger sister,' in order to raise the status of the non-subject, *sensee* 'teacher,' coded as a possessor noun. In (6), the speaker lowers his own status in order to raise the status of someone not mentioned in the sentence. As in these examples, the target of honorification is often implicit rather than explicit.

(5) imooto   ga   sensee   no   kaban   o   o-mochi   shita
    y.sister NOM   teacher   GEN   bag   ACC   PFX-carry   do:PAST
    'My younger sister carried the teacher's bag (for him).'
    (Humbling the sister's action, thereby raising the status of the other party involved, i.e. the teacher)

(6) *watashi ga   kawari ni   mairimasu*
    I   NOM   instead DAT go:HUM:NONPAST
    'I will go instead (of you/him).'
    (Humbling the speaker's action, thereby raising the status of the other party involved, i.e. 'you' or an unspecified third person)

As with the respect honorifics, the special form and the periphrastic form are usually in complementary distribution. However, when both forms are available, e.g. *haidoku-suru* and *o-yomi-suru* (two forms of 'to read'), there seems to be some semantic differentiation; while the special humble form simply adds the reserved attitude for one's own action, the *o-V suru* form indicates that one's action is done for the benefit of the other (cf. Matsumoto 2008: 94). This further explains that *haiken-suru* 'see' is prototypically heard in a request by a conductor who wants to examine passengers' ticket on a long distance train. This action is done not for the passenger but for the agent (conductor). However, this explanation does not completely work for the pair *haishaku-suru* and *o-kari suru*, 'to borrow,' as this verb inherently selects the agent (borrower) as a beneficiary.

The Japanese system of referent honorifics is a "relative honorific" system in which the same person can be marked by either a respect or a humble honorific verb or a verbal construction, depending upon the situation. The two sentences below have the same referential content; 'The (company) president said so.' However, (7a) with a respect verb is appropriate when talking to someone within one's own company, but (7b) with a humble verb is appropriate when talking to someone outside the company.

(7) a. *shachoo   ga   soo osshaimashita*
       president NOM   so   say:HON:POLITE:PAST
       'The president said so.'
    b. *shachoo   ga   soo mooshimashita*
       president NOM   so   say:HUM:POLITE:PAST
       'The president said so.'

The distinction found between (7a) and (7b) is readily explained by the concept of the "in-group" vs. "out-group" membership (Nakane 1970, Bachnik & Quinn 1994). In a formal establishment such as a business institution, the speaker must use the honorific form to address and refer to his superior, as seen in (7a). However, when he talks about the action of his in-group and higher-rank member with an out-group member, he uses the humble expression for the higher-rank person in order to exalt the status of the addressee. This is the case in (7b).

Sometimes, humble honorific verbs are used simply to increase the level of formality and politeness. This type of humble verb is called a "solemn honorific" (*soochoo-go* 荘重語). The following are modified from Kindaichi (1988: 190). Compare this example with (6).

(8) *shuumatsu wa itoo e mairimashita*
weekend TOP (PL. name) ALL go:HUM:POLITE:PAST
'(I) went to Ito on the weekend.'

Sentences with solemn honorifics such as (8) are crucially different from those with humble honorifics such as (5) and (6) in that no one other than the speaker is involved in the specified activity. It is the speaker who went to Ito, and furthermore, her action was not done for anyone else. The only motivation to use a sentence like (8) is to humble oneself in order to increase the politeness level toward the addressee. (Also see Chapter 8 §5.3 for a discussion of the *-te-itadaku/ morau* construction.) The same motivation is seen widely in expressions used in business situations. Consider (9) and (10).

(9) *honjitsu wa kyuugyo -sasete-itadakimasu*
today TOP close-do:CAU:TE-receive:HUM:POL:NONPAST
'We are closed today.'
(Lit. 'Today we humbly receive (your permission) to be closed.')

(10) *kochira de o-machi shite kudasai* (Matsumoto 2008: 99)
here LOC PFX-wait do:TE please
'Please wait here.'

(9) can be interpreted as an instance of a humble honorific, which lowers the status of the agent (the store owner) and thereby raises the status of the unspecified customers. However, applying this interpretation to (10) is problematic because, literally interpreted, (10) lowers the status of the agent of the action of 'waiting,' i.e. the status of the addressee. However, the intent of the speaker is, obviously, to make his utterance more polite. In other words, both the solemn honorific, (8), and humble honorific (10), simply index politeness towards the addressee. In fact, there seems to be a trend in modern Japanese whereby the honorific system is shifting from being referent-oriented (e.g. as with humble honorifics in their traditional sense) to being more addressee-oriented.

In some of the examples used in this section, the predicate is marked by both referent honorifics and the *-masu* and *desu* polite predicate forms. This flexibility facilitates positioning of the speaker vis-à-vis the addressee and the referent. Compare (11a) and (11b) below.

(11) a. *sensee mo irassharu?*
teacher also go:HON:NONPAST
'Is the teacher also coming?'
(A student asking his/her close friend if their teacher is coming in a respectful tone for the teacher while maintaining the friendly tone with her friend)

b. *sensee mo irasshaimasu ka*
teacher also go:HON:**POL**:NONPAST Q
'Is the teacher also coming?'
(A student either asking someone he/she is not close to, or in a more formal context, if the teacher is coming in a way that shows respect to the teacher.)

(11a) and (11b) are identical referentially. Furthermore, they both show respect to the teacher with the same honorific verb, *irasshar-*. They differ, however, in that (11b) has an extra addressee-directed form, indicating the speaker's politeness towards the addressee and/or a level of formality appropriate to the situation.[7]

5. Gendered speech

Gendered speech refers to the distinct ways in which male and female speakers talk. It is an important feature of Japanese that works together with speech level and honorific distinctions to index various speech registers. While honorific speech codes the speaker's awareness of the hierarchical status of the addressee and referent persons, gendered speech codes the speaker's awareness of their own gender identification.[8] The degrees of freedom to which one can deviate from the norm is a constant debate among scholars and members of the society alike (e.g. Okamoto and Shibamoto Smith 2004, Ide 2006; Cook 2008). It is generally observed that the novels and movie scripts are written to reflect the societal norms of gendered language, but that "actual" real life conversation doesn't always reflect these (Shibuya 2004: 73–162). This section is mostly limited to some stereotypic features of gendered speech, usually marked by lexical choices, the use of pragmatic particles (Chapter 14 §3), manipulation of the copula, and command expressions.

There are several specific words that are employed to code speaker's gender. Interjections such as *ara!* 'oh!' and *maa!* 'oh!' are used almost exclusively by adult women, but *oi* 'Hey!' almost exclusively by men. As noted in §1 of this chapter, *ore* and *boku* are first person pronouns used by males while *atashi* is typically used by females. *Kimi* and *omae* are 2nd person pronouns used by male speakers to address an equal or younger addressee, while *anata* is preferred by women in informal situations. In informal speech situations, male speakers may use "coarse" vocabulary instead of more neutral or "soft" vocabulary; e.g. *meshi* instead of *gohan* for 'rice/meal,' *kuu* instead of *taberu* for 'to eat.'

---

7. Sometimes the addressee-directed -*desu*/-*masu* forms are called addressee honorifics to contrast them with the referent honorifics. Of course, the addressee and referent can coincide. If (11b) is used directly to the teacher, the sentence means 'Are you (address and referent) going, Professor?'

8. Besides the gender based self-identity, the age and occupation based self-identities also influences speech style. Also noteworthy in this connection is the fact that speech styles defined by speaker traits have been extended to "virtual speech" (Kinsui 2003). One such example is "professor speech" (*hakase-go*). This is what (male) professors are "imagined" to use, although no real professors actually use it; *soo ja washi ga shitte oru* (professor speech) < *soo desu watashi ga shitte imasu* (normal speech) 'Yes, I know it' (Kinsui 2003:v).

Softer vocabulary items include words with *o-*, the polite prefix (or as is often called the "beautification" prefix -*bika-go* 美化語), as in *o-mizu* 'water,' *o-soba* 'noodle,' *o-sake* 'rice wine,' and *o-tenki* 'weather' (Chapter 5 §2.2).

One of the most important ways in which the gendered speech distinction is created is through the use of pragmatic particles. The particles *zo* (strong assertion) and *ze* (strong appeal) are usually used by male speakers in a restricted informal speech environment (Chapter 14 §3). The next exchange is taken from a comic book, *Major* (Mitsuda 1995). In this scene two adult baseball players are commenting on the batter named Honda.

(12) A: *oi   oi   honda-no-yatsu   shigeno no   tama ni*
         hay   hay   (name)   (name)   GEN   ball DAT

      tsuitetteru zo   (M)
      follow:ASP:NONPAST PP

      'Hey, hey. Honda is following Shigeno's (fast) ball!'

    B: *shikamo   hidari tai   hidari da   ze*
       what's.more   left   vs.   left   COP   PP

       'And it's the lefty (batter) against the lefty (pitcher), too!'

Another pragmatic particle, *wa*, indexes female speech of personal evaluation when uttered with a rising intonation (↗) (Chapter 14 §3.1).[9]

(13) *hen   da   wa* (↗) (F)
      strange   COP   PP   'It's strange!'

      oishii   wa (↗) (F)
      delicious   PP   'It's delicious!'

      yosu   wa (↗) (F)
      avoid   PP   'I won't do it.'

---

9. The pragmatic particle *wa* with the falling tone (↘) should be distinguished from the rising tone (↗) variety. While the latter is used exclusively by female speakers in limited contexts, the former may be used by both male and female speakers. Shibuya (2004: 115–6) provides the following example uttered by a Tokyo female speaker.

  (i) *de   supiido ga   deru   to   nee, kowai wa* (↘).
      and   speed   NOM   increase   COND   PP   scary PP
      'And when it picks up the speed, it is scary.'

The rising intonation variety has attained the status of exclusive femininity, and unambiguously indexes this gender in represented speech in novels. That is, readers easily imagine that the particle *wa* is pronounced with the rising intonation when they read sentences such as the following in a novel; *iya yo watashi. nanimo iitakunai. hazukashii wa* 'No. Not me. I don't want to say anything. I am embarrassed' (from *Noruwee no Mori* (*Ge*), Murakami 1991: 26).

Femininity indexing is also unambiguously observed when *wa* with a falling intonation
(↘) combines with another pragmatic particle, *ne(e)* or *yo*, or the combination, *yone(e)*,
follows an utterance (Chapter 14 §3.2 cf. Mizutani & Mizutani 1977: 150–1).

(14) *oishii*   *wa yo* / *wa nee* / *wa yonee* (↘on *wa*) (F)
    delicious PP PP / PP PP / PP PP
    'It's delicious!'

    iku wa yo / *wa ne* / *wa yonee* (↘ on *wa*) (F)
    go PP PP / PP PP / PP PP PP
    'I will go.' (with *wa yo* or *wa ne*)
    'You will go, won't you?' (*wa ne* or *wa yonee*)

Another indication of female speech is the omission of the non-past tense form of the copula, *da*, before the pragmatic particles *yo*, *ne(e)*, or *yone(e)*. The strong assertive force associated with *da* can be avoided by its omission.

(15) **Male Speech***   **Female speech**
    nihon-jin da   *yo* (M)   *nihon-jin*   *yo* (F)
    Japanese COP PP   Japanese PP
    '(She) is Japanese, you know.'   '(She) is Japanese, you know.'

    nihon-jin da   *ne* (M)   *nihon-jin*   *ne* (F)
    Japanese COP PP   Japanese PP
    '(She) is Japanese, right?'   '(She) is Japanese, right?'

    nihon-jin da   *yone(e)* (M)   *nihon-jin*   *yone(e)* (F)
    Japanese COP PP   Japanese PP
    '(She) is Japanese, right?'   '(She) is Japanese, right?'

    *These so-called male forms, especially the *da yo* sequence, have become more
    neutral, and women are found to be using it often in friendly conversations.
                                                                                    (Matsumoto 2004)

Similarly *da* can be omitted in female speech after a nominalized verb with *no*, which is glossed as SE (= Sentence Extender) in the examples below (Chapter 14 §3.3). *No* is pronounced as *n* when followed by the copula in male speech (cf. Cook 1990).

(16) *itta-n*   *da*   *yo* (M)   *itta-no*   *yo* (F)
    go:PAST-SE COP PP   go:PAST-SE PP
    '(I) went (there), you know.'   '(I) went (there), you know.'

The erstwhile nominalizer *no* has also acquired the status of a pragmatic particle associated with hyper-polite female speech. Note that as a nominalizer, *no* must follow the non-polite form, but in the following examples of hyper-polite register, it follows a addressee-directed polite form with the *desu/-masu* ending, thereby indicating its loss of the nominalizer function.

(17) (Hyper-polite female speech)
 kore ga   watakushi no   oi   desu   no
 this NOM I   GEN nephew COP:POL:NONPAST   SE
 'This is my nephew.'

(18) (Hyper-polite female speech)
 okusan   mo   irasshaimasu   no?
 wife (= you) also go:HON:POL:NONPAST   SE
 'Are you going, too?'

Syntactically, in male speech, a non-presuppositional "yes-no" question may be formed by adding the question particle *ka* to the non-polite form of verb or adjective. Female speakers at the same level of formality/politeness resort to the use of a rising intonation without *ka*, though this strategy is widely used by men also.

(19) kuu   ka ↗ (M)   taberu ↗ (F/M)
     eat (vulgar) Q   eat
     'Do you want to/shall we eat?'   'Do you want to/shall we eat?'

     umai   ka ↗ (M)   oishii   ↗ (F/M)
     delicious (vulgar) Q   delicious   Q
     'Is it delicious?'   'Is it delicious?'

For information questions, the *-n da* ending is used by men, and *no* by women (and men).

(20) dare ga kita-n   da (↗ or ↘) (M) dare ga kita   no ↗ (F/M)
     who NOM come:PAST-SE   COP   who NOM come:PAST   SE
     'Who came?'   'Who came?'

Finally, male and female speech are clearly distinguished from each other when some strong speech-act is performed in the informal register. Male speakers may use the direct imperative form (see §3 above), while female speakers tend to use one of the request forms shown earlier. The particle *yo* has the falling intonation (↘).

(21) hayaku koi   yo (M)   hayaku kite   yo (F/M)
     fast   come:IMP   PP   fast   come:TE   PP
     'Come quickly!'   'Won't you come quickly!'

     miruna   yo (M)   minaide   yo (F/M)
     see:NEG.IMP   PP   see:NEG:TE   PP
     'Don't look!'   'Don't look, please!'

The discussion so far has tried to delineate male and female speech clearly, but it should be noted that all the male vocabulary and all the sentences marked with (M) above may also be used by women, especially, but not exclusively, by young women (Matsumoto 2004). To give an example of unorthodox use of the male form used by a woman, see the next.

(22) *mata kondo sukaipu shiyoo ze*
    again next.time Skype do:VOL PP
    'Let's Skype again!'

Though this sentence unequivocally sounds like one produced by a male person due to the use of *ze*, this is an actual written sentence used by a female writer to her friend in a personal letter (provided by H. Kuwahara, November 2011). This shows clearly the male-female boundaries can be crossed by the user of the language. The writer of (22) presumably used this form to create an intimate, non-serious tone in a personal letter.

Similarly, some, if not all, of the (F) marked sentences may be used by male speakers for the purpose of mitigating strong assertions. This shows that gendered speech is strategically used to create a particular register, to express identity, and/or to negotiate their roles in a particular speech situation. It has been pointed out that male speakers tend to fluctuate their speech widely depending on the addressee due partly to their wider scope of association with different types of people ranging from family to a variety of professional contacts, but the situation has been changing in recent years with women advancing in many professional fields. Though these facts seem to suggest that speech is becoming more gender neutral, the gender distinction associated with some linguistic expressions must still be recognized. Otherwise it is impossible to explain why the non-traditional use of male speech when employed by women sounds marked; they may sound rebellious, immature, or "cute" (cf. Matsumoto 1996, 1997a). Also some (F) marked utterances cannot be used by male speakers without a marked feminine identity accompanying it. This includes *wa* with rising intonation, *wa* with *yo* etc. following it, or the hyper-polite form with *no*.[10] Thus, while it is true that in some ways speech is becoming more gender neutral, each word and sentence form mentioned in this section is still, at least to some extent, gender specific, and speakers may strategically use this aspect of language to create specific social meanings and project a particular identity.

6. Speech register creation

Speech register is a holistic linguistic atmosphere created in discourse by assembling diverse sociolinguistic marking devices mentioned above. In Japanese, even a single sentence may contain several sociolinguistic features to index complex shades of social meanings. The

---

10. Shibuya (2004), following Bodine (1975), uses the terms "sex preferential" and "sex exclusive" to distinguish two types of linguistic expressions. The former refers to linguistics expressions that are preferred by one sex, but which the other sex can also use e.g. the sentence final expression *da yo* is used often by men, but can be also used by women in certain situations. On the other hand, the latter refers to linguistic expressions that are used by one sex and are not allowed to be used by the other sex. *Wa* with rising intonation, *wa* with *yo/ne/yone* following it, or the hyper-polite form with *no* belong to this type.

following six sentences all mean, 'I will have a meal,' but the speech registers they create are quite distinct. The personal reference terms (*ore-boku-atashi-watashi-watakushi*), nouns (*meshi-gohan-shokuji* 'rice/meal') as well as the verbs (*kuu-taberu-shokuji o shimasu-shokuji o itashimasu* 'eat'), all contribute to creating speech registers.

(23) (a) *ore*   *meshi*   *kuu*   *zo*
      I (vulgar) meal (vulgar) eat (vulgar):NONPAST PP

(b) *boku*   *gohan*   *taberu*   *yo*
     I(male) rice(meal) eat:NONPAST PP

(c) *atashi gohan*   *taberu*   *wa*   (↗)
     I   rice(meal) eat :NONPAST   PP

(d) *watashi gohan*   *o*   *itadaku*   *wa*   (↗)
     I   rice(meal) ACC   eat:HUM:NONPAST   PP

(e) *watashi shokuji shimasu*
     I   meal   do:POL:NONPAST

(f) *watakushi wa shokuji o itashimasu*
     I   TOP meal   ACC do:HUM:POL:NONPAST

First, the verb form mainly codes speech levels; the verbs in (a) through (d) are in the informal form, indicating that the utterance is in the informal speech level, while those in (e) and (f) are in the *-masu* form, indicating that they are somewhat more formal/polite vis-à-vis the addressee. In addition, the verbs in (d) and (f) are humble verbs, indicating that the register is rather refined. Secondly, the chosen pronominal forms and sentence final particles indicate both the speech level and the gendered speech distinction. In particular, the pronoun in (f), *watakushi* 'I,' is a more refined form than *watashi* 'I.'

More specifically, (a) is a rough sounding sentence, most typically spoken between close male friends in an informal speech setting; (b) is soft sounding sentence spoken by a male speaker to a male or female addressee in a rather informal situation; (c) is similar to (b) but is spoken by a female speaker; (d) is also female speech, but the use of humble form without the addressee honorific form indicates that the speaker is talking in a rather refined manner to her close friend (e.g. in an expensive French restaurant where a waiter in formal attire is listening) ; (e) is a formal sentence spoken by either a male or female speaker to an addressee with whom the speaker does not share a close relationship and/or in a rather formal situation; finally (f) is also a formal sentence spoken by either sex, but in a more refined manner than (e). The linguistic features that create specific registers are usually congruent with each other in terms of the formality level and the gender distinction, but sometimes they are assembled from different categories to induce different effects (cf. Iwasaki & Horie 2000; Jones & Ono 2008).

CHAPTER 16

Sample texts

In this chapter five example texts are presented with some remarks. Section 1 is a written text. Section 2 is written, but has some features of spoken text. Section 3 is a monologue in most part, while Sections 4 and 5 are more interactive, spoken discourses.

1. Newspaper Article: "Five Assaulting Middle School Students Arrested"
2. Folk Tale: "A Crane on the Wall"
3. First Person Narrative: "Air Raid"
4. Conversation (1):   "The Northridge Earthquake"
5. Conversation (2):   "Australia"

1. Newspaper article

This newspaper article of an assault by five middle school students represents a typical reporting style found in newspapers. One notable feature of this type of writing is lengthy sentences with noticeable use of heavy modifiers. The head noun, *jiken* 'incident' (line 1.3), is modified, for example, by a long modifier starting from the first word of the article, *tookyoo-to* 'Metropolitan Tokyo' (line 1.1). Also the head noun, *utagai* 'doubt' (line 3.5), is modified by the portion starting with *nanoka gogo yoji yonjup-pun-goro* 'about 4:40 P.M. on the seventh' (lines 3.1–3.2). In this written mode of communication, elements of interpersonal concerns such as the polite ending (e.g. *desu* and *-masu*), or interpersonal particles (e.g. *yo* and *ne*) are completely lacking.

Bookoo no Chuu-san Go-nin Taiho "Five Assaulting Middle School Students Arrested" (*from Yomiuri Newspaper, September 11, 1997*)

1.1 tookyoo-to   oota-ku-nai   no   kooen de   kon-getsu   nanoka
    Tokyo-capital Oota-Ward-inside GEN park LOC this-month   seventh

1.2 kaishain   san-nin   ga   shoonen-guruupu   ni
    company.employee   three-CLS   NOM   boy-group   DAT

1.3 naguru keru no   bookoo   o   uketa   jiken   de,
    hit   kick-COP:ATT   assault   ACC   receive:PAST   incident COP:TE

1.4 keeshichoo   ikegami-sho   wa   tooka   madeni
    police-department   Ikegami-branch   TOP   tenth   TMP

1.5	*oota-ku-nai*	*ni*	*sumu*	*danshi*	*chuugaku*	*san-nensee*	*go-nin*	*o*
	Oota-Ward-inside	DAT	live	male	middle.school	third-grader	five-CL	ACC

1.6	*shoogai-no*	*utagai*	*de*	*taiho-shita.*
	bodily.injury-COP:ATT	doubt	COP:TE	arrest-do:PAST

'In the incident involving three office workers who were beaten and kicked in an assault on them by a group of boys on the seventh day of this month in a park in Oota-Ward, Tokyo, the Ikegami Branch of the Police Department made an arrest sometime on the tenth of five third year middle school students who live in Oota Ward, charging them with inflicting bodily injury.'

2.1	*kono*	*jiken*	*de*	*atama*	*no*	*hone*	*nado*	*o*	*ori*
	this	incident	INS	head	GEN	bone	and.so.forth	ACC	break:INF

2.2	*ishiki-fumee-no*	*juutai*	*datta*
	consciousness-lost-COP:ATT	serious.condition	COP:PAST

2.3	*yokohama-shi*	*no*	*kaishain*	*nakano-san* (27)	*wa*	*tooka*	*yoru,*
	Yokohama-city	GEN	company.employee	(name)-Mr.	TOP	tenth	evening

2.4	*shiboo-shita.*
	death-do:PAST

'Mr. Nakano (=pseudonym) (27 years old), a company employee in Yokohama City who had been unconscious and in critical condition since the incident in which he suffered a fractured skull, died on the evening of the tenth.'

3.1	*shirabe*	*ni*	*yoruto*	*go-nin*	*wa,*	*nanoka*	*gogo*	*yo-ji*
	investigation	DAT	according	five-CLS	TOP	seventh	P.M.	four-o'clock

3.2	*yonjup-pun-goro,*	*oota-ku*	*tamagawa*	*no*	*jidoo-kooen*	*de,*
	forty-minutes-about	Oota-Ward	Tamagawa	GEN	child-park	LOC

3.3	*benchi*	*de*	*hanashi*	*o*	*shite-ita*	*nakano-san* (27)-*ra*	*san-nin*	*ni-taishi*
	bench	LOC	talk	ACC	do:TE-ASP	(name)-Mr. (age)-PL	three-CLS	DAT

3.4	"*gan*	*o*	*tsuketa*"	*nado*	*to*	*iigakari*	*o*	*tsukete*
	eye	ACC	attach:PAST	and.so.forth	QT	claim	ACC	attach:TE

3.5	*naguru*	*keru*	*nado*	*bookoo-shita*	*utagai.*
	hit	kick	and.so.forth	assault-do:PAST	doubt

'According to the investigation, at about 4:40 PM on the seventh, the five (boys) allegedly accused Mr. Nakano (27 years old) and his friends, who had been sitting on a bench and talking in a children's park near the Tamagawa River in Oota Ward, of staring at them, and then proceeded to attack the three with blows, kicks and so forth.'

4.1	*jitensha*	*o*	*nagetsuker-are-ta*	*nakano-san*	*wa*
	bicycle	ACC	throw-PSS-PAST	(name)-Mr.	TOP

4.2	*atama*	*no*	*hone*	*o*	*otta.*	
	head	GEN	bone	ACC	break:PSAT	

'Mr. Nakano suffered a fractured skull when a bicycle was thrown at him.'

5.1	*shirabe*	*ni*	*taishi,*	*go-nin*	*wa*	
	investigation	DAT	face:INF	five-CL	TOP	
5.2	"*annani oo-kega*	*ni*		*naru*	*to*	*omowanakatta*"
	such big-injury	COP:ADV		become	QT	think:NEG:PAST
5.3.	*to*	*hanashite-iru*	*to*	*iu.*		
	QT	speak:TE-ASP	QT	say		

'In response to cross-questioning, the five (boys) are reported to have said that they had no idea that their actions would result in such a severe injury.'

2. Folk tale

This is one of the published folk tales in Tsubota Joji's three volume series, *Nihon Mukashi Banashi Shuu* "A Collection of Japanese Folk Tales." Tsubota explains that the intent of publishing these tales is to encourage mothers to read them aloud to their children, and children to read them themselves, in the hope that these stories will be preserved as part of Japanese culture into the future. The level of language, according to Tsubota, is that of the third grade.

Folk tales of this type exhibit mixture of both oral and written features of the language. One conspicuous feature of oral language in *Kabe no Tsuru* "A Crane on the Wall" below is the use of the polite (past) ending *-mashita* in almost all sentences. Other more immediate interactional features, such as pragmatic particles or sentence extenders such as *no (desu)*, however, are not present (but see line 3). On the other hand, a feature of written language can be also seen in the types of clause combining used; the infinitive form (or the *ren'yoo* form) is employed in addition to the conjunctive (TE) form. In a more interactional mode of language (such as those analyzed in §3, §4, §5 below), the infinitive is rarely used.

The organization of *Kabe no Tsuru* is typical in terms of participant introduction and tracking (Hinds & Hinds 1979). A participant introduced for the first time is marked with *ga* (*shin to yuu hito ga* 'a person named Shin' – line 1); in its second mention *wa* is used (*sono shinsan wa* 'that Shin' – line 2). Subsequently, the referent is often expressed by "zero anaphora" (Chapter 13 §2). The particle *ga* may be used again later for the purpose of discourse organization; for example Shin is marked by *ga* again in line 31 because, the story has just crossed a "paragraph boundary" (see also Maynard 1987 for other motivations for *ga* marking in folk tales).

Kabe no Tsuru "A Crane on the Wall" (from Tsubota 1975: 173–6)

(1) *mukashi, mukashi, aru tokoro ni*
old.days old.days certain place DAT
shin to yuu hito ga arimashita.
(name) QT say person NOM exist:POL:PAST
'Once upon a time, in a certain place, there lived a man named Shin.

(2) *sono shin-san wa, o-sake o utte-orimashita.*
that (name)-Mr. TOP PFX-rice.wine ACC sell:TE-ASP:POL:PAST
Shin made a living selling rice wine.

(3) *o-sakaya-san data no desu.*
PFX-liquor.shop-Mr. COP:PAST SE COP
(That is,) he was a liquor shop owner.

(4) *aru hi no koto, sono shin-san no o-mise ni,*
certain day GEN thing that (name)-Mr. GEN PFX-shop DAT
hitori-no ojiisan ga yatte-kimashita.
one.person-COP:ATT old.man NOM come-come:POL:PAST
One day, an old man came to Shin's shop.

(5) *sono ojiisan ga iimashita.*
that old.man NOM say:POL:PAST
The old man said:

(6) *zeni wa nai no da ga, chotto o-sake o*
money TOP exist:NEG SE COP but a.little PFX-rice.wine ACC
nom-asete-kudasaranai ka.
drink-CAU:TE -give:H.HON:NEG:NONPAST Q
"(I) don't have any money, but would you let me drink a little *sake* (anyway)?"

(7) *shin-san ga, sono ojiisan o mimashita tokoro,*
(name)-Mr. NOM that old.man ACC look:PAST NML
kitanai furi wa shite-orimasu ga,
dirty appearance TOP do:TE-ASP:POL:NONPAST but
nantonaku, erai tokoro ga aru
somehow great place NOM exist:NONPAST
yoo-ni omow-are-masu.
appearance-COP:ADV think-SPON-POL:NONPAST
Shin looked at the old man, and despite his dirty appearance, somehow, it seemed to Shin that he had an air of greatness.

(8) sokode,   "hai, hai, zeni   ga   nakereba,
    thus   yes   yes   money   NOM exist:NEG:COND

    nakute-mo-yoroshii."   soo itte,
    exist:NEG:TE-also-good:NONPAST so   say:TE

    sono ojiisan   ni,
    that old.man   DAT

    o-sake   o   tsuide-yarimashita.
    PFX-rice.wine ACC pour:TE-give:POL:NONPAST
    "Why, of course. If (you) don't have money, that's fine," (Shin) said and poured sake for the old man.

(9) ojiisan   wa nikkori-shite, sono sakazuki o   te   ni   tori,
    old.man TOP ssw-do:TE   that cup   ACC hand DAT take:INF

    samo uma-soo-ni,
    like delicious-appearance-COP:ADV

    gui gui-to   nomimashita.
    SSW SSW-ADV drink:POL:PAST
    The old man, smilingly, took the cup in his hand and drank it down in several great gulps.

(10) soshite nonde-shimau   to,   "aa umakatta."   soo itte,
     then   drink:TE-ASP   COND oh   delicious:PAST so   say:TE

     shitauchi   o   shite, dete-ikimashita.
     tongue.clicking ACC do:TE exit:TE-go:POL:PAST
     When (he) finished drinking (the sake), (he) said "It was good," smacked his lips, and left.

(11) shikashi, tsugi no   hi, onaji jikoku-ni   naru   to,
     but   next GEN day same time-COP:ADV become   COND

     mata yatte-kimashita.
     again come:TE-come:POL:PAST
     But the following day, (he) appeared again about the same time.

(12) soshite, "zeni wa nai   ga, chotto o-sake   o
     then   money TOP exist:NEG   but a.little PFX-rice.wine ACC

     nom-asete-kudasai."   soo ii-mashita.
     drink-CAU:TE-give:IMP   so   say-POL:PAST
     Then, (he) said, "(I) don't have money, but please let me drink some *sake* anyway."

(13) "hai, hai, zeni   ga   nakereba,
     yes yes money NOM exist:NEG:COND

     nakute   mo   yoroshii."
     exist:NEG:TE   also good:NONPAST
     "Certainly. If (you) don't have any money, that's fine."

(14) *shin-san   wa   yahari   soo itte,   sono ojiisan   ni*
     (name)-Mr. TOP expectedly so   say:TE that old.man   DAT

     o-sake   o   tsuide-yarimashita.
     PFX-rice.wine ACC pour:TE-give:POL:NONPAST

     Shin said so as before and poured *sake* for the old man.

(15) *ojiisan   wa   shitauchi   o   shite,*
     old.man TOP tongue.clicking ACC do:TE

     uma-soo-ni   nomi,
     delicious-appearance-COP:ADV drink:INF

     "*umai,   umai*"   to, *dete-ikimashita.*
     delicious delicious QT exit:TE-go:POL:PAST

     The old man smacked his lips, drank up (the sake) with great satisfaction, and said "Delicious, delicious," and left.

(16) *shikashi mata sono akuru hi,   "zeni   wa   nai   ga."*
     but   again that next day   money TOP exist:NEG but

     to yatte-kimashita.
     QT come-come:POL:PAST

     But again (the old man) came the following day, saying "(I) don't have any money, but…"

(17) *shin-san   wa   "nakute   mo   ii   desu" to*
     (name)-Mr. TOP exist:NEG:TE also good:NONPAST COP   QT

     mata nom-asete-yarimashita.
     again drink-CAU:TE-give:POL:PAST

     Shin, (saying) "It's all right if you don't," let (him) drink again.

(18) *sore kara wa   mainichi, ojiisan   wa   yatte-kite,*
     that from TOP everyday old.man TOP come-come:TE

     o-sake   no   gochisoo ni   narimashita.
     PFX-rice.wine GEN feast   DAT become:POL:PAST

     From then on, the old man came every day and was treated to *sake*.

(19) *soshite nan-nichi   tatta   deshoo ka.*
     and   how.many-days pass:PAST MOD   Q
     In this manner, countless days passed.

(20) *aru   hi   no   koto, ojiisan   ga   iimashita.*
     certain day GEN thing old.man NOM say:POL:PAST
     One day, the old man said:

(21) "*o-sake   no   dai ga   daibu tamatta   na.*
     PFX-rice.wine GEN tab NOM lot   accumulate:PAST PP
     "My *sake* tab has grown pretty high.

(22) e   demo hitotsu kaite-iku   ka."
     painting SOF one   draw:TE-go   Q
     Maybe I should just paint a picture before I go."

(23) soshite, soba ni atta   kago   no naka kara
     and   near DAT exist:PAST basket GEN inside ABL
     mikan o hitotsu tori,   sono kawa o   mukimashita.
     orange ACC one   take:INF that peel ACC peel:POL:PAST
     So saying, (he) took out one orange from a basket and peeled it.

(24) sono kawa de-motte, o-mise   no shiroi kabe ni
     that peel INS   PFX-shop GEN white wall DAT
     e   o   kakimashita.
     picture ACC paint:POL:PAST
     Using the peel, (he) painted a picture on the white wall of the shop.

(25) sas-sas-sas-to, miru ma-ni   kaita   soo desu ga,
     SSW-SSW-SSW-ADV look duration-COP:ADV paint:PAST MOD COP but
     sore wa ookina ichi-wa no tsuru deshita.
     that TOP big   one-CLS GEN crane COP:PAST
     It is said that (he) painted very swiftly, but (when he had finished) it was
     (a picture of) one large crane.

(26) mikan no kawa de kaita   no-de,
     orange GEN peel INS write:PAST so
     kiiroi tsuru ni   narimashita.
     yellow crane COP:ADV become:POL:PAST
     Since (he) had painted (it) with an orange peel, it became a yellow crane.

(27) shikashi rippa-na   tsuru de
     but   fine-COP:ATT crane COP:TE
     ikite-ru   yoo-ni   miemashita
     live:TE -ASP appearance-COP:ADV look:POT: POL:PAST
     But it was a fine crane and looked as if (it) were alive.

(28) "o-kyaku-san   ga kitara,   kono e   ni muite,
     PFX-guest-SFX   NOM come:COND this painting DAT face:TE
     te   o   tataite, uta o   utatte-morainasai."
     hand ACC clap:TE   song ACC sing:TE-receive:IMP
     "When a customer comes in, ask (him) to turn and face this picture, clap (his)
     hands and sing a song."

(29) ojiisan wa soo itte   dete-ikimashita.
     old.man TOP so say:TE leave:TE-go:POL:PAST
     The old man said so and left.

(30) to,   moo   o-kyaku-san   ga   kimashita.
     then   already   PFX-guest-SFX   NOM   come:POL:PAST
     Immediately after, a customer came in.

(31) "o-kyaku-san,   hitotsu,   te   o   tataite,   uta   o   utatte-kudasai."
     PFX-guest-SFX   one   hand ACC   clap:TE   song ACC sing:TE-give:IMP
     "Mr. Customer, please just clap (your) hands and sing a song."

(32) shin-san   ga   iimashita.
     (name)-Mr.   NOM   say:POL:PAST
     So said Shin.

(33) "hai,   hai."
     yes   yes
     "Sure."

(34) o-kyaku-san   wa   te   o   tataite,   uta   o   utaimashita.
     PFX-guest-SFX   TOP   hand   ACC   clap:TE   song ACC sing:POL:PAST
     The customer clapped (his) hands and sang a song.

(35) suruto,   fushigi-na   koto   ni,
     then   mystery-COP:ATT   thing   COP:ADV

     ima   kaita   bakari   no   tsuru -no   e   ga,
     now   paint:PAST   just   GEN   crane-COP:ATT   painting   NOM

     kabe   no   ue   de   hane   o   hirogemashita.
     wall   GEN   top   LOC   wing   ACC   spread:POL:PAST

     Then mysteriously, the picture of the crane which had just been painted spread its wings upon the wall.

(36) soshite,   atchi   e   iki,   kotchi   e   iki,   uta   ni   awasete,
     and   over.there ALL   go:INF   here   ALL go:INF   sing   DAT   match:TE

     mai   o   mai-hajimemashita.
     dance   ACC   dance-begin:POL:PAST

     And it moved here and there and began dancing in rhythm to the song.

(37) kore   ga   machi-juu   no   dai-hyooban-ni   nari,
     this   NOM   town-whole   GEN   big-reputation-COP:ADV   become:INF

     sore   kara   shin-san   no   o-mise   wa,
     that   ABL   (name)-Mr.   GEN   PFX-store   TOP

     taihen   hanjoo-itashimashita.
     very   prosperous-do:H.HON:POL:PAST

     This became the talk of the town, and after that Shin's shop became very prosperous.

(38) tokorode,   sore   kara   nan-nen   ka   tachimashita.
     by.the.way   that   ABL   now.may-year   Q   pass:POL:PAST
     Well, several years went by.

(39) o-jiisan   ga   mata yatte-kimashita.
    PFX-old.man NOM again come-come:POL:PAST
    'The old man came back again.'

(40) ojiisan   wa   tsuru-no   e   no   mae de,
    PFX-old.man TOP crane-COP:ATT painting GEN front LOC
    sono toki fue o   fuita   soo desu.
    that time flute ACC play:PAST MOD COP
    'It is said that the old man played a flute in front of the painting of the crane.'

(41) suruto, tsuru ga   e   kara dete-kite,
    then   crane NOM painting ABL   come.out:TE-come:TE
    ojiisan   no   mae ni   tachimashita.
    PFX-old.man GEN front LOC stand:POL:PAST
    'Then the crane came out of the picture and stood before the old man.'

(42) ojiisan   wa   fue o   motta   mama,
    PFX-old.man TOP flute ACC hold:PAST still
    sono tsuru ni matagari,   ten   ni   nobotte-ikimashita.
    that crane DAT climb:INF   heaven DAT climb:TE-go:POL:PAST
    'The old man, still holding the flute, climbed upon the crane, and rose up toward the heavens.'

(43) sono toki, shin-san   hajime   ooku-no   hito-tachi ga,
    that time (name)-Mr.   beginning many-DAT:ATT   people-PL   NOM
    ojiisan   to   tsuru ga   shiroi kumo no   ue   o
    PFX-old.man and crane NOM white cloud GEN top ACC
    tonde-iku no   o   mi-okutta   to yuu koto   desu.
    fly:TE-go NML ACC see-send:PAST QT say thing COP
    'At that time, Shin and many others saw the old man and the crane flying above the white clouds, so it is said.'

3. First person narrative ("Air Raid")

This is part of the "War Time Narrative" Collection recorded in August 1986, in Tokyo. The speaker (M), a housewife in her sixties, is retelling her experience of the air raid in Tokyo during World War II. The audience consists of two other housewives (N and A) who share similar experiences, and her son (J), who does not. The speaker is given the full floor at the beginning of this excerpt. The audience's participation, for the most part, is restricted to short backchanneling expressions such as *nn*. A narrative of this type is characterized by a successive chaining of clauses with the TE form and other various conjunctive forms such as *kedo* and *kara* (Chapter 12). Note, however, that no infinitive clause combining form (the *ren'yoo* form) appears. When a chain is concluded by a finite predicate form, sentence extension with *wake* often occurs.

Note the following special conventions used for this data and those in Sections 4 and 5 (See Chapter 3 §5).

1. Three major tail-pitch movements:
    ↘ = a natural falling intonation contour with final sounding
    ↗ = a rising contour with various degrees of rising with final sounding
    ∧ = a rise-fall contour with no-final sounding
2. Two minor movements:
    , = continuing contour with no-final sounding
    < = word truncation with a glottal stop
3. Pause length: Two different lengths are identified.
    … = a short pause (about 0.3 - 0.4 seconds)
    … (number) = a longer pause (longer than 0.5 seconds)
4. Overlap
    [ ] = Overlap is indicated by square brackets, [ ]. Where there are several overlapping segments in a short span of time, double square brackets ([[ ]]) are employed to avoid confusion.
5. Vowel lengthening
    : = indicates vowel lengthening
6. Other symbols used in the transcripts:
    =   latching to the previous utterance
    @   laughter token
    H   inhalation
    ⟨x words x⟩   uncertain hearing
    ⟨x x⟩   inaudible segment

Air Raid

(1) J: ato   wa   kuushuu no   koto ya   nanka
rest TOP air.raid GEN thing and SOF

oboete-masu   ka↗
remember:TE-ASP:POL:NONPAST Q

'Do you remember anything about the air raid?'

(2) M: kuushuu no   koto   wa   moo   yoku
air.raid GEN thing TOP EMPH well

oboete-[masu   yo↘]
remember:TE:-ASP:POL:NONPAST PP

'Of course, I remember the air raid very well.'

(3) A: [=*kuushuu-n toki no*] *koto wa* [[*oboete-ru*   *wa*↘]]
       air.raid-GEN time GEN thing TOP remember:TE:-ASP:NONPAST PP
       'I remember the air raid.'

(4) M: [[*are no koto ne*↗]]
       that GEN thing PP
       '(I couldn't forget) about that.'

(5) J: *nn*
       BCH

(6) M: [*son toki watashi wa ne*↘]
       that time I TOP PP
       'At that time I was…'

(7) A: [*are wa wasure-ran-nai nee,*]
       that TOP forget:POT:NEG-NONPAST PP
       'I couldn't forget that.'

(8) J: =*nn*
       BCH

(9) M: *n hatachi deshita ne,*
       yes 20.years.old COP:POL:PAST PP
       'I was twenty.'

(10) J: =*nn*
        BCH

(11) M: *hatachi desu kara,*
        20.years.old COP:POL:NONPAST so
        'I was twenty, so…

(12) M: *honde mashite kootoo-ku:…*
        and especially (place name)
        …and furthermore in Koto Ward,…

(13) M: *maa mukashi no fukagawa-kiba tte-yuu toko ne*↗
        INJ former GEN (place name) QT-say place PP
        …well, in a place that was called Fukagawa Kiba back then.'

(14) J: =*nn*
        BCH

(15) M: *maa watashi wa moo fukagawa de sodatte,*
        INJ I TOP EMPH (place name) LOC grow.up:TE
        'Well, I was raised in Fukagawa, and…

(16) M: =*mo fukagawa de umareta tte jibun de*
        EMPH (place name) LOC be.born:PAST QT self INS

```
              jifu-shite-ru                  kurai    da         kara↘
              proud-do:TE-ASP:NONPAST        extent   COP:NONPAST SO
```
…why, I'm even proud to say I was born there.

(17) M: *ma fukagawa   ni   ite,*
         INJ (place name) LOC   exist:TE
         Anyway, I was in Fukagawa, and…

(18) M: *mm   dai-ichiban-me   gurai-ni   yarareta-n-da   kara↘*
         INJ PFX-first-SFX   about-COP:ADV   do:PSS:PAST-SE-COP SOF
         …it was just about the first place that was hit.

(19) M: *…de   kiba   no   san-choome   tte-yuu tokoro wa   ne↗*
         and   (place name)   GEN   third-district   QT-say   place   TOP   PP
         And, the place called the Third District in Kiba, you know,…

(20) M: (0.7) *ano: are sonde sono toki uchi ni   wa   nee↖*
               INJ   INJ and   that time home LOC   TOP   PP
         … Uh, well, at that time, in our house…

(21) M: *ano: okkii   ane   to   ne↗*
         INJ   big   older.sister   COM   PP

         …okkii ane   fuufu   to,
         big   older.sister   husband.wife   COM

         sono   ima   yu   iwayuru   ano.   ne,
         INJ   now   FRG   so.called INJ   PP

         ano sa   kimura-san   no   are   to↘
         INJ PP   (name)-Mr.   GEN   that   and

         kyoodai   to   atashi   no   ane   to↖
         sibling   and   I   GEN   older.sister   and

         …nan-nin   ita-n   da,
         how.many-CLS   exist:PAST-SE   COP

         …there was, uh, my eldest sisters, and she and her husband and, uh, you know…that, uh, Kimura's (=pseudonym) you know, brother and my sister and…hmm, how many people were there?'

(22) M: *chichi   desho,*
         Father   MOD

         chichi   desho,
         father   MOD

         … kara   ane   fuufu   desho,
         then   older.sister   husband.wife   MOD

         =imooto   desho,
         younger.sister   MOD

>   *atashi   desho,*
>   I   MOD
>
>   *mee   shichi-nin imashita   ne,*
>   niece   seven-CLS   exist:POL:PAST   PP
>
> 'My father, right? My father, right? And there was my older
> sister and her husband, right? My younger sister,
> right? Myself, right? My nieces... there were seven people.'

(23) M: *soshite:... nenjuu   (0.9) kuushuu   kuushuu   de,*
         and   always   air.raid air.raid COP:TE
         'And there were always... constant air raids, and'

(24) M: =*an toki wa:... yuki wa: futta   no   wa   sono mae   ne↗*
          that time TOP   snow TOP fall:PAST NML TOP that before PP
          '...at that time... It had snowed before, hadn't it.'

(25) A: =*atashi ano ne↘*
          I   INJ PP
          'I, you know...'

(26) M: *sangatsu-n toki wa   furana[katta   ne↗]*
         March-GEN   time TOP fall:NEG:PAST   PP
         'It didn't snow in March, did it?'

(27) A: [⟨x x⟩] *furanai   furanai↘*
                  fall:NEG:NONPAST   fall:NEG:NONPAST
          'No, it didn't, it didn't.'

(28) M: *nn   furanakute*∧
         BCH   fall:NEG:TE
         'No, it didn't, and...'

(30) M: *moo   nankai-mo   nankai-mo: kite-ta-n   da   kedo:,*
         already many.times   many.times come:TE-ASP:PAST-SE   COP   SOF
         '...they kept coming and coming.'

(31) M: *chichi tte-yuu no   wa   o-sake   ga   suki de   ne,*
         father QT-say   NML TOP PFX-rice.wine   NOM like COP:TE PP
         'My father liked *sake*, you see, and...'

(32) M: *o-sake   nonde,*
         PFX-rice.wine   drink:TE
         '...(he) had drunk *sake*, and...'

(33) M: *ne-chat-teta   no   ne↗*
         sleep-ASP:TE-ASP:PAST   SE   PP
         '...was already sleeping, you see.'

(34) J: *nn*
BCH

(35) M: ...*de hoka-no   hito   wa   moo*
and other-COP:ATT people TOP already

hayaku: nige-chatta-n   da   kedo,
early   escape-ASP:PAST-SE   COP but

'The others had already escaped, but...

(36) M: *atashi to   chichi wa   moo   saigo made uchi   ni*
I   COM father TOP EMPH last ALL home LOC

ita   wake ↘
exist:PAST   SE

...my father and I were in the house until the end.

(37) M: *dooshite ru   ka   tte,*
why   FRG   Q   QT

It's because...

(38) M: *chichi wa   o-sake   nonde:* ↘
father TOP   PFX-rice.wine   drink:TE

...my father had drunk his *sake* and...

(39) M: *gussuri ne-chatte-ta* ↘
deeply sleep-ASP:TE-ASP:PAST

...fallen fast asleep.

(40) M: *de atashi mo   dotchi ka   tsu   to* ↘
and   I   also which Q   QT:say QT

... *anmari   odorokanai   hoo-da   kara*∧
not.very surprise:NEG:NONPAST side-COP:NONPAST so

And I'm the type who doesn't get surprised easily, so...

(41) M: *nete-teta   [wake* ↘]
sleep:TE-ASP:PAST   SE

...I was also sleeping.'

(42) A: [*n:n*]
BCH

(43) M: *soode doo-shiyoo   mo   nakute* ↘
and   how-do:VOL   also exist:NEG:TE

'There was nothing else they could do, so...

(44) M: *yobi-ni   ko-rarete,*
call-PURP   come:PSS:TE

...they called out to us and...

(45) M: = dete-tte-ta   no ne↗
          exit:TE-go:TE-ASP:PAST SE PP
          '...we left (the house).'

(46) J: =nn
          BCH

(47) M: (1.0) demo son toki wa moo::,
                but that time TOP already
          'But by then it was...

(48) M: soshite... chichi wa moo
          then   father TOP already
          shinsai   ni mo   atte-ru   kara,
          earthquake DAT also meet:TE-ASP:NONPAST so
          '...and my father had already experienced the Great Earthquake, so...

(50) M: =mo   hi   no naka   wa
           already fire GEN inside TOP
          keikensha   da   kara ne↗
          experiencer COP:NONPAST so   PP
          '...he'd already lived through a major fire.'

(51) A: ==n:n
          BCH

(52) M: kaza-shimo e: kaza-shimo e
          wind-down ALL wind-down ALL
          nigetara   dame tte yuu wake ne↗
          escape:COND   bad QT say SE   PP
          'He said we shouldn't run downwind, you see.

(53) M: hantai-ni   kaza: [kaze: no naka
          opposite-COP:ADV   wind   wind GEN inside
          hi   no naka   o] kugutte
          fire GEN inside ACC go.under:TE
          nigero   tte yuu   wake.
          escape:IMP QT say:NONPAST SE
          'Instead, he said we had to run into the wind and into the fire and under it to escape.'

(54) A: [⟨x x⟩]

(55) A: n:n
          BCH

(56) M: *soide kugutte   nigeta   kara,*
       and go.under:TE escape:PAST so
       'That's how we ran under the fire and escaped, and so…'

(57) M: =*moo sono shito-ri   de   taihen-na*
        EMPH INJ   one-CLS   INS   tough-COP:ATT
       omoi-shite   nigeta   wake ne↗
        experience-do:TE escape:PAST SE   PP
       '…I was the only one who escaped with great difficulty, you see?'

(58) J: =*nn*
       BCH

(59) M: …*soo deshoo*↗
         SO   PP
       'Don't you agree?'

(60) M: *kaza-shimo ni   nigerunara,*
        wind-down DAT escape:COND
       If you run downwind,…

(61) M: *kotchi   kara hi   ga   ku-n*   [*dattara,*]
        this.way ABL   fire NOM come:NONPAST-SE COP:COND
       …if the fire comes from this direction,…

(62) A: [*n:n*]
                                                             BCH

(63) M: *kotchi   e   niger*[[*eba*↘]]
        this.way ALL escape:COND
       …escaping this way…

(64) A: [[⟨x x⟩]]

(65) M: *raku desho*↗
        easy PP
       '…is much easier, right?'

(66) J: =*nn*
        BCH

(67) M: *sore o… kotchi   e…   hi   o*
        that ACC this.way ALL fire ACC
       kugutte-ta-n   da   kara↘
        go.under:TE-go:PAST-SE COP SOF
       'But I went this way, I went under the fire.'

(68) J: =[*nn*]
        BCH

(69) A: [nn]
           BCH

(70) M: sono toki no: kaze ne↗
           that time GEN wind PP
           'At that time, you know, the wind,…

(71) J: =[n:n]
           BCH

(72) A: =[n:n]
           BCH

(73) M: kaze wa   sugokatta   desu   yo↘
           wind TOP fierce:PAST COP:POL PP
           …the wind was very strong, I tell you.'

(74) M: moo   atashi-tachi futon   ko   mo   shotte,
           EMPH   I-PL   bed.clothes like.this EMPH carry.on.back:TE
           'We carried our *futon* on our shoulders like this,…

(75) M: =nigeta-n   da   kedo,
           escape:PAST-SE   COP   but
           …and escaped, but…

(76) M: =futon   wa   tob-asare-chau↘
           bed.clothes   TOP fly-PSS-:ASP:NONPAST
           …the *futon* was blown away.'

(77) J: n:n
           BCH

(78) M: de: nde: ue-no   ane   wa
           and and   up-COP:ATT older sister   TOP

           sukoshi…   hosokatta mon da   kara↘
           a.little   thin:PAST SE   COP:NONPAST so
           'And since my older sister was rather thin,…

(79) M: …kaze ni   fukitobas-arete,
           wind   DAT blow.away-PSS:TE
           …the wind blew her down, and…

(80) M: taore-chau↘
           fall-ASP:NONPAST
           …she fell.'

(81) J: n:n
           BCH

(82) M: *de motte-ta   ano::* (1.0)
        and carry:TE-ASP:PAST INJ
        'That thing I was carrying...

(83) M: *ko zatsunoo   tte fukuro ga an   no ne*↗
        INJ miscellaneous.bag QT bag   NOM exist:NONPAST SE PP
        '...a bag, it was a duffel bag...

(84) M: *son naka e   hijoo-shoku   to shite mame toka,*
        that inside ALL emergency-food as do:TE bean SOF
        '...I had put some emergency food in it, like beans.'

(85) J: *nn*
        BCH

(86) M: *ano:... soo-yuu mono* [*zenbu keetai-shite-ta-n   da kara ne*↗]
        INJ   such   thing all   carry-do:TE-ASP:PAST-SE COP SOF PP
        'I carried everything like that in it, you know.'

(87) A: [⟨x x⟩] *yoo-na   mono ne*↗
               like-COP:ATT thing PP
        'Things like ().'

(88) M: *so* ↘
        right
        'Right.'

(89) M: *kan*[*zume   toka chotto,*]
         canned food SOF a.little
        'A few canned foods and...'

(90) A: [*katsuobushi   toka,*]
         dried.fish.flakes SOF
        'Dried bonito flakes and...'

(91) M: [[*tabe-r*]]*areru   mono iret-oite,*
         eat-POT:NONPAST thing put-ASP:TE
        'I had put things to eat inside.'

(92) N: [[*n:n*]]
        BCH

(93) M: *dakedo sore o   boroboro boroboro... koboshi-nagara itta   no*
        but   that ACC ssw   ssw   spill-while   go:PAST NML
        oboe-teru   wa ne ↘
        remember:TE-ASP:NONPAST PP PP
        'But I remember spilling things left and right as I escaped.'

(94) J: n:n…   kekkyoku   tasukatta-n   desho↗
           BCH   finally   be.saved:PAST   -SE IP
           'But in the end you were saved, weren't you?'

(95) M: kekkyoku   moo   [zeiin,]
           Finally   EMPH   all.member
           'Yes, everyone was saved.'

(96) A: [demo mi:nna]   zeiin   tasukatta ↘
           but   all   all.member   be saved:PAST
           'Everyone?'

(97) M: ==zeiin   tasukari[[mashita ↘
           all.member   be.saved:POL:PAST
           'Everyone was saved.'

(98) M   =hitottsu   mo   kega   nashi ↘]]
           one   also   injury   no
           'Without a single injury.'

(99) A: [[⟨x x⟩]]   [erakatta: ∧]
                       be.splendid:PAST
           'That was brave of you all.'

4. Conversation (1): "The Northridge earthquake"

This conversation is taken from one of the five Japanese discourses collected as part of the "Northridge Earthquake Conversation" Project. In this portion of the transcript, two female college students are talking about their experiences of the magnitude 7.6 earthquake which hit Los Angeles in January, 1994. The conversation was recorded approximately two weeks after the earthquake (see Iwasaki (1997), Iwasaki & Horie (1998)). In the first half of this excerpt, mainly Y speaks, while S gives a variety of backchannel expressions, ranging from minimal vocalization such as *nn* to more elaborate ones ('Is that right?' – line 8; 'I see.' – line 11; or 'What floor are you on?' – line 5). The roles in conversation shift at line 44, and S becomes the primary floor holder. In this transcript, each line represents one unit of prosody mainly demarcated by a pause and tail pitch movements. Observation of such prosodic units reveal that Japanese speakers often produce phrases rather than clauses, making this type of conversation more "fragmentary" (Clancy 1982; Maynard 1989; Iwasaki 1993a).

Northridge Earthquake Conversation.

---

(1)   Y: (H) ato   daidokoro   ga   sugokat.   ⟨x te ne x⟩
                and   kitchen   NOM   messy:PAST
                '…and the kitchen was a mess.'

(2) S: *sugokatta* ⟨x *desu ne* x⟩
         messy:PAST   COP PP
         'It was messy.'

(3) Y: *mo   osara ga   zenbu ochi-chatta   desho*↘
         EMPH dish   NOM all   fall-ASP:PAST PP
         'All the dishes fell down, didn't they?'

(4) Y: [[*nanka*<
         SOF
         'It's like,…'

(5) S: [[*nan-gai-na-n   desu ka*↗
         what-floor-COP:ATT-SE   COP Q
         'What floor are you on?'

(6) Y: *iya ni-kai-na-n   desu kedo*↘
         SOF 2nd-floor-COP:ATT-SE COP but
         'We're just on the second floor, but…

(7)   [*hurui-n   desu yo*↘
          old:NONPAST-SE   COP PP
          …it's old.'

(8) S: [*soo-na-n   desu ka:*↘
         SO-COP:ATT-SE   COP   Q
         'Is that right?'

(9) Y: =*chiku sanjuu:* (H) *go-nen toka soo yuu:::   kanji   da   kara::*↘
          built thirty-five-year   SOF   so say   feeling COP so
          'It looks like it's at least thirty-five years old, or something.'

(10) S: *naruhodo nee*↗
         I.see   PP
         'I see.'

(11) Y: *de   nanka   anoo*↘
         and   somehow   INJ
         'And somehow, uhm…

(12)   …*takosu no   bin:*↗
          taco   GEN   bottle
          …a bottle of taco sauce?'

(13) S: *hai hai hai hai*↘
         yes yes yes yes
         'yes, yes, yes, yes.'

(14) Y: *ga:* ∧
         NOM

(15)   ochita-n   da   kedo: ∧
        fall:PAST-SE COP   but
        '(It) fell down, and…'

(16) S: oo oo.
        oh oh
        'Oh, my…'

(17) Y: konagona-na-n   da   kedo: ∧
        break.into.pieces-COP:ATT-SE COP but
        '…(it) was broken into pieces.'

(18)   …anoo… () takosu ka na↘
        INJ   tacos   Q   PP
        'Let's see…was it taco sauce?'

(19)   takosu   ja-nai   ya↘
        Tacos   COP:NEG   PP
        '(It) wasn't taco sauce.'

(20) S: sarusa soosu↗
        salsa-sauce
        '(Was it) salsa sauce?'

(21) Y: sarusa no   bin↘
        salsa   GEN   bottle
        '(Yeah,) a bottle of salsa.'

(22) S: nn   nn
        BCK BCK

(23)   ⟨x nioi ga   sugo< x⟩
          smell NOM strong
        '(It has a) strong smell.'

(24) Y: dakara sono↘
        so   that

(25)   ochita↘
        fall:PAST

(26)   … kiseki doori kabe ni   akaku   [⟨x baatte x⟩ @@@
          trace same wall DAT   red:INF SSW
        'Anyway, there was this red streak on the wall right along where (the bottle) had fallen.'

(27) S: [@@@@@@

(28) Y ⟨@ batten-ni @ ⟩
        cross-COP:ADV
        'It was like a cross.'

(29)   da wa<
       so
       '...so...'

(30)   wa<
       ...kuchi ga   ai...te   ochita   no kamoshinnai-n da   kedomo nee↘
          mouth NOM open:TE   fall:PAST SE maybe-SE   COP but   PP
       '...maybe it fell without the cap on.'

(31) S: nnn @@
       BCK

(32) Y: dakara koo   atarijuu   ma-k... ka mitai-na↘
       so   this.way all.around   PFX-red   look-COP:ATT
       'So it was like, all red everywhere.'

(33) S: @@@

(34) Y: demo ⟨x x⟩
       but

(35)   mi-enai   deshoo∧
       see-POT:NEG   PP
       'But, I couldn't see, right,...

(36)   [yoru da   kara↘
        night COP so
       '...because it was night time.'

(37) S: [⟨x sugoi x⟩
        terrible
       'That's terrible.'

(38) Y: da kaichuudentoo de   batto terasu to   koo↘
       so flashlight   INS   SSW   shine   COND   like.this

(39)   (H)... koo   moo   nee.
              like.this EMPH   PP

(40)   ...konagona   mitai-na↘
          break.into.pieces   look-COP:ATT
       'When I shined a flashlight in the kitchen, it was like everything was, you know, all broken into pieces.'

(41) S: aa soo-na-n   desu ka:↘
       oh so-COP:ATT-SE   COP Q
       'Is that right?'

(42) Y: kabin ga   ochi-tari toka↘
       vase NOM   fall-REP SOF
       'Like, the vase had fallen.'

(43) S: () h< hee↗
        BCK
        'Really?'

==== [Floor shifts to S from Y here] ====

(44) S: uchi   wa   nanka nee∧
        house TOP SOF   PP
        'Well, like at our place,...

(45)   ... ano atashi wa,
            INJ I   TOP

(46)   ...ano shooyu   o   takusan... tsukau deshoo↗
           INJ soy.sauce ACC lot   use   PP
        ...I use lots of soy sauce, right?'

(47) Y: [(H) aa shooyu   nee↗
             INJ soy.sauce   PP
        'Oh, soy sauce.'

(48) S: [de   korian-no↘
         and Korean-COP:ATT
        'And the Korean...

(49)   ... soo korian-no   kanojo wa: ∧
            INJ Korean-COP:ATT   she   TOP
        ...yeah, the Korean girl...

(50)   ... ano... ittsumo ninniku to: ∧
            INJ   always   garlic   and
        ...uhm, always (uses) garlic and...

(51)   (H) sesamioiru tte nan   te yuu-n   da   kke↘
            sesame.oil QT   what QT say-SE   COP PP
        ...oh, how do you say "sesame oil" (in Japanese)?

(52)   gomaabura   ka↘
        sesame.oil   Q
        It's gomaabura, isn't it?

(53)   [[gomaabura   o   tsukau-n desu yo↘
          sesame.oil   ACC use-SE   COP   PP
        Well, (she) uses sesame oil.'

(54) Y: [[aa hai hai hai↘
         INJ yes yes yes
        'Oh, yes, yes, yes.'

(55) S: de   kanojo no   ne↘
         and she   GEN PP

(56)   *gomaabura to:* ∧
       sesame.oil and

(57)   *atashi no   ne,*
       I   GEN   PP

(58)   *shooyu   ga   ne* ↘
       soy.sauce NOM PP

(59)   *taorete* ∧
       fall:TE

(60)   *ya< warete   [sug... goi   nioi   datta* ↘
       no break:TE   terrible smell COP:PAST
       'And so her sesame oil and my soy sauce fell down, no, broke, and the smell was terrible.'

(61) Y: *[aaa nioi   ga   sugoi   yo ne* ↗
       INJ smell NOM terrible PP PP
       'Yeah, the smell is terrible, isn't it?'

(62)   *[[daidokoro wa   nioi   ga   sugokatta* ↘
       kitchen   TOP smell NOM terrible:PAST
       'The kitchen smelled terrible.'

(63) S: *[[moo<*
       EMPH

(64)   *nnn mak-kuro-kuro   da   shi   nee* ↘
       INJ PFX-black-black COP and PP

(65)   *nanka... sugokatta   desu yo* ↘
       SOF   terrible:PAST COP   PP
       'Oh, uh, it was all black and just...a terrible mess.'

5. Conversation (2): "Australia"

This except, in which the wife (W) tells her husband (H) that her female relative ended up canceling a trip to Australia, quite dramatically shows the flexibility of conversational language. W announces in line 1 the main theme ('her female relative didn't go there'), then adds more information about the destination and the agent (line 3). She checks to see if H completely understands the story by producing line 5 ('She said she was going, don't you remember?'), then again adds more information about who she was planning to go with and when. See Iwasaki and Ono (1998) for an analysis of this conversation. This conversation is from a collection of natural conversations by Tsuyoshi Ono.

Australia

(1) W: *soo soshitara oo< asoko ikanakatta-n da tte* ↗
so then FRG there go:NEG:PAST-SE COP QT
'So then (she) didn't go to Au-, there, I heard.'

(2) H: [*doko e*] ↗
where ALL
'Where?'

(3) W: [*oosutoraria.*]
Australia
'Australia.'

(4) W: ...*tokkochan.*
(name)
'Tokko-chan.'

(5) H: *a soo-na no.*
oh SO-COP:ATT SE
'Oh, is that right?'

(6) W: *iku tte itte-ta deshoo* ↗
go:NONPAST QT say:TE-ASP:PAST PP
'She said (she was) going, don't you remember?'

(7) [*kareshi to gooruden-uiiku.*]
boyfriend COM golden-week
'With (her) boyfriend, (during) Golden Week.'

(8) H: [*nn nn nn*]
BCK BCK BCK
'Yes, yes, yes.'

(9) W: ...*soshitara kekkyoku nanka kareshi ga:,*
then finally SOF boyfriend NOM
'Then, the boyfriend finally (said)'

(10) H: *nn.*
BCK

(11) W: *shigoto ga ne* ↗
work NOM PP
'his work is'

(12) ...*nanka taihen de:*^
SOF hard
'rather demanding and'

(13) ...*isogashikute:*^
busy:TE
'busy and'

(14)   de   yasumi ga   torenai   toka itte,
         and off   NOM take:POT:NEG   SOF   say:TE
         'and (he) said he can't take time-off'

(15) H: arara.
         BCK
         'Oh my...'

(16) W: ...nde:... iku: ↗
         And   go
         'and (before) going'

(17) H: nn
         BCK

(18) W: isshuukan mae   toka itta   kana ↗
         one.week   before QT   say:PAST PP
         'Did they say it was one week before?'

(19) H: kyanseru.
         cancel
         'Cancelled?'

(20) W: nn.
         BCK
         'Yes.'

(21) H: ...[shita-n.]
         do:PAST-SE
         '(They) did it?'

(22) W: [shita]-n   da   tte.
         do:PAST-SE   COP Q
         '(They) did it (she) said.'

(23)   nn
         BCK
         'Yes.'

(24)   ...de:: ...kyanseru-ryoo   to-shite,
            and   cancellation-fee as
         'and as the cancellation fee

(25)   nn   ...juugoman   kakatta   wake [ne] anoo.
         HES   150.thousand   take:PAST NML   PP   HES
         'uhm... it took 150,000 yen, you see.'

(26) H: [nn].
         BCK

(27) W: ...*ryohi   ga.*
         travel.expense NOM
         '(for) the travel expense,'

(28) H: *nn.*
        BCK

(29) W: ...*juugoman   kakatte* ^
         150.thousand take:TE
         'It took 15,000 yen.'

(30) H: *nn.*
        BCK

(31) W: *honde:...   kyanseru-ryoo   to-shite* ^
        then   cancellation.fee as
        'and as the cancellation fee'

(32) H: [*nn*].
        BCK

(33) W: [*moo*]... *dakara... mooshikon-jatta   wake   okane   mo   zenbu   ne.*
        already   so   submit-ASP:PAST   SE   money   also all   PP
        'so they had submitted (the paper) and paid all'

(34) *juugoman   harae- cchatta   wake.*
     150.thousand   pay-   pay:ASP:PAST   SE
     'they paid all of the 150,000 yen fee.'

(35) H: *nn.*
        BCK

(36) W: *de   kyanseru-ryoo   to-shite goman   toraretan   da*
        and cancellation.fee   as   50.thousand   take:PSS:PAST-SE   COP

        tte   so[k- kara].
        QT   there from
        'and they were taken 50 thousand yen from the total.'

(37) H: [*e::*]?
        'What?'

(38) W: *dakara juuman   wa   kaette   kita   ttsutteta.*
        so   100.thousand   TOP   return:TE come:PAST   QT:say:PAST
        '(she) said 100 thousand yen was returned.'

(39) H: ...*a soo.*
         BCK
         'Oh, really.'

(40) W: *nn*
        BCK
        'Yeah.'

References

Abe, Hideko. 2004. "Lesbian bar talk in Shinjuku, Tokyo." In *Japanese Language, Gender, and Ideology: Cultural Models and Real People*, Shigeko Okamoto and Janet S. Shibamoto Smith (eds.), 205–221. New York: Oxford University Press.
Akatsuka, Noriko. 1985. "Conditionals and the epistemic scale." *Language* 61: 625–639.
Akatsuka-McCawley, Noriko. 1978. "Another look at *no, koto*, and *to*: Epistemology and complementizer choice in Japanese." In *Problems in Japanese Syntax and Semantics*, John Hinds and Irwin Haward (eds.), 172–212. Tokyo: Kaitaku-sha.
Akatsuka, Noriko and Clancy, Patricia M. 1993. "Conditionality and deontic modality in Japanese and Korean; Evidence from the emergence of conditionals." In *Japanese/Korean Linguistics 2*, Patricia M. Clancy (ed.), 177–192. Stanford: CSLI.
Akatsuka, Noriko and Tsukamoto, Atsuro. 1998. *Modaritī to hatsuwa kōi* [Modality and Speech Act]. Tokyo: Kenkyū-sha.
Alfonso, Anthony. 1966. *Japanese Language Patterns: A Structural Approach* (volumes 1 & 2). Tokyo: Center of Applied Linguistics, Sophia University.
Aoki, Hiromi. 2008. *Hearership as Interactive Practice: A Multi-modal Analysis of the Response Token Nn and Head Nods in Japanese Casual Conversation*. Unpublished doctoral dissertation, University of California, Los Angeles.
Asato, Susumu and Doi, Naomi. 1999. *Okinawajin wa doko kara kita ka: Ryukyū-Okinawajin no kigen to seiritsu*. [Where Did the Okinawan People Come From?: The Origin and Formation of Ryukyu-Okinawan People]. Naha: Bōdā Inku.
Bachnik, Jane M. and Quinn, Charles J., Jr. (eds.). 1994. *Situated Meaning: Inside and Outside in Japanese Self, Society, and Language*. Princeton, NJ: Princeton University Press.
Bedell, George. 1972. "On *no*." *UCLA Papers in Syntax 3: Studies in East Asian Syntax*: 1–20.
Bellwood, Peter and Renfrew, Colin. (eds.). 2002. *Examining the Farming/Language Dispersal Hypothesis*. Cambridge: McDonald Institute for Archaeological Research, University of Cambridge; Oxford: Distributed by Oxbow Books.
Bentley, John R. 2008. *A Linguistic History of the Forgotten Islands: A Reconstruction of the Proto-Language of the Southern Ryukyus*. Kent, UK: Global Oriental.
Blake, Barry J. 1994. *Case*. Cambridge: Cambridge University Press.
Bodine, Anne. 1975. "Sex differentiation in language." In *Language and Sex: Difference and Dominance*, Barrie Thorne and Nancy Henley (eds.), 130–151. Rowley, Massachusetts: Newbury House.
Bybee, Joan, Perkins, Revere and Pagliuca, William. 1994. *The Evolution of Grammar: Tense, Aspect, and Modality in the Languages of the World*. Chicago/London: The University of Chicago Press.
Camp, Maggie. 2009. *Japanese Lesbian Speech: Sexuality, Gender Identity, and Language*. Unpublished doctoral dissertation, University of Arizona, Tucson.
Chafe, Wallace. 1976. "Givenness, contrastiveness, definiteness, subjects, topics, and point of view." In *Subject and Topic*, Charles Li (ed.), 25–56. New York: Academic Press.
Chafe, Wallace. 1987. "Cognitive constraints on information flow." In *Coherence and Grounding in Discourse*, Russel Tomlin (ed.), 21–52. Amsterdam: John Benjamins.
Chafe, Wallace. 1994. *Discourse, Consciousness, and Time: The Flow and Displacement of Conscious Experience in Speaking and Writing*. Chicago/London: The University of Chicago Press.

Clancy, Patricia M. 1980. "Referential choice in English and Japanese narrative discourse." In *The Pear Stories: Cognitive and Linguistic Aspects of Narrative Production*, Wallace Chafe (ed.), 127–202. Norwood, NJ: Ablex.

Clancy, Patricia M. 1982. Written and spoken style in Japanese narratives. In *Spoken and Written Language: Exploring Orality and Literacy*. Deborah Tannen (ed.), 55–76. New York: Academic Press.

Clancy, Patricia M., Akatsuka, Noriko and Strauss, Susan. 1997. "Deontic modality and conditionality in discourse: A cross-linguistic study of adult speech to young children." In *Directions in Functional Linguistics*, Akio Kamio (ed.), 19–57. Amsterdam: John Benjamins.

Clancy, Patricia M., Thompson, Sandra A., Suzuki, Ryoko and Tao, Hongyin. 1996. "The conversational use of reactive tokens in English, Japanese, and Mandarin." *Journal of Pragmatics* 26: 355–387.

Comrie, Bernard. 1976. *Aspect*. Cambridge: Cambridge University Press.

Cook, Haruko. 1990. "An indexical account of the Japanese sentence-final particle *no*." *Discourse Processes* 13: 401–439.

Cook, Haruko. 1999. "Situational meanings of Japanese social deixis: The mixed use of the masu and plain forms." *Journal of Linguistic Anthropology* 8 (1): 87–110.

Cook, Haruko. 2008. "Style shift in Japanese academic consultations." In *Style Shifting in Japanese*, Kimberly Jones and Tsuyoshi Ono (eds.), 9–38. Amsterdam: John Benjamins.

Couper-Kuhlen, Elizabeth and Ono, Tsuyoshi. 2007. "'Incrementing' in conversation. A comparison of practices in English, German and Japanese." *Pragmatics* 17 (4): 513–552.

Dixon, Robert M.W. 1977. "Where have all the adjectives gone?" *Studies in Language* 1: 19–80.

Downing, Pamela. 1996. *Numeral Classifier Systems: The Case of Japanese*. Amsterdam: John Benjamins.

Dryer, Matthew S. 2008a. "Order of subject, object and verb." In *The World Atlas of Language Structures Online*, Martin Haspelmath, Matthew S. Dryer, David Gil and Bernard Comrie (eds.). Munich: Max Planck Digital Library, chapter 81. Available online at http://wals.info/feature/81. Accessed on 2010-09-15.

Dryer, Matthew S. 2008b. "Order of adjective and noun." In *The World Atlas of Language Structures Online*, Martin Haspelmath, Matthew S. Dryer, David Gil and Bernard Comrie (eds.). Munich: Max Planck Digital Library, chapter 87. Available online at http://wals.info/feature/87. Accessed on 2010-09-15.

Dryer, Matthew S. 2008c. "Position of interrogative phrases in content questions." In *The World Atlas of Language Structures Online*, Martin Haspelmath, Matthew S. Dryer, David Gil and Bernard Comrie (eds.). Munich: Max Planck Digital Library, chapter 93. Available online at http://wals.info/feature/93. Accessed on 2010-09-15.

Dryer, Matthew S. 2008d. "Relationship between the order of object and verb and the order of relative clause and noun. In *The World Atlas of Language Structures Online*, Martin Haspelmath, Matthew S. Dryer, David Gil and Bernard Comrie (eds.). Munich: Max Planck Digital Library, chapter 96. Available online at http://wals.info/feature/96. Accessed on 2010-09-15.

Dryer, Matthew S. 2008e. "Polar questions." In *The World Atlas of Language Structures Online*, Martin Haspelmath, Matthew S. Dryer, David Gil and Bernard Comrie (eds.). Munich: Max Planck Digital Library, chapter 116. Available online at http://wals.info/feature/116. Accessed on 2010-09-15.

Du Bois, John. 1986. "Self-evidence and ritual speech." In *Evidentiality: The Linguistic Coding of Epistemology*, Wallace Chafe and Johanna Nichols (eds.), 313–336. Norwood, NJ: Ablex.

Du Bois, John, Schuetze-Cobun, Stephan, Paolino, Danae and Cumming, Susan (eds.). 1992. *Discourse Transcription. Santa Barbara Papers in Linguistics* 4. Santa Barbara: University of California, Santa Barbara, Department of Linguistics.

Ezaki, Motoko. 2010. "Strategic derivations: The role of kanji in contemporary Japanese." *Japanese Language and Literature* 44: 179–212.

Fillmore, Charles. 1966. "Deictic categories in the semantics of 'Come'." *Foundations of Language* 2: 219–227.

Fillmore, Charles. 1972. "How to know whether you're coming or going." *Descriptive and Applied Linguistics* 5: 3–17.

Fillmore, Charles. 1975. *Santa Cruz Lectures on Deixis 1971.* Bloomington: Indiana University Linguistics Club.

Fillmore, Charles. 1982. "Frame semantics." In *Linguistics in the Morning Calm*, Linguistic Society of Korea (eds.), 222–254. Seoul: Hanshin Publishing Co.

Foley, William A. and Van Valin, Robert D., Jr. 1984. *Functional Syntax and Universal Grammar*. Cambridge: Cambridge University Press.

Ford, Cecilia and Mori, Junko. 1994. "Causal markers in Japanese and English conversations: A cross-linguistic study of interactional grammar." *Pragmatics* 4 (1): 31–61.

Fry, John. 2003. *Ellipsis and Wa-marking in Japanese Conversation*. New York and London: Routledge.

Fujii, Noriko and Ono, Tsuyoshi. 2000. "The occurrence and non-occurrence of the Japanese direct object marker *o* in conversation." *Studies in Language* 24 (1): 1–39.

Givón, Talmy. 1980. "The binding hierarchy and the typology of complements." *Studies in Language* 4 (3): 333–377.

Givón, Talmy. 1982. "Logic vs. pragmatics, with human languages as the referee: Toward an empirically viable epistemology." *Journal of Pragmatics* 6: 81–133.

Goodwin, Charles. 1981. *Conversational Organization: Interaction between Speakers and Hearers*. New York: Academic Press.

Goodwin, Charles and Heritage, John. 1990. "Conversation analysis." *Annual Review of Anthropology* 19: 283–307.

Gottlieb, Nanette. 2000. *Word-processing Technology in Japan: Kanji and the Keyboard*. Richmond, Surrey: Curzon Press.

Gottlieb, Nanette. 2005. *Language and Society in Japan*. Cambridge: Cambridge University Press.

Greenberg, Joseph. 1972. "Numeral classifiers and substantival number: Problems in the genesis of a linguistic type." *Working Papers on Language Universals* 9: 1–39.

Habein, Yaeko S. 1984. *The History of the Japanese Written Language*. Tokyo: University of Tokyo Press.

Habu, Junko. 2004. *Ancient Jomon of Japan*. Cambridge, U.K.; New York: Cambridge University Press.

Haig, John. 1996. "Subjacency and Japanese grammar: A functional account." *Studies in Language* 20 (1): 53–92.

Hamano, Shoko. 1998. *The Sound-Symbolic System of Japanese*. Stanford/Tokyo: CSLI/Kuroshio.

Hanihara, Kazuo. 1991. "Dural structural model for the population history of the Japanese." *Japan Review* 2: 1–33

Harada, Shin'ichi. 1971. "Ga-no conversion and ideolectal variations in Japanese." *Gengo Kenkyu* 60: 25–38.

Harada, Shin'ichi. 1973. "Counter equi NP deletion." *Annual Bulletin, Research Institute of Logopedics and Phoniatrics. University of Tokyo* 7: 113–147.

Harada, Shin'ichi. 1976. "*Ga-no* conversion revisited: A reply to Shibatani." *Gengo Kenkyu* 70: 23–38.

Harada, Shin'ichi. 1976. "Honorifics." In *Japanese Generative Grammar*, Masayoshi Shibatani (ed.), 499–561. New York: Academic Press.

Hasegawa, Yoko. 1989. "Questioning vs. identifying: A functional analysis of the [A candidate that which professor recommended was hired?] construction in Japanese." *BLS* 15: 138–149.

Hasegawa, Yoko. 1996. *A Study of Japanese Clause Linkage: The Connective TE in Japanese*. Stanford: CSLI.

Hashimoto, Shinkichi. [1931] 1969. *Joshi-jodōshi no kenkyū*. [A Study of Particles and Auxiliary Verbs]. Tokyo: Iwanami-shoten.

Hashimoto, Yuria. 2009. "Clause chaining, turn projection and marking of participation: Functions of TE in turn co-construction in Japanese conversation." In *Japanese/Korean Linguistics* 16, Yukihiro Takubo, Tomohide Kinuhata, Szymon Grzelak and Kayo Nagai (eds.), 250–264. Stanford: CSLI.

Hattori, Shiro. 1954. "'Gengo nendai gaku' sunawachi 'goi tōkē gaku' no hōhō ni tsuite [On the method of glottochronology and the time depth of proto-Japanese]." *Gengo Kenkyu* 26/27: 29–77.

Haugh, Michael. 2008. "Utterance final conjunctive particles and implicature in Japanese conversation." *Pragmatics* 18 (3): 425–451.

Hayashi, Makoto. 2003. *Joint Utterance Construction in Japanese Conversation*. Amsterdam: John Benjamins.

Hayes, Bruce. 2009. *Introductory Phonology*. Madden, MA: Wiley-Blackwell.

Hibiya, Junko. 1995. "The velar nasal in Tokyo Japanese: A case of diffusion from above." *Language Variation and Change* 7: 139–152.

Hinds, John. 1982. *Ellipsis in Japanese*. Edmonton, Alberta: Linguistic Research, Inc.

Hinds, John. 1983. "Topic continuity in Japanese." In *Topic Continuity in Discourse: A Quantitative Cross-Language Study*, Talmy Givón (ed.), 47–93. Amsterdam: John Benjamins.

Hinds, John. 1986. *Japanese*. Dover: Cloom Helm.

Hinds, John and Hinds, Wako. 1979. "Participant identification in Japanese narrative discourse." In *Explorations in Linguistics*, George Bedell, Eichi Kobayashi and Masatake Muraki (eds.), 201–212. Tokyo: Kenkyu-sha.

Hinds, John and Howard, Irwin (eds.). 1978. *Problems in Japanese Syntax and Semantics*. Tokyo: Kaitaku-sha.

Hiraiwa, Ken. 2002. "Nominative-genitive conversion revisited." In *Japanese/Korean Linguistics 10*, Noriko Akatsuka and Susan Strauss (eds.), 545–558. Stanford: CSLI.

Hirayama, Teruo. 1968. *Nihon no hōgen* [The Dialects of Japan]. Tokyo: Kōdan-sha.

Hoji, Hajime. 1997. *Otagai* ["Each other"]. Paper presented at the 16th West Coast Conference on Formal Linguistics, University of Washington, March 2, 1997.

Hokama, Shuzen. 2007. *Okinawa no kotoba to rekishi* [Language and history of Okinawa]. Tokyo: Chuō Kōron Shin Sha.

Horie, Kaoru. 1993. *A Cross-Linguistic Study of Perception and Cognition Verb Complements: A Cognitive Perspective*. Unpublished doctoral dissertation, University of Southern California, Los Angeles.

Horie, Kaoru. 1997. "Three types of nominalization in Modern Japanese: *no*, *koto*, and zero." *Linguistics* 35: 879–894.

Horie, Kaoru and Taira, Kaori. 2002. "Where Korean and Japanese differ: Modality vs. discourse modality." In *Japanese/Korean Linguistics 10*, Noriko Akatsuka and Susan Strauss (eds.), 178–191. Stanford: CSLI.

Hudson, Mark. 1999a. "Japanese and Austronesian: An archaeological perspective on the proposed linguistic links." In *Interdisciplinary Perspectives on the Origins of the Japanese*. Keiichi Omoto (ed.), 267–279. Kyoto: International Research Center for Japanese Studies.

Hudson, Mark. 1999b. *Ruins of Identity: Ethnogenesis in the Japanese Islands*. Honolulu: University of Hawai'i Press.

Hudson, Mark. 2002. "Agriculture and language change in the Japanese islands." In *Examining the Farming/Language Dispersal Hypothesis*, Peter Bellwood and Colin Renfrew (eds.), 311–318. Cambridge: McDonald Institute for Archaeological Research, University of Cambridge.

Ide, Sachiko. 2006. *Wakimae no goyōron*. [Pragmatics of *Wakimae*-Discernment]. Tokyo: Taishū-kan.

Ikuta, Shoko. 2008. "Speech style shift as an interactional discourse strategy: The use and non-use of desu/masu in Japanese conversational interviews." In *Style Shifting in Japanese*, Kimberly Jones and Tsuyoshi Ono (eds.), 71–89. Amsterdam: John Benjamins.

Inoue, Fumio. 1998. *Nihongo uwotchingu* [Language (Japanese) Watching]. Tokyo: Iwanami.

Inoue, Kazuko. 1976. *Henkei bunpō to nihongo* [Transformational Grammar and Japanese]. Tokyo: Taishū-kan.

Inoue, Kazuko. 1983. "*Bun no setsuzoku* [Sentence conjunctions]." In *Kōza: Gendai no gengo I: Nihongo no kihon kōzō* [Series: Modern languages I: The Basic Structure of Japanese], Kazuko Inoue (ed.), 127–151. Tokyo: Sansei-do.

International Phonetic Association. 1999. *Handbook of the International Phonetic Association*. Cambridge: Cambridge University Press.

Inukai, Takashi. 2006. "*Nihongo o moji de kaku* [To write Japanese with letters]." In *Gengo to moji: Rettō no kodai-shi* [Language and Letters: The Ancient History of the Archipelago], Mahito Uehara, Taichiro Shiraishi, Shinji Yoshikawa (eds.), 11–44. Tokyo: Iwanami-shoten.

Iori, Isao. 1995. "*Ga shitai to o shitai: chokusetsu mokuteki-go no kaku-hyoji no yure* [On *ga shitai* and *o shitai*: Fluctuation of case marking for direct objects]. In *Nihongo ruigi hyōgen no bunpō (jō)* [Grammar of Synonymous Expressions in Japanese], Tatsuo Miyajima and Yoshio Nitta (eds.), 53–61. Yokyo: Kuroshio-shuppan.

Itani, Reiko. 1992. "Japanese sentence-final particle NE: A relevance-theoretic approach." *UCL Working Papers in Linguistics* 4: 215–237.

Ito, Junko. 1990. "Prosodic minimality in Japanese." *CLS* 26: 213–239.

Ito, Junko and Mester, Ralf-Armin. 1986. "The phonology of voicing in Japanese: Theoretical consequences for morphological accessibility." *Linguistic Inquiry* 17: 49–73.

Iwasaki, Shimako. 2008. *Collaborative Construction of Talk in Japanese Conversation*. Unpublished doctoral dissertation, University of California, Los Angeles.

Iwasaki, Shoichi. 1986. "The 'Given A constraint' and the Japanese particle *ga*." *Proceedings of the First Annual Pacific Linguistics Conference* 1: 152–167. University of Oregon.

Iwasaki, Shoichi. 1987. "Identifiability, scope-setting, and the particle *wa*: A study of Japanese spoken expository discourse." In *Perspectives on Topicalization: The Case of Japanese 'Wa,'* John Hinds, Senko Maynard and Shoichi Iwasaki (eds.), 107–141. Amsterdam: John Benjamins.

Iwasaki, Shoichi. 1993a. "The structure of intonation unit in Japanese." In *Japanese/Korean Linguistics* 3, Soonja Choi (ed.), 39–53. Stanford: CSLI.

Iwasaki, Shoichi. 1993b. *Subjectivity in Grammar and Discourse: Theoretical Considerations and a Case Study of Japanese Spoken Discourse*. Amsterdam: John Benjamins.

Iwasaki, Shoichi. 1993c. "Functional transfer in the history of Japanese language." In *Japanese/Korean Linguistics* 2, Patricia M. Clancy (ed.), 20–32. Stanford: CSLI.

Iwasaki, Shoichi. 1997. "The Northridge earthquake conversation: The 'loop' sequence and mutual dependence in Japanese conversation." *Journal of Pragmatics* 28: 661–93.

Iwasaki, Shoichi. 2000. "The Functions of the attributive-finite in poetry and prose in Heian Japanese." In *Textual Parameters in Older Languages*, Susan C. Herring, Pieter van Reenen, Lene Schøesler (eds.), 237–272. Amsterdam: John Benjamins.

Iwasaki, Shoichi. 2009. "*Intonēshon tan'i* (IU) [Intonation unit (IU)]." In *Chi no kagaku: taninzū intā akushon no bunseki hōhō* [Science of Wisdom: Methods of Analysis of Multi-party Interaction], Katsuya Takanashi and Mayumi Bono. (eds.), 35–51. Tokyo: Oum-sha.

Iwasaki, Shoichi. (to appear). "Grammar of the internal expressive sentences in Japanese: Observations and explorations." In *Functional Approaches to Japanese Grammar*, Kaori Kabata and Tsuyoshi Ono (eds.).

Iwasaki, Shoichi and Horie, Preeya Ingkaphirom. 1998. "The 'Northridge earthquake' conversations: Conversational patterns in Japanese and Thai and their cultural significance." *Discourse & Society* 9 (4): 517–545.

Iwasaki, Shoichi and Horie, Preeya Ingkaphirom. 2000. "Creating speech register in Thai conversation." *Language in Society* 29: 519–554.

Iwasaki, Shoichi and Ono, Tsuyoshi. 1999. "'*Bun*' – *saiko* ['The sentence' – revisited]." In *Gengogaku to nihongo kyōiku: jitsuyōteki gengo riron no kōchiku o mezashite* [Linguistics and Japanese Language Education – Aiming at Advancing a Practical Theory of Linguistic], Yukiko Sasaki Alam (ed.), 129–144. Tokyo: Kuroshio-shuppan.

Iwasaki, Shoichi and Ono, Tsuyoshi. 2002. "'Sentence' in spontaneous spoken Japanese discourse." In *Complex Sentences in Grammar and Discourse: Essays in Honor of Sandra A. Thompson*, Joan Bybee and Michael Noonan (eds.), 175–202. Amsterdam: John Benjamins.

Izui, Hisanosuke. [1953] 1985. *Nihongo to nantoo shogo – keifu kankei ka, kiyo no kankei ka* [Japanese and the languages of the southern islands – Is it a genealogical or contributory relationship?]. (Original work published in Minzokugaku Kenkyuu 17.2., 1953). In *Nihongo no keito – Kihon ronbun-shuu 1. [Genealogy of the Japanese language – Basic research papers (1)]*, Susumu Shiba et al. (eds.), 239–55 Osaka: Izumishoin.

Jacobsen, Wesley M. 1992. *The Transitive Structure of Events in Japanese*. Tokyo: Kuroshio-shuppan.

Jones, Kimberly and Ono, Tsuyoshi (eds.). 2008. *Style Shifting in Japanese*. Amsterdam: John Benjamins.

Josephs, Lewis S. 1976. "Complementation." In *Syntax and Semantics 5: Japanese Generative Grammar*, Masayoshi Shibatani (ed.), 307–369. New York: Academic Press.

Jun, Sun-Ah (ed.). 2005. *Prosodic Typology: The Phonology of Intonation and Phrasing*. Oxford/New York: Oxford University Press.

Kageyama, 1982. "Word formation in Japanese." *Lingua* 57: 215–58.

Kamio, Akio. 1997. *Territory of Information*. Amsterdam: John Benjamins

Kanamaru, Fumi. 1997. "*Ninshō daimeishi/koshō* [Personal pronouns and address terms]." In *Joseigo no sekai* [The World of Women's Language], Sachiko Ide (ed.), 15–32. Tokyo: Meiji-shoin.

Karimata, Shigehisa. 2011. Ryukyū hōgen no shōtenka joji to bun no tsūtatsuteki na taipu. [On the focus marking particle and the communicative type of sentences]. *Nihongo no Kenkyū*. 7–4: 69–81.

Kawanishi, Yumiko. 1994. "An analysis of non-challengeable modals: Korean *canha(yo)* and Japanese *janai*." In *Japanese/Korean Linguistics 4*, Noriko Akatsuka (ed.), 95–112. Stanford: CSLI.

Keenan, Edward. 1976. "Towards a universal definition of 'subject'." In *Subject and Topic*, Charles Li (ed.), 303–333. New York: Academic Press.

Keenan, Edward L. 1985. "Relative clause." In *Language Typology and Syntactic Description 2: Complex constructions*, Timothy Shopen (ed.), 141–170. Cambridge: Cambridge University Press.

Keenan, Edward L. and Comrie, Bernard. 1977. "Noun phrase accessibility and universal grammar." *Linguistic Inquiry* 8 (1): 63–99.

Kemmer, Suzanne. 1993. *The Middle Voice*. Amsterdam: John Benjamins.

Kin, Bunkyo. 2010. *Kanbun to higashi ajia: Kundoku no bunka-ken* [*Kanbun* and East Asia: The Cultural Sphere of *Kundoku*]. Tokyo: Iwanami-shoten.

Kindaichi, Haruhiko. [1942] 1967. "*Ga-gyo bionron* [On *ga*-column nasals]." In *Nihongo on'in no kenkyu* [Studies in Japanese Phonology], 168–197. Tokyo: Tokyodo-shuppan.

Kindaichi, Haruhiko. [1950] 1976. "*Kokugo dōshi no ichibunrui* [A classification of Japanese verbs]." *Gengo Kenkyū* 15: 48–63. (Reprinted in *Kokugo dōshi no asupekuto* [Aspect of Japanese verbs], 1976. Haruhiko Kindaichi (ed.), 5–26).

Kindaichi, Haruhiko. 1988. *Nihongo (Ge)*. [Japanese – Vol. 2]. Tokyo: Iwanami-shoten.

Kinsui, Satoshi. 1997. "The influence of translation on the historical development of the Japanese passive construction." *Journal of Pragmatics* 28: 759–779.

Kinsui, Satoshi. 2003. *Bācharu nihongo – yakuwari-go no nazo*. [Virtual Japanese – The Mystery of Role-defined Language]. Tokyo: Iwanami-shoten.

Kinsui, Satoshi and Takubo, Yukinori (eds.). 1992a. *Shijishi* [Demonstratives]. *Nihongo kenkyū shiryō shū* [Collection of Research Materials of Japanese]. Tokyo: Hitsuji-shobō.

Kinsui, Satoshi and Takubo, Yukinori. 1992b. "*Danwa kanri riron kara mita Nihongo no shijishi* [Japanese demonstratives from the perspective of discourse management]." In *Shijishi* [Demonstratives]. *Nihongo kenkyū shiryō shū* [Collection of Research Materials of Japanese], Satoshi Kinsui and Yukinori Takubo (eds.), 123–149. Tokyo: Hitsuji-shobō.

Kinsui, Satoshi, Inui, Yoshihiko and Shibuya, Katsumi. 2008. *Nihongo-shi no intāfēsu*. [Interface in the History of the Japanese Language]. Tokyo: Iwanami-shoten.

Kiparsky, Paul and Kiparsky, Carol. 1971. "Fact." In *Semantics: An Interdisciplinary Reader in Philosophy, Linguistics, and Psychology*, Danny D. Steinberg and Leon A. Jakobovits (eds.), 345–369. New York: Cambridge University Press.

Kita, Sotaro and Ide, Sachiko. 2007. "Nodding, *aizuchi*, and final particles in Japanese conversation: How conversation reflects the ideology of communication and social relationships." *Journal of Pragmatics* 39 (7): 1242–1254.

Kitahara, Yasuo. 1981. *Nihongo no sekai 6, Nihongo no bunpō* [The World of Japanese 6, Japanese Grammar]. Tokyo: Chūō Kōron.

Kobayashi, Yoshiharu. 1938. *Joshi 'ga' no hyogenteki kachi*. [Expressive values of the particle '*ga*']. *Kokugo to Kokubungaku* 15–10; 198–213.

Koike, Chisato. 2001. *An analysis of increments in Japanese conversation in terms of syntax and prosody*. Paper presented at the 11th Japanese/Korean Linguistics Conference, University of California at Santa Barbara.

Koike, Chisato. 2009. *Interaction in Storytelling in Japanese Conversations: An Analysis of Story Recipients' Questions*. Unpublished doctoral dissertation, University of California, Los Angeles.

Kokuritsu Kokugo Kenkyūjo [National Language Research Institute]. 1964. *Gendai-zasshi 90-shu no yōgo yōji* [Words and letters in 90 contemporary magazines] (3). Report 25.

Konoshima, Masatoshi. 1973. *Kokugo jodōshi no kenkyū* [A Study of Japanese Auxiliary Verbs]. Tokyo: Ofu-sha.

Koori, Shiro. 1997. "'*Tōji no murayama shushō*' no futatsu no imi to futatsutsu no yomi [Two readings and two meanings of '*Tōji no murayama shushō*']." In *Bunpō to onsei* [Speech and Grammar]. Onsei bunpō kenkyūkai (ed.), 123–146. Tokyo: Kuroshio-shuppan.

Koyama, Tetsuharu. 1997. "*Bunmatsu-shi to bunmatsu intonēshon*. [Sentence final elements and sentence final intonation]." In *Bunpō to onsei* [Speech and Grammar], Onsei bunpō kenkyūkai (ed.), 97–119. Tokyo: Kuroshio-shuppan.

Kubozono, Haruo. 1993. *The Organization of Japanese Prosody*. Tokyo: Kuroshio-shuppan.

Kubozono, Haruo. 2002. *Shingo wa kōshite tsukurareru*. [How New Words Are Created]. Tokyo: Iwanami-shoten.

Kuno, Susumu. 1973. *The Structure of the Japanese Language*. Cambridge: MIT Press.

Kuno, Susumu. 1987. *Functional Syntax: Anaphora, Discourse and Empathy*. Chicago/London: The Chicago University Press.

Kuno, Susumu and Kaburaki, Etsuko. 1977. "Empathy and syntax." *Linguistic Inquiry* 8 (4): 627–672.

Kuroda, S.-Y. 1965. Causative forms in Japanese. *Foundations of Language* 1: 30–50.

Kuroda, S.-Y. 1973. "Where epistemology, style and grammar meet: A case study from Japanese." In *A Festschrift for Morris Halle*, Stephen R. Anderson and Paul Kiparsky (eds.), 377–391. New York: Rinehart and Winston.

Kuroda, S.-Y. 1974. "Pivot-independent relativization in Japanese I." *Papers in Japanese Linguistics* 3: 59–93.

Kuroda, S.-Y. 1978. "Case-marking, canonical sentence patterns and counter equi in Japanese" In Hinds and Howard (ed.). 30–51.

Kuroda, S.-Y. 1979a. "On Japanese passives." In *Explorations in Linguistics*, George Bedell, Eichi Kobayashi and Masatake Muraki (eds.), 305–347. Tokyo: Kenkyu-sha.

Kuroda, S.-Y. 1979b. "*(Ko,) so, a ni tsuite* [On *(ko,) so*, and *a*]." In *Eigo to Nihongo to: Hayashi Eiichi Kyōju Kanreki Kinen Ronbunshū* [English and Japanese: Collected Papers for Professor Eiichi Hayashi's Sixtieth Birthday], Hayashi Eiichi Kyōju Kanreki Kinen Ronbunshū Kankō Īnkai (eds.), 41–60. Tokyo: Kuroshio-shuppan.

Kuroda, S.-Y. 1984. *The categorical and the thetic judgment reconsidered*. Paper presented at the Colloquium on Anton Marty's philosophy and linguistic theory. Fribourg, Switzerland.

Kuroda, S.-Y. 1987. "A study of the so-called topic *wa* in passages from Tolstoy, Lawrence and Faulkner (Of course, in Japanese translation)." In *Perspectives on Topicalization: The Case of Japanese 'Wa,'* John Hinds, Senko Maynard and Shoichi Iwasaki (eds.), 143–161. Amsterdam: John Benjamins.

Kuroda, S.-Y. 1992a [1979b]. "*'(Ko), so, a' ni tsuite* [On '(ko), so, a']." In *Shijishi* [Demonstratives], Satoshi Kinsui and Yukinori Takubo (eds.), 91–104. Tokyo: Hitsuji-shobō.

Kuroda, S.-Y. 1992b. *Japanese Syntax and Semantics: Collected Papers*. Dordrecht/ Boston & London: Kluwer Academic Publisher.

Kurumada, Chigusa. 2009. "The acquisition and development of the topic marker *wa* in L1 Japanese: The role of NP-*wa* in mother-child interaction." In *Formulaic language 2. Acquisition, loss, psychological reality, and functional explanations*, Roberta Corrigan, Edith A. Moravcsik, Hamid Ouali and Kathleen M. Wheatley (eds.), 347–374. Amsterdam: John Benjamins.

Kurumada, Chigusa and Iwasaki, Shoichi. 2011. "Negotiating desirability: The acquisition of the uses of *ii* 'good' in mother-child interactions in Japanese." In *Japanese/Korean Linguistics* 19, 511–525. Stanford: CSLI.

Labrune, Laurence. 2012. *The Phonology of Japanese*. Oxford: Oxford University Press.

Ladefoged, Peter. 2001. *A Course in Phonetics* (4th ed.). Fort Worth, Texas: Harcourt College Publishers.

Lambrecht, Knud. 1994. *Information Structure and Sentence form: Topic, Focus, and the Mental Representations of Discourse Referents*. Cambridge: Cambridge University Press.

Langacker, Ronald. 1999. "Double-subject constructions." In *Linguistics in the Morning Calm*, The linguistic society of Korea (ed.), 83–104. Seoul: Hanshin Publishing Company.

Lewis, Paul M (ed.). 2009. *Ethnologue: Languages of the World*, Sixteenth edition. Dallas, Tex.: SIL International. Online version: http://www.ethnologue.com/.

Li, Charles and Thompson, Sandra A. 1976. "Subject and topic: A new typology of language." In *Subject and Topic*, Charles Li (ed.), 457–489. New York: Academic Press.

Li, Charles and Thompson, Sandra A. 1981. *Mandarin Chinese: A Functional Reference Grammar*. Berkeley: University of California Press.

Longacre, Robert. 1983. The grammar of discourse. New York: Plenum Press.
Lurie, David B. 2011. *Realms of Literacy: Early Japan and the History of Writing* (Harvard East Asian Monographs). Cambridge, Massachusetts: Harvard University Press.
Lyons, John. 1977. *Semantics* (2 volumes). Cambridge: Cambridge University Press.
Maekawa, Kikuo. 2010. "Coarticulatory reinterpretation of allophonic variation: Corpus-based analysis of /z/ in spontaneous Japanese." *Journal of Phonetics* 38: 360–374.
Martin, Samuel. 1966. "Lexical evidence relating Korean to Japanese." *Language* 42 (2): 185–251.
Martin, Samuel. 1991/1975. *A Reference Grammar of Japanese*. New Haven: Yale University Press.
Maruyama, Shichiro. 1976. "The Mayalo-Polynesian component in the Japanese language." *Journal of Japanese Studies* 2 (2): 413–431.
Masuoka, Takashi. 1981. "Semantics of the benefactive constructions in Japanese." *Descriptive and Applied Linguistics* 14: 67–78.
Masuoka, Takashi. 1993. *Nihongo no jōken hyōgen*. [Conditionals in Japanese]. Tokyo: Kuroshio-shuppan.
Masuoka, Takashi. 1994. "*Meishi shūshoku setsu no setsuzoku keishiki: naiyō-setsu o chūshin ni* [The conjunctive form of noun modification with a focus on content phrases]." In *Nihongo no meishi shūshoku hyōgen* [Noun modification in Japanese].Yukinori Takubo (ed.), 5–27. Tokyo: Kuroshio-shuppan.
Matsuda, Yuki. 1997. *Representation of Focus and Presupposition in Japanese (predication)*. Unpublished doctoral dissertation, University of Southern California, Los Angeles.
Matsui, Tomoko. 2000. "Linguistic encoding of the guarantee of relevance: Japanese sentence-final particle YO." In *Pragmatic Markers and Propositional Attitude*, Gisle Andersen and Thorstein Fretheim (eds.), 145–172. Amsterdam: John Benjamins.
Matsumoto, Yo. 1988. "From bound grammatical markers to free discourse markers: History of some Japanese connectives." *Berkeley Linguistics Society, Fourteenth Annual Meeting*: 340–351.
Matsumoto, Yo. 1998. "Semantic change in the grammaticalization of verbs into postpositions in Japanese." In *Studies in Japanese Grammaticalization: Cognitive and Discourse Perspectives*, Toshio Ohori (ed.), 25–60. Tokyo: Kuroshio-shuppan.
Matsumoto, Yoshiko. 1996. "Does less feminine speech in Japanese mean less femininity?" *Gender and Belief Systems: Proceedings of the Fourth Berkeley Women and Language Conference*: 455–467.
Matsumoto, Yoshiko, 1997a. "Generation and gender in media representation of young Japanese women's speech," presented in the panel "Japanese linguistic ideology and socially-situated language practice." Paper presented at the 49th Annual Meeting of the Association for Asian Studies, Chicago, March 13–16, 1997.
Matsumoto, Yoshiko. 1997b. *Noun-modifying constructions in Japanese*. Amsterdam: John Benjamins.
Matsumoto, Yoshiko. 2004. "Alternative femininity." In *Japanese Language, Gender, and Ideology*, Shigeko Okamoto and Janet S. Shibamoto Smith (eds.), 240–255. Oxford: Oxford University Press.
Matsumoto, Yoshiko. 2008. "Variations in Japanese honorification – deviations or a change in making." In *Constructional Reorganization*, Jaakko Leino (ed.), 89–104. Amsterdam: John Benjamins.
Maynard, Senko. 1986. "The particle *-o* and content-oriented indirect speech in Japanese written discourse." In *Direct and Indirect Speech*, Florian Coulmas (ed.), 179–200. Berlin/New York: Mouton de Gruyter.
Maynard, Senko. 1987. "Thematization as a staging device in the Japanese narrative." In *Perspectives on Topicalization: The Case of Japanese 'Wa,'* John Hinds, Senko Maynard and Shoichi Iwasaki (eds.), 57–82. Amsterdam: John Benjamins.

Maynard, Senko K. 1989. *Japanese Conversation*. Norwood: Ablex.

Maynard, Senko K. 1991. "Pragmatics of discourse modality: A case of *da* and *desu/masu* forms in Japanese." *Journal of Pragmatics* 15: 551–582.

Maynard, Senko K. 1992. "Cognitive and pragmatic messages of a syntactic choice: The case of the Japanese commentary predicate *n(o) da*." *Text* 12 (4): 563–613.

Maynard, Senko K. 1993. *Discourse Modality: Subjectivity, Emotion, and Voice in the Japanese Language*. Amsterdam: John Benjamins.

Maynard, Senko K. 2002. *Linguistic Emotivity: Centrality of Place, the Topic-comment dynamics and an Ideology of Pathos in Japanese Discourse*. Amsterdam: John Benjamins.

Maynard, Senko K. 2007. *Linguistic Creativity in Japanese Discourse: Exploring the Multiplicity of Self, Perspectives, and Voice*. Amsterdam: John Benjamins.

Maynard, Senko K. 2008. "Playing with multiple voices: Emotivity and creativity in Japanese style mixture." In *Style shifting in Japanese*, Kimberly Jones and Tsuyoshi Ono (eds.), 91–129. Amsterdam: John Benjamins.

McCawley, James. 1968. *The Phonological Component of a Grammar of Japanese*. Hague: Mouton.

McCawley, James. 1978. "Notes on Japanese clothing verbs." In *Problems in Japanese Syntax and Semantics*, John Hinds and Irwin Howard (eds.), 68–78. Tokyo: Kaitaku-sha.

McGloin, Naomi. 1989. *A Students' Guide to Japanese Grammar*. Tokyo: Taishukan.

McGloin, Naomi. 2002. "Markers of epistemic vs. affective stances: *Desyō* vs. *janai*." In *Japanese/Korean Linguistics 10*, Noriko Akatsuka and Susan Strauss (eds.), 136–149. Stanford: CSLI.

Mikami, Akira. 1953. *Gendai gohō josetsu*. [Introduction to Modern Grammar]. Tokyo: Kuroshio-shuppan.

Mikami, Akira. 1960. *Zō wa hana ga nagai* [The Elephant Has a Long Trunk]. Tokyo: Kuroshio-shuppan.

Miller, Roy Andrew. 1967. *The Japanese Language*. Chicago: University of Chicago Press.

Miller, Roy Andrew. 1971. *Japanese and Other Altaic Languages*. Chicago: University of Chicago Press.

Miller, Roy Andrew. 1980. *Origins of the Japanese Language*. Seattle: University of Washington Press.

Miller, Roy Andrew. 1986a. "Linguistic evidence and Japanese prehistory." In *Windows on the Japanese Past: Studies in Archaeology and Prehistory*, Richard J. Pearson, Gina L. Barnes and Karl L. Hutterer (eds.), 101–120. Ann Arbor, MI: Center for Japanese Studies, University of Michigan.

Miller, Roy Andrew. 1986b. "A modest proposal on the origin of Japanese." In *Nihogo no kigen* [Origins of the Japanese Language: An International Collection of Essays], Kazuo Mabuchi (ed.), 57–103. Tokyo: Musashino-shoin.

Mio, Isago. 1948. *Kokugo-hō bunshō-ron* [The Grammar of Japanese and a Theory of Discourse]. Tokyo: Sansei-do.

Misumi, Tomoko. 2011. *A Relevance Theoretic Analysis of Japanese "NP1 wa NP2 da."* Unpublished doctoral dissertation, International Christian University, Tokyo.

Miyagawa, Shigeru. 1983. "Pragmatics of causation in Japanese." *Papers in Linguistics* 16: 147–184.

Miyagawa, Shigeru. 1989. "Light verbs and the ergative hypothesis." *Linguistic Inquiry* 20: 659–668.

Miyagawa, Shigeru. 1989. *Structure and Case Marking in Japanese. Syntax and Semantics 22*. New York: Academic Press.

Mizutani, Osamu. 1979. *Hanashikotoba to Nihonjin – Nihongo no seitai*. [Spoken Language and Japanese – Ecology of the Japanese Language]. Tokyo: Sotaku-sha.

Mizutani, Osamu and Mizutani, Nobuko. 1977. *An Introduction to Modern Japanese*. Tokyo: Japan Times.

Mori, Junko. 1999. *Negotiating Agreement and Disagreement in Japanese: Connective Expressions and Turn Construction*. Amsterdam: John Benjamins.

Morioka, Kenji. 1987. *Goi no keisei* [Lexicon Formation]. Tokyo: Meiji-shoin.

Morishige, Satoshi. 1965. *Nippon bunpō: shugo to jutsugo* [Japanese Grammar: Subject and Predicate]. Tokyo: Musashino-shoin.

Morishige, Satoshi. 1971. *Nihon bunpō no shomondai.* [Issues in Japanese Grammar]. Tokyo: Kasama-shoin.

Morita, Emi. 2005. *Negotiation of Contingent Talk: The Japanese Interactional Particles Ne and Sa.* Amsterdam: John Benjamins.

Nagahara, Hiroyuki and Iwasaki, Shoichi. 1995. *Tail Pitch Movement and the Intermediate Phrase in Japanese.* Unpublished manuscript. (Originally presented at the Linguistic Society of America, Annual Meeting, Boston, MA, January 6–9, 1994).

Nakane, Chie. 1970. *Japanese Society.* Berkeley/Los Angeles: University of California Press.

Nakasone, Seizen. 1961. *Ryūkyuū hōgen gaisetsu. Hōgengaku kōza dai 4 kan* [Introduction to Ryukyu Dialects. Dialect Study. Vol. 4]. Tokyo: Tokyo-do.

Nakau, Minoru. 1976. "Tense, aspect, and modality." In *Syntax and Semantics 5: Japanese Generative Grammar*, Masayoshi Shibatani (ed.), 421–482. New York: Academic Press.

Nakau, Minoru. 1991. "*Chūkan-tai to jihatsu-tai* [The middle voice and the spontaneous voice]." *Nihongo-gaku* 10 (2): 52–64.

Nakayama, Toshihide and Ichihashi-Nakayama, Kumiko. 1997. "Japanese *kedo*: Discourse genre and grammaticization." In *Japanese/Korean Linguistics 6*, Ho-min Sohn and John Haig (eds.), 607–618. Stanford: CSLI.

Nichols, Johanna. 1986. "Head-marking and dependent-marking grammar." *Language* 62: 56–119.

Nihongo no keitō o kangaeru kai [An association of concerned scholars to consider the genealogy of Japanese] (eds.). 1985. *Nihongo no keitō – kihon ronbun shū 1* [Genealogy of Japan – A Collection of Fundamental Resources 1]. Osaka: Izumi-shoin.

Nishigauchi, Taisuke. 1992. "Syntax of reciprocals in Japanese." *Journal of East Asian Linguistics* 1 (2): 157–196.

Nomura, Masaaki. 1977. "*Zōgo-hō* [Word-formation]." In *Nihongo 9 (Goi to imi).* [Japanese 9 (Lexicon and Semantics)], ed. by Susumu Ohno and Takeshi Shibata (eds.), 247–284. Tokyo: Iwanami-shoten.

Norman, Jerry. 1988. *Chinese.* Cambridge: Cambridge University Press.

Ochs, Elinor, Schegloff, Emanuel A. and Thompson, Sandra A. 1996. *Interaction and Grammar.* Cambridge: Cambridge University Press.

Oehrle, Richard and Nishio, Hiroko. 1981. "Adversity." In *Coyote Papers: Working Papers in Linguistics from A to Z 2*, Ann Farmer and Chisato Kitagawa (eds.), 163–185. Tucson: University of Arizona.

Ohno, Susumu. 1980. *Nihongo no seiritsu* [Establishment of the Japanese language]. Tokyo: Kadokawa-shoten.

Ohno, Susumu. 1988. *Nihongo no bunpō: koten-hen* [Japanese Grammar: Classical]. Tokyo: Kadokawa-shoten.

Ohno, Susumu. 1993. *Kakari musubi no kenkyū* [A Study of *Kakari Musubi*]. Tokyo: Iwanami-shoten.

Ohta, Kaoru. 1994. *Verbal Nouns in Japanese.* Unpublished doctoral dissertation, University of California, Los Angeles.

Ohye, Saburo. 1975. *Nichi-ei-go no hikaku kenkyū – shukansei o megutte* [A Comparative Study of Japanese and English – On Subjectivity]. Tokyo: Nan'un-do.

Oishi, Hatsutaro. 1983. *Gendai keigo kenkyu* [A Study of the Honorific System of Modern Japanese]. Tokyo: Chikuma-shobo.

Okada, Hideo. 1999. "Japanese." In *Handbook of the International Phonetic Association*, International Phonetic Association (eds.), 117–119. Cambridge: Cambridge University Press.

Okada, Judy. 2002. "Recent trends in Japanese causatives: The *sa*-insertion phenomenon." In *Japanese/Korean Linguistics 12*, William McClure (ed.), 28–39. Stanford: CSLI.

Okada, Judy. 2003. "Morpheme insertions in Japanese causative and potential expressions." In *Japanese/Korean Linguistics 13*, Mutsuko Endo Hudson, Peter Sells and Sun-Ah Jun (eds.), 347–357. Stanford: CSLI.

Okamoto, Shigeko. 1985. *Ellipsis in Japanese Discourse*. Unpublished doctoral dissertation, University of California, Berkeley.

Okamoto, Shigeko and Shibamoto Smith, Janet S. 2004. *Japanese Language, Gender, and Ideology*. Oxford: Oxford University Press.

Okuda, Yasuo. 1978a. "*Asupekuto no kenkyū o megutte*, I [On the study of aspect, I]." *Kokugo Kyōiku* 53: 33–44.

Okuda, Yasuo. 1978b. "*Asupekuto no kenkyū o megutte*, II [On the study of aspect, II]." *Kokugo Kyōiku* 54: 14–27.

Okutsu, Keiichiro. 1978. *"Boku wa unagi da" no bunpō* [The Grammar of *boku wa unagi da*] Tokyo: Kuroshio-shuppan.

Omoto, Keiichi and Naruya Saitou. 1997. Genetic origins of the Japanese: A partial support for the dual structure hypothesis. *American Journal of Physical Anthropology* 102: 437–446.

Onishi, Takuichiro. 2008. "Proto-Japanese and the distribution of dialects." In *Proto-Japanese: Issues and Prospects*, Bjarke Frellesvig and John Whitman (eds.), 57–78. Amsterdam: John Benjamins.

Ono, Tsuyoshi. 1990. "*Te, I, Ru* clauses in Japanese recipes: A quantitative study." *Studies in Language* 14 (1): 73–92.

Ono, Tsuyoshi. 1992. "The grammaticization of the Japanese verbs *oku* and *shimau*." *Cognitive Linguistics* 3 (4): 367–390.

Ono, Tsuyoshi and Suzuki, Ryoko. 1992. "Word order variability in Japanese conversation: Motivations and grammaticization." *Text* 12: 429–445.

Onodera, Noriko O. 2004. *Japanese Discourse Markers: Synchronic and Diachronic Discourse Analysis*. Amsterdam: John Benjamins.

Onoe, Keisuke. 1981. "'*Zō wa hana ga nagai*' to '*boku wa unagi da*'. [On '*zō wa hanaga nagai*' and '*boku wa unagi da*' sentences]." *Gengo* 10 (2): 10–15.

Oshima, Shoji. 2006. *Kanji denrai* [Arrival of Kanji]. Tokyo: Iwanami-shoten.

Otsu, Y. 1980. "Some aspects of *rendaku* in Japanese and related problems." In *Theoretical Issues in Japanese Linguistics. MIT Working Papers in Linguistics*, Yukio Otsu and Ann K. Farmer (eds.), 207–227. Cambridge: MIT.

Pardeshi, Prashant. 2000. *Transitivity and Voice: A Marathi-Japanese Contrastive Perspective*. Unpublished doctoral dissertation, Kobe University, Kobe.

Perlmutter, David and Postal, Paul. 1983. "The 1-advancement exclusiveness law." In *Studies in Relational Grammar 2*, David M. Perlmutter and Carol Rosen (eds.), 81–125. Chicago: The University of Chicago Press.

Pierrehumbert, Janet and Beckman, Mary. 1988. *Japanese Tone Structure*. Cambridge, MA/London, England: The MIT Press.

Polivanov, Evgenii Dmitrievich. [1924] 1974. "Toward work on musical accentuation in Japanese (in connection with Malayan languages)." (Daniel Armstrong. Trans.) In A. A. Leonte'v. *Selected Works. Articles on General Linguistics*. The Hague/Paris: Mouton.

Poser, William J. 1984. *The Phonetics and Phonology of Tone and Intonation in Japanese*. Unpublished doctoral dissertation, MIT, Cambridge, MA.

Poser, William J. 1990. "Evidence for foot structure in Japanese." *Language* 66: 78–105.

Radford, Andrew, Atkinson, Martin, Britain, David, Clahsen, Harald and Spencer, Andrew. 1999. *Linguistics: An Introduction*. Cambridge, UK/New York: Cambridge University Press.

Ross, John R. 1967. *Constraints on Variables in Syntax*. Bloomington: Indiana University Linguistic Club.

Sacks, Harvey, Schegloff, Emanuel A. and Jefferson, Gale. 1974. "A simplest systematics for the organization of turn-taking for conversation." *Language* 50 (4): 696–735.

Sadler, Misumi. 2007. *Deconstructing the Japanese 'Dative Subject' Construction*. Amsterdam: John Benjamins.

Saiga, Hideo. 1995. "*Kanji no jisū, jishu* [The number and types of kanji]." In *Nihongo to nihongo-kyoiku vol. 8 – Nihongo no moji-hyōki (jo)* [Japanese and Japanese Language Teaching vol. 8 – Writing in Japanese (Part I)], 28–62. Tokyo: Meiji-shoin.

Saito, Mamoru. 1985. *Some Asymmetries in Japanese and Their Theoretical Implication*. Unpublished doctoral dissertation, MIT, Cambridge, MA.

Sakakura, Atsuyoshi. 1970. "*'Hiraita hyōgen' kara 'tojita hyōgen' e: Kokugoshi no arikata shiron* [From the 'open structure' to the 'closed structure': a view on the history of the language]." *Kokugo to Kokubungaku* 47 (10): 22–35

Sakata, Yukiko. 1992 [1971]. "*Shijigo 'ko, so, a' no kinō ni tsuite* [On the functions of the demonstratives 'ko, so, a']." In *Shijishi* [Demonstratives]. *Nihongo kenkyū shiryō shū* [Research materials for the study of Japanese], Satoshi Kinsui and Yukinori Takubo (eds.), 54–68. Tokyo: Hitsuji-shobō.

Sakiyama, Osamu. 1990. "*Kodai nihongo ni okeru osutoroneshia gozoku no yōs* [Austronesian elements in old Japanese]." In *Nihongo no keisei* [The Formation of Japanese], Osamu Sakiyama (ed.), 92–122. Tokyo: Sansei-do.

Sakiyama, Osamu. 2001. "Genetic relationships between Austronesian and Japanese." *National Museum of Ethnology Research Report* 25 (4).

Sawada, Osamu and Sawada, Jun. 2011. *The meaning of modal affective demonstratives in Japanese*. Paper presented at the 21st Japanese/Korean Linguistics Conference, Seoul National University, October 20–22, 2011.

Schiffrin, Deborah. 1986. *Discourse Markers, Studies in Interactional Sociolinguistics 5*. Cambridge: Cambridge University Press.

Seeley, Christopher. 1991. *A History of Writing in Japan*. Leiden/ New York/ København/ Köln: E. J. Brill.

Selting, Margaret and Couper-Kuhlen, Elizabeth (eds.). 2001. *Studies in Interactional Linguistics*. Amsterdam: John Benjamins.

Serafim, Leon A. 1994. "A modification of the Whitman Proto-Koreo-Japonic vocalic hypothesis." *Korean Linguistics* Korean Linguistics8: 181–205.

Serafim, Leon. 1999. *Reflexes of Proto-Korea-Japonic mid vowels in Japonic and Korean*. Paper presented at the Workshop on Korean-Japanese Comparative Linguistics, XIVth International Conference on Historical Linguistics, Vancouver, British Columbia

Serafim, Leon. 2003. "When and from where did the Japonic language enter the Ryukyus? – A critical comparison of language, archaeology, and history." In *Perspectives on the Origins of the Japanese Language*, Toshiki Osada and Alexander Vovin (eds.), 463–476. Kyoto: International Research Center for Japanese Studies.

Serafim, Leon A. and Shinzato, Rumiko. 2005. "On the old Japanese *kakari* (focus) particle *koso*: Its origin and structure." *Gengo Kenkyu* 127: 1–49.

Serafim, Leon A. and Shinzato, Rumiko. 2009. "Grammaticalization pathways for Japonic nominalizers: A view from the Western periphery. In *Japanese/Korean Linguistics 16*, Yukihiro Takubo, Tomohide Kinuhata, Szymon Grzelak and Kayo Nagai (eds.), 116–130. Stanford: CSLI.

Serafim, Leon A. and Shinzato, Rumiko. (forthcoming). *Synchrony and Diachrony of Okinawan Kakari Musubi in Comparative Perspective with Premodern Japanese*.

Shibamoto, Janet. 1984. "Subject ellipsis and topic in Japanese." In *Studies in Japanese Language Use*, Shigeru Miyagawa and Chisato Kitagawa (eds.), 233–265. Edmonton, Canada: Linguistic Research Inc.

Shibatani, Masayoshi. 1975. "Perceptual strategies and the phenomena of particle conversion in Japanese." In *Papers from the Parasession on Functionalism*, 469–481. CLS.

Shibatani, Masayoshi (ed.). 1976a. *Syntax and Semantics 5: Japanese Generative Grammar*. New York: Academic Press.

Shibatani, Masayoshi. 1976b. "Causativization." In *Syntax and Semantics 5: Japanese Generative Grammar*, Masayoshi Shibatani (ed.), 239–294. New York: Academic Press.

Shibatani, Masayoshi. 1977. "Grammatical relations and surface cases." *Language* 53: 789–809.

Shibatani, Masayoshi. 1978a. *Nihongo no bunseki* [An Analysis of Japanese]. Tokyo: Taishu-kan shoten.

Shibatani, Masayoshi. 1978b. "Mikami Akira and the notion of 'subject' in Japanese grammar." In *Problems in Japanese Syntax and Semantics*, John Hinds and Irwin Howard (eds.), 52–67. Tokyo: Kaitaku-sha.

Shibatani, Masayoshi. 1985. "Passives and related constructions: A prototype analysis." *Language* 61: 821–48.

Shibatani, Masayoshi. 1990. *The Languages of Japan*. Cambridge: Cambridge University Press.

Shibatani, Masayoshi. 1994. "Benefactive constructions – A Japanese-Korean comparative perspective." In *Japanese/Korean Linguistics 4*, Noriko Akatsuka (ed.), 39–74. Stanford: CSLI.

Shibatani, Masayoshi. 1995. "A. A. Xolodovic on Japanese passives." In *Subject, Voice and Ergativity*, David. C. Bennett, Theodora Bynon and B. George Hewitt (eds.), 7–19. London: School of Oriental and African Studies, University of London.

Shibatani, Masayoshi. 2000. "Non-canonical constructions in Japanese." In *Kobe Papers in Linguistics 2*, 181–218. Kobe: Kobe University.

Shibatani, Masayoshi. 2009. "Elements of complex structures, where recursion isn't." In *Syntax Complexity: Diachrony, Acquisition, Neuro-cognition, Evolution*, Talmy Givón and Masayoshi Shibatani (eds.), 163–198. Amsterdam: John Benjamins.

Shibatani, Masayoshi. (forthcoming). "What can Japanese dialects tell us about the function and development of the nominalization particle *no*?" In *Japanese/Korean Linguistics 20*, Bjarke Frellesvig and Peter Sells (eds.). Stanford: CSLI.

Shibatani, Masayoshi and Chung, Sung Yeo. 2002. "Japanese and Korean causative revisited." In *Japanese/Korean Linguistics 10*, Noriko Akatsuka and Susan Strauss (eds.), 32–49. Stanford: CSLI.

Shibuya, Katsumi. 1993. "*Nihongo kanō-hyōgen no shosō to hatten* [Aspects and development of Japanese potential expressions]." Osaka Daigaku Bungakubu Kiyō 33 (1): 1–262.

Shibuya, Rinko. 2004. *Synchronic and Diachronic Study on Sex Exclusive Differences in the Modern Japanese Language*. Unpublished doctoral dissertation, Uiversity of California, Los Angeles.

Shinzato, Rumiko. 2003. "Wars, politics, and language: A case study of the Okinawan language." In *At War with Words*, Mirjana N. Dedaić and Daniel N. Nelson (eds.), 283–313. Berlin: Mouton de Gruyter.

Shinzato, Rumiko. (forthcoming). "Okinawan *kakari musubi* in historical and comparative perspective." In *Handbook of the Ryukyuan Languages*, Patrick Heinrich and Shinsho Miyara (eds.). Berlin: Mouton de Gruyter.

Shinzato, Rumiko and Serafim, Leon A. 2003. "*Kakari musubi* in comparative perspective: Old Japanese *ka/ya* and Okinawan *-ga/-i*." In *Japanese/Korean Linguistics 11*, Patricia M. Clancy (ed.), 189–202. Stanford: CSLI.

Shirai, Yasuhiro. 1998. "Where the progressive and the resultative meet: Imperfect aspect in Japanese, Chinese, Korean and English." *Studies in Language* 22 (3): 661–692.

Smith, Carlota S. 1991. *The Parameter of Aspect*. Dordrecht/Boston/London: Kluwer Academic Publishers.

Sugamoto, Nobuko. 1982. "Transitivity and objecthood in Japanese." In *Syntax and Semantics 15: Studies in Transitivity*, Paul Hopper and Sandra A. Thompson (eds.), 423–447. New York: Academic Press.

Suzuki, Satoko. 1997. "The relevance of factivity to complementizer choice in Japanese." *Studies in Language* 21 (2): 287–311.

Suzuki, Satoko (ed.). 2006. *Emotive Communication in Japanese*. Amsterdam: John Benjamins.

Takashima, Toshio. 2001. *Kanji to Nihonjin* [Kanji and the Japanese people]. Tokyo: Bungei Shunjū.

Takeuchi, Lone. 1999. *The Structure and History of Japanese*. London and New York: Longman.

Tanaka, Hiroko. 1999. *Turn-Taking in Japanese Conversation: A Study in Grammar and Interaction*. Amsterdam: John Benjamins.

Taylor, Yuki. 2010. "Approximative *tari* in Japanese: Focus on interaction and information." In *Japanese/Korean Linguistics 17*, Shoichi Iwasaki, Hajime Hoji, Patricia M. Clancy and Sung-Ock Sohn (eds.), 533–546. Stanford: CSLI.

Terakura, Hiroko. 1983. "Noun modification and the use of *to yuu*." *Journal of the Association of Teachers of Japanese* 18 (1): 23–55.

Teramura, Hideo. 1980. "*Meishi-shūshoku-bu no hikaku* [Comparison of noun modifications (in Japanese and English)]." In *Nichi-eigo hikaku kōza, dai 2 kan, bunpō* [The Comparative Study of Japanese and English Series, Vol. 2, Grammar], Tetsuya Kunihiro (ed.), 221–266. Tokyo: Taishūkan.

Teramura, Hideo. 1982. *Nihongo no sintakkusu to semantikusu I*. [The Syntax and Semantics of Japanese I]. Tokyo: Kuroshio-shuppan.

Teramura, Hideo. 1984. *Nihongo no shintakusu to imi II*. [The Syntax and Semantics of Japanese II]. Tokyo: Kuroshio-shuppan.

Thompson, Sandra A. and Longacre, Robert. 1985. "Adverbial clauses." In *Language Typology and Syntactic Description, Vol. II*, Timothy Shopen (ed.), 171–234. Cambridge: Cambridge University Press.

Tomasello, Michael. 2003. *Constructing a Language: A Usage-based Theory of Language Acquisition*. Cambridge, Massachusetts/London, England: Harvard University Press.

Traugott, Elizabeth C. and Dasher, Richard B. 2005. *Regularity in Semantic Change*. Cambridge/New York: Cambridge University Press.

Tsujimura, Natsuko. 2007. *An Introduction to Japanese Linguistics*. (2nd ed.). Cambridge: Blackwell.

Uehara, Satoshi. 1998. *Syntactic Categories in Japanese: A Cognitive and Typological Introduction*. Tokyo: Kuroshio-shuppan.

Unger, J. Marshall. 2001. "Layers of words and volcanic ash in Japan and Korea." *Journal of Japanese Studies* 27 (1): 81–111.

Vance, Timothy J. 1987. *An Introduction to Japanese Phonology*. Albany: State University of New York Press.

Vance, Timothy J. 1996. "Sequential voicing in Sino-Japanese." *Journal of the Association of Teachers of Japanese* 30 (1): 22–43.

Vance, Timothy J. 2008. *The Sounds of Japanese*. Cambridge: Cambridge University Press.

Venditti, Jennifer. 2005. "The J_ToBI model of Japanese intonation." In *Prosodic Typology: The Phonology of Intonation and Phrasing*, Sun-Ah Jun (ed.), 172–200. Oxford: Oxford University Press.

Vendler, Zeno. 1957. "Verbs and times." *The Philosophical Review* 66: 143–160. (Reprinted in *Linguistics in Philosophy*, 1976. Zeno Vendler (ed.), 97–121. Ithaca: Cornell University Press.)

Vovin, Alexander. 1993. *A Reconstruction of Proto-Ainu*. Leiden/New York: E.J. Brill.

Vovin, Alexander. 2003. "The Genetic Relationship of the Japanese Language: Where do We Go from Here?" In *Perspectives on the Origins of the Japanese Language*, Toshiki Osada and Alexander Vovin (eds.), 15–40. Kyoto: International Research Center for Japanese Studies.
Washio, Ryuichi. 1993. "When causatives mean passive: A cross-linguistic perspective." *Journal of East Asian Linguistics* 2: 45–90.
Watanabe, Akira. 1996. "Nominative-genitive conversion and agreement in Japanese: A cross-linguistic perspective." *Journal of East Asian Linguistics* 5: 373–410.
Watanabe, Minoru. 2001. *Nihongo-shi yōsetsu* [Introduction to the History of the Japanese Language]. Tokyo: Iwanami-shoten.
Watanabe, Yasuko. 1994. "Clause-chaining, switch-reference, and action/event continuity in Japanese discourse: the case of 'te,' 'to' and zero-conjunction." *Studies in Language* 18 (1): 127–203.
Whitman, John. 1985. *The Phonological Basis for the Comparison of Japanese and Korean*. Unpublished doctoral dissertation, Harvard University, Cambridge, MA.
Yamaguchi, Nakami. 2006. *Nihongo no rekiki* [A History of the Japanese Language]. Tokyo: Iwanami-shoten.
Yanagita, Kunio. 1908. *Kagyū-ko*. [On the words for "snail"] Tokyo: Tokyo-shoin.
Yanagida, Seiji. 1975. *Mumomachi-jidai no kokugo* [The Language of the Muromachi Period]. Tokyo: Tokyo-do.
Yanagida, Yuko and Whitman, John. 2009. "Alignment and word order in Old Japanese." *Journal of East Asian Linguistics* 18: 101–144.
Yoshida, Kanehiko. 1971. *Gendaigo jodōshi no shiteki kenkyū* [A Historical Study of Modern Auxiliary Verbs]. Tokyo: Meiji-shoin.
Yoshimura, Noriko and Nishina, Akira. 2010. "'Ga-no' kōtai genshō no haikei [A background of the 'ga-no' conversion." In *Gengogaku to Nihongo Kyōiku* VI. Masahiko Minami (ed.), 9–27. Tokyo: Kuroshio-shuppan.

Texts

Mitsuda, Takuya. 1995. *Major*. Vol. 1. Episode 5. Tokyo: Shogaku-kan.
Miyamoto, Teru. 1994. *Hotaru-gawa, doro no kawa* [A firefly river, a muddy river]. Tokyo: Shincho-sha.
Murakami, Haruki. 1991. *Noruwē no Mori* [Norwegian Wood]. Tokyo: Kodan-sha.
Murakami, Haruki. 2002. *Umibe no Kafuka (jō)* [Kafka on the Shore – I]. Tokyo: Sincho-sha.
Shibuya, Rinko. 1988. *Tabi-neko kuma no monogatari* [A Story of Kuma, the Traveling Cat]. Nagoya: Dabi-tsūshin.
Takamura, Kaoru. 1997. *Lady Joker* Vols. 1 & 2. Tokyo: Mainichi Shinbun Sha.
Tsubota, Jōji. 1975. *Nihon mukashi banashi shū* 1 [A Collection of Japanese Folktales 1]. Tokyo: Shinchō-sha.

Index

A

ablative 66, 115, 117, 119–120, 155, 163
abrupt verb form 14
absolute tense 129
accent 46–49, 62, 91
accent patterns for verbs and adjectives 47
accent reduction 52
accentual phrase 51–53
accomplishment 134, 138
accomplishment verb 138–139, 147
accusative 12–13, 25–26, 28, 60, 63, 66, 110–111, 114, 125, 153–154, 172, 175, 180, 193, 195, 200, 202, 216, 229, 235
accusative marker 111
accusative case marker 119
accusative case marking particle 25, 193
accusative case particle 172
achievement 134, 137–141, 145–146
achievement verb 141, 143, 146, 148
active stative sentence 163
active sentence 153–161
active voice 153
activity verb 139, 146, 164
addressee 60, 67, 92, 219–220, 222, 224, 239–240, 247–248, 252, 255, 284, 290–292, 294, 296, 300, 303–306, 309–312, 318–320, 323–325, 327, 329–330
addressee honorific 255, 325, 330
addressee proximate 291 *see* demonstrative
adjective 15, 21, 57, 61–65, 72, 78–79, 86–93, 95–96, 104–105, 107, 126–127, 131, 148, 150, 187, 199, 227, 247, 288, 298–300, 318, 328
adjectival complex 247
adjectival predicate 105, 227, 250
adjunct 219, 223, 229, 237, 248

adjunct noun phrases 116–120
adnoun 57, 60, 65, 187
adverb 57, 63–64, 66, 71, 87, 139–140, 206, 221, 237, 268, 290, 297, 308
adverbial clause 82, 130, 215, 241, 245
adverbial clause forming noun 61
adverbial clause forming formal noun 131
adverbial deictic demonstrative expression 291
adverbial expression 98–99
adverbial form 79 *see* infinitive
adverbial form of adjective 64, 83
adverbial form of copula 88–89, 148
adverbial function 71
adverbial head 201, 208, 213, 217
adverbial numeric expression 195
adverbial numeric phrase 196–197
adverbial particle 16, 67
adverbial phrase 119, 127, 189, 191–194
adverbial relation 97
adverbial subordinate clause 129
adverbial subordination 259, 263–270, 274
adverbial suffix 63
adverbial topic 238
adversity 160–161, 173–174, 301
adversative causative 173–174
adversative passive 160–162, 173–174
affix 57, 67, 90
affixation 58, 78, 92
agency 156–157, 184
agent 63, 105, 113–114, 138, 142–143, 147–148, 153–157, 159, 163, 175, 187, 207, 266, 292, 322–324, *see* also without the intervention of agent 164, no agent caused intervention 166

agent-causer 168–169
agent-less stative-potential sentence 167
agent suffix 94
agentive-potential sentence 168
ageru 125, 155, 294–296, 322 *see* verb of giving
agglutinating suffixation 78
agglutinating verb morphology 4, 7
agglutinative language 15
aida 61, 263, 265–266
Ainu 2–3, 5–6
aizuchi 221, 306–308
allative 66, 113, 201
Altaic languages 4
Altaic hypothesis 3–4
anaphora 276, 290
anaphoric relation 286
animate 9, 57, 75, 87, 107, 134, 145, 156, 233
animate agent 157
animate causee 173
animate causer 185
animate semantic head 234
animate subject 162
anterior 132–133, 140, 287
appositive clause 202, 210–212
argument 12, 15, 57, 63, 104–105, 113, 116, 119–120, 124, 159, 161, 184, 188, 193–194, 207, 219, 223, 236, 279, *see also* core argument 195, one argument predicate 242
argument case particle 175
argument focus 248–251, 256, *see also* narrowly focused argument 248
argument structure 81, 104–106, 108–109, 114, 117, 120–121, 123–124, 159, 165, 180, 234, 237, 243, 280
aspect 12, 81, 126, 132–152, 263, *see also* marked aspect 143–151
aspect adverb 64
aspect marker 294

aspectual auxiliary 96, 108, 111, 143–144, 148, 174
assertion 67, 237, 243, 247–249, 262, 302–304, 326
assistive causative 171
assistive causation 171–172
associative phrase 198
associative plural 57
ato 61, 131–132, 263, 265
attributive form 8–9, 62, 65–66, 93, 199, 200
attributive phrase 198–201
-*au* 190
Austronesian languages 4
Austronesian "substratum" hypothesis 4
auxiliary 57, 65, 133, 147
auxiliary verb 8, 24, 78, 96, 145, 148–149, 151, 177
auxiliary suffix 79–82, 86–88, 144, 153

B
-*ba* 79, 266
backchannel 280, 349
"beautification" prefix 326
benefactive 65, 153, 179–186
benefactive auxiliary 180, 184, 186, 302
benefactive verb complex 179–181, 183
bilabial fricative 8, 32
bilabial stop 68
blending 78, 90, 100, 103
binding force 225
body-part 189
Buddhist monks 23, 25

C
CA *see* Conversation Analysis
case marking 11, 153, 195, 234
case particle 7, 9, 11–13, 20, 66–67, 232, 236, see
case particle ellipsis 13
case particle *ga* 120, 193
case particle *ni* 125
cased head 201–202
cataphoric relation 286
"categorical" judgment 239
causative 63, 79–82, 85, 121, 153, 168–179
causative-benefactive 170, 184–186

causative-passive 178–179
causative suffix 186
causative verb complex 183
cause 168–178, 185, *see also* cause/reason 263, 269, 304
causee 168–178
causee-object 169, 171
causer 168–173, 176–177, 185
causer-subject 169, 171
chained clause 271
challengeability 223
change-of-state 134, 148, 150–151
Chart of 50 Sounds 25
-*chau see te-shimau*
China 18, *see also* southern China 23
Chinese 6, 18–22, 24–25, *see also* Middle Chinese 8, literary Chinese 19, Chinese pronunciation 22, topic construction in Chinese 124
Chinese character 10, 18–24, 27, 47, 54, 56
Chinese compound 26
Chinese loan word 9, *see also* non-Chinese loan word 20, non-Chinese foreign origin 21, 56
Chinese syntactic pattern 19
Chinese translation 10
Chinese word 55, 83
Chinese writing style 274
Chinese writing system 55
"Chronicles of Japan" *see* Nihonshoki
circumstantials 270
Classical Japanese 144, 203
classifier 38, 68, 72, 74–76, 201
clausal comment 242
clausal noun modification 201–212, 216
clause 64, 67, 116, 126, 131, 198, 219, 242–243, 251, 273, 279, 306, 333, 339, 349, *see also* non-finite clause 274, same-subject clause 272
clause chaining 17, 80, 87, 270–272, 274
clause chaining form 80, 87
clause chaining language 17
clause combining 17, 259–260, 274, 333, 339

clause-forming formal nouns 131
clause structure 120
cleft argument focus construction 250
cleft focus 15 *see* pseudo-cleft
cleft sentence 229, 250–251
clipping 45, 78, 90, 100–103
"closed" structure 274
"clothing" verb 177
coercive causative 172
"Collection of Myriad Leaves" *see Man'yōshū*
combined pragmatic particle 304
comitative 66, 117, 119, 154, 206
comitative construction 116, 188–193
"comma crossing" 241, 264, 273
comment 12, 65, 67, 217, 228, 238–239, 241–243, 245, 248–252, 256, 258, 297, 309
comment focus 248–251
comment focus structure 249
commenting predicate 228
"common" language 1
common noun 58–59
communication 309, *see also* communication process 306, 308, 313, mass communication 1, mode of communication 331, speech communication 22, text communication device 20
comparative 62
complement 234, 236 *see* object complement, subject complement
complement clause 61, 175, 215, 223–224, 227, 229, 270, 277
complement taking verb 225
complementation 90, 219, 223, 229, 236
complementizer 203, 210, 223–230, 233–236, 293
completive aspect 145–146, 152
complex adjunct phrase 67
complex postpositional phrase 67, 179
complex predicate 168
compound adjective 96

compound noun 48, 72, 91, 95–96, 198
compound verb 71, 95–96, 144
compound word 40, 55, 95
compounding 45, 78, 90, 95, 99, 101–103
concessive 268, 304
concessive conditional 268
conclusive form 8–9, 66, 199
conditional 17, 79–80, 82–83, 87–88, 266–268, 271–272
conjoined subject construction 188–189, 193
conjoining 188, 259, 269, 274
conjunction 43, 54, 64, 235, 260, 263–266, 287, 304, 309
conjunctive 79, 82, 87–88, 144, 152, 170, 259, 262, 333
conjunctive form 80, 271, 339
conjunctive particle 64, 67, 260, 262
conjunctive suffix 81, 83
consciousness 277
consequence 260, 266, 269
consonant verb 78–81, 83–85, 87, 165–166, 170, 178, 319
consonant root verb *see* consonant verb
constituent order 4, 13–15
content label head 202, 210, 212, 214, 216
content noun 210
content word 20–21
continuative 134, 138–140, 142, 145, 147
contrast 67, 237, 244–246, 259, 261–262, 269
contrast particle 88
contrastive argument 244–246
contrastive structure 243–244
contrastive topic 245
contrastiveness 237, 245
conversation 237, 280–281, 287, 306–309, 311, 313, 315, 325, 327, 331, 349, 354
Conversation Analysis 14, 274, 306
coordinate compound 98
coordination 259
copula 10–11, 57–58, 62, 64–66, 78, 87–90, 93, 104, 126–127, 148, 199, 268, 288, 298–300,

305, 309, 318, 325, 327, *see also* attributive form of copula 88, adverbial form of copula 88–89, 148
core argument 195
counter 74
counterfactual 266–268
coupling 259–260, 262, 270

D
da see copula
dakara 64, 309–312, 351–352, 357
daroo 65, 88, 129, 297–298, 304
-dasu 147–148
datte 67, 311–312
dative 13, 63, 66, 112, 117, 122, 154, 163, 180, 195, 200–202, 207, 220, 222, 229
dative case marker 225, 295
dative case particle 125, 172
dative marked phrase 163
dative subject 106, 122–125, 147, 150, 165, 168, 196
dative topic 238
declarative sentence 239, 252, 257
declarative statement 297
declarative utterance 49
definite 12, 15, 57, 196–197
deictic expression 60, 257, 287, 290–294, 315
deixis 257, 283, 287
demonstrative 54, 196, 202, 276, 283–286, 290–293
demonstrative pronoun 60, 206
deontic modality 296
dependent marking language 12
derivation 90
derivational suffix 81–83
derived stative 141
deshoo 50, 297, 304
desiderative 8, 79, 81 82, 288
desu see copula
dialect 1–3, 8–10, 23, 35, 46, 87
diphthong 43, 70
direct object 11, 13, 60, 97, 125, 153–154, 159, 168, 176, 193, 203, 214, 216, 231, 233–235, 237, 245, 270
direct object relative 202
direct passive 153, 158–160
direct quotation 220–221
directional auxiliary 294

"directive" causation 171, 175
discernment 318
discourse 60, 104, 139, 237, 239, 244, 252, 255–256, 259, 275–277, 279, 284–287, 290, 308–311, 313–315, 318, 329, 333, *see also* spoken discourse 262, written discourse 221, 261, 272–273
discourse boundary 280
discourse connective 64, 308–309, 313, *see also* discourse conjunction 287
discourse deixis 283, 290
discourse marker 64, 287, 306, 308, 311, 313, *see also* English discourse marker 308
discourse process 240
discourse reference 283, 285
discourse saliency 156–157
discourse strategy 274
ditransitive 11, 63
double nominative 105–106, 168, 121, 123–125, 213, 243
"double-*o* constraint" 176
"double" judgment 239
"Dual structural model" 5
duplication 58
Dutch 10, 56
"dvandva" compounds 98
dynamic event 136
dynamic predicate 104–105, 109, 126, 128
dynamic verb 130, 141, 250, 263

E
Edo dialect 江戸方言 10
"eel" sentence 241
ellipsis 12–13, 17, 197, 220, 276, 279–280, 318
embedded clause 276
embedded interrogative word 217
embedding 236
emotion 87, 106, 111, 161, 164, 225, 253, 258, 287–288
emotion induced human behavior 136–7
epistemic modality 287, 297, 301
evaluation 144, 227, 297, 301, 326, *see also* negative evaluation 265
evaluative modality 301

eventive passive 162–163
evidential 8, 65, 79–80, 82, 87–88, 287–289, 297, 299–300
exclamation 8, 221, 287
exclamatory sentence 249, 252, 255–257, 287–288
exclusive argument focus interpretation 249
existential 89, 107, 118, 122–125
existential construction 107, 122–123, 125
existential verb 89, 107
experiencer 105, 165, 172, 258, 287–289, 345
exploratory aspect 147
external subject 124
extra argument 124, 159, 161
"extra-thematic" argument 243

F
fact supporting predicate 227
factivity 224–225
feeling 287–288, see also negative feeling 146
female speech 326–328, 330
first person pronoun 277–278, 280, 316, 325
first person subject 65, 223, 288
focus 237, 247–252, 256, 314
 see also obligatory focus 250
focus concord 8
focus construction 15, 250
focus domain 248–251
focus particle 9
focus reading 249
focus structure 247

G
gendered speech 314, 325–326, 329–330
generic 200, 240, 251, 256–257, 266, 315
generic interpretation 250
generic noun phrase 240
generic/habitual sentence type 126–129
generic sentence 256
generic situation 250
generic state 257
generic statement 158
genetic affiliation 3
genitive 9, 51, 66, 76, 117, 120, 198, 203–204, 214, 239

genitive/associative phrase 198
genitive case marker 203, 212
genitive case particle 9, 76, 197
genitive construction 200
genitive interpretation 200
genitive marker 214
genitive marking 214
genitive noun 204
genitive particle 198
genitive phrase 51, 194–196, 198, 204, 239
gerund 80
gerundive form 80
gi-joo-go 擬情語 69
gi-on-go 擬音語 69
gi-see-go 擬声語 69
Gishi Wajinden 魏志倭人伝 6
gi-tai-go 擬態語 69
glide 31–32, 35–36
glottal stop 68–69, 340
go- 67, 92
gojuu-on-zu 五十音図 25
grammatical particles 21, 24, 26, 54

H
habitual 126–129, 266
haiku 俳句 44–45
-hajimeru 147
hazu da 65, 298
head final language 15
head noun 15, 51, 198–203, 205–210, 216–217, 229, 231–232, 236, 331
headless relative clause 229
hearsay evidential 65, 300
hearsay expression 210
high vowel devoicing 29, 39
hiragana 20–21, 24–27, 54, 68
homophonous word 22, 41, 46
honorific 9–10, 58, 60, 94, 122, 164–165, 177, 230–231, 255, 295, 314, 320–325, 330, see also non-honorific overtone 230
human 57, 75, 106–107, 114–115, 123, 156–157, 160, 181, 185, 189–190, 207, 234, 279, 306
human propensity 61
humble honorific 321–324
hybrid language 4
hybrid word 57
hyōjun-go 標準語 1
hyper polite adjective form 87

hyper-polite form 329
hypothetical 266–268

I
ichi-go bun 一語文 252
identifiable 12, 15, 57, 59, 196–197, 202, 239–240, 243–244, 246, 251–252, 255–256, see also non-identifiable 15, 240, 243–244, 252, 255
identifiability 237, 239–240, 244, 246, 252
IHR see internally headed relative clause
illocutionary act 302, 304
immediate speaker 219
imperative 79–80, 82, 221, 305, 319, 328
imperfective 132–133, 143
inanimate 9, 75, 89, 107, 115, 134, 138, 145, 156, 173, 233
inanimate agent 157
inanimate causee 173, 175–176, 185
inanimate patient 157
inanimate subject 134, 175
inceptive aspect 96, 147
inchoative aspect 148–149
indefinite 9, 15, 240
independent conjunctive 262
indirect object 11, 125, 181, 202–203, 207
indirect passive 158–161, 163, 301
indirect quotation 220–221
infinitive 17, 63, 79–80, 82–83, 87–89, 91, 144–145, 147–148, 247, 259–260, 266, 273, 299–300, 319, 321–322, 333, 339
inflectional category 57, 78, 86, 88–89
inflectional suffix 68, 83, 126
informal register 62, 328
informal speech 325–326, 330
information question 14, 328
information structure 217, 237, 247–249
in-group 323
initial /r/ 8
inner clause 123
inner-speech 252, 255, 293
innovative causative form 79
instantaneous 134–138, 140–141, 143–146

Index

instrumental 12, 49, 66, 117–118, 163, 205, 208
interjection 57, 68, 325
interjectional particle 306
interactional features 333
interactional linguistics 14, 306
interactional modality 297, 302
internal state expression 287–288, 305
internally headed relative clause 229, 231–232, 234–235
interrogative noun 14, 60
integrated adverbial clause 219, 234–236
intonation 14, 29, 49–53, 280, 303–305, 307, 326–329, 340
intonation phrase 51–52
intonation unit 52–53, 280
intransitive 85–86, 136–139, 141, 142–143, 145, *see also* semantically intransitive 60
intransitive-based morphological causative 169, 171, 176–177
intransitive non-volitional verb 142
intransitive predicate 170, 208
intransitive sentence 12, 169
intransitive verb 63, 85, 136, 152, 168, 214
intransitive vs. transitive pair 86
irregular verb 78, 80–81, 165–166
irregular root verb 78
iterative 137, 139, 141, 143–144, 148, 152
IU *see* intonation unit

J

janai 304
jibun 60, 121–122, 140, 192, 224, 238, 276–278, 280, 309, 315, 341
Jōmon period 縄文時代 4–5
Jōyō Kanji List 常用漢字表 24

K

kakarimusubi 係り結び 8
kanji 漢字 *see* Chinese character
kanojo 58–59, 315
Kan-on 漢音 23
kantoo joshi 間投助詞 306
kara 'because, so' 228, 269, 304, 309

kara 'from' 66, 115, 117, 119–120, 155, 163, 194, 197, 206, 230, 274
kare 57–59, 276–277, 315
katakana 20–21, 24–28, 54, 56, 76
kedo 64, 246–247, 261–262, 269, 274–275, 281, 304–305, 308–310, 339, 343–344, 347, 351
kenjoo-go 謙譲語 321
keredo see kedo
keredomo see kedo
Kindaichi's four-way verb classification 134
kke 8, 67, 144
Kojiki 古事記 19
ko-so-a words 292, 294
ko-so-a-do 60, 64–6
kundoku 訓読 18–19
kun-reading 訓読み 22–23

L

layered clause structure 123–124
layered structure 123–124
lexical causative 168–169, 171, 174–177, 186
lexical nominalization 90
LGBT 278
List of Characters of General use 24 *see Jōyō Kanji* List
"location" verb 136
locative 12, 22, 66, 117–118, 205, 237
logical inference 65, 298
logophoric pronoun 276–277
long vowel 30–31, 33, 69
Lyman's Law 40–41

M

mae clause 264
made 117, 119
madeni 120
main clause 129, 131, 211–213, 221, 229, 241, 262–264, 280
main clause tense 130–131
male speech 327–329
malefactive meaning 183–184
manipulative causation 176
Man'yōshū 万葉集 19
Man'yōgana 万葉仮名 22, 24
-masu ending 327
matrix clause 232, 269
measure word 74–75
medial clause 17, 270–271

medial verb form 80
mental activity 164
mental process 225, 239, 289
mimetic word 26, 68
mirativity 303, 305
mitai 65, 299, 352
mixed-type sentence 256–258
modal adverb 308
"modal affective" demonstratives 293
modal auxiliary 65, 297, 304
modal expression 211, 267, 298
modal information 8
modal judgment 257
modal stance 64
modal verb in English 16, 297
modality 16, 82, 287, 296–297, 301–302
modifier 4, 7, 15, 60, 62, 197–199, 201–202, 207, 209–211, 217, 229, 239, 263, 331
modifying clause 201, 208, 211, 217
mokkan 木簡 19
mora 8, 25, 28–29, 37, 38–39, 42–49, 51–52, 62, 70, 72, 100–102, 166
moraic nasal 7, 25, 35, 37–38, 42–43, 48, 54, 69
moraic obstruent 38–39, 42–43, 69
-morau 177, 184
morphological causative 170–171, 174–177
motion verb 104
"movie director" causative 173

N

-n 84, 257, 305, 328, 356
-n da see no da
-nagara 79, 82
nara 67, 266–268
nasal assimilation 42
national language 1, 10, 54, 56, 237
native vocabulary 9, 41, 54
negative 2, 15–16, 64, 68, 72, 79–81, 87–90, 107, 126, 148, 200, 263–265, 299, 319–320
negative conjecture 65
negative effect 173
negative emotion 161
negative evaluation 265

negative feeling 146
negative overtone 146
negative past 133
negative perfect 133
negative predicate 245, 247
negative prefix 93
negative response 68, 133
negative suffix 319
new information 249, 305
-ni chigainai 298
(ni/-ku) naru 148
Nihon Shoki 日本書紀 19
nihon-go 日本語 1
ni-yotte 157–158, 163–164
no see formal noun, genitive, pronominal, sentence-final no
no da 277, 305
no-de 337
no-ni 261
(no) ni wa 270
nominal 80, 131, 199, 227, 291, 209, see also predicate nominal 251
nominal adjective 55, 57, 61–63, 65–66, 87–88, 90–93, 104–105, 123, 148, 150, 199, 227, 267, 298–299
nominal compound 98
nominal ellipsis 276, 279
nominal equivalent 80
nominal predicate 105, 243, 250
nominal reference 283
nominal referent 240
nominalization 90–91, 127, 250, 257
nominalized adjectival base 96
nominalized verb 91–92, 327
nominalized verbal base 96
nominalizer 14, 95, 148, 166, 216, 250, 257, 269, 327
nominalizing complementizer 229
nominative 9, 11–12, 21, 47–48, 63, 66, 104–105, 175, 200, 208, 272
nominative-accusative language 12
nominative case marker 9, 21, 121
nominative case marking particle 47, 195
nominative case particle 63, 212
nominative marked phase 207

nominative marker 153, 203
nominative subject 207, 216
non-activated concept 255
non-generic 200, 251, 315
non-inflectional category 57
nonidentifiable 246
nonfactive 225
"non-interventive" causative 173, 176
nonpast 31, 61, 63, 87–89, 91, 100, 104, 126, 128–131, 137, 221, 223, 250, 263, 264, 265, 270, 289, non-polite form 327–328
non-referential 200, 240, 251
non-restrictive relative clause 203
non-self-controllable 185
non-stative predicate 153
non-topic marking particle 248–249, 252
non-visual perception 212, 225
non-volitional 109, 138, 141–142, 152, 164–165
non-volitional causee 170
non-volitional intransitive 109, 164–165
non-volitional verb 142, 152, 172
noun 21, 47–48, 51, 54–63, 65, 70, 72, 75–76, 8889, 93, 95–97–98, 106–107, 131, 148, 199–217, 223, 231, 248, 258, 264, 270, 276, 279, 298, 300, 318, 322, 330–331
noun complementation 229, 236
noun equivalent 79, 87, 90–92, 94, 96, 99
noun phrase 9, 11–15, 17, 66–67, 104–105, 109–110, 113–116, 120–123, 125, 157, 168, 173, 175, 179, 180–181, 188, 194–198, 202–204, 207, 213–216, 220, 232, 237, 239–240, 242–243, 245–246, 249–252, 263, 272, 307
noun phrase accessibility hierarchy 203–204
noun phrase conjoining 188
noun phrase ellipsis 13, 220
numeral 68, 72, 74–75, 153, 201
numeral classifier see classifier
numeric expression 195, 197
numeric phrase 65, 74–76, 194–197

O
object complement 223–225, 227
object of comparison 203–204, 207
object-topic 238
objective ga 213
obligation 16, 319
obligatory focus 249–250
oblique 202–203, 207, 214
offers see speech act
on reading 音読み 22–24
onbin 音便 80, 82–85, 87
one-word sentence 252
one-argument predicate 242
one-place predicate 182
onomatopoeia 20, 68–69
open class category 57
open clausal structure 274–275
opinion 17, 320
order see speech act
original speaker 219
otagai 191–194
otagai-ni 191–193
out-group 323
outer clause 123
-oeru 145
-owaru 145

P
palatalization 36–37, 39, 68, 84
palatalized consonant 26, 37, 84
partitive construction 197
passive 79–82, 85, 153–164, 165–166, 170, 173–174, 178–179, 184–185, 234, 301, 321
passive-benefactive 185
past tense 65, 80, 83, 130, 133, 144, 199, 221–222, 263, 287, 290, 327
patient 60, 110, 153–157, 159, 168–169, 185, 187, 189, 292, 298
patient-causee 168–169
perception verb 149, 254
perfect 8, 132–133, 140, 144, 287
perfective 8, 132–133, 141, 143
perception 149, 151–152, 211–212, 225–227, 252–255, 257–258, 287–288, 299
"period crossing" 244
periphrastic causative 177, 185
permission 16, 320
permissive causation 171
permissive causative 172

personal indexical term 314–315, 318
personal names 58, 200, 316–317
personal pronoun 57, 59, 276, 279, 290, 314–315
phenomimes 69
pitch accent 62
pitch accent language 46
pivot independent relative 229
plain register 62
plural subject 116, 141
plurality 58, 99
poetry 42, 44
point-of-view 19, 277, 296
polar question 14
polarity 15, 62, 64, 81
polarity contrast 245
polite form 203, 294, 297, 304, 327–329
polite prefix 67, 92, 191, 326
polite suffix 14, 221
politeness 10, 59, 186, 304, 318, 323–325, 328
Portuguese 56
"position" verb 136
possessive construction 107, 122–125
postpositional case particle 104
postpositional phrase 67, 179, 200, 246
potential 106, 148, 150–153, 161, 164–168, 171
pragmatic particle 50, 67, 255, 262, 287, 302, 304–308, 325–327, 333
pragmatics 207, 287, 306
predicate 11–12, 14, 16, 57–58, 62, 65–66, 67, 70, 80, 87, 104–106, 108–109, 111, 117, 119–121, 123–124, 126, 128–129, 131, 148, 153, 168, 170, 180–182, 195, 201–203, 207–208, 227–229, 232, 234–235, 238, 241–243, 245–247, 250–252, 254, 256–257, 259, 260, 262, 264, 279–280, 289, 293, 303, 318, 324, 340
predicate adjective 62
predicate combining 260
prefix 4, 67–68, 92–94, 191, 326
pre-nominal genitive phrase 194
preparatory aspect 146–147
presentational sentence 252, 255

presupposition 237, 247–250
prime addressee 219–220, 222
prime speaker 219–221, 224
progressive 12, 109, 133, 135–140, 142–144, 152, 172, 223, 265
prohibition 16, 319
pronominal 203, 215, 230
pronoun 4, 13, 15, 57, 59–60, 106, 121–122, 193–194, 203–204, 206–207, 260, 276–279, 280, 284, 290, 314–317, 325, 330
proper noun 58, 202
propositional contrast 246
propositional modality 297
proto-Japanese 4–6, 8
proximate addressee 219
proximate speaker 211, 219–221, 224
pseudo-cleft 229, 250–251
psychomimes 69
purposive 221

Q
quantifier 74–76, 122, 195–196
quantifier float 122, 195
question particle 14, 116, 222, 328
question word 14–15, 60, 217
quotation 219–222, 224, 289
quotative 21, 67, 71, 116, 210, 219–225, 236, 297, 300
quotative clause 223–224
quotative construction 225, 236, 297
quotative particle 67, 71, 220, 222, 300

R
rashii 65, 79–80, 82–83, 87–88, 94, 289–290, 299–301, 312
reactive expression 68
reality conditional 266
rebus principle 24
rebus reading 22, 25
reciprocal 153, 187–194
reciprocal pattern 115–116
reciprocal pronoun 193–194
reciprocal suffix 193
reciprocal verb 113, 119, 206
reduplication 4, 70, 78, 90, 99–100
reference term 316, 317–318, 330
reference time 136

referent honorific 320, 323–325
referent tracking 276, 283
referential 67, 200, 240, 251, 277, 315, 321, 323
reflexive 60, 121–122, 140, 276–278, 315
reflexive pronoun 60, 121–122, 276–278, 315
reflexivization 121–122
register 17, 62, 80, 87, 89, 92, 203, 318, 327–330
relational head 202, 209, 213, 216–217
relational noun 209–210
relative clause 15, 104, 129–130–131, 201, 202–208, 212–213, 216–217, 219, 229, 231–232, 236, 241, 245
relative clause formation in English 216–218
"relative honorific" system 323
relative tense 129, 131, 221
reminiscent suffix 144
rendaku 連濁 39, 42
ren'yoo-kee 連用形 79, 319
reportative verb 116
representative 67, 79, 82, 87–88, 261
request 319
respect honorifics 321–323
resultative 109, 133, 135–144, 151–152, 199, 223
resumptive pronoun strategy 207
right-branch condition 41
rising intonation 14, 49, 303–305, 326, 328–329
root 8, 31, 69–71, 78–81, 83–88, 90, 299
Ryukyu 琉球 3, 9

S
salience of a concept 237
-san 94, 221, 315, 317
sandhi 80, 83
sashiageru 125, 179, 294–295, 322
sensation 87, 106, 210, 212, 253–254, 258, 287–288, 299
scrambling 13
second person 280, 288, 314–315, 317
self-controllability 63
self-speech 252, 255

semelfactive 134–135, 137, 139–141, 143–146
semi-vowel 78
sentence conjoining 188
sentence extender 14, 257, 305, 327
sentence final *no* 305
sentence final particle 67, 302, 304, 330
sentence focus 249, 252
sequential voicing 29, 39–41
shi 67, 260–261, 274, 311, 332
shuu joshi 302
simple attributive phrase 198–199
simultaneous 79, 82
Sino-Japanese compound 10, 41, 101
Sino-Japanese numeral system 72
Sino-Japanese vocabulary 9, 27, 55
slang 57, 100, 102
Smith's five-way classification of situation type 134
solemn honorifics 324
sonkei-go 尊敬語
see referent honorific
soo₁ 79–80, 82, 87–88, 288–289, 299–300
soo₂ 79–80, 82, 87–88, 299–300
soochoo-go 荘重語 *see* solemn honorific
sound euphony 83
sound-symbolic word 20, 21, 54, 63–64, 68–72, 83, 99
spatial deixis 290
speaker proximate 291
speaker's attitude 68
specific conditional 267
specific sentences 126, 128, 130, 158
specific statement 128
specifier 76
speech act 64, 319
speech level 59, 278, 315, 318–319, 325, 330
speech register 92, 325, 329, 330
speech style 314, 318, 325
spoken language 9, 11, 14, 279
spontaneous 150–153, 164–167, 173
"staging" effect 240
"standard" language 1

stative 63, 104–105, 111, 126, 128–129, 131, 134–136, 142–146, 148, 170, 288, *see also* derived stative 141
stative passive 162–163
stative potential 166–167
stative predicate 104–105, 111, 126, 128, 148, 153, 170, 242
stative sentence 105, 163
stative verb 61, 111, 123, 136, 141, 145–146, 148, 250, 263
stativizer 162
stem 78–79, 81–83, 86–87
stereotyping 301
subject 11–13, 15, 65, 97, 106, 108, 116, 120–125, 134, 141, 147, 150, 153, 155, 158–163, 165–166, 168–169, 171, 173, 175–176, 178–180, 184–185, 188–191, 193, 196, 202–203, 207–208, 212, 216, 220, 229, 231, 235–237, 242, 246, 249–250, 252, 260, 264, 266, 271–272, 276, 278–280, 288–290, 295–296, 322
subject complement 223, 227
subject honorific 321
"subject prominent and topic prominent" language 12
subjectivization 146
subjectivity 287
subject-topic 238, 241
subordinate clause 9, 129–131, 221, 263, 280
subordination 259, 263, 274
suffix 10, 14–16, 31, 48, 57–58, 63, 67–68, 71–72, 74–75, 78–83, 86–89, 92, 94, 126, 133, 144, 146–147, 152–153, 158, 164–165, 170, 174, 178, 186, 190, 193, 221, 255, 276, 288, 315–317, 319
suffixation 78
superlative 62
switch reference 120, 271
syllable 4, 7–8, 19, 24–26, 28–29, 32–33, 35–38, 42–46, 48–49, 80, 100, 166, 290, 307
syllable structure 7, 42–43, 100
syntactic role 120, 202, 231

T
-tai 8, 288
tail pitch movement 49–50, 53, 280, 349

Tale of *Genji* 源氏物語 274
tame-ni 179–181, 270
-tara 79, 82–83, 266–267, 271–272, 274
target of honorification 321–322
-tari 8, 79, 82–83, 261
-te form 16–17, 65, 80, 144, 177, 179, 265, 268–269, 271–274, 319
-te-ageru 65, 179, 302
-te-aru 65, 142–143, 144, 147, 152
-te-iku 65, 149, 151
-te-iru 65, 129, 133, 134–142, 143–145, 147, 152, 162, 223
-te-kara 263, 265
-te-kuru 65, 149–151
-te-miru 147
-te-morau 65, 168, 184–186
temporal adverbial clauses 215, 241, 263
temporal chaining 259
temporary event 136
tense 8, 12, 15, 17, 31, 57, 62–63, 65, 80–81, 83, 87, 104, 126–133, 137, 144, 199, 221–222, 263–265, 287, 289–290, 300, 327
-te-oku 146–147
terminal 117
termination suffix 81–83, 87–88
territory of information 303
-te-shimau 65, 145–146, 301
textual information 285
-te-yaru 65, 184
thetic judgment 252
third person pronoun 276–277
third person subject 65, 223, 288–289
three place predicate 181
title 94, 314–318
ToBI 21, 51
to conditional 266, 272
to yuu 210–212, 214–215, 218, 223, 226–228, 277, 283, 333
toki clause 263
tokoro 61, 223–227, 229–230, 233–236, 240–241, 256, 270, 279, 334, 342
Tokyo accent 46
Tokyo dialect 東京方言 2, 10, 35
tone 22–24, 34, 46–47, 51, 61, 67, 146, 231, 284, 304, 312, 324, 326, 329
tone language 46

topic 12–13, 15, 22, 26, 47, 65–67, 87–88, 123–124, 153, 203, 211, 217, 229, 237–249, 251–252, 255–258, 260, 272
topic-comment 65, 67, 217, 238–239, 241, 243, 251–252, 256, 258
topicalization 237, 240, 245
topic-less sentence 252, 255–256
topic marking 22, 26, 47, 66, 153, 203, 211, 248–249, 252, 272, see also deletability of the topic-marking particle 257
topic-prominent 12, 124, 242
Tōsō-on 唐宋音 23
"tough" sentence 81
transitive 136–139, 145, 147, see also semantically transitive 60, transitive-intransitive opposition 85
transitive-based morphological causative 169, 176
transitive change 114
transitive event 110, 153
transitive form 177
transitive-intransitive pair 85, 169
transitive-intransitive opposition 85–86
transitive movement 110
transitive predicate 170, 208
transitive sentence 11–12, 156, 168–169, 176
transitive situation 189–190
transitive structure 110
transitive verb 60, 63, 85–86, 136, 142–143, 152, 168, 171, 176, 190, 214, 279
transitive volitional verb 142
transitivity 63, 85, 123, 138–139, see also transitivity and aspect 138–139
transitivity marking 85
Tungusic language 6
Type IV verbs 134, 141

U
unaccented word 46, 52
unaccusative 109, 172

unagi-bun 241
unassimilated information 305
undergoer 105, 172
unergative 109, 136–137, 168
unidentifiable 239
unreality conditional 266

V
valency 104–105
Vendler's four-way verb classification 134
verb 4, 7, 10–16, 21, 31, 47, 49, 54, 56–57, 60–61, 63–65, 67–68, 71–72, 79–87, 88–92, 95, 100, 104, 107, 110–111, 113–116, 119, 120–123, 125–127, 130–131, 133–144, 146–147, 150, 152–155, 158–161, 164–166, 168, 170–173, 175–176, 178–184, 187, 190, 194–195, 197, 199, 203, 206, 214, 220–225, 227, 229, 231, 233–237, 245, 247, 250, 253–254, 261, 263, 265–266, 270–271, 273, 277, 279, 288–289, 294–297, 297–300, 307, 318–323, 325, 327–328, 330
verb morphology 4, 7, 78, 83, 85, 153, 321
verb of communication 114–115
verb of giving 114
verbal adjective see adjective
verbal ellipsis 13
verbal noun 55, 60, 72
verbal predicate 259
verbal suffix 15, 57
visual evidential 8, 65
visual perception 212, 225, 227, 254–255, 299
vocative expression 68
voice 16, 41–44, 69, 81–83, 153, 165–166, 210, 212
voice derivational suffix 81–83
voiced-voiceless contrast 70
voiceless stop 32
volition 63, 172–173, 175
volitional 109–111, 136, 141–143, 152, 165, 170, 172, 289
volitional agent 138
volitional even 136
volitional form 79–80, 82

volitional intransitive 109–110, 136
volitional verb 142, 147, 152
vowel 4, 7, 25, 29–31, 33–34, 35–39, 42–43, 48–50, 56, 69–71, 74, 78, 80–81, 84–86, 164–166, 170, 178, 280, 307, 319, 340
vowel harmony 4
vowel-lengthening 37, 70
vowel root verb see vowel verb
vowel verb 78, 80–81, 85, 165–166, 170, 178, 319

W
wa see topic
wa see female speech, pragmatic particle
"-wa -ga" sentence structure 242–243
waka 和歌 44, 61, 72
Weizhi 6 see Gishi Wajinden
women's speech see female speech
written discourse 221, 259, 261, 272–273, 279
written language 9–11, 237, 241, 279, 333
Wu dialect 23

Y
yaru see ageru
Yayoi period 5–6
yes/no question 14, 222
yo 302–305, see pragmatic particle
yo ne(e) 327, see pragmatic particle
yoo da 65, 299, 300–301
yoo ni 149, 165, 221–222, 270, 278, 334, 337
yori 62, 120, 204, 207

Z
ze 67, 302, 326, see pragmatic particle
zero anaphora 240, 279, 280, 333
zo 8, 67, 302–303, 326, 330, see pragmatic particle
-zyau see -chau, -te-shimau